America's Dirty Wars

Irregular Warfare from 1776 to the War on Terror

RUSSELL CRANDALL
Davidson College

CAMBRIDGE
UNIVERSITY PRESS

32 Avenue of the Americas, New York, NY 10013-2473, USA

Cambridge University Press is part of the University of Cambridge.

It furthers the University's mission by disseminating knowledge in the pursuit of education, learning, and research at the highest international levels of excellence.

www.cambridge.org
Information on this title: www.cambridge.org/9780521176620

© Russell Crandall 2014

This publication is in copyright. Subject to statutory exception and to the provisions of relevant collective licensing agreements, no reproduction of any part may take place without the written permission of Cambridge University Press.

First published 2014

Printed in the United States of America

A catalog record for this publication is available from the British Library.

Library of Congress Cataloging in Publication Data
Crandall, Russell, 1971–
America's dirty wars : irregular warfare from 1776 to the War on Terror / Russell Crandall.
pages cm.
Includes bibliographical references and index.
ISBN 978-1-107-00313-2 (hardback)
1. Irregular warfare – United States – Case studies. 2. Intervention (International law) – Government policy – United States. 3. Counterinsurgency – United States – Case studies. 4. Insurgency – Case studies. 5. Atrocities – Case studies. 6. United States – History, Military – Case studies. 7. United States – Military policy – Moral and ethical aspects. 8. Strategic culture – United States. I. Title.
U167.5.I8C73 2014
355.02′18–dc23   2013029629

ISBN 978-1-107-00313-2 Hardback
ISBN 978-0-521-17662-0 Paperback

Cambridge University Press has no responsibility for the persistence or accuracy of URLs for external or third-party Internet Web sites referred to in this publication and does not guarantee that any content on such Web sites is, or will remain, accurate or appropriate.

Cover image: Lt. Matthew Stuhler visits with Haji Najibullah at his home in western Marjah, Helmand Province, Afghanistan, Sunday, August 1, 2010. Many compounds were empty in the area that was hotly contested between marines and Taliban fighters and Lt. Stuhler visited to offer his support. "I don't want anything. I just want to stay at home, feed my family, and work on my farm," Najibullah said. Photo by Victor J. Blue, used with permission.

America's Dirty Wars
Irregular Warfare from 1776 to the War on Terror

This book examines the long, complex experience of American involvement in irregular warfare. It begins with the American Revolution in 1776 and chronicles big and small irregular wars for the next two and a half centuries. What is readily apparent in dirty wars is that failure is painfully tangible while success is often amorphous. Successfully fighting these wars often entails striking a critical balance between military victory and politics. America's status as a democracy only serves to make fighting – and, to a greater degree, winning – these irregular wars even harder. Rather than futilely insisting that Americans should not or cannot fight this kind of irregular war, Russell Crandall argues that we would be better served by considering how we can do so as cleanly and successfully as possible.

Russell Crandall is a professor of international politics and American foreign policy at Davidson College. His previous books include *The United States and Latin America after the Cold War* (Cambridge, 2008); *Gunboat Democracy: U.S. Interventions in the Dominican Republic, Grenada, and Panama* (2006); and *Driven by Drugs: U.S. Policy Toward Colombia* (2008). Interwoven with his academic career, Crandall has held several high-level foreign policy appointments within the U.S. government, including the Joint Chiefs of Staff and Office of the Secretary of Defense at the Pentagon and the National Security Council at the White House.

To my brother and hero, Bill Jr.

Never, never, never believe any war will be smooth and easy, or that anyone who embarks on the strange voyage can measure the tides and hurricanes he will encounter. The statesman who yields to war fever must realize that once the signal is given, he is no longer the master of policy but the slave of unforeseeable and uncontrollable events.

                        Winston Churchill

Contents

List of Figures	page ix
Acknowledgments	xi
1 Introduction	1
2 Irregular Warfare 101	15

PART ONE. THE AMERICAN REVOLUTION TO CHASING SANDINO, 1776–1930S

3 The American Revolution	29
4 Confederates and Indians	46
5 Intermezzo: The Boer War, 1899–1902	63
6 America, Aguinaldo, and the Philippines, 1898	72
7 Chasing Villa, 1916	89
8 A Cold Winter in Siberia	100
9 The Banana Wars, 1898–1930s	109
10 Intermezzo: T. E. Lawrence and the Arab Revolt, 1916–1918	127
11 Chasing Sandino, 1927–1932	136

PART TWO. THE COLD WAR, 1940S–1989

12 Cold War Counterinsurgencies	153
13 Intermezzo: Mao Zedong	157
14 Fighting Communism in Greece	165
15 Intermezzo: France in Algeria, 1954–1962	174
16 Intermezzo: David Galula	185

17 Intermezzo: Malaya Emergency, 1948–1960 — 190
18 Ramón Magsaysay and the Hukbalahap Rebellion in the Philippines, 1946–1956 — 199
19 Vietnam — 209

PART THREE. LATIN AMERICA AND THE COLD WAR, 1950s–1980s

20 From Guatemala, 1954, to Cuba and the Bay of Pigs, 1961 — 239
21 Guatemala, Post-1963 — 258
22 Cuba, Post-1963 — 269
23 Intermezzo: Che Guevara and Guerrilla Warfare — 277
24 Carter, Reagan, and the Sandinista Revolution in Nicaragua, 1979–1990 — 280
25 El Salvador, 1979–1992 — 304

PART FOUR. POST–COLD WAR, 1990s–2000s

26 Dirty Wars after the Cold War — 339
27 Colombia — 345
28 Iraq — 363
29 Intermezzo: The *Counterinsurgency Field Manual* and Postmodern Insurgencies — 393
30 Post-9/11 COIN in the Philippines — 398
31 Intermezzo: Afghanistan, Graveyard of Empires — 404
32 The Longest War: America in Afghanistan — 412
33 The Fall of Muammar Qaddafi, 2011 — 442
34 Intermezzo: JSOC Raids and Drone Strikes — 457
35 Conclusion — 467
Epilogue: "I Feel More Like a Monster" — 471

Notes — 473
Bibliography — 519
Index — 547

List of Figures

3.1	Map: The American Revolution in the South	*page* 30
3.2	General Francis Marion	42
4.1	Colonel John S. Mosby	48
4.2	George Crook	58
4.3	Geronimo	59
5.1	Map: The Boer Wars, 1880–1902	65
5.2	A blockhouse in the Transvaal	68
6.1	Map: The Philippines	73
6.2	Destroyed Spanish ship, Manila Bay, 1898	87
7.1	Map of the Punitive Expedition, 1916	90
7.2	American fliers during the Punitive Expedition	97
8.1	Map: Key sites of the Allied Intervention in Russia, 1918–1920	101
8.2	U.S. Marines in Vladivostok, 1918	103
9.1	Map: The Banana Wars, 1898–1930s	110
10.1	Map: The Arabian Peninsula in the early twentieth century	128
10.2	T. E. Lawrence and Sir Herbert Samuel, 1921	132
11.1	Map: Chasing Sandino, 1927–1932	137
11.2	U.S. Marines in Nicaragua, 1920s	143
13.1	Map: China, 1930s–1940s	158
13.2	Mao and the Long March, 1934–1935	160
14.1	Map: Greece, 1940s	166
15.1	Map: Algeria	175
17.1	Map: Malaya, 1948–1960	191
17.2	Men with rifles in Malayan New Village	194
18.1	Map: The Philippines	200

18.2	Ramón Magsaysay	204
19.1	Map: Vietnam 1960s and 1970s	210
19.2	General Vo Nguyen Giap and Ho Chi Minh, September 1945	213
20.1	Map: Cuba	245
21.1	Map: Guerrilla fronts in Guatemala, early 1980s	264
21.2	Exhumation at a mass grave near Comalapa, Guatemala, 2003	267
22.1	Che Guevara in Bolivia, 1967	275
24.1	Map: The Contra War, 1980s	292
24.2	Contra fighters in Yamales, Honduras, 1988	298
25.1	Map: Guerrilla fronts in El Salvador, 1980s	305
25.2	Map: Clandestine arms shipments to the FMLN in El Salvador, 1982	317
27.1	Map: Colombia	346
27.2	FARC leaders Manuel Marulanda and Mono Jojoy	355
27.3	Aerial eradication of illicit drug crops in Colombia in the 1990s	357
28.1	Map: Iraq, 2003	364
32.1	Map: Afghanistan	413
32.2	Lt. Matthew Stuhler visits with Haji Najibullah, 2010	430
33.1	Map: Libya	443
34.1	Countries where American drone strikes occurred, 2003–2012	463

Acknowledgments

This book was decidedly a group effort and it would never have been possible without the energy and wisdom of many family members, friends, colleagues, and students. I am of course responsible for any mistakes or oversights, but whatever end result you see in these pages is far beyond my own capabilities.

I would first like to thank Britta Crandall, my professional collaborator and, more important, my soulmate. She was at my side for the life of this project and gave me the encouragement to make it see the light of day. Even more than her keen copyediting, she kept sanity in our household while I indulged my bad habit by working on this project on more weeknights than I should have. Our three children, Nolan, Dane, and Eli, spent numerous hours in the family study patiently waiting for Dad to stop writing and go outside to play sports. The boys were also intrepid participants on two academic staff rides with Davidson College students to Kings Mountain Battlefield in South Carolina.

I benefited tremendously from the extraordinary talents of two copy editors and researchers, former Davidson students Marshall Worsham and Iain Addleton. Marshall's keen writing and editing talents made the overall narrative infinitely more logical and forceful. Coming to the book in its second half, Iain's sharp pen and countless "all-nighters" got the manuscript in publication shape before looming deadlines. William Crandall Jr. read a dizzying number of drafts and always provided wise insights and edits. His intellectual thumbprints appear on every page.

Others who discussed topics with me, read all or parts of the manuscript, or assisted with research include Rob Bose, Paul Ream, Natalie Tagher, Coleen Jose, Pete Benbow, Francisco Morales, Augusto Chian,

Allie Francis, Hunter Williams, Lauren Khater, Caroline McDermott, James Atkins, Katie Hunter, Chris Chivvis, Dan Kurtz-Phelan, Nate Shestak, Michael Bachman, Liam Miner, Peter Roady, Riordan Roett, Dane Erickson, Richard Feinberg, Patrick Baetger, Kevin Whitaker, Brian Kline, Daniel Krantz, Tom Shannon, Kevin Whitaker, Dan Troy, Guadalupe Paz, and Andrea Becerra.

Research assistants Marshall Worsham (American Revolution), Richmond Blake (Confederates and Indians), Lauren Khater (T. E. Lawrence and Russia campaign), Iain Addleton (Libya and Philippines post-9/11), Paul Ream (Nicaragua), and Pete Benbow (Iraq) wrote or co-wrote stellar drafts of listed chapters. All of these students began their research with me while undergraduates at Davidson. To my good fortune, my collaboration with them continued after graduation and right up to the book's publication.

Andy Rhodes drew fantastic maps of Nicaragua and the American Revolution in the South. The team at the University of Wisconsin-Madison's cartography lab did an outstanding job of drawing all the other maps.

I am also grateful to the several semesters of Davidson students who have taken my seminar on insurgencies and counterinsurgencies or traveled with me to Colombia in 2008, 2009, 2012, and 2013 for staff rides. In all of these instances, the students provided valuable insights and questions; many also read most of this book in a much rougher manuscript form long before it was ready for public viewing.

I would also like to thank others who were critical to my research efforts. These include the wonderful team of librarians at Davidson's Little Library. Joe Gutekanst and Susanna Boylston continued to work miracles in tracking down elusive sources. The staff at the National Archives in College Park, Maryland, and the special archives at the Universidad Centroamericana in San Salvador, El Salvador, were also extremely accommodating of my requests.

Kari and Denis McDonough provided their normal wonderfully hospitable accommodations – including batch after batch of homemade biscotti – so that I could remain a stone's throw away from the National Archives in College Park, Maryland.

At Davidson, research dean Verna Case provided critical funding on multiple occasions, including the faculty research grant and Duke Endowment group investigation research grant. Chris Alexander and the Dean Rusk International Studies Program also provided crucial funding for international research trips. Brian Shaw and Shelley Rigger provided support and funding from the McNeil Fund to assist with my international research. The redoubtable Lindsay Voegele helped prepare the manuscript for submission. Patterson Lamb did an outstanding job on the final copyedit. Janis Bolster, Shaun Vigil, and Mark Fox were very supportive in the production phase. Lew Bateman remains a staunch supporter of my scholarship and I remain immensely grateful.

My intellectual mentor and Davidson colleague, historian Ralph Levering, read through most of the manuscript with his exacting pen. His attention to detail and ability to see the big and small pictures in so many things reminded me of why I love diplomatic and military history.

My literary agent and friend Gillian MacKenzie has been a source of continuous encouragement for a good while now and thankfully she knows how much I have appreciated and benefited from her tireless talents and attention.

Last, I owe the deepest gratitude to my parents, Janet and William, whose unconditional love and encouragement over the years helped guide a youth toward his ultimate vocation of teaching and scholarship.

Summit Coffee, Davidson, North Carolina
October 2013

I

Introduction

"YOU NOW STAND AMONG THE GIANTS"

When David Petraeus took over in 2007 as the leading American general in Iraq, he had already served one year as a commander in northern Iraq and another as the head of the campaign to train Iraqi security forces. The journalist Greg Jaffe, who accompanied the American general at the time, concluded that Petraeus's knowledge of Iraq was "astonishing." On any given morning, Petraeus might investigate the status of a neighborhood bank that the Shiite-controlled Finance Ministry had closed to punish Sunnis. A moment later, he would inquire about a downed electrical transmission tower outside of Baghdad or the status of an Iraqi commander he was eager to replace. As one observer commented, "Petraeus understood Iraq from the most granular level to the most strategic.... He was monumentally well-prepared for that job."[1]

Three years later, Petraeus moved from Iraq to Afghanistan, replacing General Stanley McChrystal as top American commander after McChrystal was swiftly dismissed by President Obama after a bombshell article in *Rolling Stone* magazine quoted the American general and his staff being highly critical of White House officials.[2] In Afghanistan, Petraeus often briefed reporters using a PowerPoint slide that illustrated his "Anaconda strategy," which in Iraq had entailed a relentless combination of military, economic, and political campaigns to annihilate the Islamic insurgency. In fact, while he readily admitted the two countries were different, Petraeus apparently talked with such fervor about his Iraq experience to make points about the best approach in Afghanistan that he drew eye rolls from seasoned Afghan hands.

Given that he had only hours to prepare for his Afghan assignment after his predecessor's snap resignation, perhaps Petraeus could be forgiven for relying on the Anaconda slide to guide his thinking in the latter case. Remarkably though, the busy Anaconda graphic that consisted of concentric circles and a dozen arrows remained a key part of Petraeus's briefing throughout his tour in Afghanistan. As the effort in Afghanistan continued to drag on, it is possible that his many positive experiences in Iraq actually led him to misjudge the Afghan war.

When Petraeus was in command in Iraq, the country was mired in a violent sectarian war between ethnic Sunni and Shiite forces. Mutilated corpses were ubiquitous on Baghdad streets. Residents blocked entry into their neighborhoods with debris and charred automobiles in an attempt to keep out suicide bombers and roving death squads. Petraeus successfully addressed this dire situation by placing his troops on the key lines between the warring factions. He also provided ammunition and money to more than 100,000 former Sunni insurgents, a group that had theretofore been a direct foe of U.S. forces but was now increasingly amenable to such incentives. Civilian deaths that had peaked at more than 3,500 a month dropped by more than 60 percent, a key improvement in Iraq's security situation at the time that helped legitimize President George W. Bush's controversial "surge" strategy.

In Afghanistan, by contrast, levels of violence were considerably lower than in Iraq, which led many of Petraeus's subordinate commanders to conclude that the rapacious national, regional, and local Afghan governments – and not the Taliban insurgency – were in many ways the main sticking points to prosecuting a successful counterinsurgency and nation-building effort. Petraeus faced a choice: he could attempt to reform the government by wresting power away from the most brutal provincial warlords or he could focus on improving security by targeting Taliban insurgents, an approach that entailed cooperating with the warlords' despised militias.

Following the Iraq playbook, Petraeus opted to go for security first, an approach that during his tenure produced only modest gains in the targeted southern regions. In some instances, Petraeus's embrace of the warlords may have even led villagers back into allegiance with the Taliban. One top American general recalled, "He seemed to think that if you killed enough [enemy fighters], that would be good enough. He brought that with him from Iraq."[3]

Just over a year after he arrived in Afghanistan in 2010, Petraeus left military service to become director of the Central Intelligence Agency.

During his own retirement ceremony in Fort Myers, Florida, Petraeus stood before hundreds of guests where he was recognized for his extraordinary thirty-seven-year military career. Admiral Michael Mullen, chairman of the Joint Chiefs of Staff, told his colleague, "You now stand among the giants, not just in our time, but of all time, joining the likes of Grant and Pershing and Marshall and Eisenhower as one of the great battle captains."[4] Petraeus's remarkable successes in the late, desperate stages of the Iraq war alone validate Mullen's claim about Petraeus's place in the pantheon of brilliant American military leaders. Yet his mixed record in Afghanistan demonstrates that even giants have a hard time learning the right lessons from the last dirty war as they fight the next.

TWO CENTURIES OF DIRTY WARS

From 1776 to the present, the United States has been engaged in irregular wars almost without interruption. This book examines the ways in which the United States learned – and failed to learn – across two centuries of fighting these wars. It considers the major cases, including the prolonged conflicts in Vietnam, Afghanistan, and Iraq, alongside lesser-known campaigns such as El Salvador in the 1980s, Greece in the late 1940s, and the Philippines in the 1950s, which have been largely neglected in our historical and political memory.[5]

Across cases new and old that constitute the American experience, this book explores the seemingly inexorable pendulum swings between pledging not to get into any more dirty wars and inevitably getting pulled back in, at which point we forget the lessons of the prior campaigns in the first place. At times, American officials and commanders learned the wrong lessons from prior conflicts. For example, the wrenching and far-from-decisive campaigns against elusive and lethal guerrilla forces in Iraq at the outset of the twenty-first century led to a renewed focus on counterinsurgency and nation-building in American strategic doctrine – a direction that brought some clarity and stability to the Iraq situation but may have, before our eyes, proved unsuitable for subsequent dirty wars. The apparent failure in Afghanistan of a similar U.S. counterinsurgency strategy to defeat, once again, an elusive and committed enemy after a decade of American involvement prompted yet another pendulum shift toward a more modest assessment of what this form of involvement in irregular warfare can achieve.

The book's first section addresses the early years of this story, including the American Revolutionary War, the Civil War, Indian pacification campaigns, the bitter experience of imperial pacification in the Philippines and Cuba, and "bandit chasing" in Mexico and Nicaragua in the early twentieth century. The focus then turns to the Cold War when the United States was either directly or indirectly involved in several dirty wars in Asia and Latin America as part of its protracted struggle "on every front" against the Soviet Union.[6] The book's last section looks at the American experience since September 11, 2001, a time that has included, in addition to the large, controversial wars in Iraq and Afghanistan, relatively overlooked dirty war engagements in Colombia, the Philippines, and elsewhere.

While the discussion of the American experience in dirty wars is cumulative, each section of the book is designed to stand alone so that readers with more interest in specific U.S. historical periods can access these chapters directly. The narrative of the American experience is interspersed with short *intermezzi* that focus on non-U.S. experiences that provide international historical context and additional insights.

Panjwai District, Kandahar Province, Afghanistan, March 11, 2012, the Tenth Year of the Taliban Insurgency against the United States and NATO

Before dawn, a heavily armed U.S. staff sergeant named Robert Bales quietly left the outpost of Camp Belambay in southern Afghanistan. Wearing night-vision goggles and traditional Afghan clothes over his combat fatigues, he walked a mile to a nearby village, where he massacred seventeen Afghan civilians, including nine children. Eleven of the victims were from the same family. Bales reportedly assembled most of the bodies, covering them with blankets before attempting to burn the corpses. He then returned to Camp Belambay and turned himself in.[7]

Bales, who had received numerous military decorations before the incident, was attached to a unit based at Joint Base Lewis McChord, a large army and air force installation near Tacoma, Washington. With more than a decade in the Army, he had served three tours of duty in Iraq and was deployed to Afghanistan for the first time in December 2011 as part of a village stabilization operation in which teams of Army Special Forces, supported by other troops, attempted to develop close relationships with village elders, organize local police units, and hunt down Taliban leadership. Panjai, located near the city of Kandahar, was the center of a U.S. military offensive in 2010 and had experienced heavy fighting. Bales's defense attorney contended that his client reported suffering from nightmares, flashbacks of war scenes, and persistent headaches after his multiple combat tours in Iraq – a severe case of post-traumatic stress disorder (PTSD), the condition with which many military veterans in the United States had become so painfully familiar.

The atrocities committed by Bales, which Afghan president Hamid Karzai denounced as an "inhumane act," were only the latest of a long string of incidents in which American soldiers, many of whom had behaved honorably and courageously over years of combat, had suddenly committed a heinous act or snapped into some out-of-control cruelty. Only a month after Bales's killing spree, for example, the bad news for American officials continued when the *Los Angeles Times* published a front-page photograph of a soldier from the U.S. Army's 82nd Airborne Division with a dead insurgent's hand on his shoulder. The insurgent reportedly died planting a bomb. The article reported that the photograph was one of several similar images of troops posing with the body parts of insurgents they had killed.[8]

Sand Creek, Near Fort Lyon, Colorado Territory, United States of America, November 29, 1864, the Fifty-third Year of the Intermittent Native American Insurgency West of the Mississippi River

On this November morning, a 700-man column of the Colorado Territory militia led by the aggressive Colonel John Chivington stormed the camp of Cheyenne chief Black Kettle. The surprise attack, known as the Sand Creek massacre, left 100 Cheyenne and Arapaho dead, at least two-thirds of whom were women and children. One of the American soldiers testified, "I saw the bodies of those lying there cut all to pieces, worse mutilated than any I ever saw before; the women cut all to pieces.... With knives; scalped; their brains knocked out; children two or three months old, all ages lying there, from sucking infants up to warriors.... By whom were they mutilated? By the United States troops."[9] Another witness observed, "Fingers and ears were cut off the bodies for the jewelry they carried. The body of White Antelope, lying solitary in a creek bed, was a prime target. Besides scalping him the soldiers cut off his nose, ears, and testicles – the last for a tobacco pouch."[10] Chivington's men returned later to steal horses and kill many of the wounded before they left the camp. They also allegedly dressed their weapons and gear with scalps and other body parts, including human fetuses; they displayed these "trophies" in Denver's Apollo Theater for the public to see.

Revelations about the Sand Creek massacre sparked a substantial public outcry back on the East Coast. Peace groups began to lobby

Washington to adopt more humane Indian policies. In 1870, abolitionist and social activist Wendell Phillips called three prominent American officers in the Indian Wars – George Custer, Phillip Henry Sheridan, and Eugene Baker – the "true savages on the great plains."[11]

VARIOUS LEVELS OF DIRTINESS

The Roger Bales and Sand Creek massacres, separated by 150 years, together serve as a chilling reminder that the United States has and will almost certainly continue to commit excesses in dirty wars. Indeed, the very nature of dirty wars often leads to excessive and even barbaric behavior, something that all participants, including democracies like the United States, are not immune from. Yet, contrary to what these two instances of apparent savagery suggest, the United States, where it has involved itself in dirty wars, has in fact done so on widely varying levels of engagement, and with various levels of commitment and dirtiness. In terms of levels of involvement, Vietnam in the 1960s and 1970s and Iraq and Afghanistan this century are conflicts that America has fought directly, with combat boots on the ground. At other times, though, American involvement in dirty wars has been by proxy or otherwise indirect, often entailing the provision of economic aid and military training and materiel, as was the case in Colombia in the first decade of the twenty-first century.

Likewise, in the instance of El Salvador in the 1980s, America was deeply involved in a dirty war but fought fairly "cleanly." On the other hand, examples such as the Indian removal campaigns and the war in the Philippines beginning in 1898 are stark examples of times when the United States fought "dirty" dirty wars, engaging in such ruthless tactics as forced population removal and direct targeting of civilians. In addition, in the more recent wars in Iraq and Afghanistan there was much talk about a "new kind of war" more able to avoid, say, civilian casualties. Yet these two wars were very much like the wars the United States has been fighting since its beginning.

The objective of this book is neither to condemn nor justify America's track record in dirty wars; rather, it is to examine their characteristic political dynamics in order to illuminate salient trends, lessons, and warnings. This book thus treats the "good, the bad, and the ugly" of the American experience in a form of warfare as controversial as it is constant – a history that continues to be written today and will likely continue to be written well into the future.

Introduction 7

CONTEXT AND DEFINITIONS

Irregular wars are generally considered the conflicts that include guerrilla insurrections, insurgencies, and counterinsurgencies. Irregular wars include all of the military and nation-building campaigns in which American forces have attempted to defeat elusive and informal foes as well as bolster friendly forces and governments. The concept of a class of warfare as "irregular" derives from the first internationally accepted definition of "regular" war in the Third Geneva Convention of 1949; that is, a war fought primarily between regular forces. According to the Convention, "regular armed forces" satisfy five criteria:

- Are commanded by a person (or persons) responsible for the decisions, movements, and actions of subordinates in matters relevant to the conflict
- Bear uniform markings or insignia that are recognizable from a distance
- Carry arms openly
- Conduct operations in accordance with the international laws and norms of war
- Act as representatives of states[12]

Broadly speaking, irregular warfare is the opposite of regular warfare. But suggesting contrasting qualities is not a definition, and indeed the international community's current understanding of what irregular warfare is has grave limitations. Irregular wars tend to differ from archetypal "regular" wars in one or more of the ways that the Geneva Conventions highlight. Irregular wars, therefore, are conducted by forces that generally

- Lack clear hierarchies of command
- Do not bear soldierly markings
- Do not carry weapons openly
- Do not fight according to the period's laws and norms of war
- Do not act as representatives of a particular state
- Do not display other familiar markers of conventional wars: official diplomatic engagement, formal declarations of war, formal surrenders, and signed peace treaties

For America, these irregular wars have involved a host of states and "non-state actors," including insurgent bands, civilian collaborators, and paramilitary forces. To be sure, these wars are not necessarily small-scale or brief, as was the case in the protracted campaigns in Vietnam and, more recently, Afghanistan; indeed, these two conflicts demanded U.S. attention and involvement for much longer than the two world wars. Afghanistan gained the distinction as the longest-running war in American history in 2010.

Moreover, as the Sand Creek and Roger Bales massacres illustrate, these types of wars tend to be, in a word, dirty. Irregular warfare often involves atrocities – or, in contemporary terms, human rights violations, crimes against humanity, and unjustified targeting of civilians. While massacres form the extreme and relatively rare instance of these abuses in the American experience, all of these irregular wars have some unsettling elements. In recent years, even though much attention has been given to the "surgical" tactics of remote drone strikes, quick-insertion special operations raids, and precision-guided munitions in Iraq and Afghanistan, counterinsurgency also has shown a much less clean side, as made abundantly clear by the grim reality of Roger Bales's rampage in Panjwai and the Abu Ghraib prison scandal in Iraq a decade earlier.

Taking this observation further, as demonstrated by the strong public reactions against the massacres, it is usually immensely difficult for the U.S. government to sustain support for such wars. Worse, these wars challenge America's self-image as a liberal democracy predicated on respect for human rights and the rule of law. Finally, and contrary to what we sometimes might assume, these irregular wars are ones that America tends to win – even if most of the attention goes to the occasional monumental defeats like Vietnam.

Although conflict of this sort is sometimes called "guerrilla warfare," this label is misleading in a couple of ways. As we will see, the term "guerrilla" generally refers to a set of tactics and strategies for overcoming the power disparity against a superior, often conventional, adversary. The term "irregular" is both more capacious and more accurate, in that it emphasizes the difference between this type of war and war involving established conventions such as uniforms and avoiding intentional civilian casualties that we consider "regular" war. One or more sides in an irregular war may deploy guerrilla tactics; or they may not.

At the same time, this book often uses dirty war as an even more vivid and expansive term for the kinds of conflicts it examines. Perhaps the value of referring to these conflicts as dirty wars instead of irregular warfare is that it instantly reminds us that these conflicts are not simply defined by their irregularity but also their greater tendency for controversy, opacity, and moral dilemmas.

CATEGORIZING IRREGULAR WARFARE

There are some problems with setting the category of conflicts we are dealing with up against prevailing norms or conventions of war in a given historical period. One is the assumption, often implied, that the conventions of warfare embody a moral consensus on acceptable and unacceptable types of conduct. Warfare that fails to satisfy this consensus is, by logical argument, irregular. More accurate is that the norms of war in any historical period are mutable, often contested – and only very recently in internationally accepted courts of law.

By the same right, it is not easy to think of a war that has satisfied all the conventions of law or morality that prevail in a particular era. But does that make every war irregular? Another problem is that there are times when irregular conflicts – those that fail overwhelmingly or entirely to satisfy the prevailing norms – actually *are* the norm, as in the post–Cold War era.

An attempt to classify conflict in rigid academic terms has merit, but we must take into account the dynamic, convoluted, and ever-evolving nature of warfare. A more useful approach is to recognize that war occurs across a spectrum, extending from the unconventional to the conventional and encompassing a vast array of tactics, strategies, and approaches that, even within the same conflict, can intertwine and co-exist. This kind of thinking can help to distinguish the differences *between* conflicts but can also be used to examine the dynamics *within* a conflict, as a single conflict will often operate at different levels of the spectrum simultaneously.

Both regular and irregular conflicts can in some cases be considered "total," when one or more of the warring factions fights using a full mobilization of domestic society and places national survival and victory over all else (including questions of morality and the laws of war), as was the case for most countries involved in World War II. Thus, to provide a contrast, World War II was a total war and largely a regular war while the Persian Gulf War in 1991 was a regular but not total war.

The line separating regular warfare and dirty war is thin and often not clearly visible. World War II, for example, is often remembered as being, despite its horrible lethality and destruction, a classic case of a regular total war since the fighting took place between conventional forces fighting in conventional manners. Yet this potentially simple interpretation overlooks the fact that all the key belligerents conducted themselves "irregularly." Japanese and German troops, for example, frequently placed booby traps on dead bodies, shot medics, or pretended to give up and then jumped aside while hidden guns showered bullets at Allied troops moving in to receive the surrender.[13] The atomic bombs dropped on the Japanese cities of Hiroshima and Nagasaki instantly killed 105,000 people – mostly civilians.[14]

Another key issue is that some conflicts have been at once regular and irregular. The long and bloody war in postcolonial Vietnam that started in the late 1950s and ended nearly twenty years later in 1975 is such a case. While it often manifested the characteristics of a dirty war, Vietnam was primarily an international war between three recognized nation states – Hanoi's Democratic Republic of Vietnam (DRV), aided by the Soviet Union and China; Saigon's Republic of Vietnam (ROV), supported by the United States and other Asia-Pacific allies; and the United States. China was also a fourth de facto participant in the 1960s, when it sent hundreds of thousands of troops and support personnel to aid the DRV war effort.

American involvement in Vietnam began in the late 1950s as an irregular war between the U.S.-backed government in Saigon and largely southern irregular forces (known as the Vietcong) supplied by North Vietnam. Following France's ignominious defeat in its protracted campaign to maintain its colonial possessions in Indochina in the early 1950s, North Vietnam, America, and China came into the war heavily in the following decade when both regular and irregular warfare escalated, primarily in the South. The war ended between 1973 and 1975 as a largely conventional battle between the DRV and ROV. Vietnam was a special case of regular/irregular war. Although Vietcong guerrillas aided the DRV cause substantially, in the final analysis America and its allies lost a largely regular war against a determined DRV foe and its two main backers, the Soviet Union and China.

ZEITGEIST-LIKE MOTIVES OF A PARTICULAR ERA

By examining a large number of American episodes plus counterpoints from other countries, this book aims to rebalance our understanding of what can be learned from two centuries of American involvement in unconventional military campaigns. The United States has an extensive history of both fighting irregular wars abroad and dealing with their consequences at home. While the lessons of past conflicts have shaped the responses to each new war, every conflict brings unique challenges and successes that add to the U.S. experience with irregular warfare. These challenges and successes – at home and abroad – do more than just add to

Introduction

the unfolding narrative; they also force a reconsideration of America's self-perception as a noble world power and nudge the U.S. military's institutional "center of gravity" – at times toward and at other times away from preparing for further irregular war fighting.

Casual and professional observers have often made the mistake of concluding that all we need to know about American involvement in these irregular wars is contained in the experience of previous conflicts (overwhelmingly Vietnam); too quickly the lessons from one conspicuous historical anecdote are cut and pasted onto a present-day conflict. To give one example of this tendency, during the first year of American involvement in Afghanistan in 2001, the *New York Times* ran 245 stories that mentioned Afghanistan and Vietnam. During the first year in Iraq, it published 584 stories mentioning Iraq and Vietnam.[15]

Yet, while history and the particular histories of the more sensational episodes are vitally important to our narrative and national psyche, a more robust review of history shows they are by no means the entire story of the American experience. For example, just as significant are the ways in which past lessons have failed to prepare Americans for the next conflict.

When studying the American experience in dirty wars, it is tempting to look for a meta-explanation for why the United States has been involved in these maddening and often seemingly undesired conflicts. The distinguished foreign policy scholar Gideon Rose asserted, "The fact is that over the centuries ... the United States has been engaged in nothing less than an ongoing campaign of global pacification – clearing, holding and building in region after region around the world."[16]

One potential problem with this interpretation is that in attempting to reduce the American experience to an ongoing campaign, we risk oversimplifying the myriad factors that have driven U.S. actions over the past two centuries. In addition to the historic tendency for America to become involved in dirty wars, for example, there have also been important isolationist and anti-imperialist movements that have shaped the American experience in dirty wars – especially the desire to extricate U.S. troops from these conflicts.

Noted scholar Dominic Tierney writes that the scenario in which Americans are comfortable fighting is in fact quite narrow: "the enemy must be a state and not an insurgency, and we need to march on the adversary's capital and topple the government." When American leaders deviate from sticking to these "transformational crusades" in conventional war, Tierney contends that the connective tissue binding together public support tears apart, an insight that "explains why people back some conflicts but not others, how the United States fights, why Washington wins and loses, and how Americans remember and learn from war."[17]

While Tierney might be correct that American leaders and the broader public prefer the cleanliness of more conventional wars (e.g., storming the beaches of Normandy; a lightning-swift invasion of Iraq to topple Saddam Hussein in 2003), there are numerous cases – both old and new – in which American involvement in irregular warfare has neither failed nor been unpopular. In addition, the line between fighting the glorious conventional war and the irregular dirty war can be blurred, as the 2003 Iraq War demonstrated when within months of the initial U.S. invasion, the occupation turned highly unconventional.

A more modest but certainly accurate argument is that for reasons largely specific to the individual cases themselves, the United States has made repeated conscious and unconscious decisions that have led the country into irregular wars – often due to the zeitgeist-like motives of a particular era (e.g., Manifest Destiny in the nineteenth century; anticommunism during the Cold War; or antiterrorism in the decade after September 11, 2001). It has then been forced to deal with the consequences of those decisions in very different ways in each case. Thus, contrary to what casual observers tend to argue, history does not repeat itself every time the United States finds itself in a messy irregular conflict: there has never been, nor is there likely ever to be, "another Vietnam."

Past experiences in irregular warfare do of course influence future decisions and events. Once a war has begun, similarities emerge between new military campaigns and old, which, somewhat paradoxically, American officials and military commanders often overlook. But it is the unique factors of each particular era that define the greater part of the nature of America's involvement in these sorts of conflicts.

Over the past two-and-a-half centuries, many observers in every era have contended that the best way for the United States to avoid pitfalls in the future is to simply stay out of these sorts of ill-defined conflicts. Yet the very nature of America's military might, its unique leadership role in the world, its political and military leaders' willingness to exercise its power, and the inclination of less powerful adversaries to wage irregular wars against it have made it difficult for the United States to avoid this sort of warfare. Rather than insisting that Americans do not or cannot fight this kind of irregular war, we would be better served by considering how we can do so as cleanly and successfully as possible.

AN AMERICAN WAY OF DIRTY WAR?

As one might expect, examples taken from the American experience reveal that fighting – and, more so, winning – all types of wars is extraordinarily complex, frustrating, controversial, and bloody. But the nature of dirty wars adds an extra layer of complexity. What is readily apparent in dirty wars is that failure is painfully tangible while success is often amorphous, a vicious cycle that makes winning these conflicts an elusive goal. In fact, in some instances dirty wars that eventually produce relatively optimal outcomes are not even reported as victories at the time.[18]

Successfully fighting these wars often entails striking a critical balance between military victory and politics; how the balance falls depends on the war. In addition, regardless of military strategy in the field, the historical record suggests that how these wars are portrayed (or not) at home and abroad strongly influences their outcome.

What American leaders have often forgotten at their peril is that, by definition, dirty wars are dirty: civilians are disproportionately targeted, the line between combatant and innocent is often intentionally blurred, and there is a great temptation to "fight fire with fire" against foes who refuse to play by the "rules" of warfare. Time and again, the outcomes of these wars have been nebulous, domestic support for them has been precarious, and in them American forces have committed atrocities.

America's status as a democracy only serves to make fighting – and, to a greater degree, winning – these irregular wars even harder. The entrenched tradition of American exceptionalism complicates this issue even more. America's political rhetoric surrounding conflict claims that the country only fights wars selflessly and for the "right" reasons like promoting democracy, championing human rights, and combating terrorism. This exceptionalism habit begs the question as to whether it becomes even more damaging to the American psyche to fight dirty wars – which the United States tends to do often.

Some observers have argued that democracies like the United States are unable to unleash the levels of violence and brutality necessary to ensure victory in dirty wars because they are restricted by domestic constitutions and social injunctions against aggressive military action.[19] With a free press, for example, journalists shed light on the necessary violence and excessive atrocities inherent in these conflicts, thus (often rightly) undermining public support.[20] In the American experience, a "discouraged electorate" has proved to be detrimental to the ability to wage these irregular wars.[21] This in some instances has limited the scope of America's military engagements;

but it has also sometimes had the effect of protracting dirty wars and making them politically messy, creating backlash among those who prefer wars to be "quick, dirty, and violent," as one Army Special Forces veteran of Vietnam and El Salvador commented in 1983.[22]

Noted military historian Russell Weigley wrote during the height of the Vietnam War in the 1960s, "Guerrilla warfare is so incongruous to the methods and habits of a stable and well-to-do-society that the American Army has tended to regard it as abnormal and to forget about it whenever possible. Each new experience with irregular warfare has required then, that appropriate techniques be learned all over again."[23] Weigley's admonition about a particular conflict nearly half a century ago leads us to a central premise of this book about American history more broadly over the past two centuries: even when it is possible to do so, the United States does not properly learn from its involvement in dirty wars. We now turn to the broad historical and philosophical roots of irregular warfare that form the foundation for our central task of exploring the American legacy in such conflicts.

2

Irregular Warfare 101

Victory through policy is as much a mark of the good general as victory by the sword.

– Julius Caesar[1]

If one side uses force without compunction, undeterred by the bloodshed it involves, while the other side refrains, the first will gain the upper hand. That side will force the other to follow suit; each will drive its opponent toward extremes, and the only limiting factors are the counterpoises inherent in war. This is how the matter must be seen. It would be futile – even wrong – to try and shut one's eyes to what war really is from sheer distress at its brutality.

– Prussian military philosopher, Carl von Clausewitz, 1820s[2]

DEFINING COUNTERINSURGENCY, INSURGENCY, GUERRILLA WARFARE, AND TERRORISM

Most contemporary discussions of irregular warfare concentrate on three core concepts – counterinsurgency, insurgency, and guerrilla warfare – and this book proceeds in that convention. Let's begin by setting out definitions of each of these concepts. A counterinsurgency, quite simply, is defined as all measures adopted to suppress an insurgency. When we say a state is engaged in counterinsurgency, we generally mean that it is attempting to use some combination of political, administrative, military, psychological, and civic actions to maintain the status quo against an insurgent force that is trying to upend that order. To cite a well-known example, Fulgencio Batista's regime in late-1950s Cuba waged a counterinsurgency to maintain its ascendancy while confronted with Fidel Castro's ragtag rebel band in the Sierra Maestra mountains. Counterinsurgent forces can usually count on superior armies and overall might; however, they are not always able to count on the support of the civilian population – often a crucial factor in the outcome of this class of conflicts. In both political and military terms, counterinsurgencies tend to adapt to the nature of the insurgent threat. That is, the insurgents tend to determine the "rules of the game" and the style of fighting. Or, as one military theorist has surmised, "[as] insurrection changes, so does counterinsurgency." Almost by definition, then, one must first understand an insurgency before understanding its counterinsurgent response.

In the same spirit, we should outline a conception of insurgency and the means by which it is carried out. There is often considerable confusion as to exactly what insurgency and guerrilla warfare involve, how these phenomena have evolved throughout history, and to what extent they overlap. An insurgency is often but certainly not always an organized attempt to overthrow a central government or state by subversion or force of arms. The problem, however, is that, given the murky reality of this sort of warfare, it is often difficult to categorize a particular conflict objectively and accurately. For example, at what point does the armed resistance of an antifederal government "militia" in the U.S. state of Idaho qualify as an insurgency? Are these armed groups simply criminals or "bandits"? And who gets to decide this? Indeed, much of the labeling of insurgent and counterinsurgent forces is inherently political. The oft-quoted aphorism that "one man's terrorist is another man's freedom fighter" is especially apt for understanding the inherent political nature of classifying insurgencies.

No matter how or if we label certain groups as insurgents, insurgency is the most common form of warfare in history, something that remains true today. One scholarly database maintained since 1963 cites 464 wars between 1816 and the end of the twentieth century, of which only 79 (or 17 percent) were "conventional," defined as conflicts between countries' regular armed forces. The other 385 conflicts (or 83 percent) were either civil wars or insurgencies.[3] Thus, we must remember that insurgencies are not uncommon; rather, they are "against the rules."[4] As one contemporary observer has written, insurgencies, like cancers, exist in thousands of forms. Thus, the treatments to eliminate them range considerably as well. What history has painfully taught practitioners is that a single panacea for the insurgency malady is as "unrealistic as the idea of a universal cure for cancer."[5]

It is important to remember that insurgents are not synonymous with terrorists if we define the latter as targeting noncombatants in order to sow fear in a population for political ends.⁶ Insurgents certainly resort to terrorism, which often earns them the label "terrorist." Think of the case of the Revolutionary Armed Forces of Colombia (or FARC) that for decades was labeled an insurgency until it began carrying out attacks on civilians, at which point it became (at least in the eyes of critical observers) a terrorist organization. As we will see in chilling detail, there is nothing to keep counterinsurgent or conventional forces from using terror as well.⁷

THE LONGEVITY ADVANTAGE

What is also particularly fascinating about insurgencies is that, on the whole, they seldom succeed. While history celebrates the stunning victories of guerrilla insurgents led by inimitable figures such as Cuba's Fidel Castro, China's Mao Zedong, and Vietnam's Ho Chi Minh, the record is replete with insurgencies that were wiped out by counterinsurgent forces. When these inferior forces do succeed, we often consider their victories "revolutions" because of the dramatic political, social, and economic shifts that they effect. And often, external assistance to the guerrillas plays an indispensable part in promoting the rare insurgent victory. More commonly, however, successful guerrilla insurrections allow the rebels to break away from a central state to form separatist governments or autonomous regions. In this sense, we can define insurgency by its objectives and guerrilla warfare as the means of accomplishing them.

Insurgent groups often, but certainly not exclusively, pursue their objectives through unconventional military tactics to gain advantages over the forces of the more powerful state. It is important to note that "guerrilla" is a relatively novel term that emerged from a particular conflict (the Peninsular War of the early nineteenth century, discussed later) and therefore carries with it associations specific to that context. In contemporary usage, guerrilla warfare refers to a subset of irregular strategies and tactics, usually attributed to the deployment of a small, mobile force that aims to attrite or "bleed" a larger, more cumbersome force through small-scale skirmishes and harassing maneuvers. That said, guerrilla warfare should be understood neither to exhaust the full universe of irregular strategies and tactics nor to describe a static set of warfare tactics. Guerrilla fighting tends to change alongside developments in technology, across geographic regions, and according to counterinsurgency responses. For the sake of parsimony, though, this book at times uses the term "guerrilla warfare" as shorthand for the kinds of irregular strategies and tactics that insurgents commonly employ.

Most of the time, guerrilla warfare emerges as a matter of pragmatism, after an insurgent group realizes that more conventional forms of fighting are ineffective against a superior foe. That is, guerrilla warfare is rarely the preference of the weaker force; instead, it is dictated by their very weakness.[8] Thus, guerrillas deploy tactics that minimize their acute vulnerabilities. Guerrillas tend to be highly mobile, avoiding direct military contact with their more powerful foes. They often lack adequate arms and proper uniforms. They can be indistinguishable from their civilian counterparts, not least because they attempt to compensate for their inferior numbers by enlisting – sometimes coercively – the support of the civilian population. Guerrillas also often enjoy the "longevity advantage," meaning that unlike the "expeditionary" counterinsurgents pursuing them, they are often indigenous to the area in question and will be present in this area once the conflict is over – something local civilians readily understand.[9] This explains why counterinsurgency doctrine, in Iraq and Afghanistan in particular, cites the need to build and train local security forces as a central pillar of a successful counterinsurgency. While expeditionary forces will often have an exit date in mind, they must leave behind local allies that can match the insurgent's level of long-term investment and outlook.

A further hallmark of guerrilla fighters is that they tend to have charismatic leaders. With the high risk of death and frequently intolerable living conditions, a charismatic leader is often necessary to inspire a band of fighters to commit to what appears to be a futile and lethal cause.

A final important characteristic of guerrilla groups is that, contrary to what is sometimes assumed, they do not necessarily represent some ideological "evil." Individuals and groups across the ideological spectrum resort to guerrilla war when conditions merit. To be sure, there have been nefarious groups such as the savage Khmer Rouge in Cambodia in the 1970s and the nihilist Shining Path insurgency in Peru a decade later. But there are also cases, such as anti-Nazi partisans in World War II and American patriots resisting the British during the American War of Independence, that history tends to view favorably.[10]

IRREGULAR WARFARE IN HISTORICAL PERSPECTIVE

The stronger side usually wins; the best strategy, therefore is to be strong. – Clausewitz[11]

Given that weaker groups have battled more powerful groups since antiquity, it is not surprising that guerrilla warfare has been around for thousands of years. The Hebrew scriptures, for example, detail the efforts of

Joshua, who led a "guerrilla" band against the more powerful city-state of Jericho in modern-day Palestine. In fact, much of the Hebrew experience during biblical times involved irregular civilian armies fighting against superior forces.[12] (Perhaps unsurprisingly, guerrilla wars have a tendency to break out when imperial powers attempt to conquer and rule other societies.) Alexander the Great (356–23 BC) met serious guerrilla opposition during his conquests in Central Asia.[13]

Another salient case occurred roughly 2,000 years ago in what is today southern Spain, where the Phoenicians and Carthaginians had ruled for centuries. By 200 BC, conquering Rome had gained control of the region's major towns. But, as is often the case, military superiority and control of urban centers did not ensure the pacification or submission of rural populations. The Romans were able to hold the cities but confronted bitter resistance in the countryside. The more powerful Romans considered the local resistors to be barbarians; they dealt with them through savage means.[14] And in what is also painfully common in irregular warfare, both sides committed horrible atrocities.

The earliest known codification of guerrilla-style principles, however, was conceived far from the Mediterranean. The military philosopher Sun Tzu is considered one of the seminal thinkers on what we now call guerrilla warfare. His treatise, *The Art of War*, written around 500 BC when Chinese warlords were in constant conflict with each other, is best known for its pithy maxims, many of which provide critical insights for weaker guerrilla fighters. One example is the idea that "all warfare is based on deception" while another advises generals to "feign disorder, and crush him."[15] In the nineteenth century, British Field Marshal Lord Roberts of Kandahar spoke for many counterinsurgency commanders when he commented from Central Asia that "many of Sun Tzu Wu's maxims are perfectly applicable to the present day. The people of this country [Britain] would do well to take heart."[16]

Perhaps Sun Tzu's most crucial and innovative contribution was the idea that sometimes the most stunning victories occur without engagement in combat. "To win one hundred victories in one hundred battles is not the acme of skill. To subdue the enemy without fighting is the acme of skill."[17] For weaker foes, this means avoiding the sort of battles that expose your glaring weaknesses in personnel and arms. Sun Tzu writes, "If equally matched, we can offer battle; if slightly inferior in numbers, we can avoid the enemy; if quite unequal in every way, we can flee from him. Hence, though an obstinate fight may be made by a small force, in the end it must be captured by a larger force."[18] Sun Tzu also believed that deception was a critical component in keeping your foe off balance: "Thus one who is skilled at keeping the enemy on the move maintains deceitful appearances, according to which the enemy will act. By holding out habits, he keeps him on the march; then with a body of picked men he lies in wait for him."[19]

Sun Tzu's insights continue to resonate for the simple fact that they seem applicable to so many conflicts across history. As we will see, the twentieth century was a veritable hotbed for guerrilla insurgencies. Yet many of the supposed insights of modern "guerrilla philosophers" such as Mao or Argentine revolutionary Ernesto "Che" Guevara are mostly updates on Sun Tzu's timeless observations. Sun Tzu's perspicacity is worth considering in its own right; yet his influence on modern guerrilla leaders is even more salient given the lives and treasure lost and gained in these sorts of revolutionary wars.

THE SPANISH ULCER

Napoleon's incursion into Spain in 1808 – and the unconventional conflict it provoked – exemplifies guerrilla warfare. It is also the conflict that coined the term "guerrilla"; the diminutive of *guerra* (war) denotes its irregular nature. By 1807, Napoleon had won crucial military victories allowing him to gain control of virtually the entire European continent. But Britain remained his most lethal rival. To deny the British a strategic foothold in continental Europe, the French emperor wanted to close all ports to the British. Napoleon subsequently negotiated a dubious treaty with Spain that gave his troops an "access route" through the Iberian Peninsula.[20]

Napoleon took advantage of internal divisions within Spanish political society. In late November 1807, a 25,000-man French force commanded by General Jean-Andoche Junot – nicknamed "the Tempest" for his violent and courageous behavior – crossed into Spain; about a week later and after a brutal 300-mile march, Junot and his men entered Lisbon. Back in Spain, many Spaniards initially saw Napoleon's incursion as a welcome opportunity to remove their despised ruler, King Charles IV; Charles quickly abdicated the throne to his son, Prince Ferdinand. But sensing a strategic advantage, Charles appealed to Napoleon to intervene to restore him to power. Napoleon, for his part, had other plans than simply replacing one Spanish monarch with another. In a classic case of nepotism, Napoleon forced Ferdinand to abdicate, ostensibly in favor of the return of Charles IV, before declaring his brother, Joseph, to be King of Spain.

Napoleon's machinations sparked a bitter response among the Spanish population. Among other miscalculations, Napoleon and Joseph underestimated the loyalty of Spain's conservative *campesinos* (peasants) to their feudal lords and priests. In hindsight, it is clear that the conditions for an anti-French revolt were in place. The Spanish *campesinos* were historically xenophobic, so the arrival of French troops did little to win them over to Joseph's side. This anti-French sentiment persisted despite Joseph's relatively enlightened reforms – reforms that otherwise might have appealed to a Spanish population that for centuries had been exploited by the Catholic Church. For example, in 1808 Joseph presented a draft constitution that offered an independent judiciary, free press, and the abolition of the feudal privileges of the church and landowners. Yet, instead of supporting these reforms, the *campesinos* obeyed the priests, who called on them to fight the foreign invaders.[21] The Spaniards' loyalty to the Catholic Church led Napoleon to refer to the guerrillas as "bandits led by monks."[22] In turn, many Spaniards considered Napoleon to be the devil incarnate.

Note that even in this early instance of irregular warfare, each side's naming of the other had important political ramifications. That one of the world's most technologically advanced and best organized armies labeled its opponents "bandits" underscored the asymmetry of the conflict and won Napoleon a certain degree of domestic political support during the conflict. On the other hand, the Spanish resistance's labeling of the French as unwanted invaders – and promulgating this label through rhetoric, media, and propaganda – helped to galvanize public support around the anti-French movement. This art of labeling, as we will see, endures as a significant component of insurgencies and counterinsurgencies, on both political and military-strategic levels.

By the end of 1808, French forces routed the poorly led and unpopular Spanish army.[23] Then in early 1809, the French defeated a British army that had attempted to support the fledgling Spanish forces. Napoleon mistakenly declared the "Spanish business" to be over despite the fact that loosely organized anti-French bands continued to hamper the invaders.[24] Meanwhile, Spain's exiled monarchy met in the port city of Cádiz to discuss what to do about the French occupiers and Joseph's illegitimate rule. They called for the establishment of "guerrillas," a new sort of militia that would continue to fight the French. Now the effective Spanish tactic against the French had a name.

Ruthless and fanatic, the guerrillas started out with around 8,000 fighters, a number that ultimately swelled to 35,000–50,000. The Spanish guerrillas were an eclectic horde of priests, landowners, and *campesinos* that began to harass the French forces incessantly. The heaviest fighting took place in the regions of Navarre, Catalonia, and Aragon. As the Romans had experienced in Spain 1,600 years before, the French were able to hold the towns, but little else. The guerrillas, organized in small, independent units, also forced the French to use large numbers of troops to protect convoys. In fact, in the early phases of the conflict the French deployed around 200 cavalrymen to protect one courier carrying correspondence from one town to another. A few years later, the French were using 90,000 troops to keep the vital Burgos to Bayonne roadway open. In a setback to the French that sent shockwaves across the capitals of Europe, at the Battle of Bailén in 1808 the French surrendered roughly 18,000 men, a stunning defeat for Europe's most powerful military.[25]

By 1810, the combination of guerrillas, Spain's regular army, and British troops was able to pin down a French army of 350,000 men. Soon after, Napoleon began to draw drown his troops in Spain to send them to the Russian theater. As occurred with the Americans in Vietnam, the Soviets in Afghanistan, and numerous other episodes, Spanish guerrilla activity killed French morale in Spain. Desperate to turn the tide, the French responded with severe measures. In classical counterinsurgency fashion, the French attempted to defeat the guerrillas by denying them support and sustenance from the civilian population. They introduced oaths of allegiance and banned public meetings and holidays. In 1810, French commanders issued a decree that four guerrillas would be hanged for every Frenchman killed and that civilians would be substituted if guerrillas were not available.[26] The strategy anticipated harrowingly the dirty war practices characteristic of many twentieth-century counterinsurgencies.

But the French were not alone in resorting to dirty war. The Spanish irregular fighters committed their share of abuses in their effort to expel the foreign invaders. For those suspected of collaborating with the French, punishments of torture or burning at the stake were common. The guerrilla bands killed an estimated 30,000 suspected collaborators. In a taste of what the invading forces were up against, French general Mathieu Dumas wrote about the insurgents: "These men are brigands; they kill us when we march alone. I shall always remember how I was afflicted with great anxieties; every day I saw the murder of several French men, and I traveled over this assassins' countryside as warily as if it were a volcano."[27] Another French commander, General Gouvion St. Cyr, wrote:

Ready for all sacrifices, free from "soft" needs or prejudices ... they formed irregular corps, chose their leaders, operated by whim, attacked anywhere that numbers or conditions favored them, fled without shame when they were not the strongest, and disappeared by a combined dispersion.... In the long term, such a system of implacable hostility must suffice to destroy the most numerous and valiant of armies, obliged as they were to fritter their strength away in mobile columns and convoy escorts.[28]

This account could have described any number of guerrilla groups throughout history. True to the portrait, between 1808 and 1814 the Spanish guerrillas inflicted debilitating blow after debilitating blow upon the French, leading some historians to refer to this campaign as Napoleon's "Spanish ulcer." Yet at the end of the day, it was the formidable force of British regulars under the command of Arthur Wellesley, the future Duke of Wellington, that brought the French army to its knees in Spain. After Wellington retook Lisbon, Napoleon was forced to recall 200,000 troops from central Europe to help lance this ulcer. When it was finally over, the French lost a stunning 180,000 men while the insurgents lost a fraction of that with around 25,000 dead. Spain did not finish Napoleon, but it did inflict more losses than the devastating Russian campaign.

Wellington's intervention into the Peninsular War probably was the decisive factor in the French defeat in Spain, at least in terms of the opposition Napoleon and his generals faced there. Thus, a key historical insight: guerrilla forces seldom win without the assistance of outsiders. Yet, though Wellington has received much credit for his Iberian operations, he was well aware that his success owed much to the guerrilla bands that so relentlessly harassed French forces.

ON WAR

Historians may debate the geopolitical outcomes of the Napoleonic wars for centuries to come. What is certain, though, is that they produced one of the world's most venerated theorists of warfare, Carl von Clausewitz, who fought against Napoleon in France and Prussia. Clausewitz never completed his seminal work, *On War*, written between 1815 and 1830, yet its impact on Western military thinking is immense. His reflections focused mainly on traditional warfare, which dominated the international arena at the time of his writing. Yet his observations on the nature of war have nonetheless influenced scores of insurgent and counterinsurgent strategists. For Clausewitz, the key question was not so much how best to wage war but rather what exactly the phenomenon and essence (in German, *Wesen*) of war was.[29] That is, to what purpose do states engage in such a costly and often devastating endeavor as war?

The unwavering answer, the Prussian strategist contended, was that war is an extension of what he calls "policy" – which we may also depict as a country's national interests. Given the horrors of combat, which he describes with facility and experience, national leaders tend to pursue war only as a necessary "means" to achieve broader "policy" ends. Thus, Clausewitz believed, war becomes "an act of force to compel our enemy to do our will."[30] Force was only "the means of war; to impose our will upon the enemy is its object."[31]

Apart from his extensive treatment of traditional warfare as it was fought at the time, Clausewitz had been fascinated by the way poorly equipped peasant "armies" effectively harassed the retreating French army after its failed Russian campaign. Buffeted by geography, climate, and the strong will of the Russian people, among other factors, Napoleon's armies of roughly 600,000 at the start of the campaign dropped to only 20,000 at its end.[32] Clausewitz's observations of this episode helped him to develop his theory of the "defensive strategy," a radical departure from the military philosophies at the time that emphasized *l'offensive à l'outrance* (offensive at all costs). For Clausewitz, a strong defense was strictly temporary due to its having a "passive purpose," meaning that it should be "abandoned as soon as [armies] are strong enough to pursue a positive objective [e.g., conquest]."[33] In the twentieth century, Mao and other revolutionaries turned the "defensive strategy" theory into what they called "prolonged warfare." Rather than focusing their energies on positive objectives that conventional forces could surely dominate, these guerrillas found strength in wars of exhaustion that would lead conventional forces to cease operations, withdraw, and ultimately give up

Clausewitz also emphasized the strategic role that militias – irregular forces almost by definition – can play in war. "They are not supposed to pulverize the core but to nibble at the shell and around the edges," he wrote. As a peripheral force, Clausewitz argued, popular insurrections must remain "within the framework of a war conducted by the regular army and coordinated in one all-encompassing plan" with conventional tactics and strategies tackling key military operations and objectives. Emphasizing this cooperation, Clausewitz saw the ideal operating role of insurrections to be "in areas just outside the theatre of war – where the invader will not appear in strength – in order to deny him this area altogether. Thunder clouds of this type should build up all around the invader the farther he advances.... The flames will spread like a brush fire."[34] As historical experiences have demonstrated, the ability for militias, guerrillas, and insurgents to continually frustrate a conventional opponent, through tactics that aimed to "irritate" rather than dominate, allowed for unconventional victories over opponents with greater traditional military strength.

Albeit brief, Clausewitz's discussion of the "people in arms" presents several critical insights into the role of insurgencies in traditional warfare. Based upon his observations of these popular uprisings as "nebulous," "elusive," and built on "small detachments," Clausewitz highlighted the irregular nature of a style of warfare that included not only popular support but also popular involvement.[35] Clausewitz understood the critical role that the domestic population can play in supporting a war effort, both in terms of morale and materiel.[36] In his view, a key condition for the success of insurgent movements was that "the national character must be suited to that type [irregular] of war," suggesting that insurgencies flourish among scattered populations that provide willing support in both word and deed to the political cause of the uprising.[37]

Eerily foreshadowing a Cold War–era maxim about guerrilla warfare, Clausewitz argued that an insurgency wins a war by not losing. Expanding his point, Clausewitz contended that warring parties make peace when victory is impossible and the costs of continued fighting are too high. Specifically, an insurgency's victory lies in the "retreat of the army ... no matter how complete the defeat of a state."[38]

In this way, Clausewitz hinted at the comparative advantage of waging irregular wars against conventional forces: while traditional armies demand decisive and clear victories, insurgencies and guerrillas need only succeed in enduring warfare without being utterly decimated. Thus, while their relative strength, access to materiel, and ability to conquer territory may pale in comparison to the strongest conventional military, an insurgency's ability to endure at even the most meager levels of support translates to an ability to protract conflict and exhaust the opponent. Writing roughly 150 years later, Henry Kissinger commented, "The conventional army loses if it does not win. The guerrilla wins if he does not lose."[39] Interestingly, though, we will see at least some examples where guerrillas in fact lost by not losing and the conventional armies won by not winning.

SMALL WARS

Theories about how to fight guerrilla wars have been matched by theories of how to defeat guerrillas. In the late nineteenth century, the British strategist C. E. Callwell served in the Boer War and other British colonial conflicts.⁴⁰ He drew on the British Empire's experience in myriad colonial wars to write an influential "how-to" manual on counterinsurgency warfare. Many of Callwell's conclusions still form the core of contemporary counterinsurgency doctrine. For example, he urges that counterinsurgency success is much more than military victory: "Expeditions to put down a revolt are not put in motion merely to bring about a temporary cessation of hostilities. Their purpose is to ensure a lasting peace."⁴¹ Callwell divided the campaigns into three categories – campaigns of conquest and annexation, campaigns of pacification to suppress insurrections, and punitive campaigns intended as retaliation for certain offenses.⁴² He knew all too well what conventional troops faced in such dirty wars: "Guerrilla war is what the regular armies always have to dread, and when this is directed by a leader with a genius for war, an effective campaign becomes well-nigh impossible."

To defeat the insurgents, Callwell recommends that the counterinsurgent force must become more irregular itself: "The guerrilla mode of war must in fact be met by an abnormal system of strategy and tactics. The great principle that forms the basis of the art of war remains – the combination of initiative with energy; but this is applied in special form. The utmost vigor and decision must be displayed in harassing the enemy and in giving him no rest."⁴³

The U.S. Marine Corps duplicated Callwell's approach in the early 1940s; later, in 2006, the U.S. Army and Marine Corps brought the genre into the twenty-first century with the publication of the widely received *Counterinsurgency Field Manual* when the Iraq War was raging.⁴⁴ All such "manuals" represent attempts by conventional militaries to learn from past wars and, by extension, past mistakes. Indeed, "learning" from what went right and what went wrong in previous contacts greatly determines how militaries will fight their next war, and counterinsurgency is no exception. With this learning process in mind, we now turn to the irregular tactics and strategies that defined much of the war that gave birth to the United States of America.

PART ONE

THE AMERICAN REVOLUTION TO CHASING SANDINO, 1776–1930s

3

The American Revolution

> The cursed [American Patriot] rebels came upon us, killed, and took every soul... and so my dear friends I bid you farewell for I am started to the warm country.
>
> – Last entry in a [pro-British] Loyalist's diary found on the battlefield, King's Mountain, South Carolina, 1780[1]

The summer of 1780 was a harrowing one for American forces in the South. On May 12, Major General Benjamin Lincoln of the Continental Army surrendered Charleston, South Carolina, after two weeks of nearly constant bombardment by the British; the assault employed several tons of hotshot – superheated cannonballs – that left large swathes of the city in ashes. Then, on May 29, a force of 350 Continental Army soldiers under Abraham Buford met 150 Loyalists and British regulars led by the legendary British cavalryman, Banastre Tarleton, near Lancaster, South Carolina. In what later became known in British reports as the Battle of Waxhaws and in American history as the "Waxhaws Massacre," the Americans suffered 113 killed, 53 imprisoned, and 150 so badly wounded they had to be left behind. By August the American forces were on their heels, and many observers believed the American cause in the South would not survive the winter. On August 16, the acclaimed British commanders Charles Cornwallis and Tarleton routed Horatio Gates and Thomas Sumter at Camden, South Carolina. Just two days later Tarleton caught up with Sumter's retreating division and inflicted heavy losses at Fishing Creek, South Carolina: over 150 men killed and 300 captured. The British lost fewer than 16 men.

That the American forces were able to turn around the dismal situation of summer 1780 and ultimately liberate the former colonies through

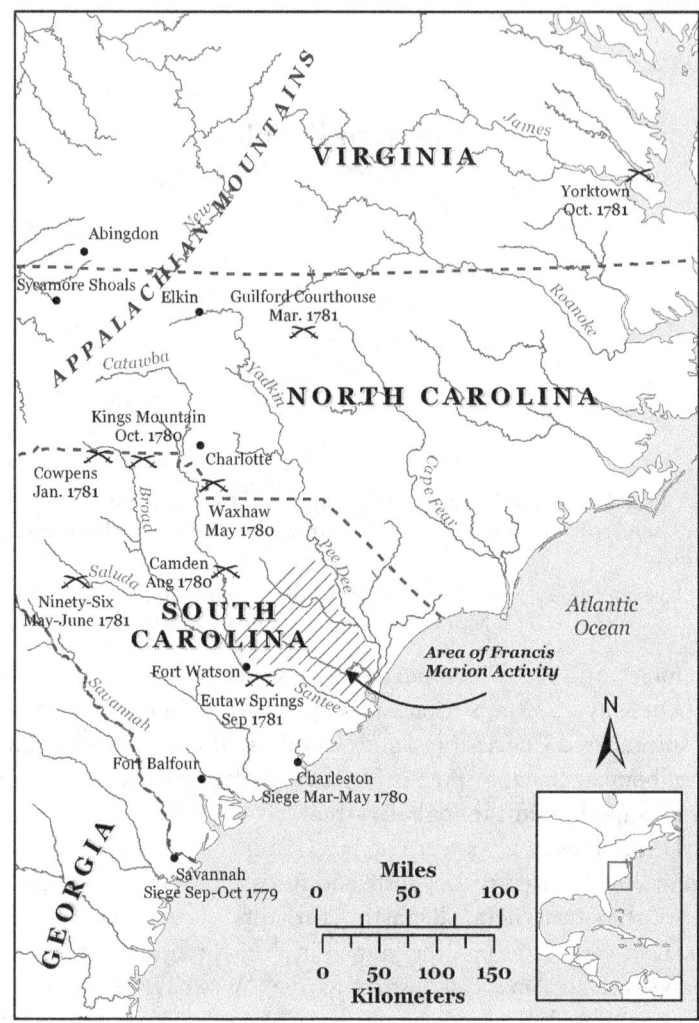

FIGURE 3.1. The American Revolution in the South. Map prepared by Andrew Rhodes. Reprinted with permission

armed struggle remains one of the great military feats in Western history. This chapter traces some of the strategic decisions that made such a feat possible, emphasizing the key role played by irregular American forces, including militia and partisan bands. It then suggests that the Continental Army's success after 1780 owed a great deal to its adoption of more irregular styles of war fighting. The fledgling American state's first experience with war set important historical precedents for its engagement in insurgency and counterinsurgency operations in the next two centuries. It is worth remembering now, given the United States' heavy involvement in counterinsurgency operations through the more than 200 years that followed, that its first experience as a state at war was on the side of the insurgents.

KINGS MOUNTAIN, NORTH CAROLINA/SOUTH CAROLINA BORDER, 1780

On a cold autumn morning in 1780, Colonel William Campbell ordered his 1,500-man column to halt a half-mile west of Kings Mountain in the far northern backwoods of South Carolina. The troops, a ragged band of volunteer militia, marched in ten companies. Campbell's own company had come from Virginia to Quaker Meadows, North Carolina, in the past week. Sensing a critical opportunity, Campbell had ordered the long march to pursue Colonel William Ferguson, commander of a large force of British and Loyalists – indeed, a full third of the British presence in the South at that time. Campbell rendezvoused with Colonels Isaac Shelby and John Sevier, frontiersmen from Kentucky and Tennessee; Benjamin Cleveland and Joseph McDowell met them a short time later.

Meanwhile, Ferguson, with about 120 British regulars recruited from New York and New England and a 1,000-volunteer Loyalist militia, had been chasing Major Joseph McDowell through South Carolina, to little end. On October 6, he positioned his men on the eastern crest of the Kings Mountain ridge. Upon reaching the ridge, Ferguson is reported to have said, "I am the king of this mountain, and God Almighty and all the Rebels out of hell could not drive me from it!"[2] One might have been inclined to agree with him. Kings Mountain rose steep and solitary from the piedmont, and at that time was covered with nearly impenetrable primeval forests, making an organized line of attack on the mountain next to impossible. Ferguson had sent messengers to Tarleton, encamped at the Wateree River just north of Kings Mountain, and Cornwallis, in nearby Charlotte, in the hope that they would join him at this spot. Though Ferguson did not know it at the time, neither of his comrades had any intention of moving.

It was October 7 when Campbell's militia reached Kings Mountain. As the sun rose, Campbell divided up his force into two lines, telling them, "If any of you, men or officers, is afraid, quit ranks and go home."[3] Cleveland gave similar advice:

When you are engaged you are not to wait for the word of command from me. I will show you, by my example, how to fight; I can undertake no more. Every man must consider himself an officer and act from his own judgment. Fire as quick as you can, and stand your ground as long as you can. When you can do no better, get behind trees, or retreat; but I beg you not to run quite off. If we are repulsed let us make a point of returning and renewing the fight; perhaps we may have better luck in the second attempt than the first.[4]

Campbell ordered the companies of Sevier, Shelby, Williams, Lacey, Cleveland, and Chronicle to take the north side of the ridge, and Campbell, McDowell, and Winston to take the south end. They surrounded the mountain, and Campbell ordered the first attack, exhorting them: "Here they are, my brave boys; shout like hell, and fight like devils!"[5] The Americans charged up the hill using any cover they could find, but Ferguson met them with two stiff bayonet charges. The rebels retreated to the bottom of the hill, regrouped, and renewed the charge. Fighting tree to tree, they picked their way to the top of the ridge.

The battle lasted only an hour. Ferguson, realizing he was hemmed in, attempted to make a quick escape through a weak spot in the American lines, but he caught heavy fire. Seven musket balls toppled him from his horse, rendering him unconscious before he hit the ground. When the Americans regrouped at the top of Kings Mountain, they surrounded the surrendering Loyalists and continued firing. As one observer wrote, "A dreadful havoc took place until the flag was sent out the second time when the work of destruction ceased."[6]

The rebel forces at Kings Mountain eliminated Ferguson's entire 1,100 man detachment, taking 689 prisoners. They buried the dead in shallow graves on the hillside. The Patriots themselves suffered only twenty-eight killed and sixty-two wounded. They left Kings Mountain quickly, fearing a reprisal from the infamously retaliatory Tarleton. Over the next few weeks, the Patriots summarily tried and hanged nine of the prisoners for looting and other war crimes, lost another hundred who escaped during the march, and dispatched the remainder to Charleston. Three months later, most of the men who fought at Kings Mountain would again see combat with General Daniel Morgan at Cowpens, South Carolina.

A classic case of irregular warfare due to the tactics employed, the Battle of Kings Mountain became a rallying victory for the American forces throughout the colonies. Although it was a relatively small success in comparison with the full scale of the Revolution, it was a critical turning point in the southern theater and served as precisely the sort of morale boost that General George Washington needed for his armies in the North.

General Sir Henry Clinton, the commander of British forces in America, later called Kings Mountain "the first link in a chain of events that followed each other in regular succession until they at last ended in the total loss of America."[7] As news of Kings Mountain spread across the eastern seaboard, confidence in the American cause surged, while Loyalists came to the sobering realization that the British forces in North America were not invincible.

Kings Mountain is also a prime example of the unconventional strategies and tactics that Americans used to force the British hand throughout the war. Given the political aims of the revolution and the maneuvers that commanders deployed on both sides, the American war of independence can be considered one of the first unconventional wars of the modern era, and the region east of the Appalachians a proving ground for some of the first modern guerrilla and partisan strategies, many of which have since become common denominators in dirty wars. Indeed, this early American conflict provides many examples typical of insurgencies and, on the part of the British, counterinsurgency responses. This reality may seem surprising because the United States has devoted so much blood and treasure to deterring insurgencies throughout its history.

Common Sense

In this section, we consider several aspects of the American Revolution that support the view that it was an early example of modern insurgency and counterinsurgency. The first aspect has to do with the relationships of power and identity between England and her former colonies. For the revolutionaries, this evolution might be summarized as a conflict between English citizens and their own government that developed into a conflict between people who identified themselves as Americans and an occupying state. These types of transitions, both actual and perceived, often characterize a successful insurgency movement.

Second, the American Revolution was also characterized by the effectiveness of militia and irregular combatants in supporting the Continental Army. We can measure this success both in battlefield outcomes and in the Continental leadership's changing attitudes toward the militia.

Third, the Revolution involved battlefield tactics that cut against the grain of the highly regimented and ordered military conventions of eighteenth-century Europe. These included Washington's use of the element of surprise in the battles at Trenton and Princeton and Francis Marion's capitalization of terrain and cover in the almost total guerrilla war in the South. It also included several instances in which frontier commanders decentralized *in bello* decision-making authority down to the level of individual soldiers, General Campbell at Kings Mountain being one such example. Finally, the American Revolution, as an insurgency, gave particular attention to off-the-battlefield political strategies and tactics, aimed at cultivating loyalty – or in some cases, fear – among civilians. As General Washington and other Patriot commanders came to realize, in an echo of classic guerrilla doctrine, the revolutionaries did not need to gain large, decisive victories to win the war, but rather needed to fight not to lose.

In its earliest expression, the war of independence was seen as the last recourse for protecting the rights and freedoms of then-English nationals. This idea resonated in the rhetoric of the early revolutionary movement: in a letter to George Mason in 1769, George Washington wrote,

> At a time when our lordly Masters in Great Britain will be satisfied with nothing less than the deprecation of American freedom, it seems highly necessary that some thing shou'd be done to avert the stroke and maintain the liberty which we have derived from our Ancestors. ... That no man shou'd scruple, or hesitate a moment to use arms in defence of so valuable a blessing, on which all the good and evil of life depends; is clearly my opinion.[8]

This popular mindset, with its emphasis on the Americans as British subjects, informed the greater part of the Americans' diplomatic and pre-belligerent strategies leading up to the first conflicts at Lexington and Concord, Massachusetts. It also helps to explain the hesitancy of even some of the most ardent firebrands to make a first strike against the British army. For one, if North America were to remain a part of the British Empire after protest and negotiation had alleviated some of the grievances that the American colonists expressed, then it would be unwise to take up arms. Furthermore, American political leaders recognized their gross disadvantage in military conflict. With no standing army and a sizable domestic opposition, the Americans' small probability of victory against the world's most powerful military was enough to discourage most.

Yet once the fighting finally broke out in April 1775, the American commanders still justified their military involvement in terms of their status as British subjects. As one scholar put it, "Between American politicians defending English liberty as it ought to be, and British politicians defending English law as it really was, the two sides had taken positions from which they could not back down without shame."[9] In the early days of the war, the question remained among the American leadership whether they were fighting to gain independence or to defend the political rights to which they were entitled as British citizens. This question translated on the battlefield into waging a primarily defensive war early on. As Washington described in a letter to his brother, John A. Washington, following his appointment as commander in chief of the Continental Army in 1775, "To prevent [the British] from penetrating into the country with fire and sword, and to harass them if they do, is all that is expected of me."[10]

As the war progressed, though, the perception that the American fighters were English subjects attempting to pressure their own government shifted dramatically. Particularly after the signing of the Declaration of Independence in 1776, the war quickly became an American effort at expelling an illegitimate occupier. By the second year of the war, the rebels increasingly considered Great Britain a foreign state operating among a hostile domestic population. Such a transformation in the psychology and self-perception of the people affected by a conflict is often critical for an insurgency movement. In the case of the American Revolution, those who supported the insurgency increasingly came to identify themselves as Americans with their own particular collective history and narrative. Yet, perhaps just as significantly at that time, a large contingent of American Tories, or loyalists, remained committed to the British side and continued to see themselves as British subjects. The American national transformation during the revolution thus was not a total one; as is often the case in insurgencies, shifting self-identities and loyalties created a polarized social milieu that often erupted into communal violence.

This kind of fundamental questioning and redefining of social and political priorities often accompanies insurgent conflicts. In fact, the transformation is often driven explicitly and intentionally, for instance, through propaganda in the form of print media (and later radio, television, and Internet) or through populist political efforts aimed at cultivating the sympathies of neutral or noncombatant civilians. During the American Revolution, Thomas Paine's widely circulated pamphlet, *Common Sense*, helped to shift the thinking of many colonists from merely opposing the excesses of British rule to supporting independence outright.

THE UNCONVENTIONAL AMERICANS

Another way to reflect on the American Revolution as an insurgency is to look "on the ground." As this book emphasizes, it is important to examine the specific tactics, strategies, and outcomes that make an insurgency or, in many cases, a counterinsurgency, a successful operation.

The American victories in the Revolution came about because of the Patriots' willingness to use tactics considered unconventional compared to the European standards of engagement of the day. The unwritten rules of war in the eighteenth century, perfected by Frederick the Great's Prussian army, were unequivocally regimented. This was a system of fighting characterized by strict military hierarchy and rigid battlefield formations.[11] Armies faced one another in long lines across open fields, exchanging volleys of musket fire with artillery bombardments providing support from the rear. Though it seems almost senseless now, it was the only acceptable style of war fighting among armies in the European tradition – a tradition heavily steeped in particular conceptions of honor, valor, and civility. In 1759, the British had crushed the French in the Plains of Abraham near Quebec with brutal frontal attacks and complex flanking maneuvers. Indeed, the British in the latter half of the eighteenth century were the champions of this hyper-structured system of warfare.

American Continentals could not match the British on the traditional battlefield. Amazingly, General Washington never won a major victory over the core ranks of the British army in open battle.[12] In what was perhaps the most telling example of American weakness in this regard, Washington nearly lost the entire Continental Army at Long Island, New York, at the end of August 1776. In two days of open field assaults, the British successfully cornered the Americans at the northern point of the island. Had Washington not ordered a daring nighttime evacuation, he would have almost certainly been forced to surrender. As many commanders on both sides realized, the core of the problem was that American soldiers lacked discipline, were poorly trained, and had little experience in European styles of warfare.

What gave the Americans the advantage was their ability and willingness to break the European rules. Many Patriots – commanders and soldiers alike – had cut their teeth fighting the French and Indians on the Appalachian frontiers. There they learned to move quietly and to use a battlefield's natural surroundings to give cover and to aid in surprise. As the war progressed, several commanders realized that these realities necessitated a subtler military strategy. Using these tactics would provide them the best chance for victory.

In consequence, American generals adapted in several ways. For one, they devolved greater responsibility for battlefield decision making to smaller groups of soldiers and, as we saw at Kings Mountain, even to individual soldiers. This shift away from rigid organization on the American side, while counterproductive in conventional encounters, was a tremendous asset when it could render conventional doctrine irrelevant.[13] American bands would attack at night in secret, or ambush a party of British or loyalist soldiers along a densely wooded trail. After inflicting heavy losses on the enemy, they retreated swiftly and quietly to avoid total rout.

Considering the foregoing description, it might be easy to think of the battlefield dynamics in the Revolutionary War in terms of what the eminent Max Boot calls "one of the cherished myths of American history." The vision of "plucky Yankees [winning] independence from Great Britain by picking off befuddled redcoats too dense to deviate from ritualistic parade-ground warfare" Boot rightly describes as caricature.[14] As he notes, in reality the British did actively attempt to adapt to the mode of war fighting of its rebel enemy, drawing on extensive experience countering irregular warfare in conflicts throughout Europe, the Caribbean, and Canada. The point that Boot perhaps glosses over too quickly, however, is that on the ground, they simply did not adapt well enough, or quickly enough. As a result, the Patriots enjoyed a decisive advantage when it came to irregular tactics.

The Patriots' unconventional strategy wore down the British forces, both in terms of numbers and morale. As one scholar explains, the American fighting style led to "the demoralization of the British troops. [The Americans] did not constitute an army, but rather a horde or a swarm of individuals who stung and flew on to sting again."[15] Applying the lessons and skills learned in the backwoods to the fight for independence, commanders in the Continental Army were able to adapt and generate a sense of tactical superiority over their British counterparts.

Due in large part to this adaptability, the Americans won several of the war's early victories. On April 19, 1775, colonial militia turned out to stop a British force marching from Lexington, Massachusetts, to destroy arms and munitions in Concord. The Americans approached Concord in rank but then scattered and took positions in the town, on a nearby hill, and on the Concord River. According to British Lieutenant John Barker's account, as the British companies marched into the town, they took fire

from all sides but mostly from the rear, where people had hid themselves in houses till we had passed and then fired. The country was an amazing strong one, full of hills, woods, stone walls, etc., which the Rebels did not fail to take advantage of, for they were all lined with People who kept an incessant fire upon us, as we did too upon them, but not with the same advantage, for they were so concealed there was hardly any seeing them.[16]

The militiamen shot from behind stone walls, bridges, barns, and trees. It was no regimented battle, and in the eyes of several British observers, it was cowardly. One soldier was surprised to find at Concord that "even women had firelocks. One was seen to fire a blunder bus between her father and her husband from their windows."[17]

A few months later, in June, the newly formed Continental Army met the British regulars at Breed's Hill outside Boston. American militia were positioned behind rocks, trees, embankments, and improvised rail fences. As the British approached the hill, they fired volleys, and then retreated up to the fortifications at the top of the hill. One company of American Continentals was said to have taken a post behind a rocky patch along the shore and picked off the British as they landed. The British did not expect the concealed onslaught and suffered dearly; though the British took the hill in the end, they absorbed more than twice the number of American casualties.

A COLD AND DESOLATE WINTER AT VALLEY FORGE

Throughout the war, General George Washington's priorities seemed to oscillate between meeting the British on their terms and attempting to capitalize on those strengths that the Americans had against the British – mobility, speed, and persistence. His results were mixed. In March 1777, British Colonel William Harcourt wrote that the Americans seemed to be "ignorant of the precision and order, and even of the principles, by which large bodies are moved, yet they possess some of the requisites for making good troops, such as extreme cunning, great industry in moving ground and felling of wood, activity and a spirit of enterprise upon any advantage."[18] During the early years of the revolution, Washington favored conventional tactics for his own divisions, leaving the use and arrangement of militia to his subordinates. In fact, in a letter to John Hancock dated September 24, 1776, he wrote, "To place any dependence upon militia is assuredly resting upon a broken staff." Yet, even with his commitment to the European conventions of war and his early skepticism toward militia, Washington still incorporated nontraditional tactics into his campaigns.

To cite a famous example, Washington's raid on the German Hessians in winter quarters at Trenton, New Jersey, demonstrates rather well the conventional-unconventional dualism of the Continental Army. On December 26, 1776, Washington led 9,000 men across the Delaware River. His army surrounded Trenton at dawn, blocking off all roads into the town and inflicting a sound defeat on the surprised Hessian troops. Shortly after the encounter, Washington met the British at Princeton, but led a stealthy withdrawal in the early morning of January 3, 1777. Keeping the sentries at post and the campfires burning, Washington ordered the wheels of the cannon carriages and supply wagons, as well as the horses' hooves, to be wrapped in rags to muffle sound. This is largely regarded as a strategic success for Washington, because he was able to maneuver around a British flank, escape a direct attack, and ensure that there would be no great battle before the winter quarters.

The New Jersey campaign, moreover, served an important demoralizing blow to the British cause. A Hessian chaplain in nearby Elizabethtown wrote after the battle, "One can no longer go to sleep without thinking this night is the last of your freedom. Previously we had been accustomed to undressing every night for bed. Now, however, is just the opposite. We go to bed completely clothed, for we are to be ready for battle."[19]

The core of Washington's force was most effective in gradually wearing down the enemy as part of a grand strategy that may best be described as erosion or attrition.[20] Ultimately, what made this successful was Washington's ability to minimize the defects of his army and to avoid confrontations that would risk catastrophic losses. This ability became most pronounced after the winter of 1777–8, spent at cold and desolate Valley Forge, Pennsylvania, twenty miles northwest of Philadelphia. By this time, Washington and the Continental commanders had become aware of their relative strength in unconventional strategies and tactics, and they developed plans to work actively with it. Valley Forge was a pivotal moment in the conflict because it signified a shift toward a war of overwhelmingly unconventional and partisan strategies on the part of the Americans.

As Joseph J. Ellis writes, after the trials leading up to and during the winter at Valley Forge, Washington became convinced that "space and time were on the American side . . . so that the only way to lose the war was to try to win it."[21] At Valley Forge, Washington recruited the aid of the Prussian Baron von Steuben to retrain the Continental Army. Like his tactics in the field, the Baron's pedagogical methods themselves were unconventional. He organized a "model unit" of 120 soldiers, whom he drilled for weeks at a time. He then instructed that company to train other units, which he, along with Washington's staff, organized according to ability and experience. This strategy thus left a great deal of battlefield command to the small-unit leaders.

At Monmouth Courthouse, New Jersey, in June 1778, Washington's officers, including Generals Lee, Wayne, and Knox, suggested a full-on attack against General Henry Clinton's British forces. Yet Washington, unwilling to risk a major defeat, opted for a partial attack on Clinton's rear guard, coupled with small militia attacks on the flanks. The hit-and-run maneuver at Monmouth succeeded in forcing the British back north, into New York.

CONTROLLING THE COUNTRYSIDE

In the three years between the battles of Monmouth Courthouse and Yorktown, Washington's emphasis in the North would be on controlling the countryside. He held the Continental Army in a massive arc that began in Philadelphia, continued up through New Jersey, around New York City, and into western Connecticut. This strategy both deepened and publicized the American presence in the mid-Atlantic and New England countryside, where the majority of the population lived. This shift in particular, from large battles near urban centers to small, "stinging" skirmishes in the farm country, literally brought the war to the doorsteps of American civilians. According to one historian, "If there were proportionately few homes in which the loss of a father, son, or brother was mourned, all were touched by economic dislocation and inflation."[22]

The collateral damage of a protracted "small war" – incidental property damage, plundering, looting, and the indelible strain on private farms of an army (or two) needing food – coupled with the endless printing of money by all thirteen states and by the Continental Congress combined to make the war an inescapable presence in civilians' lives. This fact, in turn, served to mobilize the American public to an unprecedented degree. While loyalties remained divided, it became increasingly clear that there would be no such thing as neutrality in this long war.

THE WAR IN THE SOUTH

Thus far this chapter has devoted the bulk of its attention to the Continental Army fighting in the mid-Atlantic and Northeast. The war's southern campaigns, however, deserve a deeper look because they were so dramatically different from those in the North and unfolded even more closely along the lines of guerrilla and partisan movements of later insurgencies. In fact, the South saw only two major operations before the summer of 1780: the British sieges of Savannah, Georgia, and Charleston, South Carolina, which fell in December 1778 and May 1780, respectively.

In the early years, the war in the South was characterized by intermittent skirmishes throughout Georgia and the Carolinas. The British forces, comparatively smaller than their counterparts in the North, found it exceptionally hard to hold positions in the Southeast's expansive coastal plains and wooded foothills. The Americans, for their part, focused primarily on interrupting British movement and harassing their adversaries. During this period, Francis Marion, the "Swamp Fox," led a "grimy and bizarrely attired little band of patriots" through the swamps of eastern and central South Carolina.[23]

Headquartered at Snow's Island, a small, densely forested ridge bordered by the Pee Dee River in the east, Lynch's River to the north, and Clarke's Creek on the south and west, Marion launched most of his strikes on British and Loyalist forces under the cover of darkness. Often grossly outnumbered, he and his volunteer militia – whose number fluctuated from as few as 5 to as many as 500 men throughout the course of the war – would inflict heavy damage on the enemy and then disappear again into the lowland swamps. To maximize their mobility and secrecy, Marion and his fighters used their knowledge of the terrain to access secret trails and unknown roads that zigzagged through the swamps, never camping in one spot for more than a single night. In the revealing episode that gave Marion his nickname, Banastre Tarleton chased the rebel commander through the swamps for a full twenty-six miles without catching him. Reporting to General Cornwallis, Tarleton said indignantly, "As for this damned old fox, the Devil himself could not catch him."[24]

Marion's various sorties included a raid on a Tory recruiting station, where 150 of his men killed 3 British and Tory soldiers, took 23 prisoners and 80 horses, and made off with muskets and other supplies. Marion suffered no casualties. In another covert maneuver, Marion cut off British supply trains to and from Charleston at Singleton's Mill on the Santee River. A few months later, he ambushed a force of 400 Tories on the march between Georgetown and Camden. Withdrawing a safe distance from the company of British cavalry they had observed, Marion and his men concealed themselves in a patch of woods 400 yards up a knoll. As the enemy approached, Marion charged and "slew a goodly number of them."[25] When the British retreated, Marion's troops spread out and "guarded the bridges and swamps in [their] route, and annoyed and killed [them] as they passed."[26] In April 1781, Marion and Lieutenant Colonel Henry Lee took Fort Watson on Scott's Lake, burning the outpost and taking 120 prisoners with 2 losses of their own.

Although Marion was the most renowned, he was not the only partisan leader in the South. Other militia leaders deployed similar strategies. John

FIGURE 3.2. General Francis Marion, the Swamp Fox, offering to share his meal of sweet potatoes and water with a British officer. Marion and his small band of followers, experts in partisan warfare, were the scourge of British forces in South Carolina during the American Revolution. Currier & Ives, 1876. Courtesy of the Library of Congress, Prints and Photographs, Division, LC – USZC2–2405

Dooly, the commander of several hundred Patriot militia, pestered British flanks in the marshes and swamps around the Savannah River between Savannah and Augusta, Georgia. Colonel John Sevier, who figured prominently in the Kings Mountain battle detailed in the beginning of this chapter, spent the years leading up to 1780 fighting unconventional campaigns against Cherokee and Loyalist forces in the backwoods of North Carolina and Tennessee.

The role that guerrilla and partisan strategies played in the war in the South brings forth a number of important concepts for analyzing insurgencies and counterinsurgencies. The first of these are what observers now refer to as, respectively, hearts and minds and scorched-earth approaches, both of which are discussed at length elsewhere in this book. To summarize briefly, hearts and minds refers to efforts to cultivate the support and sympathy of civilians by means such as minimizing collateral damage, undertaking projects that benefit local populations, and providing incentives for their affiliation; scorched earth refers to efforts to eliminate civilian populations or the means of their subsistence, or otherwise to intimidate them into supporting one's aims. On the Patriot side, commanders such as Colonel William Campbell were known to be scrupulously merciful to enemy soldiers and to civilians. Campbell was meticulous in his handling of prisoners and forbade his men to take any more provisions from civilian farms than they absolutely needed to subsist. While there may have been an element of idealistic honor in his conduct, his was a textbook hearts-and-minds insurgency, aimed at winning the backing of local citizens who could aid his cause.

On the other hand, Francis Marion was perhaps equally well known for his ruthlessness. He rarely hesitated to plunder a captured enemy, and he did not tolerate British sympathizers in the areas that he frequented. This often meant burning farms and homesteads and allowing his men to loot the condemned properties. So effective was Marion's scorched-earth strategy that General Charles Cornwallis wrote, "Col. Marion has so wrought on the minds of the people, partly by terror of his threats and cruelty of his punishments, and partly by the promise of plunder, that there was scarce an inhabitant between the Santee and Peedee that was not in arms against us."[27] Cornwallis's words might have been hyperbolic; more likely, perhaps, Marion's brutality simply galvanized southern populations, driving civilians to back the cause with which their sympathies already lay. If this inference is accurate, it may help to explain why communal violence in the South was so much more prevalent and fierce than in the North.

The British contributed their own share of brutality to southern battlefields. In an early instance of counterinsurgency adaptation, the British learned to fight on insurgents' terms and even became willing to forgo European conventions to win the war. The cavalry commander Banastre Tarleton was particularly merciless in this regard: in a May 1780 operation mentioned at the opening of this chapter, Tarleton pursued Colonel Abraham Buford to Waxhaw Creek, near Lancaster, on the South Carolina border with North Carolina, riding 105 miles in two days. Approaching Buford's rear guard, Tarleton demanded a surrender; when Buford refused, Tarleton attacked, charging straight through the lines and all but destroying Buford's rear column. According to one account, Buford raised a white flag and ordered his men to surrender, but a late shot felled Tarleton's horse. Suspecting duplicity, Tarleton ordered another attack, and the Loyalists in his command killed indiscriminately, even searching the grounds for wounded Patriots and executing them where they lay. Later, in August 1780, Cornwallis and Tarleton cornered Generals Horatio Gates and Thomas Sumter at Camden, South

Carolina. Gates offered surrender, and his men called for quarter, but Tarleton and his cavalry continued firing until they had killed nearly 1,000 Patriots. Although this was a gruesome setback for the Americans, "Tarleton's Quarter" became a popular rallying cry heard at Kings Mountain and other battle sites where Patriot insurgents exacted revenge.

Are these scorched earth campaigns ultimately successful or are hearts-and-minds strategies more effective in the long run? Taken as a whole the American Revolution does not provide definitive evidence one way or another, but history is replete with instances in which brutality redoubles the violence, generating revenge conflicts, meta-operations, greater instability, and outright civil war; to a certain extent, this was the outcome in the South. Although we rarely hear about it, the partisan campaigns in the South were as incendiary as some of those in the dirty wars of the twentieth century, and they were marked by disturbing levels of intra-community violence.

The proportion of British-born to American-born combatants fighting at any given time in the South was surprisingly small. Colonel Ferguson, for example, was the only soldier in his division recruited in Great Britain; the rest of his men were local volunteers and Loyalist regulars from the American Northeast. Different allegiances split communities and families in half, and accounts abound of returning soldiers and known sympathizers on both sides being tarred and feathered, beaten, hanged, or otherwise abused.

The war was also devastating for noncombatants. In one harrowing instance, William "Bloody Bill" Cunningham led a group of Loyalists in a 1779 massacre of revolutionary sympathizers at Ninety-Six, South Carolina. They acted in retaliation for the alleged killing of Cunningham's brother by a Patriot a week earlier. On the ride back to Charleston, Cunningham and his band executed and burned the homes of anyone they knew to support the Patriot cause.

THE "FLYING ARMY"

Like their counterparts in the North, the southern Continental forces compensated for their inferiority in conventional warfare with unconventional strategies. After 1780, and after devastating defeats on the field as well as the fall of Charleston and Savannah to British occupiers, American commanders in the South avoided large-scale battles almost entirely.

In a small but important battle in March 1779, American troops under General John Ashe suffered a severe rout at Briar Creek, Georgia, marking the end of large-scale conventional warfare in the South. A year later, in October 1780, Ashe and General Benjamin Lincoln were replaced by a lapsed Quaker from Rhode Island named Nathanael Greene, who streamlined the southern forces and began to harass Cornwallis's flanks and communications with a small "flying army."[28] Coordinating with the now well-experienced and battle-hardened militias, he depended on quickness, secrecy, and surprise to weaken Cornwallis's forces without having to risk his men in direct engagements with the main British lines.

The new strategy proved highly effective for other commanders as well. For example, in the January 1781 battle of Cowpens, South Carolina, American General Daniel Morgan "defied most accepted rules of contemporary warfare," taking a cornered position between the Broad and Pacolet Rivers, which made a retreat impossible and thereby ensured that the militia would not turn tail when the battle began.[29] Guessing that his opponent, Banastre Tarleton, would make a frontal attack, he placed militia on the front lines and the full body of regular infantry and cavalry behind the crest of a high hill. This left his flanks exposed, but also gave Morgan the much-needed element of surprise. He instructed the militia to fire two volleys into the British lines, exhorting them to "pick off the epaulets!" to disrupt the hierarchy of command. Then, they were to retreat to the top of the hill, behind the awaiting regulars. This was highly imaginative positioning that maximized both the autonomous strength of the militia and the sheer force of the Continentals. After the first barrage, the militia fell back behind the stronger lines waiting at the top of Cowpens ridge, while a large reserve posted half a mile behind advanced when the attack on the main lines began. The strategy worked brilliantly. The Patriots took the field, exacting losses of 110 British killed and 900 captured compared to only 25 American deaths.

VICTORY

When the forces of Washington, Lincoln, and the French Commander Rochambeau converged on Charles Cornwallis at Yorktown and finally defeated the British, it was thanks to a vast number of historical and strategic factors. While Yorktown proved to be the decisive battle – it was here that Cornwallis formally surrendered his 7,000-man army – this conclusion came only after years of a brutal war characterized largely by partisan insurgency strategy.

4

Confederates and Indians

> Unarmed none cared to stir abroad
> For berries beyond their forest-fence:
> As glides in seas the shark,
> Rides Mosby through green dark ...
>
> And five gigantic horsemen carved
> Clear-cut against the sky withdrawn;
> Are more behind? an open snare?
> Or Mosby's men but watchmen there?...
>
> Mosby speaks from the undergrowth –
> Speaks in a volley! Out jets the flame!
> Men fall from their saddles like plums from trees;
> Horses take fright, reins tangle and bind;
> "Steady – dismount – form – and into the wood!"
> – Herman Melville, "The Scout toward Aldie"[1]

THE "GRAY GHOST"

During the Civil War, Confederate insurgent bands used classic guerrilla tactics to enervate the massive Union armies. Northern Virginia, in particular, was a "hotbed" of rebel insurgent activity.[2] Local Confederate guerrillas harassed Union flanks and scouting parties, cut telegraph lines, burned railroad cars, intimidated civilian populations, and otherwise made life miserable for the northern armies. These Virginia guerrilla units often acted independently, usually without official sanction from the Confederate command in Richmond.[3] The most famous of these Confederate guerrillas was John S. Mosby, nicknamed the "Gray Ghost" for his stealthy operations behind Union lines. Mosby joined the Confederacy in 1861. Two years later, after accompanying Jeb Stuart on a cavalry raid in northern Virginia, his request was granted for a group of six men and permission to conduct clandestine and destabilizing operations behind enemy lines.[4]

Perhaps John S. Mosby's small stature – a mere 125 pounds – explains this lawyer-cum-warrior's natural propensity for asymmetric insurgent warfare. In his own words, Mosby's ambitious agenda was "to diminish ... the aggressive power of the Army of the Potomac, by compelling it to keep a large force on the defensive." He claimed that he "wanted to use and consume the Northern cavalry in hard work," and he was wildly successful.[5] Within a few months, Mosby had staged several daring and successful raids and commanded over two hundred men.

His actions quickly won the attention of the Union army, which was unprepared for this guerrilla strategy. Since insurgency violated the rules of proper warfare, which well into the nineteenth century "still declared that large forces move against one another en masse," the Union command did not expect an irregular southern resistance.[6] In fact, and perhaps because the northern commanders had lost General Washington's insurgent recipe from a century earlier, the English-born Union Colonel Sir Percy Wyndham was so accustomed to nineteenth-century European conventions of war that he first thought the Confederate insurgents' attacks on the cavalry outposts were executed by local thieves.

Benefiting from superior stealth and mobility, a firm understanding of the local territory, and small, lightweight weapons, such as the innovative Colt .44 six-shot revolver, Mosby's men carried out more than one hundred attacks against Union positions and resources. "We had to make up with celerity for lack of numbers.... If you are going to fight, then be the attacker," Mosby said.[7]

One of Mosby's most daring and celebrated raids resulted in the capture of a Union general in his quarters at Fairfax Courthouse, only about twelve miles from the Union capital in Washington. After the raid Mosby wrote to his commander, Stuart, to report:

> I kept the pike until I got within about a mile and a half of the Court-House, where I turned to the right in order to avoid some infantry camps, and came into Fairfax Court-House from the direction of the railroad station. The few guards stationed around the town, unsuspecting danger, were easily captured.... The fruits of this expedition are 1 brigadier-general (Stoughton), 2 captains, and 30 men prisoners. We also brought off 58 horses ... belonging to officers; also a considerable number of arms.[8]

Mosby's successful raid prompted an exasperated General Ulysses S. Grant to issue the stern order that "when any of Mosby's men are caught, hang them without trial."[9] Grant's attention to the insurgent band actually increased the rebels' tenacity and encouraged pride among the southern population. In fact, the Confederate army read Mosby's

FIGURE 4.1. Colonel John S. Mosby, Confederate States of America, 1860–5, nicknamed the "Gray Ghost" for his stealthy operations behind enemy lines. Robert E. Lee once proclaimed, "I wish I had a hundred like him." Courtesy of the Library of Congress. Prints and Photographs Division, LC – BH831-2473

account of the raid to every cavalry regiment to encourage Confederate pride, and Robert E. Lee wrote to Stuart: "Mosby has covered himself with honors," and "Hurrah for Mosby! I wish I had a hundred like him!"[10] In this case, the insurgency served not only to destabilize the enemy but also to invigorate the southern population.

Mosby's operations behind the Union lines also exemplify the powerful insurgent strategy of sowing fear among the enemy. Mosby's sudden hit-and-run raids instilled dread in the Union army, even in areas of low danger.[11] One Union officer wrote in May 1863 that "bands of guerrillas like so many ravenous beasts and birds of prey, hover around our lines, attacking wherever an opportunity offers plunder."[12]

The Union army adapted to the Confederate insurgency by launching its own guerrilla operations. One of its early successes was in western Virginia, where General John C. Fremont, commander of the Union Mountain Department, ordered his men to pursue the rebels in small groups and allowed each to employ its own modes of operation. Many of these bands engaged in deceptive yet effective practices, such as dressing in Confederate uniforms. Creating small antiguerrilla patrols did prove effective against the small Confederate insurgents. However, the divide-and-conquer counterinsurgent tactic also weakened the Union army's conventional defense of the Baltimore and Ohio Railroad, exposing the forces deployed along its length to attacks by the Confederates' main forces.[13]

In adopting stringent counterinsurgent policies, the Union Army did commit errors. For instance, General Fremont foolishly invited a group of Jayhawkers – Kansans with counterinsurgent experience from their confrontations with pro-slavery "Border Ruffians" in Missouri – to western Virginia. Instead of working as effective Union counterinsurgents, the Jayhawkers alienated the local population. They "set about a campaign of lawlessness so notorious that most were either driven from the state or arrested and placed in local jails."[14] By the same token, the Confederate guerrillas occasionally turned out to be a nuisance for Richmond. Many southern generals came to loathe the vicious guerrilla raids that often antagonized the very civilian populations they were supposed to be defending. For historians and analysts in later generations, these unintended consequences offer a reminder that alienating the local population through abuse greatly weakens the support and efficacy of the counterinsurgency operation. In more general terms, it also points to the disconnect that sometimes emerges in counterinsurgencies between tactics and high-level strategy. Often the tactics deployed on the ground work at cross-purposes with aims at the operational level.

INSURGENCY IN MISSOURI

Although Mosby mounted a daring and colorful insurgency campaign in northern Virginia, the bloodiest and most vengeful guerrilla warfare occurred in the western United States. Border clashes between abolitionist Kansas and pro-slavery Missouri erupted in 1854 and continued until the end of the Civil War. In 1861, Union forces occupied Missouri and even organized a new pro-Union government, but bands of Missourians began to launch hit-and-run attacks against the occupying forces. Over the course of 1862, a group of guerrillas, totaling between 3,000 and 4,000, held down a Union force of 60,000 men.

One of the Union's principal weaknesses in this theater was its resistance to even acknowledging that the Missouri guerrilla insurgency was a serious concern. Like Napoleon's view of Spanish guerrillas fifty years earlier, conventional Union military commanders refused to recognize the irregular fighters as anything more than cowardly bandits. Perhaps echoing General Washington's regard for his own militia, the Confederate military establishment dismissed the Missouri guerrillas. In 1864, one Confederate general wrote, "They will only fight when they have all the advantages and when they can run away whenever they find things too hot for them. I regard them as but one stage better than highwaymen."[15]

In time, the Union commanders came to understand the serious threat that the Missouri insurgency posed, and they responded with a time-tested counterinsurgency policy. In 1863, the Union command approved a selective removal of the Missouri population. With a special focus on those who lived within a mile radius of Union army posts, those suspected of being guerrillas, along with their families, were relocated to Arkansas.[16] Relocation and expulsion became extremely effective American counterinsurgent tactics; the U.S. Army later repeated them near the end of the Civil War and during the western Indian Wars.

MARCH TO THE SEA

Arguably, the readiest example of the Union's ruthless counterinsurgency tactics is General William Tecumseh Sherman's Savannah Campaign, otherwise known as the March to the Sea. Sherman's path of destruction through the underbelly of the South was not only a sage military tactic employed to destroy the economy and infrastructure of his Confederate enemy; it is also one example of the central role that civilian populations play in counterinsurgent warfare. Sherman had to break the spirit of the

South. For his part, President Lincoln understood the power of public support in a time of war, and he advocated a strong military effort to demoralize the southern population. He gave considerable license to his military commanders, as is evident in a letter to his newly appointed lieutenant general, Ulysses S. Grant, on April 30, 1864:

The particulars of your plan I neither know nor seek to know. You are vigilant and self reliant; and pleased with this, I wish not to obtrude any constraints or restraints upon you.

The message, though simple and concise, served as Lincoln's official sanction for the U.S. Army to execute a harsh counterinsurgent campaign. However, there was some level of conflict between the politically minded executive and the war-focused military leaders. General Sherman's Order No. 6 in April 1864 to reserve the railroad for military use only serves as such an example. This order rejected President Lincoln's plea for a shipment of foodstuffs for Union supporters in Tennessee, as a way to win more southern sympathizers.[17]

Sherman understood the strength and power of the southern resistance and knew that it would take a muscular effort to break it. In a March 1864 letter to his wife, the general wrote:

The devils seem to have a determination that cannot but be admired. No amount of poverty or adversity seems to shake their faith – niggers gone – wealth and luxury gone, money worthless, starvation in view within a period of two or three years, are causes enough to make the bravest tremble, yet I see no sign of let up – some few deserters – plenty tired of war, but the masses determined to fight it out.[18]

Sherman adopted extremely harsh policies, most notably the burning and pillaging of southern cities and plantations. The Union soldiers, often referred to as "Bummers," plundered material goods. In Georgia alone, Major General Oliver O. Howard burned 3,523 bales of cotton, took 9,000 head of cattle, and destroyed 191 miles of railroad, while General Henry Warner Slocum commandeered 4,090 horses and mules, 17,000 bales of cotton, and 119 miles of railroad. Although estimates vary, Sherman believed that his army destroyed $100,000,000 of goods in Georgia, of which $80,000,000 was left ruined and unused even by the Union force.[19] The strategy of razing and stealing not only cut off the Confederates' supply chain; it also increased public discontent for the war.

Sherman's most controversial tactic, though, was the forced removal of civilian inhabitants from Atlanta. Although estimates of the number expelled vary greatly, Colonel Le Duc's probably overstated claim that he "turned 12,000 people out of their Atlanta homes," suggests that the tactic was extreme. Civil War historian Albert Castel wrote that Sherman's action against the civilian population in Atlanta was "the harshest measure taken against civilians by Union authorities during the entire Civil War."[20] The Union generals, though, argued that the relocation was essential to ending the war and that it was only a response to the South's persistence. Sherman wrote: "If the people raise a howl against my barbarity and cruelty, I will answer that war is war, and not popularity-seeking. If they want peace, they and their relatives must stop the war."[21]

Le Duc's inflated expulsion number also supports the idea that the Union army sought to sensationalize the capture of Atlanta. By spreading exaggerated news about Atlanta's fall, the Union Army strengthened the belief that the South's final defeat was imminent. This use of propaganda proved to be a wise counterinsurgent strategy; simple and inexpensive, it persuaded many people in South that the war was no longer worth fighting.

Despite the extreme nature of Sherman's actions in the South, the Union commanders did show some restraint. Their forbearance, in part, grew out of the recognition that the southern population would have to be reintegrated into the country after the war. There was also a belief among many Union commanders on upholding certain moral imperatives. The Union army embraced a responsibility to protect southern women from vicious abuse and rape. For instance, when Private James Preble of the New York Cavalry raped Letitia Craft during Sherman's march through North Carolina in March 1865, he was court-martialed and sentenced to death by firing squad. An account of his trial and execution was published in papers across the country. Preble's execution helped to restore a sense of morality and decorum to the Union army, to discourage other soldiers from abusing the civilian population, and to begin the healing process of southern reintegration.[22] William Dunn, a surgeon from a Pennsylvania regiment, described the good conduct of Union troops in Atlanta in terms of the righteousness of the Union cause:

> Every man has seemed to be on his good behavior since we entered Atlanta. The women have been dressed up waiting for our men to commence raping but they have waited in vain. There has not been a single outrage committed in this city, a circumstance that the people say they cannot say for the Rebel Army.[23]

At the heart of this honest effort was a strategic appeal for the support of the vulnerable southern population.

Sherman's march, most particularly the fall of Atlanta, had a profound psychological effect on the country, in that it convinced the nation that the

South's chances of permanent secession were weak. Headlines of the time illustrate the Union states' elated mood. The *Chicago Daily Tribune* wrote, "The Dark Days are Over ... we can see our way out."[24] The Union victory in Atlanta and the subsequent march through Georgia rallied the Union troops. In November 1864, Wisconsin chaplain George Bradley wrote:

> The soldiers seem cheerful and happy, and all, or nearly all, are pleased to have a part in this, the *grandest affair* of the whole war. I heard one say, a day or two since, that he would not have missed it for fifty dollars.[25]

Sherman's campaign also had a profound effect on the southern civilian population, especially southern women, who had already begun to lose faith in the cause of secession in the face of fear, deprivation, and the deaths of their husbands. One North Carolina woman pleaded to the Confederate generals to end the war for the sake of her children and other women:

> Here I am without one mouthful to eat for myself and five children and God only knows when I will get something now you know as well as you have a head that it is impossible to whip they Yankees, therefore I beg you for God sake to try and make peace on some terms, and let they rest of the poor men come home and try to make something to eat, my husband has been killed, and if they all stay till they are dead, what in the name of God will become of us poor women and children?[26]

Through Sherman's southern campaign, the U.S. military learned that breeding discontent among the adversary's population is an effective counterinsurgent tool. Increasing political and social pressure on an insurgent enemy can wear it down and moderate its actions.

THE SECOND SEMINOLE WAR

The U.S. military's transition from an insurgent to a counterinsurgent force actually began before the Civil War, when the U.S. government sought to enforce its "Indian removal" legislation. The most infamous American counterinsurgency effort during this period was the Second Seminole War. Waged to expel the Seminole nation from its Florida territory, the conflict spanned a total of seven years between 1835 and 1842, making it the longest Indian war in American history.[27] The war also took a tremendous toll on the blood and treasure of the United States. The U.S. government lost almost 1,500 soldiers, 55 militiamen, and at least 100 civilian settlers to military actions and disease.[28] For its length, high number of causalities, and extreme cost, historians widely consider the Second Seminole War an American counterinsurgency failure.

Although most of the Seminoles were eventually removed from Florida, they mounted a very successful insurgency during the early years of the war. Unlike other American Indian nations that emigrated peacefully under the U.S. government's removal plan, or those that suffered from prolonged internal division, the small 5,000-person Seminole nation held to the central tenets of insurgent warfare, population unification, and guerrilla tactics. Seminole leaders united the population through violent pressure and propaganda, and they waged tactical guerilla warfare through brutal surprise attacks. In short, the Seminoles executed a brilliant insurgency.

The Seminoles used violent intimidation and pressure to prevent internal conflict and to mitigate allegiance to the U.S. removal plan. The aim was to separate the population from the counterinsurgent, control it, and obtain its active support. The Seminole nation also benefited from the unified desire to protect the Florida homeland, an impulse to which Mao Zedong refers in his treatise *On Guerrilla Warfare*.[29] "When a nation is invaded," he explains, "the people become sympathetic to one another and all aid in organizing guerrilla units."[30] The Seminoles' unified nationalist ideology certainly motivated many Indians to contribute to the insurgency.

One of the Seminoles' greatest advantages was Florida's geographic condition. Insurgency doctrine suggests that "rugged and difficult" terrain, "either because of mountains and swamps or because of vegetation," greatly strengthens an insurgent force.[31] One prime example of the Seminoles' use of their swampy terrain is the manner in which they strategically prepared and hid their villages from American military attacks. The standard U.S. military tactic against American Indians, as President Jackson stated, was to find "the deposit of women and children" and to "proceed at any hazard and expense" to that location to draw the Indian warriors out of hiding and force them into open, conventional warfare.[32]

This very effective U.S. military strategy was able to quell an Indian nation with one strong, decisive battle. However, early Seminole unification and planning prevented this style of U.S. military operation. In Withlacoochee Cove, which consisted of both swamp and prairie, the Seminoles collectively relocated their communities from the open banks of the rivers and water sources to swampy islands and wooded hammocks of the Lake Tsala Apoka area.

Moving the villages provided protection from clandestine American military attacks. The U.S. soldiers would have to wade through the unfamiliar swampy terrain to find the villages. Slowing down the Americans' approach would give the Seminole women and children time to escape into the swamps before they could be taken hostage. Relocating the villages to the protected swamps also prevented the U.S. military from drawing the Seminole warriors into open combat.

The American counterinsurgency was not wholly unsuccessful, though. General Thomas Sidney Jesup, supreme commander of the Florida militia, employed harsh military tactics to force the Seminoles into negotiations. He dispatched his 8,000-man force to monitor and destroy the Seminoles' farmland. Preventing the Indians from harvesting their principal food source, corn, led to massive starvation and forced several of the Indian leaders to sign a cease-fire accord at Fort Dade in March 1837.[33] Although controversial, Jesup's brutal tactics led to the capture of 1,978 Indians and the deaths of 400 others – almost half of the Seminole population in Florida at the beginning of the war.[34]

Jesup's controversial tactics also illustrate the issue of public support for American counterinsurgencies, a problem that continued to surface throughout similar U.S. efforts in the nineteenth and twentieth centuries. By the end of the Second Seminole War, nearly 80 percent of the American population opposed the conflict.[35] This early evidence of waning public support gives credence to the contemporary observation that a democratic public will not long maintain its support for a conflict that it perceives as immoral or excessively harsh.

THE SAVAGE WEST

After the Civil War, several Indian nations in the western territories waged insurgencies against the United States, and the American military responded with drastic counterinsurgency campaigns. Unlike the years prior to the Civil War, though, when the U.S. Army's main objective was to remove Indians from Eastern states, the new aim was principally to destroy Indian resistance. Buoyed by the messianic message of Manifest Destiny, which urged Americans to realize their God-given right to settle the North American continent, settlers moved westward to claim their spiritually, politically, and racially sanctioned dominion.

But conquering and settling the West was complicated by the presence of the indigenous groups already living there. Between 1865 and 1898, U.S. forces engaged in roughly 1,000 tactical actions with various Indian nations, notably the Sioux, the Navajo and the Apache. Collectively, the operations are now known as the Indian Wars. These conflicts are easily classified as insurgencies, since the nations employed mostly irregular combat tactics against a technologically superior American adversary.

These tactics included stealth, speed, mobility, knowledge of the terrain, and hit-and-run–style ambush attacks.

Many of the Indian groups' own experiences with warfare prepared them well for an asymmetric fight against the Americans. Many historians and anthropologists note that in warfare, most Indian tribes encouraged bravery, not simply killing. To win honors and war pride, Indian warriors would have to show considerable levels of skill and bravery. Since some tribes, like the Apache and Comanche, believed that disfiguration remained with the victim in his afterlife, their warriors often scalped and defaced their victims. For this reason, the axiom, "keep that last bullet for yourself," was a common expression among the American Indian fighters. This hyper-gruesome perception of Indian warriors created a heightened sense of fear within the American ranks, which may have actually served as a formidable insurgent tactic.

The Indian warriors were also well respected for their insurgent skills. Most notably, the Lakota, Cheyenne, and Arapaho were skillful on horseback, often able to ride at full speed while simultaneously engaging in an attack. The warriors were also extremely aware of their terrain and were adept at using it to collect intelligence. As Lieutenant Colonel George Custer wrote:

They can count an army within a score of its number by the depth that a trail is worn; they can give within a dozen the number of horses in a column by the amount of turf nibble at the last feeding place. They can tell the speed, the direction, and the strength of armies far as the dust that rides from its feet is perceptible.[36]

The Indians also used their knowledge of the terrain for dispersion and concealment. The groups used natural features to protect women and children and to set up ambush attacks on uninformed American soldiers. The ability of the warriors to blend into the terrain also increased the level of fear and insecurity among the American soldiers. An unidentified officer fighting in Arizona remarked, "they sink into the ground or somehow vanish; look behind and they are peeping over a hill at you."[37]

Despite the insurgent nature of the conflicts, the U.S. Army did not immediately adopt counterinsurgent tactics. More enamored with the "Napoleonic glories" of European war than by "grubby skirmishes" against the Indians, the U.S. Army continued to rely on conventional military combat techniques.[38] Foremost among these was the "fort system," wherein hundreds of forts scattered throughout potentially belligerent territory served as a sort of grand fortress for the 25,000-soldier cavalry. Yet, this strategy proved problematic. The sheer scale and sparse population of the American West were two of the army's greatest challenges. Great distances between forts and watering holes slowed the movement of supplies and men.

Before the railroad lines connected East and West, it was not uncommon for troops to have to carry "one hundred pounds of clothing, equipment, and rations."[39] It also took years for explorers and cartographers to fully map the vast expanses of land. Without reliable maps and atlases, the army was very susceptible to Indian ambushes. Finally, the distance slowed communications between the commanding officers on the east coast and the soldiers on the ground.

With the advent of telegraphs and the expansion of the railroad system, the U.S. military began to employ its superior technology to fight the Indian insurgencies. One key example of this superiority was the American military's ability to maintain a supply of provisions in all seasons. This allowed the ground forces to take advantage of the Indians' limited mobility and dependence upon food stores during the snowy Great Plains winters and to coerce the groups to move onto reservations. General Sherman, who led western forces after his Civil War campaigns, was a key executor in this regard. He was convinced that a patient and defensive strategy of deploying superior technology and inexorable migration into the West would overwhelm the myriad Indian tribes. And, as in his Savannah campaign, his predictions proved accurate.

Nevertheless, the Indian Wars were extremely dirty. Appalling atrocities abounded. Among the most notorious was the American-perpetrated massacre at Sand Creek, Colorado, on November 29, 1864. A Colorado Territory militia attacked a village of Cheyenne and Arapaho Indians, killing between 150 and 200 women, children, and elderly. Although the brutal American army tactics were accepted and even celebrated by the American pioneer populations, Americans back East often protested the brutality of the conflicts. Revelations about the Sand Creek massacre sparked a substantial public outcry. This early public controversy against the American counterinsurgency strategy again illustrates the difficulty of maintaining public support for nontraditional and harsh forms of combat.

The famed "Indian fighter" General George Crook, a graduate of West Point, intimately understood the complexities of public opinion. Many of the western settlers labeled him an "Indian lover," for his moderate views that the U.S. government should negotiate with indigenous nations by fair means rather than by battle. Were it not for the fact that General Sherman named him the best Indian fighter in the Army, Crook might have well

FIGURE 4.2. George Crook, 1870–80. Although he was sometimes criticized for his willingness to negotiate with Indian tribes, General Sherman called him "the best Indian fighter in the Army." His innovative counterinsurgency tactics were instrumental in the eventual defeat of the Apache chief Geronimo. Courtesy of the Library of Congress, Prints and Photographs Division, LC – BH826–2600

FIGURE 4.3. Geronimo, 1886. Courtesy of the Library of Congress, Prints and Photographs Division, LC – USZ62–46637

lacked the public support to lead his campaign against the elusive Bedonkohe Apache named Geronimo.[40]

Crook's success as a counterinsurgent was the result of his unorthodox and radically innovative military tactics. Since he knew that he could not compete with the territorial knowledge of his Apache adversaries, he appealed to disaffected tribe members, who served as his scouts. His allies performed numerous reconnaissance missions for him to locate Apache positions. Crook also sought to develop a total-war strategy by studying the Apache's cultural habits and mentality. According to one scholar, Crook's innovation of small counter-Apache patrols applied coercion "not only to the body, but to the mind and soul."[41]

Crook also embraced the counterinsurgent tactic of increased mobility. To cope with the harsh Arizona conditions, he trained his men to use mules and to operate in small, fast units. His patrols, which tirelessly pursued their enemies, sapped the security and morale from Geronimo's Apache warriors in New Mexico, just as General Jesup had done against the Seminoles a few decades prior. Last, Crook built a sense of camaraderie among his counterinsurgency unit by enduring the same hardships as his men. In contrast to traditional military units, he did not pack special supplies for himself, and he even cooked and ate with his subordinates. Creating a stronger community by appealing to unity and loyalty inevitably strengthened his campaign.[42]

The stunning defeat and surrender of Geronimo illustrates the eventual success of the U.S. Army in adopting counterinsurgency tactics. In the twilight of his career, after decades of harassing and fighting U.S. forces, Geronimo commanded a small band of Apache in the rugged Sierra Madre Mountains of northern Mexico. At least two of his Apache contemporaries, Mangas Coloradas and Cochise, were known as far better military leaders than Geronimo. Yet he was able to elude the 5,000 American troops who were pursuing him by hiding in the difficult terrain. Geronimo eventually grew tired of the constant, vigilant American pursuit. Like his counterinsurgent foe, Geronimo also faced political pressure from his population. As support for his hideout and ambush operations began to fade among his tribe, Geronimo was forced to end his resistance. Ultimately, he surrendered to Crook's replacement, General Nelson A. Miles, at Skeleton Canyon, Arizona, in September 1886. In a military report in October of the same year, Charles Gatewood wrote that "[the Apache] could have no rest and they feared no treachery; hence delivered themselves to a foe they knew superior to themselves."[43] The U.S. Army had simply made the Apache's evasiveness too difficult to sustain.

LESSONS OF THE INDIAN WARS

> As a war cry, "Geronimo" has certainly stood the test of time. Paratroopers in World War II yelled it as they hurled themselves into the void, and, more recently, our lethal team of killers were said to have uttered it when they surprised the bin Ladens in their compound in Pakistan. – Larry McMurtry[44]

As in the Seminole case four decades earlier, the U.S. Army again launched a forced expulsion strategy. The most dangerous Apache were relocated with their families to distant Florida, where they were unfamiliar with the swampy terrain. An officer defended the U.S. government action:

> This was the only practical solution of the question, for as long as the blood-thirsty Apaches were on their familiar ground, which offered them an easy opportunity to escape and hide in inaccessible mountains, after committing an outrage, so long would they continue their bloody work.[45]

Although the Indian Wars of the nineteenth century were without a doubt morally objectionable by today's standards, the policies and strategies developed from these conflicts significantly shaped the American military's counterinsurgency structure in future conflicts. The Indian Wars and the insurgency elements of the Civil War gave the U.S. Army invaluable experience in the art of irregular warfare for the "imperial" and "banana" wars of the early twentieth century. Among the most important lessons in these nineteenth-century operations is that public support is essential to a military's ability to effectively wage a counterinsurgency. Time and again, the U.S. Army bore witness to the fact that although extremely harsh dirty war tactics may be effective in the short run, they alienate large segments of society in the long term. The issue of public support poses a great obstacle to military commanders and policymakers in the United States, since dirty tactics are sometimes the only viable military option. The question then becomes how to mitigate the negative reaction among the population.

The U.S. military also learned that effective counterinsurgency strategy often involves measures to actively weaken public support for adversaries. This can be done through direct appeals to the enemy population to cease supporting its military or severe repression of this same civilian population. That is, both the carrot and the stick can be used to compel civilians to cease their collaboration. Sherman, for one, wielded a ferocious stick against the southern population to increase pressure on the Confederate government to end the war. As true then as it is now, in counterinsurgency, people matter.

Another lesson that the U.S. military learned from its nineteenth-century experiences was that denying an insurgent population life-sustaining resources can quickly end a conflict. Preventing the Seminoles from harvesting their crops, for instance, greatly weakened their ability to resist and to wage battle. This very basic idea continues throughout the development of counterinsurgent practice and thought. Today, for example, the U.S. government freezes the bank accounts of international terrorist groups to limit their ability to survive. Attacking the resource system rather than people may also be a more viable option, politically speaking, against contemporary insurgencies.

Since some of the nineteenth century's most effective tactics, such as population relocation, are no longer morally appropriate, the U.S. military must rely more heavily on ending the supply of resources to enemy combatants. At the same time, the creation and continuation of the combatant detention facility in Guantanamo Bay, Cuba, following the terrorist attacks of September 11, 2011, suggest that the United States still remains willing to take extreme and controversial measures in these dirty wars. Last, the American military of the nineteenth century learned that the effective deployment of technology greatly enhances counterinsurgency campaigns. Increased technological capabilities improve the military's ability to collect intelligence; to increase stealth, speed, and mobility; and to augment the intimidation leveled against the insurgents.

5

Intermezzo

The Boer War, 1899–1902

> This war is fast degenerating into the same kind of dacoit hunt we used to have in Murmah. The Boer is becoming just as cold-blooded a ruffian as the dacoit was and his wholesale slaughter of Kaffirs [Africans] ... has I think forfeited his right to be considered a belligerent. I found the bodies of four Kaffir boys none of them over 12 years of age with their heads broken in by the Boers and left in the Kraal [Afrikaans for cattle enclosure] of their fathers. Strong measures will be required to stop this slaughter.
> – British Colonel Rawlinson to Field Marshall Lord Roberts, August 28, 1899[1]

The Boer War that raged across present-day South Africa from 1899 to 1902 was Britain's costliest and bloodiest war in the century between 1815 and 1914.[2] It was arguably the most humiliating of the nation's colonial history. The Boer conflict was a dirty war with atrocities committed on both sides. The conflict also witnessed the advent of key military innovations on a large scale. Repeating rifles and machine guns turned the strategic balance in favor of defense, a trend that would see its full, devastating manifestation in the muddy trenches of France a dozen years later. The commander of Britain's military forces in the campaign, Lord Kitchener, was also one of the most controversial figures of his time. He succeeded in waging a counterguerrilla campaign against a hard-fighting enemy, despite numerous tactical defeats and an outraged opposition at home. The Boer War is also instructive for our study of the American experience in irregular warfare given that it provides an important comparison of how another imperial power fared in similar circumstances. At the very time that the British were mired in the Boer War, U.S. political and military forces were attempting to quell an insurgency and "nation-build" in the Philippines.

It is worth reflecting on the similarities and differences between this case and contemporaneous ones in the American context. As in the American Civil War and Indian Wars, part of the British success came as a result of a harsh relocation policy; the British authorities forced Afrikaner civilians into concentration camps where many of them died of starvation and disease. There is also a comparison to be drawn between the U.S. Army's fort system in the undeveloped West, as we saw in the last chapter, and the British "blockhouse" strategy, which aimed to create a fortified line of defense across the Transvaal. Both systems encountered similar limitations.

The story of the Boer War starts in 1652, with the establishment of a shipping station at the Cape of Good Hope by the Dutch East India Company. Over the next fifty years, around 2,000 European settlers, mostly Dutch Calvinists, moved to the newly formed colony and became the first "white Africans." They named themselves *Afrikaners* ("the people of Africa") and spoke a variant of Dutch that was eventually called *Afrikaans*.[3] A large number of the Afrikaners formed part of a group of semi-nomadic pioneers and agriculturalists known as *Boers* (Afrikaans for farmers).

Amid the Napoleonic Wars in the early nineteenth century, the British took possession of the Cape Colony in 1806. Most Afrikaners were willing to live under British rule, but many Boers on the frontiers of the Cape Colony were unhappy with the new political arrangement. Seeking to escape British laws and institutions, the Boers embarked on the Great Trek, a massive relocation of over 12,000 *Voortrekkers* (pioneers) eastward into unsettled areas in the 1830s and 1840s. The Crown quickly moved to annex these newly settled areas to enhance its control over the broader region. The territory was traded between British and Boer hands over the next three decades, with the British ultimately annexing the region known as the Transvaal in 1877 to create a united South Africa and consolidate its control over newly discovered diamond deposits. The Boers soon rebelled against the move, inaugurating the four months of fighting that became known as the First Boer War. The two sides reached an agreement that resulted in Boer self-government in the Transvaal, with nominal British control.

The discovery in 1886 of another precious natural resource – gold – in the Transvaal once again heightened British interest in the region. In the

Intermezzo: The Boer War, 1899–1902

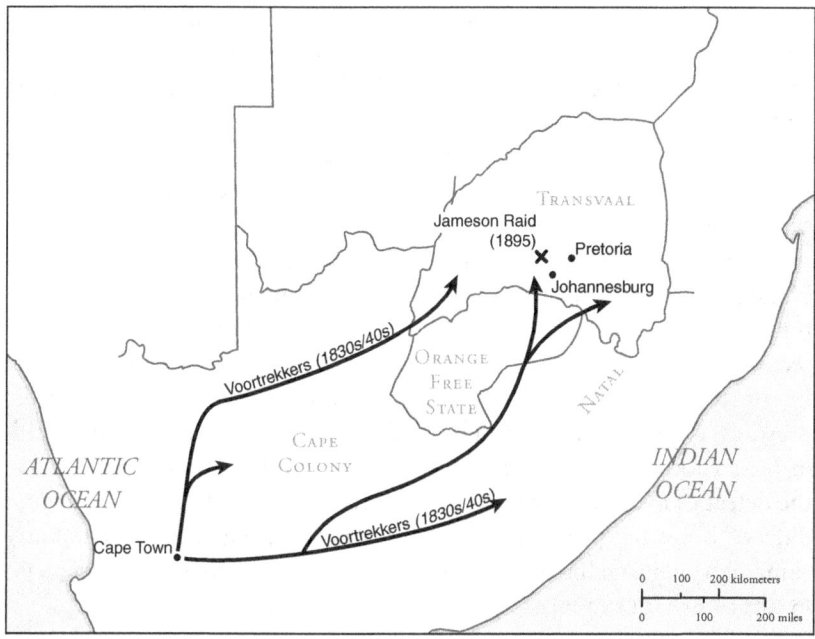

FIGURE 5.1. The Boer Wars, 1880–1 and 1899–1902. Map prepared by the University of Wisconsin-Madison Cartography Lab©. Reprinted with permission

ten years following the discovery of gold, roughly 60,000 mostly British *Uitlanders* ("foreigners") had relocated to the Transvaal, almost doubling the population of "native" Boers. In late December 1895, Cecil Rhodes, then prime minister of Cape Colony, supported an attack on the Transvaal to clear the way for British mining interests. The three-day operation – known as Jameson's Raid for the British colonial commander Leander Starr Jameson – was a dismal failure, as the expected uprising against the Transvaal government by the Uitlanders never mobilized. Disputes over the Uitlanders across the next several years helped precipitate the outbreak of the Second Boer War.

WAR BREAKS OUT

In 1899 negotiations continued between the British and Boers regarding political rights for the Uitlanders; observers have since concluded that this objective on the part of the British was likely a front that disguised their deeper interest in obtaining access to the mining region. Looming over the talks was the threat of war as a way to solve this political impasse. In September of the same year, the British issued an ultimatum demanding full political rights for Uitlanders in the Transvaal; Boer leaders rejected the British demand, and war immediately followed.

The initial outbreak of hostilities in the Second Boer War (now widely but erroneously known simply as the Boer War) proceeded according to the standard military conventions of the time. The Boers launched strikes on British positions and laid siege to cities within the British-controlled Natal and Cape Colony territories. A British counteroffensive to push back the sieges failed; bolstered by massive reinforcements, a much larger second effort in 1900 led by Field Marshall Lord Roberts allowed the British to secure both Natal and Cape Colony, effectively restoring the prewar territorial status quo. The British then invaded the Transvaal and, in June 1900, captured both Johannesburg and the capital, Pretoria. Yet the defeat of the Boer army and the subsequent occupation of their capital did not bring the peace that the British had expected. A short military campaign against a highly inferior foe soon gave way to a very dirty phase in one of Britain's more inglorious imperial wars.[4]

THE INSURGENCY TAKES HOLD

Over the next eighteen months, the Boers deployed a guerrilla strategy that maximized their relative strengths vis-à-vis their enemy. These strengths are by now familiar: they included intimate knowledge of the landscape, mobility on horseback, civilian sympathy, and exceptional military leadership from commanders such as Christiaan de Wet and Louis Botha. The Boers relied upon militia units known as "commandos" that had originally been intended to protect frontier settlements from attacks by African tribes.[5]

These farmers-cum-guerrillas usually relied on their own firearms, pieces normally reserved for hunting and personal defense. The resilient Boer guerrillas were excellent shots and horsemen, dangerous and highly mobile. In short, they were the perfectly suited to "light cavalry" forces that so often harangued the ostensibly superior British military. Like Mosby, the "Gray Ghost" who tormented Union forces in the American Civil War, the Boers unleashed a strategy of intermittent flying raids directed against British troops, communications, and, most critically, the railway system.

The British now found themselves in a classic guerrilla war. In November 1900, just as the conventional phase of the war was concluding and the guerrilla phase beginning, Field Marshall Horatio Herbert Kitchener replaced Roberts as the top commander of British forces. While the British had adopted some heavy-handed policies, such as the burning of houses near telephone lines, railways, and bridges before his arrival, Kitchener deduced that he would need to fight fire with fire to defeat the elusive enemy. To begin, Kitchener responded to Boer attacks on trains by placing Boer civilians on them as "human shields."[6]

By 1901, as Boer incursions continued across the Orange Free State and the Transvaal and even into Cape Colony, Kitchener mobilized a force of roughly 500,000 British and colonial troops (including 17,000 Australians) and adopted a "scorched-earth" policy that, while controversial, proved extremely effective in isolating and ultimately defeating the Boer guerrillas. As the term suggests, scorched-earth warfare attempts to eliminate anything in the theater of conflict that could possibly be used to aid the enemy. For the duration of the war, the British systematically burned Boer crops and houses (around 30,000 farmhouses destroyed in all), forced tens of thousands of Boer women and children into desolate concentration camps, and committed untold atrocities. Strictly in terms of military objectives achieved, the strategies yielded a "successful" counterinsurgency campaign.[7]

The British military's hallmark counterinsurgency tactic during the war was the "blockhouse" system. Originally designed as a fortified line to protect railways in early 1901, the blockhouse system eventually became an offensive weapon against Boer commandos. Built quickly with stone, wood, and corrugated iron, and manned by around a half dozen soldiers per edifice, blockhouses were usually built about 1,000 yards apart, each within sight of the other, and connected by trenches a few feet deep and protected by barbed wire and trip wires rigged with rock-filled tin cans.[8] Interestingly, the barbed wire itself proved to be a very effective weapon, albeit unintentionally: where it first served to keep the enemy "fenced out," once the enemy had breached the lines, it hemmed them in for easy elimination.

By the end of the conflict in 1902, over 8,000 blockhouses extended for 3,700 miles, with 50,000 white troops and 16,000 African scouts manning the fortifications. Life inside the blockhouses was often numbingly tedious, given the tight confines and remote locations. Long periods of solitude on the *veld* were interrupted only occasionally by Boer attacks.

All told, the blockhouses were a stunning success. Yet, like most elements in an irregular war, they were not without problems. At times, for example, the houses were constructed too far apart, defeating one of the system's main intentions: to alert one blockhouse to any attack on an

FIGURE 5.2. A blockhouse in the Transvaal. Designed as a fortified line to protect railways in early 1901, the blockhouse system became an offensive weapon against Boer commandos. Built quickly with stone, wood, and corrugated iron, and manned by around a half dozen soldiers per edifice, blockhouses were usually built about 1,000 yards apart, each within sight of the other, and connected by trenches a few feet deep and protected by barbed wire and trip wires rigged with rock-filled tin cans. Fusilier Museum, Bury, Manchester, UK

adjacent structure. Recall that this was also one of the damning limitations of the fort system deployed in the American West in the late 1800s. Legendary Boer commander De Wet called the blockhouses the "blockhead system"; his forces routinely slipped across the wire fences intended to corral them. Moreover, while they were effective as a defensive tactic, the blockhouses never allowed the British forces to deliver a decisive blow against the Boers.[9]

Another key strategic development was Kitchener's increased use of mobile columns in an effort to match the mobility of his enemy. Eventually, some of his commanders demonstrated that they could leave behind tents and food wagons for up to six days, relying only on what men could carry on their saddles. As we will see, the U.S. Army adopted a similar approach when pursuing Pancho Villa in northern Mexico in 1916.

Intermezzo: The Boer War, 1899–1902   69

IMPERIAL CONCENTRATION CAMPS

Kitchener's decision to "reconcentrate" Boer women and children into camps was not an unprecedented counterinsurgency tactic in its time, although the euphemistic term "concentration camp" originated in the British instance. Within the same thirty-year period, both the Spanish in Cuba and the Americans in the Philippines and during the Indian Wars were experimenting with their own variations of concentration camps. The British justified their decision to build the camps by claiming that they would protect the women and children left vulnerable by destroyed households and property. It was lost on few observers, however, that the camps were an essential element of the scorched-earth policy.

At first, Boers and Africans who had taken an oath of neutrality were admitted as "residents" into the camps.[10] Later, though, civilians were rounded up and brought to the camps against their will to deprive the Boer commandos of provisions and intelligence. Between 115,000 and 150,000 Boer and African civilians populated the camps. By far the most shocking and controversial aspect of the camps was the horrific health and sanitation conditions. Due more to British incompetence than cruelty, deaths in the camps are estimated to have run as high as 3,000 per month. Most of the deceased were children. There were few medical doctors, and poor hygiene practices wreaked havoc in the cramped confines; detainees often used home remedies to combat their illnesses, a practice that actually served to spread the diseases more quickly. Epidemics of typhoid, enteric fever, and measles were rampant. In fact, more civilians may have died in the concentration camps than combatants on both sides during the entire war. All told, an estimated 15,000 to 28,000 Boer civilians died in the camps.

Accounts of the conditions within the camps infuriated the Boer guerrillas. Remarkably, though, when the Boers attacked the lightly armed camps they took supplies and left the women and children. As in the case of the contemporaneous American intervention in the Philippines, the strategically effective concentration camps were a bitterly controversial subject at home. By October 1901, enough information about the camps had leaked to cause a scandal in London. One English woman, Emily Hobhouse, visited the camps and interviewed Boer women, many of whom were wives of commandos. She returned to England to launch a vocal public campaign against the camps. Henry Campbell-Bannerman, leader of the opposition Labor party, declared that the British were employing "methods of barbarism" in the camps.[11]

ATROCITIES AND REPRISALS

Beyond the camps' confines, soldiers on both sides committed atrocities and reprisals. Just as the British troops during the American Revolution believed that colonial forces fought ingloriously, their imperial successors in Africa considered the Boers to be dishonorable and cowardly combatants. British troops were especially peeved that the Boers did not wear uniforms and, in some instances, even wore captured British uniforms when their own clothes had worn out, giving them a potentially lethal edge in the initial stages of an encounter. This is part of the reason that Boer prisoners were sometimes shot soon after being captured. Not surprisingly, the British high command attempted to limit the dispersion of such embarrassing information coming in from the battlefield. Yet, as was also the case with American troops stationed in the Philippines, soldiers' letters home depicted to an often-disbelieving public the shocking day-to-day reality of this dirty war.

Some of the worst offenders were the colonial irregulars – Australians, Canadians, and South Africans. One of the most widely known episodes involved an Australian-run anticommando unit called the Bushveldt Carbineers that patrolled in the wild northern Transvaal, about 180 miles north of Pretoria. Six of the regiment's officers (five Australians, one Englishman) were court-martialed for ordering the murder of twelve Boer prisoners. The Australians argued that shooting prisoners had become an accepted practice.

In February 1902, Kitchener ordered that two Australian officers, Lieutenants Harry "Breaker" Morant and P. J. Handcock, be executed. An outcry erupted back in Australia. Critics argued that the British command had made scapegoats of the two Australians. While this argument endures in the classic Australian film *Breaker Morant*, the full story is that Kitchener was in fact irate about his own army's lack of discipline and wanted to make an example out of the Australians.[12]

BRITISH VICTORY

By the spring of 1902 the British scorched-earth strategy had defeated the Boers. Facing starvation and lacking ammunition, Boer commandos began surrendering in droves, a sure sign of a demoralized and doomed insurgency. The British had indeed drained the sea. Yet, even after the outcome had been effectively decided, the British continued to engage Boer guerrilla bands, sometimes suffering humiliating defeats. In one such case, a column of 1,200 British soldiers was virtually annihilated. Yet, as was the case throughout the war, the Boers could never translate impressive localized actions such as this one into broader strategic victories.

In May 1902, the war officially ended with the Treaty of Vereeniging that placed the two Boer republics under British rule. It was a costly dirty war. All told, roughly 22,000 British imperial troops were killed in battle; another 16,000 died from disease. The Boers lost up to 7,000 fighters from an irregular force of 60,000 to 90,000 men. Finally, in an often unspoken consequence of this costly war, 40,000 Africans died in battle or in the camps.

6

America, Aguinaldo, and the Philippines, 1898

The most ultimately righteous of all wars is a war with savages, [which establishes] the foundations for the future greatness of a mighty people.
– Theodore Roosevelt[1]

Only a few days after the United States declared war against Spain on April 25, 1898, Commodore George Dewey, on his flagship the USS *Olympia*, guided the American fleet from Nagasaki to Manila Bay to confront the antiquated Spanish navy.[2] Washington's orders to Dewey's were short but clear: "War has commenced between the United States and Spain. Proceed at once to Philippine islands. Commence operations at once, particularly against the Spanish fleet. You must capture vessels or destroy. Use utmost endeavors."[3]

The fighting in Manila Bay began on the morning of May 1, when for posterity Dewey reportedly shouted, "You may fire when ready, Gridley."[4] After several hours of shelling, Dewey's men took a break for breakfast and then resumed.[5] When one American gunner heard that Dewey had ordered the cessation, he apparently pleaded, "For God's sake, Captain, don't stop us now. To hell with breakfast."[6] By lunch on a hot and windless day, the Americans had soundly defeated the Spanish fleet of battle-seasoned Rear Admiral Patricio Montojo. In one of the most lopsided victories in naval history, the Americans had lost only one man, from heatstroke. All the main Spanish ships were sunk; other auxiliary ships were captured or scuttled. A total of 381 Spanish sailors were left dead or wounded. When news of Dewey's victory reached Washington, it stunned U.S. officials, who had not expected that victory in the highly strategic Pacific region would come so fast or so easily.

America, Aguinaldo, and the Philippines

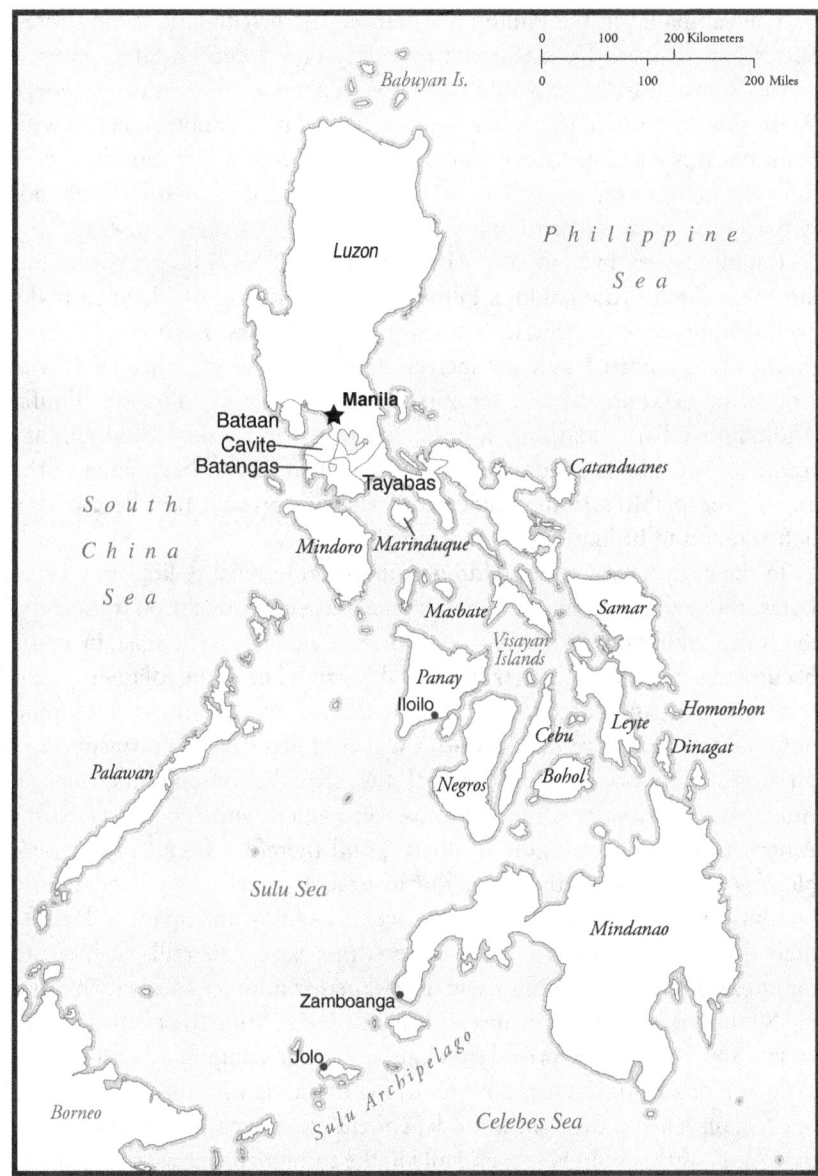

FIGURE 6.1. The Philippines. Map prepared by the University of Wisconsin-Madison Cartography Lab©. Reprinted with permission

The campaign in the Philippines marked the first time that the United States had deliberately attempted to pacify and occupy a large piece of territory overseas. That would not happen again until President George W. Bush's invasion of Iraq more than a century later. Though it began with triumph, this sustained dirty war descended within a few months into a military nightmare, as well as a domestic polarization of a kind not witnessed again until Vietnam.[7]

Joining Dewey in Manila Bay by way of a U.S. Navy escort two weeks later was Emilio Aguinaldo, a Filipino nationalist who would soon make an indelible mark in America's history of small wars. Born in 1869 to a politically connected and prosperous family in the province of Cavite (south of Manila on the country's largest island, Luzon), Emilio Aguinaldo y Famy had only a basic education and little formal military training. Yet, like the redoubtable Augusto Sandino in Nicaragua in the 1920s, Aguinaldo's formal deficiencies did not prevent him becoming a deft leader and brilliant military strategist.

In the early 1890s, Aguinaldo was involved in local politics in Cavite. Later, the young Filipino nationalist joined a secret revolutionary society, the Katipunan, and ultimately took up arms against the Spanish in 1895, becoming a general soon after the actual fighting began the following year. Interestingly, Aguinaldo and other *ilustrados* (reform-minded Filipino nationalists) looked to the American war of independence for inspiration on how a nation could throw off the shackles of colonial rule. In Aguinaldo's estimation, the Filipinos were allied with the "great North American nation, the cradle of liberty, and therefore friend of our people."[8] As is so often the case, the insurgent forces were divided into factions, which weakened their effectiveness against the Spanish. Despite their divisions, the *insurrectos* attempted, in classic guerrilla fashion, to minimize direct confrontations against superior military forces by harassing Spanish troops in the countryside instead of fighting to occupy towns.[9]

In 1897, the Spanish bribed the charismatic and cunning Aguinaldo into exile in Hong Kong; he was now returning in league with the Americans to once again take up the fight for independence from Spain. Dewey believed that Aguinaldo would be a useful ally in the campaign against the Spanish. The effect of this alliance, precipitated by the sudden American victory in Manila Bay, was to add a new element – the United States – into a Spanish-insurrecto conflict that had already been ablaze for several years.[10]

The American commander immediately understood that he did not have enough troops to take Manila from the Spanish. He also had to contend with Aguinaldo's nationalist forces, which were camped just outside Manila and were equally eager to capture the city from the Spanish. Thus, Dewey did what all good commanders would do in such circumstances: he allied his forces with the enemy (Aguinaldo) of his enemy (the Spanish in Manila). Yet, contrary to what is sometimes assumed, Dewey did not wish to defeat the Spanish in order to seize the Philippines for his country; rather, he hoped that a victory in the Philippines would help force a Spanish surrender in Cuba.[11] The American commander, using the loaded language of his time, also considered the insurgents "friends" who were "far superior in their intelligence and more capable of self-government than the natives of Cuba."[12]

Meanwhile, Dewey also petitioned Washington for a larger army force to help take Manila. Back home, the U.S. military responded by sending out of San Francisco an almost 13,000-man expeditionary force under the command of Major General Wesley Merritt. Merritt was one of the Union's "boy generals" during the Civil War and had also commanded in the Indian Wars. With his experience fighting Indians, Merritt thought he would be better equipped to deal with the "savages" than the naval commander Dewey. While eager to take on both the Spanish and insurrectos, Merritt was under strict orders to avoid a "rupture with insurgents" given their utility against the more immediate Spanish foe.[13]

Most of the American troops were volunteers from the western states; they tended to make up in enthusiasm what they lacked in discipline. Like some of their compatriots fighting the Spanish in Cuba, the initial expeditionary force dispatched to steamy Manila was fitted with heavy wool clothing and equipped with obsolete black-powder Springfield rifles rather than the modern Krag-Jorgensons.[14] Aguinaldo, for his part, strongly believed that the Americans would provide the necessary military might to make his dream of Filipino independence (from the Spanish, that is) finally possible.

The "showdown" with the Spanish took place on August 13, 1898, with the Battle of Manila, a few months after the Manila Bay rout. This time, knowing the fate that awaited them if they attempted to hold the city, the Spanish quickly surrendered to the jubilant Americans after only a token effort to defend the city. The Battle of Manila is perhaps most noteworthy for what did *not* happen after this battle: the Americans did not turn over control of Manila to their ostensible Filipino allies who were conducting their own siege of the Spanish positions. In fact, the Spanish commander in Manila agreed to surrender only after U.S. forces promised to keep Filipino troops out of the city. The American forces soon entered a city of 400,000 residents that verged on epidemic and anarchy;

Aguinaldo's forces had cut off the water supply, schools were closed, and garbage filled the streets.[15]

The Battle of Manila was another easy success for the Americans, but it was a bitter pill for the humiliated Filipino nationalists who now realized that the Americans had no plans to share power. Yet, while shut out of Manila, Aguinaldo still commanded a formidable army and political organization, even if large elements of Filipino society, especially the elites who tended to be privileged under the Spanish rule, remained dubious of his rebellion.

Throughout the fall of 1898, the American troops held Manila while Aguinaldo's nationalist forces controlled the regions outside the city in what was a tenuous and tense truce between the ostensible allies. Communication between the two sides had steadily decreased since May as both sides realized that their respective interests were not only distinct, but potentially incompatible. On December 10, American and Spanish diplomats signed the Treaty of Paris, which, in addition to other imperial "cessions" including Guam and Puerto Rico, transferred from Spain to the United States the massive archipelago of the Philippines for the eventual sum of $20 million. The United States, it seemed, had gained a global empire at Spain's expense. Yet, for the United States, this was an opportunistic form of imperialism.

From May to December 1898, President McKinley had shifted his objectives from solely defeating the Spanish to aggressively supporting the acquisition of a global empire.[16] Before Manila Bay, President McKinley had made it publicly clear that he was not interested in building an American empire, although at this point the subject of both his statements and his attention was Spain's precarious hold over Cuba. Yet the dramatic victory at Manila Bay irrevocably changed this view as suddenly, it seemed, the difficult work of acquisition was already done. Some contend that McKinley was forced to consult a globe to locate those "darned islands" in the Pacific.[17] Public pressure to retain the entire archipelago certainly weighed on the mind of McKinley, who was up for reelection in November 1900. One theme in this book is that the messiness of American democracy has often made prosecuting dirty wars more difficult. At the same time, American democracy has at times clamored for this sort of war. Yet as the Philippines episode illustrates, American battlefield defeats, atrocities, casualty levels, and length of conflict can turn public sentiment against previously popular dirty wars.

Another key element was the oft-cited "White Man's burden," the paternalistic assumption that it was now America's God-given responsibility to "civilize" the "primitive" peoples. In the words of Knute Nelson, a Republican senator from Minnesota, "Providence has given the United States the duty of extending Christian civilization, we propose to execute it."[18] In a debate that found its restatement in the disputes over American intervention in Vietnam in the 1960s and Iraq in 2003, some politicians expressed worry about the likely cost of empire regardless of the ends it was meant to achieve. Republican William E. Mason of Illinois stated, "God almighty help the party that seeks to give civilization and Christian liberty hypodermically with thirteen inch guns."[19] Another senator predicted that 50,000 troops would be a "very conservative estimate" for the number of troops needed to pacify the archipelago.[20]

What almost all American politicians agreed upon at the time, though, was the belief that the Filipinos were completely unprepared to govern the islands themselves. Ultimately, pro-imperialist politicians such as President McKinley pitched the Philippines' annexation to the American public in terms of freedom and national honor.[21] This would not be European-style imperialism but a new form of protection for a grateful people. Within days of the signed treaties, the McKinley administration attempted to demonstrate that American dominion would bring liberty to its newly subjected population. In the American president's words,

Finally, it should be the earnest and paramount aim of the military administration to win the confidence, respect, and affection of the inhabitants of the Philippines by assuring them in every possible way that full measure of individual rights and liberties which is the heritage of a free people, and by providing to them that the mission of the United States is one of benevolent assimilation, substituting the mild saw of justice and right for arbitrary rule.[22]

Part of what drove McKinley and others was the firm belief that America would succeed where Spain had miserably failed. In contrast to Spanish conquest and exploitation, America would be a beneficial occupying force. If force were ever necessary, proponents believed, Americans would use it without resorting to the cynical barbarity so typical of European powers.

As in the lead-up to the Second Boer War, as late as December 1898, both Filipino insurrectos and American generals thought that an accommodation could be reached. In part, the Filipinos believed that anti-imperialist senators in the U.S. Congress would defeat the Treaty of Paris, effectively killing annexation. They were nearly right; the treaty passed the Senate 57 to 27 – only one vote more than the required two-thirds. Then on the fateful day of February 4, 1899, Private William Grayson of Nebraska opened fire at Filipino soldiers who did not respond to his call. This seemingly isolated skirmish immediately prompted more violent exchanges, and the United States' real war in the Philippines had begun.[23]

Remarkably, the ensuing counterinsurgency war, which the United States effectively inherited from Spain, lasted three years – fifteen times longer than the war in Cuba, which receives the majority of historical attention.[24] It was the United States' biggest and bloodiest dirty war following independence but before Vietnam. In fact, the war in the Philippines has often been compared to Vietnam since they were both instances of a sizable American counterinsurgency campaign in an Asian theater; they also share, among other elements, the dubious legacy of bitter controversy back on the domestic front and instances of horrible atrocities committed against the civilian population. Like Vietnam, the Philippines from 1898 to 1902 was an instance of full-scale American intervention, of combat boots on the ground – or, to use a modern term, a "heavy footprint" approach. At its height, the U.S. Army had a force of 70,000 in the Philippines, about half the number of American troops active at one time in Iraq after the invasion in 2003; it was only a fraction of the 537,000 American troops in Vietnam at the end of 1968. One key distinction, though, is that the Philippines campaign is largely considered to be a counterinsurgency and nation-building success while Vietnam remains a bitter and humiliating failure.

Some scholars believe that the American effort in the Philippines represents a sort of "model" counterinsurgency and nation-building in that it successfully balanced the "carrots and sticks" needed to defeat the insurgency. Yet, surveying the shocking extent of America's prodigious use of scorched-earth counterinsurgency "sticks," such as concentration camps and the intentional targeting of civilians in military operations, must put any measure of "success" in sobering context.

AMERICA TAKES ON AGUINALDO

The American forces quickly established military superiority in the months following the outbreak of hostilities in February 1899. As in the British experience in South Africa, the U.S. Army was initially involved in a conventional operation against Aguinaldo's army. The Filipino forces often dug down in entrenchments that the American troops could easily locate and destroy. Through May, General John Otis, Merritt's replacement, witnessed his 30,000-man force rack up a string of victories that cost the lives of around 3,000 insurrectos, compared to fewer than sixty American deaths. At this initial stage, it appeared to most U.S. commanders that "pacification" in the Philippines was going to be easy. Much like George Bush's claim of "Mission Accomplished" in Iraq a century later, Otis believed that the virtual destruction of Aguinaldo's conventional Republican Army meant "war in its proper meaning had ceased to exist."[25]

The problem, though, was that the Americans would engage and defeat Aguinaldo's men, occupy a key territory or city, and then retreat back to Manila in a sort of early "search-and-destroy" tactic that Americans would later use with little success in Vietnam. In fact, it was only in late 1899 that American troops ventured more than sixty miles beyond Manila.[26] A good share of the problem resulted from the wholly inadequate size of the U.S. force. To address this deficiency, in March 1899 the U.S. Congress approved the recruitment of 35,000 volunteer soldiers to be used exclusively for the Philippines.[27] By November 1899, fresh troop reinforcements signified that the first wave of American soldiers was not going to be able to finish the conflict. Their arrival also meant that Otis now had an even larger force with which to finish off the Filipino army.

Thus, in a result that is common to counterinsurgency, Otis's battlefield victories did not translate into a strategic success.[28] The poorly trained and equipped American army was also quickly learning that war in the tropics was a far cry from war in the comparatively hospitable American West. Disease and poor sanitation were proving to be deadlier enemies than the Filipino insurgents. One particularly affected division suffered 515 casualties, almost all of them from malaria and heat exhaustion; in another regiment, 60 percent of the troops were in the hospital with illnesses instead of fighting Filipinos.

At the same time that the Americans were gearing up for a decisive battle, Aguinaldo realized that he could not continue to withstand the American punishment for much longer. He clearly understood that if the insurrectos were to have a chance, they would have to resort to guerrilla warfare to minimize their military weaknesses vis-à-vis the modern American force. Aguinaldo also believed that it was critical to maintain the support of the Filipino people, both the *principales*, or native elites, and the mass population. And Aguinaldo was most definitely not beyond using violence to punish and intimidate civilians and others suspected of betrayal. To these ends, the insurgents went as far as burning alive and cutting the tongues out of suspected American sympathizers, or *americanistas*. Last, Aguinaldo hoped to prolong the war to the extent that the American public would turn against this misguided imperial adventure.

Over the course of 1899, in the same way that the *ilustrados* had organized against the Spanish a few years earlier, Aguinaldo abandoned the Republican Army in favor of a guerrilla approach. Aguinaldo's forces now left behind the major cities and towns, operating in mobile bands of a few dozen men deep in the mountains of the Luzon island. Like the Boers, they sometimes operated as "part-time militias": farmers one day, fighters the next.

For the American soldiers, the Filipinos' new strategy ushered in an entirely new and much more frustrating phase in the war. According to one U.S. captain "One day we may be fighting with thousands of their people [and] the next day you can't find an enemy, they are all 'amigos.' They have hidden their rifles and may be working for you, for all you know."[29] The historian William Sexton described the insufferable conditions that American troops were now enduring as they sought out the elusive enemy:

Many of the men's clothes had not been dry for two weeks. Constant wetness had rotted leather and stitching shoes, and many of the men were barefoot. The majority were suffering from malarial fevers and chills. Many faces were pale and emaciated, the indication of dysentery. . . . Everyone was hungry.[30]

Further hindering the U.S. Army's counterinsurgency efforts, the American forces were scattered throughout roughly 400 garrisons that were often isolated from each other and unable to communicate. Frequently, Army headquarters in Manila would send out orders that would not arrive at the garrisons for weeks, if at all. One unanticipated benefit of this system, however, was that U.S. troops tended to remain in the same region for sustained periods of time, which allowed them to get to know the terrain and people more intimately.[31]

Even early in the war, before most reports of atrocities began to trickle back to American readers and politicians, American journalists covering the war repeatedly complained about misleading information coming from U.S. government sources. A group of eleven foreign correspondents sent a cable back to the United States critical of what they considered censorship of the war,

We believe that, owing to official dispatches from Manila made public in Washington, the people of the United States have not received a correct impression of the situation in the Philippines, but that these dispatches have presented an ultra-optimistic view that is not shared by the general officers in the field. We believe the dispatches incorrectly represent the existing conditions among the Filipinos in respect to internal dissension and democratization resulting from the American campaign and to the brigand character of their army. . . . We think the tenacity of the Filipino purpose has been under-estimated. . . . The censorship has compelled us to participate in this misrepresentation by exercising or altering uncontroverted statements of the facts on the plea that "they would alarm the people at home" or "have the people of the United States by the ears."[32]

THE BOY COLONEL

In May 1900, General Arthur MacArthur, known as the "Boy Colonel" during his time with the Union in the Civil War and father of future general Douglas MacArthur, replaced Otis as commander of U.S. forces in the Philippines. MacArthur believed that Otis had been too lenient in his counterinsurgency campaign, including his treatment of the civilian population. MacArthur now commanded a force of 70,000 as well as scores of local Filipinos who opposed Aguindaldo's insurrection for a variety of reasons. Instead of a weakened conventional foe, American commanders saw the "renewal of war everywhere."[33]

The war was only beginning to heat up now that Aguinaldo had moved to a guerrilla stance and MacArthur was responding even more aggressively. The McKinley administration back home announced that the United States was making real progress in the pacification campaign. Bearing a striking resemblance to President George W. Bush's rhetoric in his reelection campaign in 2004 as the war in Iraq raged, after some eighteen months of counterinsurgency warfare in Philippines, McKinley's optimistic rhetoric was intended to reassure the American public that this fight would soon come to an end.

Many of the realities on the ground in the Philippines failed to corroborate McKinley's confidence in the course of the war. By all estimates, Aguinaldo's guerrilla forces were getting stronger. Nonetheless, McKinley's pro-imperialism stance aided his presidential campaign against Democratic candidate William Jennings Bryan. Aguinaldo had hoped the protracted conflict would convince U.S. voters to elect Bryan, who would then subsequently work to end the conflict. In fact, insurrectos launched an offensive throughout Luzon in the fall of 1900 for the very purpose of influencing the election. Yet this did not happen as McKinley won with a comfortable majority that even improved on his 1896 victory over Bryan.

GUERRILLA HUNTING AND REPRESSION

Soon after McKinley secured his second term, Secretary of War Elihu Root ordered American forces to resort to the "methods, which have proved successful in our Indian campaigns in the West."[34] For his part, MacArthur decided that it was time to take the gloves off. In a clear demonstration that the U.S. Army was adopting a "zero tolerance" approach to the insurgency, in December MacArthur declared martial law. Now civilians caught aiding guerrillas would receive the death penalty. The same sentence was given to combatants caught out of uniform.

Known as "repression," the new counterinsurgency approach focused on mass arrests, deportations, and aggressive food denial campaigns. The Americans' chief aim was to separate the guerrillas from the towns and rural populations that could abet them. In the case of food denial, the army authorities instructed the civilian population in a certain area to move with their families and possessions into a designated town by a specific date.[35] The U.S. targeted the *principalía* suspected of sympathizing with the insurgents who might have heretofore been seen as immune from American pressure given their social status. U.S. commanders in the Philippines wanted to send a clear signal that, in this new war, there were no neutrals.[36]

One American general summed up the U.S. Army's chilling but militarily expedient thinking when he said that in the inevitable horror of war, "the innocent must generally suffer with the guilty" and that "a short and severe war creates in the aggregate less loss and suffering than a benevolent war indefinitely prolonged."[37] To this end, in provinces such as Batangas, U.S. troops rounded up rural populations outside the cities into strategic village encampments and then destroyed everything nearby: animals, foodstuffs, and houses. Once the villages were secured, men outside the perimeters could be arrested as guerrillas. Inside the villages, Americans distributed vaccinations and conducted other public health campaigns in an attempt to improve the often dire living conditions. Despite these attempts, around 11,000 Filipinos died in the camps, mostly to disease.

As in the hunt for Geronimo during the Indian Wars, one of the U.S. Army's key "repression" tactics in the Philippines conflict was the use of indigenous "scouts." Ethnic groups such as the Macabebes (known as Macabebe Scouts by the U.S government), who had performed similar "services" for the Spanish in the preceding years, proved to be especially capable and effective intelligence agents. One key advantage of using Macabebes was that they were at times indistinguishable from other Filipinos, making it easy for them to operate amid the guerrillas.[38] Suddenly, the Americans had indispensable "local knowledge," a key element of almost any successful counterinsurgency. The Macabebes were notorious for their skill as well as their ruthlessness against Tagalog insurgents or anyone else whom they suspected as sympathetic to the rebel cause. One American officer, Gregory Batson, worked the scouts and reflected, "They are terrors.... Word reaches a place that the Macabebes are coming and every Tagalog hunts his hole."[39] All told, roughly 15,000 Filipinos worked as scouts.[40]

In another key development, as the conflict continued to drag on, the U.S. troops on the ground were more likely to be veterans than raw recruits and were thus much less likely to be fooled by guerrilla tactics. Nevertheless, the U.S. Army was never fully comfortable in this "guerrilla hunting" mode. As one American soldier complained, "it is as easy to hunt quail with an old-fashioned horse pistol and without a dog, as it is to encounter the enemy under circumstances favorable to our success."[41]

The brutal irony of America's involvement in the Philippines was that, like Vietnam in the 1960s and 1970s, El Salvador in the 1980s, and the Iraq War two decades later, the longer it went on, the better the U.S. military became at learning how to fight it—even if this fact alone is not a guarantee of success. Given that it is hard to have perspective while still caught up in the fighting, military "learning" normally takes place after a conflict is completed, whatever the outcome. Thus, we have the well-known saying that "generals tend to fight the last war," meaning that they tend to learn and apply the lessons of a previous conflict, whether or not they are applicable to their present situation. In the Philippines, however, the U.S. Army's inability to defeat Aguinaldo's force quickly and decisively helped ensure that there would be ample time for the Americans to learn how to beat them. The Americans learned that they had to be tougher at the counterinsurgency game than the guerrillas if they were going to win this war.

Like so many counterinsurgency strategies, repression was not glamorous. Indeed, many American soldiers complained that they had been reduced to police officers in their monitoring of food production and patrolling pacified villages. And, like so many counterinsurgency strategies, the results were only fully apparent after they had succeeded. The U.S. Army realized that it did not need to defeat the insurgency but simply deflate it. In the simplest terms, it attempted this by increasing the "cost of membership" of being a guerrilla. So while finding a rifle here or capturing a guerrilla there did not appear to be much of a war, repression in sum ended up being remarkably successful in undermining Aguinaldo's guerrilla strategy.

Yet MacArthur's initial approach was not all sticks. He implemented a widespread amnesty program to get the insurrectos to lay down their arms. In this program, insurgents who surrendered and took an oath of allegiance to the United States could return to civilian life without harm. Only 5,000 Filipinos took up the offer, a small fraction of the overall insurrection force of roughly 80,000. Moreover, from the beginning of the conflict, the U.S. government and army promoted efforts such as building schools and sanitation campaigns to win the hearts and minds of the local population as well as to "civilize" the country. The schools were especially successful; American soldiers often served as teachers in regions that had sorely lacked any sort of formal education. In September 1898, General Otis established a public school system that started with seven schools in Manila. Within six months of occupation, the U.S. Army built 203 schools in northwestern Luzon that were attended by over 10,000 children. While "repression" was the "stick" of U.S. counterinsurgency strategy, this policy of "attraction" became the "carrot."

In March 1900, President McKinley appointed William Howard Taft to oversee the Second Philippine Commission. By September, the commission was operating to promote the political institutions and policies needed for stable government. While far from perfect, regions of the country pacified militarily were transferred to Taft's political administration. The end game of Taft's work was that, through innovative efforts such as bringing Filipinos (including former guerrillas) into local government, it ultimately gave many Filipinos a serious stake in U.S.-led pacification and nation-building. Also, in establishing political institutions such as a supreme court, the policies demonstrated to Filipinos that American rule would be substantially different from that of the Spanish colonial predecessors.

A HOWLING WILDERNESS

Repression and attraction were the two main components of the U.S. counterinsurgency and nation-building (read, colonial) efforts. There is considerable disagreement among political historians as to whether this combination represented a brilliant combination of counterinsurgency carrots and sticks or another instance of the ends justifying reprehensible means. What scholars do agree upon, though, is that the particular strategy adopted – and the very nature of the guerrilla conflict in this far-away archipelago – did seem to promote an unusually high number of American atrocities.

Again like the British experience in the Boer War, soldiers' letters home were the main media through which the American public became aware of the atrocities. Newspapers routinely published the shocking accounts; anti-imperialist editors and others back at home were outraged that Americans were doing exactly what the Spanish had done in Cuba and the British had done in southern Africa. The public was reading in vivid detail that the Philippines was a dirty war and that Americans were often doing the dirty work. In one soldier's account, "We snuck through the grass as high as a man's head until both platoons had flanked them. We opened fire and killed all but one. They were unarmed."[42] Boston's *Evening Post* ran a soldier's account recalling the "people's shrieks and torments" as the villages were being burned.[43] We will see these sorts of atrocities committed in El Salvador. The difference, though, is that in the Philippines it was as often as not the Americans, and not local forces, who were carrying out the killings.

One especially notorious American practice in the Philippines was an interrogation technique called the "water cure." An account by A. F. Miller of the 32nd Volunteer Infantry Regiment was published in the Omaha *World-Herald* in May 1900. In it, Miller explains how his unit was able to uncover hidden weapons from intelligence gained from the water cure. He also described what the treatment entailed. "Lay them on their backs, a man standing on each hand and foot, then put a round stick in the mouth and pour a pail of water in the mouth and nose, and if they don't give up pour in another pail. They swell up like toads. I tell you it is a terrible torture."[44]

The pro-imperialist euphoria that had followed Dewey's cakewalk at Manila Bay now seemed a relic of a far-off time. In an effort to stop what they believed was an unjust war, some antiwar activists actually corresponded with guerrilla leaders and sent pamphlets to American troops urging them to abandon the fighting.[45] This infuriated imperialists such as President Theodore Roosevelt, who had no patience for what he believed were terribly naive and dangerous sympathies:

If the so-called anti-imperialists ... would honestly ascertain the truth on the ground and not in distant America, they would be convinced of the error of their statements and conclusions, and of the unfortunate effect of their publications here. If I am shot by a Filipino bullet it might just as well come from one of my own men, because I know from observations confirmed by captured prisoners that the continuance of fighting is chiefly due to reports that are sent out from America.[46]

Some of the most egregious of the estimated one hundred atrocities committed by American forces resulted in military trials. One of the more publicized instances stemmed from the reprisals ordered after Filipino insurgents ambushed American troops in late September 1901, in the town of Balangiga on the southern coast of Samar island, killing over half of the seventy-four-man company in hand-to-hand combat.[47] The Filipino attack, known as the Balangiga massacre, was considered the U.S. military's worst defeat since the Battle of Little Big Horn. Brigadier General Jacob "Hell-Roaring Jack" Smith (his nickname came from his boastfulness, not ruthlessness) ordered one of his majors to make the island a "howling wilderness," stating that "I want no prisoners, I wish you to burn and kill; the more you kill and burn, the better it will please me."

American soldiers conducted yet another scorched-earth campaign, but this one was on an entirely different order. Under Smith's directive, the Americans targeted Filipinos over the age of ten, including women and children. One major reported destroying more than 250 dwellings over an eleven-day period. Within six months, Samar was "quiet as a cemetery."[48] Scholarly estimates on the number of civilians killed during the reprisal period was between 2,500 and 50,000. Smith faced court-martial in 1902; he was found guilty but only forced to retire.

While the Roosevelt administration did deplore some of the American atrocities, it also went to great lengths to put such behavior in context. In 1902, Secretary of War Elihu Root responded to accusations of American excess by pointing out that the Filipino insurgency had been "conducted with the barbarous cruelty common among uncivilized races." He continued that U.S. operations had been enacted with "scrupulous regard for the rules of civilized warfare, with careful and genuine consideration for the prisoner and the noncombatant, with self-restraint, and with humanity never surpassed, if ever equaled, in any conflict, worth only of praise, and reflecting credit on the American people."[49] Root's vigorous defense of American actions highlights a key element of any dirty war: some will see the counterinsurgency actions as just and appropriate while others will view the same actions much more critically.

AGUINALDO CAPTURED

In late March 1901, the U.S. counterinsurgency effort scored a victory that dealt a lethal blow to the Filipino insurgency. Employing Macabebe Scouts who pretended to be their captors, the disguised "prisoners" (General Frederick Funston and some soldiers) marched over 100 miles, deep into Aguinaldo's hidden lair at Palanan. Once close enough, they surprised the Filipinos and took Aguinaldo prisoner, killing several guards in the process. U.S. commanders did not want to make a martyr of the Filipino nationalist, so they treated him well. Fortunately for the Americans, within a few weeks Aguinaldo swore allegiance to the United States and urged his erstwhile guerrilla comrades to lay down their arms.[50] Aguinaldo later ran for president of the Philippine Commonwealth in 1935, when he was badly defeated. In the weeks and months following Aguinaldo's declaration, 13,000 Filipino guerrillas surrendered.

America, Aguinaldo, and the Philippines

FIGURE 6.2. Stereopticon card showing part of the destroyed Spanish fleet following the Battle of Manila. The American war against Spain in the Philippines quickly turned to a U.S counterinsurgent campaign against Filipino nationalists led by Emilio Aguinaldo. This bloody conflict polarized public opinion back home in the United States. Aguinaldo was eventually captured, which helped seal the American victory. Courtesy of the Library of Congress, Prints and Photographs Division, LC-USZ62-19547

A "SUCCESSFUL" CONCLUSION

By July 1902, the Filipino insurrection was effectively over. During this month, President Roosevelt congratulated his armed forces on the "successful conclusion" of the military operations in the Philippines. The war claimed over 4,000 U.S. soldiers' lives in combat; an equal number fell from disease. Over 125,000 American troops served in the conflict. Some estimates place the number of Filipinos killed at 16,000, with another 200,000 civilians dying from disease, famine, and American-led massacres. The war lasted roughly as long as the Civil War. Almost all of the U.S. generals who held commands in the Philippines had also fought in the Indian Wars.

Like most failed insurrections, the Filipino insurrection did not die all at once. Rather, it petered out over several years, long after it represented any serious challenge to the standing government. There are several reasons for the American success. For one, the insurrectos' brutal policies antagonized many Filipinos. Thus, when they compared the insurgents' heavy-handedness with American "attraction" policies, they considered the American strategy to be more benign and preferable. Moreover, lacking a global or neighboring power to supply it with materiel and funding, Aguinaldo's force also suffered from a complete dearth of the external assistance that can often be the "make or break" factor in determining an insurgency's success.

Aguinaldo did have his advantages. For one, he had the benefit of fighting on home soil. The American force was far from its shores and, at least initially, was unprepared to fight in the unfamiliar and hostile jungle terrain. Aguinaldo also had the nationalist cause on his side. Despite the collapse of the Filipino insurrection, one should hesitate to conclude as writer Max Boot does that the American campaign was "one of the most successful counter-insurgencies by a Western army in modern times."[51] Since this point obviously depends on who defines success, perhaps a more fitting conclusion is that the United States eventually achieved its political goals despite many fits and starts in what was a searing dirty war campaign followed by a relatively benevolent colonial administration.

After realizing how difficult quelling the nationalist insurgency would be, pacification, not conquest, became the goal and in this regard the United States was successful. By the war's end, the United States eventually got the nation-building right through a patient and comprehensive set of policies that included building roads, railways, ports, dams, and irrigation plants; expenditures on health and education led to a doubling of the Filipino population between 1900 and 1920, and literacy rose from 20 to 50 percent within roughly the same time.[52] Yet the ultimately "successful" pacification was still a dirty business in the Philippines. Not surprisingly given the historical evidence of excessive force, to some contemporary observers the United States owes the Philippines a belated apology for the atrocities and outrages committed during the war. A century ago, Teddy Roosevelt certainly believed that America's aims and efforts in the Philippines were noble. By "dissolving cruelty" [through defeating Aguinaldo's forces], he once said,

> our armies do more than bring peace, do more than bring order, they bring freedom. ... The warfare that has extended the boundaries of civilization at the expense of barbarism and savagery has been for centuries one of the most potent factors in the progress of humanity. Yet, from its very nature it has always and everywhere been liable to dark abuses.[53]

7

Chasing Villa, 1916

This book is dedicated to the officers and men of the Old Army whose gallant services, whether in the deserts of Arizona, the snows of the far north, the jungles of Cuba, the rice swamps of the Philippines, or the plateaus of Mexico, have added many a brilliant page to our National Identity.
– Major Frank Tompkins, author of *Chasing Villa*[1]

Intervention must be avoided until a time comes when it is inevitable, which God forbid!
– President Woodrow Wilson to his wife[2]

In the morning darkness of March 9, 1916, a band of 400 to 500 troops under the command of the legendary revolutionary general, Francisco "Pancho" Villa, raided the small American cavalry outpost of Camp Furlong, near Columbus, New Mexico, three miles north of the Mexican border. While Villa had become well known for heading bold charges throughout the Mexican Revolution, still raging in 1916, this time he led from the rear, dividing his forces and sending an advance guard of eighty men ahead into the town. Although the raid was not a total surprise – Villa had not been sighted for a month and there had been reports that he was planning a raid on a border town – the cavalry at Camp Furlong were caught unprepared.[3] Many of the troops had been up reveling late into the night, and most of their rifles and ammunition were under lock.[4]

The cavalry finally mobilized and set up two machine guns on opposite sides of the town, trapping the Villistas in the crossfire. Interestingly, the army camp did not receive the brunt of Villa's attack; it was instead a classic plundering and pillaging venture, as Villa's men went house-to-house searching for precious stores of weapons, horses, and money that they

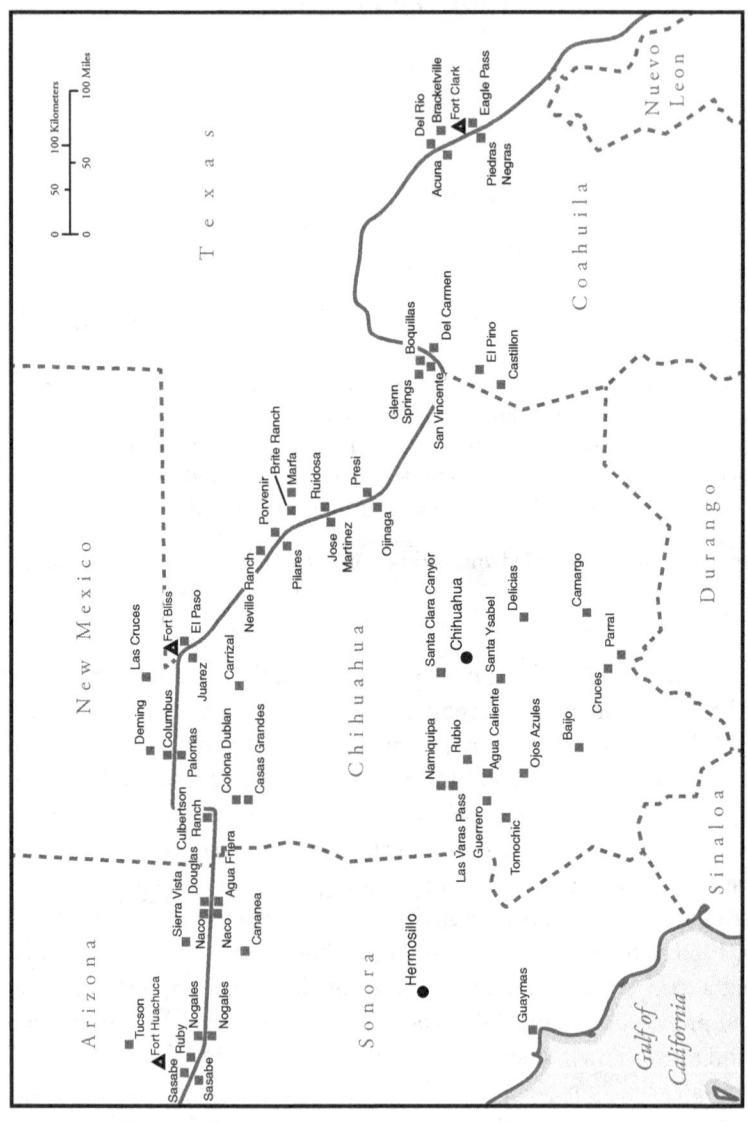

FIGURE 7.1. Punitive Expedition, 1916. Map prepared by the University of Wisconsin-Madison Cartography Lab©. Reprinted with permission

could shunt back across the border. Yet, with a population of roughly 350 men, women, and children, Columbus had little to offer in terms of treasure for these desperate Mexican revolutionaries. Instead, the settlement was a "cluster of adobe houses, a hotel, a few stores and streets knee deep in sand, combined with the cactus, mesquite, and rattlesnakes."[5]

Historians still debate whether Villa's main rationale for the daring raid was indeed to capture booty or rather retaliate against the *gringo* government that had stopped supporting him in favor of his arch-rival and president of the "preconstitutional" Mexican republic, Venustiano Carranza. In fact, following a recent failed battle against Carranza's U.S.-supplied forces the previous October, a vengeful Villa threatened, "from this moment on, I will devote my life to the killing of every Gringo I can get my hands on and the destruction of all Gringo property." In the ensuing months, Villa targeted vulnerable U.S. citizens in both Mexico and across the border.[6] In strictly military terms, the raid was a disaster for Villa. A brilliant but congenitally compulsive military strategist, Villa lost 100 men to bullets; 30 more were captured, and he failed to seize any weapons, money, or supplies. It was a devastating turn of fate for the vaunted revolutionary general.

Back in February 1914, an ambivalent American president Woodrow Wilson had openly opposed the government of Victoriano Huerta despite that fact that the U.S. Ambassador in Mexico, Henry Lane Wilson, had conspired with Huerta to overthrow the civilian president Francisco Madero the previous year. Wilson now decided to lift the arms embargo that had cut off arms to the "Constitutionalist" (effectively Carranza's) forces opposing Huerta. Two months later, Wilson went a step further when he instructed the U.S. Navy to occupy the port of Veracruz to prevent the Huerta regime from receiving a shipment of German arms. U.S forces were able to gain control of the city but only after they inflicted hundreds of casualties on Huerta's troops as well as civilians. Both "Hueristas" and Constitutionalists reacted angrily to the American military intervention.

Based in the northern region of Chihuahua and commander of the feared División del Norte, Villa helped the Constitutionalists battle the Huerta forces, which helped lead to the dictator's ouster in August 1914 and Carranza's ascension to power. To make matters even more confusing, Carranza was subsequently forced from Mexico City by Villa's forces, who then occupied the capital. However, Constitutionalists returned Carranza to power in August 1915, forcing Villa on the defensive. Needless to say, the erstwhile allies were now bitter enemies.

Initially, the Wilson administration favored Villa over Carranza as the future post-Huerta president. Yet, by late 1915, Villa had suffered several battle defeats including the decisive Battle of Celaya, in which 4,000 of his soldiers were killed and another 6,000 were captured. Carranza also promised to protect U.S. property, which further prompted Woodrow Wilson to recognize his government. Villa's once formidable army, which had entered triumphantly into Mexico City only months earlier, was now a shadow of its former self. As both a bandit and a revolutionary, Villa seemed to be on his last legs. And, like so many other Mexican revolutionaries who succumbed to acts of political betrayal, Villa would ultimately meet his fate in battle. Yet the Columbus raid was at least one indication that the seasoned rebel had some fight left in him.

AMERICA RETALIATES

In addition to the destruction and plunder, Villa's men killed seventeen Americans in the raid on Columbus. Most of the American defenders came from the U.S. Army contingent stationed at Camp Furlong on the outskirts of Columbus. The 13th U.S. Cavalry was led by Colonel Herbert J. Slocum. After Villa's troops had fled, Major Frank Tompkins reported to Slocum, requesting permission to pursue the Villista raiders. Permission was granted and Tompkins and thirty-two men rode off in hot pursuit.[7]

Within hours, Tompkins's men had violated the War Department's restrictions on crossing the Mexican border. Yet, following the Columbus raid, few Americans would be upset to hear that vengeful Americans had crossed into Mexican territory to apprehend and even to kill the cold-blooded Villa. This was especially the case since the images of horror along the border were published on the front pages of newspapers across the United States. William F. "Buffalo Bill" Cody quickly integrated Villa's raid into his Wild West Show. Men from all parts of the country volunteered to head south to protect American soil and dignity.

Tompkins's pursuit failed to locate the wily and elusive Villista forces. Meanwhile, back in Columbus, the American cavalry treated the surviving Mexican prisoners harshly. Colonel Slocum offered these unflinching words to a dying prisoner: "Let him bake in the sun."[8] The burial party that encountered this doomed Villista prisoner immediately beat him, threw him into the wagon, and continued to the cremation site. Several Mexican residents of Columbus were tried and hanged as conspirators. While they certainly did not start this particular fight, the civilian and military residents of Columbus were eager to play dirty in their response to Villa's provocation.

As the dust settled in Columbus, American President Woodrow Wilson made a fateful decision. After meeting with his cabinet to discuss the thorny issue of how to respond without provoking a reaction from the Mexican government, then led by Venustiano Carranza, he instructed the army to pursue Villa inside Mexican territory. The War Department sent an unequivocal order to General Funston, Major General in the southern United States, "You will promptly organize an adequate military force of troops from your department under the command of General John J. Pershing and will direct him to proceed promptly across the border in pursuit of the Mexican band which attacked the town of Columbus, New Mexico, and the troops there on the morning of the ninth."[9]

Given that he had fought in the Indian wars for five years and against insurgents in the Philippines, the battle-seasoned "Black Jack" was a reasonable pick for command of this "hot little campaign."[10] Yet, unlike the conflict waged by the British in the Boer War or the Spanish in Cuba, this was not to be an especially nasty dirty war. American objectives were not about occupation of foreign lands or pacification of a hostile population but rather capture of a bandit. Not that any plans were on file for this sort of "counter-bandit" operation, however.[11]

Wilson's decision to launch Pershing's "Punitive Expedition" was driven by an American public clamoring for revenge. One contemporary, Mary Means Scott, recalled the patriotic fervor she felt when witnessing the Punitive Expedition's incursion into Mexico near Columbus:

And then the day arrived when General Pershing planned to enter Mexico! Men, horses, field artillery, trucks, supplies, repair units, all poised for the start. As usual, the townspeople were caught up in the great moment – retribution was at hand. It would be the culminating show. Early, at the border, marked by a barbed-wire fence, families began to gather.... We watched for hours, it seemed as the horses and riders passed in a giant parade: flags and guidons flying; pistols at the waist, sabres at the saddle, all enveloped in a canopy of dust. There was applause, whistles, waves, and shouts of "goodbye" as friends came into view. Then men and boys volunteered much advice on what to do with Pancho Villa when caught. It was a great exodus – an historic hour. The might of the United States army departing on a punitive expedition to right a wrong visited upon an unsuspecting border town – the cavalry to the rescue! It was a thrilling sight to us.[12]

Yet despite the emotion and expectations of a speedy triumph that accompanied the invading troops, the expedition almost immediately became a much-maligned effort by a sizable American military force to apprehend one man and his small cadre of followers. While quite wary of the prospect of a general war with Mexico, the War Department did not set limits on the depth of Pershing's penetration. And as historian Rachel St. John has written, while there was no declaration of war, the United States seemed to be going to war.

The Wilson administration's decision to act unilaterally against Villa inside Mexico turned into an effective assault on Mexican sovereignty, something that infuriated Carranza. Wilson's Secretary of State Robert Lansing informed the Carranza government that if it was "unwilling or unable to give this protection by preventing its territory from being the rendezvous and refuge of murderers and plunders, that does not relieve this Government from its duty to take all steps necessary to safeguard American citizens on American soil."[13] That is, if Mexico City would not act, Washington would. And a century later, American president George W. Bush articulated a rationale similar to Lansing's. But instead of the Carranza government's provision of sanctuary for Villa's band, for Bush it was the Taliban regime in Kabul providing a safe haven for the perpetrators of the terrorist attacks on September 11, 2001, and they needed to be called to task.

BANDIT CHASING

While the Americans learned many lessons about new modes of war, fighting in its extended pursuit of a mobile foe with intimate knowledge of the local terrain, the expedition nonetheless ended in humiliation for the United States. What is more, Washington's initially limited operation to punish a *bandido* nearly spiraled into a full-scale war with its southern neighbor.

From the outset, numerous obstacles beset the operation. Not least among these was Villa's strategic advantage in having spent the last several years fighting federal troops across the rough terrain of the Sierra Madre region; plus, he had a nine-day head-start on the American forces. For another thing, the U.S. planners had no strategic plans at the top level for a "counter-bandit" operation. Instead, the War Department had only full-scale invasion plans that included seaborne operations at the port cities of Guaymas and Veracruz.[14] With communications with Washington slowed by technological deficiencies, the expedition had little campaign-level oversight. Although horribly frustrated by these factors and by Villa's elusiveness, the Punitive

Expedition was nonetheless noteworthy for the U.S. Army's unexpected yet remarkable innovations on the battlefield, many of which soon acquired dramatic – and more organized – relevance in the muddy trenches of France.

Pershing's force consisted of three brigades: two of cavalry and one of infantry. In the first serious U.S. Army action since the Philippine insurrection fifteen years earlier, the American force of approximately 10,000 troops established its main camp in the Mexican town of Casas Grandes, 120 miles south of Columbus. From the very beginning, the Punitive Expedition faced formidable logistical obstacles. Medical equipment and medicine, for starters, were constantly in short supply; communication across the border was sporadic as there was no functioning telegraph line. Supplies such as food, water, and ammunition were readily available in the United States and easily transported to Columbus and El Paso, but problems arose as the Americans attempted to bring these materials over the border to a force that was continuously pushing deeper into Mexican territory in search of Villa. Matters were not made any easier by Mexico's railway network being off-limits to the Americans. Carranza was worried that allowing the foreign troops to use the railways would incite a backlash against his government for not standing up to the gringos.[15]

Left without access to the trains, the Americans turned to a novel form of transportation, the automobile. In fact, the use of motorized transport had not yet been formalized in U.S. military doctrine, but by the end of the campaign the innovation was marked as a breakthrough in waging war. At times, truck parts arrived "disassembled without directions, tools, or anyone who knew how to fit them together."[16] Hence, using automobiles (in addition to wagons and mules) forced the Army to employ civilian mechanics in its ranks, since they were the only ones who knew how to repair the machines. Eventually, the U.S. Army used trucks to carry 10,000 tons of supplies into Mexico, much of it fodder for the animals that carried the equipment southward from Casa Grandes.

The Punitive Expedition's other historic innovation was the deployment of air power. Led by Captain Benjamin D. Foulois, the First Aero Squadron consisted of eight Curtiss JN-3 biplanes known as "Jennies." Interestingly, although the pilots were more than up to the task, the planes themselves could fly only in calm weather and suffered innumerable breakdowns. Also, the expedition's area of operations was primarily over the jagged Sierra Madre Mountains, which made the airplanes almost worthless. Within a month, all of the Jennies had crashed.

Despite the logistical obstacles, Pershing maintained a strategy of using cavalry to strike deep into Villa's ever-shifting mountain hideouts. The contingent never captured Villa, although it came close on a few occasions. The American troops did, however, break records for the fastest and longest marches in U.S. cavalry history. One key element was the use of "flying columns," wherein troops carried only the supplies they could hold on their backs. In some instances and echoing the British tactics in the Boer War, the pursuing Americans lived off the land in order to prolong the duration of their missions. The idea was to get American troops to be as mobile and dispersed as possible in pursuing the evading Villistas.

In this sense, the Punitive Expedition was mirroring the strategy and tactics of General Crooks's innovative "counterinsurgency" force against the Apaches. Major Frank Tompkins described the conditions during a prolonged operation: "We were rapidly losing all outward resemblance to regular troops. We were ragged, shoes almost gone and nearly everyone had a beard. We certainly presented a hard-boiled, savage appearance."[17] In what is often a necessary counterinsurgency tactic, the Americans had adapted to their enemy's disciplines (or, perhaps in this case, the lack thereof) in their tireless pursuit of the Villistas. Yet no level of gumption or acclimatization could fundamentally change the reality that the U.S. troops were searching for Villa on his home territory: an arid, rocky region the size of Virginia, North Carolina, and South Carolina combined that was horribly inhospitable to foreigners lacking good maps and surveillance. It is worth noting that these three factors – a discrepancy between the two forces in familiarity with the theater of operations, a large geographical space, and terrain that is difficult to traverse – are often decisive for the success of insurgent and counterinsurgent activities. In modern history, counterinsurgency forces have tended to have the disadvantage in each of these factors. Pershing's expedition was no exception.

It was perhaps inevitable that once Pershing failed to quickly catch Villa, his "invasion" would cause a political row between Washington and Mexico City. This was largely because Mexican public sentiment was overwhelmingly opposed to the presence of American troops on their soil. As one analyst put it, they were "about as eager to help the Americans in capturing their hero as were the people of Sherwood Forest to help the Sheriff of Nottingham capture Robin Hood."[18]

As the campaign wore on, tensions rose between the U.S. troops and the "Carrancista," or federal government troops, who had initially been at least a tense ally with the Americans given their mutual enemy. A series of skirmishes and battles between the two forces ensued. The most salient of

FIGURE 7.2. American fliers Edgar Staley Gorrell and Herbert Arthur Dargue at the Mexican front during the Punitive Expedition into Mexico, 1916. During this campaign in 1916, American forces pursued elusive revolutionary bandit Francisco "Pancho" Villa deep into Mexican territory. Washington's expedited limited intervention almost led to a broader war between the two countries. Led by General John "Black Jack" Pershing, the campaign failed to capture Villa but the irregular war tactics learned helped prepare American forces for their involvement in World War I a few years later. Courtesy of the Library of Congress, Prints and Photographs Division, LC-USZ62-92483

these took place in Carrizal, Chihuahua, on June 21, 1916, about three months after the Punitive Expedition first entered Mexico. Captain Charles T. Boyd ordered an aggressive march through Carrizal. The Carrancista commander of the town refused entry, knowing he had hundreds of men in well-defended positions to back up his intransigence, not including the numerous armed civilians who were also willing to take on the gringo invaders. Boyd ordered the inferior American forces, about 100 men, to attack in two groups over open ground. In the ensuing fight, which lasted two hours, 10 Americans were killed (including all of the officers), and 23 were taken prisoner.[19]

The Battle of Carrizal was a disaster for both the U.S. Army and the Wilson administration. Instead of fighting Villistas, now it seemed that the Americans were fighting (and losing) against their erstwhile Carrancista allies and spiteful villagers. This was not the easy and dramatic success for which the Wilson administration and military planners in Washington had hoped. Carrizal also helped increase the likelihood of a full-scale war between Mexico and the United States. Public sentiment back in the United States only served to heighten the war fever. Americans wanted to see Villa face justice, but they were also frustrated that Carranza had not done more to accommodate the invading troops. Editorials published at the time in William Randolph Hearst's *New York Journal* were indicative of the American fervor:

Is it not the time for soldiers of the U.S. to do something PERMANENT? ... Nothing worthwhile will be accomplished by occasional "punitive expeditions." ... The way to IMPRESS the Mexicans is to REPRESS the Mexicans.... The way to begin is to say to them "We are no longer planning to catch this bandit or that. We are GOING INTO MEXICO. And as far as we GO, we'll stay.[20]

In response to the demand to avenge the episode at Carrizal, as well as other humiliations, the War Department ordered General Funston to seize all international bridges across the Rio Grande in order to prepare for a full-scale American invasion into Mexico.[21] While he too was frustrated with Carranza, President Wilson knew that an all-out war with Mexico was the last thing the United States needed at the time. Germany, not Mexico, was the real threat, and America's military force needed to be ready to battle the European power. Thus, Wilson ordered his men to effectively "lie low" to lessen the chance that the American troops would engage Carrancistas without appearing to have retreated in defeat. Thus, while Pershing's force would remain in Mexico for another seven months, the hunt for Pancho Villa had all but ended.

Chasing Villa, 1916

The Punitive Expedition lasted less than a year, from March 1916 to January 1917. Like the case of the Americans against the Viet Cong in Vietnam, Pershing's troops defeated the Villistas in the major encounters. Yet despite these tactical victories, the campaign was a miserable failure. Instead of capturing or killing Villa, the Americans enhanced his strength and aura. His depleted band of 400 men had now risen to perhaps 5,000 fighters during the same short period. Soon after crossing back onto U.S. soil, a despondent General Pershing wrote privately, "Having dashed into Mexico with the intention of eating the Mexicans raw, we turn back at the very first repulse and are now sneaking home under cover like a whipped cur with his tail between his legs."[22]

Yet, more than this, the Punitive Expedition was the end of one era and the beginning of another for the U.S. Army. The campaign was the last U.S. military operation whose critical element was the mounted cavalryman. Another unanticipated benefit of this frustrating mission was that it gave Pershing and his men ample time to train and practice. This experience and learning came in handy in Europe soon after the Punitive Expedition had ceased its mission. More central for our purposes in this book, the Punitive Expedition foreshadowed the sorts of dirty wars that would occupy and often stymie American forces – as well as political leaders – in Central America and the Caribbean for the next two decades.

8

A Cold Winter in Siberia

We have no heart for the fight.
  – Message written anonymously and shared among American troops awaiting their withdrawal, Siberia, 1920[1]

If nothing else, the Russian intervention is one of the classic examples of where war starts: in war rooms all over the world; warm, well-appointed rooms where men can play politics and dwell on the certainty of results rather than the magnitude of catastrophe.
  – Richard Goldhurst[2]

After a bittersweet experience in the imperial pacification campaign in the Philippines after 1898, as well as the more recent mission to apprehend Pancho Villa in 1916, American troops found themselves involved in the epic conflagration of World War I. The United States' belated military entrance into this war, in April 1917 with the declaration of war on Germany, proved decisive in the outcome of the conflict, helping to ensure the victory of America's key allies, Britain and France.

While the collective memory of participation in this great conflict has naturally declined over time, Americans continue to evoke what they perceive as a generally noble involvement and a war fought largely in muddy trenches in France; yet, as World War I began its denouement, American soldiers deployed in Russia were only just embarking on a remarkable but forgotten dirty war that received scant attention compared to the American campaign in France.

Begun in 1918, the American intervention in Russia was part of a broad Allied campaign aimed at maintaining Russian military forces in combat against the Central Forces (most critically Germany and Austria-Hungary)

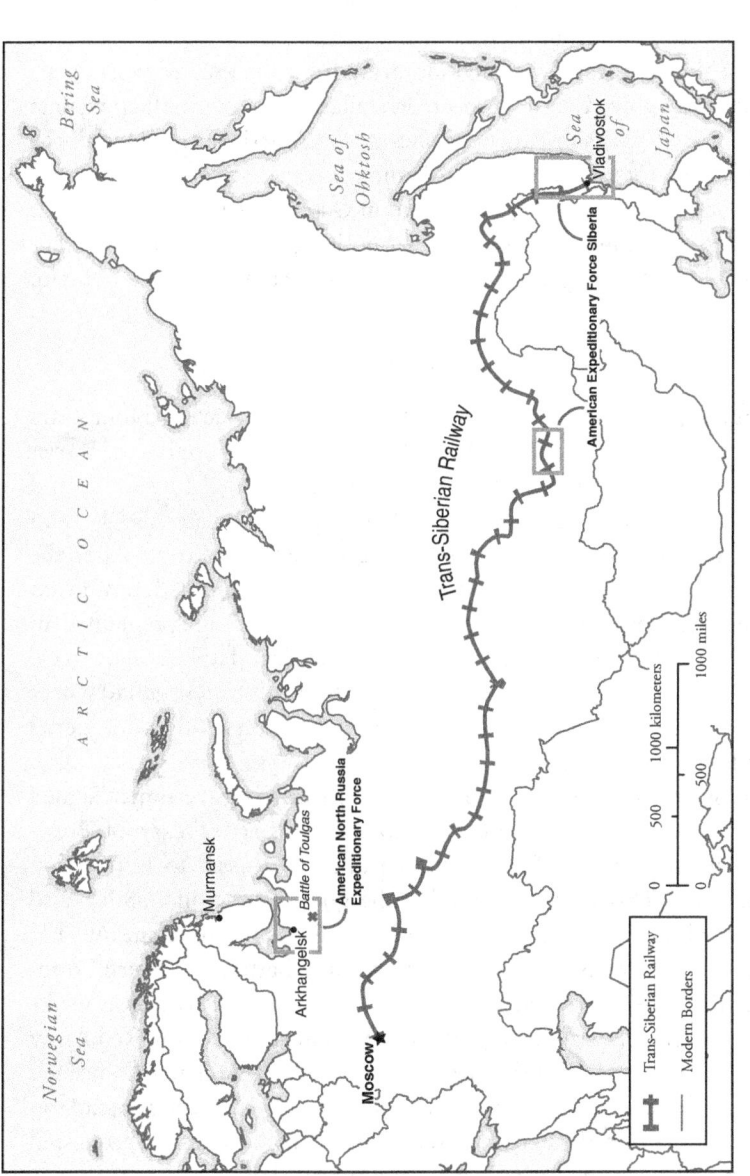

FIGURE 8.1. The Allied and American intervention in Russia, 1918–1920. The boxes represent the theaters of operation for the two distinct American campaigns: the American North Russian Expeditionary Force, which fought in North Russia, near Arkhangelsk, and the American Expeditionary Force Siberia, which served near the port of Vladivostok, focusing their operations on the protection of the Trans-Siberian Railroad. Also marked, the Battle of Toulgas was the site of a fierce offensive by Bolshevik guerrillas over which the Allied forces managed to triumph only after incurring severe casualties. Map prepared by the University of Wisconsin-Madison Cartography Lab©. Reprinted with permission

while Russia faced internal turmoil. Starting in 1918, nearly 13,000 American soldiers were sent to the tumultuous country as part of this multinational campaign.[3] American forces would remain in Russia, awaiting a withdrawal forestalled by a severe winter, until 1920. While the impetus behind the Allied intervention grew from the greater world war, the campaign evolved into a more irregular form of conflict against Bolshevik forces. The subsequent clashes of the American troops with the ruling Bolshevik forces – who, led by Vladimir Lenin, had seized power after overthrowing the provisional government in October 1917 – exposed them to age-old guerrilla tactics as they fought an irregular war rooted in communist ideology. It was a war the Americans and the Allies would not win.

ORIGINS OF THE ALLIED INTERVENTION

The beginnings of the two-year American intervention occurred four years previously, in 1914, when the Allies began shipping supplies to tsarist Russia through key ports in Arkhangelsk (Archangel), Murmansk, and the remote Pacific city of Vladivostok in an effort to bolster the Russian military campaign against Germany along the Eastern Front. After the initial revolution in February 1917, these shipments continued, now given to the Russian Provisional Government, to ensure that Russia remained an ally for the Triple Entente. Pursuant to the sociopolitical upheaval of 1917, the European Allies and some in the Wilson administration began to worry about the millions of dollars of economic and military aid and materiel falling into Bolshevik hands.[4]

Upon assuming power in late 1917, the new Soviet government signed an initial armistice with Germany followed by 1918 Treaty of Brest-Litovsk with the Central Powers, which allowed Russia to fully resign from the war.[5] This decision appalled the governments in London and Paris, for whom the disintegration of the Eastern Front meant that Germany could refocus its efforts on the already battered Western Front. Additionally, fear increased among the Allies that if the Bolsheviks obtained the war materiel their governments had supplied, the Red Army might then use it to support the Germans. By 1918, Britain and France felt they had no choice but to intervene militarily. However, already spread too thin in the European theater, the French and British militaries requested reinforcements from the United States and other allies.[6]

In general, the initial Allied intervention was conceived to achieve three critical objectives: first, to ensure that Allied materiel did not end up with Bolshevik or German forces; second, to assist the Czech allies stranded

A Cold Winter in Siberia

FIGURE 8.2. U.S. Marines landing in the Pacific port city of Vladivostok in 1918. This city served as the central focus for one of two American campaigns in Russia, the American Expeditionary Force Siberia, as part of the Allied intervention into the Russian civil war. These American troops fought to safeguard Allied weapons, materiel, and equipment as well as the Trans-Siberian Railroad from Bolshevik control. AFP Collection, Permission by Getty Images, 96518590

along the Trans-Siberian railroad; and third, to revive the Eastern Front and defeat Bolshevism in cooperation with the White forces, a combination of anti-Bolshevik and pro-tsar groups that "banded themselves together secretly and sent repeated calls to the Allies for help in ridding their territory of" Bolshevik control.[7] The first two goals of the intervention spoke clearly to the Allies' drive to win World War I; yet the final objective diverged slightly toward an ideological conflict with the Bolsheviks and opened the door to irregular warfare with their Red forces.

Given that the newly ascendant Bolsheviks enjoyed political control of the government, relative popular support, and well-organized forces, it may appear odd that they used guerrilla tactics at all. Notwithstanding these advantages, the Bolsheviks fought to unseat lingering pockets of White Russians who opposed them throughout the vast country. Both the Red and White armies bolstered their ranks through peasant volunteers and were relatively evenly matched until the Whites began receiving Allied munitions and supplies. While their clashes focused in western Russia, chiefly in the north Caucasus region, pockets of fighting also occurred in

Siberia and North Russia, where the American campaigns would be sent and ultimately drawn into the war.[8] The deep ideological divisions between the Red and White factions, and the battle for Russian hearts and minds, inevitably contributed to the irregularity of the Allied intervention and participation in the Russian civil war.

WILSON'S FATEFUL DECISION

In large part, it was this ideological conflict that made President Wilson wary of the Allies' proposed intervention, and so his decision to commit troops presumed American neutrality, at least at the outset. While both American campaigns – the North Russia and Siberia expeditions, as they were called – began as missions to safeguard those weapons and supplies from the Bolsheviks, they both, to varying extents, evolved into irregular warfare against Red forces employing guerrilla tactics.[9] The veil of neutrality the two expeditions assumed would dissipate under pressure from the other Allied forces and their commanders, as well as the increasing participation in direct combat with Bolshevik forces.

Before this descent into irregular warfare, President Wilson first had to sanction the use of American military personnel in the Allied intervention. Weighing his decision, Wilson struggled with a dilemma: as a rhetorical champion of self-determination, and having already pursued recent problematic interventions in Mexico and the Caribbean, he was wary of intervening in Russia given the uncertainty of the outcome and general war-weariness felt by his people.[10] Ultimately, British and French leaders, as well as domestic advisers, successfully coaxed the reluctant president into joining the intervention. However, Wilson's reservations manifested themselves in the campaign's vague and confusing policies – for example, the conflict between the "neutrality" promised by Washington and the other Allies' intention to confront Bolshevik forces directly. The American approach failed to address the realities on the ground, such as the inevitable conflict between the Bolshevik and Allied forces that ensued over the railways, which played an integral role in shipping war materiel.[11]

At the urging of French and British allies, who could not field a full intervention with their depleted troops and who still bore substantial responsibilities on the Western Front, Wilson agreed to contribute American forces to a joint intervention. In July of 1918, Wilson authored his famous aide-mémoire, a document that was both a directive to American troops and their leaders and also a promise of American support

A Cold Winter in Siberia

to the Allied officials. The edict approved the United States' involvement in the intervention but gave only vague direction to the mission:

> Military action is admissible in Russia ... to steady any efforts of self-government or self-defense in which the Russians themselves may be willing to accept assistance. Whether from Vladivostok or from Murmansk and Archangel, the only legitimate object for which American or allied troops can be employed ... is to guard military stores.[12]

Despite its vague language, the aide-mémoire clearly made no direct challenge to Bolshevism as a political party; it did not explicitly reject the anti-Bolshevik sentiment that drove the French and British policies for the intervention. While Wilson intended the United States' involvement to remain neutral and limited to the protection of war materiel supplied by the Allies, the scope of the French and British objectives for the intervention extended into a direct challenge to Bolshevism, in the hope that it might be defeated, and with it, communism.[13] With these stark differences in purposes, the U.S. forces entered Russia as part of a mission that soon shifted from materiel safeguarding to an irregular war as external parties became entrenched in the Russian civil war.

BLOOD ON THE ICE

From Washington's policymaking, two separate, though similar, campaigns emerged that embodied the American role in the Russian intervention: one that would focus on protecting the Trans-Siberian Railway in Siberia from Red control as well as guarding Allied materiel stockpiles; the other that would guard similar equipment and munitions at the ports of North Russia. Neither campaign was intended to engage in direct combat with Red forces, but both campaigns faced a reality entirely different from the one described in Wilson's missive once they landed in Russia.[14] For instance, the Trans-Siberian Railroad served as a key site for transforming the intervention from weapons guarding to defense against and combat with the Bolshevik forces. Initially, the American Expeditionary Force Siberia had been charged with guarding the railway to assist with the evacuation of stranded Czech Legionnaires, who had already faced the Red guerrilla forces on the railways. Further into the intervention, the Inter-Allied Railway agreement, signed between the United States, Great Britain, France, Russia, Japan, Italy, and China on January 9, 1919, gave the Allies critical control of the railroads via a commission to which each signing nation sent a representative.[15]

The effect on the Siberian campaign was drastic. Suddenly "the primary concern of American forces ... became the restoration and protection of the railways ... [which] served to aid the anti-Bolshevik cause" and transformed the American presence in Russia into a partisan faction that summoned, in conjunction with the other Allies' anti-Bolshevik operations and propaganda, the Red insurgency from the civil war.[16] Notably, Red forces saw these railways as crucial targets upon which to focus their guerrilla tactics.

Under these conditions, U.S. Army commander General William S. Graves and his 8,000 troops in Siberia ended their neutrality, transforming their roles into those of counterinsurgents: a role familiar to those who had used similar tactics when they fought in the Philippines. For instance, General Graves and his soldiers focused on expanding their stronghold over villages in the Suchan valley as resistance to Bolshevik encroachment and in an effort to combat Bolshevism by winning the Russian people's allegiance.[17]

Although it was shorter than the Siberian campaign, which lasted nearly two years from the late summer of 1918 to the late spring of 1920, the North Russia campaign, whose troops were deployed from September 1918 to July 1919, also initially set out to protect weapons stockpiles.[18] Likewise, the American North Russian Expeditionary Force was inescapably pulled into guerrilla warfare with Red forces. These 5,000 American soldiers, who nicknamed themselves the "Polar Bears," faced the same "unknown tenaciousness" – the relentless attacks and constantly evolving tactics – of the Bolshevik fighters as did their Siberian-bound brothers-in-arms.[19]

Ironically, the deadliest battle for the American campaigns, occurring at Toulgas, southeast of Arkhangelsk, fell on Armistice Day, November 11, 1918; the Bolshevik guerrillas launched a surprise offensive against the Allied forces that turned into a days-long battle between insurgent Reds and counterinsurgent Allied and American forces.[20] The Bolsheviks used a plethora of guerrilla tactics that included attacking the Allied hospital in order to push the troops away from their own artillery guns and into the line of Bolshevik fire.[21] As American troops throughout Europe celebrated the end of the Great War, their fellow soldiers in North Russia fought against a brutal Bolshevik insurgent attack, incurring significant casualties on both sides, with the Allies ultimately emerging victorious as they pushed the Bolsheviks back from their position.[22]

American troops in both North Russia and Siberia "had fought a grim fight against terrible odds"; they had been spread far too thin across the vast territories of Russia and were unprepared for the guerrilla tactics used

A Cold Winter in Siberia

by Bolshevik forces.[23] In large part, the American campaign rhetorically rested on the concept of neutrality and appealing to the hearts and minds of the Russians, which stood in opposition to the other Allies' overt attempts at fighting Bolshevism by supporting the White forces; instead of focusing their efforts on anti-Bolshevik operations or propaganda, like the other Allied forces, the American troops initially directed their efforts toward helping Russian citizens and maintaining space between the Red and White forces.[24] Nevertheless, the Americans were inexorably drawn into the factionalism of the intervention and ended up clashing repeatedly with Bolshevik forces. So often in dirty wars counterinsurgents try to be the arbiter among different factions but end up becoming a faction themselves.

Even though many of these American soldiers, especially those stationed in North Russia, had previously experienced guerrilla warfare elsewhere, the Bolsheviks fought with new strategies and tactics that the American forces were unprepared to combat, often targeting economic aspects of the country that were less easily repaired and replaced than soldiers (i.e., infrastructure and transportation). In fact, these revolutionary techniques appeared in Mao Zedong's definition of guerrilla warfare in later years.[25] Additionally, the Red Army held the critical advantages typical of guerrilla forces: knowledge of the geography and terrain, intelligence on their enemies, confusion of the guerrillas with the general populace, and the ability to move swiftly through the country.[26] As the Allied troops faced increasing hardships, the Red insurgents "grew more adept [and] they began to take more desperate and damaging measures" that ultimately drove the U.S. and Allied forces to defeat.[27]

From its inception, the American intervention faced insurmountable challenges ranging from inconsistent policies to harsh climates to logistical obstacles. Indeed, President Wilson's initial decision to restrict American involvement had stemmed from concerns in the administration that overt military action would backfire – by casting anti-Bolshevism as a Western capitalist-supported endeavor – and would concomitantly grant the Bolsheviks more extensive popular support throughout Russia, increase their already great power, and push them toward an alliance with Germany in the Great War.[28] However, upon American withdrawal from Russia in 1920, this decision to limit American involvement emerged as most ironic, for the Bolshevik victory over the Allied forces' intervention had indeed bolstered their power.[29] Ultimately, the American and Allied intervention failed "completely and ignobly," and the experiences of the two American Expeditionary Forces in North Russia and Siberia became one of America's forgotten dirty wars.[30]

At the close of World War I, the various reasons used to justify the intervention became moot, resulting in a full withdrawal of all Allied forces, weary and defeated, by 1920. Scholars continue to debate the lasting effects of the failed intervention: some argue that the Allies' campaign catalyzed negative relations between Russia and the West that would characterize U.S.-Soviet relations for decades, while others contend that the Cold War inevitably resulted from political and economic tensions between the two superpowers.[31] Ultimately, the military failure has faded into history, the campaigns in Siberia and North Russia often forgotten as experiences in American counterinsurgency.

9

The Banana Wars, 1898–1930s

I fervently hope that we will have no more elections in Latin America to supervise.

– American diplomat, 1928[1]

History tends to remember well the Punitive Expedition because of the inimitable character of Pancho Villa and his revolutionary bandits. Yet, as we have seen, the expedition was an atypical dirty war in that it was a limited expedition rather than a broader pacification or counterinsurgency operation. This is not to say, though, that the United States did not deal with more "orthodox" dirty wars during this era. In fact, the so-called Banana Wars of the 1910s and 1920s in nations such as Haiti, the Dominican Republic, and Nicaragua were quintessential dirty wars of the American imperial variety.

Here were all the trappings of America's involvement in irregular conflict throughout its history: occupation and nation-building, jungles and mountains, elusive and sometimes charismatic rebels, atrocities, and bitter controversy back in the United States. The imperial Banana Wars of the early twentieth century were also some of America's first experiences with nation-building defined as establishing government ministries and holding elections, however imperfect or ephemeral these "indigenous" institutions often proved. In later decades, Vietnam and El Salvador and, subsequently, Iraq and Afghanistan would become the germane examples, but before these more recent efforts, the massive undertakings in the United States' own hemisphere involved many of the same strategies and obstacles of guerrilla and counterinsurgency warfare that the U.S. military is still learning to deal with today.

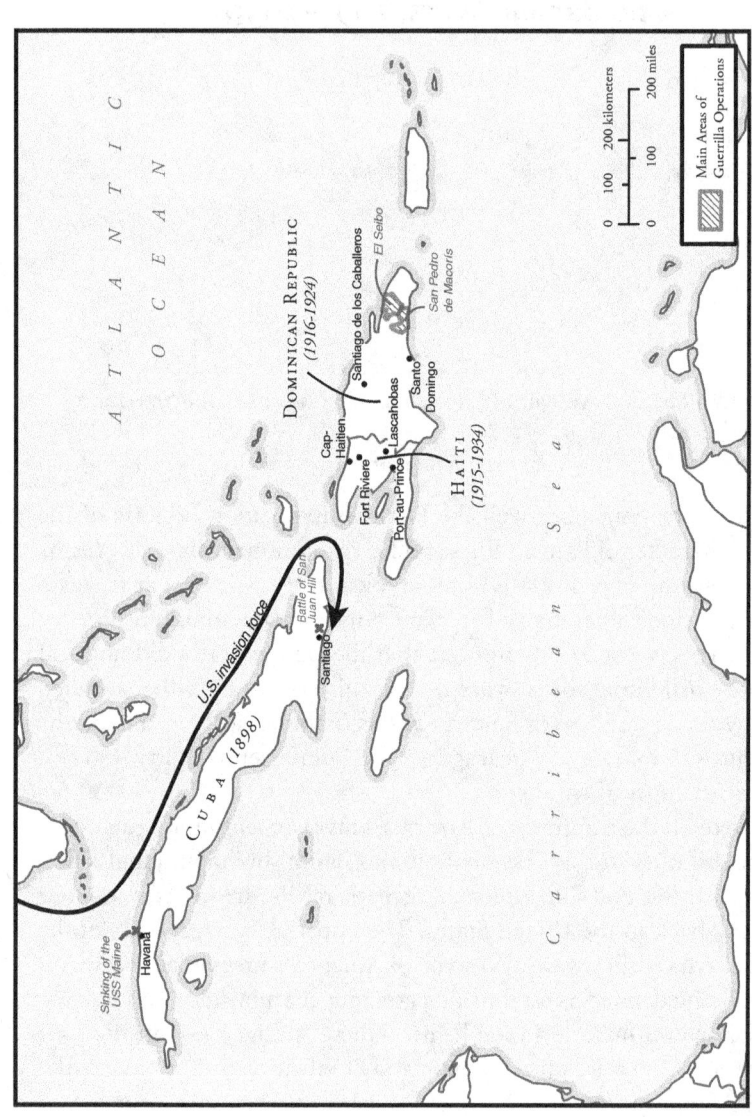

FIGURE 9.1. The Banana Wars, 1898–1930s. Over three decades, the United States repeatedly intervened in Cuba, Haiti, and the Dominican Republic in an attempt to protect U.S. interests in the region. Map prepared by the University of Wisconsin-Madison Cartography Lab©. Reprinted with permission

Americans' deep faith in the inevitability and righteousness of Manifest Destiny, which helped them settle the American West rapidly and enduringly, did not end after continental expansion was exhausted in the latter part of the nineteenth century. Instead, driven by a quickly growing industrial base in the 1890s, the United States began to flex its military and diplomatic muscles abroad, especially in the Caribbean and Central America. Interestingly, as U.S. policy in the region became increasingly militarized, successive administrations in Washington from 1898 to the early 1930s adopted rhetoric that strove to elevate the moral component of U.S. involvement in the region. Yes, they would admit, there was a strategic element that motivated American action; but there was also the moral imperative of promoting democracy. Washington struck a fine balance between its realist desire to keep its neighbors from becoming threats and its quasi-ethical imperative not to colonize or otherwise control these same countries.

Recognizing these seemingly conflicting objectives – intervening to promote pro-U.S. outcomes but also letting the countries govern their own affairs – helps explain the highly ambivalent attitude that Americans, including Presidents Theodore Roosevelt and Woodrow Wilson, the U.S. Congress, and the general public, held about America's flirtation with imperialism in the early decades of the twentieth century.

It should come as little surprise that maintaining American hegemony in its "backyard" required the use of military force. With the exception of the much larger war in the Philippines and the 1916 intervention to apprehend Mexican bandit Pancho Villa, both cases in which the U.S. Army did the fighting, America's imperial "shock troops" in the early twentieth century were the U.S. Marines. The marines applied the guerrilla warfare and counterinsurgency lessons they learned in the jungles and mountains of Nicaragua and Hispaniola to future battles in the South Pacific during World War II and, to a lesser extent, in Vietnam. In fact, some observers of the U.S. military's experience in Vietnam believe that the war's outcome might have been far more positive had the U.S. Army done a more thorough job of emulating the style of combat that the marines had used from 1898 to the early 1930s.

While the marines were the "boots on the ground" for the Banana Wars, it was the emergence of the U.S. Navy as a global force that also allowed the United States both to project and deploy what we now call "hard power." Alfred. T. Mahan's oft-cited 1890 publication *The Influence of Seapower upon History* helped to change the way that states around the world viewed their navies.[2] The most dramatic breakthroughs in ideas often appear simple and self-evident in hindsight; no less for Mahan, whose innovative observation was that global powers needed global navies. As a faculty member at the Naval War College, where he formulated the series of lectures that were the book's basis, Mahan befriended a young visiting lecturer named Theodore Roosevelt in 1897. Needless to say, Roosevelt became an ardent proponent of Mahan's doctrine, best demonstrated in December 1907, when, as president, Roosevelt sent off the sixteen battleships of the Great White Fleet from Hampton Roads, Virginia, for a tour around the world. Roosevelt correctly believed that the fleet's tour would send a strong message that the U.S. Navy was a force to be reckoned with.

The early Banana Wars did not require massive numbers of U.S. troops on the ground. Instead, deployments usually comprised fewer than 1,000 marines. From 1898 to 1933, the U.S. military was involved in over thirty operations in the Caribbean and Central America. Sometimes, the marine interventions would last only a few months before the situation was stabilized – often when debtor states made their payments to American creditors, or when the marines had defeated a certain faction. At the other end of the spectrum, the United States kept a military presence in Haiti for nineteen years!

While these actions were not conventional imperialism, we should not underestimate Washington's depth of involvement during many of these interventions. Washington trained police forces, supervised elections, and restructured customs houses. When needed, the U.S. military fought dirty wars against nationalist and anti-American guerrilla forces. The country's imperial nation-building project was conducted in an atmosphere of deep paternalism and racism. Few American policymakers questioned the premise that one major reason for the interventions was that the Latin Americans were incapable of governing themselves. And while not everyone stated this publicly, most U.S. officials also believed that the Latin "race" was not an inconsequential factor in explaining their chronic instability.

As in the Indian Wars, contemporary standards would hold the Banana Wars to be wholly politically incorrect, if not outright immoral. And like the Punitive Expedition, the Banana Wars took place amid fierce public debate at home. Interestingly, domestic opinion helped precipitate the war with Spain in 1898 as well as the effort to annex the Philippines shortly thereafter. But by the same right, American public opinion – in particular the belief that American troops were committing atrocities abroad – was also largely responsible for the increasing pressure to bring the troops home from Central America and the Caribbean in the 1920s.

Ironically, the Banana Wars reached their height during the administration of Woodrow Wilson, a president who based his 1916 reelection campaign on keeping America out of a war with Germany. Yet Wilson's messianic paternalism and desire to stamp out instability south of the border outweighed any of his pacifist instincts. Wilson twice ordered the U.S. forces into Mexico during its tumultuous revolution (the marines landed in Veracruz in 1914, and the U.S. Army tracked Pancho Villa in 1916); he also ordered marine occupations in Haiti (1915), the Dominican Republic (1916), and Cuba (1917).

"VIVA CUBA LIBRE! VIVAN LOS AMERICANOS!"

American high school students are taught that the sinking of the USS *Maine* in Havana harbor February 15, 1898, helped precipitate America's war with Spain in Cuba and the Philippines. What they are less aware of, however, is that Cuban insurgents, or *insurrectos*, had been fighting for independence since 1895 against more than 200,000 Spanish colonial troops. Realizing that they could never defeat the superior Spanish forces in conventional combat, the insurrectos adopted a guerrilla strategy that involved what we now call "scorched earth" tactics: forced displacement of civilians and brutal treatment of Spanish troops. According to one diplomatic historian, the insurrectos took such an approach because they were "determined to unfurl triumphantly, even over ruin and ashes, the flag of the Republic of Cuba."[3] The insurrectos also believed that they merely needed to hold against the Spanish, as it would be only a matter of time before the Americans would intervene and effectively guarantee Cuban independence.

In 1896, Madrid sent General Valeriano Weyler to Havana to serve as governor and commander in chief, and more to the point, to seize control of the insurgency. On October 21, 1896, Weyler issued an infamous order that established *reconcentrados* (concentration camps) in Spanish-controlled towns across the island. Cuban civilians were forced into the towns where, to an even greater degree than the British during the Boer War or the United States in the Philippines, the Spanish were unable to provide basic sustenance and sanitation for the civilians held there.[4] Thousands of Cubans died of disease and starvation. It merits mentioning that the Spanish army itself lost an estimated 44,000 men between 1895 and 1898, almost all to disease.[5] Weyler also revived a system from the 1870s that employed a series of fortified lines across the islands from west to east, not unlike the British blockhouse system in southern Africa.[6]

All told, despite these measures, the Spanish used poor tactics against their Cuban adversaries. Most notable was the army's propensity to remain entrenched in provincial towns instead of promoting mobile detachments of cavalry and mounted infantry that could have struck at the insurrectos' rural strongholds.[7] This is a remarkable case for our purposes because the Spanish excesses against Cuban insurgents infuriated Americans to the point that public opinion helped to instigate war against Spain. Thus, while these iron-fisted counterinsurgency tactics might have made some advances against the rebels, the strategy failed in that it greatly hastened an intervention that resulted in a swift and humiliating defeat for Spain. What is also remarkable is that, only a few years later, the U.S. Army implemented counterinsurgency tactics in the Philippines that were strikingly similar to what the Spanish had attempted in Cuba.

The insurrectos' cause was warmly received in the United States. Once again, the American public saw this as a classic small power's struggle for liberty against a colonial foe. The insurrectos received most of their funding from U.S. sources. In 1897, forty-eight resolutions passed the House and Senate, either in favor of recognizing Cuba's independence or making a show of force or otherwise intervening in that island nation.[8] This eagerness for a confrontation was fueled in part by the "yellow journalism" of publishers such as William Randolph Hearst, who sent reporters to Cuba to chronicle Spanish abuses. There was also a more strategic interest at play: the prospect of acquisition. Since the early nineteenth century, Cuba had been the "low-hanging fruit" for the United States, and now the time seemed right to snatch the golden apple from the hands of the decrepit Spanish empire.

Though the U.S. public and congressional opinion demanded action, Republican president William McKinley was still reluctant to go to war with Spain. The shocking news about the USS *Maine* ultimately persuaded him otherwise. On April 11, 1898, McKinley sent his war message to Congress:

I ask the Congress to authorize and empower the President to take measures to secure a full and final termination of hostilities between the government of Spain and the people of Cuba, and to secure in the island the establishment of a stable government, capable of maintaining order and observing its international obligations, insuring peace and tranquility and the security of its citizens as well as our own, and to use the military and naval forces of the United States as may be necessary for these purposes.[9]

The war with Spain in Cuba lasted 113 days. Overall, it was an easy victory for the rising American power against a declining European empire. After a decade of naval expansion, the United States had a larger navy than did Spain, allowing it to dominate the seas around Cuba. On the ground, though, it was a rather different situation. American troops arrived on the island outfitted in blue, winter service dress. With only 28,000 officers and troops at the beginning of 1898, moreover, the American force was woefully unprepared to face 150,000 Spanish regulars and 40,000 irregulars.

Confirming the initial assumption that the U.S. forces and Cuban rebels were united against the Spanish, when U.S. troops first met up with Cuban insurgent forces, they shouted "Viva Cuba libre!" and were met by Cuban cries of "Vivan los americanos!" Within months of McKinley's war message and despite their glaring shortcomings in training and size, the Americans decisively defeated the Spanish forces. Major General John R. Brooke told a Cuban audience when the last Spanish were departing the island that the United States had intervened "to give protection to the people, security to person and property, to restore confidence ... to resume the pursuits of peace, and to afford full protections in the exercise of all civil and religious rights."[10] Brooke's words touting Washington's ostensibly noble and altruistic objectives in Cuba were reflective of an emerging American self-identity as a different sort of imperial power. Indeed, Brooke's text could have been pasted into any number of other official American pronouncements justifying interventions in foreign countries over the next several decades. The moral component has persisted, at least in American political rhetoric, through more recent interventions such as Vietnam, El Salvador, Iraq, and Afghanistan.

Soon, though, it became increasingly clear that the triumphant Americans were not going to hand over power to the insurrectos readily. In April of 1898, the U.S. Congress enacted the Teller Amendment, which stipulated that the U.S. could not annex Cuba but instead could only "pacify" Cuba to leave "control of the island to its people."[11] Quickly, though, the euphoria surrounding America's dramatic victory led Washington to believe that it should play a substantial role in now "independent" Cuba. After the heady victory against the Spanish, the United States now wondered whether empire was such a bad thing after all.

With Cuba now firmly under its military control, Washington needed to figure out how it would balance its stated desire not to act as a "conventional" European-style colonial master with its equally strong desire to control events in a manner favorable to U.S. interests. The Platt Amendment, passed by Congress in 1901, authorized the U.S. president to grant sovereignty to Cuba only if several provisions were adopted.[12]

Not surprisingly, these conditions included, among others, the lease and sale of naval stations and an American right to intervene to restore order. U.S. officials had told the Cuban nationalists that the American military occupation would not end until these provisions granting the United States exceptional powers were included in Cuba's new constitution. This unyielding demand led the Cubans to incorporate the Platt Amendment almost verbatim into the new constitution.

Thus, an extremely qualified Cuban "independence" was born. The constitution that encoded this new independence also formalized America's entry into the imperial game. Historians have labeled this era one of "protective imperialism" or "benevolent imperialism" to distinguish it from the simultaneous European variants on empire. Yet, while successive administrations were hoping that the United States could determine favorable outcomes in its sphere of influence in the Caribbean and Central America without having its military directly involved, events would prove otherwise. Indeed, putting "boots on the ground" in various quantities and durations became a somewhat counterintuitive hallmark of benevolent imperialism through the early 1930s.

Before 1898, Washington had largely been interested in keeping European powers out of the hemisphere, Central America and the Caribbean in particular. But after Theodore Roosevelt entered the White House in 1901 following McKinley's assassination, the United States would actively work to address the "chronic wrongdoing" that plagued its neighbors' internal political systems and threatened U.S. security and economic interests in the region.

In Roosevelt's message to Congress of December 6, 1904, the American president declared:

All that this country desires is to see the neighboring countries stable, orderly, and prosperous. Any country whose people conduct themselves well can count upon our hearty friendship. If a nation shows that it knows how to act with reasonable efficiency and decency in social and political matters, if it keeps order and pays its obligations, it need fear no interference from the United States."[13]

In September 1906, Roosevelt wrote to the Cuban ambassador in Washington expressing his reluctance to send in troops to quell an uprising in Cuba. "Our intervention in Cuban affairs will only come if Cuba shows that she has fallen into the insurrectionary habit, that she lacks the self-restraint necessary to secure peaceful self-government, and that her contending factions have plunged the country into anarchy."[14] In reality, Roosevelt and his presidential successors appeared more than willing to send troops into Cuba and elsewhere. One cause of this enthusiasm was the enormous power imbalances between the continuously industrializing United States and its Latin neighbors. Using military force to determine favorable outcomes was all the more appealing when the prospects of success were so great.

NATION-BUILDING IN HAITI

Just over a century after its earth-shattering, slave-led revolution and independence from France in 1804, Haiti was a veritable economic and political basket case. During this time, the country experienced over one hundred civil wars and revolutions, which were devastating for the country's development. What made Haiti particularly unstable at the turn of the twentieth century was the ongoing activity of rural mercenary bands known as *cacos*. Descended from runaway slaves, their name derived from the "kaa-ko," a local bird of prey. During peacetime (which, unfortunately was not all that often) these men lived as bandits, extorting money and goods from landowners or just about anyone else who came their way. Yet they were also willing to accept money from a political faction in return for their ruthless support against any of the faction's enemies. In this sense, they habitually acted as a sort of a "rent-a-revolution" band in Haiti's tortured history as an independent nation. And, as one might suspect, caco leaders were more than willing to change their allegiances at the drop of a hat if the price was right.[15]

In early 1915, the pro-U.S. Jean Vilbrum Guillaume Sam assumed the presidency. One of the few black Haitians ever to hold the position at that time (most executives were members of the mulatto elite), Sam was no stranger to revolts, as he had participated in several successful presidential ousters. This time, the cacos were working on behalf of mulattos eager to restore their rule. In office, Sam moved quickly to dampen dissent, suppressing political opposition and ordering the executions of almost two hundred political prisoners. The next day, after hearing of the mass executions, mulatto rebels infiltrated the French legation where Sam had sought refuge. They apparently found the Haitian leader hiding in a bathroom, where they executed him and then dragged his body out into the street, where it was ripped to shreds by a furious mob. The crowd then paraded pieces of Sam's body through neighborhoods in the Haitian capital.

Once again, Haiti was engulfed in violence and chaos. The difference in 1915, though, was that now the United States had become a formidable economic and military power and it was concerned about the political and economic chaos erupting so close to its shore. The somewhat overestimated belief that Germany might exploit Haiti's misfortunes only heightened the Wilson administration's resolve to take action. When Wilson gave the order to intervene in Haiti for the first time, his fateful decision to go after Pancho Villa was still nine months away. Thus, Haiti was one of Wilson's first and most challenging opportunities to reconcile his opposing desires to uphold the principle of self-determination and American humility in foreign affairs and to address chronic instability in the backyard.

In this instance, Wilson opted for security. In a memo to Secretary of State Robert Lansing, Wilson wrote, "The more I think about the situation, the more I am convinced that it is our duty to take immediate action.... I mean to send a commissioner there ... and to say to them as firmly and definitely as is consistent with courtesy and kindness that the United States cannot consent to stand by and permit revolutionary conditions to constantly exist."[16] Wilson was deeply concerned that *not* intervening would lead to chaos in Haiti.

Only days after Sam's execution, Rear Admiral William B. Caperton deployed 340 sailors and marines from the USS *Washington* into Port-au-Prince; other troops from the USS *Nashville* and USS *Eagle* landed at Cap-Haïtien. The American troops rapidly occupied Port-au-Prince and other small towns. The force quickly grew to around two thousand. From the initial battlefield reports, this appeared to be a relatively easy operation. Within a few months, the Americans had taken control over the customs houses and worked to establish democratic elections. In a typically paternalistic tone, Secretary Lansing commented on the situation: "the intelligent Haitians should feel gratified that it was the United States rather than some other power whose motives might not be as unselfish as ours."[17]

The U.S. government negotiated the U.S-Haiti Treaty of 1915, which gave Washington the right to supervise government finances, control customs houses, and create a U.S-officered constabulary. The problem, however, was that the cacos were not eager to go along with this U.S.-mandated plan. In very short order they were executing yet another revolt, although this time it was against the American occupiers instead of the Haitian elites.

Caperton's forces easily removed the cacos from the areas surrounding Port-au-Prince. But when the 1st Marine Brigade attempted to pursue the mercenaries into their hideouts in the northern and central mountains, they were stymied. Led by such legendary marines as Major Smedley Butler, who had come to fame doing similar "imperial housekeeping" in Nicaragua a few years earlier, the Americans hoped to settle the caco issue once and for all.[18] What distinguished the Americans' fighting against their Haitian foes was their initial willingness to go on the offensive through highly mobile operations.

Like their caco adversaries, the marines were ruthless, hunting the bandits like animals. In one battle in the northern mountains, only a few dozen marines killed fifty cacos without taking a single prisoner. The caco threat effectively ended after the Butler-led marines captured the caco stronghold at Fort Rivière, an unusually conventional battle in a very unconventional conflict that earned Butler and two other marines the Medal of Honor. Thus, within just a few months, the two thousand or so marines had effectively ended the caco threat to the U.S. custodial government in Haiti. Unlike in most dirty wars, the casualty rate for the United States was minuscule. The first caco revolt left 3 marines dead and 18 wounded. An estimated 200 cacos were killed.

The Americans proceeded to focus on the nation-building side of the occupation. One of the first priorities was to establish a native constabulary force that would, it was hoped, maintain order long after the American forces had returned home. The Gendarmerie d'Haïti was outfitted with uniforms and weapons supplied by the marines. What became effectively a facsimile of the U.S. Marine Corps was initially commanded by Americans such as Lieutenant Colonel Butler.

By February 1916 the gendarmerie consisted of 1,500 enlisted men; six months later that number rose to 2,500. The idea was to deploy U.S. and Haitian units as complementary forces. The marines would continue to secure main towns while the gendarmerie would carry out rural patrols. The U.S. Department of State authorized the gendarmerie to build roads and schools and to act as de facto regional civil servants: judges, school superintendents, tax collectors, and police chiefs. Yet the gendarmeries were never the fully apolitical force that the Americans had hoped for. In fact, American training and equipment had effectively created an army, as opposed to the expected constabulary, and the incipient force was often more powerful than the weak national governments in Port-au-Prince, placing even greater stress on an already highly precarious situation.[19] Smedley Butler, for one, was proud of this U.S.-led force, or what he called the "little chocolate soldiers." The American added that he wanted to do his "level best to make a real and happy nation out of this bloody crazed Garden of Eden."[20] It was only in the early 1930s, on the eve of the American military's departure from Haiti, that the gendarmerie transitioned to full Haitian command.

Another element of American nation-building in Haiti was the attempt to construct a constitutional democracy. President Wilson's assistant secretary of the navy, none other than Franklin Delano Roosevelt, acknowledged that he had written the constitution imposed on Haiti during the American occupation. Roosevelt later said of the experience, "You know, I have had something to do with the running of a couple of little republics. The facts are that I wrote Haiti's constitution myself, and if I so say it I think it is a very good constitution."[21] The new constitution was approved overwhelmingly (98,225 in favor, 769 against) in a 1919 plebiscite, although only 5 percent of the Haitian population voted.

The U.S. government also pushed aggressively to improve the country's physical infrastructure, especially roads. In 1915, there were only two paved roads in the entire country. Three years later, U.S.-supported programs had built 470 miles of road, including the first highway linking Port-au-Prince with Cap-Haïtien.[22] Yet these dramatic road-building gains had a sordid flip side: they were predicated on a hated forced labor system. Eager to see quick results, U.S. officials reinstated the *corvée*, a nineteenth-century law that required rural farmers to perform labor on roads instead of paying a tax. The U.S.-imposed corvée was ended in 1918, but only after thousands of farmers had been forced from their villages to work in distant parts of the country.[23]

Predictably, before it ended, the corvée provoked widespread resentment among Haiti's rural population, the very citizens who were most likely to support and join the cacos. One mulatto and Haitian nationalist, Charlemagne Masséna Péralte, was arrested in 1917 for assaulting the home of a U.S. officer and sentenced to five years at hard labor. Ever resentful of the American domination of his country, the charismatic Péralte escaped to the northern hills and established an insurgent force in the style of the traditional cacos. The Haitian fighter led a force of over 3,000 men that fought a bloody series of battles with U.S. Marines between April and October of 1919.[24] He also commanded the support of an estimated 20 percent of Haiti's population, so that at one point there were more than 40,000 fighting, to some degree, under his banner.

With his legendary cry, "Drive the invaders into the sea and free Haiti!" Péralte executed a revolt that was much bloodier than the first caco insurgency in 1915.[25] The gendarmerie was unable to contain the cacos, forcing the American forces to confront them directly. This time, instead of sending a light, mobile force after the rebels, the American marines responded with considerably more firepower. During 1919, the marines and gendarmerie launched almost two hundred engagements against Péralte. One key innovation in the offensive was the use of coordinated air-ground attacks through the use of six Curtiss "Jennies," the very make of planes that had proved so ineffective and frustrating during the Punitive Expedition in Mexico in 1916. In the first six months of 1919, the marines and gendarmerie defeated numerous caco bands. But this alone was not enough to eliminate the insurgency. In early October, Péralte launched a daring raid on Port-au-Prince, assisted by clandestine rebels hidden inside the capital. Péralte's operation was a military failure, but it reinforced the impression that Haiti was a complete mess. Péralte's days as an insurgent leader were numbered, however; that same October one of his commanders, Jean-Baptiste Conze, betrayed him by leading a marine officer disguised as a prisoner to his lair. A firefight flared and Péralte was killed. The Americans snapped a photograph of the deceased Péralte and distributed it on a flyer throughout the country to dampen support for the fallen Haitian. The scheme had precisely the opposite effect, however: it helped establish Péralte as a martyr killed at the hands of the American invaders. Even today, Péralte remains a beloved symbol of Haitian nationalism.

By 1920, the second caco revolt was over. The fighting yielded over 2,500 cacos dead (ten times the number in 1915); another 12,000 or so surrendered to American and gendarmerie forces as part of an amnesty program. The Americans had won a decisive victory in the early Banana Wars, or so it seemed. Back at home, the American public began to question what increasingly appeared to be sordid American involvement in Haiti. Reports of atrocities committed by the marines reached U.S. shores as the military campaign intensified. But it was not only the marines who were playing dirty. A chilling instance of caco excess occurred in 1920 when a patrol of four marines was ambushed by a caco band near the town of Lascahobas. A marine sergeant, Lawrence Muth, was wounded and left for dead as the other marines withdrew. Later, the marines returned to look for him. They found his body naked and according to one account; "the head and heart had been taken away and the latter probably eaten."[26]

In 1920, Republican presidential candidate Warren G. Harding stated that he would not "empower an assistant secretary of the navy to draft a constitution for helpless neighbors in the West Indies and jam it down their throats at the point of a bayonet."[27] In 1922, a special Senate committee headed by Republican senator Medill McCormick of Illinois spent almost a year working on a report on the occupation. While it did not find widespread atrocities, the report criticized blunders made by the Wilson administration and abuses committed by the marines.

Taken at one level, the nineteen-year occupation of Haiti from 1915 to 1934 was a remarkable victory for the Americans. A few thousand marines pacified a tumultuous island of 3 million people. For five of these years, U.S. Marines were fighting aggressively and successfully (if at times shamefully) against caco bands. Hundreds of miles of roads were built, 1,250 miles of telephone lines were installed, 82 miles of irrigation dug, and 11 hospitals and 147 rural clinics were built.[28] U.S. engineers built a national college and provided clean water to 10 cities and 64 villages. After the second caco revolt ended in 1919, the American military force was reduced to the point that only 800 marines were patrolling the country.

Yet, despite these successes in counterinsurgency and nation-building, this was not a glorious dirty war.[29] As was also the case in Nicaragua and the Dominican Republic at roughly the same time, the infrastructure and democratic institutions disintegrated soon after the Americans departed. Moreover, both the U.S. government and public were weary of these sorts of endless occupations, even if by the final years they involved only a fraction of the original force. And after the carnage of World War I, the United States did not have much stomach for "splendid little wars." When the marines finally left Haiti in 1934, the *Denver News* commented, "Neither the Haitians, the American public, nor the Marines themselves will feel very badly about it if they never go back."

DISORDER IN THE DOMINICAN REPUBLIC

> We went into San Domingo [the Dominican Republic], into that distracted country, whose finances were utterly disordered, and with what result, pray? For the first time San Domingo soon found herself endowed with something that might be called a real civilization. – Sen. William Bruce[30]

If the U.S. military did not already have its hands full with the Haitian occupation, it certainly did when, in 1916, Haiti's neighbor on the island of Hispaniola, the Dominican Republic, descended into terrible disorder. With striking parallels to the Haitian intervention, the Americans soon found themselves attempting to create decidedly pro-U.S. political and economic stability while fighting rebels who detested the American occupation of their country. And like Haiti, the Dominican Republic was more than once on the receiving end of American imperial might. What usually sparked a U.S. intervention was the failure of the Dominicans to pay their debt to American interests. Washington would dispatch gunboats to Dominican shores, and the situation was usually resolved to the Americans' satisfaction. Yet, at the same time, American presidents such as Theodore Roosevelt had a certain reluctance to intervene, as they knew that getting out of such a political and economic quagmire could prove much harder than getting in. During a dispute in 1903 that led to the promulgation of Roosevelt's famous "Corollary" justifying intervention to stamp out "chronic wrong-doing," the president revealed that he had "about the same desire to annex it [the Dominican Republic] as a gorged boa constrictor might have to swallow a porcupine wrong-end-to."[31]

After a decade of assassinations, coups, and negotiated power transitions, secretary of war General Desiderio Arias took control of the military and Congress, ousting the relatively pro-American president, Juan Isidro Jiménez. U.S. officials distrusted Arias, as they suspected him of being a German sympathizer as well as running arms across the border to cacos fighting the American occupation in Haiti. As he had done in Haiti, Rear Admiral William Caperton, the commander of the Navy's Special Services Squadron, sent 150 marines into the capital, Santo Domingo. They were immediately able to secure the city; Arias fled to the nation's second-largest city, Santiago de los Caballeros, under threat of an American naval bombardment. Within months a contingent of over 1,300 marines had seized Santiago as well.

U.S. military officials soon opted for complete military control of the country. However, by 1917, the American involvement in World War I increased pressure to withdraw troops from the Dominican Republic and send them to fight in Europe. In fact, marine levels fell below 2,000 men for the duration of the European war. And like Haiti, a big part of keeping opponents of the U.S. intervention in check was to create a domestic constabulary, the Guardia Nacional Dominicana. The establishment of the Guardia was hindered by the Dominican rebels' major 1917 offensives. While it was still insufficiently trained and suffering from low morale, the Guardia was forced to rush into service against resilient insurgents, who kept the American troops and their Guardia counterparts occupied for a stunning six years.

By 1919, the Americans and Guardia had made little progress against the rebels who continued to control parts of the countryside, especially the eastern provinces of El Seibo and San Pedro de Macorís. There were likely only about 600 rebels active full-time, but irregular militias often provided additional men under arms. In time though, the Americans and their counterparts in the Guardia employed more severe, and more effective, tactics. For one, U.S. forces used a cordon system, whereby troops would block off an area, round up the males, and line them up so that concealed informants could indentify insurgents.³² The cordon approach caught hundreds of rebels in its net. Yet, not surprisingly, innocent civilians who were also apprehended became bitter and resentful toward the Americans and their Dominican colleagues. The Americans faced a dilemma: the same tactics that were proving effective in defeating insurgents were also extremely ineffective in winning Dominican hearts and minds. Writing after the fact, the prominent American diplomat, Sumner Welles, described an outcome that today we call "blowback":

> it is a fact that a policy of repression was carried out by the forces of occupation over a protracted period in the eastern provinces of the Dominican Republic, which was inherently unwise, which reacted primarily upon peaceful civilians, and as the result of which many atrocities were undoubtedly committed."³³

As Welles indicates, the American counterinsurgency effort, while ultimately effective, was hindered by instances of atrocities and abuses. Marine captain Charles F. Merkel became known as the "Tiger of Seibo" for his ruthless tactics. In one instance, the American officer reportedly tortured a prisoner by cutting him with a knife, pouring salt and orange juice on the wounds, and cutting off his ears.³⁴ Interestingly, though, American troop excesses in the Dominican Republic never provoked the level of domestic controversy and revulsion that those in Haiti did.

Aided by an amnesty program that served as a "carrot" to get rebels to lay down their arms, the Dominican insurgency had ebbed considerably, although it did not disappear altogether. U.S. Marines and Guardia troops killed over 1,000 rebels while the marines suffered only 20 killed and 67 wounded. As in Haiti, American officials wanted to leave behind a professional constabulary and democracy to ensure that Washington would not have to send more imperial boots into the country.

In 1924, Horacio Vásquez won the national election, after which the marines departed for home. Renamed the Policia Nacional Dominicana and later the Fuerzas Armadas de la República Dominicana, the national police force assumed the marines' duties as enforcers of peace and security. Yet Vásquez was unable to keep them under his control. He had named Rafael Leonidas Trujillo y Molina as chief of staff of the force. Trujillo was a member of the first class of officers who had graduated from the country's Haina Military Academy, which had been founded by the marines three years earlier. In 1930, Trujillo used his control of the national police to slingshot himself into the presidency, where he ruled with an iron first for three decades.

The U.S. military left the Dominican Republic with a relatively stable political and economic structure.[35] Yet slightly beneath the veneer of this Caribbean democracy lay all of the seeds for continued violence and tyranny. The Dominican intervention was certainly not a glamorous war. In contrast to the much romanticized fighting of the Rough Riders at San Juan Hill in Cuba almost two decades earlier, the marines' anti-rebel campaigns in the Dominican Republic were hot, often godlessly uncomfortable, and largely devoid of heroism and glory. Soon after the American departure, one observer astutely observed the dilemma of so many dirty wars: "The Marine Corps is intended to be a fighting body and we should not ask it to assume all sorts of civil and political responsibilities unless we develop it within a group of specially trained men."[36]

"ONE OF THE MOST DIFFICULT OPERATIONS IN THE WORLD"

Even if in some cases it took almost two decades, U.S. forces in the Banana Wars were eventually able to quell insurgent forces, hold elections, and train national constabularies.[37] The real problems came after the U.S. troops returned home. Instead of the shining examples of democracy and stability that some American leaders expected or hoped for, strongmen (often emerging from the very constabularies that U.S. forces established) over time seized national power and ruled as dictators. While the United States may not have been directly responsible for creating these Frankenstein monsters in every case, Washington subsequently came to rely upon them as predictably reliable and docile "allies" in the struggle against fascism in the 1930s and 1940s and subsequently communism during the Cold War.

Central America and the Caribbean around the turn of the twentieth century proved an important testing ground for the U.S. military.[38] For the rest of the century the United States engaged in a series of what came to be known by the U.S. military as "small wars," both in its traditional imperial "lake" in Central America and the Caribbean and also in far away theaters such as Southeast Asia in the 1960s and early 1970s. By way of conclusion, it is worth reflecting on one American commander's view of small wars, penned in 1906, just before the second intervention into Cuba. Using the racist language of the times, army chief of staff General J. Franklin Bell wrote to Roosevelt warning him that it is one of the most difficult operations in the world, to completely disarm a hostile population as skillful in the arts of concealment and deception as is the Latin race. The heartbreaking feature of it all is that you organize an army and it goes forth with military ardor, with all the pomp and panoply of war, enthusiastically to meet and conquer the enemy, only to discover it can find nothing to fight.[39]

Bell had fought in the Indians Wars and was promoted to general during the Philippine campaign, so he was under no illusions about dirty wars in Cuba or anywhere else in the world. The bigotry of his language aside, there was some truth in his observation about the difficulty of fighting a small counterinsurgency, a fact with which the United States is still coming to terms.

10

Intermezzo
T. E. Lawrence and the Arab Revolt, 1916–1918

> It [my account] does not pretend to be impartial. I was fighting for my hand, upon my own midden.
> – T. E. Lawrence, preface to *Seven Pillars of Wisdom*

British officer Thomas Edward Lawrence, known professionally as T. E. Lawrence, forever joined the pantheon of insurgency and counterinsurgency thinkers with his efforts as a military liaison during the Arab Revolt (1916–1918) against the dominion of the Ottoman Empire. Lawrence published his account as *Seven Pillars of Wisdom: A Triumph*,[1] part travelogue and part insurgency "how-to" manual. An Arabic speaker, Lawrence actually had limited formal officer training, but he was an avid reader of military theory. The man was certainly a larger than life character whose successes had an outsized impact on the history of World War I and the Middle East.

Part of what makes Lawrence's experiences so influential is the extent to which this Western officer adopted the culture, habit, and even dress of his Arab counterparts. Lawrence was long accustomed to focusing on the "counterinsurgency" side of irregular warfare, and through his eyes Western military thinkers could glimpse the life of an insurgent. One contemporary who encountered Lawrence described his unique qualities: "This man is different from the rest of the Englishmen whom we have seen so far, [in] that he listens attentively to the political organization of the Arabs and his questions show a depth in the subject, which is not present except with one who has in it a pleasure and a passion."[2] Not content

128 Part One. The American Revolution to Chasing Sandino

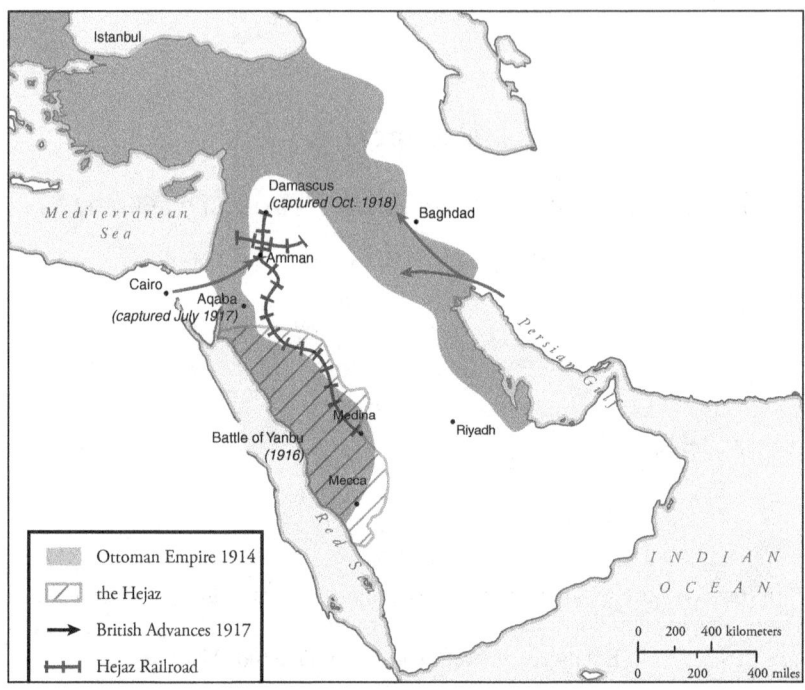

FIGURE 10.1. The Arabian Peninsula in the early twentieth century. The map depicts the region as T. E. Lawrence would have experienced it. Over the course of the two-year revolt, Lawrence and the insurgents, who began their uprising in the holy city of Mecca located in the central part of the Hejaz, moved northward to Aqaba, a critical port on the Gulf of Aqaba that fed into the Red Sea. This capture of Aqaba and other key coastal cities allowed the British government to supply naval and air-based military assistance to the insurgents, helping lead to a decisive removal of Ottoman forces and influence from the region. Map prepared by the University of Wisconsin-Madison Cartography Lab©. Reprinted with permission

simply to conclude his assessment of the Arabs' fighting prowess and return to the British ranks, Lawrence remained with the rebel forces and effectively became an insurgent. Despite his role as a British emissary, Lawrence became as dedicated to the Arab nationalist cause as the Arab insurgents, committing himself to the goal of realizing an Arab nation even when the British government reneged on its promises to the insurgents.

LAWRENCE AND FAISAL JOIN FORCES

Lawrence had studied history at Oxford and was well versed in such legendary military theorists as Clausewitz and France's Ferdinand Foch.[3]

Additionally, his education in archaeology, Arabic, history, and the Middle East in general led him to work extensively in the region on behalf of the British Museum.[4] Living in the region, his views changed radically, and he developed a romanticism about the Arabs that led to his desire for deeper cultural immersion.[5]

With this considerable experience, Lawrence became the ideal candidate for the British Government's newly established Arab Bureau in Cairo, which would serve as a counter to German-Turkish influence in the region.[6] His deployment came at a time of deep instability in the region, as Arab nationalists began to seek independence from the Ottoman Empire. The British had recently begun to consider the region, from present-day Syria to Yemen, a focal point in the balance of power; endorsing the Arab Revolt would pose a counterweight to Ottoman and, by extension, German geopolitical influence. The British developed a policy of partitioning the Ottoman empire into "spheres of influence" that it could then manipulate to suit its interests.[7] Essentially, the British aimed to use the Arabs' rebellion as a way to topple the Ottomans – after which Britain would assume control of the region through a system of indirect governance known as the "mandate."

Lawrence initially served as an intelligence officer, although his mission quickly evolved into one of direct, on-the-ground engagement with the Arab insurgents.[8] Living among the Arabs and studying their society, culture, and power structures, Lawrence came to understand that the best military approach for them was not direct, conventional confrontation but indirect, guerrilla-style warfare that drew on their "irregular skills."[9] Lawrence understood that the Arabs' superiority lay in their ability to stage quick attacks and raids, and to use the harsh desert terrain to their advantage.[10]

Operating largely in what is now Jordan, Lawrence convinced Faisal – the third son of Sharif Husayn of Mecca and future king, albeit briefly, of Greater Syria and then of Iraq – to join the insurgency as its local leader. For Lawrence, Faisal was "the leader who would bring the Arab Revolt to full glory" not only as the indigenous leader of this foreign-sponsored insurgency but also because of his considerable experience in political and military affairs:

His training ... had made him past-master in diplomacy. His military service with the Turks had given him a working knowledge of tactics. ... He was a careful judge of man ... If he had the strength to realize his dreams he would go very far.[11]

In Lawrence's view, "here, as it seemed, was offered to our hand ... a prophet who, if veiled, would give cogent form to the idea behind the activity of the Arab revolt."[12] With Faisal at the helm of the insurgents, Lawrence successfully counseled him and other Arab leaders to avoid costly frontal attacks on Turkish positions such as the fortified city of Medina.[13] This "strategic avoidance" allowed the Arabs to use their mobility over the arid deserts in order to strike at Turkish vulnerabilities such as the remote and largely undefended railway lines. According to Lawrence, "We could develop a highly mobile, highly equipped striking force of the smallest size, and use it successfully at distributed points of the Turkish line, to make them strengthen their posts beyond the defensive minimum. ... This would be a short cut to success."[14]

In one such instance, the Arab insurgents moved to take a critical pass that would lead to Aqaba, which British officials saw as a path to new bases with access to the Hejaz (in Arabia bordering on the Red Sea) railway.[15] They staked out positions in the hills that surrounded the Turks' valley in the hot desert sun – "the hill-belt was a paradise for snipers; and Arabs were artists in sniping."[16] While the Turks fired erratically at the Arab snipers, their shots often missed due to the insurgents' ability to "move with speed, eccentrically," and their superior knowledge of the terrain.[17] Changing tactics quickly, the snipers mounted camels and, now a flash cavalry unit, rode full-speed into the Turkish camp. In combination, these tactics caught the Turkish off guard and brought the Arabs a significant victory in their revolt.

The battle embodied Lawrence's characterization of the Arab Revolt as a war "of dervishes against regular troops," in which the Arabs, with their unusual tactics, figuratively danced circles around the Ottoman forces.[18] Lawrence's approach foreshadows those tactics that such influential twentieth-century figures as China's Mao Zedong and Argentine cum Cuban revolutionary Che Guevara would later embrace in their treatises on guerrilla warfare. In fact, some scholars have suggested that the Arab Revolt, specifically Lawrence's military approach, serves as the foundational framework for modern guerrilla warfare.[19]

"THE GENIE OF THE ARAB EMPIRE"

Initially it seems odd that the British would work with an unorthodox movement such as the Arab insurgency to achieve their strategic and political goals for the Middle East, given the British strength as a conventional force. However, British officials came to realize the advantages of catalyzing an indigenous movement to challenge the Ottomans. Theoretically, irregular warfare presented advantages to the Arabs against the conventional Turkish forces; however, its execution proved slightly more challenging.

One of the more pressing issues facing the insurgency was recruiting and unifying guerrilla fighters; Arabia at the time had a tribal and fiercely divided society, which threatened the fundamental unity of the movement.[20] Britain countered these schisms in three ways: first, it heavily endorsed the economic benefits of the revolt (e.g., looting) as a way to encourage participation; second, it strove to construct a unifying ideology, Arab nationalism, under which the guerrilla fighters might rally; and third, it used preexisting tribal divisions to create a vast network of guerrilla militias, increasing the insurgency's territorial presence.

Lawrence emphasized the need for the Arab revolt to have more than just adequate material support; it needed a strong ideological base that would boost the Arabs' morale in the face of Turkish attacks.[21] Arab nationalism, a minority movement that had recently begun to emerge in the Levant, a region in the Arabian Peninsula's northwest, filled this ideological vacuum neatly. It would galvanize the Arabs to challenge the Ottoman seat of power and help further British interests in the region. However, the insurgency's foundations served as a key point of divergence for the Arab and British parties.

Ultimately, nationalism would come to represent the ends for the Arabs, and the means for the British. Yet, at the outset of the insurrection, the two parties seemed to have reached a general consensus about overthrowing Ottoman hegemony. Planning the insurgency, Lawrence recognized the need to work with the irregular guerrilla-style tactics that the Arabs would use. However, despite this tactical direction and cooperation, at the strategic level British and Arab interests still diverged. Wartime alliances serve strategic purposes; they form around similar interests and bring together different sources of power to achieve a common goal.[22] But differences in political interests provide a source of friction between allies. The Arabs and the British had different visions for the Middle East, which would emerge as incompatible over the course of the insurgency; yet these two different visions stemmed from similar motivations of territorial gains, imperial prowess, and ridding the region of Ottoman rule.

At the political level, British and Arab interests and goals neither overlapped nor complemented one another at any point prior to, during, or after the insurgency. For a while, the alliance against the Ottomans helped these disparate policies to temporarily coexist. However, even the shared success that Britain and the Arabs found in ousting the Ottomans could not prevent the alliance from

FIGURE 10.2 Stereopticon card showing British politician and diplomat Sir Herbert Samuel (right) beside T. E. Lawrence. The image was taken right before takeoff to Al-Azraq, located in the Transjordan territory of the British Mandate (modern-day Jordan) in 1921. From 1920 to 1925, Samuel served as High Commissioner of the British Mandate of Palestine, which covered territories both east and west of the Jordan River (formally known as Palestine and Transjordan). This political entity was carved out of the remnants of the Ottoman Empire by the British government pursuant to the end of World War I. American Colony, Jerusalem, 1921. Courtesy of the Library of Congress, Prints and Photographs Division, LC-DIG-matpc-02317

crumbling. With this approach, by 1919 Britain had unwittingly backed itself into a political corner. Unprepared for the success and momentum of the Arab nationalist movement, Britain was equally unready to fulfill its promises to the Arabs of independence, sovereignty, and territorial expansion.[23] Its temporary rhetorical support for the Arabs directly conflicted with the secret negotiations that British officials had been conducting with the French to partition up the Ottoman imperial carcass.[24] Rather than uphold its alliance with the Arabs, Britain had instead maintained its loyalty to Europe and returned to its desire to bring the Middle East under British control through the mandate system.[25]

This problematic revelation of Britain's political maneuvering brought to light the quintessential danger when an external force is involved in another party's affairs: at the political level, parties necessarily look out for their own interests, regardless of the promises, support, or assistance they have given. As a key leader of the insurgency, Lawrence felt as slighted by the British government as did the Arabs, despite his role as a British representative. Upon learning London's decision to renege on its promises to the Arabs, Lawrence declared, "I vowed to make the Arab Revolt an engine of its own success."[26] After all, the success of the revolt reflected on Lawrence's leadership, and his hopes rested on the successful establishment of an Arab nation.[27]

Having sponsored a nationalist uprising on false pretenses as a strategy for achieving its own political ends, the British government now faced the consequences of inciting a revolt it naively believed it could control. This policymaking reflected not only considerable shortsightedness but also an ignorance of the power of nationalist ideology: "once the genie of the Arab empire was set free, it could not be bottled again."[28] Even Lawrence, a non-Arab British citizen, found himself consumed by the nationalist fervor, dedicated to making "a new nation, to restore lost influences, to give twenty million Semites the foundations on which to build an inspired dream-palace of their national thoughts."[29] Although Lawrence was a foreigner, his dreams for an Arab nation mirrored those of the Arabs themselves, indicating the severe disappointment and anger felt by the insurgents in the Hejaz at the British betrayal.

"27 ARTICLES"

The success of the Arab Revolt canonized Lawrence's theory of guerrilla warfare, establishing his tactical approach as quintessential to successful insurgencies and influencing the principles found in the later writings of Mao. Because of his role as both an emissary of the British government and fellow insurgent of the Arabs, London officials worried that Lawrence might be killed in action and sent him a request to condense his experience with the Arabs into a document for the British officers joining with Faisal's forces.[30] Lawrence published his observations and analyses as a series entitled "27 Articles" in the *Arab Bulletin*. Echoing his own emphasis on understanding the national character of the Arabs, Lawrence's missives mostly concern manners of dress and behavior when in the presence of Arabs. Moreover, he repeatedly cautioned that the principles in the "27 Articles" could not act as a panacea for future endeavors but applied to a specific people in a specific context.[31] Nevertheless, his recommendations provide valuable advice regarding the Arabs' approach to nation-building and war making, as well as the role of a foreign power in aiding such endeavors.

Article 15, in particular, became one of the most frequently quoted principles, especially among American leaders in the Iraq and Afghanistan wars in the first decade of the twenty-first century sobered by the difficulty of leading counterinsurgency campaigns in the Middle East and Muslim world. Lawrence's experiences led him to advise foreigners with the following wisdom:

> Do not try to do too much with your own hands. Better the Arabs do it tolerably than that you do it perfectly. It is their war, and you are to help them, not to win it for them ... your practical work will not be as good as, perhaps, you think it is.[32]

This deference to Arab control of their insurgency implies a broader principle behind a successful guerrilla movement – political support from the population. Lawrence believed that without the staunch backing of the Arab population, he could not win – but with their aid, he could not lose.[33] Echoes of this dictum have sounded in many of the American counterinsurgency efforts since the Arab Revolt.

COOPERATIVE INSURGENCIES

The British experience in the Hejaz in the early twentieth century was not unique. Other historical examples mirror this phenomenon of tenuous alliances and misaligned policies. One case, that of the United States and Afghanistan, stands as a strikingly similar iteration of the Arab Revolt and its aftermath. Initially, the United States actively supported Afghanistan's mujahideen insurgents against the occupying Soviet and its Afghan proxy forces in the 1980s.[34] The mujahideen insurgency succeeded in driving out the Soviets, a strategic success for both the insurgents and the United States. However, after the Soviet Union collapsed in the early 1990s, the Taliban eventually seized control of Afghanistan – and, implementing their own policy (one at odds with American interests and values), became a new political opponent against the United States, a rivalry culminating in the September 11, 2001, attacks and the American War on Terror.[35]

Again, the tensions between strategy and policy lay at the heart of this alliance's undoing: while supporting the mujahideen served a strategic purpose against the Soviets, the two parties' political visions differed dramatically, ending their need for cooperation once the shared interest of ousting the Soviets from Afghanistan had been achieved. What remains from this example of cooperative insurgency gone awry is a protracted war, high political tensions, and a local population under the sway of the "wrong" policies: the long-term results of American involvement with and direct support of an insurgency whose policies did not truly align with those of the United States.

With this more contemporary example in mind, the Arab Revolt seems especially salient for understanding the role and potential consequences of cooperative insurgencies. Despite tactical and strategic successes, the insurgency's resulting political quagmire presented increased political challenges for both the British and the Arabs in the long run. Moreover, it does not appear that this alliance allowed either party to achieve its political goals immediately or entirely: British policy, especially the mandate system and the promise of a Jewish homeland, catalyzed bitterness among the Arabs and eventually independence movements across the region toppled imperialism.[36]

It may be argued that the British-Arab alliance and cooperative insurgency was the most viable option for breaking Ottoman hegemony and clearing the way for a new political framework in the Middle East. However, given this analysis of the Arab Revolt and its aftermath, were these tactical and strategic successes worth the subsequent conflict that helped to set the Middle East on a treacherous political path? More broadly, we may ask whether cooperative insurgencies such as the Arab Revolt best serve long-term policy goals given the potential for dissension between the allied parties. If anything, the case of the Arab Revolt highlights a major risk involved in supporting insurgencies and, more relevant to this book, counterinsurgencies: alliances with foreign actors, especially politically charged militant factions whose political interests differ significantly from ours, may bring short-term strategic success but often lead to long-term, perhaps more complex, political challenges.

For Lawrence, the successes of the Arab Revolt spoke to his insightful use of military theory in crafting an uprising that could challenge the Ottoman forces. His experience led him to support the Arabs' policy goals, but as a British citizen he witnessed his own government renege on promises and guarantees of political sovereignty. Lawrence's vision for a sovereign Arab state disappeared under the mandate system and did not materialize until after the Second World War. In the interim, his writings not only introduced the Arab people to the Western world but broke new ground for the deployment of, and defense against, guerrilla warfare.

11

Chasing Sandino, 1927–1932

All people encountered are unquestionably strong for Sandino.... I will have to wage a real blood and thunder campaign and will have casualties every day. I will become involved in a small real war.

– U.S. Marine Corps captain Oliver Floyd[1]

Like Pancho Villa in northern Mexico, an indefatigable nationalist revolutionary by the name of Augusto César Sandino strung U.S. Marines along a multiyear chase around the Nicaraguan countryside in the latter half of the 1920s. Once again, the mighty United States found itself confounded by a Latin American "bandit." To make matters worse, Sandino's charisma and emotive denunciations of American domination of his fellow Nicaraguans made him an international celebrity and turned many against the U.S. campaign in the Central American republic. The hunt came at a time when, following World War I, both the American politicians and the public were wary of the nebulous and protracted dirty wars the United States had been involved in with frequency since its war with Spain in 1898.

The elusive hunt for Sandino is also instructive because it was easily the most important dirty war (the marines themselves called them "small wars") that the American military fought post-Philippines and pre–World War II. Many military historians attribute the fighting prowess of the U.S. Marines on South Pacific islands such as Iwo Jima to the hard-won lessons they learned over the course of years in the mountains and jungles of Nicaragua.

While the Sandino affair broke in the late 1920s, American involvement in Nicaragua had begun decades earlier. During the nineteenth century, the

FIGURE 11.1. Chasing Sandino, 1927–1932. Map prepared by Andrew Rhodes. Reprinted with permission

potential for an inter-oceanic canal across Nicaragua drew Washington's attention. Perhaps unsurprisingly, the interest diminished after the United States secured a very favorable canal route through the newly created country of Panama in 1903 and opened the passage in 1914. But for Nicaragua to lose its appeal as a potential canal route did not ensure that

Washington would ignore the tiny Central American country, especially after 1898. Beginning in 1893, Nicaragua was led by the ambitious and fervently anti-American president, José Santos Zelaya of the Liberal Party. When Washington opted for the canal route through Panama, Zelaya attempted to enlist Japan and Germany to build a route through Nicaragua, a move that infuriated U.S. officials who feared these two rival countries might gain influence in the region.

Nicaragua's two main parties, the Liberals and Conservatives, were bitter rivals during these years; disputes between these two political entities frequently erupted in violence. For better or worse, Washington often interposed American diplomats and marines to serve as "judges" to determine which side would emerge victorious in any particular dispute. The American officials were neither altruistic nor even impartial in their officiating. Rather, they almost always intervened to resolve the events in a way that promoted American security and economic interests.

In October 1909, an anti-Zelaya revolt broke out in Bluefields, a port town on the country's Caribbean coast. Bluefields was the provincial center for banana, rubber, and gold-mining companies, most of which were controlled by American, British, and other foreign entities. Fed up with Zelaya's corruption and virulent anti-Americanism, U.S. residents in the town backed the revolt. Led by an estranged Conservative Party leader, Juan José Estrada, the revolt soon had to confront the federal troops that Zelaya dispatched from Managua. In the subsequent fighting, Zelaya's forces captured two American mercenaries working for Estrada as demolition experts. The two men, Lee Roy Cannon and Leonard Groce, were given a military trial and summarily executed.

Back in Washington, the Taft administration broke off relations with the recalcitrant Zelaya government.[2] However, when it became apparent to the Taft administration that Estrada was unable to hold Bluefields, it called in the U.S. Marine Corps, headed up by the redoubtable but at this point largely anonymous officer Smedley Butler. Within days of the marine landing in Bluefields on May 27, 1910, Zelaya vacated the presidency, leaving the country in the hands of an interim Liberal government. In August, Estrada's men entered Managua victoriously and Estrada named himself president. U.S. Secretary of State Philander Knox quickly recognized the new Conservative administration.

By 1911, however, Estrada's vice president, Adolfo Díaz, had assumed the presidency. Soon after taking office, he was confronted with a revolt led by one of his main political rivals, Luis Mena. Díaz requested yet another American intervention to address the threat, a move that ensured the Washington-friendly leader's continuation in power. This time, a force of 2,700 leathernecks landed on both the Pacific and Caribbean coasts and quelled the revolt in Managua and its surrounds. While the marines were able to deal with the immediate threat in 1912, a legation of around 100 leathernecks remained in the country for the next thirteen years.

The ensuing period might have witnessed a decrease in American military operations in Nicaragua, but it did not mean that Washington stopped influencing and, in some instances, dictating events in the country. Elections were one area in particular where U.S. officials worked to ensure that "democracy" operated in a manner that suited American interests. Regarding the election of Conservative Party candidate Emiliano Chamorro in 1916, Smedley Butler remarked, "our candidates always win."[3]

A TEMPORARY WITHDRAWAL

Following the United States' successful but bloody involvement in World War I and the seemingly endless interventions in nearby Haiti and Dominican Republic, in the first half of the 1920s U.S. officials were eager to avoid deeper engagement in Nicaragua. In fact, if anything, Washington wanted to pull the marines out – to "declare victory and go home" – lest they be "invited" once more to sort out a Liberal-Conservative clash. By 1924 Managua had finished paying its loans to American creditors, a criterion whose satisfaction was usually required before American boots would leave a "banana republic," the pejorative term coined by American writer O. Henry in his 1904 novel on Honduras titled *Cabbages and Kings*. To achieve the expected pullout, the U.S. military did exactly what it attempted in Haiti and the Dominican Republic: raise a national constabulary, hold elections, and get the hell out of Dodge. In 1925, the small legation of marines left Nicaragua.

But the American withdrawal proved much more difficult than its entry into Bluefields in 1909. In 1925, Chamorro returned to power through a coup d'état that forced Liberal president Juan Sacasa into exile. Washington refused to endorse Chamorro's putsch, which resulted in his being replaced by none other than former Conservative president Adolfo Díaz. A year later, Sacasa returned to stake his claim on the presidency, establishing a new government in the town of Puerto Cabezas on the Caribbean coast. Led by the venerable Liberal military commander, General José María Moncada, Sacasa's forces almost overthrew the Díaz government in Managua.

By this time, however, U.S. boots were back on the ground in Nicaragua to prevent Sacasa's forces from seizing power, ostensibly to protect American lives and property. Less public was the U.S. government's fear that Sacasa's ascendancy would benefit his sponsor, the Mexican government. President Coolidge's secretary of state, Frank Kellogg, soon dispatched Colonel Henry L. Stimson to Nicaragua to resolve the Díaz versus Sacasa/Moncada conflict that was threatening to become a full-scale civil war.[4] Kellogg told Simpson, "I want you to go down there, and if you can see a way to clean up that mess, I want you to do it."[5]

Starting in April 1927, Stimson began discussions with Díaz to hammer out a compromise with the rebel forces. The American envoy then met with the rebel commander Moncada near the Tipitapa River, which connects the country's two massive inland bodies of water, Lake Nicaragua and Lake Managua. The talks yielded an apparent breakthrough. Known as the Espino Negro pact since it was reportedly brokered under a blackthorn tree, the resulting agreement stipulated a variety of measures intended to end the fighting: Díaz would remain in power until Washington supervised new elections in 1928; the Liberal generals would stop their rebellion as part of a general amnesty; and opposition politicians would get appointments in Díaz's interim government.

Díaz's Conservatives readily acceded to a compromise that kept them in office, albeit temporarily. More critical, though, was the support Moncada lent to the agreement, which was no doubt assisted by Stimson's thinly veiled hint to the rebel general about what would ensue if the negotiations failed – "I have instructions to attain [peace] willingly or by force."[6] Stimson's mission appeared to have averted further disaster – and the deeper U.S. military involvement that such fighting would have inevitably invited. Indeed, eleven of Moncada's military lieutenants agreed to lay down their arms and abide by the terms of Stimson's plan. Yet one rebel commander, Augusto Sandino, refused to go along with the U.S.-negotiated solution.

SANDINO REBELS

Sandino was born in 1893 in the village of Niquinohomo located between Managua and the provincial city of Granada. His father owned a coffee *finca* (farm) and was a politically moderate Liberal. In his youth, the son worked on a banana plantation in Honduras and then made his way to Mexico where he was a supervisor of gasoline sales at Huasteca Petroleum Company in the coastal port city of Veracruz. Sandino's travels and employment during this time exposed him to the burning issues of labor organization, militancy, and nationalism that defined his rebellion back in Nicaragua. He was apparently also deeply influenced by the writings of the Seventh-day Adventists. In 1926, urged by his father, Sandino returned to Niquinohoma.

At his core, Sandino was virulently anticapitalist and antigovernment. Disgusted with the political class in general, Sandino found both Liberal and Conservative leaders to be a "bunch of scoundrels, cowards, and traitors, incapable of leading a valiant and patriotic people."[7] Upon his return to Nicaragua, Sandino first displayed his newfound radicalism at the U.S.-owned San Albino mine in northern Nueva Segovia, a rugged mountain department along the border with Honduras. Sandino attempted to organize the mineworkers, urging them to rebel against an unjust government. Sandino then used some of his own money to arm the laborers with weapons purchased from gunrunners along the Honduran border. He and a few dozen miners attacked a Conservative garrison at the town of El Jícaro located in the same area. The raid failed. This setback prompted Sandino to travel to Puerto Cabezas to meet up with Moncada, who was leading another, much larger band of Liberal rebels. Moncada treated the upstart revolutionary with little respect; he told Sandino to join an existing rebel unit. Put off, Sandino forged on by himself. Within months, Sandino had established a surprisingly well-armed force of eight hundred fighters, and his military prowess won him the grudging respect of Liberal guerrilla commanders.

History often overlooks the fact that at the onset, Sandino's rebellion was against the Conservative Nicaraguan government, not the United States. In fact, Sandino initially hoped that American involvement might help the Liberal rebels' cause. The Nicaraguan commander did aim some barbed words at President Coolidge, whom he accused of persisting "in maintaining in power his lackey Adolfo Díaz, a person who enjoys the contempt of every good Nicaraguan."[8] Indeed, at his core, Sandino remained a Liberal first and an anti-imperialist second.

With the signing of the Espino Negro accords, Sandino and his rebel band appeared to be destined for a footnote in Nicaragua's tortured history. Though he first expressed support for the pact, Sandino soon moved to outright opposition and pushed deeper into the mountains to prepare his forces.

"A HANDSOME TOMB WITH SOLDIERS"

The Guardia force that U.S. Marines had trained in the previous decade ultimately succumbed to manipulation by Nicaraguan politicians. By 1927 marine officers were back on the ground, working aggressively to raise a new force that they hoped (once again) would maintain order after the American troops left. At this time, there were about two thousand marines in the country. In fact, as was the case in Haiti and the Dominican Republic, the marines initially commanded the Guardia. President Díaz also requested that the Americans help defend Managua and spread out to other cities to keep an eye on the rebel forces.

The U.S. military detachment deployed in Nicaragua in 1927 also manned rural garrisons, including one in the town of Ocotal in Sandino's stronghold of Nueva Segovia. At first, although he had seized the U.S.-owned San Abino mine, Sandino generally respected American property and citizens, not wanting to provoke the imperial giant. His stance changed, however, as he came to see the American occupiers as the real enemies to Nicaragua's sovereignty.

From the Ocotal garrison, Marine Captain G. D. Hatfield sent a note to Sandino indicating that he was an "individual outside the law" and that "Nicaragua has had its last revolution."[9] Hatfield told him to follow the example of Aguinaldo in the Philippines, who had renounced his rebellion and had become "a splendid friend of the United States."[10] He added that Sandino had two days to give up or the marines would "finish with you and your forces once and for all."[11] Sandino sent a note to Hatfield declining the offer, signing it "Your obedient servant, who wishes to put you in a handsome tomb with Soldiers." Hatfield responded, "Bravo, General. If words were bullets and phrases were soldiers, you would be a field marshal instead of a mule thief."[12]

On the morning of July 15, having plundered the San Albino mine for dynamite, the aptly named "Sandinistas" sneaked into the town where the force of forty-eight marines and a slightly smaller number of Guardia were posted. After a day of fighting, a guerrilla carried a flag of truce and approached the marines with a message from Sandino. In the note, Sandino complimented Hatfield on his "brave fight," but stated that the marines and Guardia needed to surrender within an hour or they would be destroyed. Hatfield responded that "Go to Hell" marines "did not know how to surrender and that water or no water we would stick it out until killed or captured, and that firing would be resumed as soon as the flag bearer had turned the nearest corner."[13]

The fighting lasted sixteen hours and resulted in the death of an estimated 50 Sandinistas, although the Americans claimed they had killed 300. Marine and Guardia losses together were 1 dead and 5 wounded. The marines used five DH-4 biplanes, each one outfitted with two machine

Chasing Sandino, 1927–1932

FIGURE 11.2. U.S. Marines display a captured flag from Sandino's forces. The unsuccessful American military campaign in Nicaragua to defeat Sandino's guerrilla forces sparked bitter debates back in the United States. *Source*: Time and Life Collection, reproduced with permission from Getty Images, 50596664

guns and four 25-pound bombs.[14] The planes strafed and dive-bombed Sandinista troops, sending them scattering in terror. Of particular note, German war planners studied the marine action at Ocotal carefully; the German Luftwaffe subsequently used the dive-bombing tactics to devastating success during World War II. In the end, Sandino unquestionably demonstrated that he could hold his own against marine and Guardia forces, but the battle of Ocotal was a stern setback for the insurgency.[15] Nine days later, the marines routed the Sandinistas again. Realizing that he could not continue to confront the marines in conventional head-to-head combat, Sandino adopted the age-old guerrilla strategy of hit-and-run, minimizing his direct exposure to the superior opposing force.

The marines believed Sandino was operating out of a clandestine base known as El Chipote. To find the site, American commanders dispatched hundreds of marines and Guardias to the formidable Nueva Segovia region along the Honduran border. Operating in small patrols that routinely tracked "bandit" movements, the counterinsurgent forces were nonetheless dogged for months by insurgent ambushes and raids. In a dramatic development, the Sandinistas shot down an American surveillance plane that was part of the effort to locate the elusive rebel forces. The marines sent out a search party to locate the downed fliers, but they were stopped short by an insurgent ambush. The captured pilots were placed on trial and executed by Sandino's men.

By November, marine pilots had located El Chipote, east of the San Albino mine, and had started bombing it daily. Apparently, though, at times they were bombing what turned out to be straw-stuffed dummies of Sandinistas. When a marine-led ground force descended upon El Chipote, the slippery Sandino had already fled. All told, Sandino proved to be an elusive and exasperating foe for the next five years, something that deeply frustrated the American troops. According to one U.S. reporter following the story, "The wily Sandino is a maddening problem for the Marines because of his swift shifting, and many officers declare earnestly they would give a year's pay only once to come to grips with him."[16]

Unable to capture Sandino, the American officials in Managua launched a public relations campaign that attempted to minimize Sandino's significance. Marine General Logan Feland, the commanding officer in Nicaragua, discredited Sandino as nothing more than an ordinary bandit and declared the rebellion over.

To a contemporary eye, the assessments seem premature; alternatively, they were intentional distortions aimed at downplaying Sandino's significance and cutting away at his civilian support base. In either case, Sandino was proving to be a resilient guerrilla fighter and not just a simple "cattle thief."[17] And this is exactly what President Calvin Coolidge did not want: an ill-defined, unpopular, costly, and protracted dirty war in Central America. By 1928, with the Sandinistas gaining strength, the marine contingent in Nicaragua had grown to 6,000 men.

While Sandino quickly adapted to a military strategy well suited to his rural insurgent position, the marines and Guardia also began to adapt to their frustrating adversary. Most important, they began using more mobile and coordinated patrols to minimize their vulnerability against Sandinista ambushes. The marines also took advantage of the critical intelligence provided by Sandinista defectors. They often performed best when they went on the offensive, striking the Sandinistas directly. The infamous Company N, commanded by Louis (Chesty) Puller, acted as a strike unit in the mountain region of Jinotega. The company averaged two marine officers and 30 Guardia enlisted men. Armed with automatic weapons and grenade launchers, the troops were confident and aggressive.

Puller's men defeated the rebels in over 20 engagements, prompting the Sandinistas to start calling Puller the "Tiger of the Mountains." In an example of counterinsurgency "learning," after bandit-chasing in Nicaragua, Puller became the chief instructor at Marine Basic School, where one of his first pupils was a young second lieutenant, Lewis Walt, who later became the commander of III Marine Amphibious Force and the first commander of I Corps in South Vietnam.[18]

"WHAT THE HELL ARE WE DOING THERE?"

As the hunt for Sandino dragged on year after year, voices back in the States began to question the American occupation and military campaign in Nicaragua. Senator Burton K. Wheeler of Montana accused the Coolidge administration of being guilty of a "dishonorable program of brutal bluff and bully. What right have we to send our boys into a foreign country to stamp out banditry? If we are to ask them to stamp out banditry, let's send them to Chicago to stamp it out there. As far as I'm concerned, I wouldn't sacrifice the lifeblood of one American boy for all the damn Nicaraguans."[19] Celebrated American satirist Will Rogers reflected the dubious mood of many American observers when he quipped, "Why are we in Nicaragua and what the Hell are we doing there?"[20]

Sandino's cause in the United States was aided by glowing depictions of the Nicaraguan rebel in American publications. Like American reporter Herbert Matthews, who interviewed the young and charismatic Cuban revolutionary Fidel Castro in the Sierra Maestra three decades later, the itinerant journalist Carleton Beals was the first American reporter to meet with Sandino in the remote Nicaraguan mountains. Writing for the *Nation*, Beals attempted to let Sandino speak in his own words:

"Let me repeat," declared the General [Sandino]. "We are no more bandits than was [George] Washington. If the American public had not become calloused to justice and to the elemental rights of mankind, it would not so easily forget its own past when a handful of ragged soldiers marched through the snow leaving blood-tracks behind them to win liberty and independence. If their consciences had not become dulled by their scramble for wealth, Americans would not so easily forget the lesson that, sooner or later, every nation, however weak, achieves freedom, and that every abuse of power hastens the destruction of the one who wields it."[21]

Romantic and positive depictions of Sandino helped many Americans conclude that it was the United States, not the Sandinistas, who were the real bandits in Nicaragua. In 1928, more than one hundred protestors marched in front of the White House carrying signs that read, "Wall Street and not Sandino is the Real Bandit." Letters to marines departing for Nicaragua pleaded with them not to fight for American interests but to join Sandino in his "war for freedom."[22] Sandino's half-brother, Socrates, made a speaking tour in the United States to drum up support for the rebel cause. The editors of the *Daily Worker* and *Nation* raised funds for "medical supplies" and distributed pamphlets calling on supporters to "Enlist with Sandino" and "Defeat the War against Nicaragua." Senator J. Thomas Heflin of Alabama compared the Nicaraguan nationalist to the Founding Fathers. "Sandino crying for liberty, begging for the deliverance of his country from the invader, sounds like the cries of our fathers made in the days of the Revolution," he argued. "We are seeking this man out to kill him for fighting for principles that we fought for in 1776."[23] All of this and more ensured that Sandino would be become a hero for the anti-imperialist, anticapitalist left in the United States and internationally.

An important part of the public outcry stemmed not just from glowing depictions of Sandino but also from the impression that the marines were "fighting dirty." Senator George Norris responded to the secretary of navy's acknowledgment that the Coolidge administration had "used the armed forces of the United States to destroy human life, to burn villages, to bomb innocent women and children from the air."[24] As in Haiti and the Dominican Republic, the grim reality for the U.S. Marines and their Guardia counterparts was that civilian deaths and atrocities were part and parcel of these dirty wars. And the longer the conflict dragged on, the more opportunity there was for these violations to occur.

To be sure, the excesses ran both ways. Sandino himself was a blood-thirsty fighter. To provide one example, the rebel commander ordered a variety of punishments for Nicaraguans suspected of sympathizing with marines or Guardia. One was the *corte de chaleco* (the "vest cut"), wherein victims were decapitated, their arms cut off, and a design etched on their chest.

SANDINO BETRAYED

As Espino Negro stipulated, the United States would supervise presidential elections in 1928. President Coolidge dispatched Brigadier General Frank McCoy to oversee the vote. McCoy had been described as "one of these iron-willed, super logical, single-track types whose stern jaw carried not an ounce of compromise."[25] A detachment of 900 marines and sailors acted as poll watchers in an effort to hold what they hoped to promote as a "free and fair" election that would allow the Americans finally to withdraw from Nicaragua.

Nicaraguan voters had their fingers dipped in colored ink after voting to identify them as having cast a ballot. No one with an ink-tipped finger was allowed to vote a second time. Sandino denounced the elections, but he was unable to stop them, although at one point his forces spread the rumor that the colored ink was poisoned. Amazingly, the Liberal commander and former rebel José María Moncada won the presidency. American president-elect Herbert Hoover happened to be in the Pacific port city of Corinto at the time of the election and told a marine officer who devised the ink plan, "I lived once in New York and proposed it as a cure for one of Tammany's bad habits, but everybody said it would be insulting."[26]

The relatively free and fair presidential elections provided the stability that U.S. diplomats and officers in Nicaragua believed were necessary for their desired exit. In Washington, Hoover made prompt withdrawal from Nicaragua a priority, especially now that the election had occurred. Back in Managua, though, marine officers were worried that a pullout that was too abrupt would create more chaos in a country that could not suffer any more instability. To make matters more bizarre, in May 1929, Sandino took a year's leave – a sort of guerrilla sabbatical – in Mexico where the leftist government provided him with political asylum.

Upon returning to Nicaragua, Sandino appeared to begin where he had left off: driving the marines crazy with his tenacity and elusiveness. On December 31, 1930, Sandinista guerrillas ambushed a heavily armored marine patrol near Ocotal, killing eight soldiers. Soon after the fateful ambush, President Hoover's senior officials met to discuss ways to get the marines out and home. In this instance, at least, Sandino's fortitude appeared to be weakening Washington's resolve in Nicaragua.[27] As in Iraq eighty years later, Washington eventually decided on a phased withdrawal – that is, get out but not so quickly that you would be forced to return.

Remarkably, the phased withdrawal was still in progress in 1932 when another presidential election cycle came about. The Hoover administration was under tremendous pressure to hold the elections given that congressional opponents were able to cut off funding for the vote in Nicaragua. Despite this setback, the marines and navy were still able to proceed with the election. U.S. officials hoped that this election would be like the one four years earlier – that the vote would further legitimize the Nicaraguan government, isolate Sandino, and allow the Americans to finally leave. In yet another indication of how small and exclusive the

Nicaraguan political class was at the time, the eternal enemies Liberal Juan Sacasa and Conservative Adolfo Díaz ran against each other. And once again Sandino refused to go along with the process, contending that all the marines must leave the country before the vote could be held. In November 6, the Nicaraguan people elected Sacasa as president.

As promised, the U.S. Marines finally left Nicaragua in early 1933 – as far as many American officials were concerned, not a moment too soon.[28] But it certainly was not "mission accomplished" in Nicaragua. In fact, Sandino was still active as shown by his daring attack on the Corinto-Granada railroad in 1932. During that same year leading up to the marine withdrawal there were more than 150 skirmishes between Sandinistas and marine/Guardia forces.

In a fateful decision, Sacasa announced that the first Nicaraguan commander of the Guardia Nacional would be Anastasio "Tacho" Somoza Debayle. It seemed at this point that in Somoza, the Guardia had a strong, efficient leader who would be able to command the nascent force successfully after the U.S. pullout. Marine officer Matthew Hanna commented, "I know of no one who will labor as intelligently or conscientiously to maintain the non-partisan character of the Guardia, or will be as efficient in all manners connected with the administration and command of the Force."[29]

Following the American departure, Somoza opened up negotiations with Sandino. Sandino despised Somoza, calling him the "penguin" for his rotund figure. In February 1934, Sandino met his despised counterpart in Managua. After a "farewell" dinner at the presidential palace, Sandino was apprehended by a Guardia patrol. Under Tacho's orders, the troops took Sandino and two of his generals to a military airfield and executed them.

With the death of their irreplaceable leader, the Sandinistas soon vanished as a guerrilla insurgency. In 1936 Somoza seized power, initiating a nearly four-decade period of iron-fisted rule. Far from being a pillar of the rule of law in Nicaragua, as U.S. officials had hoped, the Guardia soon became the Somoza family's personal shock troops.

Despite the requests of three former Nicaraguan presidents, the United States now refused to intervene in Nicaraguan politics to remove the new dictator. Concluding that these unpopular and long interventions in the first three decades of the twentieth century were more trouble than they were worth, in the 1930s President Franklin Delano Roosevelt's Good Neighbor Policy mandated that Washington remain clear from involvement in the banana republics.

Chasing Sandino, 1927–1932   149

THE SMALL WARS MANUAL

During the "Sandino phase" of the United States' protracted involvement in Nicaragua, 136 American troops died. Compared to the roughly 50,000 killed in Vietnam and the nearly 5,000 killed in Iraq, the casualties were relatively light. Nonetheless, this was a profoundly important dirty war for the U.S. military. The failed hunt for Sandino provided the marines with invaluable experience in jungle warfare. The intervention combined operations with local troops, close air support, and all the trappings of what we now call nation-building: civil projects and elections. The protracted and deeply frustrating experience in Nicaragua figured heavily in the conception of a seminal document, the Marine Corps' *Small Wars Manual*. Published in 1940, the manual was notable in two respects: it was the first official, strategic-level document in American history to acknowledge that small wars, such as the one in Nicaragua and those elsewhere in Central America and the Philippines, have a central role in the American warfare experience. It also was the first attempt to codify the lessons gained from these conflicts for future application.

The manual attempted to turn the key elements of dirty war fighting into military doctrine. To this end, while it did not explicitly use the term "hearts and minds," it told marines that they should show "as little military display as possible with a view to gaining the lasting friendship of the inhabitants."[30] However, when it came to future applications, as in the war in Vietnam, much of the U.S. military's "learning" from the Banana Wars was lost on strategists trying to develop an overarching template for how to fight these sorts of irregular wars. Amazingly, the author of a 1960 Marine Corps training manual was not even aware that the 1940 version existed.[31]

PART TWO

THE COLD WAR, 1940s–1989

12

Cold War Counterinsurgencies

Where there is a visible enemy to fight in open combat, the answer is not so difficult. Many serve, all applaud, and the tide of patriotism runs high. But when there is a long, slow struggle, with no immediately visible foe, your choice will seem hard indeed.
– President John F. Kennedy to West Point class of 1961[1]

While the United States had ample experience in the first half of the twentieth century, chasing Augusto Sandino up and down the mountains of Nicaragua or battling Aguinaldo's forces in the Philippines, it was the Cold War that gave the United States its deepest experience – directly and indirectly – in dirty wars. As early as 1951, Washington was beginning to conclude that communist-led guerrilla insurgencies threatened American interests. According to a draft of a high-level classified government report, "communist-controlled guerrilla warfare represents one of the most potent instrumentalities in the arsenal of communist aggression on a worldwide basis." According to this emerging estimation, the United States needed to take "practicable steps ... to counter such guerrilla warfare."[2]

This growing recognition of the need to counter guerrilla subversion contrasted significantly with the preponderant doctrine at the time, which preached "massive retaliation" as the most effective deterrent against what was assumed to be an unyielding Soviet empire. Yet, while nuclear deterrence remained a pillar of American strategy, episodes such as the Suez Crisis in Egypt in 1956 led American policymakers to conclude that the Soviets were not just building long-range ballistic weapons but also were clandestinely arming and allying with anti-Western forces across the globe. Over the next several decades, the American public would become familiar with a number of places and events such as the Bay of Pigs and Vietnam that reinforced the idea that U.S. efforts to check Soviet-backed subversion now meant getting down in the weeds of counterinsurgency operations in faraway and previously unimportant locales.

On his first day in office, John F. Kennedy is reported to have said, "What are we going to do about guerrilla warfare?"[3] Like so many at the time, Kennedy had a romantic fascination with guerrilla warfare; he was especially struck by Mao Zedong's chilling aphorism, "Guerrillas are like fish, and the people are the water they swim in. If the temperature of the water is right, the fish will thrive and multiply."[4] Kennedy's response was not surprising given the spate of guerrilla victories ranging from China to Cuba since the end of World War II. Kennedy worried that the U.S. diplomatic corps was too slow to understand the looming guerrilla threat in what was then called the Third World. The new president had read Mao and had even written the introduction to a text on counterinsurgency. The president believed that irregular warfare was never simply a military problem but always a combination of political and military factors.

When Kennedy took office in 1961, all eyes were on Vietnam, where the Viet Cong appeared ready to be the next guerrilla band to achieve a remarkable communist success by defeating the anticommunist South Vietnamese government. Interestingly, U.S.-supported irregular warfare operations had already been unleashed before the Kennedy administration took such an avid interest in the topic. Most critically, the redoubtable U.S. colonel, and later brigadier general, Edward G. Lansdale, had been promoting South Vietnam's counterinsurgency efforts against communist guerrillas ever since the Geneva Accords divided the country in 1954.[5]

For Kennedy, defeating communist guerrillas required "a whole new kind of strategy, a wholly different kind of force, and therefore a new and wholly different kind of military training."[6] Kennedy particularly believed in the ability of the U.S. Army Special Forces (SF), otherwise known as the Green Berets, to serve as the primary response to this new challenge. Against the Pentagon's reluctance due to its overall dislike of elite, unconventionally focused forces at the time, he increased the SF budget fivefold and personally selected their equipment, which included shoes with steel soles to protect against jungle booby traps. In October 1961, Kennedy took White House reporters on a trip to Fort Bragg, North Carolina, where SF soldiers performed ambushes and ate snake meat. One soldier even used a hydrogen peroxide-fueled jetpack, the Bell Rocket Belt, to fly over a lake before landing next to a smiling president.[7]

In principle, the core of the U.S. response to guerrilla insurgencies during the Cold War involved three wide-ranging objectives for "client" (or target) countries: democratization, economic development, and security. This three-pronged approach began during Kennedy's administration and endured as the primary model in U.S. policy, military doctrine, and practice, although U.S. responses at different times often emphasized one objective over the others. Most of the time security was the priority, but this is not to say that the pro-democracy and economic modernization goals were cut out of the picture.

The Kennedy administration was not simply concerned about the insurgent threats. Rather, they firmly believed that America's mission must also include robust support for democracy across the globe. For Kennedy, democracy was "the destiny of humanity." Americans must oppose the "powerful destructive forces ... challenging the universal values that for centuries have inspired men of good will in all parts of the world."[8]

Washington's "anticommunist" strategy became one of not only counterinsurgency but also support for democracy. A deeply influential trend in social science at the time, "modernization theory" involved the notion that economic dynamism would help usher in stable democracies. Kennedy and his advisers believed that this process of democratization with economic modernization thus needed to form the core of American engagement in regions where these institutions and processes were absent. Kennedy made this point eloquently when he stated, "the fundamental task of our foreign aid program ... is not negatively to fight communism: its fundamental task is to help make a historical demonstration that ... economic growth and political democracy can develop hand in hand."[9] White House adviser Walt Rostow made a similar point when he addressed members of the first class of Green Berets to graduate with specific instruction in counterinsurgency from the U.S. Army Center for Special Warfare: "You are not merely soldiers in the old sense. ... Your job is to work with ... your fellow citizens in the whole creative process of modernization."[10]

At the same time, American policymakers concluded that the economic growth that would usher in democracy could be obtained only if "internal order" was first established.[11] Thus, in their view, security was indispensable to modernization. To ensure protection from both internal and external subversion, states needed capable militaries and police forces, and the United States could and should assist anticommunist governments to arm and train their security forces. In practice, this thinking led to new assistance programs such as the International Military Education and Training Program (IMET) that provided training for local officers and soldiers. The Kennedy administration also supported the expansion of Military Assistance Advisory Groups (MAAGS) that helped consolidate both conventional and unconventional military forces in Greece and the Philippines.[12]

The region where Kennedy's "modernization through militaries" approach was most aggressively put into practice was Latin America. Indeed, Kennedy was terrified that "another Cuba" along the lines of Fidel Castro's victorious Marxist revolution could emerge in America's "backyard." And, before long, communist revolution indeed came to the region. Bolivia, Venezuela, Guatemala, Nicaragua, and Peru comprise only a partial list of countries where Cuba-inspired guerrilla insurgencies took root. And, true to form, beginning with Kennedy, American administrations responded to this threat by arming and training militaries to check this subversion.

These sections tell the story of how the democracy-modernization-security approach played out through the Cold War, emphasizing the key similarities and modulations in each case. They include a thorough treatment of the U.S. Cold War counterinsurgency experience in Greece and the Philippines. A long chapter on Indochina and Vietnam analyzes what might be considered the seminal example of the U.S. Cold War approach and its painful conclusion. Vietnam represents the point from which American counterinsurgency doctrine would have to make a large evolutionary step into the post–Cold War era: after the loss in Vietnam, it was decided, there could be no more Vietnams.

13

Intermezzo

Mao Zedong

In guerrilla warfare there is no such thing as a decisive battle.
– Mao Zedong

The Chinese revolution in the late 1940s resonated deeply across the capitals of Western Europe and the United States. Somehow, what at first appeared to be a ragtag force of Communist guerrillas had defeated a U.S.-backed ally in the Chinese Nationalists. After the onset of growing tensions with Moscow following World War II, American policymakers provided limited, largely ineffective aid to the Nationalists as the world's fourth-largest country in terms of landmass and largest country by population, with about 20 percent of the global total, "went red."

Mao Zedong's stunning communist revolution sent an urgent telegram to revolutionary movements around the globe, especially in what was then usually called the Third World. In short, Mao showed that dogged perseverance and political acumen could overcome enormous military disadvantages. Over the next several decades, numerous "Maoist" insurgencies in Asia, Africa, and Latin America broke out in attempts to replicate the spectacular success of Mao's Chinese forces.

Mao co-founded the Chinese Communist Party in 1921, at which point it advocated a largely urban-based approach to revolution modeled on the Bolshevik takeover of Petrograd in 1917. In fact, Soviet advisers counseled their Chinese counterparts on this very strategy.[1] Having spent most of his life in the countryside, though, Mao came to believe that China's overwhelmingly rural population necessitated a revolution that emanated from

158   Part Two. The Cold War, 1940s–1989

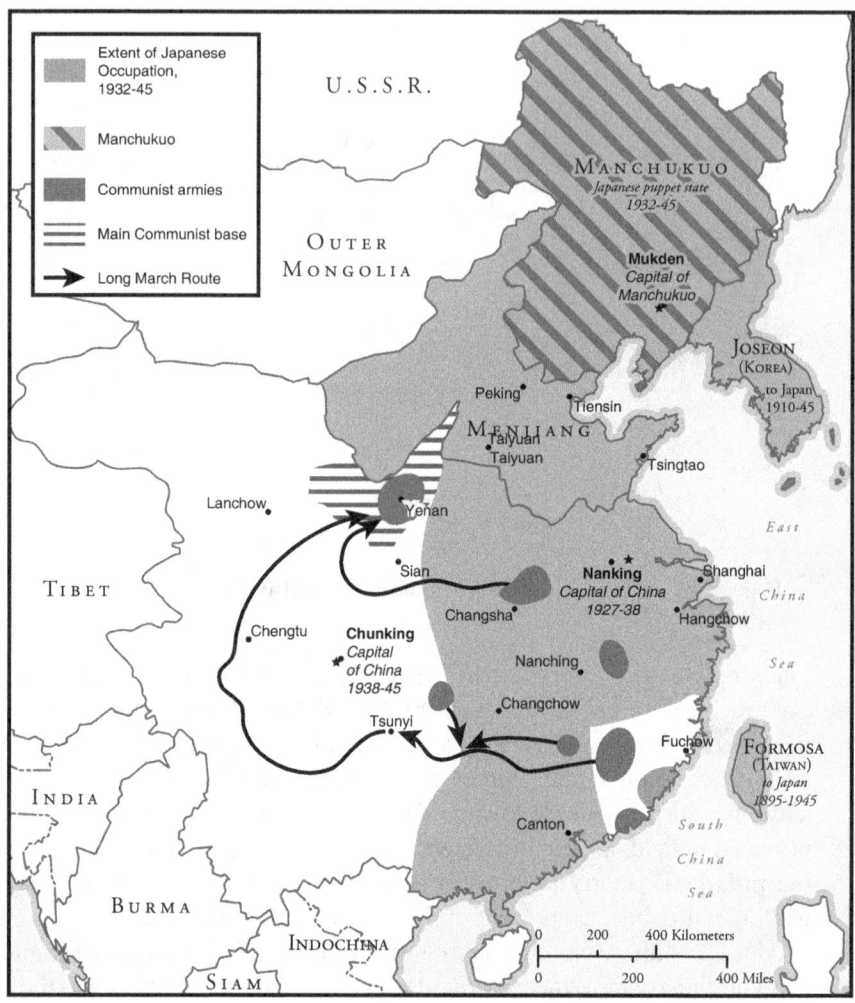

FIGURE 13.1. China, 1930s-1940s. Map prepared by the University of Wisconsin-Madison Cartography Lab©. Reprinted with permission

outside the major urban centers.[2] Mao also presciently recognized that any rural insurrection would take time to build and that patience would be paramount. In Mao's estimation, the communist forces would need to spend years organizing and fighting in the rural areas before moving to the cities for the final victory. Once again we see the longevity advantage and long-term outlook of insurgent leaders manifested in irregular

Intermezzo: Mao Zedong

warfare. These guerrilla leaders grasp these essential elements that escape the counterinsurgents who think the war can be won quickly and easily. This said, Mao did not come up with his approach on his own; instead, he avidly read Clausewitz and T. E. Lawrence. Most important, however, was the influence of Sun Tzu's *Art of War*.

Mao used the early years of his insurgency to carry out drastic land reform in the areas under communist control, often confiscating land and giving it directly to the peasants. Generalissimo Chiang Kai-Shek assumed the head of the Nationalist Party (KMT) following the death of its leader Sun Yat-sen in 1925. Initially at least tenuously allied with the communists, the idealistic Chiang of socialist leanings and Methodist faith subsequently turned on them when he thought they were strong enough to threaten his control of the KMT.[3]

From 1927 to 1933, Chiang tried to destroy Mao's rural forces and targeted leftists in Chinese cities; in Shanghai alone Chiang's forces killed an estimated 12,000 people suspected of communist sympathies.[4] The Nationalists also built railroads throughout the Chinese countryside, in part to increase their mobility and to keep the pressure on the communists. In a strategy reminiscent of the British efforts against the Boers, they also constructed blockhouses that reduced the communists' ability to move from one region to another.

By late 1934, Mao's forces were unable to withstand the Nationalist onslaught. They fled in a series of retreats to the west and north of China collectively known as the Long March. It was an appropriate name: in little over a year, starting in October 1934 the communists' First Front Army led by Mao and Zhou Enlai walked over 8,000 miles from Jiangxi in the far southeast to the northern province of Shaanxi, fighting more than 200 battles along the way. The forces walked roughly 15 miles a day and suffered enormous deprivation due to disease and constant harassment by Chiang's forces. Of the 120,000 communists who started the journey, roughly 20,000 made it to Shaanxi. Remarkably, though, the marchers acquired upward of 40,000 recruits during the arduous march.[5] Upon arriving in Shaanxi, Mao's forces established their bases in caves as protection against their enemies.

While the Long March allowed Mao's forces to escape destruction at the hands of the Nationalists, their predicament quickly became complicated by the Japanese occupation of China. Japan had seized Manchuria in September 1931. By the middle of July 1937, Japanese forces had moved deeper into Chinese territory and occupied most of the major cities. The

FIGURE 13.2. Mao Zedong with fellow communist leaders Zhou Enlai and Zhu De during the Long March. Over the course of a year, Mao and his followers traversed 8,000 miles of territory, walking 15 miles a day in extremely harsh conditions. Of the 120,000 who began the trek, only 20,000 remained. However, the Long March saved Mao's army and attracted many new followers to his cause. *Source*: Mandadori Collection, reproduced with permission from Getty Images, 141551616

communists and Nationalists suspended their hostilities against each other to focus on expelling the Japanese invaders.

The Japanese invasion came to be a gift from heaven for Mao since it greatly improved his battered army's advantage over the Nationalists. The Japanese did not consider the communists a serious threat to their occupation and so focused most of their attention on decimating the Nationalists. Nonetheless, Mao realized the communists' precarious situation required a full-scale guerrilla warfare strategy.

It was during these years fighting the Japanese that Mao published several of his classic theoretical works, including *Guerrilla Warfare* and *Basic Tactics*. These treatises were among the first "how-to" manuals for guerrilla warfare. *Basic Tactics* began by asking, "How is it that the bare-handed masses, banded together in ill-armed military units without guns or bullets, are able to charge the enemy, kill the enemy, and resolutely carry out effective action in the war?"[6] Mao's answer was both simple and highly effective, even if some of his writings come almost verbatim from Sun Tzu. Most critically, Mao insisted that the struggle was inherently political, not military. Thus, all organization, training, and fighting should be conducted with their political ramifications in mind. Thus, for Mao, "when the Red Army fights, it fights not merely for the sake of fighting, but to agitate the masses, to organize them, to arm them, and to help them establish revolutionary political power; apart from such objectives, fighting loses its meaning and the Red Army the reason for its existence."[7]

Mao believed that propaganda was a critical tool in winning over the allegiance of the rural masses, and these masses were key to the revolution's success. His vast propaganda campaign was partly intended to show that, in the most basic terms, the communists were good while the Japanese and Nationalists were bad. Mao therefore insisted that his troops treat the rural population with respect: "Do not steal from people," he wrote. "Be neither selfish or unjust."[8]

On the military front, Mao believed that guerrilla warfare was essential but that it was only one part of a total war of the oppressed against the oppressor. He also held that "there are no decisive battles in guerrilla warfare."[9] Instead guerrilla forces must maximize their strengths while masking their many weaknesses: "Attack dispersed and isolated enemy first. Concentrate forces later; Win control of rural areas first; Wipe out the enemy's effective strength; Use local superiority; Do not fight unless you are sure to win; Fear no sacrifice; Seize weak areas first; Use captured men and weapons; Rest, regroup and train between battles."[10]

Mao identified three critical phases that the revolutionary forces must pass through: the "strategic defensive," when the force is most vulnerable and political organization is key; the "stalemate," when the force is strong enough to battle the enemy; and the "strategic offensive," when the guerrilla army joins with other conventional forces to finish the job.

Sensing the inevitable renewal of hostilities once the Japanese had been defeated, the communists and Nationalists began to jostle for position even before the end of World War II. The Japanese intervention had given Mao vital breathing room to conduct his political organization in the countryside. At the time of Japan's defeat, Mao controlled an area of China with a population of 100,000,000 people. By 1945, his communist forces were much stronger than Chiang's Nationalists; in 1946, the People's Liberation

Army (PLA) was established. Three years later the communists occupied Beijing, and soon after Mao announced the creation of the People's Republic of China.

The communist revolution in China was a cataclysmic event that profoundly influenced the course of the Cold War. For many Marxists across the globe it appeared to validate the notion that a committed but small band of insurgents could overthrow stronger Western forces and their "local clients." Mao's success also prompted American and European military planners to consider more aggressively how they would counter what appeared to be a terrifyingly effective guerrilla strategy.

PROJECT CIRCUS AND KAMBA GUERRILLAS

After consolidating its victory over the Nationalist forces, in 1950 Communist China took over Tibet. Chastened about "losing" China to communism, Washington's nascent intelligence service, the Central Intelligence Agency, created a clandestine operation intended to train anti-China Tibetan insurgents and gather intelligence about the Chinese. In 1955, a group of local Tibetan leaders secretly plotted an armed insurrection, and a revolt broke out a year later, with the rebels attacking local government offices, slaughtering hundreds of Chinese. The rebel organization also targeted communist officials for assassination, disrupted communication lines, and attacked Chinese army troops stationed in Tibet.

Within this unfolding context of guerrilla warfare directed against a communist foe, Washington began supporting the insurgents through what was called "Project Circus." Tibetan guerrillas were whisked abroad for training, and weapons and ammunition were dropped inside Tibet. In 1959, the agency opened a secret facility to train Tibetan recruits at Camp Hale near Leadville, Colorado, in part because the high-altitude location approximated the Himalayas. Roughly two hundred "Kamba guerrillas" passed through the Colorado program.

While the CIA program never sparked mass uprising against the Chinese occupiers as was hoped for, the effort did produce an intelligence coup, in the form of a vast trove of Chinese army documents captured by Tibetan fighters and turned over to the CIA in 1961. These papers described the low morale among Chinese soldiers, who had learned of the vast famine that was wracking China during the Great Leap Forward. As Jonathan Mirsky wrote, over the next several years, however, there was growing disagreement in Washington over the CIA's activities in Tibet, and in 1971, as National Security Advisor Henry Kissinger prepared for Nixon's meeting with Mao, the program was wound down.[11]

KOREA: GUERRILLA WAR AMID A REGULAR WAR

Tibet was not the only area in Asia where the U.S. government was involved in training indigenous guerrilla fighters against Mao's communist forces. The Korean War began in June 1950 with the Moscow and Beijing-backed North Korean invasion of U.S.-supported South Korea (following Japan's defeat in World War II, ending its thirty-five-year occupation of Korea, the nation had been partitioned into North and South Korea). Within days of the communist invasion, Washington was shipping troops to the battle. Initial setbacks drove the U.S.-commanded forces to the very south of the peninsula, but within months General Douglas MacArthur's forces had pushed the invaders back over 38th parallel.

In early October, MacArthur's soldiers were nearing the Yalu River, which forms the border between North Korea and China. In a fateful decision, Mao decided to secretly send hundreds of thousands of Chinese soldiers across the Yalu, at times carrying pre-cooked meals so they would not be forced to set fires visible to American pilots. Yet, on October 26, American forces took their first Chinese prisoner. Still unaware of the extent of Mao's invasion, General MacArthur was confident that his boys would be home by Christmas. In late November, however, the Chinese launched a full-scale attack, which sent the American forces reeling back toward Seoul.

After months of bitter fighting, the conflict stabilized roughly along the 38th parallel, the point that had separated the two Koreas before the war began.[12] For almost the next two years, the Korean War often resembled World War I–style trench warfare with "endless artillery barrages, impenetrable defensive lines, ghoulish conditions, dead boys piling up in the snow." By the fall of 1952, a plurality of Americans considered the war a mistake.[13]

The Korean War is considered to be a conventional war with irregular elements that were not well understood (either then or now). Most critically, the United States secretly supported an anticommunist guerrilla campaign against the China-backed North Korean forces. Some of these anticommunist Korean forces acted in coordination with American military planners while an untold number acted independently to, in the word of an American general, "harass the Reds, motivated solely by hatred of the forces that had despoiled their native land."[14]

In one key operation focused on intelligence-gathering and rescue operations, American warships plied North Korean waters all the way up to the Yalu River. From these island and ship bases, U.S. forces made clandestine contact with the Korean guerrillas. Low-flying American bomber and transport planes dropped communications equipment to the underground units; Grumman HU-16 Albatross flying boats repeatedly landed in open sea and taxied up to the North Korean beaches for a rendezvous with guerrilla forces.

For the U.S. military, one of the guerrillas' most useful functions was to rescue American pilots shot down over North Korea. Amazingly, the system was so well organized that every American fighter and bomber pilot operating over North Korea was briefed on the safe areas into which he could parachute if the plane was hit. Once the flyers contacted the guerrillas, an underground network went into operation to move the Americans to the coast and to safety. One observer noted, "the system worked because it combined our American technical equipment, such as the helicopter, with the determination and daring of both the American airmen and the North Korean guerrillas."[15]

Not surprisingly, the North Korean and Chinese forces were quite aware of these guerrilla bands, and in the winter of 1951-2 began a counterinsurgent campaign to eliminate the threat. Communist cadres announced an amnesty for guerrillas on wall posters and newspapers; yet, as is so often the case in antiguerrilla campaigns, these offers were accompanied with the threats of execution for those who held out. Fearing reprisals for those trapped behind enemy lines, soon after the formal war had ended the American military conducted a full-blown amphibious evacuation of tens of thousands of partisan fighters.

14

Fighting Communism in Greece

Washington's effort to bolster the fledgling Greek government was its first experience with counterinsurgency after World War II. An American decision to back Athens came in 1947 at a time when the overarching strategic framework for countering communism, "containment," was still in its embryonic stage. Greece was one of the first "pawns" in the expanding Cold War chessboard. The country had suffered horribly during the Nazi occupation, with roughly 8 percent of its population killed, 6 percent made homeless, and much of the rest of the nation devastated by catastrophic crop and infrastructure losses. During the war, the anti-Nazi Greek communists represented some of the most dogged and successful partisans, rejecting cooperation with the Axis occupation and resorting to guerrilla warfare in Greece's formidable mountain ranges. The National Liberation Front (EAM) was one of the largest anti-Nazi groups, even if it was not entirely communist.[1] Backed by the British, by late 1944 around 1.5 million of Greece's 7.5 million inhabitants were somehow affiliated with the EAM.

Following Greece's liberation in October 1944, the EAM found itself controlling most of the country; however, it soon began to clash with the British as well as the British-sponsored, royalist former Greek government, which had been exiled to Cairo. Almost overnight, these elements decimated the EAM. Even so, the group remained a viable political entity, one that was eager to assume power in postoccupation Greece.[2] But given the fissures among the various Greek groups during the Nazi years, it was almost a foregone conclusion that the ensuing political activity would be far from harmonious.

FIGURE 14.1. Greece, 1940s. Map prepared by the University of Wisconsin-Madison Cartography Lab©. Reprinted with permission

As is so often the case with right-wing "paramilitaries" in dirty wars, these forces, whether correctly or incorrectly, identified left-leaning civilians as apologists or clandestine communist revolutionaries. In the paramilitaries' uncompromising logic, the next step was to threaten and kill these civilians. In Greece, members of the political left, even though many had fought against the Germans, began to be the targets of right-wing paramilitary attacks. From 1945 to 1946, paramilitary groups killed more than 1,000 Greek communists and leftists in what became known as the "White Terror"; in rural areas, right-wing mobs lynched suspected guerrillas.[3] Others were arrested and tortured by the Greek government. Fleeing likely death or imprisonment, thousands of leftists fled to neighboring countries: 25,000 to Yugoslavia, 5,000 to Bulgaria, and 23,000 to Albania. Following the paramilitary terrorism, many Greek communists concluded that political change could come through armed struggle alone.

In 1946, the EAM's repeated setbacks prompted the Greek Communist Party, the KKE, to organize a rural guerrilla insurgency against the newly elected Greek government in Athens. The Greek Civil War, as it is known, between the communist guerrillas and the Greek government, backed at first by the British, then by the United States, lasted from 1946 to 1949.

One might have concluded that the communist guerrillas were in an extremely favorable position vis-à-vis the fledgling Greek government. For the seasoned communist fighters, Greece's rugged mountains provided the perfect terrain for irregular warfare, with countless hideaways where the revolutionaries could find refuge and plot to ambush government forces. The communists were also a sizable guerrilla force of 46,000 fighters at the onset. Moreover, the very fact of having resisted the Nazi occupation gave the guerrillas a ready-made level of legitimacy among the Greek population, and with "hearts and minds" so often key to winning these sorts of wars, this appeared to be a tremendous asset. The guerrillas had another key element of most successful insurgencies: strong leadership in the astute military strategist Markos Vafiadis. Last, the communists enjoyed crucial external support in the form of open borders with adjoining communist countries such as Yugoslavia, Albania, and Bulgaria.

By 1946, Vafiadis's guerrillas were known as the Greek Democratic Army (DSE). Over the next year, the communist fighters operated against the poorly equipped and demoralized Greek army just as they had against the Germans: staging hit-and-run attacks on poorly defended rural villages and police stations. For the Greek government, the situation was dire. It was ultimately moved to request aid from Great Britain and the United

States. With the exhausted British Empire unable to carry the burden, the question came down to whether Washington would come to the rescue.

THE TRUMAN DOCTRINE

The Truman administration's decision to aid Greece was not an easy one. In fact, Secretary of State George Marshall, for one, worried that the aid would go to an unpopular government.[4] U.S. policymakers were also wary of picking up the slack for what had been Great Britain's responsibility in Greece. Yet the evolving strategic logic of containment began to weigh on Truman's adviser. For Marshall, the threat was not so much that the Greek communists would take power but that their success would set an alarming precedent for others who were vying for communist expansion at the expense of U.S.-backed regimes. The newly formed CIA was of a similar mind. One CIA communiqué read, "far more disastrous than the loss of Greece itself would be the psychological and political repercussions [which] could result in international panic."[5] Under Secretary of State Dean Acheson worried that Greece's fall could take with it "the whole Near and Middle East and North Africa."[6]

Thus, with Greece occupying a prominent position among American strategic concerns, the Cold War "domino theory" was born. Truman explained the main reasons for aiding the Greek government in his famous "Truman Doctrine" speech to Congress in March 1947:

The United States has received from the Greek Government an urgent appeal for financial and economic assistance. Preliminary reports from the American Economic Mission now in Greece and reports from the American Ambassador in Greece corroborate the statement of the Greek Government that assistance is imperative if Greece is to survive as a free nation. I do not believe that the American people and the Congress wish to turn a deaf ear to the appeal of the Greek Government....

[A] militant minority, exploiting human want and misery, was able to create political chaos which, until now, has made economic recovery impossible.... The very existence of the Greek state is today threatened by the terrorist activities of several thousand armed men, led by Communists, who defy the government's authority at a number of points, particularly along the northern boundaries....

Meanwhile, the Greek government is unable to cope with the situation. The Greek army is small and poorly equipped. It needs supplies and equipment if it is to restore the authority of the government throughout Greek territory. Greece must have assistance if it is to become a self-supporting and self-respecting democracy.... The United States must supply that assistance.... There is no other country to which democratic Greece can turn. No other nation is willing and able to provide the necessary support for a democratic Greek government.[7]

In May 1947 the Republican-controlled Congress approved a $400 million assistance package for Greece and Turkey, a country also considered susceptible to Stalin's machinations. When it was enacted, the Truman administration's Greece policy was largely about what is known in foreign policy circles as "engagement." The situation in Greece was grim, but Washington would now attempt to make a bad situation better by becoming more involved, not less. The costs of this sort of engagement strategy were high, given that the United States now quite visibly had its credibility on the line in Greece.

At the same time, the Truman administration had no desire to have American GIs actually doing the fighting. As Truman also suggested in his congressional address, the U.S. strategy was to bolster the Greek government by more than simple military means. According to a National Security Council memorandum,

The United States should ... make full use of its political, economic and, if necessary, military power in such manner as may be found most effective to prevent Greece from falling under the domination of the USSR through either external attack or Soviet-dominated Communist movements within Greece, so long as the legally elected government of Greece evidences a determination to oppose such Communist aggression.[8]

It quickly became apparent to American policymakers that the Greek government they were now committed to bolstering was in pathetic shape. The Greek army was particularly corrupt and ineffective, an alarming prospect given the guerrilla war that had erupted.[9]

One of the United States' most important counterinsurgency policies was the establishment of a military office that would coordinate the military assistance and training. The Joint U.S. Military Advisory and Planning Group (JUSMAPG) was established in December 1947, and General James Van Fleet arrived soon after to command it.[10] With the JUSMAPG in place, the U.S. military was active in a country threatened by formidable communist guerrillas. While still not directly involved, American forces were now much closer to the fight. In future years, Washington would establish JUSMAPGs in other countries under siege from communist guerrillas such as the Philippines, Vietnam, and El Salvador.

As part of the Truman Doctrine, Washington spent roughly $200 million on the Greek military, supplying it with critical materiel, including dive-bombers and napalm bombs. American assistance and training helped the Greek army to swell from 90,000 in 1946 to 260,000 in 1948. By 1947, U.S. aid supported the Greek army's entire budget.[11] U.S. officers also organized and trained crack commando units that began taking the fight directly to the guerrillas. Americans also worked to bolster Greece's still decimated infrastructure; they helped build roads, communication systems, railways, and airstrips in remote garrison towns.

U.S. officials also promoted aggressive counterinsurgency actions, including population resettlement, the common tactic of antiguerrilla operations. Resettlement efforts proved to be devastating for the guerrillas by depriving them of critical support from the affected civilians, especially in the southern and central parts of the country. Yet, not surprisingly, the program also antagonized rural Greeks who blamed the government for their new hardships.

Given the Greek government's spotty political and economic record, the Truman administration maintained that the aid was conditional on substantive reform. In reality, though, this was often not the case: the Greek government at times used American aid to fuel its dirty war against leftists and communists, an embarrassing revelation for Washington. Quick to dampen these allegations, one American ambassador told Congress that reports of summary arrests and murder were "half-truths, distortions of the truth, and down-right lies originating in the propaganda mill of the Kremlin."[12] At the same time, U.S. officials also pressured the Greek government to crack down on leftist political activity. In late 1947, the government shut down the communist newspaper, *Rizospastis*. It also abolished the right to strike and purged government ranks of suspected communists.

THE REBELS SPLINTER

In addition to now confronting a more robust Greek army, the guerrillas' cause was complicated by Stalin's lukewarm support. Ever the player of diplomatic realpolitik, Stalin worried that continued strife in Greece could needlessly complicate his dealings with the West. This was a move later echoed in Moscow's disagreement with Cuban initiatives to launch guerrilla insurgencies elsewhere in Latin America during the 1960s. At a meeting in 1948 with Eastern Bloc leaders, the Soviet premier revealed his doubts about the Greek insurgency:

Fighting Communism in Greece

The Americans and the British have a very strong interest in the Mediterranean. They would like to have their bases in Greece. They would use all possible means to support a government that would be obedient. This is an international issue of great importance. If the particular movement is halted, they would have no excuse to attack you.... If you are confident that the partisans have good chances of winning, that is a different manner. But I have some doubts about this.[13]

While Stalin never warmed to the Greek insurgents, Tito's Yugoslavia maintained an open border, which provided critical refuge and supplies for the guerrillas. In the summer of 1949, however, Tito closed the border after a number of disputes with the Greek communists. The insurgents had already suffered another fateful blow in 1948 when Nikolaos Zachariadis, general secretary of Greece's communist party, had Vafiades purged out of fear of his rising status. Zachariadis then became the self-proclaimed general and commander of the guerrilla force. Ever restless, Zachariadis jettisoned Vafiades's patient hit-and-run strategy for a conventional approach that he hoped would deal Athens a decisive setback.

This new strategy led the guerrilla fighters into towns and grouped them into concentrated field formations, which made them cannon fodder for the more powerful Greek army. In a postwar interview King Paul, who assumed the throne in 1947, recounted, "The bandits made a mistake. They went in for the regular military form of warfare in large units. That's when they got it in the neck. Before that, we would give them a punch and they would disappear into thin air, then reappear and attack a village to get food."[14]

The Greek military's air and artillery support proved particularly devastating to the reorganized insurgents. By late summer 1949 and after a series of conventional battles, the guerrillas began to flee into Albania. Soon thereafter, the Greek Democratic Army ceased to function as a guerrilla force. On October 16, the Greek communist radio announced a cessation to hostilities. Athens had won.

LESSONS LEARNED

Greece's civil war resulted in perhaps 50,000 combatants killed and another 500,000 civilians displaced. And this was all immediately after the terrible devastation wrought during the Nazi occupation of World War II. The war's widespread destruction was, in this case, a major factor in the guerrillas' defeat. The communists were never able to garner the crucial support of

Greece's rural farmers and laborers, who considered the guerrillas nothing more than bandits operating largely in parts of the country that had for decades been the site of lawless activity. Moreover, the guerrillas often treated civilians harshly; in one crude episode, they kidnapped thousands of children and sent them to Eastern Bloc countries to ostensibly "rescue" them from the war's harms.[15] But beyond this historical contingency and others like it – such as the closing of the Yugoslav border – it was at least as much the guerrillas' ineptitude as the government's counterinsurgency capacity that decided the war.[16]

American policymakers and military strategists came away from the Greek Civil War with a renewed belief that a light counterinsurgency footprint was all that was needed to bolster weak national governments and keep communist guerrillas at bay. There are several reasons this might have been an easy – and potentially accurate – conclusion to draw. For one, the guerrillas lacked a strong foothold among Greece's rural population. In most cases of successful communist insurgency, support of the people was a crucial element.

Second, the guerrillas did not receive substantial support in the form of funding or materiel from the USSR or another regional power. In Vietnam, a steady flow of arms, ammunition, and money in addition to training and overt ideological support from abroad made small, fleet-footed guerrilla armies much more difficult forces for America's light-footprint counterinsurgency support operations to contend with – even if those guerrilla armies were badly organized. In Greece, Stalin did not flinch. He told the Greek communists to abandon the struggle because, he believed, the United States and United Kingdom would not allow a communist stronghold an area so strategically important to Mediterranean communications and transport.

Third, while there were all sorts of setbacks and failures in Greece, U.S. support had a critical impact. Scholars continue to debate whether Athens would have emerged victorious had the Americans withheld aid, but had the outcome gone in the guerrillas' favor, the United States might have reconsidered its light-footprint approach, opting for deeper involvement. As it stood, though, the light-footprint became a critical strategy for containing the comparatively small and tangential guerrilla insurgencies that subsequently erupted as the conflict in Southeast Asia escalated.

On the other hand, the American experience fighting the Greek counterinsurgency demonstrated to American military planners that while a low-impact strategy in terms of U.S. combatants in the field could bring positive results, such a strategy was well served by heavy firepower. The overwhelming operational achievements of fighter-bombers and targeted bomb strikes in Greece no doubt influenced American generals in the initial years of the Vietnam conflict. Perhaps most important, the American success in Greece convinced then senator and future president Lyndon B. Johnson that the United States could prevail in Vietnam as it had in Greece.

15

Intermezzo

France in Algeria, 1954–1962

> The theory, the famous theory of water and fish of Mao Tse-Tung, which has achieved much, is still very simple and very true: If you withdraw the water, that is to say, the support of the population, fish can no longer live. It's simple, I know, but in war only the simple things can be achieved.
> – French General Maurice Challe[1]

After the humiliation of World War II, the French military and political class took solace in their remaining colonies, which included Indochina, Algeria, Madagascar, Morocco, French Somaliland (Djibouti), and other territories in central and western Africa. Socialist Prime Minister Paul Ramadier, for one, stated soon after World War II, "We will hold on everywhere, in Indochina as in Madagascar. Our empire will not be taken away from us, because we represent might and also right."[2] After a humiliating 1954 defeat at Dien Bien Phu in Indochina, though, it seemed that France's days as an imperial power were greatly numbered. This new reality came as a shock to many in France who assumed that French *grandeur* would continue indefinitely.

Many in the French military responded to the loss of Indochina by concluding that it was a defeat at the hands of global communism, not grassroots nationalism. Disillusioned officers posited a connection between the communist forces they were fighting in the Indochina campaign and a vast subversive threat throughout the former European empires. As one French proponent concluded, "Western civilization now faces a life or death situation." Even the imperturbable Charles de Gaulle commented, "Nationalism in Indochina is a means, the end is Soviet

Intermezzo: France in Algeria 175

FIGURE 15.1. Algeria. Map prepared by the University of Wisconsin-Madison Cartography Lab©. Reprinted with permission

imperialism."[3] This perception was the basis for the counterinsurgency doctrine that emerged in France in the late 1950s – what became known as *guerre révolutionnaire*. In this view, the French military needed a new approach to prevent more losses to global communism.[4]

The theory turned on two vital features: the importance of the civilian population and the strength of a unified civilian-military command. The French officers believed that the communists, as ideological descendants of

Marx and Mao, were able to win over domestic populations by masking their motives in the language of equality and independence – that is, by waging war on the battlegrounds of politics and psychology. French theorists took this interpretation and created a more formal, even scientific, approach to guerrilla warfare. In fact, they even developed an equation: "partisan warfare + psychological warfare = revolutionary warfare."[5]

Intellectual pioneers of guerre révolutionnaire included such French officers as General Lionel-Max Chassin, Roger Trinquier, and Charles Lacheroy, all of whom served in Indochina and subsequently Algeria. While certainly not agreeing on everything, they generally contended that the best way to counter a communist revolutionary enemy was to beat it both politically and psychologically, and that this must be achieved on three fronts: in the destruction of the armed opposition; in the construction of regions where insurgents could not operate and were cut off from civilian support; and in the broad deployment of psychological operations.

The first two of these fronts were the doctrine's most pernicious and controversial elements. The logic was that communist influence – whether it was physical infrastructure or the beliefs of rural villagers – had to be wiped out before any lasting effort to win over the population could begin. According to one guerre révolutionnaire proponent, "These two terms [destruction and construction] are inseparable. To destroy without building up would mean useless labor; to build without first destroying would be a delusion."[6] By destruction, the French meant that all means should be implemented, including the very tactics of the guerrillas such as terror and resettlement. In other words, dirty insurgencies could only be defeated with dirty counterinsurgencies. A large part of the appeal of guerre révolutionnaire was that its all-encompassing thesis helped the French military explain its humiliation at the hands of inferior adversaries. It was in Algeria that the French applied guerre révolutionnaire in its fullest and most furious form.

REVOLT AND REPRISAL

The full story of the Algerian revolt against French rule begins with France's colonial conquest of Algiers in 1830. In the hundred years of French colonial rule, thousands of settlers from France, Italy, and Spain had migrated to Algeria. Known as *pieds-noirs*, the immigrants largely lived in the cities in the north of the country, near the coast. Over time, the

Intermezzo: France in Algeria 177

indigenous, predominantly Muslim Algerian population grew disproportionately, so that by the 1940s, the pieds-noirs comprised only about 13 percent of the population. Despite their shrinking proportion in the population, the relative privilege of this group in matters of politics and society fueled resentment at a time when the idea of "national liberation" was gaining currency throughout colonized regions of the world.

While Allied forces were celebrating France's liberation from Nazi occupation, in May 8, 1945, native Algerians protesting French rule clashed with police in the market town of Sétif. A parade by Algerian Muslims, ostensibly organized to celebrate the Nazi surrender but also fueled by intense nationalist sentiments, turned ugly; marchers clashed with the French *gendarmerie*, the colonial police force. The same night, armed Muslims roamed neighborhoods, killing pieds-noirs when they located them.[7] The rioters killed more than a hundred Europeans; scores of women were raped, including an eighty-four-year-old woman. The corpses were often mutilated, with men's genitals stuffed into their mouths.

In a brutal harbinger of the impending war's mutual brutality, after the Algerian riots had embroiled the streets for several days, the French colonial forces responded ruthlessly. Estimates place the number of Algerians killed between 1,000 and 45,000.[8] During the days of reprisals, French troops raped Algerian women at will. While the savage French response succeeded in suppressing the localized rebellion, the Sétif massacre served to galvanize Algerians against both pieds-noirs prerogatives and continued French rule.

In terms of counterinsurgency, France's experience in Algeria resulted in a paradoxical outcome: France overwhelmingly won the counterinsurgency war, often using dirty tactics such as torture and forced resettlement. At the same time, though, the French also overwhelmingly lost the political battle that determined Algeria's fate. The war in Algeria lasted eight years, involved six French prime ministers, and even led to Sherman tanks being deployed in Paris to prevent a rebellion by disgruntled military officers. By the end, Algeria was an independent state and the war had ruptured French society far more than any of its other twentieth-century colonial wars had done.[9] At the same time, it became an important example for the U.S. government in the beginning years of a Cold War doctrine that would involve many small and dirty counterinsurgency wars.

Guerre Révolutionnaire

Well-organized Algerian nationalist movements, which included several nascent communist groups, began to mobilize in Algeria after World War

II. Then, on the night of October 31, 1954, Algerian nationalists unleashed scores of attacks throughout Algeria, in many instances setting off bombs and assaulting *gendarmarie* posts. Executed by small groups using crude rifles and homemade ballistics, the attacks startled French authorities, who did not think the Muslim Algerians capable of orchestrating operations of such breadth and impact. The French would soon learn that these operations were the beginning of an anti-French, pro-independence insurgency known as the Front de Libération Nationale (FLN).

The FLN and its supporting military force, the Armée de Libération Nationale (ALN), attempted to establish rural bases where they could prolong the conflict and perfect their "politics" in preparation for a decisive encounter with the French. Ideologically, the FLN was aggressively socialist and anti-imperialist but – contrary to the French tendency to consider them thus – not communist. At the very onset, the FLN hoped to draw the French into a quick, lethal battle so that it could humiliate the colonial forces into an immediate withdrawal, but this hope was quickly dashed by French fortitude. The FLN's efforts were further stymied by the lack of any sizable external sponsor who could provide much-needed support and arms shipments.

During these early years, the FLN had only a few hundred to a few thousand fighters under arms; most of the clandestine organization's operations were of the small-scale, hit-and-run variety.[10] By 1957, though, the FLN had between 15,000 and 20,000 members, even though many of these served only as part-time combatants. Despite the swelling numbers, the FLN never had sufficient weapons to arm all of its members, a lethal disadvantage vis-à-vis the French.

Yet, from the onset, the French found the FLN a formidable foe. The group benefited from a novel intelligence network that, at least initially, allowed it to keep its secrets secure. The trick was to distribute information through "cells," in which just a few men knew each other. If an FLN member was captured he would have very little intelligence to reveal to his French interrogators.

In turn, the French military's counterinsurgency strategy was quite simple. It adopted a guerre révolutionnaire approach to waging war without restraint. By the end of 1956, France had committed 400,000 troops to Algeria. The French also relied on around 200,000 *harkis* (Muslim fighters loyal to the French), who were often very lethal fighters. The FLN, in turn, targeted the harkis for particular savagery given their presumed betrayal of the Algerian independence movement.

In late 1957, under the command of General Raoul Salan, the French military adopted a *quadrillage* system as a way of establishing a military presence in as many areas as possible of the country's often remote and inhospitable terrain. The quadrillage divided the country into sectors; in each sector a permanent garrison was stationed. While the approach certainly succeeded in getting French troops out into the hinterlands and thereby cutting down on FLN raids, it committed the French to a defensive posture at the expense of more mobile operations that could take the fight directly to the enemy. On the other hand, quadrillage was much safer for the participating French troops, something not lost on French commanders concerned about the potential domestic reaction back home.[11]

While the French strategy attempted to annihilate the insurgency militarily, there was also an integral component that aimed to win over popular support. Knowing full well the "psychological value" of this ostensible humanitarianism, the French deployed the sections administratives spécialisées (SAS), a unit of trained junior officers who went out to rural areas to live with Muslims and build schools, medical clinics, and whatever else the local community might need. The French also attempted more direct forms of psychological warfare by distributing leaflets or using blaring loudspeakers to bombard local residents with pro-French slogans.[12] French troops often "rewarded" Algerians for "correct" behavior.[13]

BREAKING SOME EGGS

Beginning in late 1956, the FLN embarked on a new strategy that proved to be one of the most fateful developments of this long and brutal war. The group decided to take the war "downtown" by targeting the country's key city, Algiers. More specifically, the FLN leadership selected the infamous Casbah neighborhood, home to around 80,000 Algerians and one of the world's most densely populated slums. In addition to the resident population's strong pro-FLN sentiment, the Casbah's narrow and twisting streets made it an ideal site for urban insurgent attacks.

The FLN's strategy was to use terror against pieds-noirs and French military targets to provoke a French overreaction that would push the Algerian population toward favoring the insurgents. The FLN's terror weapon of choice was the homemade bomb. FLN commander Yacef Saadi, a loafer, soccer fanatic, and womanizer, was the head of the group's secret bombing campaign. French authorities were aware of Saadi as a political agitator, but initially did not suspect him as a terrorist. Quickly, Algiers rumbled with the sound of bomb explosions in cafes, streetcars, shops, soccer stadiums, and dance halls. Within months, the FLN's urban bomb cells had succeeded in terrifying the pied-noir population of Algiers that up to this point had felt largely immune from the war.

In early 1957, the French responded to the highly worrisome developments in Algiers by sending in General Jacques, a soldier of "dash and vigor," and his 8,000-strong 10e Division Parachutiste (10e DP) with full powers and orders to "restore power in the capital."[14] Massu and his beret and "leopard" camouflage-wearing "paras" embodied the guerre révolutionnaire approach to counterinsurgency. One of Massu's first key actions was to ruthlessly break the general eight-day strike called by the FLN for the Casbah. *Paras* went from shop to shop with stark orders from the owners: open up for business or we'll destroy your store. Massu's gambit succeeded as shop owners quickly obeyed the French threats.

Another critical French effort was the *nettoyage*, or cleansing operation. The idea was to have paras on constant patrol, setting up checkpoints and conducting house-to-house searches. The bomb-makers would be given no refuge. Given the FLN's intentionally clandestine strategy in the Casbah, Massu's chances of success depended heavily on high-quality intelligence. Muslim Casbah residents who served as informers were know as *bleus* and often provided the French with indispensable information. Another critical element of Massu's strategy was the use of massive arrests of suspected FLN members. Many of these Algerians were never seen again. In fact, a startling 30 percent of the male population of the Casbah was arrested during the siege; shockingly, 3,000 of the 24,000 total Muslims arrested during the Battle of Algiers disappeared while in detention.[15]

Massu and the paras justified torture as a "necessity" and as a matter of "efficiency." Only by breaking some eggs, the French believed, could the counterterror effort succeed in infiltrating the highly secret bombing network. It is noteworthy that Massu's strategy proved lethal against the FLN in the Casbah. Within nine months the FLN had been destroyed as a terror network in Algiers. In September 1957, Yacef Saadi was arrested while his fellow guerrilla leader, Ali la Pointe, was killed.

While the French success using torture in the Battle of Algiers might serve as a counterexample to the popular view that torture tends not to yield good intelligence since the victims invent information to avoid suffering, it nonetheless had catastrophic consequences for France's political ambitions in Algeria. The irony of this "victory" was that the French military deployed means of repression almost identical to those that they had endured during the Nazi occupation the decade before: some of the French torturers reportedly recognized techniques that had been used on them by the Gestapo when they were Resistance fighters. And once the torture began in Algiers, it left "behind a poison that would linger in the French system long after the war itself had ended."[16]

Whatever the short-term counterinsurgency gains, the French win in Algiers came at the expense of its own moral standing. What is more, Algiers focused international attention on the "Algeria question," leaving France exposed in the forum of world opinion at a time when "national liberation" movements were gaining broad sympathy. In this sense, like the American experience following the Tet Offensive in Vietnam, the Battle of Algiers wound up being a severe political setback for France.

HUNTING COMMANDOS AND THE MORICE LINE

After the Battle of Algiers, French commanders made a renewed effort to go after the Algerian insurgents in the hinterlands. One of the first efforts occurred in late 1957 when General Salan constructed a series of border protections called the Morice Line. Consisting of two rows of electric fences, barbed wire, and land mines stretching for more than 320 kilometers along the Tunisian frontier, the Morice Line aimed to cut off the Algerians' source of smuggled arms. The Line was guarded by 40,000 French troops and reinforced by radar and blockhouses in an approach not unlike the British strategy against the Boers half a century earlier. Mobile units were held in reserve to pursue any insurgent penetrations. A similar line guarded the Moroccan border as well. The French also mandated that the areas around the lines were free-fire zones where civilians could be shot on sight.

At the same time, the French relocated a startling 300,000 Muslims living along the Tunisian border to 250 inland settlements. Conditions inside the camps were appalling. Called *regroupments*, the villages aimed to keep the villagers separate from FLN violence or influence and deny the insurgents supplies or refuge. All told, a million rural peasants were resettled into these barbed wire camps across the country.

The cleared zones then gave the French military the green light to hunt insurgents crossing into Algeria.[17] Amazingly, the border interdiction efforts reduced arms and fighter trafficking by up to 90 percent. Thus, France managed to achieve in Algeria what the Americans could not do in Vietnam: secure borders.[18] Moreover, echoing a key strategic move from the Boer War, the closing of the borders also created a sort of "hunting preserve" where French mobile forces could track down trapped FLN and ALN fighters.

In 1958, General Maurice Challe, the new commander of the French army in Algeria after Salan, stepped up pressure considerably to break the back of the FLN's rural operations. Moving away from the static quadrillage, "Plan Challe" deployed highly trained mobile units equipped with French- and American-made helicopters to pursue the enemy. Interestingly, Challe was not a fanatical proponent of guerre révolutionnaire, yet his new strategy of using *commandos de chasse* (hunting commandos) and political campaigns certainly shared much with this widely held philosophy.

The new French strategy worked remarkably well. Despite the ire provoked by the forced resettlements, rural Algerian communities increasingly rejected the FLN. In fact, far more Algerians worked on the French side than with the FLN even though the number of FLN fighters had grown to about 200,000 by 1960. The French believed that they had effectively defeated the FLN. According to one French officer, "We have pacified the country so well ... [n]owadays, no one joins the guerrillas."[19]

Yet while French counterinsurgency strategy proved lethally effective on the ground, like the American experience in Vietnam, the longer the war lasted, the greater the perception grew at home that the French had committed egregious crimes in their efforts. Allegations of torture and atrocities rocked French society. In once instance, in early 1959, thirty-five priests who had served as reserve officers in Algeria issued a report stating among other things, "it emerges broadly that methods are used in the conduct of war that our consciences condemn.... Interrogations are conducted only too generally by methods we must call torture."[20] As the years dragged on, it became increasingly clear that "France was strong, militarily, in Algeria, but weak, politically, at home; the FLN was weak, militarily, at home, but strong politically, abroad."[21] In other words, what was good for France militarily was bad politically – and vice versa.[22]

FRANCE ON THE BRINK

The situation in Algeria would get far worse before it began to improve. In the late 1950s, pieds-noirs were becoming increasingly frustrated with what they believed were French concessions to the Algerians. In May 1958, disgruntled French officers revolted against the government of the 4th Republic, which they considered paralyzed on Algeria policy. None other than Jacques Massu of Battle of Algiers fame formed a "committee of civil and army public security"; General Salan, commander in Algeria, announced that he was assuming provisional powers. Meanwhile, French paratroopers from Algeria seized Corsica and set their sights on Paris. The Fourth Republic was finished.

It was only through astute statesmanship that Charles de Gaulle, the French hero of World War II, managed to avert a crisis. On June 1, he became premier of the country and won a landslide victory in the December presidential election. Charles de Gaulle presciently understood that France would have to forfeit Algeria sooner rather than later. There was simply no way, he believed, that France could withstand the demographic trends and nationalist sentiment evolving in Algeria. It is important to keep in mind, though, that de Gaulle came to this view only after he had exhausted all hope that France could hold on in Algeria.

Correctly sensing that de Gaulle's pronouncements about Algerian self-determination indicated that the insurgents were winning the political war, the FLN began to cease its attacks on French troops. But the impending demise of French rule in Algeria infuriated the pieds-noirs. Over the next two years, militant pied-noir factions as well as French military contingents launched their own campaign against the Gaullist government in a series of uprisings and revolts. This was coupled, in 1961, with the merciless targeting of indigenous Algerian civilians by a violent faction known as the Organisation de l'armée secrete (OAS).

As the OAS killing spree increased, French units began to fight these pied-noir radicals. De Gaulle had ordered the military to break the OAS "by all means" even if that meant killing Frenchmen. As thousands of pieds-noirs fled to France near the war's end in 1962, the OAS attempted to prevent the exodus through a campaign of violence that included an attempt to assassinate de Gaulle. In fact, before it was over, the OAS had spread its terrorism to mainland France. Yet, despite the desperate acts of the OAS, both France and the FLN had moved toward an agreement, which spelled the end for the paramilitary group's ability to influence events in Algeria.

A CEASE-FIRE AT LAST

The cease-fire that was signed at Evian on March 18, 1962, was the culmination of secret negotiations that began almost a year earlier. During this time there was open fighting between OAS and French troops in Algeria. Yet, amazingly, during the negotiations France capitulated on almost every major issue that it had considered critical to its national interests.[23] By this point, de Gaulle deeply feared that Algeria could push France into civil war. He wanted out. Algerian independence was declared on July 3, 1962. On the counterinsurgency side, at the time of Evian, the FLN's insurgent force was reduced to fewer than 10,000 full-time fighters, down from a peak of 60,000 in 1959.[24] The war had been a decisive counterinsurgency victory for France. But this victory came at the expense of both losing the political war and almost losing France itself. The French suffered 17,500 killed, while another 3,500 Europeans died, mostly at the hands of the FLN. The FLN also killed 30,000 Algerians during the war; afterward, an estimated 30,000–150,000 harkis were targeted for death for their alleged treason.[25] The Algerian insurgents lost around 150,000 members during this colonial war.

The FLN's protracted but ultimately stunning victory over the French galvanized other nationalist and communist movements across the world. The FLN had no interest in compromising its political objectives and ended up getting everything it had demanded from day one in 1954. The FLN's victory was not lost on the Kennedy administration in Washington. While still a senator, John Kennedy had made waves with a speech that appealed to the legitimacy of Algerian self-determination. Yet, no matter what sympathies Kennedy might have had for the Algerian nationalists, the deep fear of more "Algerias" weighed heavily on an American president deeply concerned with stopping violent revolutions around the globe.

16

Intermezzo

David Galula

[The insurgent] is everywhere and nowhere.
— David Galula[1]

We have seen how the French experience in Indochina directly led to the application of *guerre révolutionnaire* in Algeria. While crude, in hindsight these counterinsurgency principles proved ruthlessly effective against the Algerian insurgents. In fact, contrary to what is often posited today, the French counterinsurgency methods in Algeria suggest that, at least at the time, torture could pay intelligence dividends. There was one military thinker in particular, David Galula, who emerged from this conflict to have a tremendous influence on how Western government and militaries would approach counterinsurgencies.

Having served in the French Army in North Africa, Italy, and then Indochina and Algeria, Galula was certainly a seasoned practitioner of counterinsurgency warfare.[2] He even spent eighteen months in Greece just as that civil war was winding down. In 1962, Galula resigned his French commission and moved to the United States to study warfare at Harvard University. Over the next few years, he wrote books on both the French experience in Algeria and counterinsurgency warfare more broadly. His work *Counterinsurgency Warfare: Theory and Practice* subsequently became a sort of "counterinsurgency bible" for budding military strategists eager to unlock the way to defeat Marxist insurgencies across the globe. Galula's insights into the nature of insurgencies were not entirely novel; rather, they reflected the lessons gleaned from his intellectual predecessors such as Sir Charles Gwynn, a British officer who wrote a seminal 1939 text titled *Imperial Policing*, which laid out key principles for how colonial powers could quell native uprisings.[3]

If Mao and other "classical insurgency" leaders had perfected the "scientific" approach to successful guerrilla warfare in the years following World War II, Galula contended that counterinsurgent forces could be equally systematic. In other words, if there could be a "theory" of insurgency, there could be one for counterinsurgency as well. Galula contended that insurgencies arise often because one group in a particular country wants to seize power. That is, the insurgent challenges the status quo. This can happen through a full-scale revolution, as was the case in France in 1789 and Russia 1917. Yet more common during the Cold War was the type of protracted, politically deft struggle conducted over years to achieve the same revolutionary effect.

Galula warned his readers that insurgencies are often well advanced before they appear to be active. Yet even the most embryonic insurgencies hold the "strategic initiative" since they are largely able to decide when and where to fight. He also believed that a burden of the guerrillas was that they had to continue growing stronger and larger. "The insurgent thus has to grow in the course of the war from small to large, from weakness to strength, or else he fails."[4] Part of Galula's genius was his insight into the fundamental realities and dilemmas facing counterinsurgent forces. For example, he made the keen observation that in a conventional war it is a dereliction of duty for a soldier not to fire back at someone who fires at him. Yet, in counterinsurgency, this is not necessarily the case as such an action can often be counterproductive.

Another insight was that counterinsurgencies should not attempt to mimic the ways of their insurgent adversaries. That would be the "same as a giant to try to fit into a dwarf's clothing."[5] Instead, the counterinsurgency needed to utilize its "tangible assets" such as air mobility or the ability to control the economy. Galula also realized that counterinsurgent forces were inherently "conservative" as they were attempting to preserve the status quo. In this sense, insurgents were about disorder, while counterinsurgents cherished order.

Galula argued that counterinsurgent operations could not be strictly military or political, and that these "tasks and responsibilities cannot be neatly divided between the civilian and the solider, for their operations overlap too much with each other. The soldier does not stay in his garrison with nothing to do, once the early large-scale operations have been concluded."[6] At the same time, Galula readily admitted that soldiers, not judges or development experts, would do most of the counterinsurgency work. Thus, the "soldier must then be prepared to become a propagandist, a social worker, a civil engineer, a schoolteacher, a nurse, a boy scout."[7] Ultimately, though, Galula believed that the critically important civil population would respect actions, not words. Thus, more than simply talking about progress and security, counterinsurgents had to actually provide it if they expected to win over and maintain public sentiment.

Once all of the various counterinsurgent mechanisms were in place, the government needed to act quickly to seize the initiative from the insurgent. This would take the form of traditional military efforts to expel the insurgents and defend the local population. This is because, as so many counterinsurgent campaigns have bitterly learned, securing the population must come first. If that cannot be achieved, then there is no reason to waste time with other efforts to win hearts and minds. Galula's solution also involved empowering local residents by organizing self-defense units and ensuring that the "locals" were given positions of authority in the existing government.

The approach also included elections that would bolster the legitimacy of the national government. In addition, Galula believed that counterinsurgents should not use terror against their foes, no matter how frustrating the conflict had become. This was because terror was a "source of disorder, which is precisely what the counterinsurgency aims to stop."[8] One of Galula's greatest warnings is that overreacting by resorting to terror would simply generate more antigovernment animosity, replenishing the ranks of insurgent forces.[9]

While Galula was concerned about excess, he also recognized that the counterinsurgency cannot conduct its operations blindly when faced with a violent insurgency. Rather, the counterinsurgents would necessarily have to crack down on civil liberties and suspend the regular rule of law if doing so was advantageous, especially since insurgents so often refuse to play by the established rules of the game.

Once these sorts of activities were fulfilled in one area, counterinsurgent forces could start all over again elsewhere, and so on. Galula's counterinsurgency recipe was not glamorous, but it has proven remarkably influential since it was written. When coupled with the observations of other practitioners such as Great Britain's Robert Thompson, Galula's work is fundamental to what is known by scholars and military practitioners as classical counterinsurgency, the mostly informal Cold War era philosophy on how to defeat Marxist guerrilla insurgencies.[10]

Galula's "classical" maxims, such as prioritizing the safety of the local population over killing the enemy, deeply influenced American policymakers who, through the 1960s, confronted guerrilla movements across the globe.[11] Almost fifty years after Galula's writing, American strategists like General David Petraeus, faced with seemingly unstoppable insurgencies in Iraq and Afghanistan, turned to Galula's work for lessons on what needed to be done. Indeed, a lot of what can be considered "postmodern" counterinsurgency in Iraq, Afghanistan, and elsewhere has its roots squarely in the Cold War era "classical" approach.

THE LEGACY OF CLASSICAL COUNTERINSURGENCY

Seen through contemporary eyes, "classical counterinsurgency," prevalent during the Cold War and made popular by theorists such as Galula, might appear politically incorrect. With its emphasis on population resettlement, curfews, food control, and other stringent methods, the strategy could seem overly harsh or even criminal. We should not forget that the mostly Marxist revolutionary theorists of classical insurgency and the "classical counterinsurgency" responders who thrived in the second half of the twentieth century built their understanding of irregular warfare on the works of earlier thinkers such as Sun Tzu, Clausewitz, T. E. Lawrence, and C. E. Callwell.[12] Yet the influence of classical counterinsurgency nonetheless endures largely because it proved itself to be a relatively successful response to communist movements. However, there is debate as to whether the classical strategy is still relevant now that, with the end of the Cold War, we have entered a "postmodern" phase of insurgencies and counterinsurgencies.

One reason the classical approach still matters is that even if some of its harsher edges are removed, its unyielding emphasis on securing the population over destroying the enemy remains an appealing approach to dealing with insurgencies.[13] At the same time, more contemporary insurgencies look nothing like their Cold War predecessors in many fundamental ways – for example, Al-Qaeda's emphasis on religious fanaticism and "leaderless resistance."[14]

Some counterinsurgency scholars have written that classical insurgencies were set apart by their reason for taking up arms: to seize power. Thus, classical insurgents normally needed a physical refuge from which to launch their operations. Too often, though, adherents of the classical approach assumed that the conflicts in question involved a direct struggle between insurgent and counterinsurgent, when the reality in cases like

Algeria and Indochina revealed much more nuanced insurgent movements and motivations.[15]

Classical counterinsurgency developed as a response to almost exclusively Marxist guerrilla revolutions across the globe during the Cold War. If almost all of those revolutions were either defeated or fizzled out with the end of the Cold War, we have to ask whether the classical approach still applied when addressing postmodern insurgencies like Al Qaeda or the Taliban in Afghanistan.

17

Intermezzo

Malaya Emergency, 1948–1960

On Saturday, October 6, 1951, the British High Commissioner in Malaya Sir Henry Gurney and his wife left the steamy administrative capital of Kuala Lumpur for the relative cool of Fraser's Hill, a mountain retreat about forty miles away. While they were passing through a narrow stretch of road on the way to the hill station, a platoon of thirty-eight communist guerrillas ambushed the car. Gurney fled the vehicle, but was mowed down by bullets as he attempted to seek cover on the side of the road. Gurney's wife and secretary remained inside the car and miraculously escaped the ambush unharmed.[1] Three weeks after the Gurney assassination, a convoy in the same area was also hit, this time with sixteen killed and scores injured. With the escalated raids, the guerrillas appeared formidable and terrifying. After three years of counterinsurgency warfare, the British effort to defeat the communist insurgents in its Asian colony was at its most despondent moment.

As in many of the cases we have already seen, observers began to question controversial policies, such as forced resettlement, that formed part of the British counterinsurgency repertoire.[2] Yet over the course of the next several years the British were able to handily defeat the insurgents. The story of the British counterinsurgency "success" stands as a firm reminder that dirty war victories are usually not very clean. And as the British learned so well, setbacks tend to be dramatic while progress is usually invisible. This would become an important insight for the United States as it began to navigate its own dirty wars, especially in Vietnam.

THE EMERGENCY

During the Japanese occupation of Malaya, the British army trained an indigenous guerrilla force which they called the Malayan People's

Intermezzo: Malaya Emergency

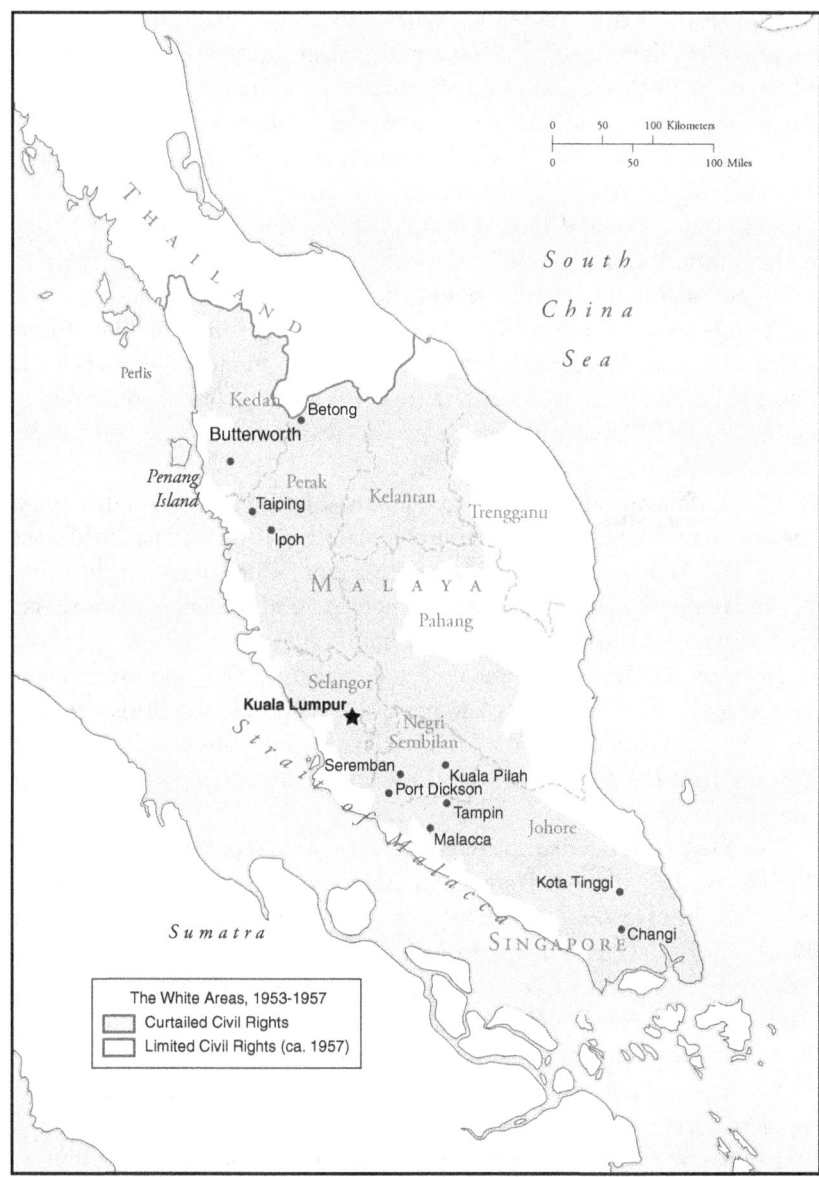

FIGURE 17.1. Malayan Emergency, 1948–60. In 1953 General Sir Gerald Templer introduced "white areas" as part of the counterinsurgency campaign in Malaya. These regions were designated free of insurgent activity in which there were relaxed restrictions on food and travel. By contrast, black areas continued to enforce all regulations and restrictions. Map prepared by the University of Wisconsin-Madison Cartography Lab©. Reprinted with permission

Anti-Japanese Army (MPAJA). While ultimately unable to defeat the Japanese on their own, the force gained legitimacy in the eyes of the Malayan people (and British commanders!) by putting up a dogged fight. They also received critical experience in guerrilla warfare, as well as arms, from their British "allies." After the occupation, the MPAJA came into contact with the Malay Communist Party (MCP), which had been organized in the 1920s and soon transformed into the armed wing of Malay communism. Ironically, this British-trained cadre would become the very insurgent faction the British would fight in the coming decade.

Perhaps around half a million of the more than three million ethnic Chinese in Malaya supported the MCP. The communists were especially effective at riling up Chinese resentment regarding British promises to ensure their full citizenship in the newly created but still not fully independent Federation of Malaya.

When Malaya was liberated from Japanese occupation in August 1945, the British were eager to reclaim the colonial possession they had held since 1874. The Alabama-sized territory supplied one-third of the world's rubber and tin, both in drastically short supply in the aftermath of the war. Yet Malayan communists, almost all of whom were ethnic Chinese, were not eager to see the British resume their colonial rule. This opposition came even though the communists had generally supported the British against the Japanese. Now the aim of the Malayan communists switched from how to defeat Japan to how to expel any foreign force aiming to control the island.

The MCP believed that the moment was ripe to repeat the revolution in Malaya. In fact, the MCP's general secretary, Chen Peng, called for an expedited insurrection to take advantage of British weakness right after World War II. The plan was to use terror and intimidation against the Malayan population, especially targeting laborers in tin mines and rubber plantations. Soon enough, the communist commanders expected, the British would simply abandon their colonial possession.

By 1946, rebellion was brewing as communist-hatched strikes broke out across the country. The MCP had penetrated deep into labor unions in order to sow the seeds of revolution. They were also now patrolling in detachments of 100 to 200 men, hitting isolated police outposts, conducting sabotage, and targeting civilians.[3] On June 16, 1948, MCP guerrillas murdered three British rubber plantation workers. Two days later, British authorities responded to the unfolding unrest by declaring the start of an "Anti-Bandit Campaign" – later to be known, simply and infamously, as the "Emergency."

At this early stage, there were perhaps 4,000 communist guerrillas roaming the dense jungles that covered 80 percent of the colony's territory. The Malayan Security Forces then had 9,000 police officers and 10 infantry battalions. The British Army garrison in 1948 consisted of a Gurkha brigade, for a total of 6 battalions.[4] For the first two years of the Emergency, the British attempted to use brute force to check the guerrillas' growing activity and influence, pursuing them using large sweeps and "search-and-destroy" missions. The approach was simple: find the enemy and kill him.

The strategy encountered obstacles from the start. One major problem was that the counterinsurgents had to find a way to manage an estimated 400,000 largely self-sufficient peasants – dubbed "squatters" by the British – who lived on the fringes of the jungle, in the heart of communist territory. The number of squatters had risen exponentially during World War II as the rural Chinese community fled to the fringes of the jungle to elude the Japanese.[5] Many of the squatters shared ethnic and cultural ties with the largely Chinese communists. They were easily influenced by the guerrillas' message of economic and social equality and were quickly converted into sympathetic civilians or armed fighters. Focusing on their attempts to eliminate the guerrilla bands in the jungles and the countryside, the British failed to take this growing relationship into account – as well as the communists' more sinister campaign of intimidation and terror.

LIEUTENANT GENERAL SIR HAROLD BRIGGS

In 1950, Lieutenant General Sir Harold Briggs was appointed director of operations in Malaya. A veteran of the British campaign in Burma, Briggs developed a key innovation that turned the British operation into a successful counterinsurgency. In his view, killing guerrillas could not be the only goal; rather, the British must instead focus on protecting vulnerable rural populations (read, the squatters) and thereby isolate the guerrillas. By April 1950, the "Briggs Plan" was under way, the hallmark being a massive effort to resettle squatters to protected villages far away from communist influence. Within a year over 100,000 squatters had been resettled into what eventually became more than 500 "new villages." At first, most of them were protected with rudimentary barbed wire barriers and guarded by a detachment of special constables, until the villages were able to mount their own guard units.[6]

There were problems with the villages as well. For one, the village sites were usually chosen for their defensive location, not for their arability, a

FIGURE 17.2. Men with rifles in Malayan New Village of Pokok Asam. Central Office of Information, 1953. Courtesy of the Library of Congress, Prints and Photographs Division, LC – LOT 7671

major setback for the largely agrarian population. Another problem was that villagers often needed to venture out to work on crops or on plantations, making them more vulnerable to guerrilla targeting. As time went on, though, many of the villages received electricity, schools, and water supplies. The villages were controversial from the very beginning, and the living conditions within them varied tremendously. But the British might have dodged a bullet in that the villages could have easily turned into breeding grounds for guerrilla recruits but didn't. Instead, by the 1960s, many of the new villages had become sustainable, "normal" villages, despite their dubious origins.

In the middle of 1951, a new component of the Briggs Plan, "Operation Starvation," was unveiled. The frankly titled program used restrictions on food and medicine to achieve its objective of denying the guerrillas sustenance. Shopkeepers were made to keep all records of food sales, and workers were not allowed to take food out to work with them; rice rations were delivered cooked so that they remained edible for only a few days. Colonial police and other troops guarded rice convoys.[7]

Intermezzo: Malaya Emergency 195

By the end of 1951, the British still faced a determined insurgency. The Malay population was believed to be more or less equally split in its support for the communists and the colonial government. The British counterinsurgency yielded few obvious successes, and critics claimed that the new villages were replete with communist spies. With Gurney's assassination a month earlier, the guerrillas still seemed to operate with impunity. Victory was elusive for the British. With his efforts to quell the insurrection having yielded so little, an exhausted and disillusioned Briggs left Malaya for a retirement in Cyprus.[8]

"WINNING THE HEARTS AND MINDS"

> I'll shoot the first bastard who says this Emergency is over. There are probably as many communist terrorists in the jungle as there were two years ago. – Sir Gerald Templer[9]

Gurney's death during the ambush was a sobering blow to the British effort in Malaya. Yet, while tragic, it also gave London a chance to renew its efforts to bring order to the country. The British took a gamble by appointing Sir Gerald Templer as both high commissioner of Malaya and director of operations, giving him authoritarian control over the civilian and military efforts. Templer remained in office for twenty-eight months. Wiry and neat, he was initially criticized for having no previous experience in Malaya. Others questioned the suitability of combining the civil and military posts, and doubted whether a military man could handle the intricate politics of civilian government.[10] To his credit, though, Templer did possess an acute sense of how to run a military government as a result of his tenure as commander of the British Zone in occupied Germany after World War II.[11]

Templer's approach did not diverge too much from the Briggs Plan but rather attempted to improve it. The British had to "win the hearts and minds" of the rural population. The phrase is Templer's; it would become inseparable from the concept of modern counterinsurgency.[12] Templer estimated that he needed to win over two-thirds of the population to win the war.

For Templer, the path to winning these hearts and minds lay in large part in giving the Malay population a stake in the British effort. And this meant a British pledge that it would allow Malayan independence once the communist threat had been eliminated. Of course, pacification would need to come before independence. For Templer, the "carrot" of independence would only complement, not replace, the "stick" of continued harsh counterinsurgency policies.

One key innovation Templer introduced was a collection of "lessons learned" from the British jungle training school that he compiled into a small book known as *The Conduct of Anti-Terrorist Operations in Malaya*. Twice a year, both British and Malayan soldiers received a portable, updated edition that provided refreshers on the best tactics to counter the guerrillas.[13] Templer often traveled across the territory with a large show of force to remind friend and foe alike that the colonial effort was formidable. On the railways, for example, he moved about in an armored train followed by two armored vehicles on rails. Templer was a "can do" commander, often visiting new villages where he would inspect the local police, school, and home guard; he would give pep talks to the villagers through his interpreter.

Only a few months after his arrival in February 1952, Templer began to put his bare-knuckled imprimatur on the British campaign. In one instance, a guerrilla ambush killed 12 British officers inspecting a sabotaged waterline about 50 miles north of Kuala Lumpur. Three days later, Templer arrived in the area and summoned scores of community leaders to meet with him. The British commander called them cowards, berating them for not fighting guerrillas themselves. In Templer's words, "It does not amuse me to punish innocent people, but many of you are not innocent. You have information which you are too cowardly to give."[14] Templer then used his emergency powers to impose a collective punishment on the communities through a 22-hour per day curfew and reduction in the rice ration by almost half. Villagers violating the new rules were subjected to heavy fines and jail terms.

But Templer also gave the villagers a way to make amends. Households were given a sheet with instructions from the high commissioner on which they could list information about communists in the area. A day later, the papers were collected and dropped unopened into sealed boxes. Templer then opened them himself at the Government House in Kuala Lumpur in the presence of village representatives. The intelligence provided quickly led to the arrest of 40 suspects. A few weeks later, the curfew was lifted. Soon after this, Long Pin, a famous guerrilla, was killed in the same vicinity. Templer visited the village again, but this time to congratulate them on a job well done.[15]

While his strategy was controversial and unquestionably painful to the rural population, Templer succeeded in forcing the guerrillas deeper and deeper into the jungle, often starved and desperate for food. Some captured guerrillas admitted that their rations had been cut to a cigarette-tin of rice a day.[16] When British authorities learned about an area where guerrillas were on the verge of starvation, they would tighten the rice rationing. British authorities even issued a Tin Puncturing Order whereby tins distributed to villagers had to be punctured to ensure that the contents were consumed immediately and not hoarded to feed insurgent fighters. Templer's food policies were not without their problems. In fact, the very essence of the program – to provide barely enough food "to keep a person in good health" – was morally questionable. Critics claimed that the approach was intentionally creating millions of "half-starved" rural residents.

If food control was the counterinsurgency's fundamental "stick," the signature "carrot" was what came to be called "white areas." The British declared a 220-square-mile area in the central district of Malacca "communist-free"; they lifted emergency restrictions and dismantled police roadblocks for the population of 160,000. Over time, the white area increased in size until, in 1957, it covered 30,000 of Malaya's 51,000 square miles and included around half of Malaya's population.[17]

At the same time, in a flash of unyielding counterinsurgency doctrine, Templer beefed up the security forces so that they could more aggressively pursue their adversaries. When combined with the resettlement and food denial policies, this new approach proved brutally effective. Desperate guerrillas were relentlessly harassed by "hunter-killer" platoons that forced scores of surrenders and defections. Air mobility in the form of helicopters was also crucial. So was stronger fortification of the new villages and the more aggressive protection afforded to truck convoys on remote roads. At its maximum height, Britain had 40,000 troops in the Malayan theater: 25,000 British, 10,000 Ghurkas, and 5,000 from other Commonwealth countries.[18]

Under Templer's watch, the British also attempted to break the guerrillas' will through psychological warfare. They dropped almost 100 million leaflets in areas infested by the Malayan Races Liberation Army (MRLA). Sometimes the leaflets showed pictures of captured emaciated guerrillas in captivity with their "well-fed grins" a few weeks later after they had agreed to cooperate.[19] The Commonwealth authorities also offered rewards for capturing guerrillas: $250,000 for the MCP's secretary general, down to US$2,500 for a rank-and-file fighter. At times the British even used former guerrillas to man small platoons that hunted their former comrades-in-arms. After eighteen months of service, the former combatants were released unconditionally. Back in the new villages, films and dramas performed by ex-guerrillas aimed to demonstrate how much better life was away from communist control.[20]

Even with this new successful strategy, it still took an estimated 1,800 man-hours of "jungle-bashing" for every encounter with communist insurgents. And, lest we forget that this was in fact a war, it merits mentioning that the British also dropped 3,500 tons of bombs along with their leaflets. All told, since the Briggs days, the British showed a remarkable capacity to adopt a new military approach after realizing that their initial large sweeps had failed to dent the insurgency. That effort was now bearing fruit.[21]

On August 31, 1957, the British granted independence to Malaya. By this time, 3,500 civilians had died in the conflict, alongside around 2,000 security forces and 10,000 guerrillas. The MCP/MRLA had proven formidable adversaries, and the British had made countless mistakes while they prosecuted a war that did not officially end until 1960. However, the British were able to learn from their mistakes. They were patient and painstaking in how they adapted their counterinsurgency efforts, but they were also merciless in the implementation.

ROBERT THOMPSON AND THE LESSONS OF MALAYA

One of Templer's closest counterinsurgency advisers was a British lieutenant colonel named Robert Thompson. Thompson came away from Malaya with sharply defined beliefs about what was necessary to defeat communist guerrilla insurgencies. Unlike the iron-fisted French theory of guerre révolutionnaire that followed the humiliation in Indochina, Thompson's theory contended that the key to successful counterinsurgency was to defeat "political subversion," not the guerrillas themselves. He made several corollary points. First, he asserted, a government must show that it has the confidence and know-how to win the war. Second, Thompson believed that the force of arms alone was insufficient to win; the government must use strong judicial systems and police forces to win the allegiance of the population. Third, the government must be as patient as its adversaries. In his view, "the very nature of a communist-inspired insurgency, where force of arms alone will not prevail, dictates that a long-term view must be taken of all the problems which arise."[22]

Thompson's missives were read widely in the early 1960s and deeply influenced American officials in Vietnam, who were trying to figure out how to approach the Viet Cong. In fact, in the early 1960s Thompson went to Saigon to advise the fledgling regime of Ngo Dinh Diem. One of the first things that he realized was that challenges in Malaya paled in comparison to the tempest brewing in Vietnam, something his American colleagues would tragically learn in the years to come.

18

Ramón Magsaysay and the Hukbalahap Rebellion in the Philippines, 1946–1956

[We] can only hold out as long as it is supported by the masses. No more, no less.
– Luis Taruc, leader of the communist insurgency in the Philippines, 1948[1]

After the victory over Aguinaldo's guerrillas in the Philippines in 1902, the United States governed the archipelago for the next half-century. Japan's occupation of the Philippines during World War II led to the ignominious surrender of 15,000 American troops at Bataan and forced American general Douglas MacArthur to evacuate his forces to Australia. While the United States regrouped and prepared to win back the Pacific, over 250,000 Filipinos participated in some form of guerrilla activity against the Japanese occupiers during the course of the war as part of the People's Anti-Japanese Army, the Hukbalahap.

While their name suggests that they were singularly focused on fighting the Japanese, the Huks did not lay down their arms following independence. Rechristening themselves the People's Liberation Army, they returned to guerrilla warfare, this time to overthrow what they considered a corrupt and illegitimate government in Manila. While much of the Huk leadership came from the educated urban class, the Huk cause was bolstered by the miserable labor and land conditions in much of rural Luzon; malnourishment was rife and few *campesinos* owned their own land. After fighting the Japanese, many in the Philippines felt that they deserved a greater voice in political affairs as well as control of their land.[2] Even General MacArthur admitted the Huks' appeal in the countryside: "If I worked in those sugar fields, I'd probably be a Huk myself."[3]

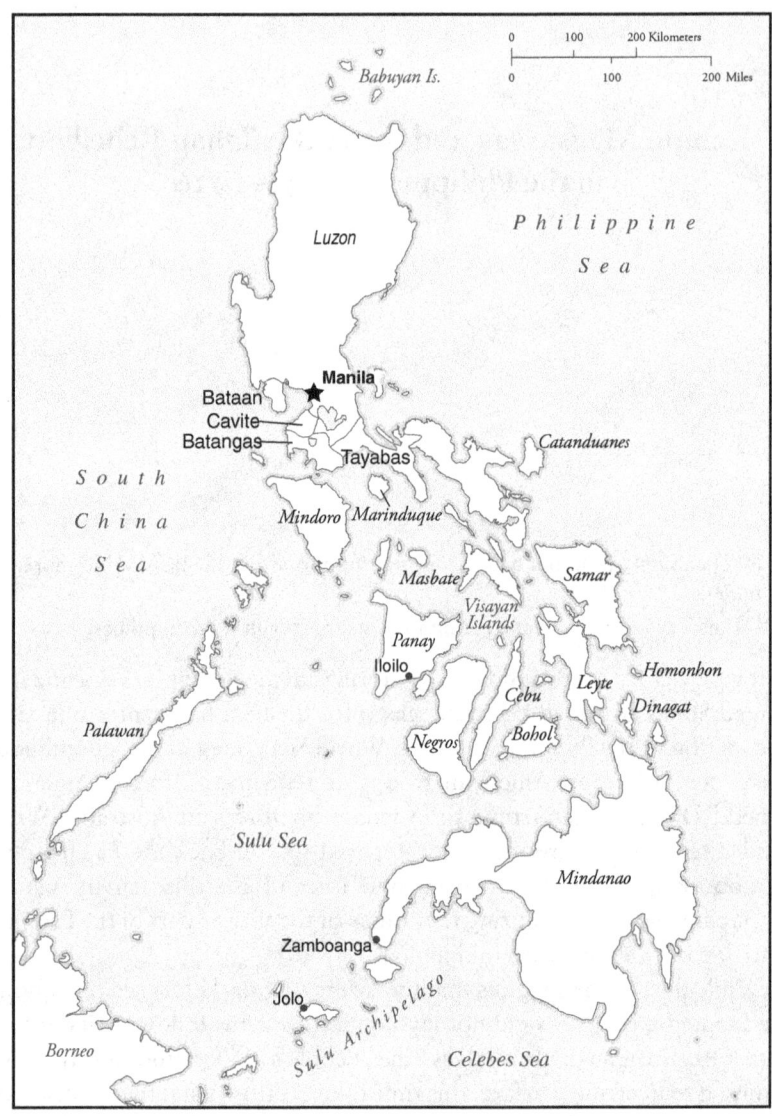

FIGURE 18.1. The Philippines. Map prepared by the University of Wisconsin-Madison Cartography Lab©. Reprinted with permission

By 1949, the Huks had become a formidable guerrilla insurgency; they were soon capable of launching operations on the outskirts of Manila. In 1951 the group was stronger than ever, with at least 12,000 men under arms;[4] some put the actual number at twice this figure. But the communist insurgency was not without its weaknesses. Like so many guerrilla groups throughout history, the Huk ranks were riddled with internal dissension, jealousies, and poor military coordination. Another debilitating problem was that while they had more than enough men under arms, the Huks lacked a potent external sponsor who would provide scarce weapons and ammunition.[5] For the most part, they could rely on weaponry left over from World War II, but as the duration of the conflict lengthened it became harder and harder for the insurgents to acquire the munitions they needed to effectively combat government forces.[6] Despite these problems, the Huk rebellion spread rapidly and soon had a strong foothold in the Philippines, controlling much of the islands of Luzon and Mindanao.[7]

Beset with the problem of a popularly supported rural insurgency, the Roxas administration responded with a fierce counterinsurgency campaign known as the "mailed fist."[8] Of particular note, the generally ineffective security forces attempted a system of cordons ("zonas") similar to what the British had attempted against the Boers in South Africa. This approach only further antagonized an already embittered rural population. In short, Manila's initial, heavy-handed counterinsurgency backfired.

Roxas's death in 1948 launched vice president Elpidio Quirino into the presidency. Despite some fleeting attempts at "soft-glove"[9] reform in the countryside, Quirino's counterinsurgency strategies remained largely unchanged. Quirino campaigned in the presidential election of 1949 and won in an unquestionably fraudulent vote. For the Huks, the rigged election was further evidence that the Filipino government did not represent the people.[10]

"HOLD THE PHILIPPINES WHATEVER THE COST"

At this point, the United States had very little direct involvement in the increasingly lethal guerrilla conflict in the Philippines. Since the end of World War II, it had sent small amounts of military and economic aid to the Philippines, totaling $72.6 million between 1945 and 1948, without making the country a priority.[11] As Manila's position grew more precarious, Quirino pleaded for both more aid and the introduction of American combat troops. Preoccupied with an icy relationship with Moscow and the anticommunist campaign in Greece, the Americans were initially reluctant to expand their involvement.

However, the Truman administration's unfolding "containment" strategy made this position more and more difficult to maintain. The administration tended to view the Huks, like the Greek insurgents, as pawns of international communism. In this case, the worry was less Soviet plotting and more the ideological and financial influence of Beijing.[12] The Joint Chiefs of Staff concluded, "The situation in the Philippines cannot be viewed as a local problem.... [T]he strategic importance of the United States' position in the Philippines is such as to justify the commitment of United States forces for its protection should circumstances require."[13] Dean Rusk, the State Department's top diplomat for Asia concurred: "If we fail there, the rest of Asia will surely consider we have nothing to offer elsewhere.... [I]t is vital that we hold the Philippines whatever the cost – unless we are prepared to write off Asia."[14]

Given the successful outcome in Greece, which avoided the introduction of U.S. combat troops, it appeared as though the United States had a ready model for preventing other dominoes from falling to communist insurrection. However, this model was complicated substantially by the historically paternalistic relationship of the United States in the Philippines. While the Truman administration desired to defeat the Huk insurgency, it also did not want to appear to be acting like a colonial power. American officials hoped that the light-footprint approach that had proved so successful in Greece could be replicated halfway across the world in the jungles of Luzon and Mindanao.

Further complicating the American counterinsurgency strategy in the Philippines, the government and security forces in Manila were weak, corrupt, and deeply unpopular in many parts of the countryside. As in Greece, the American effort would combine conventional security-focused counterinsurgency with technical and development assistance designed to make the Filipino government more efficient and responsive. In practice, Washington's involvement meant taking extensive control of the Filipino government. In addition to economic assistance, the State Department sent officials to serve as field officers to the Philippine army, while the CIA also opened up a station in Manila. According to one U.S. official, "we must control to the maximum every *centavo* of aid of any character that we send to this country."[15] American engagement had returned to the Philippines.

RAMÓN MAGSAYSAY

By late 1950, President Quirino recognized that his government's counterinsurgency strategy was failing to rein in the Huk threat. In September, Quirino appointed a former anti-Japanese guerrilla leader, Ramón Magsaysay, as his secretary for national defense in order to change the dynamics of the conflict. Magsaysay was the right person in the right place at the right time. His arrival, coupled with the almost simultaneous U.S. decision to support the Filipino government, was the turning point of the Huk Rebellion. Magsaysay had a keen understanding of his enemy, having grown up impoverished on a rural farm and fought as a guerrilla against the Japanese occupation. Magsaysay was deeply familiar with the desperation among the rural population that the Huks had so successfully exploited.

Magsaysay went to work on a new strategy that attempted both to reform the corrupt Filipino government and security forces and to enact sorely overdue land reform in the countryside. Capitalizing on his folksy manner, reputation for honesty, and indefatigable work habits, Magsaysay quickly personalized his policies. Indeed, the defense minister with the keen political ear seemed to be everywhere, making unannounced "lightning visits" to inspect troops or checking in with rural villagers.[16] He was known for his pithy slogans. With some, like "Honesty comes first," and "If you really want to please me, spend any money you would spend on me on the poor," he intended to reinforce his simple but steadfast effort to strengthen the government's relationship with the Filipino people.[17] With others he aimed to motivate his troops: "The army is no place for hooligans. Your uniform is the symbol of our national sovereignty and you must treat it with respect and see that it is respected." Magsaysay would also punish troops for stealing in front of affected villagers to demonstrate that he meant what he said; this became one way of repairing the relationship between the Filipino population and the army. Magsaysay also refused to tolerate the military's reticence to fight the Huks. Once, after being told how long it would take to make a unit combat ready, he replied, "Three weeks? These units aren't going to waste three weeks! They move out of here in three hours!" Three hours later, the army was on the march.[18]

Magsaysay was relentless in his efforts to root out the deep-seated corruption and lack of offensive spirit within the military's ranks. He recruited aggressive young officers to replace ones that he had personally fired. He made sure that his soldiers were paid on time, were fed well, and were promoted when they did good work. Magsaysay also attempted inventive ways to bolster the rural population's faith in the government. Most notably, he instituted a program in which farmers could send a reduced-rate telegram to his ministry and usually receive an answer within a day. Another innovation involved providing legal counsel at cost to peasants who were pursuing cases against rural landowners. In an early state employment program, he organized the construction of thousands of partially prefabricated rural schools, using local laborers as builders.

FIGURE 18.2 Ramón Magsaysay served as the Philippines' defense minister and president during the Huk Rebellion (1946–56). His relentless energy and innovative leadership were some of the most important factors in defeating the insurgency, and he formed a close partnership with Colonel Edward Lansdale. He died in a plane crash in 1957. *Source*: Time and Life Pictures, reproduced with permission from Getty Images, 50879483

A devout anticommunist, Magsaysay's unconventional but unyielding commitment to winning over the rural population did not mean that he was also unwilling to confront the guerrillas aggressively. In his words his troops needed to be "ambassadors of goodwill and Huk hunters – in that order."[19] One of Magsaysay's keenest insights was that winning the population's support was key to defeating the communists. The 1951 general elections became a symbol of his campaign to demonstrate that the Filipino government had the population's best interests at heart. Magsaysay was determined to prevent a repeat of the rigged elections of 1949, which had greatly bolstered public support for the Huk movement. Captured documents revealed that the Huks, for their part, fully expected the elections to be fraudulent, which in turn would further delegitimize an already unpopular government. Thus, the Huk leaders suffered a blow when it became apparent that Magsaysay's efforts to protect ballot boxes and other policies ensured a remarkably free and fair election. Interestingly, the peaceful election served to enhance Magsaysay's political stature, not that of President Quirino.[20]

COLONEL EDWARD G. LANSDALE

Ramón Magsaysay was not alone in his efforts to bolster the Philippine's campaign against the Huks. In fact, many of his most effective reforms were coordinated in conjunction with U.S. Air Force Lieutenant Colonel Edward G. Lansdale, who worked as part of the Joint U.S. Military Advisory Group (JUSMAG) established in late 1947. Lansdale, appointed to his position only a week after Magsaysay became defense minister, struck up an instant partnership with the Filipino politician.[21] Lansdale had direct access to Magsaysay and helped generate the creation of the Civil Affairs Office, a psychological operations outfit intent on landing "blows" on the enemy.[22]

In addition to creating new agencies, Lansdale also accompanied Magsaysay on his lightning visits to the countryside. In fact, they often met in Lansdale's Manila bungalow to discuss policy.[23] In his memoirs, Lansdale described his counterpart as

a burly and energetic civilian wearing a floppy straw hat and a vividly colored aloha sport shirt who seemed always to turn up on the scene almost magically when the going got rough, his eyes spotting the details of the situation at once.... [S]ome soldiers who had shown unusual qualities under fire were promoted on the spot; some who had been cowardly or negligent were relieved of the duties promptly and sent to face investigation and trial.[24]

Lansdale was also instrumental in reorganizing the Philippine security force's counterinsurgency strategy. Most critically, and similar to what the British were attempting against communist guerrillas in Malaya, Lansdale helped reorganize parts of the army into self-sufficient Battalion Combat Teams (BCTs). At the same time, increased U.S. military aid made it possible to create additional BCTs that allowed the Filipino security forces to operate in a much larger geographic area.

In a sharp departure from previous tactics, Magsaysay often hand-picked the BCT commanders who led forces that were as much about protecting the rural population as killing guerrillas. The BCTs were deployed on a long-term basis in a particular region and conducted aggressive patrolling and even food-denial efforts. Civil affairs officers were attached to each BCT in order to carry Magsaysay's critical political message to the battlefield. Troops even carried extra food so that they could distribute it to rural villagers if needed.[25]

Another highly effective Lansdale-supported program attempted to resettle and provide land to former Huk guerrillas. Known as the Economic Development Corps (EDCOR), the program provided participating "settlers" with a loan for startup capital to create businesses or construct residences or villages. Ultimately, the program resettled 5,200 Filipinos, even if only a fraction of these were in fact demobilized Huks. EDCOR became a public relations bonanza for the government as it promptly stole the Huks' message about being the champion of the landless.[26] In the Philippines, at least, resettlement proved to be an effective and relatively clean counterinsurgency tactic.

In addition to the American advisory effort, an assistance package of $500 million – of which $400 million was economic aid – provided Manila with badly needed resources. Faustino Tenorio, a former Huk, admitted that the assistance played a large part in turning the tide against the insurgency. In his words, the "money from the American government financed Magsaysay's programs, including cash handouts to barrios to buy people's support."[27]

Two years into Magsaysay's new strategy, the Huks were on the run, retreating deeper and deeper into the jungle. As well as making life increasingly miserable for the guerrillas, Magsaysay's aggressive tactics had the added benefit of pushing the insurgents away from their main source of support – the local population. In turn, this made his efforts to win over Filipino citizens even more effective. By 1954 almost 10,000 Huks had been killed, 5,000 had been captured, and another 16,000 had surrendered. The Filipino security forces had suffered only 1,500 casualties.

In one memorable episode, after Magsaysay made it known that he would speak with any Filipino willing to provide information on the Huks, the insurgents sent an operative posing as an ordinary citizen to assassinate Magsaysay. When the guerrilla arrived to meet his target, he was so taken by what Magsaysay said that he decided to switch to the Philippine leader's side. Even better for the government, the former Huk informed Magsaysay that the guerrilla leadership could be located by tracking the route of a young girl in Manila who passed clandestine messages while selling meats and vegetables from a basket. Putting the girl under surveillance, Philippine authorities soon arrested over 100 insurgents.[28]

TARUC SURRENDERS

In 1953, the immensely popular Magsaysay resigned from the ministry of defense. His letter of resignation to President Quirino described his frustration with the reform process: "My purpose was to shift our attack on communism to one of its basic causes in our country: land hunger. In this, as in many other matters, the administration has met the people's need with inaction."[29] He immediately announced his campaign for the presidency and defeated Quirino in a landslide election later that year. While he likely would have won anyway, Washington quietly funneled funds into his campaign. As president, Magsaysay now had full command of the counterinsurgency effort, which doomed the Huks' already dismal chances of victory. In May 1954, the Huk leader Taruc surrendered, marking the end of the Huk Rebellion. According to Taruc, "the government began to respect the civil liberties of the people. Consequently, as the army's public relations improved, the people cooperated more willingly with government troops. The people were weary of war and badly in need of some sort of democratic peace."[30]

Magsaysay's remarkable story reinforces the critical role that leadership can play in counterinsurgency efforts. In this case, Magsaysay used his accumulated power not to enrich himself but to combat the insurgents and address the people's needs. Part of this was due to Magsaysay's belief that taking advantage of his situation would doom his beloved country.[31] Magsaysay died tragically in a plane crash in 1957. By this time, though, his dream of stopping the Huk advance had been achieved.

For the United States, the Philippines represented another Cold War counterinsurgency victory coming on the heels of the experience in Greece. Communist guerrilla insurgencies, it seemed, could be defeated by proxy. At the same time, the United States undoubtedly got a little bit lucky in both instances. Like the Greek communists, the Huks never enjoyed the support of an external power such as China. In addition, Magsaysay's unique leadership ensured that the Philippine government's response was infinitely better than it would have been otherwise. Manila's crude counterinsurgency efforts before Magsaysay's ascension are an indication of what might have continued had he not changed course – a dirtier dirty war instead of the relatively clean one that resulted after Magsaysay.

19

Vietnam

We, the French, have experience [in Vietnam]. You, the Americans, wanted to take over our place in Indo-China. Now you want to take over where we left off and restart the war that we ended. I predict that you will sink bit by bit into a bottomless military and political swamp however much you pay in men and money.
– Charles de Gaulle[1]

This is a grubby, dirty method of fighting. If we could corner all the Viet Cong operating on the highland on an open ground we could lay them flat in twenty-five minutes. But it takes weeks to find even fifty of them.
– American military officer in Vietnam[2]

That is true. It is also irrelevant.
– The postwar response from a North Vietnamese when told the United States never lost in battle in Vietnam[3]

In September 1945, American policymakers were in an understandably triumphant mood. On September 2, Japanese representatives on the USS *Missouri* signed the surrender papers that ended World War II. At this point, the Huks had not yet turned their ire toward the newly independent Philippine government, and Mao Zedong was still a few years away from defeating the Nationalists. However, the events on Tokyo Bay overshadowed another vital strategic development in East Asia. On the same day, Vietnamese leader Ho Chi Minh issued a declaration establishing the Democratic Republic of Vietnam in what was then known as French Indochina.

A communist since the early 1920s, Ho opened his remarks by directly placing the Vietnamese people's struggle in the context of the American

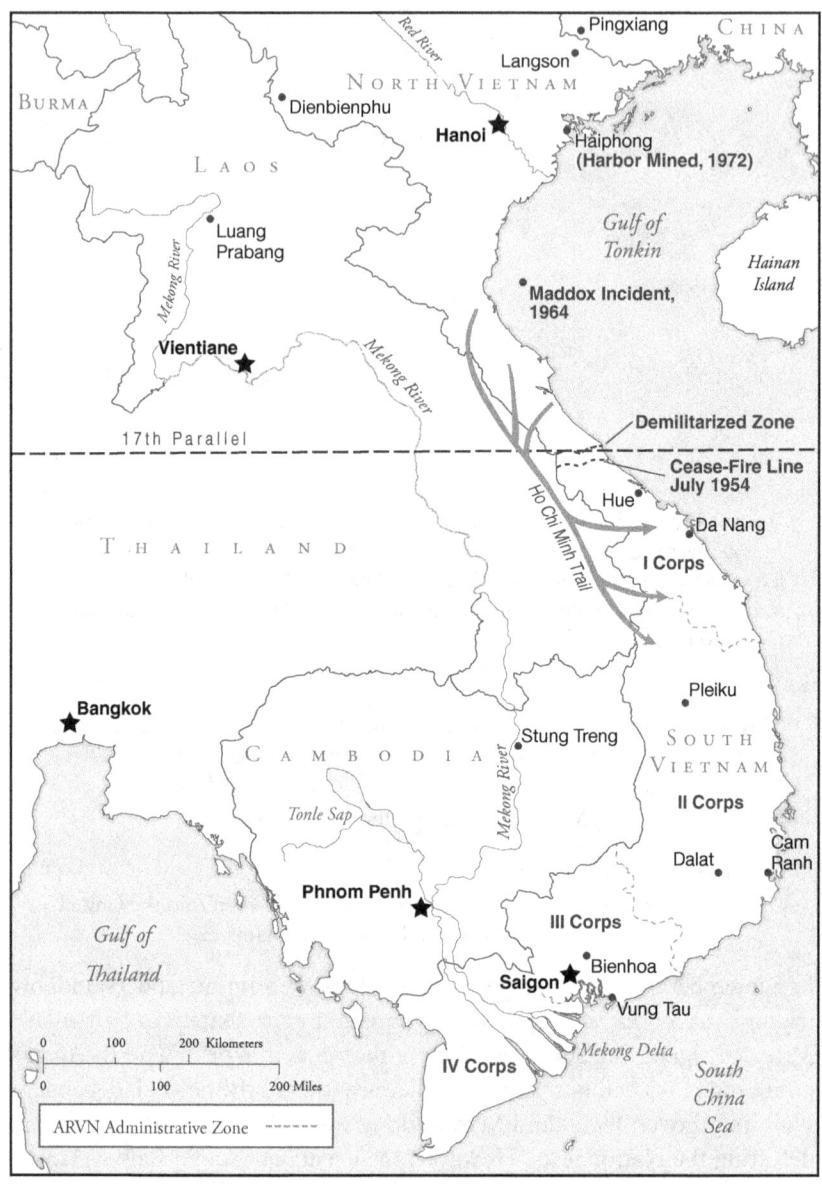

FIGURE 19.1. Vietnam, 1960s and 1970s. Map prepared by the University of Wisconsin-Madison Cartography Lab©. Reprinted with permission

Declaration of Independence. Having been "subjected to the double yoke of the French and the Japanese," Ho argued, the Vietnamese people were "determined to mobilize all their physical and mental strength, to sacrifice their lives and property in order to safeguard their independence and liberty."[4] Yet, as the Vietnamese would quickly learn, France was not eager to grant its colony independence. In fact, after the Japanese ended their occupation of the region at the end of World War II, France reestablished its colonial rule in Indochina, granting only minor political concessions to the nationalists.[5]

Over the next year, the French and Vietnamese failed time and again to broker a mutually acceptable solution to the colony's status, leading Ho to declare war on the French on December 19, 1946, staging an attack on Hanoi that killed thousands of French citizens. At this point, the unfolding "war of national liberation" involved about 20,000 French troops and fewer than 50,000 guerrillas operating as the "League for the Revolution and Independence of Vietnam," abbreviated to "Viet Minh." As an armed faction, the Viet Minh had been active since the early 1940s, opposing French rule, then fighting the Japanese, and now once again resisting the French colonial forces.

By 1950, French forces had swelled to about 150,000 troops, although with the exception of the officers, most of these were not actually French nationals but members of the vaunted Foreign Legion or drawn from colonies like Algeria, Morocco, Laos, and Vietnam. The Viet Minh had increased their numbers at a similar rate and now stood at 250,000. French counterinsurgency strategy during the late 1940s was quite simple. The goal was to force the Viet Minh guerrillas into a series of "pincer" encounters in which superior French firepower would annihilate the enemy. Sending its best generals to the theater, Paris believed that the war would be won in fifteen months. The French never achieved a decisive battle during these first years, though they did inflict repeated blows on the Viet Minh. The problem was that by the early 1950s their "inferior" adversary had become considerably less inferior.

A major factor contributing to this change was the support that the Viet Minh received from communist regimes in recently victorious Maoist China as well as the Soviet Union. Indeed, the nature of the Viet Minh's struggle against the French colonial forces changed dramatically following China's communist revolution in 1949. In prior years the Chinese had allowed the Viet Minh to cross the border to seek refuge in China. Now, however, this permissiveness had shifted toward much more aggressive forms of support for the anti-French fighters, which further increased after the Korean War ended in 1953. Swollen with Chinese aid and training, Viet Minh battalions began to appear in full field formations, often equipped with mortars, anti-artillery guns, and other modern weapons.[6] Following China's lead, the Soviets began to provide assistance as well.[7] Guerrilla bands of 40 to 60 men had become battalions, then regiments, then 10,000-man divisions. The French were fighting an army, one that had increasing reason to believe that it could defeat its imperial masters on the battlefield.

The Viet Minh were blessed with a brilliant military commander in Vo Nguyen Giap. Eager to defeat the French before anticipated American aid arrived, Giap largely adopted Mao's strategy of protracted warfare to wear down the French. Like Mao, Giap was also greatly influenced by T. E. Lawrence's writings. In fact, in 1946, Giap told French General Raoul Salin, "My fighting gospel is T. E. Lawrence's *Seven Pillars of Wisdom*. I am never without it."[8] But, unlike Mao, who faced a relatively demoralized National Revolutionary Army under Chiang Kai-shek between 1947 and 1949, Giap had to contend with a robust and ruthless French force.

As the war continued, French officers became increasingly frustrated by their inability to lure the Viet Minh forces into conventional battles. They also failed miserably at undermining the communists' influence among the rural population. Hoping to turn the corner in a war that they called "la guerre sans fronts" (war without fronts), one French general, the World War II military hero Marshall de Lattre de Tassigny, attempted to boost French morale by mobilizing French civilians living in Indochina for guard duties, a move that opened up garrison troops for combat. Tassigny also sent many French women and children home so that troops could concentrate on the fighting.

Another complication for the French was that the war was steadily losing popularity at home. At a time when France was attempting to rebuild its war-torn economy, the effort to retain Indochina represented a severe drain on national coffers. In fact, by the early 1950s this war had already cost double the sum that the French had received from the United States through the Marshall Plan. After seven years, there was no victory in sight, and the French political left was increasingly sympathetic to the aspirations of the Vietnamese fighters. They began to cast the French position as immoral, with the French Communist Party referring to the Indochina campaign as a "dirty war." Paris responded to these setbacks by ramping up its effort to win the war decisively. General Henri Navarre took over command of French Union forces in the Far East on May 28, 1953. Navarre's mission was to strike a fatal blow against Giap's forces,

FIGURE 19.2. General Vo Nguyen Giap and Ho Chi Minh, September 1945. In 1945 Vietnamese independence leader Ho Chi Minh announced the formation of the Democratic Republic of Vietnam. France refused to recognize this movement and fighting broke out between the French-led forces and the domestic insurgency known as the Viet Minh. Following its humiliating defeat at the hands of Viet Minh forces in the remote garrison of Dien Bien Phu in 1954, France withdrew from Vietnam. Over the next two decades, the United States assumed the role as the key external actor fighting to prevent a communist takeover of its allied government in South Vietnam. Reproduced with permission from Associated Press, 00042902369

and he brought with him additional fresh French troops and the promise of increased American aid.[9]

Before 1950, even though it was bolstering Manila against the Huks, the Truman administration had little desire to get involved in France's colonial reconquest in Indochina. The Korean War changed its stance, however. Suddenly, American policymakers understood the geopolitical power that a Red China wielded. With the threat of "losing more Chinas," few in the upper levels of Truman's cabinet wanted to appear soft on stopping communism. Washington was also concerned that a French defeat in Indochina might weaken French military resolve back in Europe, where it was needed to stave off any Soviet advances.

This apprehension led U.S. officials increasingly to view France's mission as less of a colonial venture and more of a strike against communism. Confident that its ally would prevail, Washington began to assist the French effort soon after the Korean War's nebulous conclusion. American aid began to flow in after 1950; within a few years, American dollars were financing over three-quarters of French operations in Indochina. At first, American officials believed that U.S. aid alone would help turn the tide. President Eisenhower's secretary of state, John Foster Dulles, told Congress that he expected the French to "break the back" of Viet Minh forces by 1955.[10]

These sorts of rosy scenarios reminded U.S. diplomat George Kennan of what he once described as "that curious trait of the American political personality which causes it to appear reprehensible to voice anything less than unlimited optimism about the fortunes of another government one had adopted as a friend and protégé."[11] By 1954, Americans were now on the ground in the form of over 300 American advisers in Vietnam working as part of a Military Assistance Advisory Group (MAAG), the military footprint approach that had worked successfully in both Greece and the Philippines.

DISASTER AT DIEN BIEN PHU

The crux of General Navarre's renewed offensive stance was a risky campaign that aimed to lure the Viet Minh into a pitched battle at Dien Bien Phu, a locale in the Muong Thanh valley in the remote western highlands. The French plan was to insert a large contingent of troops into the region to construct an air-supplied garrison and wait for the Viet Minh to attack them. They selected Dien Bien Phu in part because of its proximity to Laos, at that time still a French ally. The French hoped to cut off guerrilla supply routes into Laos that had allowed the Viet Minh to operate actively along the border. Once the encounter ensued, the French believed, the garrison artillery would become a "meat grinder" for the hapless Viet Minh – a remarkable assumption given the French experience only four decades earlier in the muddy trenches of Verdun and elsewhere during World War I.

In late November 1953, the French dropped three parachute battalions across the valley. It was an inauspicious landing. Viet Minh in the area lobbed mortars at the landing soldiers, and the massive size of the valley prevented the French from occupying the surrounding hills, which would soon become Giap's base. The French garrison consisted of 13,000 soldiers, but only half were combat ready. Yet they endured for four months before the Viet Minh attacked. During this time American military advisers visited the base and declared it secure, noting in particular the defenses of the French base's lifeline: the runway. Indeed, it appeared that the camp was fortified "almost to Verdun standards."[12]

Based on this evaluation and their own estimates, the French commanders fatally assumed that the garrison could be indefinitely resupplied from the air.[13] However, they grossly underestimated Giap's logistical ability to amass forces – especially heavy artillery – around Dien Bien Phu. French intelligence initially projected Viet Minh artillery strength of 40 to 60 guns capable of firing 25,000 rounds. Giap, on the other hand, estimated that he had 250 to 350 guns, including Soviet heavy rocket launchers, all capable of firing around 350,000 rounds. Using bicycles, Chinese-provided vehicles, and a massive human labor effort, the Viet Minh were able to transport several divisions (up to 60,000 men) to the valley.

Giap indeed gave Navarre his coveted "set battle." But now the French were the inferior force in an inferior position on the valley floor. In a reversal of conventional guerrilla strategy, Giap also aimed for a head-to-head encounter. In March 1954, the Viet Minh's siege of Dien Bien Phu began with a ferocious artillery barrage from the surrounding high ground. Over the course of three days, the Vietnamese overran three outposts and left the critical runway inoperable.

In addition to the highly accurate and relentless artillery barrages from the surrounding higher ground, the Viet Minh launched "human wave" assaults reminiscent of trench warfare during World War I. Losing the airstrip was an immediate and dramatic setback given that the fortress initially had only thirteen days of supplies and fewer than ten days of ammunition and fuel. Despondent that he had little ability to respond to the Viet Minh's punishing barrages, the commander of French artillery, Colonel Charles Piroth, committed suicide with a hand grenade. He was buried in secrecy so as not to harm the French troops' morale.

The French attempted to compensate by air dropping supplies. Due to cloud cover and relentless anti-aircraft fire, these drops often ended up in the hands of the enemy, a setback that only worsened as the Viet Minh's cordon continued to tighten around the besieged garrison. Over the next 56 days, the French forces endured hellish conditions in their futile attempt to hold off the attacking forces.[14]

Despite the initial French and American estimates that Dien Bien Phu's defenses were impenetrable, the garrison did not have a single concrete emplacement. The earth and log bunkers that it did have were decimated by the withering bombardments. After a while, the Viet Minh bombing had turned the ground soil into fine sand, which made it almost impossible to dig and repair bunkers and trenches.[15] General Navarre's reflection on the siege provides an apt description of the conditions:

All around our positions, the enemy had created a network of camouflaged paths which permitted the [unhindered] transport of ammunition ... to the vicinity of the batteries.... We knew that a large number of artillery and AA [anti-aircraft] gun emplacements had been prepared, but their camouflage had been so perfect that only a small number of them had been located prior to the beginning of the attacks.... Under the influence of [Communist] Chinese Advisers, the Viet-Minh command had used processes quite different from the classical methods. The artillery had been dug in by single pieces. The guns had been brought forward dismantled, carried by men, to emplacements where they had direct observation of their targets. They were installed in shell-proof dugouts, and fired point blank from portholes or were pulled out by their crews and pulled back as soon as our counterbattery fire began. Each piece or group of pieces was covered by massed antiaircraft artillery put into position and camouflaged in the same manner as the guns. This way of using the artillery and AA guns was possible only with the "human ant hill" at the disposal of the Viet-Minh and was to make shambles of all the estimates of our own artillerymen. It was the major surprise of the battle.[16]

In the late afternoon of May 7, 1954, a Viet Minh platoon commander planted a red flag with a gold star atop the headquarters bunker of Dien Bien Phu. The bloody siege had come to an end, and an army that had come into existence only a decade before had dealt the French a humiliating defeat at this faraway outpost.[17] Of an estimated 15,000 men who fought on the French side during the siege, 3,000 lay dead, 2,000 had deserted, and most of the rest were captured and placed in horrible conditions. The Viet Minh had suffered roughly 23,000 casualties, with 8,000 dead.

The French defeat owed much to the strategic unfeasibility of Navarre's campaign-level approach. The chief problem, of which Dien Bien Phu formed only part, was that Navarre never had the mobility necessary to cover Indochina – a field of combat four times the size of Korea. The French never had more than ten helicopters available at any given point during the war. Arguably, Navarre overextended his forces, leaving them vulnerable to an unexpectedly lethal and determined adversary.

Dien Bien Phu broke the will of the French to fight the Indochina war, though perhaps not their ability. But that is all that Ho and Giap needed to accomplish. The Maoist approach to fighting superior foes had been corroborated in Indochina, a fact not lost on budding revolutionaries around the world over the coming decade. Indeed, as we have already seen, Algerian and Malayan revolutionaries looked to Giap's victory as a source of affirmation for their own struggles.

A few months later, negotiations at the Geneva Conference resulted in the formal independence of Laos and Cambodia. Interestingly, the hawkish secretary of state John Foster Dulles contended that the United States should take the place of France and continue the war.[18] Eisenhower, however, who had a good sense of what war was all about, refused to send American combat troops into Vietnam. So he agreed with others at the conference to partition the country: Ho Chi Minh's communist Democratic Republic of Vietnam was given control of Vietnam north of the 17th parallel, while an election to reunite the country under a single government was promised for 1956 – an election that never took place.[19]

The eight years of war had cost the French around what then amounted to $10 billion, including substantial American aid. At the same time, a startling 77,000 were killed or recorded as missing. Another 40,000 were taken prisoner with fewer than half of these ever repatriated. This sum included three generals and over 2,000 other officers. Viet Minh losses during the war were estimated to be as high as 200,000.

THE NORTH INFILTRATES THE SOUTH

The 1954 Geneva Accords laid out a political path for Indochina in light of France's humiliating withdrawal. With its population advantage in the communist-influenced North, Ho's regime in Hanoi was confident that it would win a plebiscite to unify the country in 1956. Interestingly, though, many of the "voters" in the North – up to one million of them – were fleeing south to escape communist indoctrination and control. Most of the refugees were Catholic, a group U.S. officials believed to be reliably anticommunist and thus more likely to vote in favor of the South. U.S. advisers, including the redoubtable Colonel Edward Lansdale, who was fresh off his decisive deployment in the Philippines, conducted propaganda campaigns to encourage as many Vietnamese as possible to cross over.

While many Vietnamese deeply feared communist consolidation of the entire country, the environment in the South was not much better. The French-backed Catholic Ngo Dinh Diem had ascended to power in Saigon in 1955, but the nascent state was a political, economic, and social basket case. Citing the inevitability of Hanoi conducting fraud, Diem rejected the plebiscite. Hanoi's response was to opt for national unification through armed action.[20]

This move brought to bear another crucial element of the Geneva Accords, which mandated that Viet Minh troops and operatives in the South relocate to the North after the establishment of the 17th parallel. Yet, under orders from Hanoi, many of these cadres remained behind, clandestinely training and planning for the conflict. They hid arms and supplies all over the South for quick access in a guerrilla war against Diem's regime in Saigon. Ho also trained over 75,000 former Viet Minh who had come up from the South to fight the French. Ho subsequently sent these politically "purified" cadres back across the 17th parallel to bolster the secret communist ranks in these strategic areas.

This communist organization in the South was called the National Liberation Front for South Vietnam (NLF). Right after the 1954 accords, the still informal guerrilla group numbered around 10,000, mostly former Viet Minh. But within a couple of years the group's numbers doubled. And then doubled again. In just this short time, the group was collecting taxes, murdering "traitors," targeting rural politicians and teachers, and gaining deep influence through the southern countryside.

A good part of what made the communists so effective was that they were perfectly willing to use any level of terror to ensure their political and military dominion in the countryside.[21] In 1954 alone, communists killed more than 11,000 Vietnamese living in the South. By 1957, the communists had killed almost 500 local officials, a rate that doubled over the next several years. The guerrillas first targeted their activities in the Mekong Delta, the central highlands, and coastal plains. This was guerrilla dirty war at its most brutal. Almost overnight, the NLF had become, as John Tierney has noted, "one of the best led and organized paramilitary outfits in history."[22]

At first, despite the growing NLF activity in the countryside in the late 1950s, Diem appeared to have the situation under control. Communist violence was certainly a nuisance, it seemed, but Diem seemed to be the "can do" Magsaysay-like figure who could convince the rural population to believe in the Saigon government. One American senator, Mike Mansfield, later optimistically predicted that "Diem's star is likely to remain in the ascendancy and that of Ho Chi Minh to fade – because Diem is following a course which more closely meets the needs and aspirations of the Vietnamese people."[23]

Diem's first counterinsurgency effort, the "Anti-Communist Denunciation Campaign," started in 1956 and intended to destroy communist organization in the South. Yet the efforts were haphazard, effectively conceding the political organizing and "hearts and minds" impetus to the relentless communists. Diem's military tended to resemble a "palace guard," a weak force that rarely left Saigon lest it find itself in "enemy territory."[24]

With the Viet Cong's (VC) aggressive organization and mobilization, U.S. officials entered a situation that might have been already lost. First, there was nothing to indicate that U.S. military and economic aid to Diem's regime would make any difference. The $4 billion that Washington pumped into the French effort against the Viet Minh had been unable to stop its inexorable slide toward defeat. Nevertheless, Washington was committed to preventing the communists from turning South Vietnam into another "domino" in the global Cold War geopolitical game. Bolstering the MAAG deployed before Dien Bien Phu, Washington dispatched hundreds of military and development advisers – both overt and covert – to keep South Vietnam from falling.[25] Overall, U.S. advisers had a high opinion of Diem's counterinsurgency strategy and initiative.[26]

Diem realized that success was predicated on his government's ability to stabilize the situation in the countryside.[27] One problem, though, is that, unlike in Athens or Manila, the U.S. advisers were not actually focusing primarily on the counterinsurgency. In 1957, the MAAG went to work training Diem's military, known as the Army of the Republic of Vietnam (ARVN), in the mold of the U.S. military. In 1959, the Eisenhower White House approved U.S. advisers to accompany South Vietnamese army battalions to provide "combat guidance," although actual combat was still forbidden.[28] Hundreds of Vietnamese officers attended training courses in the Philippines, Okinawa, and the United States, all to learn the ins and outs of American military doctrine.[29] U.S. advisers created a largely conventional military since, at that time, the greatest threat was considered to be an invasion from the North. However, as both advisers and trainees would come to realize, it was inadequate for the type of war Ho was planning to fight. And the situation was already dire.

By the end of 1959 sizable areas of South Vietnam – including some threateningly close to Saigon – were under communist control. A U.S. intelligence agent told Senator Mansfield at the time, "if you drew a paint brush across the South, every hair of the brush would touch [an insurgent.]"[30]

EARLY ATTEMPTS AT PACIFICATION

When John F. Kennedy took office in early 1961, there were 685 American troops in Vietnam, mostly advising the ARVN to use massive firepower to repel a Hanoi-led invasion just as the United States had done in Korea. Early on, Kennedy was deeply influenced by a report written in January 1961 by Edward Lansdale, then head of the Office of Special Operations in the Defense Department. Contending that the "real war" in Vietnam, which the U.S. was losing, was the guerrilla insurgency in the South, Lansdale's view dissented from the MAAG's concern with Hanoi's invasion.[31]

Kennedy took special note of Lansdale's report and even tried to offer him the Vietnamese ambassadorship. In fact, in the incoming Kennedy administration, a sort of cult of guerrilla warfare was developing. Kennedy apparently kept a copy of Mao's treatise, *Guerrilla Warfare*, on his desk in the White House. Entering the presidency, Kennedy had pledged "to bear any burden, meet any hardship, support any friend and oppose any foe to assure the survival and success of liberty."[32] In May 1961, Kennedy warned the U.S. Congress of this new and terrifying communist guerrilla threat, active in Vietnam and throughout the world:

> For the adversaries of freedom did not create the revolution; nor did they create the conditions which compel it. But they are seeking to ride the crest of its wave – to capture it for themselves. Yet their aggression is more often concealed than open. They have fired no missiles; and their troops are seldom seen. They send arms, agitators, aid, technicians, and propaganda to every troubled area. But where fighting is required, it is usually done by others – by guerrillas striking at night, by assassins striking alone – assassins who have taken the lives of four thousand civil officers in the last twelve months in Vietnam alone – by subversives and saboteurs and insurrectionists, who in some cases control whole areas inside of independent nations.... It is a contest of will and purpose as well as force and violence – a battle for minds and souls as well as lives and territory. And in that contest, we cannot stand aside.... This nation was born of revolution and raised in freedom. And we do not intend to leave an open road for despotism.[33]

The Kennedy administration believed that it had belatedly but accurately identified the guerrilla threat. It pushed the U.S. military to conduct counterinsurgency courses at an unprecedented clip. In an eighteen-month period, the military taught counterinsurgency doctrine and tactics to over 2,000 of its officers; 500,000 enlisted men received some sort of special training. Even civilian government agencies had their own "guerrilla schools."[34]

Kennedy sent NSC aide Walt Rostow and General Maxwell Taylor to Saigon in October 1961 to determine how the United States might help South Vietnam against the insurgent threat. A week later, the two Americans sent a sober but optimistic cable to Kennedy describing a deteriorating situation, one that could easily be lost if more U.S. support was not forthcoming. They added that current military operations against the Viet Cong were ineffective due to lack of intelligence and a poor chain of command within the South Vietnamese armed forces. Victory was possible, they projected, but only through careful escalation.[35]

Interestingly, though, Rostow and Taylor did not emphasize the need to address the phenomenon of guerrilla warfare despite President Kennedy's prior call for a "whole new kind of strategy" focused on irregular warfare. Instead, the report's emphasis on freeing the South Vietnamese army from a posture of static defense and giving it mobility by providing American helicopters and pilots suggested a conflict more like Korea than the broad outlines of a sustained counterinsurgency campaign, which entailed increasing special forces for antiguerrilla training and economic development for nation-building.[36]

Kennedy responded to the report by substantially increasing the number of advisers, but not combat troops. His administration looked to the Malaya Emergency as the model of how to win in Vietnam. In fact, backed by U.S. advisers, in 1961 the South Vietnamese government began constructing policies intended to mirror controversial but ultimately successful "New Village" programs in Malaya.[37] Saigon even turned to British military advisers who had worked in Malaya, including Robert Thompson, the former minister of defense during the Emergency. In late 1961, Diem requested that Thompson produce a plan for "pacification," the now infamous term for securing the countryside and quelling insurgent violence. Thompson's resulting "Strategic Hamlets" plan sited the Mekong Delta for the massive resettlement effort because it was believed to have relatively weak Viet Cong influence.

First known as the Delta Pacification Program, the resettlement effort began by using hundreds of ARVN troops to relocate 70 families from the Viet Cong stronghold province of Binh-Duon, directly North of Saigon. The villagers left only after being forced at gunpoint. By 1962, the South

Vietnamese government had established over 3,000 strategic hamlets with a startling total population of 4.3 million. They had plans for over 11,000 hamlets. Diem himself might not have actually been all that excited about the effort. He is reported to have told Thompson, "It makes the Americans happy and it does not worry either me or the Viet Cong."[38]

Under pressure to show results, Vietnamese officials often inflated the numbers of "secure" hamlets. In reality, most of the hamlets were not viable and many were even controlled by the Viet Cong. Supplies intended for the new villages ended up in enemy hands. At the core, there was simply little incentive for villagers to move to these poorly guarded and undersupplied hamlets. Villagers were often expected to provide the building materials themselves. As one American adviser put it, "No wonder the Viet Cong looked like Robin Hoods when they began to hit the hamlets."[39]

American reporters covering Vietnam began to poke holes in the hamlet program almost as soon as it began. One *Wall Street Journal* reporter wrote that visiting a hamlet left one with the impression of having "blundered into some sort of prison camp."[40] Another critic dismissively wrote that "if you stand long enough down there, they'll throw a piece of barbed wire around you and call you a strategic hamlet."[41] Another problem confronting the American and South Vietnamese effort was the inescapable fact that the Viet Cong were able to bolster their local support through promises, often specious, to give land to peasants.

At this early point, U.S. military commanders mounted serious objections to the counterinsurgency focus in Vietnam, arguing that it distracted from the real mission of developing the ARVN as a conventional force. General Lyman Lemnitzer, chairman of the Joint Chiefs of Staff, had visited Vietnam in 1961 and reported that "the new administration was oversold on guerrilla warfare and ... too much emphasis on counterguerrilla measures would impair the ability of the South Vietnamese Army to meet a conventional assault like the attack on South Korea by the ten or more regular North Vietnamese divisions."[42]

Despite the vocal opposition from his generals, Kennedy remained adamantly against a "total war" involving U.S. combat troops. Yet under the young president's watch the American-backed effort was not going well. South Vietnamese army sweeps failed to catch the elusive guerrillas; firepower was killing innocent civilians rather than Viet Cong commandos; and strategic hamlets were playing easily into the Viet Cong's hands. To many observers at the time, Vietnam appeared to be spiraling out of control. Whatever the direction of the war, the direction of U.S. policy remained escalation. In 1962, vast amounts of America's finest jet planes, helicopters, and armored personnel carriers were being delivered to South Vietnam. U.S. advisers now numbered 8,000 and jumped to over 11,000 by the end of the year. By the time of Kennedy's assassination in 1963, the number had reached 16,000.[43]

THE WAR ESCALATES

> This is not a jungle war, but a struggle for freedom on every front of human activity.

Lyndon B. Johnson spoke these words in 1964, after Diem's regime had fallen on November 2, 1963; by then, a small percentage of the estimated 8,000 hamlets were viable and could realistically be defended against Viet Cong attacks. And though there would be subsequent resettlement efforts in these early years of the 1960s, none would come close to achieving what the British did in Malaya: cutting the insurgent "fish" off from the "sea" that was Vietnam's rural population. By 1964, the Viet Cong controlled half of South Vietnam.

The Kennedy administration gave up on Diem almost as quickly as it had come around to him in 1961. The United States would continue to "engage" in Vietnam, but a new point man would have to be found. The end of Diem's regime also marked the beginning of the end of the U.S. government's Greece/Philippines-style approach to Vietnam. Even if the exclusively "advisory" role for American troops had been something of a charade, by 1964 Lyndon Johnson's White House had begun to speak more candidly about the prospect of American troops fighting in Vietnam. The Joint Chiefs of Staff wrote in a report in January 1964 that the United States "must be prepared to put aside many of the self-imposed restrictions which now limit our efforts."[44]

Two days after Kennedy's assassination, the U.S. Ambassador in Saigon, Henry Cabot Lodge, told Johnson, "The picture is bad. If Vietnam is to be saved, you, Mr. President, are going to have to do it." Johnson apparently replied, "I am not going to lose Vietnam. I am not going to be the president who saw Southeast Asia go the way China went."[45]

On August 2, 1964, three North Vietnamese torpedo boats engaged the USS *Maddox*, a U.S. Navy destroyer, followed by a second dubious attack on August 4. In response three days later, the U.S. House of Representatives passed the Gulf of Tonkin resolution 414–0; the Senate followed, 88–2. The congressional action gave Johnson extraordinary leeway in prosecuting the war, but fell short of officially declaring war.

Johnson tasked General William C. Westmoreland, a distinguished commander from World War II who had deployed to Vietnam in June as Commander of the United States Forces, Military Assistance Command, Vietnam (COMUSMACV), to develop a new battlefield strategy. The number of military advisers in Vietnam was now 23,000.[46]

While it is misleading to assume that Westmoreland had total command over American efforts in Vietnam, he was nonetheless the general who spearheaded the strategy that entailed a much deeper American military commitment.[47] Westmoreland believed that the war could not be won by gaining victories in key locations or taking control of strategically important areas, but only by reducing the enemy's numbers. The logic was simple: we will kill more of them than they will kill us, and eventually they will give up. Indeed, as American military commanders had long insisted, it was time to unleash America's overwhelming advantage in firepower to decimate the Viet Cong.[48] The name for this new approach was "attrition."

The central operation-level tool in this new approach was a "search-and-destroy" strategy, in which U.S. patrols would pursue VC units through the dense jungles, attempting to corner them or draw them into an engagement where, assuredly, American bullets and bombs would inflict heavy casualties. The problem with the strategy, though, was that the enemy refused to fight the way the United States wanted it to do. The Viet Cong continued to hide among the rural population, building clandestine political networks and exploiting external support through supply chains such as the famed Ho Chi Minh Trail, which brought indispensable materiel from North Vietnam via Cambodia and Laos. For much of the war, though, when the Viet Cong did confront American forces in open combat, they were almost always routed.

In retrospect, one strong argument against attrition was not that it did too little, too late, but that it did so much that it relieved the South Vietnamese government, people, and military from the responsibility of getting the counterinsurgency right.[49] This is the case even though the war in South Vietnam was never purely a counterinsurgency. Rather, Hanoi was substantially involved in aiding and directing the war efforts in South Vietnam well before its sizable numbers of regular troops started fighting in the South in the 1960s.

Another consequence of attrition was that it caused many American civilian and military leaders to become overly dependent on statistics. For example, "body counts" – rather than the viability of the enemy, or progress toward a political solution between the two halves of Vietnam – became the metric for how well the attrition strategy was working.

Secretary of Defense Robert McNamara, for one, was obsessed with statistics on the war. This focus on the raw numbers likely distracted American officials from a more "holistic" sense of the real progress being made in Vietnam. Future Nixon adviser Henry Kissinger later lamented "the degree to which our heavy, bureaucratic, and modern government creates a sort of blindness in which bureaucracies run a competition of their own with their own programs and measure success by the degree to which they fulfill their own norms, without being in a position to judge whether the norms made any sense to begin with."[50]

The formal entry of American combat troops into the Vietnam theater occurred on March 8, 1965, when 3,500 U.S. Marines landed on the beaches north of Da Nang, 85 miles south of the demilitarized zone dividing the two countries. The marines' initial mission was to protect the key air base used by South Vietnamese and American forces. According to Westmoreland, the marines had a second mission: to play a mobile counterinsurgency role in the vicinity. Not surprisingly, within a month of coming ashore the marines were directly fighting Viet Cong guerrillas. At this fateful moment, President Johnson decided to send ashore two more marine battalions, which increased U.S. "support" forces in South Vietnam by 18,000 to 20,000 men.[51]

General Westmoreland also believed that a massive bombing campaign against North Vietnam was necessary to support the new efforts. The campaign, Operation Rolling Thunder, began in March 1965 and lasted until November 1968. The campaign had three aims: to bolster the morale of the weak regime in Saigon, to interdict supplies to the Viet Cong, and to send a strong message to Hanoi to persuade it to abandon its efforts to destabilize the South. Interestingly, during the war most of the bombs were dropped in South Vietnam, not North Vietnam, and a clear majority were dropped in close-air operations protecting U.S. troops on the ground. In 1965, the United States conducted about 4,800 bombing raids per month; in 1966, the frequency increased to 12,000 per month. Each B-52 sortie could drop 60,000 pounds of ordnance.

In the end, the United States dropped more than 8 million tons of bombs over Vietnam, twice the amount dropped by British and American bombers during World War II.[52] September 24, 1965, stands as a good example of the scale of the bombing campaign: in a single day, the U.S. Air Force sent 167 bombers against North Vietnamese targets, dropping thousands of bombs. It also flew an additional 317 bomber sorties "in country" in the South, dropping an additional 270 tons of bombs. All told, the attacks delivered more bomb tonnage than the French Air Force did during the entire 56-day siege of Dien Bien Phu.[53]

FROM ATTRITION TO PACIFICATION

Just remember this, communist guerrillas hide among the people. If you win the people over to your side, the communist guerrillas have no place to hide, and you can find them. Then, as military men, fix them ... finish them! – Edward Lansdale[54]

On the ground, the Marine Corps continued to bear the weight of American operations in Vietnam. Interestingly, Marine commanders' views on how the war could be won diverged significantly from the attrition mainline. Officers such as Major General Victor H. Krulak, a student of marine action in the Banana Wars, lobbied for promoting the "spreading inkblot" strategy whereby small American and South Vietnamese units would focus on "clear and hold" as opposed to search and destroy. Krulak came to understand that an overwhelmingly large proportion of the South Vietnamese population lived in a small area of the country. Thus, he believed that the key to winning was to provide security and keep communist influence out of these areas. His conclusions bore a striking resemblance to the "hearts-and-minds" strategy that had failed under Kennedy, and it was roundly criticized. Another Marine Corps commander questioned Westmoreland's body count strategy, saying that it "can be a dubious index of success since, if the killing is accompanied by devastation of friendly areas, we may end up having done more harm than good."[55]

Much of the marines' opposition to the attrition approach derived from two difficult realities on the ground. First, the American enlisted troops received very little counterinsurgency training and were therefore ill-prepared to fight the kind of war that the Viet Cong was pursuing. Second, the troops rotated into Vietnam on one-year tours. As an American adviser put it, "The United States has not been in Vietnam for nine years, but for one year nine times."[56] In the spring of 1965, U.S. Army Chief of Staff General Harold K. Johnson commissioned a study entitled "A Program for the Pacification and Long-Term Development of Vietnam" (PROVN), which repudiated Westmoreland's strategy of search and destroy. Instead, it called for a renewed emphasis on population protection, winning the war at the "village, district, and provincial" levels.[57]

The marines were willing to deviate from the attrition strategy not only theoretically but also operationally. One noteworthy marine effort that began at roughly the same time was the deployment of Combined Action Platoons (CAPs). Organized by General Lewis Walt (who had studied as a second lieutenant at the Marines' Basic School under Chesty Puller, at one point the legendary leader of the U.S. effort against Sandino in Nicaragua), the CAPs were tasked with attacking the Viet Cong's infrastructure, protecting the population, collecting intelligence, and training militias. They were hugely innovative. They used small cadres of troops – usually twelve to fifteen marines – who lived among and fought alongside locals and militia forces, focusing not only on combat but also population security and gathering intelligence.

By 1966, around seventy-five CAPs had been established in the I Corps Tactical Zone, which encompassed South Vietnam's five northernmost provinces but represented only a small percentage of total marine forces in Vietnam. Involving only 2,500 marines at the peak of implementation, the CAP program never became a major part of the American military effort, especially since General Westmoreland roundly opposed it. In fact, only about 15 percent of marines were engaged in counterinsurgency efforts at all in 1966. They also had to deal with the reality that they were stuck working with the often corrupt South Vietnamese government and its sluggish military. In these conditions, even the best policies might not have been nearly enough to turn the tide. In the end, the CAPs were a short-term fix that achieved tactical victories but not strategic success.[58]

As the war raged on without an end in sight, it became increasingly clear to American planners that no matter how sophisticated its statistical analyses might be, the United States still had not figured out how to win in Vietnam. It also became apparent that the South Vietnamese government was an unreliable ally and that U.S. engagement had created a crisis of dependence. One observer wrote, "The failure to understand the capabilities and limitations of our ally in Vietnam is probably the single most important explanation of what went wrong with U.S. policy there."[59] In 1967, one response to the desperate situation came in the form of a new program with yet another U.S. government acronym. This was the Civil Operations and Revolutionary Development Support, or CORDS.

Led by Army Lieutenant Colonel Robert Komer, who was known as "Blowtorch Bob" for the heat he put on civil servants and others who did not cooperate with him, CORDS attempted to integrate all of the civilian and military counterinsurgency agencies and strategies into a more concerted unit. For too long, Komer believed, one agency or military service would pursue a development or counterinsurgency objective while others would do something entirely different, often at cross-purposes to the efforts of the first. CORDS would attempt to streamline the process.

CORDS was also noteworthy in bringing a renewed focus to "pacification." Komer reiterated the two central tenets of the concept: secure the rural population and keep the guerrillas from returning. Now, in clear contrast to attrition, U.S. development technicians and soldiers would provide the funding and know-how, but the Vietnamese would take charge of the actual implementation. Komer did not create pacification; rather, he resurrected it from the early 1960s before it had been largely displaced by attrition and "Americanization." The American effort had come full-circle: once again, the U.S. command believed the South Vietnamese would need to win the war themselves.[60]

U.S. combat units began organizing South Vietnamese outfits, such as the locally recruited peasant militias known as Regional Forces (RF) and Popular Forces (PF). By 1973, the RFs and PFs accounted for around 500,000 men spread across 1,600 RF companies and an equal number of PF platoons. CORDS also prioritized continued economic development backed up by targeted military operations and intelligence gathering to keep the Viet Cong from disrupting the newfound gains.[61]

In late 1969, there were around 7,600 American advisers working on pacification, up from approximately 1,000 three years earlier. Between 1966 and 1970, money spent on pacification and economic programs rose from $582 million to $1.5 billion. This shift was important for several reasons. For one, it was an instance of American military planners evaluating the effectiveness of their strategies mid-conflict, thinking critically about what was and was not working, and attempting to apply new strategies to address prior shortcomings.

However, the return to a counterinsurgency support approach in Vietnam likely came too late. It proved an ineffective response to the Viet Cong's deft and sustained use of intelligence and political "infrastructure." The deep communist presence in villages all over the country provided critical supplies and sanctuary to the Viet Cong guerrillas. The U.S. counterinsurgency support approach could do little to disrupt this relationship. So, beginning the same year as CORDS, American commanders decided to supplement their counterinsurgency support efforts with a mostly clandestine offensive strategy known as the Phoenix Program (Phung Hoang). Designed by the Central Intelligence Agency, the program tasked U.S. Special Forces and South Vietnamese operatives with aggressively scouring the countryside and hunting down an estimated 75,000 Viet Cong targets across South Vietnam.[62]

In a sense, American officials and Saigon were playing the lethal game that the Viet Cong had first perfected in the late 1950s. In August 1969, a quota for "neutralized" Viet Cong was added to the program, leading many observers to conclude that Phoenix was simply a murky assassination agenda. It was further marred by two obstacles: first, the South Vietnamese were extremely reluctant to share intelligence with the Americans; second, the Viet Cong began to respond by aggressively targeting South Vietnamese whom they believed to be involved in these neutralization efforts. Nevertheless, Hanoi later admitted that the program landed a nasty blow against the VC infrastructure. Some claim that by 1972 Phoenix had taken 81,000 operatives out of action, with 26,000 of those killed and another 22,000 "turned" to work against their former comrades.[63]

LOSING THE WAR AT HOME: MY LAI AND THE TET OFFENSIVE

To the extent that it was a counterinsurgency, the war in Vietnam was now the most controversial one in American history. What is more, the U.S. government increasingly faced intense public opposition at home, driven by media that showed, often in graphic detail, how badly American efforts were going. As was the case in the Banana Wars of the early twentieth century, the public response is often a fundamental element of dirty wars: if there is any success on the ground, it is often difficult to measure, and there is usually a notable lag before any "good" news reaches home.

Perhaps the low-water mark for domestic support of the war came in the winter of 1968. Between midnight and 3 AM on the morning of January 30, 1968, the day marking the celebration of the new lunar year, Viet Cong and North Vietnamese Army (NVA) forces attacked a series of cities across South Vietnam. Nineteen Viet Cong soldiers detonated a hole in the wall surrounding the American embassy in Saigon. The invaders traded fire with American military police for several hours before being subdued. Over the next 24 hours, Viet Cong forces attacked 36 out of 44 provincial capitals and 100 towns, as well as the South Vietnamese military headquarters, and the presidential palace in Saigon.[64] Within a few days, the "Great Offensive" as Hanoi and the Viet Cong called it, had been beaten back. Yet Tet had instantly become the largest military offensive in the war.

While initially startled by their stealthy adversaries, the ARVN and American forces quickly regained their footing. Contrary to what many had predicted, the ARVN did not surrender or retreat when the Viet Cong onslaught came. Nor did the villagers in the South Vietnamese countryside rise up in support of the communist guerrillas in their midst; many joined the South Vietnamese forces in repelling the guerrillas and NVA. Saigon might not have fully won the hearts and minds of the Vietnamese population, but neither had the Viet Cong.

For their part, the Viet Cong abandoned the long-standing irregular approach to the war during Tet in favor of much more conventional tactics. In most cases, VC forces were annihilated in these sorts of engagements. One notable exception, however, was in the ancient imperial city of Hué. Viet Cong and North Vietnamese regular forces seized the city and subsequently rounded up South Vietnamese soldiers, government officials and others sympathetic to the American forces, killing up to 6,000. The fighting lasted for over a month, the majority of it comprised of Stalingrad-esque house-to-house battles. When U.S. Marines and soldiers retook the town a month later, it was "a shattered stinking hulk, its streets choked with rubble and rotting bodies."[65] The American forces killed an estimated 5,000 of the enemy and expelled another 5,000 from the city while only losing 147 killed and 857 wounded – remarkable tactical results that nonetheless failed to cover the unfolding political defeat linked to Tet.

As observers back home began to appreciate the full extent of the damage the first phase of Tet had done to the American mission, an even more shocking event occurred that would prove a devastating blow to its moral and political standing in Vietnam. In the hamlet of My Lai, members of "Charlie" Company of the 1st Battalion, 20th Infantry Regiment, 11th Brigade of the 23rd Infantry Division killed between 347 and 504 unarmed civilians. Many of them were killed at close range, and many of the bodies exhumed later were found mutilated. Early battlefield reports indicated that 128 Viet Cong and 22 civilians had been killed in a daylong firefight, and General Westmoreland praised the company for an "outstanding job." However, the events came to light when 11th Brigade veteran Ron Ridenhour wrote a detailed report documenting the tragedy and sent it to President Richard Nixon, the State and Defense Departments, Congress, and other agencies. When the story broke in the national press in spring 1969, My Lai became one of the most ignominious names in American counterinsurgency history, and the brutality with which it was associated turned out to be a major point for the war's opposition.

The Viet Cong and NVA launched two more phases of the offensive in May and August of the same year, but in September the operation ceased. As the dust settled, Hanoi and the Viet Cong began to realize the extent of their losses. A stunning 45,000 of an initial 84,000 guerrilla fighters had been killed. About 2,000 Americans died in the fighting. The North Vietnamese politburo admitted: "We failed to seize a number of primary objectives and to destroy mobile and defensive units of the enemy. We also failed to hold occupied areas. In the political field, we failed to motivate the people to stage uprisings."

Amazingly, the Viet Cong ceased to be an effective fighting force after the Tet setback, almost completely ending its typical guerrilla-style attacks. Reports of hunger and desperation among the Viet Cong ranks echoed what had happened to the Malayan communists after the British put their counterinsurgency strategy into place. We now better understand that Tet was a military debacle for the Viet Cong – and, by extension, an impediment to Hanoi's designs for toppling the government in Saigon. However, Tet was also a political coup for the Viet Cong and North Vietnamese because of how the devastating defeat was interpreted by the American public.

It is understandable that American reporters stationed in South Vietnam and back home observed the apparently prodigious guerrilla offensive and concluded that it signaled an American failure in Vietnam. Images of communist fighters penetrating the U.S. Embassy in Saigon and footage of burning houses provided strong evidence that little progress was being made. Venerable CBS anchor Walter Cronkite wondered aloud what so many Americans were thinking after the attacks: "What the hell is going on? I thought we were winning this war."[66] It is also not surprising that the American media's negative interpretation of events led many Americans to doubt U.S. efforts in Vietnam.

The full record of pacification programs during the war was replete with wasteful spending and poor execution. Yet there is no question that by the late 1960s and early 1970s the Americans and Vietnamese had been able to convert some small successes into broader strategic gains, especially after the Tet offensive. At the end of 1967, less than half of the rural South Vietnam population was considered "secured." By the end of 1971, this number had risen to 97 percent. And the remaining 3 percent was almost completely "contested," which meant that there were almost no South Vietnamese under total Viet Cong control.[67]

VIETNAMIZATION AND "PEACE WITH HONOR"

Following Tet, American and South Vietnamese forces might have had the upper hand against the Viet Cong, but driven by growing impatience and bitterness back home, the incoming Nixon administration expedited the "Vietnamization" of the conflict. Under this doctrine, the United States would gradually remove its combat forces from the theater while the South Vietnamese counterparts filled the ensuing vacuum. Less studied, however, is the fact that the American combat troops who remained also began to adopt new strategies and tactics that mirrored what the marines and other doctrinal "heretics" had been encouraging for years.

Like his predecessor Westmoreland, the new commander in Vietnam, General Creighton Abrams, had a conventional army background, but he had come to understand pacification's fundamental role in any successful strategy. To this end, Abrams split up divisional forces and sent them out on sustained patrols (often at night) in platoon and company strength. There were conventional battles in Vietnam after 1968, such as the futile assault of Hamburger Hill in May 1969, but the U.S. approach was now far more about "clear and hold" than victory through annihilation.[68]

President Nixon pursued Vietnamization to achieve what he called "peace with honor," which we may view in retrospect as a diplomatic euphemism for "getting the heck out and calling it a draw." By the end of 1971, most American combat forces had been withdrawn; total troop strength was now just under 200,000. The war was also beginning to fade from the American consciousness. In one poll, 41 percent of the American public listed the economy as their main concern while only 15 percent listed Vietnam. Yet, while Americans were no longer doing the ground-level fighting, Nixon actually drastically escalated the bombing campaign to gain leverage over Hanoi in negotiations. In other words, if Westmoreland had earlier wanted to bomb the Viet Cong and NVA to the "Stone Age," Nixon and his trusted national security adviser Henry Kissinger wanted to bomb them to the peace table.

The U.S. campaign also helped to institute a land redistribution program in South Vietnam. Diem's original land reform in the late 1950s had been a profound failure, but the second time around in Vietnam proved to be a charm. Undertaken by South Vietnamese president Nguyen Van Thieu with American "technical" support, the "Land-to-the-Tiller" program introduced in March 1970 redistributed 2.5 million acres over three years.[69] By 1973, over half of the rural population had acquired land from the reforms.

The U.S. Agency for International Development (USAID) played a key role in designing the reform program. Sophisticated for its day, USAID used computerized procedures for rapid surveying; it also worked to expedite issuing land titles. Interestingly, the civil-military CORDS program also had an important part, often pressing villages to participate in the land reform efforts. The American media and public might have become tired of the war in Vietnam, but because of efforts like Thieu's land reform program the people of South Vietnam were now just beginning to believe in their government.

THE EASTER OFFENSIVE

On March 30, 1972, Hanoi launched its so-called Easter Offensive, unleashing 125,000 conventional troops into South Vietnam to strike a decisive blow and end the war. The invaders supplemented their massive ground forces with hundreds of tanks and artillery pieces. Still reeling, the Viet Cong played almost no role in the offensive. General Giap hoped that even if the invasion did not topple the government in Saigon, it would allow the North Vietnamese to occupy territory in the South and put a halt to pacification. Yet, even Giap's more cautious expectation did not materialize.

Although the North Vietnamese were able to quickly occupy key provinces, President Thieu replaced key commanders and subsequently the tide began to change. South Vietnamese forces regained the initiative and, with support from U.S. air power, repelled the invading forces.[70] The offensive soon collapsed; roughly half of the invading troops were captured or killed. The offensive ended in a stunning defeat for the vaunted NVA and its commander, who had humiliated the French at Dien Bien Phu and exasperated the Americans for years. Now that it was his turn to be humiliated, Giap removed himself as commander of the North Vietnamese forces.

The Nixon administration responded to the Easter Offensive by once again escalating the bombing campaign, this time targeting Hanoi. Known as Operation Linebacker, the bombing campaign, as one lieutenant general described, it was "not Rolling Thunder – it was war."[71] In conjunction with Linebacker, the U.S. Navy staged Operation Pocket Money, in which naval aircraft dropped dozens of Mark 56 mines in Haiphong Harbor. It took them only a few minutes to cripple the port, but doing so reduced North Vietnam's vital imports – mostly from China and the Soviet Union – by 80 percent.[72]

ESCAPE FROM SAIGON

In January 1973 the United States and South Vietnam signed a peace agreement with North Vietnam, thus ending America's direct involvement in the war. This withdrawal was predicated on Hanoi's promise to cease its offensive hostilities and repatriate American prisoners of war. Nixon also promised Thieu that the United States would come to Saigon's aid if the North did launch another offensive. Two years later in 1975, however, and with Nixon having already left office in disgrace, the U.S. Congress was in no mood to provide additional aid for a war effort that it felt had been a tragic and deceptive error.[73]

Led by Senior General Van Tien Dung, North Vietnamese forces captured Saigon on April 30, 1975, a month after the offensive had begun, thus ending the war in Vietnam. Buoyed by the ARVN's thorough repulsion of NVA forces in the Easter Offensive, American and South Vietnamese officials were taken aback by how quickly the ARVN forces crumbled.

In the days leading up to the NVA's final victory, the American public was inundated with images of a massive helicopter evacuation of American and certain Vietnamese personnel from Saigon. If there was ever an image that captured the ignominious end to the American experiment in Vietnam, it was the footage of Americans on the roof of the U.S. Embassy evacuating to helicopters overhead on that fateful April day.

Winning the war in Vietnam was never going to be easy. The Americans and their South Vietnamese counterparts faced a ruthless, multifaceted enemy in the Viet Cong and North Vietnamese military. They also benefited tremendously from foreign aid, mostly from China and the Soviet Union. And for most of the war, the South Vietnamese government was largely an artificial and illegitimate entity, kept alive primarily through massive infusions of American aid.

The U.S. military managed to win almost every conventional battle during its long years fighting in Vietnam. By the late 1960s, U.S. commanders and politicians in Washington came to embrace a more "hearts-and-minds" counterinsurgency approach to the war – an approach that appears to have borne considerable fruit. Despite its glaring deficiencies, the American counterinsurgency strategy had largely defeated the Viet Cong, one of the most formidable guerrilla forces in modern history.

Yet winning the war was a classic dilemma of too little, too late. By the time the counterinsurgency support strategy was instituted, the American public and political class wanted nothing to do with this tiny country across the globe that had inflicted so much pain on the United States. Though there were notable victories on the ground by the early 1970s, the goal of keeping South Vietnam "independent and non-Communist" was out of the question.[74]

The costs of the "American" phase of the Indochina War were great. The ARVN lost 275,000 in combat; another roughly 500,000 South Vietnamese civilians were killed, many assassinated by the Viet Cong or killed by American bombs and shells. The Americans lost 58,209 lives, just under 47,500 due to enemy actions. By most estimates, the North Vietnamese lost over 1,100,000 troops – about 251,000 of them Viet Cong and the rest NVA.

The United States and France each spent eight years fighting in Indochina against an elusive enemy, but the American effort, in both manpower and cost, was ten times larger than that of the French. Both evacuated the region before achieving their respective military objectives, and both countries saw their home fronts torn apart by the controversy over these increasingly unpopular dirty wars.

In recent years, scholars have argued that the U.S. Congress and public pulled the plug on Saigon and the ARVN at the moment that the South had finally gotten its act together and that another influx of aid to South Vietnam would have kept it viable in the face of North Vietnamese attacks. We will of course never fully know the answer to this historical counter-factual. Yet we do know that the American public's perception of the war was a critical factor and that after Tet it began to diverge from the reality on the ground in Vietnam. Thus, even if more aid might have made a difference, a key obstacle would have been the political will to make this happen in such a negative political climate.

Despite this view that America had finally gotten it right, the United States' most important "lesson learned" from Vietnam was that it did not want any more Vietnams: these ill-defined morasses that suck in American dollars and blood. Next time, many American officers who served in Vietnam concluded, the U.S. military would use overwhelming force to pursue clearly defined political objectives.[75] And then get out, as quickly as possible.

PART THREE

LATIN AMERICA AND THE COLD WAR,
1950s–1980s

20

From Guatemala, 1954, to Cuba and the Bay of Pigs, 1961

In Latin America, Communist agents seeking to exploit that region's peaceful revolution of hope have established a base on Cuba, only 90 miles from our shores. Our objection with Cuba is not over the people's drive for a better life. Our objection is to their domination by foreign and domestic tyrannies. Cuban social and economic reform should be encouraged. Questions of economic and trade policy can always be negotiated. But Communist domination in this Hemisphere can never be negotiated.
– President John F. Kennedy, State of the Union address, January 30, 1961

[Washington] will not be able to hurt us if all of Latin America is in flames.
– Fidel Castro[1]

The years between 1953 and 1962 bore witness to two of the United States' most notorious counterinsurgency ventures. Aimed at overthrowing the leftist governments in Cuba and Guatemala, the two operations employed American-supported covert "indigenous" proxy forces made up of disaffected citizens and exiles of each country seeking to spark popular uprisings against the regimes. Both operations were led clandestinely by the CIA and deliberately designed to appear as though they were entirely Latin affairs. The Guatemala operation succeeded entirely in achieving its goal of removing the country's leftist leader, a result that strongly influenced the decision to launch the doomed Cuba operation intended to repeat the magic against Fidel Castro's regime. Its failure was likely a major reason that Washington largely abandoned this type of intervention in Latin America for the rest of the Cold War.

This chapter analyzes the Operation PBSUCCESS in Guatemala in 1954 and the Bay of Pigs operation in Cuba seven years later, weighing the policy priorities and miscalculations that led the United States to undertake them. This discussion provides a sharp contrast to the U.S. counterinsurgency efforts in Latin America treated in the chapters that follow: by 1964, the United States had moved more toward supporting and training on-the-ground domestic counterinsurgent forces as well as providing economic development assistance to stem the Marxist revolutionary tide sweeping the Americas.

THE FALL OF ARBENZ

In the late 1940s and early 1950s, the small Central American country of Guatemala was enjoying an unprecedented period of democracy and social reform after decades of strongman rule and oligarchic control over the economy. In 1944, demonstrations by teachers, students, and others led to the departure of the particularly repressive dictator Jorge Ubico. A few months later, young army officers revolted against Ubico's selected successor, sparking the reformist movement of the "October revolution." The intellectual Juan José Arévalo returned from exile to win the presidency with the freest vote in the Central American country's history. Arévalo cited Franklin Roosevelt's New Deal as the inspiration for his administration in Guatemala. A new constitution greatly expanded enfranchisement (save illiterate women) and banned military officials from holding office. Arévalo's government also gave new liberties to labor unions, defended press freedoms, and promoted literacy campaigns, especially in the mountain highlands dominated by the indigenous Mayan people. Despite his unprecedented reforms, Arévalo was unable to meet many of the expectations associated with his presidency.

In the 1950 democratic election, the quiet, serious, and left-leaning army colonel Jacobo Árbenz took 65 percent of the vote and succeeded Arévalo to continue Guatemala's unprecedented and remarkable "Decade of Spring." More aggressively than his predecessor, Árbenz unapologetically promised to "convert Guatemala from a backward country with a predominantly feudal economy into a modern capitalist state."[2] This effort focused on land reform, a topic that instantly brought him into conflict with the United Fruit Company (UFC), the largest landholder in the country. In 1899, United Fruit had acquired a ninety-nine-year concession over a large area of jungle from Guatemala's then-strongman, which gave the Boston-based entity the right to construct and operate a railroad to the Caribbean coast. United Fruit's port at Puerto Barrio was the country's only Atlantic port, while its railway was the only way to ship freight to and from the port.

Even by Latin America's historically skewed standards, land distribution in Guatemala was highly unequal: 2 percent of owners held three-quarters of all arable land, while more than half of all farmland was locked in large plantations (over 1,100 acres), much of it fallow. The reforms initiated by Árbenz impacted farms larger than 670 acres that were not fully worked, or those greater than 223 acres on fallow plots.[3] Compensation was provided in interest-bearing bonds based on the land's declared tax value. In only two years, a million acres were distributed to roughly 100,000 families. Árbenz called for the expropriation of 380,000 acres of United Fruit land, around 40 percent of its holdings in Guatemala. Almost 85 percent of the land was fallow, ostensibly to guard against any outbreaks of banana diseases. Árbenz's government offered compensation of $1.1 million, far below United Fruit's claim that the land was worth $16 million. By making such a large claim, United Fruit inadvertently revealed the extent of its previous tax evasion. By the time Árbenz fell in 1954, his government had expropriated roughly 1.5 million acres.[4] Interestingly, though, when United Fruit officials plotted a coup against him in 1952, the Truman administration helped put a stop to the plotting.[5]

While not a communist himself, Árbenz was deeply influenced by the ideology, and key members from Guatemala's communist party entered his government. For the Eisenhower administration – which was increasingly concerned about communist expansion around the world – the composition of Árbenz's cabinet reinforced the fear that his government could become a "Soviet beachhead in the Western Hemisphere." What is ironic about Eisenhower's stance against Árbenz is that within several years Washington would be promoting the very type of land reform throughout Latin America and Asia that it had condemned as "communism" in Guatemala.

The American entity with the most to lose in Árbenz's reform program, United Fruit, exerted considerable pressure on Washington to act, even if Washington's initial decision to oust Árbenz came before the expropriation of UFC lands. Even at the time, it was well known that the banana giant had extremely close contacts with the Eisenhower administration. The brothers Allen and John Foster Dulles, for instance, were directors of the CIA and secretary of state, respectively, and both had ties with United Fruit through their work with the Sullivan and Cromwell law firm. Moreover, the family of the State Department's top diplomat for Latin America, John Moors Cabot, owned stakes in United

Fruit, and Eisenhower's personal secretary was the spouse of the company's public relations director.[6] Yet leading scholars, including Richard Zimmerman, argue persuasively that the U.S. government's main reason for opposing Árbenz was concern about the spread of communism into the Americas.

By the end of 1953, the tensions between Washington and Guatemala City had escalated dramatically. Leaders in Guatemala's neighboring states, including the pro-U.S. strongman Anastasio Somoza in Nicaragua and his counterpart in Honduras, were also concerned about communist infiltration into their countries. The CIA had been hatching a covert operation to address this threat in Guatemala, and by January 1954 the operation had a code name, Operation PBSUCCESS. An undistinguished Guatemala ex-army colonel and furniture salesman named Castillo Armas was picked to lead the anti-Árbenz "Liberation Army," and his paramilitary force began to train in Somoza's Nicaragua.

Only recently, Washington had dispatched a new ambassador to Guatemala City, John Peurifoy, who had been selected for the key purpose of coordinating Operation PBSUCCESS. The fiercely anticommunist Peurifoy had worked in Greece in the late 1940s during the successful effort to support the anticommunist regime in Athens. Indeed, the relatively easy counterinsurgency win in Greece contributed to Washington's belief that a similar outcome could be achieved in the mountains of Central America. This time, though, it would entail removing a pro-communist government rather than, as in Greece, keeping communists from overthrowing an American-backed government.

U.S. government officials continued to deny the veracity of published reports of secret armies and unfolding plots. Then, in March 1954 at a meeting of the Organization of American States (OAS) in Caracas, Venezuela, John Foster Dulles was able to obtain a majority resolution that effectively justified armed intervention in any member state that was "dominated by Communism" and therefore a "hemispheric threat." With its diplomatic "backing" enhanced, the CIA proceeded with the training of the exile force in Nicaragua. A variety of psychological operations were planned, including taped recordings of disinformation for broadcasting and printed leaflets dropped over Guatemalan cities. Soviet-issued weapons were purchased, to be planted in Guatemala as "evidence" of Árbenz's strong ties with global communism. In April, Eisenhower used aggressive language in an address to Congress, warning that "the Reds" were already in power in Guatemala and were now eager to spread their "tentacles" to other Central American republics.

Soon after, Árbenz's government accepted the delivery of a cache of arms from Czechoslovakia. The clandestine shipment had originated from the Polish port of Szcecin, packed inside the Swedish freighter *Alfhem*. It arrived in Guatemala's Atlantic port of Puerto Barrios on May 15, 1954. The delivery, which the U.S spy agency had tracked as it crossed the Atlantic and altered its course repeatedly, was proof positive for the CIA of Árbenz's communist bona fides. CIA Director Allen Dulles quickly convened senior administration officials and received support to set the invasion date for the following month. On May 17, the U.S. State Department issued a statement denouncing the arms delivery; Eisenhower followed with a public message that the developments in Guatemala could allow a "Communist dictatorship" there. On May 20, a ground unit of CIA saboteurs set explosives on the railroad tracks outside Puerto Barrios in a failed effort to prevent the *Alfhem*'s supplies from leaving the port. Interestingly, Washington had already imposed an arms embargo on Guatemala since 1948 and the Czech arms were of limited use.

Over the ensuing weeks, the CIA placed alarmist articles in newspapers across the region and handed out booklets warning of the growing communist threat in Guatemala. On June 2, a coup against Árbenz was foiled, but the pressure was on. A few days later, Árbenz suspended constitutional guarantees for thirty days. On June 17, American mercenaries began bombing missions over Guatemala. Castillo Armas soon led his 300-man "army" across the Honduran border into Guatemala. At first, it appeared as though Árbenz would be able to repel the invading forces, as his army largely remained loyal and fought back against the invaders. Castillo Armas entered the provincial city of Esquipulas, but he had greater difficulties elsewhere. With his advisers concerned about the possibility of failure, Eisenhower authorized the use of two more fighter-bombers to strike targets throughout the country.

At the same time, psychological and propaganda efforts made the "revolt" appear much more widespread than it actually was. The CIA filmed anti-Árbenz propaganda in a studio in Miami, and then broadcast it from Nicaragua after falsely claiming that the studio was located "deep into the jungle." Castillo Armas's planes buzzing over Guatemala City dropped leaflets intended to convince army troops to defect to the "rebel" side. Written on the pamphlets were slogans such as "Struggle against communist atheism, Communist intervention, Communist oppression.... Struggle with your patriotic brothers! Struggle with Castillo Armas!"[7] Richard Bissell, a CIA official, came up with the inventive ploy of using a small, ragtag air force to fly over Guatemala City and drop relatively harmless Coca-Cola bottles, which sounded like artillery shells when they exploded. The psychological operations were highly effective in spreading fear and uncertainty throughout the country.

On June 24, having seized the town of Chiquimula, Castillo Armas proclaimed it the capital of his "provisional government." Momentum had turned against Árbenz. Further sealing the Guatemalan president's fate, Washington won a 5–4 United Nations (UN) vote against an official inquiry into the events unfolding in the Central American country.

This CIA-hatched episode of "regime change" never sparked a wide-scale insurrection against Árbenz. Yet within two weeks Árbenz was unable to rely on his military's loyalty, and the Guatemalan president fled into exile in late June. Over the next two weeks, five provisional governments attempted to restore some semblance of order. As the dust settled, Castillo Armas himself assumed the interim presidency; several months later his administration was "endorsed" in a dubious plebiscite, in which he won 99 percent of the vote.

Just a few weeks after the operation, President Eisenhower attended a reception for senior CIA officials and commented, "Thanks to all of you. You've averted a Soviet beachhead in our hemisphere."[8] In the months immediately following Árbenz's ouster, police, military and ad hoc vigilante militias killed 3,000 to 5,000 "Arbencistas."[9] Within three years, the share of Guatemala's lands that had been redistributed during Árbenz's tenure had all been taken away from the beneficiaries. Over the next three decades, military generals and their civilian lackeys maintained power in Guatemala. The Decade of Spring was over. Yet Washington's lesson from Guatemala was that targeted covert operations could help check communism in the hemisphere without the deep commitment or risk of American boots on the ground. At the same time, however, Washington paid a high price in public esteem throughout Latin America for its blatant "Big Stick" ouster, as shown by protests outside U.S. embassies in several Latin American capitals.[10]

THE QUIXOTIC CASTRO

Cuba will not be Guatemala. – Ernesto "Che" Guevara[11]

Fatefully, a young, idealistic, Argentine doctor was living in Guatemala during Árbenz's ouster. Although Guatemala did not fulfill all of Ernesto Guevara's high expectations about what a communist revolution should

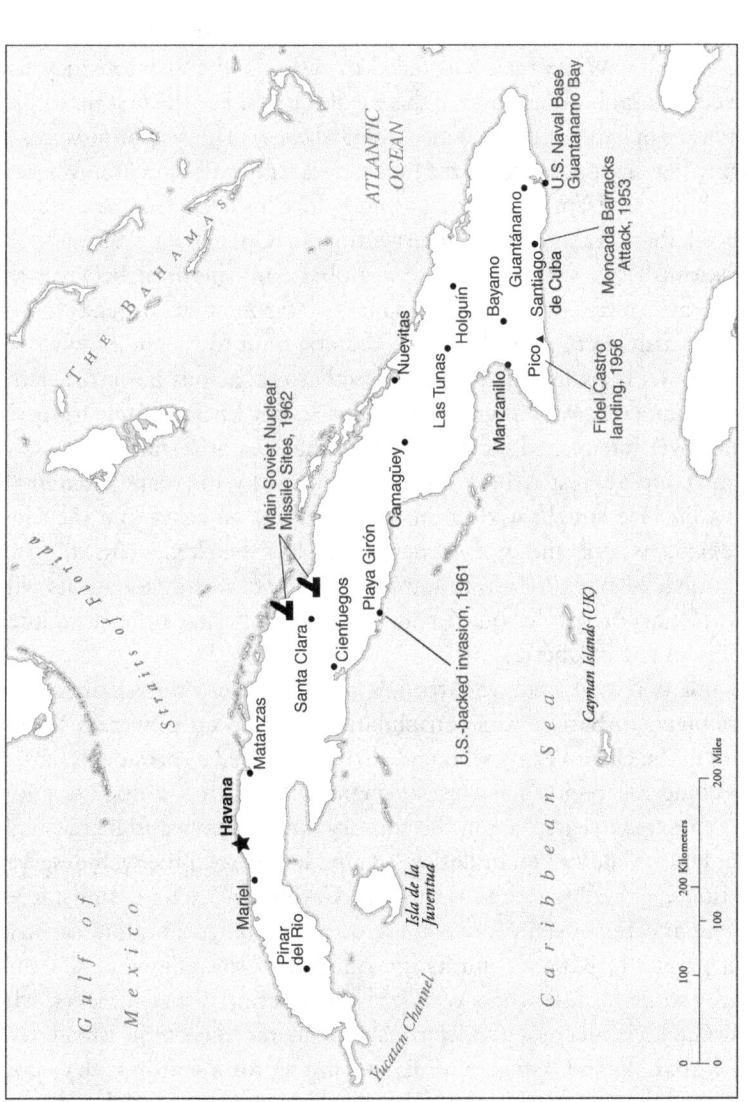

FIGURE 20.1. Cuba. Map prepared by the University of Wisconsin-Madison Cartography Lab©. Reprinted with permission

look like, a biographer has noted that Arbenz's reformist aspirations made the country "a compelling place to be in 1954."[12] Almost daily, Guevara met with revolutionaries and communists from across Latin America, including well-respected Cubans who stood out from the other political expatriates. Many of them were veterans of an armed uprising against Fulgencio Batista's regime in Cuba. While they had failed to dislodge the dictator, they had gained considerable admiration in these exile circles. For the first time in his life, Guevara openly identified with a political cause. The Argentine wrote to his family that he could breathe the "most democratic air" in Latin America.

Watching the dramatic events unfold before his eyes, Guevara became convinced that Washington's intervention in Guatemala was only the "first skirmish" in what would be a global confrontation between the United States and communism.[13] Guevara wrote that Árbenz "could have given arms to the people, but he did not want to ... and now we see the result." Only by taking the fight directly to rapacious Latin American elites and imperial Washington could the region liberate itself from the "hostile governments and social conditions that do not permit progress."[14] After the coup against Árbenz, Guevara was lucky to escape Guatemala with his life. He sought asylum in the Argentine embassy and then fled to Mexico, where the government, led by the leftist Institutional Revolutionary Party (PRI), was admired by leftists worldwide for its willingness to harbor revolutionaries and dissidents fleeing rightist regimes, especially in Latin America.

Rewind two years before Árbenz's ouster. Across the Caribbean in Cuba, Fulgencio Batista was consolidating his grip on power. A former sergeant in the Cuban army who had also once served as president, Batista had become the region's newest strongman through a bloodless coup. Over the next six years, he ran the country with a heavy and increasingly corrupt hand.[15] Before long, Batista's Cuba had earned the well-deserved reputation as the "whorehouse of the Caribbean" where sun-starved American and European tourists traveled to gamble, drink, and carouse. Not surprisingly, Batista's autocratic rule began to antagonize Cubans, especially students and others with leftist and nationalist sentiments, who saw the Cuban leader as a puppet for American interests on the island. One young Cuban, Fidel Castro, considered running for a seat in Cuba's congress. But Batista's return to power prompted him to abandon the crooked political system for a quixotic attempt to seize power through the force of arms.

Fidel Castro and his brother Raúl, along with 135 other insurrectionists, launched their first attack against the Moncada army barracks in

Santiago de Cuba on July 26, 1953. The aim was to seize the barracks' weapons and to use them to foment and arm a revolt against the Batista regime. The attack failed. Sixty-one rebels were killed and more than half of the survivors were captured or executed. A week after fleeing into the mountains with a small group of the conspirators, Castro was captured and subsequently sentenced to fifteen years in prison.[16] This did not prevent him, however, from making his famous "History Will Absolve Me" speech, in which he presciently laid out how violent struggle would be necessary to make the social and economic changes that he believed were necessary for Cuba. Castro's predictions aside, Batista released the rabble-rouser as part of an amnesty in early 1955. Castro then moved to Mexico where he founded the July 26 Movement, named for the date of the failed raid on the barracks.

It was in Mexico that Ernesto Guevara – later to be known best as "Che" – first met Castro's growing band of revolutionaries. They were laying plans to overthrow the despised Cuban dictator once again. Che was to be their doctor. Guevara wrote in his diary in July 1955: "A political occurrence is having met Fidel Castro, the Cuban revolutionary, a young man, intelligent, very sure of himself and of extraordinary audacity; I think there is a mutual sympathy between us."[17]

The July 26 Movement remained largely secret, known only to its hardened inner core of mostly middle-class, reform-minded Cubans who were united by their hatred of Batista. Most of the *moncadistas* were communists but there were some activists from the youth wing of the Ortodoxo opposition party. Above all, Castro's followers were nationalists driven by the lofty rhetoric of the great martyr of Cuban independence, José Martí. In fact, Castro had not studied the works of Lenin, Mao, or other notable revolutionary communists before embarking on his own insurgency. He was influenced by one of his favorite novels, Ernest Hemingway's *For Whom the Bell Tolls*, an account of the adventures of a Republican guerrilla in the Spanish Civil War. In his own words, "That book helped me conceive of our own irregular war."[18]

While Castro and others have subsequently mythologized the role of the July 26 Movement in these remarkable historical moments, several other revolutionary groups were simultaneously organizing to oppose Batista's rule, including the important Directorio Revolucionario, based at the University of Havana. In March 1957, the Directorio and another clandestine group attacked the presidential palace in Havana to assassinate Batista. In the aftermath of the failed attempt, Batista's security forces hunted down most of the Directorio operators. At the same time, in the eastern province of Oriente and its capital of Santiago de Cuba, underground revolutionary Frank País and his colleagues planned another significant secret operation known as the *llano*.

Castro's July 26 Movement was not a monolithic revolutionary force in Cuba as myth might say. Its role was divided between the underground llano and the guerrilla forces, known as the *sierra*. The role of the llano has traditionally been less recognized but this group played a central part in the logistics and planning of the revolution and increasing the guerrilla fronts in the mountain ranges in Oriente province. The main idea behind the llano was to establish an urban militia and create a general strike throughout Cuba, which would then be strengthened by the sierra guerrillas in the mountains. The llano members were from the middle and professional class of Cuban society, and Frank País, until his death in mid-1957, was almost singlehandedly in charge of these underground forces. País was also responsible for bringing important social and political figures into agreement with the insurrectional aims of the guerrilla movement that continued in his absence.

In November 1956, Che, Fidel and Raúl Castro, and roughly eighty other fighters had cast off from the port of Tuxpan on the coast of Veracruz, sailing from Mexico to Cuba on the creaky yacht *Granma*. Over the miserable week-long crossing, the men suffered from horrible seasickness and were forced to jettison most of their supplies during a storm. The plan was for País to lead an uprising in the provincial city of Santiago that was to coincide with the *Granma*'s arrival, but the País uprising started early and was quickly stifled. It was thus no use to the invading force. As the *Granma* neared the Cuban shores, a coast guard patrol spotted it and alerted the Cuban military, which attacked the men while they attempted to disembark. The revolutionaries finally managed to land at Playa de los Colorados on the eastern part of the island. Batista's air force made swift work of many of Castro's men, killing them before they could find relative safety in the mountains. In all, fewer than two dozen revolutionaries made it from the beaches to the rugged Sierra Maestra mountains.

The guerrillas' subsequent military operations were largely failures. Their tactics mostly conformed to the major revolutionary trends of the era. As in China and Vietnam, the Cuban rebels wanted to organize a rural insurgency that "educated" the local populations about the revolution. The Cuban army was remarkably reluctant to engage the guerrillas. Only 200 government troops were killed between December 1956 and January 1959, indicating their unwillingness to try to flush out and exchange fire with the guerrillas. After less than a year of operations in the Sierra Maestra, the Cuban army had effectively conceded the mountains to the rebels.

By 1957, the tiny rebel force had survived the initial phase of establishing a position in the mountains. That is precisely when luck turned in its favor. In February, Herbert Matthews, a senior *New York Times* reporter and press veteran of the Spanish Civil War, Benito Mussolini's Abyssinian campaign, and World War II, arrived in the rebels' clandestine camp. Matthews mistakenly concluded that Castro had large numbers of guerrillas under his control, while the real number was closer to twenty. He published glowing articles about the Cuban insurgents. Castro "is alive and fighting hard and successfully in the rugged, almost impenetrable vastness of the Sierra Maestra, at the southern tip of the island," Matthews wrote. "Thousands of men and women are heart and soul with Fidel Castro and the new deal for which they think he stands.... Hundreds of highly respected citizens are helping Señor Castro ... [and] a fierce Government counterterrorism [policy] has aroused the people even more against General Batista.... From the look of things, General Batista cannot possibly hope to suppress the Castro revolt." Matthews went on to portray the "Rebel Army's" political leanings almost as an analogue to Rooseveltian liberalism: "It is a revolutionary movement that calls itself socialistic. It is also nationalistic, which generally in Latin America means anti-Yankee. The program is vague and couched in generalities, but it amounts to a new deal for Cuba, radical, democratic, and therefore anti-Communist.... [Castro] has strong ideas of liberty, democracy, social justice, the need to restore the Constitution, to hold elections."[19] The *New York Times* subsequently published a photo of Matthews together with Fidel, which demolished the Batista regime's claim that the journalist had invented the encounter.

By the end of 1957, the now-famous rebels had established a viable yet crude civil administration inside the Sierra Maestra. And, following the footsteps of Mao and Giáp, the guerrillas evaded the Cuban army's strategy of trapping them inside a steadily tightening noose. The rebels took great advantage of the Sierra Maestra's thick forests and deep ravines to continually attack the bogged down army units. Early the following year, they established Radio Rebelde, a clandestine radio station that spouted pro-revolutionary propaganda. At the same time, an urban insurgency against Batista helped keep the Cuban army tied up in the cities. The sagacious Castro also deftly used his men's relatively benign treatment of captured Cuban army soldiers to help cement their reputation as humane fighters.

External events also strengthened Castro's position. In early 1958, the Eisenhower administration stopped sending military supplies to Batista. In May, an increasingly worried Batista ordered a large number of raw recruits and reservists into an Operación Verano (Summer Operation) that lasted ten weeks. Yet the troops made few gains against the increasingly confident, seasoned, and popular guerrillas. The offensive ended in a humiliating failure. On New Year's Eve 1958, the despised Batista fled Cuba on a plane for the Dominican Republic and victorious rebels and throngs of Cubans celebrated in Havana.

The July 26 Movement had become the preeminent political force among the motley coalition of anti-regime groups. And Castro was unquestionably the most charismatic and adored leader of this broad-based revolt. Two key rebel leaders, Che Guevara and Camilo Cienfuegos, entered Havana to secure military facilities. Around a week later, after having sworn in the "revolutionary government's" first president, Judge Manuel Urrutia, Castro himself entered the capital. His improbable rebellion had succeeded.[20] Yet, contrary to the lore that developed around this story in subsequent years, Castro's band of *barbudos* were not the only Cubans responsible for the revolution; rather, virtually every sector of Cuban society had turned against the despised Batista. Most notable among those who deserted him was the urban middle and upper class, whose opposition made his fall infinitely more likely.

THE BAY OF PIGS

The overthrow of Batista was as important for what it represented as for what actually occurred. Castro's initially tiny band of fighters achieved a decisive victory in the face of highly improbable odds. The strategy of Mao and Giap had been adopted in Latin America and had worked brilliantly. In fact, the Cuban rebels did not even need to resort to the "protracted" component of the strategy given the rapidity of the victory. And unlike turnovers in Indochina and Algeria, this success was close to home, a development that unsettled policymakers in Washington.

Yet Castro's ascension initially enjoyed a warm reception in the United States, an outcome that seemed to point to the endurance of U.S.-Cuban ties. In April 1959 Castro paid an eleven-day visit to the United States. This helped to consolidate his image as a moderate nationalist in the eyes of the American public and media. Castro told the American Society of

Newspaper Editors, "We are not Communists," and added that his government would not expropriate private property. In Washington, Castro met with Vice President Richard Nixon, but not President Eisenhower; he visited the Lincoln and Jefferson memorials as well as Mount Vernon.[21] Tracking his extreme popularity in liberated Cuba, U.S. newspapers and television at the time were replete with stories about the charismatic and romantic Cuban leader. Even decidedly "imperialist" American conglomerates such as Texaco and Esso ran advertisements in *Revolución*, the new Cuban daily. Domestic companies such as Bacardi also paid taxes in advance as a patriotic gesture.[22]

But this honeymoon between Washington and Havana was not to last. Washington increasingly saw Castro as a communist while the Cuban leader increasingly believed that the United States was out to get him. Both were mostly correct. Reports of Cuban efforts to foment leftist revolution in neighboring countries such as Panama, Venezuela, and Haiti helped convince the Eisenhower administration that a tougher approach was necessary. Only a month after Batista had fled, Daniel Braddock, the acting American chargé d'affaires in Havana, sent out a classified memo to the CIA and State Department titled "Cuba as a Base for Revolutionary Operations against Other Latin American Governments." It read, "A number of leaders of the successful revolutionary movement in Cuba consider that efforts should now be undertaken to free the people of some other Latin American nations from their dictatorial governments."[23]

While Che Guevara was generally regarded as the principal force behind such thinking, and was indeed active in the planning, he was far from alone. Fidel Castro had reportedly made remarks along such lines, particularly during his recent visit to Venezuela. As Braddock noted presciently, "it can be expected that Cuba will be a center of revolutionary scheming and activities for some time, with consequent concern and difficulties for various governments including our own."[24] Vice President Nixon issued a memo that rejected attempts to "get along with" and "understand" Castro. Eisenhower had even accused Castro of being a "madman" and discussed a blockade of the island to make the Cuban people hungry and move them to "throw Castro out."[25]

To borrow a sports metaphor, by 1960 U.S. policy toward Castro had turned to hardball.[26] In keeping with the Eisenhower administration's estimations, even some politically moderate Latin American leaders such as Costa Rica's José "Pepe" Figuere and Venezuela's Rómulo Betancourt, who had initially supported Havana, began to agree that communism was consolidating in Cuba and ripe for export to the rest of the Americas. Soon the CIA group that had overthrown Jacobo Arbenz in Guatemala in 1954 was reconstituted to replicate its magic in Cuba.

In the same year, then-Senator John F. Kennedy wrote a political book, *The Strategy of Peace*, wherein he accused the Eisenhower administration of stoking antipathy toward Cuba. Remarkably, Kennedy added that the White House should have given Castro a "warmer welcome," which would have helped him steer toward "a more rational course."[27] During that year's presidential campaign, though, Kennedy publicly said that his administration would aid anti-Castro groups in exile. Republican candidate Nixon, whose colleagues in the government had privately been doing exactly this with covert programs, reluctantly took the public position that Kennedy was being reckless in risking a World War III over Cuba. At the same time, the secret plans for an invasion of Cuba continued. Chairman of the Joint Chiefs of Staff General Lyman Lemnitzer told Eisenhower that the exiles in training were "the best army in Latin America."[28]

U.S. officials had come to view Castro as a serious threat to its interests in the hemisphere. CIA Director Allen Dulles, for one, briefed President Eisenhower that Castro's "cautious attitude" toward Moscow had shifted toward "active support." And American officials believed that time was working against them, given the influx of Soviet and Eastern Bloc arms that was bolstering the Cuban armed forces. Having made so much of Eisenhower's apparent inaction against Castro in that fall's presidential election despite his private understanding that covert operations were afoot, Kennedy entered the White House feeling pressure to finish the job against the Cuban leader.

On Saturday, April 15, 1961, the secret operation to overthrow Fidel Castro's regime was launched from Happy Valley, the CIA code name assigned to a village on Nicaragua's Atlantic coast. Under the glow of floodlights, eight B-26 Douglas Invaders lined up for takeoff. The planes had recently been acquired from a U.S. Air Force bone yard near Tucson, Arizona, and then refurbished and painted to resemble the B-26s in Castro's air force, down to the FAR (Fuerza Aérea Revolucionaria) markings on their fuselages. The idea was that the disguised planes would enter Cuban air space and sow confusion as the defending forces mistook the "C-26s" for friendly forces.

As the operation unfolded, newspapers in the United States ran front-page stories with headlines such as "Castro's Pilots Bomb Their Own Bases"; others claimed that the Cuban air force was in ruins, which was far from the truth. One anti-Castro pilot, Mario Zúñiga, ran interference by landing a "distressed" plane at Miami International Airport and immediately stating his rehearsed

Guatemala to Cuba and the Bay of Pigs

line: he was a Cuban air force officer who had defected from Cuba and perpetrated the recent attacks. Almost immediately reporters began to doubt Zúñiga's account. For one, his plane had the machine-gun barrels on the nose, unlike Castro's B-26s, which had them mounted on the wings.[29]

Two days later, in the early hours of April 17, an assortment of 1,400 men, mostly Cuban exiles, attempted to invade their homeland and oust Fidel Castro. Over the previous week, infantrymen from the Cuban Expedition Force (Brigade 2506, as the men called themselves) had flown into Nicaragua from training camps near Guatemala's Pacific coast. Before their initial departure from Nicaragua, the infamous dictator Luis Somoza (son of Anastasio) told the troops to bring him a "a couple of hairs from Castro's beard."

The military campaign, known as Operation Zapata, had three landing points adjacent to the Bay of Pigs. The first and most significant site was Playa Girón on Cuba's southern coast. Contrary to what is often remembered, the goal was never to take over Cuba militarily but rather to use the small force to hold a piece of Cuban territory long enough to allow massive anti-Castro uprisings to erupt across the island. What the CIA did not fully appreciate, however, was that Castro had already imprisoned many of the very individuals who would have been likely targets to join and lead the insurrection.

The operation at the Bahía de Cochinos (Bay of Pigs) quickly unraveled. A day into the invasion, the brigade of exiles was actually holding its position fairly well, but there was little ammunition left and the maritime supply chain was under attack by Castro's planes. This dire situation quickly came to the attention of the White House. National Security Advisor McGeorge Bundy wrote to Kennedy that "The Cuban armed forces are stronger, the popular response is weaker, and our tactical position is feebler than we had hoped."[30] Three days after the landing, the force was forced to flee to the ocean or swamps; over a thousand survivors were quickly captured by Castro's celebrating forces. Meanwhile, the CIA officers who were overseeing the operation in Washington listened to radio transmissions from the counterrevolutionaries in Cuba. After being powerless to send the Cuban brigade the supplies and air support it had requested for three days, the officers listened to the brigade commander's last message: "I have nothing left to fight with," he said. "Am taking to the woods. I can't wait for you." Then the radio was silent.[31] Though it lasted only five days, the operation cost almost $500 million and over one hundred lives (a handful of whom were U.S. citizens) on the exile side, as well as an untold number of Castro's troops.

One of the biggest mistaken assumptions was that Castro's air force would have been crippled before the invading forces hit the Cuban beaches. Kennedy permitted only one raid against parked Cuban planes, an attack that largely was ineffective with only eight B-26s. Castro, on the other hand, realized that taking out the transport ships supporting the operation would be the key to repelling the invasion. Without them no supplies could reach the beachhead.

Not surprisingly, as time went on and the full extent of the disaster dawned on the White House, there was greater pressure for Kennedy to respond with increased military force. This would have been a bitter irony since Kennedy had originally rejected the plan to take out Castro's planes with U.S. forces. At this tense moment, Kennedy was forced to decide between deploying military strength to save the brigade, thereby risking a larger conflict, and cutting his losses by accepting the debacle. While he did approve more expanded but still highly restricted military operations over the beaches of Cuba, Kennedy effectively opted for recognizing his loss.

The operation was designed to appear as an entirely Cuban-on-Cuban affair. The expectation was that a week or so after the full beachhead was established, a provisional government would be flown in and declare itself the de facto authority in Cuba. Washington would then offer critical aid in an unfolding "civil war." Kennedy's secretary of state Dean Rusk later put the thinking in perspective when he quipped, "It doesn't take Price Waterhouse to figure out that fifteen hundred Cubans aren't as good as twenty-five thousand."[32]

Tellingly, the Kennedy administration initially denied that the United States had anything to do with the operation. Yet the stark reality was that U.S. officials had organized and funded the entire effort, and both the Joint Chiefs of Staff and the president had approved the plan. Not only had Washington been caught lying about its involvement, but it had also been humiliated by an infinitely weaker *communist* foe. One American general called it the greatest American defeat since 1812; historian Theodore Draper deemed it "a perfect failure."

The complicated truth about the Bay of Pigs operation is that it was not "ginned up by a nefarious band of agents within the bowels of the CIA" but instead produced by two presidential administrations, cheered on by numerous members of Congress, and ultimately approved by brilliant and well-meaning men. As journalist Jim Rasenberger wrote, "until it failed, the plan made a kind of sense."[33]

For Richard Bissell, the CIA's deputy director for plans in charge of the anti-Castro operation, these sorts of covert schemes were "distasteful" but not "immoral." Bissell himself had cut his teeth in the covert operation against Árbenz, one of a cadre of American intelligence officials who leaped at the opportunity to "lead armies and install governments, to create small air forces and devise wondrous chimeras, to break and make rules as needed, and to do all of this in the name of a cause they sincerely believed to be noble and just."[34] The Bay of Pigs invasion, these confident American covert operatives might have dreamed, would simply be another feather in their caps. Instead, the fiasco wound up strengthening the Soviet-Cuban alliance, manifested by Moscow's increased arms shipments that included state-of-the-art jet fighters and air defense systems.[35]

"MURDER, INC. IN THE CARIBBEAN"

While the Bay of Pigs operation ended in humiliation for the Kennedy administration, this did not deter it from pursuing subsequent anti-Castro operations in late spring and summer of 1961. Among the operatives brought in to help coordinate these programs was Colonel Edward G. Lansdale, whose exploits in the Philippines and Vietnam had caught the White House's attention. Another specially designated operative was William Harvey, the former station chief of Berlin, who had masterminded a remarkable tunnel operation in which Americans dug from West Berlin into East Berlin to tap Soviet transmissions. Interestingly, though, Lansdale had strong reservations about Washington's ability to overthrow Castro, contending "there's no way you can overthrow Castro without a strong, indigenous opposition. And there is no such opposition, either in Cuba or outside of it."[36] Apparently, though, Lansdale never shared his views with President Kennedy.

In November 1961, Kennedy approved Operation Mongoose, which further tarnished the CIA's image with morally and operationally dubious efforts to oust the Cuban leader. Remarkably, the president's brother, Attorney General Robert Kennedy, told the CIA that Mongoose was to be "the top priority in the United States government – all else is secondary – no time, money, effort, or manpower is to be spared."[37] His idea was to "stir things up on [the] island with espionage, sabotage, and general disorder." Mongoose subsequently engaged in dozens of plots to depose Castro. Some of these involved conventional methods, such as industrial sabotage and burning sugarcane crops. Others were more far-fetched, such as the attempt to spread a rumor around Cuba that Castro was the

Antichrist. Of particular salience, Mongoose was so aggressive and off-putting that later on President Lyndon Johnson called it "a damned branch of Murder, Inc. in the Caribbean."[38]

Despite these covert efforts, and after several months of severe toil, the Kennedy administration secured the release of over 1,100 men captured during the brief Bay of Pigs operation. In December 1962, Robert Kennedy told a private group of business representatives, "My brother made a mistake.... These men fought well; the disaster was no fault of theirs. They are our responsibility."[39]

On the morning of October 14, 1962, an American U-2 plane flying high above Cuba took photographs that would, within a matter of days, lead the CIA's National Photographic Interpretation Center to confirm the presence of at least two medium-range ballistic missiles capable of hitting American cities east of the Mississippi River with nuclear payloads. President Kennedy's steady performance during the Cuban Missile Crisis likely had much to do with the bitter lessons he learned from the Bay of Pigs, not least among them, to take the advice of aggressive military advisers with a healthy dose of salt. In this instance, Kennedy opted for a quarantine of the island nation despite the Joint Chiefs of Staff's riskier call for aerial bombing and subsequent ground invasion. Interestingly, Castro and Che were incensed with Khrushchev after he cut a deal with Kennedy to pull the missiles out of Cuba in exchange for an American promise not to invade the island and a withdrawal of its Jupiter missiles from Turkey.

GUATEMALAN SUCCESS, CUBAN FAILURE

The American-led operations against suspected communist foes in Guatemala in 1954 and in Cuba in 1961 were remarkably similar. One was a mock-insurgency against Árbenz. The other was a counterrevolutionary operation against Castro. They both involved CIA-backed guerrilla forces that were supposed to depose the leadership in the country, install transitional governments, and foment popular opposition to the former regime and support for the new regime. The Árbenz coup was successful largely because of the extensive psychological and propaganda efforts; American operators thought it could be replicated in Cuba but grossly underestimated the popular approval of Castro's regime. It also made strategic errors in not eliminating the Cuban air force, but that was possibly the inevitable result of Kennedy's wanting to keep the operation clandestine and avoid large-scale U.S. military force.

What is interesting is the legacy that the Bay of Pigs left for U.S. involvement in the region. As we will see in the next chapter, the United States avoided similar interventions in Guatemala and Cuba after the early 1960s, opting instead for a policy of proxy counterinsurgency training and arming when a Cuba-inspired Marxist insurgency erupted in Guatemala; and a very similar militarization policy fighting the insurgencies that emanated from Cuba, first promoted by Che Guevara.

21

Guatemala, Post-1963

The duty of a revolutionary is to make revolution.
– Che Guevara, 1962[1]

There are some indications that Fidel Castro is planning to increase his support of the Guatemalan insurgency, perhaps to the point of dispatching a small force of guerrillas now undergoing training in Cuba.
– U.S. classified intelligence report, 1960s[2]

If you [the Guatemalan people] are with us, we'll feed you; if not, we'll kill you.
– Guatemalan General Ríos Montt[3]

To bring the story forward, six years after Operation PBSUCCESS, junior army officers in Guatemala attempted a coup against the ruling authoritarian regime headed by General José Miguel Ramón Ydígoras, who had taken power after Castillo Armas had been murdered. The year was 1960. Interestingly, the revolting officers were upset that the CIA was using Guatemala to train anti-Castro Cuban exiles.[4] When the uprising foundered, a few of these officers retreated to the hills to organize a guerrilla insurgency, which they believed would be the surest avenue to radical social and economic change. Not surprisingly, they soon established contact with Havana. This incipient insurgent group became the Havana-backed MR-13 (Movimiento Revolucionario 13 de Noviembre), founded in 1960 with its base in the mountainous *oriente* (east) – in and around villages, such as Zacapa, whose names would become synonymous with the campaign of terror and atrocity that the country's unfolding guerrilla conflict would produce. This group became the nexus of the insurgent forces that engaged in armed insurrection against the Guatemalan

Guatemala, Post-1963   259

government for the next four decades. In addition to the MR-13 that soon integrated into the Guatemalan Labor Party (PGT), a motley alphabet soup of revolutionary acronyms such as Guerrilla Army of the Poor (EGP), the Revolutionary Organization of Armed People (ORPA), and the Rebel Armed Forces (FAR) comprised the total guerrilla force attempting to spark "another Cuba" in Guatemala. Over the next several decades, all sorts of communists, workers, activists, and other leftists joined these guerrilla bands.

The groups often conducted economic sabotage and targeted government buildings and officials for assassination or kidnapping. By the late 1960s, the Marxist insurgents began bolder operations, including the 1968 killing of American Ambassador John Gordon Mein after he resisted a kidnapping attempt. That same year, insurgents also killed two U.S. embassy military attachés in the capital of Guatemala City. Two years later, rebels assassinated the West German ambassador when the regime rejected their demands of $700,000 in ransom and the release of twenty-five political prisoners. Carlos Arana assumed the presidency in 1970 and, supported by American military advisers, further escalated the counter-insurgent pressure against the disparate Cuban-inspired guerrilla groups.

THE DEATH SQUADS

In 1966, Guatemalan troops entered the province of Zacapa, hunting for MR-13 (Revolutionary Movement 13th November) fighters. Quickly and meticulously, soldiers eliminated approximately 400 guerrillas. They also killed more than 1,000 villagers. Following the operation, each member of the involved brigade received a "ZACAPA" badge as an honorary military decoration. Tragically, the Zacapa massacre foreshadowed what became a horribly long and bloody counterinsurgency war. When the war formally ended in 1996, an estimated 200,000 Guatemalans had been killed out of a population of less than 10 million. And in a firm indication of the Guatemalan army's scorched earth strategy, 95 percent of the deaths came at the hands of the country's security forces.

During these years dozens of paramilitary terrorist groups – increasingly called "death squads" – went into action to eradicate what the Guatemalan state considered a scourge of leftist subversion. Operating under such names as the White Hand, the Purple Rose, or the New Anti-Communist Organization, the groups would often distribute leaflets bearing the names and sometimes the photographs of their prospective victims, whose corpses – and those of many others – were later found grotesquely mutilated: deceased men with their eyes gouged out, their testicles in their mouths, without hands or tongues, and female victims with their breasts cut off. The brutality shocked Guatemalans and the international community, and it prompted Guatemala's Catholic bishops to write in 1967,

> We cannot remain indifferent while entire towns are decimated, while each day leaves new widows and orphans who are victims of mysterious struggles and vendettas, while men are seized in their houses by unknown kidnappers and detained in unknown places or are vilely murdered, their bodies appearing later horribly disfigured and profaned.[5]

CASTRO, GUEVARA, AND FOCO THEORY

Meanwhile, Fidel Castro's Cuba was at the forefront of a major push to ignite 26-of-July–style revolutions throughout the Western Hemisphere. In addition to the MR-13, several other groups in Latin America received inspiration as well as funding and training from the Cuban government. Such groups included Nicaragua's "Rigoberto López Pérez" guerrilla column, an anti-Somoza brigade named for the poet and assassin of long-time dictator Anastasio Somoza in 1956.

Before long, the organization was carrying out bank robberies, propaganda operations, and surprise attacks, but it was destroyed in the summer of 1959 in an ambush near El Chaparral, Honduras. Among its members was Carlos Fonseca, the founder of the Frente Sandinista de Liberación Nacional (FSLN), which ousted Somoza in 1979 and assumed complete control two years later after a long and bloody conflict. By 1962, Cuba had become a sort of "guerrilla central": its revolutionary influence extended as far as the Dominican Republic, Venezuela, Bolivia – and even into Africa. One American intelligence official, active in espionage against Havana, explained Cuban methodologies:

> Castro tells revolutionaries from other Latin American countries: "Come to Cuba; we will pay your way; we will train you in underground organization techniques, in guerrilla warfare, in sabotage and in terrorism. We will see to it that you get back to your homeland. Once you are there, we will keep in touch with you, give you propaganda support, send you propaganda materials for your movement, training aids to expand your guerrilla forces, secret communications methods, and perhaps funds and specialized demolition equipment."[6]

The face of this new Cuban export was Che Guevara, whose *foco* strategy provided the theoretical and practical framework for instigating revolutions abroad. The doctrine held that a general revolution could be prompted by small, quick-striking guerrilla vanguards that created a "focus" (hence, *foco*) of discontent with the status quo. However, as we will see later in this chapter, the approach failed in most cases, and Guevara met his demise in Bolivia, perhaps in part because he and his forces failed to follow the strategy's central principles. Even still, Guevara's writings proved influential and his operations formidable. They certainly attracted Washington's attention.

All other factors aside, given the United States' interest in preventing communist successes in the region, and given its track record of using military force to promote counterrevolutionary outcomes around the world, Guatemala and Cuba post-1963 would have seemed nearly ideal opportunities for a large-scale counterinsurgency intervention. Yet, the U.S. did not intervene – at least, not much. Instead, these cases mark an important moment in the story of the U.S. experience in guerrilla war. At the core of the American response to the Guatemalan conflict and the Cuban-directed foco movements was the deployment of small Special Forces teams to serve as military trainers and advisers.

The reasons for this approach were many, and historians continue to debate them.[7] For one, while communism remained a primary concern for the U.S. government, the Johnson administration had embraced once again the Truman-era strategy of containment, aiming to stop the spread of communism elsewhere rather than attempting to reverse the ideology's gains where it had already succeeded. Second, the failure of CIA-led ventures like PBSUCCESS and the Bay of Pigs operations to create enduring strongholds against communism, along with the damage those ventures did to American prestige, were strong disincentives against pursuing similar options in the mid-1960s. And third, the building conflict in Vietnam and the disaffection it provoked domestically made it increasingly difficult for the U.S. government to justify military interventions in the rest of the world. As a result, this era of U.S. counterinsurgency involvement became the beginning of "counterinsurgency by instruction" – providing training, supplies, and operational support to local counterinsurgent forces – without significantly compromising American lives or prestige. It became a central feature of U.S. counterinsurgency strategy that endures into the twenty-first century. While it remains controversial, U.S. counterinsurgency policy did succeed in checking Castro's revolutionary machinations in Latin America, including Guatemala

"SCORCHED COMMUNISTS"

By the 1960s Latin America was awash in foco guerrilla insurgencies. Yet Washington considered Guatemala to be the hottest case, or at least the one for which a Cuba-like outcome was most likely. For example, a secret U.S. intelligence report predicted that it was Guatemala where "the short-term opportunities for the insurgents now seem the most promising – because of the weaknesses of the government rather than the strength of the insurgents, who are few in numbers and divided by factional rivalry."[8] In response, the Pentagon deployed light Special Forces teams to serve as military trainers and advisers. Between 1966 and 1968, over 1,000 Green Berets served in the country, attempting to teach their Guatemalan counterparts the ins and outs of counterinsurgency warfare. All told, 28 American soldiers died during their deployments, mostly in skirmishes with guerrillas. Yet American efforts did not lead to the defeat of the Marxist rebels; instead, new groups such as the Cuban-inspired Ejército Guerrillero de los Pobres (Guerrilla Army of the Poor) organized themselves to continue the banner of armed revolution in the country.

By the early 1970s, the Green Berets had helped to develop the Guatemalan army into a much more serious counterinsurgency force, one increasingly able to stem guerrilla advances in the country. Yet U.S. military operatives on the ground had little sense of the strategy behind their efforts other than that it was to stop communism. One young American adviser, who later became a U.S. Army general, stated in a later interview with the author, "We did not have a strategy.... We had little or no leverage on the Guatemalans. Our approach of our advisory effort was tactical rather than even operational or strategic. [Our message was that] the guerrillas are really bad and we'll potentially be good. That was about as strategic as we got."[9]

This absence of strategy had a number of important consequences for the situation in Guatemala and for American interests there. One was that the country remained unstable, with the guerrillas attempting all sorts of bold missions such as targeting foreign ambassadors. Another consequence, which American policymakers and military advisers did not fully realize, was that Washington was helping to create a sort of "Frankenstein" military in Guatemala. Guatemalan commanders were happy to have U.S. supplies, but they resisted advice and training. A CIA report in 1970 labeled the government led by Carlos Arana, of Zacapa massacre infamy, to be "the most extreme and unyielding in the hemisphere." The "client" government in the fight against communist insurgents was becoming an embarrassment for American policymakers. The consequence of this drift is that the United States became "half involved" in

Guatemala: not deep enough to significantly influence the increasing bloodthirsty counterinsurgency campaigns but also just enough to be sullied by the long-standing association with this repressive regime.

Adding to this sense of the misalignment of U.S. and Guatemalan aims was the unavoidable brutality of the Guatemalan government and paramilitary factions. In a candid confidential to his superiors written in 1968, American diplomat Viron P. Vaky worried about "counter-terror" in Guatemala because it was "indiscriminate." "We cannot rationalize that fact away," he wrote confidentially. "The official squads are guilty of atrocities. Interrogations are brutal, torture is used and bodies are mutilated." Vaky saw this as a serious political and moral problem for U.S. objectives:

> One can easily see there how counterterror has blurred the question of Communist insurgency and is converting it into an issue of morality and justice.... We are associated with this tactic in the minds of many people, and whether it is right or wrong so to associate us is rapidly becoming irrelevant.... Have our values been so twisted by our adversary concept of politics in the hemisphere? Is it conceivable that we are so obsessed with insurgency that we are prepared to rationalize murder as an acceptable counter-insurgency weapon?[10]

Given the Guatemalan army's growing barbarity, it is perhaps not surprising that its commanders, for their part, were not eager to have American officials scrutinizing their actions. In one stark example of how Guatemalan and American expectations had diverged, when the Carter administration threatened to cut off military aid to Guatemala to censure its human rights abuses, the Guatemalans preemptively rejected the aid even before Carter was able to suspend it. The country's foreign minister told American diplomats at the time, "Guatemalans had to protect their vital interests" and that meant breaking from Washington's orbit if necessary.[11] At the same time, Guatemalan generals and the conservative business class heaped scorn on Carter for having gone soft on communism and abandoning their natural ideological ally in Guatemala.[12]

A U.S. Senate report in 1971 summarized U.S. policies in Guatemala from 1954 to 1970 and revealed that what seemed like an appropriate counterinsurgency response in the 1960s had turned into a major headache given the nature of the Guatemalan military. The report noted the wisdom of the adage that it's easier to get into a bear trap than to get out.[13]

Guatemala's counterinsurgency war had always been bloody. But in the late 1970s, it became a "dirty" dirty war. In fact, by the time the final peace accords emerged in 1996, a United Nations report labeled the Guatemalan security forces' actions "genocidal," given that the killing was directed so

FIGURE 21.1. Declassified U.S. intelligence map of Guatemala from the early 1980s indicating location of various fronts of the Marxist insurgency, Guerrilla Army of the Poor (EGP is the Spanish initials). Map prepared by the University of Wisconsin-Madison Cartography Lab©. Reprinted with permission

much toward the country's indigenous Mayan population. In only two years in the early 1980s, 100,000 Guatemalans were killed, mostly as part of the ruthless and extremely effective counterinsurgency campaign.[14] The brunt of this widespread killing came in the late 1970s and early 1980s when the Guatemalan army adopted a "scorched-earth" approach to fighting the guerrillas. Whereas before the "Zapaca strategy" had involved relatively isolated incidents, now it had become institutional military doctrine. As is often the case, the army's logic was simple: eliminate the civilian support for the guerrillas and they will wither away.

In the early 1980s, rebel fighters organized the National Revolutionary Union (URNG) to bring together the various guerrillas groups under one command. General Fernando Romero Lucas García, who had become president in 1978, responded with harsh measures, including the escalation of the rapid counterinsurgency campaign that disproportionately targeted the Mayan indigenous population. Critics alleged that Lucas García ordered the deaths of over seventy-five political leaders as well as thousands of other extrajudicial executions. Despite the military onslaught, the now united URNG rebels remained resilient, considerably stronger than they had been during the previous two decades. In fact, they were able to levy "war taxes" and issue "travel passes" just outside of the capital.

Then, in March 1982, junior military officers demanding an end to electoral fraud and corruption led a coup against Lucas García and his hand-picked successor, General Ángel Aníbal Guevara. The coup leaders asked retired general Efraín Ríos Montt, now an evangelical pastor, to lead a three-member military junta that subsequently annulled the 1965 constitution and dissolved Congress. Despite implementing a smattering of human rights reforms, cleaning up the notoriously corrupt Guatemalan state bureaucracy – he helped publicize his campaign by requiring public officials to wear pins that said, "I don't steal, don't lie, don't abuse" – and bringing some indigenous political figures into his government, Ríos Montt remained committed to using a heavy hand to quell the insurgency.[15] For Montt, the conflict was total and victory would come at any cost: "I must do what I must.... We here are fighting the Third World War." In late 1982, Ríos Montt famously denied accusations that his government was conducting a dirty war: "We have no scorched-earth policy; we have a policy of scorched Communists."

Ríos Montt soon declared a state of siege and launched an assault on the URNG. One major problem the military faced was that the guerrillas, who occupied villages and towns throughout rural Guatemala, would often flee before the army (now doubled in size to 30,000 men) attacked, leaving the local villagers to bear the brunt of the violence. The cold-blooded counterinsurgency logic was at play. Don't target the fish but instead take away the sea. Hundreds of Mayan villages simply vanished; beheadings, garroting, immolation, and summary massacres were conducted throughout the alleged guerrilla strongholds.[16]

Ríos Montt also wanted to bring the predominantly Mayan rural population more fully under state control. In a program known as *frijoles y fusiles* (beans and guns), cores of resettlement "strategic hamlets" were established to relocate Mayan peasants away from guerrilla influence. Once again, resettlement became an integral component of a harsh counterinsurgency strategy. As one American official noted: "Those who are perceived to support the government are rewarded with food for work, housing if they have been displaced, and other forms of government largesse. Those perceived not to be in support of the government are met with whatever force is considered necessary."[17]

Another critical element in Ríos Montt's plan was the establishment of *patrullas de autodefensa civil* (self-defense patrols or PACs). In this effort, local villagers received food, water, employment, and health care if they worked on local militia patrols. In the end, roughly one million peasants from 850 villages served in the PACs. Ríos Montt was clear about this strategy, "If we close our eyes, increase the number of soldiers and policemen, and we attack the subversives, we can do it [defeat the guerrillas.] . . . Security does not consist of arms, tanks, and airplanes. This is not even five percent of the requirement for a national security policy. Security lies in the relationship between the State and the people."[18] This turned out to be very "successful" counterinsurgency policy, for the PACs eventually helped to eliminate the URNG as a guerrilla force.

Interestingly, the hawkish Reagan administration hesitated before restoring military assistance to the Guatemalan military even though many top officials sympathized with Ríos Montt's predicament.[19] Administration officials might not have been thrilled with the Guatemalan military's indiscriminate operations, but they were also fearful of "another Nicaragua" following the successful Cuban-inspired Marxist revolution in 1979. The irony, though, was that the Guatemalan army's scorched earth successes helped to ensure that Washington would not become more deeply involved in this horribly violent counterinsurgent war.

On August 8, 1983, Rios Montt was ousted by his own minister of defense, who contended that "religious fanatics" were ruining the country. With a new constitution promulgated in 1985, elections ensued and Vinicio Cerezo, a Christian Democrat, was elected and became the country's first civilian president in sixteen years. To the dismay of many human rights activists and families of victims, Cerezo granted an amnesty to members of the army that gave them immunity from prosecution for former human rights abuses.

Guatemala, Post-1963 267

FIGURE 21.2. Comalapa. Forensic anthropologists exhume the remains inside a mass grave at a former Guatemalan military base near Comalapa, Guatemala, September 7, 2003. The Guatemalan military employed a scorched earth strategy aimed at eliminating a variety of Marxist insurgencies during the 1960s, 1970s, and 1980s. The strategy targeted the country's majority but politically and economically marginalized Mayan Indian population – the very citizens who were thought to enable the small Cuba-inspired and trained guerrilla bands. Reproduced with permission from Victor J. Blue

Contrary to what is often assumed, Guatemala's counterinsurgency was at its dirtiest precisely when American influence was at its lowest point since the overthrow of Árbenz in 1954. This fact does not free the United States from any culpability in Guatemala's tragic internal war and repression. If anything, it reinforces the simple but often overlooked reality that local client governments and militaries do not necessarily hold the same objectives as U.S. policymakers. This misalignment of aims has proven to be one of the major obstacles in U.S. counterinsurgency experience since the middle of the twentieth century. In this case, the Guatemalan state adopted a "by any means necessary" approach to winning the war, one that went far beyond what Washington believed appropriate.

As a result, the hallmark of U.S. action in Guatemala became almost the opposite of what it had been in the 1950s. The United States adopted a low-impact counterinsurgency support strategy, which had an analogue in the counter-foco operations against Cuban-style revolutions across Latin America. This approach became a central feature of U.S. counterinsurgency doctrine after Vietnam and until the turn of the century, and the lessons of Guatemala influenced the character of subsequent counterinsurgency interventions. But perhaps most important, the United States learned that low-impact involvement does not always work. Guatemala's thirty-year war (that ended with a negotiated agreement in 1996) was one of the longest by far in the Western Hemisphere's modern history, and the fact that it ultimately averted a communist overthrow may have come more by the Guatemalan government's brutality and the eventual collapse of global communism than it did by American efforts.

22

Cuba, Post-1963

To our sister republics south of our border, we offer a special pledge – to convert our good words into good deeds – in a new alliance for progress – to assist free men and free governments in casting off the chains of poverty. But this peaceful revolution of hope cannot become the prey of hostile powers. Let all our neighbors know that we shall join with them to oppose aggression or subversion anywhere in the Americas. And let every other power know that this Hemisphere intends to remain the master of its own house.
– President John F. Kennedy's Inaugural Address, January 20, 1961[1]

Revolution is the order of the day *here and now*.
– Régis Debray, French intellectual who joined Che's band in Bolivia[2]

[Latin America] reminds me of an active volcano.
– Soviet Premier Nikita Khrushchev, 1960[3]

By the mid-1960s, Cuba had consolidated its communist regime in Havana, and Cuba-inspired *foco* insurrections had emerged across the region, most extensively in the Dominican Republic, Venezuela, and Guatemala. While Moscow was somewhat hesitant about exporting armed revolution lest it provoke Washington in its own backyard, Havana was bent on creating, as Che Guevara wrote in 1967, "many Vietnams" in the Americas.[4]

During these same years, Washington was adamant that there could not be "another Cuba" in Latin America. After watching the utter debacle of the Bay of Pigs and Guatemala's gradual descent into a crisis of governance and outright war, the Kennedy administration reasoned that one way to stem communism in Latin America was to avoid large-scale intervention and improbable military ventures. More effective, they thought, would be to deal instead with the root causes of inequity and injustice that led people in places like Cuba to turn to Marxist revolution in the first place. In the president's oft-quoted view, "Those who make peaceful revolution impossible make violent revolution inevitable."[5]

The hallmark of Kennedy's "peaceful revolution" strategy was the Alliance for Progress, a planned ten-year program of massive economic investment and assistance to promote sorely needed political, social, and economic reform in the region. The idea was that the funds would help the Latin Americans implement better tax schemes, promote massive land reform efforts, and give the majority poor and disenfranchised a stake in these reformist governments. For Kennedy, the Alliance would allow "us again to transform the [hemisphere] into a vast crucible of revolutionary ideas and efforts."[6]

This was the "carrot" side of the Alliance's approach. But it was not the only side. Deeply influenced by the unfolding efforts to counter communist insurgency in Southeast Asia, Kennedy ordered U.S. civilian and military officials to embark on a significant effort to train Latin American military and police forces so that they could defend American allies from communist subversion. The administration increased military aid to Latin America – by 1963, almost 50 percent over the assistance levels of the Eisenhower years. Starting in 1961, the Kennedy administration also placed Special Forces Groups (SFGs) in vulnerable Latin American countries such as Guatemala and Colombia. Some of these groups, such as the 8th SFG led by Colonel B. J. Pinkerton, had previously conducted clandestine operations in Laos.

The United States also began training Latin American military officers and soldiers at U.S. institutions, such as the School of the Americas in the Panama Canal Zone. Here they were instructed in organizational command, counterinsurgency tactics, covert and psychological operations, military intelligence, and interrogation techniques.[7] Between 1962 and 1970 roughly 22,000 military men were trained in such schools – 9,000 in 1962 alone.[8] Another 100,000 police officers were given American training in their home countries. Secretary of Defense Robert A. McNamara announced that U.S.-trained Latin American military leaders had an obligation to maintain "internal security" and to combat "domestic subversion."

Washington also established Military Assistance Advisory Groups (MAAGS) to be stationed throughout the region. Then if a Latin American country came to be considered "hot," SFGs were dispatched to help with all sorts of counterinsurgency work: civil affairs, psychological operations, intelligence, and interrogation. These deployments of combat-seasoned Green Berets and embassy-based MAAGS were often almost identical to the counterinsurgency models being tested at the same time in Vietnam.

It was perhaps inevitable that Cuba would be at the center of this dramatic scaling up of low-impact counterinsurgency. A since declassified "secret" U.S. government intelligence report published in 1961 highlighted the perception of Cuba's key role as an incubator for revolution in the region:

> Castro's Cuba has become to much of the Latin American community a living example of the radical breakup of traditional social and economic patterns. For many of these who seek to upset the *status quo* in their own countries Havana has developed into the mecca of revolutionary inspiration and conspiracy.... Castro's shadow looms large because social and economic conditions throughout Latin America invite opposition to ruling authority and encourage agitation for radical change.[9]

Indeed, by 1962 Cuba had become the primary source of manpower and resources for igniting insurgencies throughout the Western Hemisphere. And Che Guevara was at the helm. Ironically, Guevara's first "client" for the export of armed revolution was not in Latin America but Africa. In late April 1965, Che and a group of Afro-Caribbean Cubans arrived on the shores of Congo's Lake Tanganyika to bolster the political heirs of the murdered Congolese nationalist Patrice Lumumba. Yet almost from the outset, Guevara's mission fared miserably. For one, the Africans were not thrilled about an outsider lecturing them about how to start a revolution. And Guevara found the Congolese rebels led by Laurent Kabila to be undisciplined and thus unable to defeat the European mercenaries supporting the other side.[10] He wrote in his post-Congo report to Fidel:

> The soldiers are of peasant stock and completely raw, for whom the main attraction is to have a rifle and a uniform, sometimes even shoes and a certain authority in the area. Corrupted by inactivity and the habit of ordering peasants around, saturated with fetishistic notions about death and the enemy, devoid of any coherent political education, they consequently lack revolutionary awareness or any forward-looking perspective beyond the traditional horizon of their tribal territory. Lazy and undisciplined, they are without any spirit of combat or self-sacrifice.[11]

The "African safari" proved a complete disaster as Che and his African hosts wound up mistrusting and eventually loathing each other. Che returned to Cuba and set his eyes on Latin America, the region that had always been on the forefront of his revolutionary agenda. Before long Che had selected his next target country: landlocked and impoverished Bolivia. In many ways, Bolivia was a curious choice for the mission; the country had already witnessed a leftist in revolution in 1952, and many grievances, such as land distribution, had already been at least partially addressed. Nonetheless, Che and his fellows hoped that they could spark a revolt there and then turn their sights on Che's native Argentina.

A secret training camp was set up in Cuba that allowed both Cubans and their Bolivian "comrades" to prepare intensively for the foco. In November 1966, Guevara traveled to La Paz on false documents via Moscow, Prague, Madrid, Brazil, and Uruguay. He was clean-shaven and partially bald, disguised as a Uruguayan businessman. He soon realized that almost nothing had been done to prepare his proposed clandestine base camp.[12] Within days, the *guerrilleros* descended from the Andean high plains down to the country's sweltering *chaco* region to the east, where they would launch the foco uprising. Che now had an "army" of a few dozen men, principally Cubans and Bolivians but also a few Peruvians and other foreigners.

The decision to locate the foco strategy in southeastern Bolivia was another unusual and ultimately fateful decision. Far from the tin mines and the legions of poorly paid miners living high up in the soaring Andes who could have possibly served as Che's collaborating population, the base camp in the lightly populated and inhospitable region made it difficult to win over any significant civilian support. Making matters worse, the rural *campesinos* in the region sometimes called the insurgents *gringos* because of their peculiar speech and thick beards.

In February 1967, Che led the band's first expedition. They hacked away at thick jungle and traversed roaring rivers, conditions that made the Sierra Maestra seem like summer camp in comparison. The revolutionaries had no accurate maps; morale dropped quickly. A month later, Che's men ambushed an army patrol, killing several soldiers and capturing vital weapons and supplies. Yet by taking on the army the rebels revealed their position to spotter planes and helicopters. The *foquistas'* fate had been sealed. The Bolivian army doggedly pursued the Cubans deeper and deeper into the jungle. Bolivian strongman René Barrientos had seized upon evidence located at the rebels' camp to condemn them as agents for "Castro Communism" and called upon the patriotic sentiment of his fellow citizens to repel the invaders. Che's increasingly erratic and moody behavior served to diminish the guerrillas' faith in their once idolized leader. The guerrilla ranks dwindled through capture and death in the merciless terrain. In April, Che summarized the dire outlook:

[Our] isolation appears to be complete, sickness has undermined the health of some comrades, forcing us to divide forces, which has greatly diminished our effectiveness.... The peasant base has not yet been developed although it appears through planned terror we can neutralize some of them; support will come later. Not one [Bolivian] enlistment has been obtained.[13]

By August with the beleaguered Che near death, the army continued to press forward. Though it was a minute conflict in the totality of the Cold War, Bolivia quickly became a showdown between Cuban-led focos and U.S. counterinsurgency forces. With the presence of Che's band now confirmed, Barrientos requested the assistance of a U.S. Special Forces Mobile Training Team.

Sixteen Green Berets under Major Robert "Pappy" Shelton arrived in eastern Bolivia in April 1967. The son of a Tennessee dirt farmer, Shelton supervised the training of 400 Bolivian conscripts tasked to take down the focos. The Green Beret team established its operation at an abandoned sugar plantation and mill outside the small town of La Esperanza, approximately fifty miles north of the major provincial city of Santa Cruz. As in many of the United States' counterinsurgency efforts at the time, Shelton's men conducted "civic action," including building a school for the local community. One Green Beret sergeant involved in the operation described well the difference between their mission and what Che hoped to achieve: "He [Guevara] believed in his way, and we believe in our way. We ain't buyin' communism. In the United States and these other countries, it ain't movin' in ... not if I can help it."[14]

The Green Beret team confronted an enormous challenge in training its Bolivian counterparts. In the decade since the country's leftist revolution in 1952, the state had almost abolished the armed forces. A U.S. Southern Command report in May 1967 revealed the severe concerns that U.S. military planners had about the Bolivian forces, noting that "the recent outbreak of guerrilla activity ... has pointed up the serious deficiencies in the [Bolivian] armed forces organization, logistics, leadership, and intelligence capabilities and has raised the question of whether the military has the capability to counter even a small guerrilla movement."[15]

In a reflection of how seriously the Johnson administration was taking the Bolivia threat, a month later National Security Advisor Walt Rostow met with representatives from the CIA, State Department, and Defense Department to discuss the "whole guerrilla problem in Latin America." Rostow reported to President Johnson that he had made a list of seven countries, in order of the "degree of urgency" for a U.S. response. He put Bolivia at the top of the list "more because of the fragility of the political situation and the weakness of the armed forces than the size and effectiveness of the guerrilla movement."[16] But despite Washington's skepticism, the Green Berets had the Bolivian Ranger forces ready to deploy by September.

The CIA also jumped into the action, quickly rounding up operatives to head to Bolivia, including a young Cuban-American paramilitary operative named Félix Rodríguez. Since 1963, Rodríguez had run a communications unit made up of CIA-funded anti-Castro commandos based in Nicaragua. The group had over 300 members in Nicaragua, Costa Rica, and Miami, and had at its disposal two 250-foot "mother ships," two 50-foot fast boats, as well as a C-47 transport plane, several Cessnas, and a Beaver floatplane. Rodríguez subsequently revealed the logic behind the aggressive effort to check Che once and for all in Bolivia: "[The CIA] feared [what might happen if] Che grabbed Bolivia.... With a secure Cuban base there, they could easily expand the revolution to important countries like Brazil, Argentina ..."[17]

For its part, the Bolivian army continued to capture sensitive documents in its hunt for the guerrillas. They discovered scores of weapons, medical supplies, and documents that detailed the list of contacts in Bolivia, deciphered radio messages from Havana, codes, and even a cigar butt. At the end of August, Guevara suffered a major blow when ten guerrillas in his band were ambushed by an army patrol.[18] Sensing desperation within the rebel ranks, the Bolivian government grew confident, publicly announcing that Che would soon be captured.

In late September, the U.S.-trained 2nd Ranger Battalion, part of Bolivia's 8th Division, entered active duty to hunt down the guerrillas. At almost the same time, Che and his few remaining guerrillas set out for the remote town of La Higuera. Ironically for the leader who wrote a veritable textbook on guerrilla warfare, Che's men broke almost every major rule of insurgency strategy. For example, the exhausted and hungry men walked on roads instead of keeping to the forests.[19]

In early October, the Rangers surrounded Che's men at La Higuera and took the wounded Che captive. Felix Rodríguez soon arrived by helicopter and described the state of the Argentine-Cuban revolutionary: "He was a mess.... Hair matted, clothes ragged and torn." Despite Rodríguez's alleged effort to take Guevara alive, on October 9 at the age of thirty-nine, Che was executed by a Bolivian army sergeant eager to avenge the deaths of some of his fellow soldiers in the pursuit.

It took a full two days for Washington to learn of Che's capture and execution. Walt Rostow sent a memo to President Johnson indicating that

Cuba, Post-1963

FIGURE 22.1. Ernesto "Che" Guevara, the Marxist revolutionary, led a guerrilla insurgency in Bolivia. Bolivian officials said this crude photo, showing Guevara with an automatic rifle on September 22, 1967, in Bolivia while leading a band of guerrillas, was one of many similar pictures captured. Guevara hoped that his small band of guerrillas could replicate the stunning success of the Cuban revolutionaries a decade earlier. Reproduced with permission from Associated Press, 6709221359

"this morning we are about 99% sure that 'Che' Guevara is dead." Rostow added that Che's death had three significant implications:

It marks the passing of another of the aggressive, romantic revolutionaries like [Indonesia's] Sukarno, [Ghana's] Nkrumah, [Algeria's] Ben Bella – and reinforces this trend.... In the Latin American context, it will have a strong impact in discouraging would-be guerrillas.... [And] it shows the soundness of our "preventive medicine" assistance to countries facing incipient insurgency – it was the Bolivian 2nd Ranger Battalion, trained by our Green Berets from June [sic]– September of this year, that cornered and got him.[20]

During an interagency policy meeting the next day, U.S. officials concluded that the events in Bolivia represented a serious setback to "Castro's theory and practice of promoting guerrilla warfare in this hemisphere." In Washington's estimation, in Latin America it was counterinsurgency one, foco zero.

However, the officials failed to appreciate the extent to which Che's defeat was the result of the focos' own blunders. Bolivia was in so many ways unripe for revolution. Most critically, the rural population had no desire to be led by a gang of strongly accented foreigners. The group, moreover, had neglected to follow some of the central tenets of foco doctrine.

Interestingly, on October 21, 1967, twelve days after Che's death, an estimated 55,000 Americans stood in silence at the Lincoln Memorial in Washington. At the same time, in an indication of how Cuban-style focos had fallen out of favor in both Soviet and Chinese communist realms, news of Guevara's death drew cool reactions from Moscow and Beijing. Official Soviet channels deplored his taste for "adventurism." The Chinese press slammed the Argentine revolutionary for allowing the gun to control the party and not the other way around.[21]

In the lead-up to Guevara's capture, one burning question in American policy circles was whether the results could be more positive than those emerging from Vietnam at the same time. As it turned out, the Special Forces' deployment to Bolivia was a textbook example of American counterinsurgency strategy paying enormous dividends: U.S. soldiers trained the Bolivians in a very short amount of time and these native soldiers soon took care of the guerrilla problem by annihilating Che's band.

However, this new American counterinsurgency strategy brought its own problems. Whatever its counterinsurgent efficacy might have been, U.S. training and materiel often served to bolster abusive Latin American militaries and governments. Today, whether the U.S. approach to Latin America after the mid-1960s made bad situations better or worse is an open debate, but there is no question that it became irrevocably associated with militaries that often used "internal security" as an excuse to terrorize civilian populations and stifle the very type of reform that Kennedy was so eager to see take root.

23

Intermezzo

Che Guevara and Guerrilla Warfare

The unexpected ease with which the Cuban revolutionaries overthrew Batista led them to conclude that the same thing should and could be done in other countries in Latin America. Castro told the crowds gathered at a rally in Havana in 1959 that the time had come to liberate the hemisphere:

> How much America and the peoples of our hemisphere need a revolution like the one that has taken place in Cuba! How much America needs an example like this in all its nations. How much it needs for the millionaires who have become rich by stealing the people's money to lose everything they have stolen. How much America needs for the war criminals in the countries of our hemisphere to be shot.[1]

Che, in particular, became a strong proponent for exporting armed revolution to other parts of the hemisphere. Influenced by Mao's writings from three decades earlier, he and fellow Cuban leaders believed that other revolutionaries could simply follow a straightforward yet crucial textbook that could teach them how to become successful revolutionaries. In fact, by 1960 Che had authored a tome entitled *Guerrilla Warfare* that became requisite reading for budding revolutionaries across the hemisphere.[2]

Che believed that "a hard core of thirty to fifty men [was] enough to initiate armed revolution in any Latin American country." Based on the experience in Cuba, he highlighted three strategies for a successful revolutionary war. First, Che contended that this small band of committed fighters could take revolution into their own hands, providing the spark for mass revolt rather than waiting for another precipitating event to occur. He also posited that popular forces could win against a regular army. Guerrilla warfare, waged with the support of civilians, could bring a conventional army to its knees by wearing down its ability and its resolve to fight. Third, he maintained that in the Latin American context, the best place to "center" subversive activity was in the countryside, where, due to often horrible working conditions and a skewed distribution of land, "class contradictions are at their most violent."[3] These three tenets constituted the heart of *foco* theory.[4]

In a 1959 article, Guevara wrote, "The guerrilla is fundamentally ... an agrarian revolutionary. He interprets the desires of the great peasant masses to be owners of land, owners of their own means of production, of their livestock, of all that for which they have fought for years, for that which constitutes their life and will also be their cemetery."[5] If Mao's guerrilla strategies appeared to have been copied from Sun Tzu, Che's guerrilla manifesto reads like a Latin American facsimile of Mao's work. This is not surprising given that Che was an avid student of his Chinese counterpart. Moreover, Mao and Che both succeeded with the strategy; there did not appear to be much reason to tinker with the formula. Although Che took his ideas of guerrilla warfare from Mao, he attempted to draw distinctive Latin American conclusions from his experience in the Cuban Revolution – in his own words, to modify the "old dogmas" – for his own manual.[6]

Che's guerrilla recipe also unwittingly revealed a whimsical side of life as a foco guerrilla. In one section he says, "Very important in the life of a fighter are cigars, cigarettes, or pipe tobacco, for the smoke that can be enjoyed during moments of rest is a great boon to the solitary soldier. A pipe is best, for it allows the fullest use, in times of shortages, of the tobacco of cigarettes and cigar butts."[7][8]

During the early 1960s, Che was also very influential in arguing *why* such armed revolutions were necessary. His was essentially a Marxist interpretation of how Latin America's chronic underdevelopment and instability had been caused by rapacious U.S. imperialists. In the seminal *Second Declaration of Havana* in 1962, Che wrote: "In this continent of semi-colonies about four persons per minute die of hunger, curable illness or premature old age; five and a half thousand a day, two million a year.... A holocaust of lives which in fifteen years has caused twice the number of deaths produced by the First World War, and it still continues. Meanwhile from Latin America a continuous torrent of money flows to the United States, some four thousand dollars a minute, five million a day, two billion a year.... For each thousand dollars that leaves us there remains a corpse that is the price of what is called imperialism."[9]

Che dismissed social reform through the ballot box as hopelessly naive: Washington and its corporate cronies would never allow real reform to take hold. One only had to look to Árbenz's experience in Guatemala to realize that the *yanquis* would not tolerate an outcome that did not ensure their military and economic control of the region. The only effective path to social justice and equality, then, was violent revolution.

In hindsight, we now know that foco warfare was a relatively short-lived and unsuccessful footnote in the history of war. One of Che's fundamental miscalculations was a failure to ascribe the stunning success of the Cuban revolt to factors largely exclusive to Cuba. The *barbudos* were fighting against a widely hated and illegitimate tyrant in Batista, which made it infinitely easier to win over the support of both rural and urban populations. In other countries in Latin America where Cuba-style focos were attempted, the governments in power were at least sometimes partially democratic and legitimate.

Nonetheless, given the level of repression in Latin America – the very "fuel" of foco – it is surprising that almost all of the insurgencies in these countries failed, largely because of the failure of the population to rise up with the rebels in a general insurrection, as had taken place in Cuba. The miscalculations seem especially stark because the Cuban revolutionaries did realize that their victory had come far faster and far easier than the leftist takeovers in China and the Soviet Union. That its proponents expected Latin America to go the way of Cuba, and not of these other two examples, demonstrates how far removed foco theory was from the particular social, economic, and nationalistic contexts of different Latin American countries.

Another dimension in which foco theory erred was in its overestimation of the importance of the countryside. Much of the success of later leftist revolutions in Latin America came when the insurgents threatened major metropolitan areas, as when the Sandinistas seized León and Managua in Nicaragua, or when the Farabundo Martí National Liberation Front (FMLN) took positions in the mountains around San Salvador in the summer of 1983. Granted, foco did acknowledge the crucial role of urban universities as hotbeds of antiregime sentiment that could then be channeled to the broader society. Indeed, *foquistas* expected that many newly sensitized university students would flee the cities for the hills and mountains to start revolutions. Often, as in the early stages of the Sandinista insurgency in Nicaragua and throughout the Salvadoran revolution, when these vanguard intellectuals did head for the countryside, the result was often dismal failure and death at the hands of counterinsurgency forces.[10]

24

Carter, Reagan, and the Sandinista Revolution in Nicaragua, 1979–1990

> If any nation, whatever its political system, deprives its people of basic human rights, that fact will help shape our own people's attitude toward that nation's repressive government.... [W]e should use our tremendous influence to increase freedom, particularly in those countries that depend upon us for their very survival.
> – President Jimmy Carter during the 1978 presidential campaign[1]

In the early morning of January 10, 1978, Pedro Joaquín Chamorro, a prominent Nicaraguan political figure and head of the opposition newspaper *La Prensa*, was driving in Managua when a green Toyota truck suddenly swerved in front of him. Two men leaped out of the truck and fired shotgun blasts at Chamorro's vehicle, then jumped into a waiting car and sped away. Chamorro was rushed to a nearby hospital but died on the way. Nicaragua's strongman, Anastasio "Tachito" Somoza, the second son of the Somoza who killed the nationalist guerrilla Sandino and seized power in the early 1930s, claimed that the assassination had been perpetrated by opposition members themselves to implicate the increasingly despised regime.

Few Nicaraguans believed this version of the story. Instead, they blamed Somoza for the extrajudicial killing, and their eagerness to get rid of the dynastic dictatorship increased significantly. In the aftermath of Chamorro's public funeral, youth in cities across the country tossed homemade bombs at military jeeps and shot at National Guard posts with hunting rifles. In their first coordinated anti-Somoza move, business leaders called a national strike demanding that Chamorro's killers be found and tried.[2] Chamorro's death became the spark for the conflagration that sealed Somoza's dramatic downfall and initiated a Marxist revolution in Nicaragua.

The Nicaraguan insurrection is an especially salient episode in our of study of insurgencies and counterinsurgencies in Latin America during the Cold War since it is the only example of a successful *foco* revolution after the pioneering one in Cuba in 1959. As we have seen, many focos were attempted during the 1960s and 1970s, from Guatemala to Venezuela and down to Bolivia and Argentina, but almost all failed at the hands of counterinsurgent forces, often trained and funded by Washington. Despite this trend, the Sandinistas took inspiration from the Cuban foco thesis that a small group of highly dedicated insurgents could spark a triumphant national revolution. Given this historical context, the revolution was deeply influential for Marxist guerrillas operating in the jungles and mountains across the region – most notably in El Salvador and Guatemala – who witnessed the Sandinistas' rapid and total victory over what was long believed to be an impregnable Somoza regime.

The case of Nicaragua is equally salient for the American experience in irregular wars during this era. The searing experience of Vietnam had left a bitter taste in the mouths of U.S. policymakers, politicians, and the military. Few wanted to repeat the mistakes that had led to an outcome that was at once described as a stalemate, a betrayal, and an ignominious defeat. Indeed, the absence of a clear-cut victory in Vietnam dramatically reduced the U.S. establishment's appetite for irregular wars in faraway locales.[3]

For the U.S. military in particular, the lesson learned from Vietnam was to have no more Vietnams. Rather, a smaller military footprint would help ensure that the United States did not assume too much of the responsibility for winning a war. The problem, however, was that Marxist guerrillas in Nicaragua, El Salvador, and elsewhere in Central America were not going to sit out their moment to create "another Cuba" or "another Vietnam" simply to suit Washington's strategic interests.

President Jimmy Carter came into office believing that the best way to deal with the dilemma of armed revolution in Central America was to stop backing the pro-American rightist dictators whose tyranny and injustices led citizens to revolt in the first place. Instead, the United States would now be a vocal champion of human rights around the globe, even if it meant criticizing some of its reliable allies (read, tyrants) in Cold War flashpoint states. The new president urged Americans to rid themselves of their historically "inordinate fear of Communism which once led us to embrace any dictator who joined us in that fear."[4] Yet this conciliatory tone changed somewhat after the Sandinistas installed an avowedly Marxist government in Managua.

While it did not jettison its human rights agenda, the Carter administration did become more "hawkish," reinforcing the idea that the United States would continue to use military force to disrupt the leftist revolutions that threatened America's strategic interests.[5] Just as "no more Cubas" became the Kennedy administration's mantra after Castro's victory in 1959, the idea that there should be "no more Nicaraguas" drove the Carter and subsequently the Reagan administrations to disrupt revolutions in Central America in the late 1970s and 1980s. At the same time, the "no more Vietnams" injunction almost guaranteed that intervention in these cases, whether military or civilian, would be substantially different from many of the dirty wars that had come before.

There was one major difference in the Nicaragua case: in contrast to both Washington's usual counterinsurgent stance against Latin American revolutionary movements and its active engagement in neighboring El Salvador, the Carter and Reagan administrations supported an insurgent force known as *la contrarevolución* (more commonly, the contras) against the established government in Managua. It was a marked role reversal for the United States, but, interestingly, the approach taken in supporting the opposition forces in Nicaragua proved very similar to that taken *against* opposition forces in El Salvador during the same period.

SANDINO LIVES ON

Following Sandino's execution in February 1934, the rebel's mythical and ideological influence remained strong in Nicaragua. His revolutionary legacy became embodied in the idea of *sandinismo*, a combination of nationalism, popular power, anti-imperialism, and principles of radical social change along Marxist lines.[6] Middle-class Nicaraguan university students and other intellectuals gave these ideas political expression when they founded the Frente Sandinista de Liberación Nacional (FSLN) in 1961.

The Sandinistas, as they were called, operated primarily as a guerrilla vanguard, though their forces were only a fraction the size of their counterparts in Guatemala. They received backing from Fidel Castro following the 1959 revolution and Havana's decision to support foco insurgencies across the region, and were led by figures such as Tomás Borge and Carlos Fonseca. The Sandinistas aspired to finish the rebellion their beloved martyr had attempted back in the late 1920s and early 1930s. However, the Somozas' security forces were strong, and few observers gave the Sandinistas any chance of overthrowing the dictatorship. After the initial foco had faltered, Borge and Fonseca led the Sandinistas back to the mountains to establish a peasant network, an effort that would require much more time to bear fruit.

U.S. officials were not very concerned when the Nicaraguan guerrillas first appeared. In 1964, the CIA reported that the FSLN was a "Cuban-supported and Communist-infiltrated subversive group" but was not "a serious threat to the [Nicaraguan] government."[7] At this point Washington was far more concerned about Guatemala "going red." In fact, despite Washington's heavy hand in Nicaraguan affairs after the Sandino chase four decades earlier, only a few dozen American military advisers served in Nicaragua during the 1960s, while more than a thousand did so in neighboring Guatemala. The United States did provide roughly 13 percent of Somoza's annual defense budget, an amount that helped to support the regime but never proved vital to its survival.

The Somoza regime and successive Washington administrations maintained strong ties in the first decades of the Cold War. Luis Somoza, the eldest son of the Somoza dynasty's founder, ruled the country from 1957 to 1967 on a strongly pro-American platform. He realized that, at that time, American support for his regime was critical to his ability to maintain his grip on power. The same view informed the government of Luis's younger brother, "Tachito," who had himself elected president in 1967. Notably, the Somozas required all of the National Guard officers to spend one year training and studying at the U.S.-run School of the Americas in the Panama Canal Zone. In the 1950s and 1960s, this military school trained more officers from Nicaragua than from any other country in Latin America.

Forced back into the countryside after the first foco collapsed, the Sandinistas found it difficult to stay alive, much less to organize a coherent revolution. For one, Somoza's notorious National Guard (or Guardia) continued to hound the weakened rebels in the countryside, forcing them to relocate and recuperate each time they began to develop a foothold in one region. For another, the well-educated, urban Sandinista leaders perpetually struggled with their inability to connect with the poor and uneducated rural *campesinos* (farmers), who were supposed to serve as the "masses" for the revolt. By the early 1970s, all signs indicated that the Sandinistas would soon join the ranks of so many other failed foco insurgencies. But a series of breaks during the 1970s played into the Sandinistas' hands. The first event, a devastating earthquake that hit Managua in late

December 1972, raised many Nicaraguans' ire against the younger Somoza, as they watched his cronies steal much of the relief aid. The Sandinistas deftly used the earthquake to reinforce their contention that Somoza was an immoral and venal leader, one willing to allow his countrymen to suffer while he became richer and richer.

On its own, this was not enough to give the Sandinistas the upper hand; even by 1977, they were not nearly in a position to threaten Somoza's rule. Bitter factional disputes within the group hindered its ability to maximize its military and political prowess. Moreover, the Sandinistas did not actually control any territory at this point; it had no "zones of liberation" within which to train guerrillas and sensitize the local population. However, the second (grimly) fortuitous event, Chamorro's assassination, helped change that as more disgusted citizens joined the guerrilla ranks. Desperate to maintain control, Somoza ordered brutal attacks by Guardia troops in poor, urban barrios, executing young men with submachine guns at point-blank range.[8] At the same time that the Sandinistas were resurrecting themselves, a broad coalition of anti-Somoza political parties, unions, and social organizations created the Broad Opposition Front (FAO). The FAO's creation reinforced the reality that a critical mass of Nicaraguan society had turned against the hated regime.

"A REVOLUTION WITHOUT FRONTIERS"

On August 22, 1978, two dozen Sandinista commandos led by commander Edén Pastora seized the Nicaraguan National Palace where the Congress was in full session. For two days the commandos held the entire legislature hostage while Pastora – known by his guerrilla nom de guerre, "Comandante Cero" – negotiated with the despised Somoza. Fearing the death of several of his relatives, Somoza conceded to Pastora's demands, which included a $500,000 ransom and the release of fifty-eight political prisoners, including Tomás Borge. Somoza also granted Pastora's commandos safe passage out of the country, with most heading to Cuba. The raid's success sparked an uprising against the regime in the slums around Managua, which Somoza attempted to quell using his U.S.-supplied air force.[9] More important, however, the bold move showed the Nicaraguan people, Somoza, and officials in Washington that the Sandinistas were a formidable guerrilla outfit – one capable of dramatic and successful operations.

Shortly after seizing the palace, the Sandinistas issued their long-awaited call to national insurrection on Nicaragua's airwaves and throughout national newspapers, proclaiming, "A free fatherland or death!"[10] In September, the Sandinistas carried out a major military offensive in the style of the Cuban *barbudos* twenty years earlier. The guerrillas attacked Guardia garrisons in Managua, and the mountain cities of Estelí and Chinandega, among other targets. The Guardia hit back hard, but their actions often served to alienate the civilian population, leading them to shift their allegiance to the opposition.[11] Demonstrating the growing depth of their regional support, both the non-Marxist Panamanian and Venezuelan governments began providing arms and training to the Sandinista insurgents.

Somoza's popularity inside and out of Nicaragua continued to deteriorate. The influential Catholic Church increasingly opposed Somoza's rule. Many priests throughout rural Nicaragua had witnessed the Guardia's "institutional violence" firsthand; they were now eager to see him overthrown and more than a few men of the cloth joined the rebel forces. A visiting U.S. congressional delegation concluded that Somoza was the "Idi Amin" of Latin America.[12] Once a loyal "S.O.B." to Washington, Somoza was now an embarrassing liability for Carter's progressive vision of the region.

The Carter administration remained torn over what to do about Nicaragua. Since taking office in January 1977, President Carter had elevated human rights to a "fundamental tenet of our foreign policy."[13] To complicate matters further, U.S. ambassador to Nicaragua Lawrence Pezzullo noted in a memo that the FSLN-led revolution was "an authentic Nicaraguan phenomenon" and "a pluralistic movement, led by people with a wide range of backgrounds."[14] At the same time, Carter and his advisers were terrified that Nicaragua could turn into another Cuba.

The Carter White House kept holding out for a compromise approach that would depose Somoza and replace him with someone more moderate than the Sandinista leadership. But after a majority of Nicaraguans had turned against the regime, the Carter administration cut off military aid in January 1978 and imposed sanctions in February 1979. It then moved to a more neutral position, which helped the Sandinistas by further delegitimizing Somoza's teetering regime.

Carter was sincere in his belief that the United States needed to resist the temptation to become too involved in Nicaragua's unfolding revolution. He had earlier expressed hope "that our days of unilateral intervention such as occurred in Vietnam, Cambodia, and the Dominican Republic are over."[15] Now, the test case was Nicaragua; a country located squarely in America's "backyard" where Washington had historically been quick to act in interventionist and controlling ways that it would not so readily consider in other parts of the world. Yet, in his desire to deal with the Nicaragua dilemma in a new way, Carter failed to take into full account two perhaps paradoxical realities. First, while American disengagement might have been morally and pragmatically persuasive, it did not ensure a strategic success for American interests. Second, given America's deep involvement in Nicaraguan affairs, the new human rights approach was itself a potent form of intervention.[16]

In May 1979, the Sandinistas launched a "final offensive" – or "hour of the overthrow," to use the phrase of its clandestine radio broadcast. It proved a tremendous success.[17] FSLN bands hit Guardia garrisons throughout the country. They also called for a general strike that crippled the country's economy. The rebels established their own provisional capital in the provincial city of León; they even threatened to take Managua, though two weeks of fighting pushed them back to the nearby city of Masaya. This represented a remarkable turn of fortune for the Sandinistas, given that the National Guard had virtually wiped them out less than a decade before.

Interestingly, not all of the guerrilla attacks against the Guardia were actually perpetrated by the Sandinistas. Instead, hatred of Somoza and the Guardia at times led to spontaneous revolts. These impromptu insurrections reinforced the notion that the opposition to Somoza was much greater and more widespread than the Sandinista revolution. Even significant parts of the Nicaraguan business class had turned against Somoza. And, as in the general insurrection that helped oust Batista in Cuba two decades earlier, it is highly unlikely that the Sandinistas would have seized power had a strong majority of Nicaraguans not opposed the regime.

Remarkably, at the time, the CIA was still informing U.S. policymakers that the Sandinistas would not be able to defeat Somoza's forces. Dennis P. McAuliffe, the top officer at the U.S. Southern Command in Panama, told a congressional committee that Sandinista operations were solely "hit and run" attacks and "not very significant."[18] By July, Somoza had fled the country and a new five-member Provisional Junta of National Reconciliation, which included both Sandinista and non-Sandinista opposition figures, had been established. The entering regime enjoyed almost universal support within Nicaragua, as well as from the international community.

The Carter administration attempted to pressure the opposition to allow more non-Sandinistas into the junta, but U.S. officials had lost considerable credibility by taking so long to withdraw their support for Somoza. Washington still held enormous *power* vis-à-vis Nicaragua, but its ability to *influence* events in the Central American country had ebbed considerably. Before long, the Sandinistas had pushed out the more moderate members of the junta and consolidated their Cuba-inspired rule over Nicaragua, making themselves, one contemporary noted, "the real winners of the revolution."[19]

Over the ensuing years, two brothers, Daniel and Humberto Ortega, became the public leaders of the Sandinista movement, much as Fidel Castro and his younger brother Raúl had done in Cuba. Sons of a Managua businessman who served as one of Augusto Sandino's original guerrillas, the Ortegas had headed a Sandinista faction known as the Terceristas, which had become the dominant revolutionary group both militarily and politically in 1978. Daniel consolidated his position as the head of the new revolutionary government while Humberto became the minister of defense.

At the same time, despite its continued enthusiastic support in public settings for human rights, the Carter administration was increasingly concerned about the threat of a communist advance in Nicaragua via the Sandinistas. Within days of the July 1979 victory, senior American intelligence officials predicted that "the hard-core Marxists in the regime will quickly begin trying to neutralize the influence of the junta's more moderate members and seize control."[20] That year, Carter was shown high-altitude photographs and other intelligence that confirmed that the Sandinistas were sending arms shipments to El Salvador.

In 1979, Washington provided the fledgling government almost $25 million in emergency relief and recovery aid, including food and medical supplies, in an effort to influence the Sandinistas through development assistance. By January 1981, when the Carter team was leaving office, direct U.S. assistance to Managua reached $118 million; yet the effort did not work.[21] Rather, the FSLN's rhetoric of calling for a "revolution without frontiers" shocked officials already worried that the Sandinista regime was showing its true radical colors.

In early 1980, President Carter signed a classified intelligence "finding" that authorized the CIA to promote "democratic elements" in Nicaragua. This support took the form of money funneled to opposition parties to pay for expenses and propaganda. No money was provided for armed actions.[22] Nonetheless, Carter's finding served to move the United States away from its hands-off approach to dealing with revolutionary change in Nicaragua. Thus, even before the conservative Ronald Reagan took office, Jimmy Carter had become a relative hawk on Nicaragua.

Behind the scenes, a consensus was beginning to emerge among American policymakers and politicians that Managua was actively supporting the embryonic insurgency in El Salvador, the Farabundo Martí National Liberation Front (FMLN). We now know that this assessment was correct; Sandinista commanders began discussions early on about arming their Marxist *compañeros* in Guatemala and most critically, El Salvador, to expedite a repetition of the outcome in Nicaragua. However, this emerging storyline clashed with Carter's public message of support for post-Somoza Nicaragua, foreshadowing a difficult reconciliation of Managua's policies on the ground with the newly proclaimed ethos of noninterventionism in American foreign policy.

A "DISORDERLY MIX OF POLICIES"

Jimmy Carter did not have much opportunity to deal with the Sandinistas given that November's presidential elections brought in Republican challenger Ronald Reagan, an avowed foreign policy hawk who promised to combat communist expansion in the hemisphere. Reagan's administration watched as Managua began courting the global left. By the mid-1980s, more than 6,000 Cuban advisers were in Nicaragua, 2,000 of whom were security officials. Managua also began accepting shiploads of weaponry from Cuba, North Korea, Czechoslovakia, and the Soviet Union. Cuban advisers worked with new defense minister Humberto Ortega to build Nicaragua's armed forces.[23]

While there were certainly some "pragmatists" on the Reagan team such as Secretary of State James Baker, senior foreign policy officials including CIA director William Casey, Secretary of Defense Caspar Weinberger, and United Nations Ambassador Jeane Kirkpatrick pushed from the outset to combat this communist conspiracy in Central America. Key Reagan officials firmly believed that Havana and Moscow now had a beachhead in Central America, and that it was incumbent on the United States not just to prevent its expansion – but to roll it back.

For the Reagan administration and even some Democratic members of Congress, the Sandinistas' continued arms shipments to the FMLN were a major sore point. In early April 1981, the Reagan administration announced its indefinite cessation of aid to Nicaragua. Later that year, the president approved National Security Decision Directive 17 (NSDD

17), signaling a robust new attentiveness to the region, including an intent "to assist in defeating the insurgency in El Salvador, and to oppose actions by Cuba, Nicaragua, or others to introduce ... supplies for insurgents."[24]

The plan continued the Carter-era support of "democratic forces" in Nicaragua, but it also provided for the military training of indigenous units and leaders both in and out of the country. Under NSDD 17, Assistant Secretary of State for Latin America Thomas Enders embraced the ongoing covert preparations to arm and train anti-Sandinista fighters, presenting them as "a lowball option, a small operation not intended to overthrow."[25] In reality, Enders envisioned support for anti-Sandinista forces as a "bargaining chip" to pressure the Sandinistas to return to the negotiating table about El Salvador.

At the end of the year, Reagan signed a new finding centered on the creation of a proxy force of Nicaraguan exiles reminiscent of those assembled by the CIA for Guatemala in 1954 and for the Bay of Pigs invasion of Cuba in 1961.[26] The CIA would play a low-profile role in supporting anti-Sandinista forces, opting instead to have Argentina's military conduct the training. This rightist military was in power in Buenos Aires and was conducting its own campaign of torture and disappearances against suspected leftists and communists.

A July 1982 "scope paper" submitted to the National Security Council outlined the specific activities undertaken by the CIA pursuant to the seminal December 1981 presidential finding. Among these activities were the "financial and material support to democratic Nicaraguan leaders" and, more significantly, efforts "to create a paramilitary potential ... to effect changes in Nicaraguan government policies."[27] With this paper, the Reagan administration was expressing both a desire to get tough with communism in Central America and a post-Vietnam reluctance for direct U.S. military or covert actions in these sorts of proxy wars.[28]

With new, post-Watergate and post-Vietnam reforms of the intelligence oversight process, the CIA now had to inform select committees on Capitol Hill about its actions, including those in Nicaragua. Thus, the Reagan administration's unfolding "secret" war against Nicaragua was not as secret as many people now assume. Nor was it remarkably consistent in its objectives. As former Reagan official Robert Kagan reflected, the mix of new intelligence oversight, late Cold War dynamics, and historical involvement in Nicaragua made U.S.-Nicaraguan relations during the contra war a "disorderly mix of policies."[29]

A House intelligence committee report in 1982 concluded that Managua was "helping train insurgents and [was] transferring arms and financial support from and through Nicaragua to the insurgents" in El Salvador.[30] The Sandinistas also provided "the insurgents bases of operation in Nicaragua," and Cuban involvement "especially in providing arms" was "also evident." Amazingly, the Sandinistas were not denying these claims. Now head of the Sandinistas' intelligence service, Tomás Borge contended that it was their moral duty to support their revolutionary comrades in Central America. "How can we keep our arms folded in the face of the crimes that are being committed in El Salvador and Guatemala?" he asked. "If we are accused of expressing solidarity, if we are forced to sit in the dock because of this, we say: We have shown our solidarity with all Latin American peoples in the past, we are doing so at present and will continue to do so in the future."[31] Under pressure to ease its support for the FMLN in return for a softer U.S. stance toward Nicaragua, Daniel Ortega contended that his country was "interested in seeing the guerrillas in El Salvador and Guatemala triumph.... [It is] our shield – it makes our revolution safer."[32]

The scale of the continued arms shipments to the FMLN even provoked Democratic senator Paul Tsongas to remark after an intelligence briefing, "Those of us who are opposed to the policy accept the fact that there is indeed Nicaraguan involvement in El Salvador."[33] U.S. officials and politicians were also coming to a related conclusion about the Sandinistas' buildup of their own armed forces. In March 1982, the CIA released aerial reconnaissance photographs that purported to show the location of Managua's new battalion of twenty-five Soviet-made T-55 tanks, two Soviet-made Mi-17 helicopters, and four airfields being updated to accommodate fighter aircraft.[34]

If Washington was beginning to play hardball in Nicaragua, so were the Soviets. In fact, after a visit to Moscow in November 1981, Humberto Ortega helped establish an intricate system of arms deliveries to his swelling military, including supplies from Algeria (an early supporter of the Sandinistas), Bulgaria, and Vietnam, as well as direct supplies from the Soviet Union, East Germany, and Cuba.

In a last attempt to salvage the deteriorating bilateral relationship, in August 1981 the Reagan administration sent Assistant Secretary of State Thomas Enders to Managua for talks. Seeking to use "the threat of confrontation rather than confrontation itself," Enders engaged the Sandinista leaders in a frequently heated discussion of possible solutions. Enders warned that the United States would be inclined to involve itself militarily if the Sandinistas failed to halt the flow of arms to El Salvador, prompting one of Ortega's advisers to yell, "All right, come on in! We'll meet you man to man!"[35] At the end of the meetings, Enders proposed the Reagan administration's bargain: in exchange for halting the export of arms and insurrection in El Salvador and a reduction in Nicaragua's armed forces, the United States would provide Nicaragua with continued security arrangements and economic aid.[36] After a month of consideration, Ortega firmly rejected the offer.

In hindsight, given the devastating contra war that followed, the offer might have benefited the Sandinistas more than they realized at the time. However, sandinismo in its inception was an ideology of anti-imperialism, thus joining the new Nicaraguan government's domestic and foreign policies together.[37] By rejecting the American offer, the Sandinistas stayed true to their ideology and strategically solidified domestic support for their rule.

After El Salvador's highly publicized and surprising municipal elections in March 1982, when an overwhelming percentage of the population came out to vote despite FMLN threats, the Reagan administration began to emphasize democracy and the rule of law as integral components of Nicaragua policy. This approach proved beneficial over the long run with conservative Democrats in Congress who were wary of aggressive U.S. meddling in Nicaragua but also concerned about the country's increasingly hardline Marxist direction.

THE CONTRAS ARE BORN

Shortly after Reagan took office, a disparate group of former National Guardsmen, former and now disgruntled Sandinistas, peasants, and Miskito Indians collectively known as the contras began receiving American assistance. At first, the CIA's involvement was still indirect as Argentine military officers trained and at times commanded the contras from camps inside Honduras. The total number of anti-Sandinista troops at the beginning of the U.S. covert program was around 2,000, half of them Atlantic Coast Indians.[38]

The most influential contra group was the Honduras-based Fuerza Democrática Nicaragüense (FDN). At this early point, the most "visible and appealing" contra was a former Jesuit priest and university rector named Edgar Chamorro. At their height, the contras numbered roughly 15,000 soldiers, often pulled from the ranks of the rural campesinos. As the contras' ambitions increased, so did those of the Reagan administration, which saw these budding "freedom fighters" as an integral part of its global anticommunist agenda. By 1982 and 1983, the anti-Sandinista

FIGURE 24.1. The Contra War, 1980s. Map prepared by Andrew Rhodes. Reprinted with permission

guerrilla forces had become the Reagan administration's only serious tool for influencing events in Nicaragua.

The Sandinistas also had to adapt to the unexpected strength of the contra threat. Early on, the Sandinista army's strategy had been to use militia to deal with the insurgents while holding the regular troops in reserve to protect key cities and military bases. But after a series of contra offensives startled the army leadership, it was forced to send out regular battalions to the front lines in the northern regions near the Honduran border. In an indication of how seriously Managua was taking this new force, a high-ranking Cuban general, Arnoldo Ochoa, arrived in 1983 to take charge of the war. Ochoa's approach was to decimate the enemy using aggressive counterinsurgency tactics, creating a fascinating role-reversal for the Cold War Cuban military: they and the Sandinistas were employing the very sort of counterinsurgency strategy that the United States was promoting next door in El Salvador.

The Cubans began training a special counterguerrilla battalion able to remain on patrol for extended periods of time. But the Sandinistas quickly learned that they would need greater mobility if this new strategy were to succeed. Moscow immediately provided fresh weapons and equipment, including ten Mi-8 helicopter transports, more than 300 new trucks, two dozen armored fighting vehicles and tanks, and scores of rocket launchers known as "Stalin organs."[39] U.S. intelligence officials estimated that Soviet deliveries to Nicaragua doubled in 1983, from 10,000 tons of materiel to 20,000. Moscow also increased the number of advisers in-country from 70 to 100, and the Cuban presence grew from 7,500 to 9,000, of whom more than 2,000 were military and internal security advisers. Interestingly, during the Somoza era there had been no more than a few hundred secret police agents, while under the Sandinistas that number grew to more than 3,000.[40]

Fatefully, the new counterinsurgency strategy required a significant increase in the already sizable army force of 25,000. In July, Sandinista army commander Humberto Ortega announced plans for universal military conscription, a program that proved highly unpopular in future years.

THE NOT-SO-SECRET WAR

As news of the U.S. funding for the contras leaked out in the press over months and years in the early 1980s, Reagan administration officials were forced to defend a policy that was not supposed to be discussed in public. One senior official responded to a *Newsweek* article by contending, "We are not waging a secret war, or anything approaching that. What we are doing is trying to keep Managua off balance and apply pressure to stop providing military aid to the insurgents in El Salvador."[41] In late 1982, Democratic Congressman Tom Harkin referred to the same *Newsweek* article and commented that "news reports of late ... clearly indicate that we are becoming ever more mired in the jungles and swamps of Latin America.... [T]he real mistake we are making is not only in doing something that is clearly illegal, but in siding with perhaps the most hated group of Nicaraguans that could exist outside of the borders of Nicaragua, and I talk about Somocistas."[42] Another Democrat, Congressman George Miller, asked Congress to "go on record in getting control of those agencies who have convinced the White House to substitute covert action for policy, to substitute covert action for diplomacy, and take an action that without the express consent of this Congress is in fact illegal, unethical and against the best interests of this country."[43]

This opposition yielded a highly ambivalent policy, reflected in U.S. assistance to the contras that waxed and waned throughout the 1980s, sometimes cut off completely. In April 1982, Democratic representative and chairman of the House Intelligence Committee Edward Boland added a phrase to the secret annex to an intelligence authorization bill declaring that congressional funding could not be spent "for the purpose of overthrowing the government of Nicaragua or provoking an exchange between Nicaragua and Honduras."[44] However, this language focused solely on intent – not actions – leaving tremendous wiggle room for the Reagan administration to pursue its covert policies. It also allowed Boland and other congressional Democrats to escape the criticism that they had refused to prevent communist expansion in Central America, without also being accused of supporting covert machinations against a sovereign government.[45]

The 1983 congressional session, however, saw a more concerted assault on Reagan's contra policy. Another Boland amendment (officially the Boland-Zablocki amendment) struck a deal by cutting off aid to the contras, but actually increased aid to El Salvador and the other pro-American governments in Central America by $80 million. The amendment passed the house 228–195 in what Secretary of State George Shultz called "the worst legislative defeat of the Reagan administration to that date."[46] Soon after, though, the Senate rescued the covert program as the Boland amendment restrictions were dropped before the bill went forward.

BOOTS ON THE GROUND: LOW-INTENSITY CONFLICT IN ACTION

Meanwhile, operations on the ground in Nicaragua continued with little regard for the funding disputes in Congress. As politicians continued to haggle over legislative language back in Washington, the CIA went ahead with its aid and training to the contras as well as direct paramilitary operations inside Nicaragua.

The American experience in Nicaragua began to give shape to the idea of "low-intensity conflict" within U.S. policy and military circles.[47] Limited warfare and counterinsurgency as operational responses to "ambiguous warfare" in Vietnam had largely failed; yet American foreign policy in the 1980s maintained a "commitment to intervene" abroad as a matter of national security. Low-intensity conflict, defined as a political-military confrontation below conventional war and above the routine, peaceful competition among states, came to describe the protracted struggle of competing principles and ideologies occurring in Nicaragua.

In essence, low-intensity conflict served to re-brand many tried and true dirty war tactics. At the heart of this strategy was the use of contra attacks to destabilize the economic livelihood of the country piece by piece, simultaneously eroding the political capital and legitimacy of the Sandinista regime.

In early October 1983, men in motorboats attacked piers at the Pacific port of Corinto, igniting fuel storage tanks that contained over three million gallons of gasoline. The explosion reportedly left the Nicaraguan government with less than a month's supply of oil reserves. The CIA had supported the operation, which involved not contra forces, as many would have suspected, but so-called UCLAs or "unilaterally-controlled Latino assets" hired by the agency to carry out such secret missions. In some aspects resembling a mini-version of the Bay of Pigs, this operation was the closest that the United States came to a direct action against Nicaragua. The CIA also supported mining Nicaragua's harbors to deter merchant captains and to delay or cancel oil shipments, a move that later erupted in controversy when the International Court of Justice voted 15–0 to condemn the mining, with an American judge concurring. The UN Security Council discussed the issue for four days before Washington used its veto to prevent a censure.

The reaction back in Washington was no warmer. The vice chairman of the Senate Select Committee on Intelligence, Senator Daniel Patrick Moynihan, resigned his position in protest; conservative senator Barry Goldwater sent a blunt "Dear Bill" letter to CIA Director William Casey. The letter stated, "I'm pissed off.... I don't like this. I don't like it one bit from the president or from you.... This is an act violating international law. It is an act of war. For the life of me, I don't see how we are going to explain it."[48] Just when it seemed the situation could not get any worse, in the last weeks of Reagan's second presidential campaign the *Washington*

Post revealed that the CIA had produced a manual for the contras that included instructions on how to "neutralize" local Sandinista officials.

Despite policy rationale in Washington, military action on the ground often had little to do with the arms flow to El Salvador and centered instead on tactics of terror and destruction to coerce the hearts and minds of peasants in Nicaragua's mountainous border regions to give their allegiance to the contras. On the morning of August 10, 1983, 100 to 200 contras ambushed a bus carrying 18 civilians near the town of Jinotega, killing 15 of them.[49] The same contra forces were reported to have later dynamited a key bridge near Jinotega. Vivid reports of the incident surfaced in the following days, distinguished by front page photos in Sandinista newspapers of a 9-month-old girl who had been shot in the hip during the attack and whose 16-year-old mother had been killed.[50] As State Department memos later reported, the trend of contra attacks on unarmed civilians, women, and children was well documented and valuable to Sandinista rhetoric.

All told, U.S. support allowed the contras to conduct far more frequent and lethal operations against the Sandinista security forces and their civilian adherents. The contras conducted the war ferociously, frequently destroying Sandinista-run agricultural cooperatives to undermine the regime's popular support in the countryside. The contras often went into battle armed with U.S.-made M-16s, Belgian FAL automatic rifles, M-79 grenade launchers, mortars, and other sophisticated equipment. In one large-scale episode, a contra strike into the "Las Minas" area of northern Nicaragua included thousands of combatants and caused considerable damage to local infrastructure. By the end of 1985, the Nicaraguan Ministry of Health estimated that more than 3,600 civilians had been killed, roughly 4,000 wounded, and about 5,200 kidnapped during contra raids.[51]

THE REAGAN DOCTRINE

Undeterred by growing opposition in Congress, Reagan used his landslide victory in the 1984 presidential election against Democrat Walter Mondale to renew his public campaign for contra aid. For what was now being dubbed the Reagan Doctrine, the contras had become both a strategic and a moral issue. The United States, Reagan believed, needed to be on the side of freedom throughout the world; he even compared the contras to the Founding Fathers, which infuriated critics who pointed out the guerrilla insurgency's repeated violations of both human rights and the laws of war. In fact, the contras' violent ways became the new rallying cry for human rights, religious, and congressional activists opposed to Reagan's policies. What was lost in the acerbic debate in Washington was that the lion's share of the contra aid was coming from other sources, such as Saudi Arabia, especially after the strict 1984 Boland amendment restrictions began to kick in.

In 1985, Congress approved two policies that underscored its ambivalence about Nicaragua. The first was for "humanitarian" aid. The second was a trade embargo against Nicaragua, which made the country's desperate economic situation even worse. CIA sabotage efforts, the trade embargo, and the Sandinistas' inept fiscal and monetary policies had turned the country into an economic basket case, undermining the ruling junta's popular support. In 1982 roughly 19 percent of the national budget went to defense; by 1988 it was closer to 40 percent and rising. The Sandinistas were also reeling from sustained criticism from the Catholic Church, including Pope John Paul II himself, as well as the opposition newspaper *La Prensa*.

UNDER FIRE

I am down here as a job. I am not down here as a soldier, so this is not my war. I don't believe it's an American war. – Eugene Hasenfus[52]

On Sunday, October 5, 1986, a C-123K cargo plane took off from Ilopango, El Salvador, and was flying low into Nicaraguan airspace, only 700 meters off the ground to elude Sandinista radar. Deep in the jungle of the Chontales Department, José Fernando Canales and Byron Montiel, young soldiers just five months into their mandatory service in the Sandinista military, had set up a portable land-air rocket, or "arrow," several days before.

When they heard the engines of the unmarked cargo plane, José Fernando received the order to shoot. He aimed, fired, and within seconds the plane exploded in the air and fell to earth in pieces; only the tail section remained intact. Twenty-four hours later, the Sandinista mouthpiece "The Voice of Nicaragua" broke into its regular programming with a special bulletin that a plane belonging to the "counterrevolution" had been hit by an "arrow," and perhaps more important, that "North Americans" were among the crew. When Sandinista troops reached the crash site, they found 13,000 pounds of weaponry: 50,000 AK-47 rifle cartridges, 60 collapsible

FIGURE 24.2. Two Contra fighters on February 11, 1988, in Yamales, Honduras. In these sorts of regions thousands of Contras camped hoping for renewed U.S. military aid in their fight against the Sandinista regime. Reproduced with permission from Associated Press, 8802110037

AK-47s, a similar number of RPG-7 grenade launchers, and 150 pairs of jungle boots.[53]

The C-123K carried three Americans and one Nicaraguan. The pilot William Cooper, co-pilot Wallace Blaine Sawyer, and radio operator Freddy Vilches died in the crash. Eugene Hasenfus, in charge of dropping the cargo, had been able to see the incoming rocket in time and jumped from the plane with a parachute given to him by his brother before leaving the United States.

"Give up, gringo, or we'll blow you to hell!" reportedly shouted the pursuing soldier Rafael Antonio Acevedo, when he found Hasenfus in an abandoned hut, eating a squash and lying in a hammock he had made from his parachute.[54] The American was armed with a pistol and a pocketknife, but immediately surrendered to the twenty-year-old Sandinista conscript. Days later Nicaraguan Defense Minister Humberto Ortega decorated the Sandinista soldiers involved with gold medals.[55]

During a broadcast from his trial in Nicaragua, Hasenfus claimed to be working for the CIA. In fact, the fuselage of the cargo plane was a "flying file cabinet" that included logbooks with detailed descriptions of previous covert supply flights from airports in El Salvador and Honduras, including the type and quantity of weapons dropped in each flight.[56] A month later, the controversy deepened when reports revealed that funds for the contras were being illegally obtained through the sale of arms to Iran in exchange for the release of American hostages in Lebanon. Several officials in the Reagan White House including National Security Council aide and Marine Lieutenant Colonel Oliver North were implicated, and the White House was exposed in a clear end-run around Congress. President Reagan initially insisted that he "did not – repeat, did not – trade weapons or anything else for hostages." Within weeks, though, Attorney General Edwin Meese announced that his investigation into the matter had uncovered evidence suggesting that between $12 million and $30 million of the arms sales to Iran had been "diverted" to the contras.

The "Iran-Contra" scandal represented America's worst political scandal since Watergate. Sometime in 1986, North began overcharging the Iranians for the arms and using the surplus to fund the contra resupply operation that involved Hasenfus. Interestingly, former CIA official Felix Rodríguez, who had been at the Bay of Pigs and was present when Che Guevara was killed in Bolivia, had also been assisting the contra resupply effort. North also relied on his colleague Richard Secord to transfer the funds and handle other logistical details. North was attempting to get around the Boland amendment's restriction on funding the contras. Secord and North netted over $16 million in profits from arms sales to Iran, though less than $4 million made its way to contra coffers; over the same period, Saudi Arabia contributed around $32 million.[57]

By the end of Reagan's second term, even bona fide anticommunists like George Shultz wanted "to get the Nicaragua problem resolved if only because it had become too painfully divisive for the country."[58] What helped this "extraction" along somewhat was the advent of a peace process in early 1987 led by Costa Rican president Oscar Arias. The Arias plan called for immediate cease-fires in Nicaragua, El Salvador, and Guatemala and the suspension of all outside support for insurgencies and plans for future elections. Within two months of the signing of the agreement, governments were to offer amnesty to guerrillas who had laid down their weapons to start a dialogue.

While administration officials were not thrilled by the plan's implications for its contra funding, they soon realized that the democratic procedures it required would be very valuable in undermining the highly undemocratic Sandinista government. The Central American presidents met in Esquipulas, Guatemala, in early August 1987 and approved the Esquipulas II Accord, a slightly modified version of the Arias plan. The document did not call for an immediate cease-fire, but it eventually laid the broad foundations for each country to address its internal conflict.[59]

VICTORY – AT THE BALLOT BOX

> You [Sandinistas] can't beat the gringos at their own game.... The opposition will have the best U.S. campaign advisers behind it. They will clobber you. – Cuban official in Nicaragua[60]

With the now longstanding U.S. insistence on democracy in Nicaragua combined with Arias's Central America–wide peace process, there was great pressure for the Sandinistas to legitimize their rule. They were confident that they would win the vote handily, and they set presidential elections for early 1990. In September 1989, the incoming Bush administration began efforts to provide funding for the elections. Officials insisted that the aid would be used for "non-partisan technical support of the elections process" but the funding went almost exclusively to the anti-Sandinista opposition known as the Nicaraguan Opposition Union (UNO). This coalition party, which spanned the ideological spectrum, from conservative to communist, fielded as a presidential candidate Violeta Chamorro, the widow of the assassinated journalist and anti-Somoza leader. Chamorro's credentials as a legitimate political figure were also burnished by her former role in the post-Somoza revolutionary government.

The National Endowment for Democracy (NED) provided the Nicaraguan opposition with over $1 million, although a considerable amount of this money did not arrive until very late in the campaign.[61] Despite the U.S. funding, the Sandinistas remained confident of a pronounced victory at the polls. In fact, as the election grew nearer, the Sandinistas invited even more international observers to witness their expected electoral triumph.

Amazingly, at the same time, the Sandinistas began escalating their supply shipments to the FMLN in El Salvador in preparation for an offensive in late 1989. The offensive ultimately failed, but it rattled San Salvador. A month later, a small plane carrying arms from Nicaragua to the FMLN crashed in El Salvador. The shipment, recovered by Salvadoran security forces, included twenty-four Soviet-made SA-7 surface-to-air missiles, marking the first time that the Sandinistas had sent such heavy grade weapons to their Salvadoran allies. The Sandinistas' delivery might have been a deliberate message to the Bush White House that they were still willing to cause problems for the United States in El Salvador if Washington continued to fund the contras. Publicly, Humberto Ortega dismissed the "big fuss" that was being made because "some arrows have turned up in El Salvador."[62]

The elections on February 25, 1990, drew an estimated 700 official observers. By the end of the day, more than half of the almost 4,500 polling stations had been observed by teams from the UN, Organization of American States (OAS), and former president Jimmy Carter's private democracy organization. More than 2,000 unofficial observers and journalists were also in the country.

That night, the UN team's "quick count" of less than 10 percent of the vote showed Chamorro winning a decisive victory. Stunned, the Sandinista Directorate called a hasty meeting to decide its next moves. Within hours, an official from the Supreme Electoral Council read the initial results aloud, further indicating a stunning upset. When the dust had settled and all the votes were counted, Chamorro had taken 55 percent to Ortega's 41 percent. Indeed, Nicaraguans of all walks of life had given the Sandinistas a clear mandate: it was time to go. The Sandinista revolution was over, killed in the end by the ballot box.

ANOTHER "ENDLESS WAR" CONCLUDES

The contra war resulted in the deaths of around 10,000 Nicaraguans. Conservative U.S. officials and politicians argued that the Sandinistas' ouster via elections was a vindication of the Reagan administration's policies, especially as the contras kept pressure on an otherwise recalcitrant Managua. Liberals, on the other hand, contended that it was only the Bush administration's rejection of the hardline Reagan approach that had allowed for this relatively pacific outcome.

Regardless, the conflict was a forceful iteration of century-long American influence in Nicaraguan affairs. The Reagan administration's commitment to confronting Soviet and Cuban wars of national liberation was expressed as a policy that, contrary to Carter's ambivalence about using military force to check leftist revolution, Washington should unabashedly but sparingly offer assistance and deploy forces to promote U.S. interests.

In many ways, its outcome was a vindication, if not a justification, of low-intensity conflict strategy. Not surprisingly, many critics believed that low-intensity conflict was a new term for the chronic inclination of the United States to intervene in "endless wars."[63] Over the course of almost a decade, American-supported contra attacks decimated the economic infrastructure of Nicaragua and proved successful in eroding support for a once-popular Sandinista regime. The covert nature of American involvement was critical; while support for the contras may not have remained out of the public eye, it largely avoided public control, and outcries among the American citizenry over repeated accounts of human rights violations often went ignored.

There is no question that Washington also demanded that the Sandinistas pursue elections, which was something that a majority of Nicaraguans wanted as well. In fact, the Reagan administration had a tendency to pursue policies in Central America that were more pragmatic than its strident Cold War anticommunist rhetoric suggested. Even Reagan bemoaned the pressure from Republican hawks in a 1988 comment to his chief of staff, "Those sons of bitches won't be happy until we have 25,000 troops in Managua, and I'm not going to do it."[64] In his final years in office, Reagan's lack of ideological conviction got him into trouble with influential "neoconservative" foreign policy intellectuals who compared the Republican president to the British "appeaser" Neville Chamberlain.

Nonetheless, this more modest project (in comparison to El Salvador) was still a powerful form of interventionism in that the United States effectively determined Nicaragua's fate. Once the 1990s elections took place and the Sandinistas stepped down from power, Washington and the American people quickly forgot about Nicaragua and the United States' deep involvement just a few years earlier.

25

El Salvador, 1979–1992

Let's not delude ourselves, the Soviet Union underlies all the unrest that is going on. If they weren't engaged in this game of dominoes, there wouldn't be any hot spots in the world.
– President Ronald Reagan, 1983[1]

We know very little about who exactly is out there in the hills.... We know that they receive arms through Nicaragua. But beyond that I don't know very much.
– U.S. diplomatic official, San Salvador, 1982[2]

The insurgency was a many-headed thing – as most of these [Marxist insurgencies] were. You had the hard core real communists and you had the other guys who were land reformers and maybe naïve to go along with the really tough guys but who wanted change and who felt that the only way to change that system was to do it through violence.
– Reagan administration official Roger Fontaine[3]

On January 10, 1981, Marxist guerrillas operating in El Salvador's rugged mountain ranges along the Honduran border announced the launch of their "final offensive" to overthrow the central government in San Salvador. A year earlier, disparate insurgent groups across the small Central American country had united to form the Farabundo Martí National Liberation Front (FMLN), supposedly at the insistence of Fidel Castro, who demanded revolutionary unity before he would send support. Over 2,500 poorly trained Salvadoran guerrillas and a few hundred Cubans assaulted more than 80 Salvadoran armed forces' Fuerza Armada de El Salvador (ESAF) positions. This was roughly the same number of insurgents that the Sandinistas next door in

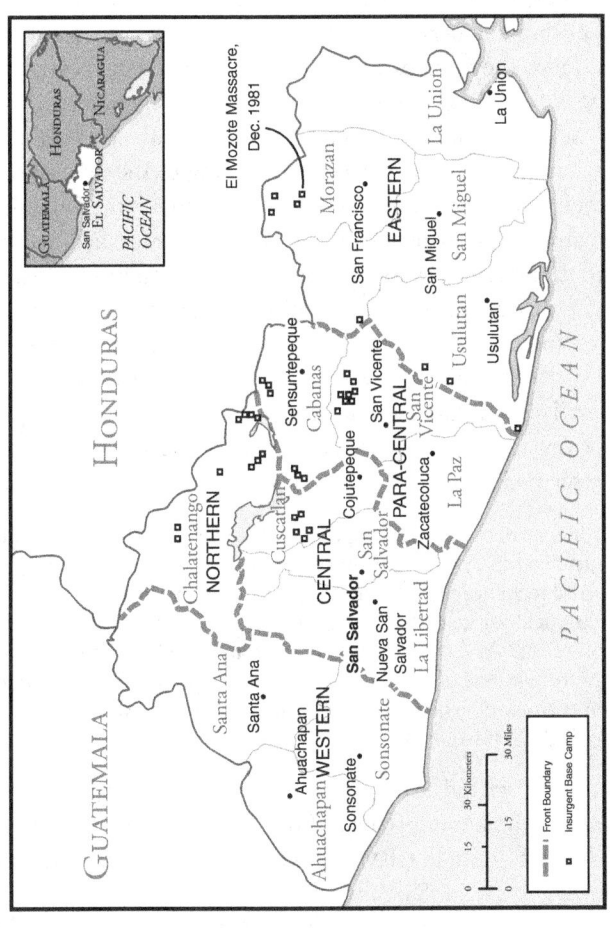

FIGURE 25.1. Map of El Salvador included in a classified 1982 U.S. government document indicating the reported locations of the different Marxist guerrilla fronts that were fighting the Washington-backed central government in the 1980s. Map prepared by the University of Wisconsin-Madison Cartography Lab©. Reprinted with permission

Nicaragua had when they unleashed the operation that ousted the widely hated Somoza regime. Given the Sandinistas' success in 1979, many Salvadoran leftists and guerrillas assumed that the insurrection would quickly triumph. In fact, the FMLN scheduled the offensive for early January so that they would be able to seize power before the hawkish Reagan administration took office a few weeks later.[4]

Much to the chagrin of the FMLN leadership, the offensive accomplished almost nothing. Guerrilla leaders had made at least two fatal miscalculations. First, they overestimated the willingness and capacity of Salvadoran citizens to take up arms in the struggle. In one interpretation, this reluctance was a result of the stranglehold that the Salvadoran military had over the civilian population. Indeed, responding to the revolutionary left's threat to their entrenched interests, in the late 1970s the Salvadoran military and oligarchy-sponsored death squads had unleashed a loosely coordinated and clandestine assassination campaign against leftist student, labor, and political movements, turning the capital, San Salvador, into a literal dumping ground for murdered victims. At the height of what became known as "death squad" savagery in the late 1970s and early 1980s, often horribly mutilated bodies could be found on the capital's streets each morning or piled up at the municipal dump. As journalist Mark Danner described:

Sometimes the bodies were headless, or faceless, their feature having been obliterated with a shotgun blast or an application of battery acid; sometimes limbs were missing, or hands and feet chopped off, or eyes gouged out; women's genitals were torn and bloody, bespeaking repeated rape; men's were often found severed and stuffed into their mouths. And cut into the flesh of a corpse's back or chest was likely to be the signature of one or another of the "death squads" that had done the work, the most notorious of which were the Union of White Warriors and the Maximiliano Hernández Martínez Brigade.[5]

The Salvadoran majority did not join the insurgents, this interpretation goes, because they understandably feared these kinds of repercussions. A contrary view suggests that the FMLN had underestimated the (albeit tenuous) legitimacy that El Salvador's ruling junta had among the Salvadoran population. While the previous decade had seen multiple presidential elections manipulated by the military to prevent winning reformist candidates from taking office, by the early 1980s the central government had consolidated some civilian support. General Carlos Humberto Romero, the country's widely hated strongman, had already been ousted in a 1979 coup and replaced by a relative centrist and reformer, José Napoleón Duarte. The junta in San Salvador at the time of the offensive may have been weak and far from universally popular, but it had embarked on several major reforms, including economic policies that were almost socialist in nature. Regardless of which interpretation is the more accurate, it is true that the final offensive failed to gain crucial support, leaving it stalled several weeks in.

At the same time, the FMLN also underestimated the capacity of the Salvadoran military and security forces. Although they were largely garrison outfits at this point, the 8,000-man ESAF and 5,000 military police proved capable of repelling the guerrilla raids. In a key indication that ESAF morale survived the offensive, military troops mutinied in only one garrison.

Shocked by their total lack of progress, FMLN leaders quickly claimed that it was not in fact a "final" offensive but a more general operation. Many within Salvadoran civil society criticized the guerrillas' decision to unleash the offensive. One senior Catholic Church official stated, "The groups on the left have made violence an absolute end in itself and magnified their adherence to Marxism. That is why most of the public has turned its back on them. . . . Terrorism is not liberation."[6]

Despite the FMLN's failure to take down the junta, El Salvador's fledgling government remained severely threatened by a surprisingly well-armed Marxist insurgency, which appeared only to be getting stronger due to the flood of aid spilling over the borders from Sandinista Nicaragua. And now Washington was paying attention. Just a month before the "final offensive" had begun, President Jimmy Carter had approved a compromise military assistance package that included a modest military training program, but he had suspended it only weeks later after reports of the grisly murder of four American church workers by Salvadoran security forces. Then, in response to the final offensive, just days before Carter left office in January 1981, the clearly ambivalent Carter administration once again reversed its decision and committed several million dollars in military assistance.[7] The administration's public announcement cited the need to "support the Salvadoran government in its struggle against left-wing terrorism supported covertly . . . by Cuba and other Communist nations."[8]

At the time, Washington and the U.S. embassy in San Salvador were aware that the Salvadoran government and armed forces were full of "bad apples" when it came to human rights abuses. Yet, after the Sandinista victory in Nicaragua, the risk of another domino falling to communism was of greater concern. The U.S. strategy for achieving anticommunist security was referred to within government circles at the time as a "grit-your-teeth" policy: it might not be pretty given the state of El Salvador's fledgling government and abusive military, but the alternatives were far worse.

The Carter administration's fateful decision to support the Salvadoran military was built on the calculus that any stable environment would require a reformed security force. It also reflected the depressing reality that the Salvadoran military called most of the shots in Salvadoran politics. According to one U.S. official, "military assistance is an essential component of any strategy in El Salvador. [The Salvadoran military] are the center of power, and most of what you want, you have to get from them or with their approval."[9] While some of its members agonized over the decision, the Carter team had come to believe that the thorough professionalization of the Salvadoran armed forces, combined with aggressive encouragement of the junta's economic and social reforms, would bolster stability and facilitate a rapprochement between the reactionary right and revolutionary left. Critics swiftly claimed that El Salvador would become "Vietnam in Spanish." Nonetheless, the Carter administration's new framework for an "engagement strategy" that would attempt to turn around El Salvador's bleak economic, political, and humanitarian climate was falling into place, just in time for the incoming Reagan administration.

The hawkish rhetoric coming from leading Reagan hardliners, such as Secretary of State Alexander Haig, UN Ambassador Jeane Kirkpatrick, and National Security Advisor William Clark, is what most analysts now associate with El Salvador policy in the 1980s. Yet the true thrust of the "engagement strategy" was developed in the Carter administration, before Reagan even took office. Indeed, the idea grew roots two years before the final offensive, when the Carter administration concluded in a classified report that the "spread of violence and radicalization – spawned by the resistance of most ruling elites to peaceful change – ... is increasing both the temptation and the ability of Cuba to penetrate the area."[10] This was hurting U.S. interests in the hemisphere, and Carter's answer was to become more, not less, involved.

Many key officials in the incoming Reagan foreign policy team, including Secretary of State Alexander Haig and Secretary of Defense Caspar Weinberger, were ideologically predisposed to see the Salvador problem as an instance of communist machination led by Moscow and Havana. The administration decided that further measures were necessary and increased the number of U.S. military trainers in the country from nineteen to forty-five and authorized an additional $25 million in military assistance.[11] This initially ad hoc approach evolved into a multibillion dollar effort to build El Salvador's democracy and restructure its highly inequitable social and economic systems. In practice, this meant embracing the center-left Christian Democratic Party and its standard-bearer, José Napoleón Duarte. At times, it also meant embracing Duarte's attempts to implement left-leaning economic reforms such as a massive land redistribution program and the nationalization of the banking system. Thus, in effect, and despite vocal opposition from hardliners, the Reagan team ultimately took up the Carter administration's strategy of engagement.

America's massive decade-long campaign in El Salvador represented its largest attempt at nation-building and counterinsurgency since Vietnam and before Afghanistan and Iraq. Two points merit notice here. First, by definition, Washington's attempts to hold the line against Marxism in El Salvador meant that it would have to jump into bed with a dubious Salvadoran government and, far more problematically, armed forces notorious for crimes-against-humanity-level brutality. Unlike the Carter administration, which had agonized over the decision to back the Salvadoran security forces, especially initially, the Reagan administration had little such compunction.

In its first few years in office, the Reagan administration did not push the Salvadoran government and military nearly hard enough on the dire human rights situation. Driven by the unyielding belief that Moscow and Havana were responsible for El Salvador's ostensible "people's revolution," the Reagan hardliners felt that pressure on the human rights question would only weaken a government already on the edge of collapse. Perhaps equally noteworthy, by the mid-1980s, after it was clear that the FMLN would not seize power, the Reagan administration belatedly began to push its Salvadoran counterparts on human rights.

The second point is that the engagement strategy was predicated on the reality that neither Congress nor the American public – nor, perhaps owing more to the latter than to the former, the Reagan administration – would condone the deployment of U.S. combat troops in El Salvador. Vietnam had ended roughly six years earlier, and American policymakers and military planners made it clear that American troops could train, fund, and advise in El Salvador, but they would not fight.

Notably, El Salvador never became the Vietnam-esque quagmire that some observers had predicted. Nor did El Salvador, despite all of its faults and violence, deteriorate into a scorched-earth counterinsurgency state (like Guatemala) or fall to a successful Marxist revolution (like Nicaragua). Instead, bolstered by U.S. military aid and nation-building know-how, stronger but still highly imperfect democracy and human rights protections slowly and painfully took root over the next decade. All told, the reasons that Guatemala or Vietnam scenarios did *not* come to fruition make the Salvador case a critical one for understanding subsequent American counterinsurgency and nation-building efforts in Iraq, Afghanistan, the Philippines, and Colombia.

THE 1972 ELECTIONS

During the 1960s, new political organizations began to test El Salvador's long repressive and often military-dominated political system. One of these, the Christian Democratic Party (PCD), was deeply influenced by the Catholic Church's teachings on social justice and emerged as a vocal advocate for reform. Presidential elections in February 1972 proved to be a watershed for the PCD. Christian Democratic leader and former three-term San Salvador mayor José Napoleón Duarte and vice presidential running mate democratic socialist Guillermo Ungo campaigned on an umbrella ticket against the military's hand-picked candidate, Colonel Arturo Molina. Interestingly, Duarte had entered politics because he was worried that the oligarchy's reactionary policies were making a communist revolt more likely.

The Notre Dame University-educated Duarte easily took the rural and urban vote, prompting the military to order a news blackout immediately after the polls closed. Three days later the regime's official election board announced that Molina had been elected president. A month later, Duarte was implicated in a failed coup against the "elected" government, then arrested, tortured (his facial bones were severely broken), and exiled to Venezuela for the next seven years.[12]

EL SALVADOR'S REVOLUTIONARY LEFT

For many on the left, any possibility of peaceful reform ended with the fraudulent 1972 elections, even if the event did not receive much attention outside of El Salvador. One future guerrilla leader lamented, "The dictatorship had shut the space for participation."[13] Another guerrilla stated a quarter of a century later in an interview with the author that after 1972 she had concluded, "Either we take the struggle into the open in the mountains, or they'll kill us here in the city."[14]

At the time of the presidential election in 1972, only one guerrilla organization was active in El Salvador, the Popular Forces of Liberation (FPL). Its operations were mostly limited to kidnappings. The FPL was

El Salvador, 1979–1992 311

founded in 1972 by a dozen young communists, including Salvador Cayetano Carpio who became the group's top commander. Carpio pushed for a Maoist "prolonged struggle" against the military. Interestingly, he was one of the few Salvadoran leaders actually advocating a people's revolt from the lower classes; the majority of El Salvador's radicals in the early 1970s were members of an educated elite who wanted a Cuban-style insurrection leading to swift victory, or who worked directly within the political system via the Communist Party. By 1980, the FPL had swelled to around 2,000 troops operating in the single mountain province of Chalatenango, where they remained for the war's duration.

In the years after 1972, the landscape of El Salvador's revolutionary left changed dramatically. Government and paramilitary repression radicalized left-leaning intellectuals, swelling the guerrilla ranks. The second large guerrilla group to emerge in the early 1970s was the People's Revolutionary Army (ERP). In 1975, the group's founder, noted essayist and poet Roque Dalton, was accused by other guerrillas of treason and executed after a kangaroo trial. His death eased the way for Joaquín Villalobos (whose nom de guerre was "Atilio"), a middle-class economist, to take over the ERP's leadership. The brilliant Villalobos opted for a Cuba-style foco strategy to promote a rapid revolution through popular insurrection. For most of the war, the ERP was active in the eastern mountain province of Morazán.

The FPL and ERP were intense rivals and they refused to merge into one coordinated insurgency. Various Salvadoran guerrilla leaders reportedly met with Fidel Castro in Cuba in 1980 to address the factions' impasse. Castro was apparently more concerned about the Sandinistas' survival in Nicaragua than about the internal jealousies of the Salvadoran revolutionaries. Eager to resolve their divisions, he made the guerrilla leaders promise to fight as a united force, leading them to form, in October 1980, the Farabundo Martí National Liberation Front (FMLN). It is worth noting that the roots of the Salvadoran insurgency were mostly domestic, not externally pushed by Moscow, Havana, or, after 1979, the Sandinistas in Managua.

The Democratic Revolutionary Front (FDR) was established in April 1980 and attempted to serve as the incipient FMLN's political wing. The charismatic socialist Rubén Zamora and Guillermo Ungo, Duarte's running mate in 1972, became two of its key members. Zamora and Ungo made numerous trips to the rest of Latin America, Europe, and the United States advocating radical social reform in El Salvador. The FDR's main contention was that the successive democratic governments in the 1980s were not in fact representative of the people's will; more radical reform had to be undertaken, by violent means if necessary, to change El Salvador. By the mid-1980s, however, the FMLN considered the FDR an increasingly useless "political" partner, preferring instead to focus efforts on winning the armed insurgency.

A NEW GOVERNMENT IN EL SALVADOR

In the early morning of October 15, 1979, several young Salvadoran Army officers notified their president and commander in chief, General Carlos Romero, that he had only a few hours to pack his belongings and leave the country. Romero had assumed power in 1977 and had ruled the country with an iron hand. He fled the country, and, without a shot being fired, the October coup succeeded. Within days, a new government formed, composed of relatively unknown junior army colonels and three civilians, including the Christian Democrat Guillermo Ungo, who had run for vice president in the 1972 sham election.

The 1979 government promised to address El Salvador's glaring social deficit aggressively. They pledged radical changes in the country's "social and economic structures," political pluralism, and an "immediate end" to military corruption and the repression of the political left and the vast rural Salvadoran population. In return, the junta asked for "patience, understanding, and the confidence of the Salvadoran people."[15] A few days after the junta was organized, San Salvador's Archbishop Óscar Romero called on Salvadorans to give the new government a chance.

For the junta's military officers, reform was a matter of pragmatism. They understandably feared a fate like that of Somoza's National Guard. Some officers also worried that they could not rely on the dovish Carter administration to come to their aid if an insurrection broke out. It was better to reform now, they thought, than to lose out later.

For the two legitimately leftist civilians on the junta, Román Mayorga from the Jesuit-run Central American University in San Salvador and the Christian Democrat Ungo, the coup was the "revolution" they had long sought, and, miraculously, it had not come through the barrel of the gun. Now, for the first time in its history, the Salvadoran government was committed to radical social change.

However, internal disputes wracked the junta from its inception. It began to lose members after only three months of existence. Leftist civilians claimed that conservatives and the military were usurping the nascent government. The armed forces resisted strict civilian control. After months of stalemate, the military finally agreed to bring in the exiled Duarte to lead the fledgling junta. In December 1980, Duarte was sworn in as president and, in a concession to conservative elements, hardline Colonel Abdul Gutiérrez became vice president. Many observers were convinced that the Duarte-led junta was no longer a reformist administration but rather a front for the oligarchy and military. As one foreign diplomat quipped, "Duarte is an adornment."[16]

Naturally, the junta struggled to define itself on the political spectrum during its years in power. Duarte wrote in his memoir, "No one seemed to be in control, neither the Junta, the security forces nor the leftists. The Army officers were fighting among themselves.... They had staged a coup, but they could not control the Army or the government. Nor did the government control them. [After October 1979] there was a power vacuum."[17] Part of Duarte's dilemma as head of the junta was that the revolutionary left accused him of being a rightist while the oligarchy and military distrusted him for being a socialist. According to guerrilla leader Fermán Cienfuegos, "The 'leadership' of Duarte is nothing but an expression of the most abject and treasonous sellout, a systemic genocide designed to assure maintenance of the circuits of capital accumulations." In contrast, one Salvadoran businessman quipped, "Duarte is just a communist who happens to believe in God."[18]

Representing a political middle ground, the new junta was almost precisely what President Jimmy Carter's Latin America team wanted for El Salvador. According to Frank Devine, Carter's ambassador in San Salvador at the time, "the finest hour that El Salvador had in its memorable history was that coup of October 15, 1979."[19] The aims of the junta and those of the Carter administration converged remarkably: both wanted elections, civilian control over the military, and drastic human rights reform.

The Carter administration decided to engage this precarious and relatively reform-minded government. Classified U.S. government documents concluded that the new junta was "well-balanced, moderate, and well-disposed toward the United States and committed to the democratic process and human rights."[20] Two weeks after the coup, U.S. officials announced that Washington would provide the new government with "significant" military aid. Thomas Enders, then the top State Department diplomat for Latin America, stated that the coup promoted "the transformation of the military from an institution dedicated to the status quo to one that spearheads land reform and supports constitutional democracy."[21]

THE ASSASSINATION OF ARCHBISHOP ROMERO

For all the enthusiasm surrounding the reformist junta, the human rights situation in El Salvador remained dismal. Right-wing paramilitary factions and death squads continued to operate with impunity in the cities, and leftists both within the government and outside it were being targeted by the thousands. More than 2,500 civilians were killed in 1978 and 1979. In May 1979, Archbishop Romero traveled to the Vatican to provide the pope with seven dossiers stuffed with reports documenting El Salvador's horrifying condition. The pope recommended "much equilibrium and prudence, especially in making specific denunciations," and added that "it was better to remain confined to principles because it was risky to fall into errors of equivocations in making concrete denunciations."[22] Romero returned to El Salvador where he continued to call for social justice and an end to the violence.

On March 24, 1980, Archbishop Romero was assassinated while celebrating mass at the small chapel of the Divine Providence Hospital where he lived. A professional assassin fired a single .22 or .223 caliber bullet from a red, four-door Volkswagen vehicle. Romero's last words were reported to be, "May God have mercy on the assassins." The cold-blooded murder took place only a day after Romero had delivered a sermon in which he called on Salvadoran soldiers, as Christians, to obey God's higher order and to stop carrying out repressive orders. He said, "I beseech you, I beg you, I order you, in the name of God, to stop the repression!"[23]

Hundreds of thousands of Salvadorans attended Romero's funeral at the National Cathedral. The procession turned chaotic when unidentified gunmen opened fire on the mourners, killing and wounding dozens. Similar to the 1972 presidential election, Romero's brutal murder galvanized many on the left, leaving them to conclude that the archbishop's message could only be realized through the barrel of a gun. Former guerrilla leader Gerson Martínez commented in a 2008 interview with the author that "this assassination was the consecration of the civil war."[24]

The infamous and shadowy former Salvadoran army officer Roberto D'Aubuisson was believed to have presided over a meeting of active duty military personnel in which they drew straws to see who would kill Romero. A few months after the archbishop's assassination, D'Aubuisson was arrested on a farm along with a group of civilians and soldiers. The raid uncovered weapons and documents that implicated the group in death squad activity, including Romero's killing. However, the arrests sparked a wave of rightist terrorist threats and other pressures on government officials that culminated in D'Aubuisson's release.

BATTLES AT THE POLLS

The first pillar of the U.S. counterinsurgency and nation-building effort in El Salvador involved propping up the besieged junta in San Salvador and pushing it toward some semblance of democratic reform. Over the course of the war, elections played a major role in this aspect of the operation – and in how the rest of the operation was executed and perceived. In March 1981, President Duarte appointed an independent election council to prepare for the following year's national election. The vote would elect a constituent assembly tasked with appointing an interim government, drafting a new constitution, and setting a date for presidential elections. The government used slogans such as "Your Vote, Your Solution" and "Because El Salvador has changed, your vote will be respected" to convince the skeptical Salvadoran population that these would indeed be free elections – the first in fifty years.[25]

U.S. agencies already active in El Salvador, such as the Agency for International Development (AID) and the quasi-official American Institute for Free Labor Development (AIFLD), spent hundreds of thousands of dollars to bolster Salvadoran efforts to ensure an orderly election process. At the same time, a covert CIA program helped fund the production of campaign materials and radio and television commercials to boost the fortunes of Duarte's centrist Christian Democrats against the guerrillas and right-wing Nationalist Republican Alliance (ARENA). In a tactic intended to bolster the government's candidates, one CIA "psychological operation" distributed flyers that showed on one side an oligarch with money spilling out of his pockets and on the other a guerrilla wearing a red bandana and carrying a rifle.[26] Washington was no doubt funding and training the ESAF to defeat the guerrillas with bullets, but it also worked aggressively to help the Salvadoran government win the hearts and minds of the population through the ballot.

A critical underlying aspect of this civilian-support program was the Reagan administration's opposition to negotiated power sharing between the junta and the FMLN. In the administration's view, such an arrangement would legitimize the guerrillas having "shot their way to power." According to the State Department's Thomas Enders, a key architect of the unfolding engagement strategy, "We should recognize that El Salvador's leaders will not – and should not – grant the insurgents through negotiations the share of power the rebels have not been able to win on the battlefield. But they should be – and are – willing to compete with the guerrillas at the polls."[27] Heading up to the 1982 elections, the Salvadoran government declared that the FMLN could participate in the vote if they first laid down their arms.

The guerrillas dismissed the offer, maintaining that power sharing had to precede any election. The guerrillas also promised that they would disrupt what they considered an illegitimate election and warned Salvadorans not to participate. One FMLN commander advised on guerrilla radio that "the people are to build barricades in the countryside to prevent free movement; the people must remain at home."[28] Media reports detailed guerrilla graffiti across the country that warned residents, "Vote in the morning, die in the afternoon." In a fit of saber-rattling intended to provide a preview of what election day would be like, a few weeks before the elections the guerrillas conducted raids across the country, including in the capital, but to little effect.[29]

During this time, the U.S. embassy notified Washington that the FMLN was "mounting a major attempt to block elections in El Salvador for March 28 [1982]" after "massive new shipments of arms for the insurgents began arriving in December." The embassy indicated that the disruptive guerrilla operations were being planned at the same time that the FMLN's civilian wing, the FDR, was telling American audiences that the guerrillas would not interfere with the vote.[30]

As the election appeared to many to be a sham, critics on the political left in the United States remained dubious about its merits. One particular point of controversy was a plan to deploy the ESAF to protect voters and polling stations. Peace activist Colman McCarthy wrote in the *Washington Post*:

> It's an odd way for the government of El Salvador to prepare for next month's election: by turning the army loose to massacre the voters. In the annals of voter-registration drives, the West has seen nothing quite like it. Presumably there will be no ballot initiative on whether citizens suspect of disloyalty prefer to be decapitated, shot behind the ear, or slain by strafing from American-supplied helicopters. All three methods have been perfected by the American-advised Salvadoran army.[31]

When the voting finally took place in late March 1982, international and domestic electoral observers were generally stunned by what they witnessed. Defying the guerrilla calls to stay away, over 1.5 million Salvadorans went to the polls, representing roughly 80 percent of the electorate. Despite chilling predictions, the FMLN did not significantly disrupt the voting process.

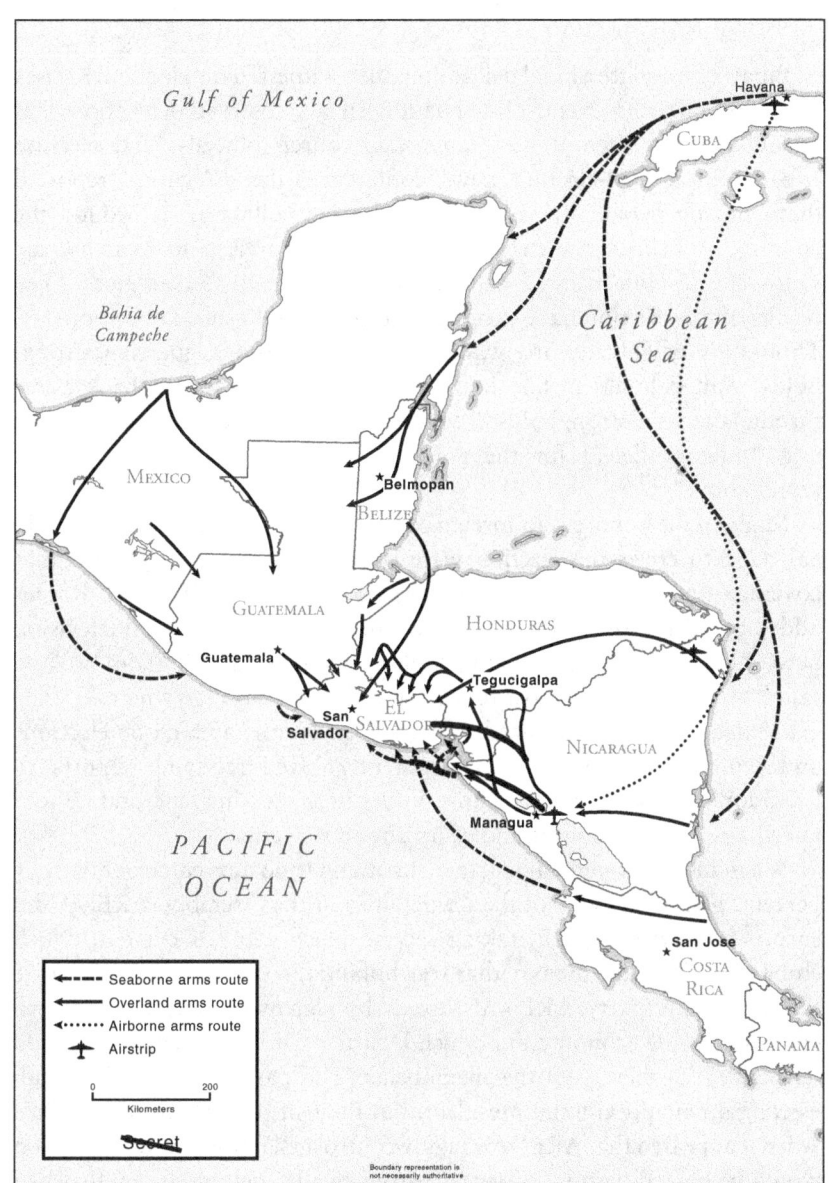

FIGURE 25.2. Map from a 1982 classified U.S. intelligence document indicating clandestine arms shipment routes to El Salvador's Marxist guerrilla group, the FMLN. Cuba was a main source of the FMLN's weapons although it also received shipments from sympathetic communist regimes such as Vietnam and Czechoslovakia. Vocal critics of the Reagan administration contended that the U.S. government intentionally inflated the threat of external communist support to Salvadoran guerrillas in order to justify a military anticommunist strategy in El Salvador – and Central America more broadly. Map prepared by the University of Wisconsin-Madison Cartography Lab©. Reprinted with permission

Bipartisan congressional delegations also witnessed the election. Kansas Senate Republican Nancy Kassebaum led an observer delegation that included fellow members of Congress, church officials, and election experts. In a post-election news conference, the delegation reported that "having personally visited a number of polling areas around the country, [it] believes these elections were fair and free." American ambassador Deane Hinton in El Salvador cabled back to Washington, "The results of this election have exceeded our most optimistic expectations.... Thousands of Salvadorans walked overnight through guerrilla strongholds, waited hours in line to vote, and are now walking back home through the same strongholds."[32] Secretary of State Alexander Haig called it a "military defeat for the guerrillas quite as much as a political repudiation."[33]

Many of the hundreds of foreign correspondents who had traveled to El Salvador to cover the election were surprised at the events given that coverage of the war to date had been so negative. CBS's Dan Rather added to the positive spin on the vote, announcing on national television news, "It's a triumph! A million people at the polls." NBC's Tom Brokaw said it was "one of the most remarkable election days anywhere."[34] The *Washington Post* editorialized, "The United States gambled on elections and won." President Reagan apparently loved receiving reports of Salvadoran peasants standing four hours in the baking sun, and he told anecdotes about it months and years after the election.[35]

When the votes were tallied, the Christian Democrats came out with 35 percent, giving them 24 of the 60 deputies in the assembly. ARENA did surprisingly well, though, taking second place with 26 percent, which embarrassed a U.S. embassy that was hoping the vote would marginalize the fiery rightist party. ARENA's strong showing owed much to the dismal condition of the economy, for which Duarte's Christian Democrats could be blamed as they were the incumbents. The parties were tasked with electing a new provisional president, but the Christian Democrats balked when it appeared that ARENA's highly controversial Roberto D'Aubuisson would be elected because of support from smaller rightist parties that had joined ARENA to form a majority coalition.[36]

At this point U.S. diplomats began to apply significant pressure on select Salvadoran politicians to ensure that D'Aubuisson – now the international poster figure for El Salvador's death squads – did not win the vote. Under duress, the military high command proposed a more acceptable solution in the form of independent businessman Álvaro Magaña.[37] As one State Department official put it, "[Ambassador]

Hinton jammed Magaña down D'Aubuisson's throat."[38] In a somewhat counterintuitive development, the Salvadoran military was intervening to produce an outcome that antagonized the right and bolstered the country's U.S.-backed political center. Inferring that more than simple diplomatic pressure was used to secure the deal, one U.S. diplomat noted, "That's not [U.S.] intervention. That's money talking." Denied the presidency, D'Aubuisson still ended up as president of the assembly, a sharp setback to the U.S. strategy. This was made abundantly clear when the rightist-controlled assembly, as one of its first initiatives, repealed parts of the U.S.-supported land reform program.

Reagan's expansion of the engagement strategy depended on the continued perception in Washington that massive U.S. aid and training were moving the country toward better democracy via a series of surprisingly fair elections, human rights protections, and a professional military. Following repeated and surprisingly open elections in El Salvador, many Democrats in Congress came to believe that the Salvadoran government was relatively legitimate and merited U.S. economic and military assistance. In this sense, the ballot box in El Salvador pushed the conservative Reagan administration and liberal congressional Democrats to "converge" on engagement.

THE ESAF LEADERSHIP

Even as elections in the 1980s helped to legitimize both the government in San Salvador and U.S. engagement policy, the military situation did nearly as much to discredit them. Despite the embarrassing failure of the 1981 final offensive, over the next year the FMLN became a much more powerful fighting force. In late January 1982, a guerrilla commando raid on the Ilopango air base outside San Salvador destroyed six U.S.-supplied helicopters and eleven other aircraft. Well-armed guerrilla forces, camped out on and around the Guazapa volcano, were unnervingly close to the capital. The Reagan administration responded by doubling the number of U.S. "trainers" (the term "adviser" was decidedly out of favor after Vietnam) in El Salvador and ramping up military assistance, but only by $25 million.

By Reagan's second year, it was clear that this modest escalation of engagement was not going to produce a quick turnaround.[39] Junta president José Napoleón Duarte lamented, "We are losing the fight with the guerrillas in the countryside." An American military trainer later explained, "We had to reform or we were going to lose. And it wasn't because the guerrillas were so good; it was because the [Salvadoran] Army was so bad."⁴⁰ The reality was that the ESAF's training, morale, and fighting prowess remained marginal at best.

Back in the late 1970s, before the war began, the ESAF was effectively "a mission of 11,000 that had no mission." Its lightning victory over Honduras in the short-lived "Soccer War" in 1969 helped perpetuate a conventional war doctrine geared to defeating external enemies, not internal insurgents. One lower-level ESAF officer, when asked about the military's understanding of counterinsurgency, admitted, "The only war our senior leaders ever fought was with Honduras."⁴¹ This reliance on a conventional doctrine meant, for example, that air strike capability was emphasized while internal troop mobility was not. The ESAF's culture and actions were also inextricably tied to the conservative business and land-owning class: in the early years of Marxist opposition, the military had been commissioned to stamp out the leftist subversion that threatened the country's more powerful interests.

At the same time, the military elite stayed well clear of the battlefield. In the first years of the war, one common jeer was that ESAF senior officers "don't even own fatigues." Those who ended up doing the actual fighting "tended to be the total incompetents."⁴² Officers were often accused of collecting the salaries of nonexistent "ghost soldiers" and leasing their troops to land and business owners to work as security guards and laborers. Poorly educated Salvadoran youths were picked up from the streets and conscripted for two-year stints. One U.S. officer repeated a generally held view that the ESAF spent its time "sitting in garrison or abusing civilians."⁴³

Most Salvadoran officers – whether they were army or security forces, which included the National Police, National Guard, and Treasury Police – were graduates of the Captain General Gerardo Barrios Military Academy. Named for a nineteenth-century commander and president, the military school was often referred to the as the "Escuela de los Presidentes" because so many of its graduates ended up running the country. Entry into the military school was highly competitive, and graduation as an officer meant virtually unmatched financial and social rewards. For lower-middle-class youth especially, this was an appealing enticement, despite the academy's emphasis on rote memorization and its general neglect of strategic doctrine.⁴⁴

The school graduated only about 20 percent of its first-year entrants each year, and graduating classes became known infamously as *tandas* (rotations), tightly knit groups that were commissioned and promoted together. The tandas were notorious for their insularity and for their willingness to tolerate abuses committed by members of their own ranks.⁴⁵ For one observer, "If among them there proved to be embarrassing incompetents, not to mention murderers, rapists and thieves, then those men were shielded by their classmates and defended ferociously."⁴⁶

U.S. advisers believed that the tanda culture lay at the heart of the ESAF's problems. According to one adviser, "I remember one of our guys from the MilGroup [the U.S. Military Group attached to the Embassy in San Salvador] said to me the way to reform the officer corps in the long run was to take about six thousand pounds of TNT over to the military school and blow it away. By the time they get out of military school they know how to smuggle cars without paying any duty. And the idea that they are creatures beyond the law is already in them."⁴⁷ Another U.S. military attaché in San Salvador reflected, "You're not talking about simple training; you're getting right down into military tradition."

The Pentagon attempted to address the tanda issue indirectly by training a new breed of junior officers outside of El Salvador, mostly in the United States, Panama, and Honduras. The principal aim was to extricate budding officers from their corrupt Salvadoran institutions. But the external training sites were also necessary from a capacity perspective. An informal agreement between Congress and the White House limited to fifty-five the number of U.S. military trainers who could be deployed in El Salvador at any one time. But the effort required far more trainers than this cap would permit.

In 1981, the first group of 500 Salvadoran officer candidates traveled to Fort Benning, Georgia, to take the three-month basic officer training course. By the end of 1983, the U.S. military had trained over half the ESAF officer corps – approximately 900 officers – all outside of El Salvador. But the program had its share of problems. For one, American advisers often lamented that the positive training conducted outside the country was wasted as officers reverted "to the old way of doing things with disturbing frequency once back in El Salvador."⁴⁸ For another, the system created divisions within the ESAF officer corps. ESAF officers trained in the traditional manner at Gerardo Barrios looked askance at compatriots who had become officers in these far less demanding and shorter U.S. military courses.

"COUNTERINSURGENCY BY PROXY"

At the same time, the fifty-five American trainers on the ground in El Salvador were saddled with the Herculean task of turning the rest of the corrupt and insular garrison army – the Americans' euphemism was

"9-to-5 army" – into a mobile and lethal counterinsurgency force able to check if not defeat the FMLN and, instead of terrorizing the understandably mistrustful civilian population, win its hearts and minds. The state of the Salvadoran enlisted ranks shocked many of the incoming American soldiers. The American adviser Luis Orlando, who arrived in El Salvador in 1983, told the author, "I was a member of the Cuban army when Castro was in the Sierra Maestra. I saw the deterioration and breakdown of the military as they were supporting the dictator Batista. Salvador was the same movie."[49]

The guiding principle of the U.S military effort was known as "KISSSS"; in the post-Vietnam, "light footprint" ethos this meant "keep it simple, sustainable, small, and Salvadoran." Vietnam was still fresh, and its main lesson for American advisers in El Salvador was that local forces would need to take responsibility for their own successes and failures. Contrary to what some critics assumed, the Pentagon, the Reagan administration, and a sizable congressional majority had no significant interest in escalating the "counterinsurgency by proxy" campaign in El Salvador into full-scale combat deployment, as in the bruising quagmire of Vietnam.

A major initiative that began in 1982 was the creation of a new joint general staff to serve as the ESAF's commanding body. One stinging criticism of the American adviser role was that many of the U.S. military's best soldiers and trainers were not sent to El Salvador because deployment there involved no clear combat mission. As one adviser admitted, "We have the third team here."[50] Another recurrent complaint was that the American advisers themselves received very little training for the mission. The majority passed through a two-day general security assistance course before taking off for the Salvadoran theater. Also, as for much of the Vietnam War, American advisers spent an average of one year on the ground before rotating out of El Salvador. The short timeline meant that they acquired familiarity with the theater and reached effective mission capability only months or weeks before their departure.

Further complicating the American operation was the uncertain status of congressional approval for military assistance packages. U.S. advisers were never sure that federal funding would continue; in fact, political maneuvering over the course of the war resulted in several congressional threats to cut assistance. Not only was financial assistance uncertain, but it was also uncoordinated – in 1984, military assistance to El Salvador arrived in three separate and unrelated allotments – and not always wisely used. The ESAF often used assistance credits to make ill-advised weapons and supply purchases, such as radios that did not include Spanish-language instructions.

Despite these limitations, however, U.S. training and assistance helped grow the ESAF from 16,000 troops in 1982 to 25,000 only a year later. And, in contrast to the lean years before massive U.S. assistance kicked in, when ESAF troops were equipped with old G-3 rifles, these soldiers now had M-16s and other modern weaponry. By the end of 1984, the ESAF had grown to around 30,000 soldiers and roughly two-thirds of them had received U.S. training. The rapid U.S.-sponsored growth of the ESAF continued until 1986 when the force topped out at almost 40,000 personnel. Despite these gains, an embarrassing 60–80 percent of these troops were deployed in static defense as opposed to the more necessary and effective offensive combat operations.

THE EL MOZOTE MASSACRE

In 1981, the Pentagon released a classified strategy document for El Salvador known as the Woerner Report for the American general who penned it. The report highlighted the need for a legitimate security force in El Salvador and criticized the ESAF for its flagrant prosecution of and support for wartime atrocities. It read: "Unabated terror from the right and continued tolerance of institutional violence could dangerously erode popular support to the point wherein the Armed Forces would not be viewed as the protector of society, but as an army of occupation."[51] This estimation was perhaps never more prescient than when an ESAF "rapid reaction" force massacred hundreds of civilians in and around the village of El Mozote.

The ESAF's Atlacatl Battalion was created on March 1, 1981, under the command of the daring and ambitious Lieutenant Colonel Domingo Monterrosa. Monterrosa had taken courses at the U.S. Army's controversial School of the Americas in the Panama Canal Zone in 1966, and a U.S. Army Special Forces mobile training team helped to train the elite unit to take the fight to the enemy in search-and-destroy missions throughout the countryside and jungles in late 1981. Initially capped at 600, the force soon grew to around 1,000 soldiers notorious for their violent records and lack of discipline.[52]

In early December of the same year, the battalion was deployed on what the ESAF called Operación Rescate (Rescue) to corner and annihilate FMLN cells in the guerrilla-infested eastern mountain province of Morazán. At five o'clock on the morning of December 11, soldiers of the

3rd Section of the 5th Company of the Atlacatl Battalion began to take residents of the village of El Mozote out of their houses, grouping them by gender and age in the town plaza. The Salvadoran troops then deliberately and systematically executed hundreds of men, women, and children. According to survivors, soldiers slitting throats of children shouted, "You are guerrillas and this is justice. This is justice." Scores of women were raped before being shot in the head. One witness said that a soldier told a superior that he would not kill children. The superior said, "Which son of a bitch says that?" He then went into the group of detained children, grabbed a small boy, threw him up in the air and impaled him on his bayonet on the way down.

The killing at El Mozote lasted all day and into the evening. Atlacatl conducted similar operations in nearby villages over the course of four days. All told, the ESAF killed over 800 civilians in what came to be known to history as the El Mozote massacre, although roughly half of the executions took place in other villages. More than half of the victims were children younger than eighteen, with some only a few months or days old.[53] Years later, UN investigators found 143 skeletons in a common grave, including 131 children with an average age of six.[54]

Eager not to waste such a propaganda opportunity, the FMLN went on the air with its Radio Venceremos (Radio We Will Prevail):

This genocidal military method is no happenstance. Vietnam represents its historical precedent. The U.S. Congress and people, as the world public opinion probably remember the massacre of My Lai, which had a profound impact on the U.S. people, the U.S. Army itself, and all countries around the murder.... Those responsible for these murders are the same as those at My Lai.... Imperialism admits having carried out the design and supervision of genocide in El Salvador.[55]

In late January 1982, foreign correspondents Raymond Bonner of the *New York Times*, Alma Guillermoprieto of the *Washington Post*, and photographer Susan Meiselas, who had been traveling in guerrilla-controlled areas, began reporting on the massacre. Guillermoprieto's January 27 article, "Salvadoran Peasants Describe Mass Killing: Woman Tells of Children's Deaths," reported the testimony of three survivors.[56] At the same time the news reports were appearing, the U.S. embassy in San Salvador sent a confidential cable to Washington labeled, "Report on Alleged Massacre," which concluded that "civilians did die in the Operation Rescate, but no evidence could be found to confirm that government forces systematically massacred civilians in the operations zone, nor that the number of civilians killed even remotely approached number cited in other reports."⁵⁷ Likely influenced by the embassy's reporting, back in Washington senior Reagan administration officials began to deny that a massacre had taken place. Senior State Department official Thomas Enders stated publicly, "There is no evidence to confirm that government forces systematically massacred civilians in the operations zone, or that the number of civilians even remotely approached the 733 or 926 victims cited in the press."⁵⁸

During Vietnam, many foreign correspondents came to the conclusion that American military and civilian officials often lied to conceal how poorly the war was going. Following El Mozote, this same type of "credibility gap" opened in El Salvador policy. Journalists began to dismiss official American reports as "propaganda." In 2008 Guillermoprieto recalled to the author,

I think the massacre of El Mozote consolidated my own view that U.S. involvement in the Salvadoran conflict was criminal: I had seen Deane Hinton busily trying to cover up Salvadoran government atrocities before El Mozote, and now I saw again how not only Hinton but the State Department as a whole made every effort to discredit what Ray Bonner, Susan Meiselas [a photographer] and I had seen with our own eyes.⁵⁹

The connection between U.S. training and the Atlacatl's brutality led many critics to understandably conclude that the U.S. government was responsible for these atrocities. U.S. advisers and diplomats, on the other hand, contended that their influence was intended to improve a rotten institution.⁶⁰ Knowing that a clean ESAF was key to a successful counterinsurgency strategy, U.S. advisers claimed that they had little patience with their Salvadoran counterparts who were suspected of committing or sanctioning abuses. U.S. advisers knew that an increasingly desperate ESAF could very easily adopt "scorched earth" tactics to ensure that the FMLN did not seize power. The success of the Guatemalan military's brutal yet extremely effective counterinsurgency war in Guatemala was fresh in the minds of the ESAF, U.S. advisers, and the FMLN. Yet, in trying to promote a "cleaner" counterinsurgency, U.S. advisers were confronted with all of the associated challenges of trying to win a war with minimal violence. An American trainer lamented in 1981,

If the solution here were to eradicate the guerrillas, fine, we could eradicate them. Villages sympathetic to the guerrillas, for instance, could be relocated or – as indeed happens in some cases – destroyed. The point is that we won't do it. We've all become humanists. We let the terrorists exist because what it would take to eradicate them would not be acceptable. Our hearts bleed too much.⁶¹

According to U.S. officer James Steele, who defended the U.S. approach, "No one on the U.S. team sanctioned those [abuses]; we did everything we could to get Salvadorans to recognize that you don't win people's support by being abusive." In fact, Steele contended, he and his fellow officers were actually frustrated with the restrictions that prevented them from accompanying the ESAF into combat. "If we had been able to be more out in the field with them, even in very small numbers," he explained, "we could have avoided some of those things happening periodically."[62] Moreover, according to U.S. adviser Colonel John Waghelstein, to the extent that U.S. advisers *were* engaged, they were making a bad situation better. He explained, "It was also evident from the guerrillas' writing that the more U.S. advisers that were on the scene, the less likely the Salvadoran Armed Forces were to do something really stupid, which they were prone to do.... Our presence there was instrumental to getting the Salvadorans to stop abusing their citizens."[63] U.S. officials often defended their interpretation of a positive impact on a horrid situation by citing statistics indicating that as the ESAF transformed into a professional military four times its original size, the rate of gross human rights violations dropped precipitously.

THE FMLN WINS HEARTS AND MINDS

As the Salvadoran war rolled into its third year, the situation appeared increasingly bleak for the Salvadoran government and its American sponsors. The disparities, in terms of morale, commitment, and capacity, between the ESAF and FMLN forces were now glaring. In July 1983, a *New York Times* correspondent wrote, "Whereas the Salvadoran soldier looks, at best, young and earnest, the guerrillas encountered by Western correspondents are self-confident to the point of being cocky."[64] Many observers at the time noted that while the guerrillas were fighting for a clearly defined cause that they believed in, the government and military were more reluctant participants in the conflict. A U.S. embassy official remarked, "The left is always going to be one step ahead of us because they care about the revolution."[65] An FMLN fighter boasted to a foreign reporter that if he fought and died they would name a street after him; if an ESAF soldier died, he did so anonymously.

By that summer, the insurgents had taken control of most of Chalatenango, a northern province, as well as much of the eastern half of the country. The guerrillas were also bringing the war to the cities, including San Salvador. The Pentagon was reporting that the FMLN "displayed a boldness and a level of operational competence that repeatedly embarrassed Salvadoran forces." ESAF units often surrendered en masse, while the guerrillas benefited from a policy of releasing ESAF prisoners after an interrogation, an approach that provided them with excellent enemy intelligence and encouraged ESAF deserters. Nearly a quarter of the FMLN's arms at this point were U.S.-provided ESAF weapons that the insurgents had captured or purchased.

In late 1983, FMLN forces raided El Paraíso and destroyed the quarter-mile-long Cuscatlán Bridge, sending another massive economic and psychological blow to the Salvadoran government and its American sponsors. The U.S. military group commanding El Salvador gave the Salvadoran government only six weeks to survive.[66] Other Pentagon officials expected the FMLN to control most of the countryside in a matter of months, even if they had not yet seized power by then. These dire predictions were not exaggerated, given that by this time the guerrillas controlled vast swaths of territory, especially in the mountainous third of the country.

Although their sabotage operations wreaked economic havoc, the FMLN made it a priority to avoid targeting civilians. Over 4,000 civilians were killed in 1983 alone, but fewer than 100 of these deaths were attributed to the FMLN. Most of the indiscriminate killing continued to be carried out by death squads and security forces. According to one Salvadoran political analyst, "It is one thing for the death squads to go after several hundred peasants in a decade [as was the case in the 1950s and 1960s]; it is another thing to kill more than 12,000 people in one year." To be sure, the FMLN was winning the hearts-and-minds campaign. The ESAF's strategic response was a series of comparatively indiscriminate "search-and-destroy" sweeps backed up by artillery and A-37 attack aircraft supplied by Washington, an approach that may have created as many fresh guerrilla recruits as guerrilla KIAs (killed in action).

THE NATIONAL PLAN

Frustrated by the dire state of the war, in early February 1983 high-ranking U.S. officers joined Ambassador Hinton for a visit to the ESAF's High Command, where provisional president Magaña and Minister of Defense José Guillermo García were also present. The American delegation recommended that the ESAF create a joint civilian-military entity to plan and execute an extensive "pacification" campaign in the departments of San Vicente and subsequently Usulután.[67] Loosely based on the CORDS program from Vietnam, the new National Plan directed civilian government agencies to implement agrarian reform programs, employment initiatives, and infrastructure projects and to provide emergency humanitarian services to the war-weary population. It also directed the military to organize light *cazador* (hunter) battalions for deployment in San Vicente. In classical counterinsurgency fashion, the units would "clear and hold" the areas so that the civilian programs could "build." A third key element of the National Plan was the creation of a civilian defense force tasked with keeping the guerrillas out after the heavy military presence eased.

Developed jointly in Washington, U.S. Southern Command in Panama, and Embassy San Salvador, the National Plan was initially resisted by the ESAF for its emphasis on civilian over military priorities. The Salvadoran government agency responsible for implementing these programs, the National Commission for Reconstruction (CONARA), worked in four phases: planning, offensive, development, and consolidation, an approach that strongly reflected the U.S. advisers' belief that "clear, build, hold" was a key component of a successful civilian-military strategy.[68]

After several months, most indicators suggested that the plan was proceeding well.[69] By July 1983, over 7,000 ESAF troops were in and around San Vicente, even though some key ESAF commanders wished they had instead been hunting guerrillas in the rebel hotbed departments of Chalatenango and Morazán. In one civic program, "clowns, a mariachi band and skimpily clad dancers perform between speeches by Salvadoran army officers and social workers calling on peasants to reject the guerrillas. Meanwhile, army barbers cut hair, and soldiers pass out rice, dresses and medicine." As one U.S. soldier described this program, "You see the army winning hearts and minds. . . . This is low-intensity doctrine in action."[70] Salvadoran officials reported on the results of the National Plan's first phase, Operation Well-Being, at the end of 1983. The FMLN had largely withdrawn from San Vicente, and the joint forces had set up a wide range of development projects, such as reopening forty-one schools, establishing seven cooperative farms, and distributing vaccinations in dozens of communities.

Yet while the initial results were encouraging, the National Plan soon began to flounder. The tremendous bureaucratic red tape in San Salvador forced the delay or cancellation of many planned projects. More critically, when the ESAF withdrew roughly half of its army force deployed in San Vicente, the guerrillas immediately returned. A foreign correspondent in San Vicente at the time observed that the FMLN quickly "overran civil defense outposts, forced the closure of schools and clinics, subverted the cooperatives, and chased officials loyal to the Salvadoran government back to the safety of San Salvador."[71] Another distressing outcome was the poor performance of civilian militias. Only 500 participants joined out of an expected 1,500. Those who did join had the tendency to sell their weapons to the guerrillas.

The militia effort was also crippled by memories of the feared paramilitary organization known as Organización Democrática Nacionalista (ORDEN); it began in the 1960s and 1970s as a civil defense unit but morphed into a death squad machine. While a civilian defense force was a key component of the strategy, U.S. advisers didn't want a new "Frankenstein" militia to spin out of the ESAF's control, similar to what had effectively occurred in Guatemala. Making matters worse, ESAF officers widely considered the civilian defense force a "gringo-imposed program" that was effectively useless but a necessary price to pay for continued U.S. military aid.[72] One U.S. trainer summed up the grim plight of the militias:

The hand-me-down rifle that the civil defender shares with several of his compatriots will likely be the only tangible support he receives in return for volunteering.... He will receive neither a uniform nor pay. If his unit is attacked, he will discover that the local ESAF commander has no plans to come to his rescue. If wounded, he will not be evacuated to a Salvadoran military hospital.... Volunteers for civil defense come from the ranks of those who fail to qualify for conscription: the aged, the lame, and the otherwise unfit.[73]

A few years after the National Plan was implemented, the level of guerrilla activity in San Vicente was about the same as before the program had begun. The failure of the plan, which had been intended as the template for effective counterinsurgency throughout El Salvador, became a key subject for foreign correspondents covering the war. Reporting on National Plan setbacks, the *New York Times*' Lydia Chavez wrote, "The question that hangs over the American counterinsurgency experts in El Salvador is whether any amount of training and cajoling and convincing can enable an unpopular military establishment to quell a leftist armed rebellion, and whether, in the end, the job once again will have to be taken over by American troops."[74]

"WE HAVE TO FACE THE HARD FACTS"

By the mid to late 1980s, the apparent incompetence and unpopularity of the government and the ESAF accompanied with continued FMLN activity led many in the media and elsewhere to conclude that, despite billions in U.S. aid, the situation in El Salvador was dire. Marxist revolution had been averted, perhaps, but the Salvadoran government and ESAF now appeared locked in a bloody stalemate with the tenacious FMLN.[75] The *New York Times* told its readers in early 1989, "Things are getting worse in El Salvador, a trend that is etched as usual in blood – blood shed by guerrilla attacks, bombings and killings; more bloodshed by Army sweeps and death squad murders. After eight years of savage civil war, Salvadorans seemed enraged and saddened by the terrible normalcy such violence has acquired."[76] Another U.S. journalist reported that the well-guarded Embassy San Salvador that housed U.S. diplomats, development experts, the Military Group, and certainly its fair share of spies resembled "a military bunker more than a diplomatic post." In another inference to a prolonged quagmire, the correspondent also cited the plaque located on one of the embassy's walls commemorating the fourteen Americans who had died in the conflict to date.[77]

It was not only foreign correspondents who thought that perhaps the United States had a long way to go before its side would even have a shot at winning this war. In August 1987, the former commander of the U.S. Southern Command in Panama made a gloomy assessment: "We have to face the hard facts, and we have to say this is going to be a war that will go on for years. It might go 15 years, but it can be won.... It's difficult to convince people that in the long run democracy will survive only if we are willing to sacrifice in our own hemisphere."[78] Members of Congress also expressed their concerns in late 1987 when two liberal Republicans, Senator Mark Hatfield of Oregon and Congressman James Leach of Iowa, published a report that called out the "financing failure of the U.S. policy [in El Salvador] and the urgent need to reform it." According to the report's congressional sponsors, "Congress and the administration should accept that the search for a military solution for the conflict in El Salvador has produced a stalemate." The U.S. should direct its military aid toward a resolution of what the report called a civil war.[79]

A SECOND "FINAL OFFENSIVE"

Reflecting months of planning, the FMLN's second "final offensive" began on the morning of November 11, 1989, when urban commandos launched a mortar attack against National Guard installations and ESAF General Staff headquarters in the capital. That same night thousands of insurgents launched simultaneous attacks on ESAF positions throughout the country. They also struck both the presidential palace and the private residence of the newly elected president, Alfredo Cristiani. The would-be assassination

El Salvador, 1979–1992 331

victim happened to be outside the capital at the time. Relying on hidden caches of weapons and supplies, the FMLN continued the offensive for three weeks. Commandos dispersed throughout San Salvador would wait inside houses, allow ESAF troops to pass by, and then ambush the vulnerable soldiers.

ESAF commanders were taken almost entirely by surprise by the offensive's ferocity and breadth. The ESAF had spent the past decade trying to transform into a counterinsurgency unit capable of taking the fight to the guerrillas in the mountains. In November 1989, it was entirely unprepared to fight the urban battles that the guerrillas' incursion into San Salvador forced it into. In a classified post mortem on the offensive, the U.S. embassy in San Salvador reported that after days of heavy fighting, desperate ESAF commanders requested that Cristiani approve the use of airstrikes within the cities.

Their president's approval of selected urban targets in hand, the ESAF used its A-37s and C-47s to go after guerrilla positions, especially in San Salvador.[80] The problem, however, was that the guerrillas had intentionally occupied locales in upper-class areas that it correctly believed the ESAF would be reluctant to bomb. The guerrillas also constructed trenches to withstand the air attacks. Despite these obstacles, the ESAF did hit a number of neighborhoods, a move that resulted in thousands of insurgent and civilian casualties and large numbers of buildings destroyed.

A week into the offensive, FMLN commandos began occupying positions in Colonia Escalón, one of the capital's most exclusive neighborhoods. Before long, the guerrillas infiltrated the Sheraton Hotel, where they found the startled secretary general of the Organization of American States (OAS), João Clemente Baena Soares, as well as diplomats from various countries and a dozen U.S. Green Berets. The guerrilla commandos soon released all of the hotel guests, including Baena Soares. A half-dozen or so Green Berets barricaded themselves in their rooms in order to fight it out with the guerrillas. The guerrilla commandos soon withdrew from the hotel to avoid a certain firefight with the well-armed American soldiers.[81]

The next day, the FMLN broadcast that insurgent columns were on the "skirts" of San Salvador volcano, located right above the city. The rebels proposed a "ceasefire," a move that Cristiani called "insincere."[82] Amid the unfolding chaos, U.S. military personnel criticized the ESAF's inability to respond to this serious onslaught. According to one adviser, "They [the ESAF commanders] were just completely taken off balance. Most of the [U.S.] advisers were locked down, but two of us figured we could survive and get in and work with them at the Estado Mayor [Chiefs of

Staff]. We're in there with the Salvadorans, who were saying, 'We've lost the war, can you get me to Miami?'"[83] An American diplomat working in El Salvador recalled, "Heck, we had spent a billion on the ESAF and the FMLN had walked into San Salvador."[84]

The three-week insurgent offensive was marked by the heaviest fighting of the war. By early December, the ESAF had pushed the majority of the rebel forces out of capital, but large insurgent columns remained just outside the city. Believing exaggerated reports of rebel numbers, the tentative ESAF remained in largely defensive positions. It actually took prodding from U.S. advisers for the ESAF to pursue the retreating guerrillas.

The FMLN commanders prayed that the show of force in San Salvador and other cities would spark a general revolt in support of the guerrillas. Hundreds of millions of dollars in American aid and countless hours of training had still left the ESAF entirely incapable of effectively handling a large-scale insurrection. However, as was less understood at the time, a major influence on the FMLN's decision to launch the second offensive was that its military standing was severely diminished vis-à-vis the ESAF. In a sense, the final offensive was a "Hail Mary," a last-ditch effort to break the ESAF. Its failure pushed the FMLN and ESAF into two more years of what U.S. policymakers called a "hurtful stalemate."[85]

AN INSURGENCY IN DECLINE

We had to face the reality that we could not win. – Gerson Martínez[86]

In December 1989, FMLN guerrillas forced 200 soldiers – three full companies – of the Bracamonte Immediate-Reaction Infantry Battalion to withdraw into Honduras, carrying their wounded comrades with them.[87] Soon after dawn on February 10, 1990, guerrillas deployed in the mountainous region of Chalatenango encountered a large ESAF patrol. A firefight ensued that left two ESAF officers and eleven soldiers dead, with six more captured. The guerrillas lost one in the skirmish. Then in November 1990, the FMLN mounted eleven simultaneous attacks on ESAF targets, including SAM shoot-downs of an ESAF helicopter and attack aircraft.

Despite the failure of the November 1989 final offensive to spark a mass uprising, the FMLN appeared stronger than ever, which led *The Economist* magazine to conclude, "The last of Central America's anticommunist wars has its own murderous momentum."[88] Despite these pessimistic assessments, the reality in the late 1980s and early 1990s was that the FMLN understood that it had no way of winning power. It could still hit the ESAF at will, causing embarrassing setbacks to the Salvadoran government. Yet this was a far cry from the Sandinista-like uprising that it had first expected in early 1981 and then, somewhat delusionally, again in late 1989. What is more, the demise of communism in Eastern Europe dried up much of the FMLN's external sponsorship. The Sandinistas' largely unexpected electoral defeat in 1990 removed the FMLN's closest ally from power in Managua, and another key ally, Cuba, was cutting aid after losing badly needed economic subsidies from the Soviet Union. Having relied for years on external funding and solidarity, the FMLN was now on its own.

Moreover, the Salvadoran government had held a series of elections that, despite the guerrillas' best efforts, deepened its legitimacy and popularity. Having lived on cornmeal and other meager rations for years –in some cases more than a decade – FMLN commanders were increasingly disposed to a negotiated settlement. In the words of the FMLN leader Gerson Martínez, negotiations that "started in the early 1980s as a distraction eventually became an imperative."[89] The move toward talks was bolstered by the evolution of the Central America–wide peace negotiations led by Costa Rican president Oscar Arias. The core of Arias's plan became the Esquipulas II Accord of 1987, which called for "pacification and integration" of warring societies, including El Salvador. "Pacification" meant an end to military actions; "integration" referred to the admission of guerrilla fighters into the political system.

In El Salvador, incoming ARENA president Alfredo Cristiani called for direct negotiations with the FMLN within days of his inauguration in 1989. Part of Cristiani's dilemma was that he wanted to pursue a peace process but did not want to appear to his rightist supporters to be caving in to pressure from either the guerrillas or the United States. Complicating matters even more, ARENA's business wing was increasingly wary of D'Aubuisson's militaristic platform and dogma inside the party and thus was now willing to at least consider a negotiated settlement.[90]

The first significant negotiations between the rightist Cristiani government and Marxist guerrillas took place in Mexico in September 1989. The UN, OAS, and Catholic Church served as observers. At the meetings, the FMLN presented a proposal for establishing a cease-fire by November 15 that would then end the war two months later. A follow-up meeting was held in Costa Rica in October, but the talks stalled over the Salvadoran government's insistence that the FMLN agree to an unconditional surrender.

On January 16, 1992, in a solemn ceremony at a nineteenth-century castle in Mexico City, the government of El Salvador signed a UN-brokered peace accord with the FMLN, ending the country's bloody twelve-year war. The agreement also culminated two years of highly contentious and frustrating negotiations between the Salvadoran government and FMLN. Tremendous destruction to infrastructure, 77,000 Salvadorans dead, and millions displaced (somewhat ironically, mostly to the United States) left neither side victorious on the battlefield. Today, former government and guerrilla negotiators readily admit that the impetus for the negotiated settlement came only after both sides realized that they could not defeat the other militarily. In the U.S. military's terminology, the conflict had reached a "hurtful stalemate."

The final agreement drastically reduced the Salvadoran military oligarchy's decades-long iron grip over politics and society. Among other things, the settlement cut the size of the armed forces in half, abolished notoriously abusive intelligence and national police forces, established a truth commission to investigate abuses during the war, and allowed the FMLN to transform itself from a revolutionary Marxist insurgency into a political party. Given that many of these key accords were also similar to at least some of the FMLN's original demands in return for a cessation of their insurgency, the Salvadoran peace agreement represented a sort of "negotiated revolution." For students of conflict management and peace studies, El Salvador now represents a fascinating and unique model for a negotiated settlement to a brutal civil war.

In subsequent years, and especially amid the wars in Iraq and Afghanistan, the Pentagon repeatedly held up the Salvador experience as a model counterinsurgency and nation-building effort. For its proponents, Salvador served as proof that a small-footprint advisory force, combined with tremendous patience and persistence in the face of vociferous domestic criticism, can indeed bolster a fledgling regime, professionalize a rogue armed force, and defeat a formidable insurgency. The problem with this glowing interpretation, however, is that it overlooks the critical impact on the final outcome of other factors outside of Washington's immediate control, such as the end of the Cold War. That is, there was more than a bit of good timing and fortune in America's "successful" effort in El Salvador. It also downplays the large price that Salvadoran civilians had to pay in human rights abuses, economic stagnation, and the traumatic effects of living with long-term structural violence.

Over the next two decades and spanning the Clinton, George W. Bush, and Obama administrations, the U.S government pursued a surprisingly bipartisan yet largely overlooked Salvador-like operation in Colombia, a country that had suffered for years from a weak state, a garrison-style military, and unchecked illegal violence from both the right and left. As was the case in El Salvador, the better the situation became in Colombia, the less media attention it received. Perhaps one way to know when a dirty war is going well is when it disappears from the headlines.

PART FOUR

POST-COLD WAR, 1990s–2000s

26

Dirty Wars after the Cold War

When the Berlin Wall fell and the Soviet Union collapsed in the late 1980s and early 1990s, the world hoped that an era of peace was finally at hand. With the forces of capitalism and communism no longer clashing, no longer vying for territories on their peripheries, no longer financing and arming revolutions and counterrevolutions, it seemed that the bitter battles and divisions of the Cold War might be replaced by a new world order based on personal freedom, open markets, and democracy. The United States, it appeared, had emerged from the harrowing Cold War unscathed and stronger than ever, and was now entrusted with leading the world into the next millennium.

But, alas, there was always someone left to fight. Ethnic nationalism and discontent in Eastern Europe flooded into the vacuum that the Soviets had left in Eastern Europe. The Middle East had just seen the end of the horrific Iran-Iraq War and was still enduring the trauma of the Israeli-Palestinian conflict. And as Africa continued to shrug off its former colonial masters, violence escalated to epic levels in countries such as Sierra Leone, Rwanda, and the Democratic Republic of the Congo. The celebration in Western capitals of the Soviets' demise was brief and punctuated by the realization that the work of democratic reform and economic liberalization was far from complete in much of the world. Indeed, if anything, the problems of the Cold War era in certain ways seemed simple compared to those of the years that followed.

Some believed that in the post-Vietnam era in the 1970s and into the 1980s the U.S. military leadership both wittingly and unwittingly rejected irregular warfare as a key component of future wars. Thus, rather than trying to figure out what went wrong in the jungles of Vietnam and work to fix it, the U.S. Army in particular banished it from its key field manuals. When "counter-insurgency" or "low-intensity" (as it was called in the 1980s) operations did come to prominence in Africa and Central America, the military tended to regard them as the exclusive domain of special forces.[1]

In fact, while low-intensity operations raged in Nicaragua and El Salvador, American strategic doctrine underwent a change reflecting the concerns that Americans, military and civilian alike, had in the wake of Vietnam: namely, that military force was being used without full consideration of its objectives and limitations. The beginning of this doctrinal shift can be pegged to a precise date. On November 28, 1984, Caspar Weinberger, secretary of defense under President Ronald Reagan, gave a speech entitled "The Uses of Military Power." With Vietnam in mind, Weinberger called for more circumspection in the deployment of U.S. troops. He specified three requirements: (a) that the United States should not commit its forces to any endeavor unless vital national interests were perceived to be at stake, (b) that troops should be committed wholeheartedly and with the intention of achieving full victory, and (c) that full victory should be defined in terms of clear political and military objectives. Weinberger argued emphatically that this signal set of objectives and restrictions had to be established before troops could be committed to any conflict, lest the United States find itself entrenched in another losing fight.

In a lethal presage of the nature of dirty wars in the twenty-first century, one of the most searing episodes for America at the dusk of the Cold War occurred in October 1983 when a yellow Mercedes Benz truck packed with explosives plowed through barbed wire and concertina fences into the main entrance of the U.S. Marines barracks in Beirut, Lebanon. The suicide attack killed 241 marines and sailors, the corps' greatest single-day loss since the Battle of Iwo Jima in 1945.[2] A clandestine group calling itself Islamic Jihad claimed responsibility for the attack. This was a radical breakaway faction of the Shiite Amal movement that would soon be known as Hezbollah, an insurgent and terrorist group born in Lebanon's Bekaa Valley via trainers from Iran's Revolutionary Guard.[3]

THE POWELL DOCTRINE

In 1990, General Colin Powell, chairman of the Joint Chiefs of Staff, expanded on Weinberger's views, enshrining a set of principles that eventually came to be known as the Powell Doctrine. He asserted that the

United States should never settle for less than overwhelming force to bring about a swift conclusion to any conflict, that every available resource should be committed to this end, and that American casualties should be as minimal as possible.

The first test of these new parameters for the use of American military force was profoundly successful. In August 1990, Iraqi president Saddam Hussein accused Kuwait of waging economic warfare against Iraq and invaded the tiny neighboring country. The act ignited immediate indignation from other Arab nations and the United States, which quickly formed a coalition and demanded Iraq's withdrawal from Kuwait. Hussein ignored the ultimatum, and the United States led a full-scale attack against Hussein's military to push the invaders out of the tiny coastal country. With an overwhelming force of close to one million troops from thirty-three countries, and with the unparalleled technological prowess of the United States, the coalition devastated Iraq's military with a sustained aerial campaign. Ground forces rolled over the remnants and liberated Kuwait in just 100 hours.

The objectives of Operation Desert Storm, which became known as the Persian Gulf War, were clear, and the execution was nearly flawless, although thousands of Iraqi civilians were killed as "collateral damage." Fewer than 200 coalition troops died from enemy fire, while Iraqi losses – estimated as high as 100,000 but more likely around 20,000 military and 2,300 civilian – were catastrophic and utterly demoralizing. Entire units, fearful of American airpower, deserted their fortifications and either fled into the desert or surrendered en masse to coalition ground forces when they arrived. Even the vaunted Republican Guard, an elite force directly under Hussein's control, was dispatched wholesale by the seemingly indomitable might of the American war machine.[4]

The Gulf War signaled more than just the arrival of American military primacy, however. It was also the first conflict to witness the "CNN effect," the nearly instantaneous feed of information to the Western public from journalists and other media representatives embedded in the conflict zone. News crews in Baghdad broadcast live footage of precision-guided bombs falling on the capital city while Iraqi anti-aircraft guns lobbed streams of yellow tracers into the sky, hoping in vain to bring down the American planes. This development would come to have enormous repercussions in the post–Cold War world and would very much alter the dynamics of military intervention and dirty wars.

The technology that was put on display in the Gulf War was by far the most advanced ever used in combat. American generals publicized infrared gun camera footage from AH-64 Apache attack helicopters as they strafed Iraqi convoys, and from F-117 stealth fighters as they penetrated deep into heavily defended Iraqi airspace to destroy enemy command and control centers with impunity. The fourth-largest army in the world, battle-hardened after eight years of internecine trench warfare with Iran, was annihilated by a lean and agile force armed with satellites and microprocessors. Pentagon planners and defense contractors began to have visions of unmanned aircraft and tanks fighting the wars of the future: sanitized, without friendly casualties. Perhaps, as long as America stayed at the cutting edge of technological innovation, it could remain uncontested and undefeated on the battlefield.

However, as the Gulf War ended, the doctrinal evolution that drove the American strategy on the ground in Iraq began a slow and steady decline. Through the 1990s and early 2000s, the United States engaged in numerous unilateral and multilateral military interventions around the world. Despite the prescriptions of the Powell Doctrine, the U.S. military found itself in the 1990s functioning not as an overwhelming force fighting for clear objectives and decisive victory, but rather as a scalpel, attempting to wage delicate fights in Third World countries against elusive enemies, with restrictive rules of engagement, and with Congress carefully monitoring them. Indeed, in the wake of the Powell Doctrine and the stunning victory of the Gulf War, the small, dirty wars did not end. They merely took on a different character. In some instances, they were even uglier than Marxist insurgencies with their lofty rhetoric of "people's war" and "liberation."

In Somalia, amid famine and the effective collapse of the state, tens of thousands of civilians died and anarchy reigned. Clan leaders and warlords rose up to claim power, most infamously among them Mohamed Farrah Aidid and his Habr Gidr militia in the capital city of Mogadishu. In Sierra Leone, rebels waged war against a weak government and recruited thousands of child soldiers while a lucrative diamond trade fueled the conflict. Ethnic tensions in Rwanda boiled over into civil war and genocide as Hutu militiamen slaughtered close to a million Tutsis over the span of a hundred days, often using little more than rifles and machetes. And in Colombia, the Marxist Revolutionary Armed Forces of Colombia (FARC) increasingly took over the production and trade of narcotics, while right-wing paramilitaries sprang up to defend their ranches and illicit drug routes, posing yet another obstacle to the democratic government of Colombia and its American supporters.

The United Nations humanitarian mission in Somalia ended in a humiliating withdrawal by U.S. forces after the infamous Battle of Mogadishu.

Dirty Wars after the Cold War 343

The initial intervention involved a large multilateral contingent called the United Task Force (UNITAF). Led by a substantial U.S. Marine contingent, UNITAF operated under a mandate to use violent force only to provide security for UN personnel. However, this larger expeditionary unit was withdrawn in March of 1993 and replaced by a skeleton army force with an unclear mandate and restrictive rules of engagement.

In the hunt to bring down Aidid, who had become Mogadishu's most notorious warlord, U.S. forces, consisting primarily of soldiers from the Army's 75th Ranger Regiment and the shadowy special operations unit known as Delta Force, launched Operation Gothic Serpent to bring in several of Aidid's lieutenants. The mission derailed when Somali militiamen shot down two UH-60 Blackhawk helicopters. The ensuing search and rescue efforts claimed the lives of even more U.S. personnel, who vowed to leave none of their comrades behind. Ultimately, eighteen Americans perished in the crumbled streets of Mogadishu.

In hindsight, it now appears as though the Powell Doctrine was in decline, at least in terms of how the United States actually used force abroad, as soon as it took effect. Yet the U.S. military leadership still clung to the idea that interventions in Haiti, Somalia, Bosnia, Kosovo, and elsewhere were peripheral conflicts, exceptions to the doctrine-level rules of engagement. Many believed that the real threat to American security still lay in a modernizing China, or a resurgent Russia, or an isolated North Korea. Within that paradigm, the U.S. defense and intelligence services continued to emphasize maintaining technological primacy over enemies that did not yet exist.

If the Powell Doctrine was in decline through the 1990s, the events of September 11, 2001, signaled its demise. Indeed, the devastating terrorist attacks led to a revolution in political and military affairs in the United States. In the post-9/11 world, the theater of warfare changed dramatically. The American defense community's concerns shifted from failed and failing states to states that harbored – or maintained other ostensible connections with – terrorist organizations. Moreover, fueled in part by the American media's fixation on large-scale combat, the geographic center of attention also shifted from Africa, Eastern Europe, and East Asia to the predominantly Muslim Middle East.

At the same time, America's enemies took on a new character: they seemed to operate freely and almost invisibly in a world of permeable borders. With the Internet, terrorist propaganda flowed freely, and recruitment was easier than ever. And most of all, terrorism was cheap. Like the guerrilla of the Marxist ideal, the Islamic terrorist needed little more than the shirt on his back, while his opponent depended on billions of dollars of technology, equipment, infrastructure, intelligence analysis, and support staff for the most routine field patrol.

In at least two of the major post–Cold War cases, what began as interventions with limited counterterrorism aims turned into full-scale dirty wars. In some ways, these operations were familiar to those commanders who had experience in El Salvador and the multilateral peace support operations of the 1990s. But to a significant extent, they were brand-new sorts of dirty wars for the American military, and the lessons learned earlier had only limited application to the present circumstances. The last section of this book examines five of these major U.S. engagements in the post–Cold War era: counternarcotics and counterinsurgency in Colombia, the War in Iraq, the little-reported counterinsurgency operation in the Philippines, the Afghanistan war, and the overthrow of Muammar Qaddafi in Libya in 2011.

27

Colombia

On February 7, 2003, a car containing 200 kilograms of explosives blew up in the parking garage of the exclusive El Nogal social club in one of Bogotá's most upscale neighborhoods. The blast killed 36 and wounded more than 200. No one claimed responsibility for what was Colombia's worst terrorist attack in over ten years in its decades-long internal war. Yet, the government soon declared that it had evidence linking the attack to the Revolutionary Armed Forces of Colombia (FARC), the country's oldest and largest guerrilla insurgency.

The rebels had apparently recruited a young squash champion, John Freddy Arellán, to join the club as a squash instructor. While it is not clear whether Arellán was willingly carrying out the terrorist attack, he drove the car into the garage on that fateful day. A FARC operative detonated the bomb remotely while Arellán was still inside; Arellán and his uncle, Oswaldo Arellán perished in the explosion and the operative was captured three weeks later. The El Nogal bombings shook the nation's elites, who had become accustomed to living largely normal lives despite the low-level guerrilla presence that had existed for more than forty years. But the violent and brazen blast made it appear as though no place was safe from the guerrillas' reach.

As the twenty-first century began, Colombia held the dubious distinction of having the longest-standing insurgency war in the modern era. Some of the country's first Marxist revolutionaries began armed operations as early as the late 1940s. The formal organization of the two major rebel groups, the FARC and National Liberation Army (ELN) – occurred in the early 1960s. For the next three decades, though, these two

FIGURE 27.1. FARC-controlled areas in Colombia in the late 1990s and early 2000s. Also marked is the FARC liberated zone in the center of the country, which effectively amounted to an autonomous guerrilla-held enclave within Colombia. Map prepared by the University of Wisconsin-Madison Cartography Lab©. Reprinted with permission

groups – along with several other smaller factions – did not pose much of a threat to the Colombian government. During the 1970s, for example, the FARC had only nine operative fronts, and while the exact number of its members at any one time has never been released publicly, its ranks then likely totaled only in the hundreds.

By the 1990s, some of Colombia's guerrilla groups had conducted successful negotiations with the government, allowing them to lay down their arms and enter the political process. Yet the FARC and the ELN remained active in the country's vast jungles and mountain areas, far away from the reach of a Colombian state that had never effectively governed in such regions. But they still did not threaten the Colombian government in any serious way. Making matters worse, murky "paramilitary" forces – some loosely or more closely sanctioned, funded, and connected with the Colombian state – roamed the country's vast countryside, committing scores of massacres and other abuses.

By the late 1990s, though, fueled by its rapid entry into the booming and lucrative drug trade, the FARC had vastly increased its illicit revenues; it used these windfall funds to acquire sophisticated weaponry and increase its ranks by thousands of fresh recruits from Colombia's impoverished provincial regions. Now numbering over 20,000 men, women, and children under arms, the FARC began attacking army and police outposts.

They even threatened and in several instances seized larger towns across the country. In one case in the southern part of Colombia, the guerrilla army killed and captured over 100 soldiers. In 1998, Colombia's elite combat brigade – the 52nd Counter-Guerrilla Battalion – was defeated by a larger FARC force near El Billar gorge in Caquetá department, a highly embarrassing setback for the Colombian military. With time, the insurgents began to set their sights on the major cities, including Bogotá. The FARC's offensive served as a literal attack on democracy: in 1997, guerrillas killed 200 candidates for office and forced another 2,000 to withdraw from campaigns.

That same year, an estimated 13 percent of mayors had links to guerrillas.[1] In July 1999, a Gallup polling firm asked Colombians, "Do you think it is possible that one day the Colombian guerrillas will take power by force?" A stunning two-thirds of respondents said yes. The FARC rampage was abetted by then-Colombian president Andrés Pastrana's decision upon taking office in 1998 to grant the rebel group an El Salvador-sized *zona de despeje* (liberated zone) in the southeastern departments of Meta and Caquetá. A formal agreement between the FARC and the Colombian government established the despeje on November 7, 1998; it was extended in February 1999 for another ninety days. Pastrana naively expected that the FARC would consider the concession an act of the government's goodwill; in turn, this trust would help ensure progress in the ongoing government-FARC peace talks.

At the time, many observers firmly believed that the FARC was likely to negotiate in good faith since it appeared that the group had maximized its military position vis-à-vis the Colombian government. Interestingly, members of the U.S. Congress, the head of the New York Stock Exchange, and AOL's Steve Case, among many other luminaries, made pilgrimages to the area to see the revolution firsthand and, in some cases, to help promote a negotiated settlement to the war. Yet, instead of engaging in serious peace talks with the government, the FARC used the despeje to arm and train legions of soldiers, import dozens of Irish Republican Army (IRA) bomb-making teams, cultivate coca (the plant that provides the raw material for cocaine), and plan new offensives throughout the country. What did not exist in Colombia at this time was a "hurtful stalemate" – like that which had emerged in El Salvador by the later years of its bloody internal war – that might have forced the FARC to genuinely accept the talks. Instead of trying to broker a deal that would ensure the end of their insurgency, the FARC used their remarkable "gift" from Pastrana to unleash a military offensive across Colombia.

By 2002, the FARC was stronger than ever, its eyes now on the big prize of Bogotá and the eventual seizure of national power. The group's wing of urban militias began more aggressive efforts to "strangle" Bogotá by stationing sizable numbers of troops in inaccessible mountain areas not far from the capital. Kidnappings, extortion, and terrorist attacks against civilians reached levels shocking even for Colombia. The FARC kidnapped a leftist presidential candidate from that year's election, Ingrid Betancourt. It was within this deteriorating climate that Colombians turned in droves to hardline rightist presidential candidate Álvaro Uribe, who won office in a landslide vote in 2002. In sharp contrast to the conciliatory approach his predecessor Pastranas had tried with the rebel groups, Uribe's signature policy was to use all aspects of state power (especially the military) to protect citizens from illegal violence.

As the evidence confirms, 2002 was a horrible year for Colombia. Six years later, though, the Andean country had undergone a profound positive transformation. The Colombian government's turnaround started in March of 2008, when the Colombian military attacked a FARC jungle camp just over the border in Ecuador.[2] The operation killed veteran "guerrillero" Edgar Devía, also known as Raúl Reyes, the FARC's second-in-command. The raid was highly controversial because it crossed into foreign territory, but it became even more sensational when reports surfaced that the military had recovered three laptop computers, external hard drives, and memory sticks full of information that shed light on the organization's strategic thinking and inner dealings. In violation of the FARC's strict operational security (and apparently to assist him in writing his autobiography), Reyes had maintained files, some of which dated back decades and included records of strategies, meetings, and correspondence, a treasure trove of the FARC's past and present. The Colombian government handed the files over to an independent body, the International Institute for Strategic Studies (IISS), to help diffuse allegations of tampering and misinformation.

The IISS team produced a 240-page strategic dossier, *The FARC Files: Venezuela, Ecuador and the Secret Archive of Raúl Reyes*. The report was damning. The documents revealed longstanding and deep political and military involvement with Colombia's two most important neighbors, Ecuador and Venezuela, both at that time governed by colorful and controversial leftist administrations. To list just a few of the highlights: the FARC expected to receive about $250,000 from the Venezuelan government of Hugo Chávez; the guerrillas directly contributed $100,000 to the campaign of current Ecuadoran President Rafael Correa; and they likely helped round up an additional $300,000 for Correa's candidacy from sympathetic leftist sources.[3]

The FARC received another blow a few weeks after the 2008 Ecuador raid when the group announced that its founding leader Manuel Marulanda had died of a heart attack. Then, in July, the Colombian military conducted one of the most successful rescue operations in history: without firing a shot, it freed former presidential candidate Ingrid Betancourt, three American antidrug contractors, and several other Colombians. Deploying commandos disguised as humanitarian workers, the military's "Operation Check" appeared to "checkmate" the FARC, as the rescue deprived the guerrilla group of its "crown jewel" hostages.

The Colombian military's remarkable gains against the FARC were not simply good luck. Instead, following the nadir of the despeje debacle, under Uribe's dogged and often controversial leadership the Colombian government and armed forces pursued a strategy that brought the country back from the abyss. The involvement of the United States in the Colombia-FARC conflict carried strong echoes of its "soft footprint" experience in El Salvador in the 1980s. There, U.S. forces had backed a fledgling democratic government's military in the face of a formidable Marxist insurgency. The U.S. government played a similarly critical role in supporting the Colombians' effort. U.S. officials believed that Colombia's garrison military in fact needed to be both "militarized" and "professionalized." At the same time, though, the United States ultimately realized that any lasting effort against the FARC would require more than simply providing the Colombians with military aid and training; they would also need institutional strengthening such as greater awareness and respect for human rights. While the Americans' supporting role was far from perfect, and scores of critics lambasted Washington for turning a blind eye to Colombian security forces' abuses, this broad approach characterized the American effort in Colombia over the next decade.

The FARC had become a "narco-terrorist" organization by the turn of the century, and this would ultimately make it impossible for the United States to differentiate between counterinsurgency and counternarcotics as Washington deepened its involvement in Colombia. Also, the attacks of September 11, 2001, drastically lowered the threshold for the American public and politicians to support counterterror work around the world. Under George W. Bush's administration, and with the 2002 El Nogal bombing, the FARC quickly became a focal point of the U.S. War on Terror.

It is worth considering that any American presumption to "save" Colombia would have likely failed if Colombian politicians and citizenry had not committed themselves to rescuing their country from the insurgent groups. Colombia probably had to hit bottom before the government and economic elites woke up to the severity of the crisis. The commitment of indefatigable but highly controversial Colombian president Uribe played a critical role in what became an extraordinary societal determination to defeat a once tolerated but increasingly detested Marxist insurgency-cum-narcotrafficking organization.

Having started in earnest in the 1960s, Colombia's insurgency was initially a classic Cold War case of Cuban-inspired guerrillas attempting to overthrow a fledgling national government. Yet unlike most of the revolutionary groups in Latin America during this time, the FARC did not disappear when the Berlin Wall fell in 1989. Instead, the organization's drug revenues allowed it to continue its revolutionary activities even if such a violent path to seizing power had already been discredited. As in El Salvador in the 1980s, Washington played a largely indirect yet pivotal role in Colombia's war. But the approach was successful largely because it forced the Colombians to assume primary responsibility for resolving their seemingly endless insurgency war.

PLAN COLOMBIA

There was intense concern in the early days [of the Plan Colombia strategy], especially among Democrats with long memories of Vietnam, that

the program should not become a Vietnam-like counterinsurgency effort. –
Thomas R. Pickering[4]

When American president Bill Clinton decided to engage Colombia late in his second term, one might have assumed that the move was predicated overwhelmingly on the insurgency question, given the FARC's shocking power at the time. But there was another, more pressing, domestic policy priority to consider: drugs. U.S. officials were much more concerned about the growing evidence that cocaine production had surged in the Andean state. Thus, in many respects, the stunning "counterinsurgency" victory in Colombia was coincident with – if not a result of – Washington's eagerness to score a victory on the drug front.

By the late 1980s, the United States had begun in earnest to prosecute the longstanding "war on drugs" by going after the drugs at their source. Known in the military and law enforcement lingo as the "supply-side" strategy, U.S. interdiction efforts necessarily focused in the Andean region of South America as it was almost the sole producer of the world's cocaine. For ten years or so, Washington's efforts in Colombia were heavily focused on combating cocaine production and trafficking. Yet, by the turn of the century, Colombia's coca cultivation and cocaine production had exploded. Not surprisingly, the meteoric revenues from involvement in the cocaine trade proved too tempting for the guerrillas, in particular the FARC.[5]

As its response to the Colombian situation, the Clinton administration designed "Plan Colombia," a program that would ultimately cost US$6 billion and involve state-of-the-art helicopters and other sophisticated equipment as well as trainers. A "light footprint" would be used to "save" Colombia, a campaign intentionally based on the one used in El Salvador in the 1980s that had bolstered a weak and legitimate government against a serious Marxist insurgent threat.

For a host of reasons, Plan-Colombia attempted to "rescue" Colombia by drastically escalating the drug war, although most Colombians would have said then that the money would have been better spent going directly after the illegal groups. Despite the FARC's very real threat to the Colombian government, in accordance with Plan Colombia, the overwhelming majority of U.S. security assistance went to counternarcotics efforts.[6]

In short order, the Clinton administration was able to gain an impressive level of bipartisan support for Plan Colombia by reassuring Congress that the assistance would be used exclusively to fight drugs. This was a particularly deft political move given that it placed any opponents in the awkward position of appearing to be soft on the drug war. To placate more liberal members of Congress who believed Plan Colombia was overly "militarized," the White House increased "soft side" expenditures (read, social and economic assistance geared to indirectly bolster the antidrug fight) as well.

URIBE AND DEMOCRATIC SECURITY

After Plan Colombia had been place for several years, attention turned from U.S. efforts to action by the Colombians: what could they do with the assistance and training they had received? Much of the "heavy" and most expensive materiel from the United States had been front-loaded in the delivery schedule to Colombia. Thus, once this equipment was in country, U.S. assistance by definition turned more to maintenance of these substantial military-related "investments."

President Álvaro Uribe took office in 2002 on a simple yet fundamental promise to the war-weary Colombian population that his government would establish security in all areas of the country. For Colombian ears, this was a bold claim. Since its founding in the early nineteenth century, the Colombian state had never effectively governed in wide swaths of state territory, especially those far from the large cities such as Bogotá and Medellín. But Uribe's fundamental insight was simple but unyielding: democracy, economic opportunity, and even social justice could not come until the state could first protect its citizens from illegal violence.

One of Uribe's most decisive breakthroughs was his successful effort to get Colombia's elites to buy into the new strategy. His government levied a "war tax" on the country's richest citizens and enterprises that raised almost US$4 billion over four years. These are startling numbers when you consider that U.S. aid over this same time was roughly US$5 billion. Labeling the new strategy "Democratic Security," Uribe used this revenue windfall to increase the size of the military and police forces from 280,00 in 2002 to 415,000 five years later.[7]

Bolstered by these funds as well as billions of dollars in military materiel and training provided by Washington, Uribe pushed his military and police forces not only to clear areas from guerrilla control but to "hold" them so that the insurgents could not return. Seemingly overnight, Colombian military convoys opened up key highways by placing an armed soldier every kilometer or so along them; U.S.-provided Blackhawk helicopters gave the Colombian forces long-overdue but indispensable air mobility as they chased FARC bands across high mountain ranges and thick jungles. In 1998, the Colombian military operated 20 helicopters; by 2007, this number stood at 265.

Uribe's message to his fellow Colombians was clear and unequivocal: the Colombian state is committed to protecting you. Colombians began to talk excitedly of being able finally to "breathe" in a country that, due to the fear of political violence, had become a prison to its own people.[8] Not surprisingly, Uribe's hardline approach was not without its vocal critics, who contended that he was simply using violence to fight violence instead of addressing the root causes of Colombia's poverty, exclusion, desperation, and resulting violence.[9]

Uribe's generals did not come up with their ultimately successful strategy overnight; rather, their plan reflected years of learning how to reverse the strategic tide against the region's most formidable guerrilla insurgency. The new strategy focused on "holding" strategic areas where the military had already won control. Then, Colombian forces would deploy to "strategic operation areas" where insurgents operated with impunity.

Now much better equipped and trained than ever before – largely because of U.S. assistance – the Colombian military first put its new plan into practice in 2003 when it pushed the FARC out of the department of Cundinamarca, home to Bogotá. The armed forces then established a regional task force base that coordinated army, air force, and marine operations in the FARC's traditional strongholds in the southeastern parts of the country. Taking the fight straight to the enemy, this force of 10,000 soldiers succeeded in "clearing and holding" the areas in a manner that had been unimaginable only a few years earlier.

Colombian commanders were elated about their gains against the FARC. A military that had long been criticized for being at once an inert, Salvadoran-style "9-to-5" garrison army and an accomplice to the horrific violence conducted by right-wing paramilitary groups in prior years had been transformed into a formidable fighting force. With a standing strength of over 400,000, the Colombian military was now the most respected institution in Colombia. In addition to its increased professionalism, the Colombian military also now had assets such as U.S.-provided helicopters, providing critical air mobility.

One of the military's signature triumphs included a massive intelligence coup against the FARC. For decades, the Colombian forces seemed utterly incapable of locating, let alone eliminating, FARC leadership. When asked about the problem, Colombian and U.S. officials would often reply that the largely impenetrable triple-canopy jungle where the FARC leaders spent most of their time made bombing attacks indiscriminate and any sort of commando raid impossible. As a result, FARC commanders were able to live surprisingly comfortable lives – Scotch whiskey and Cuban cigars were preferred indulgences – knowing that their inhospitable environs ensured safety.[10] Yet, quietly backed by U.S. intelligence agencies, the Colombians gained access to the leadership by compromising the FARC's command and control structure. Pretending to be FARC commanders, military officials inserted themselves into guerrilla radio communications. In fact, this is the very device that the military used to trick the FARC captors during the daring rescue of presidential candidate Ingrid Betancourt and the other hostages.

Although these types of clandestine measures came under scrutiny for their possible violation of Geneva Conventions, the Colombian military deployed them to great effect. And, to be sure, they were the same tactics the FARC had consistently used against them during the past twenty years of this prolonged conflict.[11] At times, the military would debrief former guerrillas and then reinsert them back into FARC ranks without their commanders even noticing that the deserters had left. In turn, these FARC "plants" provided critical on-the-ground intelligence to the Colombian security forces. They also managed to leave high-tech tracing beacons. With a beacon in place, the FARC commanders became targets for precision-guided missiles, a key tactical innovation made possible by Plan Colombia.[12]

In September 2010, Colombian security forces used these tactics to infiltrate the jungle compound of FARC military leader Victor Julio Suárez (whose nom de guerre was Mono Jojoy). Once Jojoy's whereabouts were confirmed, the military launched a massive attack that employed 30 planes, 27 helicopters, hundreds of special forces operatives, and more than 30 tons of explosive (including around 50 precision-guided bombs). Operation Sodom ended in the death of Suaréz, the most feared man in the country, wanted for more than 100 separate crimes. Colombian Defense Minister Rodrigo Rivera characterized Jojoy's 300-meter-long hideout, equipped with Viet Cong–like tunnels and escape routes, as "the mother of all FARC camps." Uribe's successor, Juan Manuel Santos, ebulliently called the strike a "turning point" and "the beginning of the end for the FARC."[13] The outcome would likely have been impossible without sustained collaboration with U.S. intelligence services.

The FARC guerrillas were now indisputably on the run and, as intelligence reports suggested, increasingly unable to communicate with one another. Their presence throughout the countryside became sharply reduced. Not surprisingly, life as a "Farquista" was now far less enjoyable

FIGURE 27.2. Manuel Marulanda, center, the founder and top leader of the FARC, walks with Mono Jojoy, right, the number two in command, in guerrilla-controlled territory in the late 1990s. Billions of dollars of American military materiel and training helped swell the Colombian military that eventually devastated the FARC's rank-and-file and leadership ranks. AP Photo/Scott Dalton, reproduced with permission from Associated Press, 00042902369

than it had been when the group operated with impunity. FARC "soldiers," most of whom were forcibly recruited into the guerrilla ranks in the first place, began to desert at the startling rate of four per day. In an echo of the Magsaysay counterinsurgency strategy in the Philippines in the 1950s or the British efforts in Malaya, FARC deserters reported that hunger was often what drove them to flee even though they risked certain death if the FARC captured them.[14] In a sign that even some die-hard revolutionaries were losing the fighting spirit, the Colombian government also reported that most of the FARC deserters had already spent ten to fifteen years with the rebel group.

The Colombian military's aggressive operations also dealt the FARC a devastating financial blow. With a large share of its massive war funds generated through the cocaine trade, the FARC saw its revenues plummet from an estimated US$500 million to US$250 million. The Colombian forces reported destroying over 3,000 cocaine labs in 2009 alone.[15]

The Colombian security forces' "hard-side" operations, such as military offensives and intelligence-gathering, dealt the FARC a severe and unprecedented setback. But this is only part of the Colombian counterinsurgency story. The route to defeating insurgencies was not simply in direct confrontation but in winning the hearts and minds of the population. To this end, the Colombian government's "clear and hold" strategy enabled "soft-side" projects to flourish, especially economic development programs in regions previously overrun with coca and FARC elements.

Backed by the U.S. State Department and other international aid organizations, these programs had success in breaking the cycle of violence, even if progress came in fits and starts. This reality contrasts to prior years, when programs such as alternative crop development (e.g., promoting the cultivation of hearts of palm or coffee rather than coca) floundered because of the absence of security guarantees that would permanently keep the insurgents from returning to the area.

The "security-first" method of counterinsurgency, coupled with the programs designed to encourage citizen participation in regions once occupied by the FARC, became more and more effective as the levels of violence dropped.[16] In many respects, the program outlined by Uribe was strikingly prescient in describing what the Colombian state would be able to achieve and how it would do so: "once a basic level of security has been established," the thesis goes, "the State will embark upon a policy of territorial consolidation, re-establishing the normal operation of the justice system, strengthening local democracy, meeting the most urgent needs of the population, broadening state services and initiating medium- to long-term projects aimed at creating sustainable development."[17]

In conjunction with the destabilization of FARC leadership and finances, under the Democratic Security programs first envisioned by Uribe, the Colombian military was able to remove the FARC from its strongholds in remote parts of Colombia. One prime example of its success in this regard occurred in the town of San Vicente, just outside Serranía de La Macarena National Park in the department of Meta, where Mono Jojoy was killed several years later. This was often referred to as "FARC-landia" because of the rebel group's de facto control over all aspects of political, economic, and social life. Until 2002, the FARC ran a visitor's center staffed by female guerrillas in San Vicente. The building's walls were festooned with huge posters of famed insurgent fighters. Rebels in the region also ran a court, built infrastructure, and taxed local residents.[18]

Funded in no large part from Plan Colombia dollars, the Colombian government embarked on an aggressive effort to establish "fusion centers" in regions that the military had taken away from the rebels. In locales such as the six municipalities that comprise La Macarena, the centers attempted

Colombia 357

FIGURE 27.3. Aerial eradication of illicit drug crops in Colombia in the 1990s. The United States and Western Europe's insatiable demand for cocaine provided windfall revenues to the FARC insurgency. In turn, the FARC used these funds to buy sophisticated armaments that by the late 1990s turned the once dispersed group into the strongest insurgency in modern Latin American history. Reproduced with permission from Marcelo Salinas

to combine the critical elements of governance – judicial, security, education, and so on – to give the local population a stake in the "post-guerrilla" environment. La Macarena was a particularly interesting case since, during the guerrilla-controlled days, almost the entire economy was tied to coca cultivation. Given the deeply ingrained incentive facing farmers to grow the lucrative crop, many assumed that "La Mac," as it was called, presented a particularly challenging case for a "fusion" success story.[19] Moreover, La Macarena's sheer size – 11,000 square miles, larger than the state of Rhode Island – made the task particularly daunting. Yet, in this one instance, a strong majority of La Macarena's population enthusiastically embraced the government's efforts: both coca cultivation and violence dropped precipitously as myriad government agencies took up physical space in the fusion center to coordinate the "build" phase. A dramatic increase in dairy production complemented the nearly total eradication of coca farms. In 2006, 12,000 to 14,000 hectares of La Macarena's land area was employed in coca cultivation, accounting for almost 25 percent of all coca production in Colombia; in 2010, there was almost none.

The Colombian government invested a whopping US$320 million in the La Macarena program to bring fundamental state institutions to this remote and war-ravaged land. Interestingly, Washington provided only around 10 percent of the funding, which indicated that Bogotá was increasingly able and willing to shoulder these counterinsurgency and nation-building efforts itself. The sizable investment that brought special prosecutors, infrastructure programs, and development programs to La Macarena was vital in that it changed the local population's perception of the Colombian state. For the first time in memory, the Colombian state was both present and effective in the former FARC-controlled region.

Another key "soft side" development was the reform of Colombia's slow, corrupt, and ineffective judicial system. Backed by hundreds of millions of dollars of U.S. assistance, the most critical achievement on the judicial side was the move from an oral to a written accusatory system. This shift helped boost the conviction rate from 3 to 65 percent.[20] While still far from adequate, case loads were now being expedited in an effort to gain the Colombian citizenry's trust in the judiciary. The new system was able to conclude trials in an average of less than a year, a sharp contrast to the five-year rate at which it operated previously. U.S.-funded programs also trained over 2,000 "conciliators." The conciliators mediated over seven million cases in the first several years of their existence. Although reform efforts did not transform Colombia into a judicial paradise, they did allow citizens to gain a sense of connection with public institutions that had for so long alienated them.

TAKING ON THE PARAMILITARIES

The Uribe government's main effort to promote security focused on repelling the FARC deeper into the jungle and away from where most Colombians actually lived. Yet Uribe's ability to go after the leftist rebels was hindered by accusations that he harbored sympathy for and even actively collaborated with rightist paramilitaries notorious for their drug trafficking and human rights abuses. It was thus incumbent on Uribe to demonstrate to the Colombian people and the international community that he was seriously committed to curbing paramilitary activity. Back in the 1980s, drug kingpins such as Medellín's Pablo Escobar created personal "shock troops" to retaliate against the guerrillas' extortions and kidnappings. When the drug cartels were "decapitated" by the Colombian government in the early 1990s, their personal militias were left orphaned and morphed into the more formal and political "paramilitaries."

While the paramilitaries' primary goal was to "cleanse" areas from guerrilla control, this objective often took the form of targeting suspect civilian sympathizers. At the height of paramilitary actions in the late 1990s and early 2000s, the "paras" committed the overwhelming share of atrocities and other forms of human rights abuses. And like the guerrillas, the paramilitaries financed their brutality by trafficking narcotics.

By offering the paramilitary leaders leniency in return for laying down their arms and confessing to their illicit activities, the Uribe government succeeded in demobilizing an estimated 30,000 well-armed fighters. Uribe surprised many critics when in May 2008 he ordered the extradition to the United States of fourteen former paramilitary commanders. Claiming that they were not fully cooperating with the stipulations of the demobilization agreement, Uribe shocked the paramilitary commanders, who had assumed that their participation in the program would ensure that they would never end up in a gringo jail. Overall, while far from perfect, Uribe's demobilization efforts removed a hostile organization from the political landscape, which in turn allowed the Colombian government to focus its efforts on defeating the FARC.

In the context of the United States' history of counterinsurgency engagements, the response to paramilitary forces in Colombia provides some striking lessons. For example, as in El Salvador, perceived success for both the Colombian and the U.S. governments depended on their ability to distance themselves from and emphasize their contrast to the paramilitaries. Recognizing that any association between the government's operations and paramilitary activities would hinder its ability to win over Colombian hearts and minds, striking out against the "paras" was a key move in the strategic game. Of course, this outcome is not always guaranteed and was far from inevitable in Colombia. Given different conditions on the ground, such as deeper civilian sympathy for the paramilitary forces, the calculation might have been wrong.

"FALSE POSITIVES"

In 2008, in a key vote of confidence in the Colombian security forces' success since Uribe took office, several national magazines listed the Colombian defense minister, Juan Manuel Santos, as their "person of the year."[21] In addition to the successful targeting of several FARC leaders, during this same year kidnappings were down to fewer than 500, the lowest total in twenty years; the homicide rate was also down 44 percent from 2003 to 2008; and Colombia's security forces were largely responsible for an 80 percent decrease in both left-wing and right-wing violence. The Colombian government estimated that an astounding 68,000 lives had been saved due to the improvement in the security situation.[22]

One indication of the Colombian military's growing legitimacy was a 2002 Gallup poll, which registered 80 percent support for the armed forces, up from 42 percent in 1998. The figure remained that high for the next decade. Perhaps counterintuitively, another indication was the wave of Facebook-organized protests that rocked Colombia in early 2009. Millions of Colombians took to the streets to march against the guerrilla group's violent ways even though militarily speaking the group had been degraded to a shadow of its former self.

The United States provided over US$6 billion in military and social assistance to Colombia during the first decade of the twenty-first century. Yet, this training and the sizable war chest were not the sole keys to Colombia's dramatic turn of fortunes. Rather, the Colombian state relied on the broad public consensus that it was the state's responsibility and right to address the country's ills – a consensus that Uribe worked doggedly to promote. In this regard, it may have actually helped the Uribe administration's cause that Colombia had "hit bottom" a decade earlier as the country's political and economic class finally realized that only a concerted societal effort could save the nation from catastrophe.

As is so often the case in dirty wars, Uribe's success on the security front did not mean that he was somehow a saint. On the contrary, human rights groups continued to accuse the Colombian leader of allowing far too much impunity within the government and military ranks. A bitter reminder of the military's deficiencies came in 2008, when a scandal broke that tainted the institution's newly gained legitimacy. Facing tremendous pressure to show "positive" kills, Colombian military officers lured eleven youths from a poor town near Bogotá to a location hundreds of miles away, dressed them in guerrilla clothing, and murdered them. One victim was a street vendor named Israel Rodríguez, who went fishing one day in 2008 and never returned. Two days later, his family identified his body in a plastic bag, marked by the Colombian army as a guerrilla fighter killed in combat.[23] Prosecutors quickly had hundreds of alleged cases of "false positives" on their books. Following an inquiry, Uribe ordered the

Colombia 361

dismissal of twenty-seven soldiers and officers.²⁴ The Colombian government later claimed that another 2,300 security officials were under active investigation for crimes related to the false positives.²⁵

THE COLOMBIA OPTION

Even at its most dire point, Colombia held certain advantages in terms of its ability to counter pernicious insurgent groups.²⁶ For one, the country's democratic politics had been in place for decades before events spiraled out of control in the 1990s. Thus, unlike El Salvador, the Colombian government did not have to start from point zero to build its institutions up to a level where Colombian citizens found them credible.

Álvaro Uribe set the broad strategic framework within which Colombia's counterinsurgency effort took place. While this was indispensable to the overall success, presidential leadership was not the only decisive factor in this story. Rather, after years of dithering – to the point where critics contended that it had a tacit agreement with the FARC that neither side would target the other's leadership – the Colombian military finally made a commitment to tackling the insurgent threat. U.S. materiel and training would have done far less had Colombia's generals not made this momentous decision.

For the United States, this was in some ways a far more familiar situation than that of its other twenty-first-century counterinsurgency operations. Many of the U.S. military trainers spoke native Spanish or had served in "Salvador" in the 1980s, and American forces engaged in Colombia were better acquainted with the culture, religion, and history of that country than were their counterparts in Iraq and Afghanistan. There was also the enduring legacy of more than a decade of American counterinsurgency experience in Latin America.

Another key element of the Colombia case is that most of the U.S. assistance came after the September 11, 2001, terrorist attacks, which changed the way American policymakers looked at "terrorism" globally. In this sense, 9/11 proved to be devastating for the FARC, as the group became an unwitting enemy in George W. Bush's global war on terrorism.

Contrast this case to that of El Salvador in the 1980s. The recent memory of Vietnam had led many in the Carter and (more hawkish) Reagan administrations to conclude that the United States should not commit combat troops to El Salvador. Even though El Salvador did not turn into the Vietnam-like quagmire that many observers predicted at the conflict's onset, this fear plagued the Colombia case as well. Indeed, like El

Salvador, Washington's decision to send everything short of combat troops was predicated on the assumption that it was essential that the "host government" take responsibility for the effort. Colombia's dramatic gains, supported by robust American assistance, suggested that American engagement could actually make a bad situation better, not worse.

In the late 1990s Colombia's government needed to put an end to impunity and violence in the country's large ungoverned areas. The road to its pacification was one of U.S.-supported militarization, which included "fusion centers," counternarcotics operations, and coca-alternative development assistance. Yet one should be wary of concluding that American hardware and training or Uribe's leadership irrevocably transformed Colombia into a land of milk and honey. In many areas where the FARC and other belligerents instituted their own forms of governance, the Colombian government's reach still exceeds its grasp. Bogotá could finally begin to claim that the FARC has imploded – as defense minister Rivera promised would happen at the end of Santos's term in 2012. While levels of violence and impunity – not to mention drug trafficking – sadly remained higher than normal for a pacific democracy, as far as successes go in dirty wars, many military observers considered the U.S.-backed effort a win.

28

Iraq

The Iraq War was a war of choice, not necessity.
– Thomas Ricks and Bernard Trainor[1]

[The U.S. military] has developed over time a singular focus on conventional warfare ... which left it ill-suited to the kind of operation it encountered as soon as conventional war-fighting ceased to be the primary focus in [Iraq].
– Brigadier Nigel Aylwin-Foster, British Army[2]

Be polite, be professional, but have a plan to kill everybody you meet.
– General James Mattis to a group of Marines

On the morning of March 21, 2003, the U.S. military launched its invasion of Saddam Hussein's Iraq. It was familiar territory for American commanders, given that the U.S. military had devastated Hussein's forces in the Gulf War a decade earlier. In many respects, U.S. planners expected a sort of "Gulf War Redux," believing that the Iraqi military's vaunted Republican Guard would be their main foe in the push to take the capital of Baghdad and remove Hussein from power. Five divisions (three U.S. Army, one U.S. Marine, and the British 1st Armoured Division with attached Royal Marine Commandos) led the way in what was called a blitz-like operation, using vastly superior mobility, technology, and training to take Baghdad in two weeks. Interestingly, the invading force was roughly 150,000 troops, about half the number that some senior U.S. planners had advocated in the lead-up to the war.

The chief operational strategy in the invasion, known as Operation Iraqi Freedom, was "shock and awe," designed to overwhelm the enemy's defenses, decapitate Saddam Hussein's command infrastructure, and

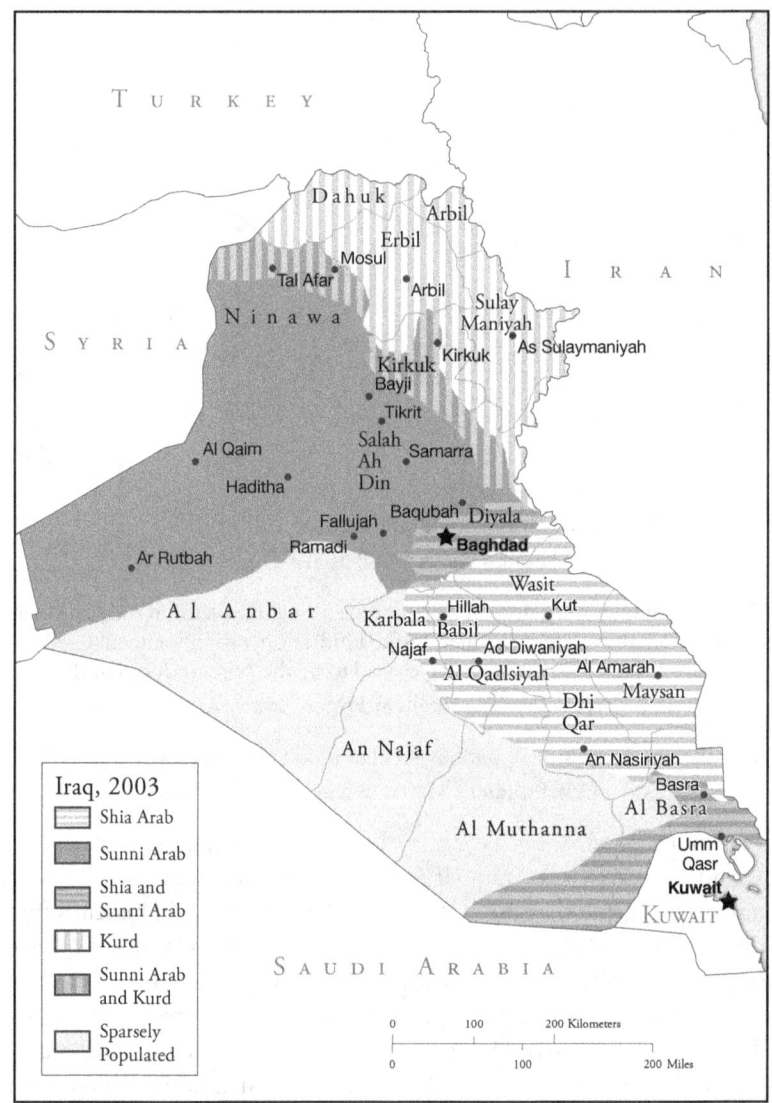

FIGURE 28.1. Iraq, 2003. Between 2004 and 2007, the U.S. military struggled to rein in vicious sectarian violence that threatened to tear the country apart. Map prepared by the University of Wisconsin-Madison Cartography Lab©. Reprinted with permission

bomb the apparatus of the Iraqi state into submission. On the highways leading to Baghdad, infrared gun camera footage and night-vision devices transmitted sanitized images of the war back to the West. Friendly casualties were light, and Iraqi troops abandoned their positions and surrendered to the Coalition en masse. Precision-guided munitions dropped from the air eliminated the Iraqi troops who remained at their posts.

A textbook example of maneuver warfare, the operation had all the appearances of a complete conventional victory. Covering 400 desert miles from Kuwait to Baghdad and rolling over a demoralized enemy, Coalition forces outflanked and isolated the heaviest pockets of resistance.[3] Tanks and infantry rolled with impunity; bombing attacks were selective and devastating. To supporters, the approach's success seemed like the ultimate vindication: a light and maneuverable army using overwhelming force, it seemed, could accomplish anything. When the 3rd Infantry Division took the Saddam International Airport on the western end of Baghdad on April 3, it then proceeded to launch the first of two "thunder runs" across the capital – charges of tanks and other vehicles intended to intimidate the Iraqi defenders, as well as gain an understanding of how the enemy intended to fight. Iraqi resistance in the capital quickly dissipated. The war appeared to be over.

This "leaner and meaner" force was partly the brainchild of U.S. Defense Secretary Donald Rumsfeld. He had spent years advocating the creation of a "transformed" military that could accomplish rapid and decisive military missions and make a quick exit. There were several points to Rumsfeld's military vision. The primary thrust was to increase force readiness by developing units that could be deployed swiftly and to great effectiveness and to decrease the force footprint by reducing the number of troops in theater and, hence, the amount of labor and materiel needed to support them.

This would be accomplished by using small, agile ground forces and heavy air support, working in concert with cutting edge technology and a unified command structure. Rumsfeld's military doctrine was in part a response to the massive, resource-draining peacekeeping efforts that he believed had previously plagued the U.S. military in such locales as Kosovo and Haiti. To a certain extent, the effective use of small numbers of specially trained CIA and Special Forces soldiers to topple the Taliban and pursue Al Qaeda in Afghanistan had validated the doctrine over the preceding eighteen months. However, although the two branches shared the broader, light footprint doctrines, the composition of their forces and the way they thought were drastically different.

History will likely record that the American-led Coalition succeeded in using this lighter force in the Iraqi invasion. Indeed, Saddam Hussein was overthrown just three weeks after the invasion began. A toppled statue of the dictator fell in Firdos Square on April 9; images of jubilant Iraqis led many around the world to conclude that the war had come to a rapid conclusion. Yet, further scrutiny of the invasion's first several weeks reveals that the seeds of much greater problems were already germinating.

These seeds were perhaps first evident in the resistance that Coalition forces faced in their notorious thunder runs. While the high-intensity patrols forced Iraqi defenders to flee without the house-to-house fighting that American planners expected would turn Baghdad into another Stalingrad or Mogadishu, irregular forces operating in small groups – and often consisting of foreign jihadist fighters – used tactics such as taking warheads from rocket-propelled grenades, wrapping them in cloth, and tossing them in the middle of roads to blow up Bradley fighting vehicles and tanks. The tactic was a crude precursor to the use of highly-lethal improvised explosive devices (IEDs) that would plague U.S. troops in ensuing years.

The unexpected fighting effectiveness of Iraqi paramilitary fighters known as Fedayeen Saddam (Saddam's "Men of Sacrifice") foreshadowed the bitter counterinsurgency war in which U.S. forces would soon become embroiled. A loosely trained and poorly equipped irregular force, the Fedayeen were overseen by Hussein's son Uday, known for his cruelty and excess, and were fiercely loyal to Hussein's ruling Ba'athist regime. The fighters often dressed in civilian clothing, ignoring the rules of conventional warfare and instead using deception and ambush to bloody the invading force.

In remarks that earned him rebukes from more senior officers, General William Wallace, commander of the Army's 5th Corps, told the *New York Times* and *Washington Post* that these irregular forces were using "bizarre" tactics such as charging American tanks and Bradley vehicles with light trucks and .50-caliber weapons. "The enemy we're fighting is a bit different than the one we war-gamed against, because of these paramilitary forces," he said. "We knew they were here, but we did not know how they would fight."[4]

Intense face-offs in southern cities such as Nasiriya revealed the Fedayeen's willingness to die for their cause and their ability to use comparatively unsophisticated tactics to score blows against the Coalition forces: for example, a common means for disabling high-tech U.S. Apache helicopters flying overhead was to fire waves of AK-47 bullets at them. The Fedayeen were also able to debilitate vulnerable supply lines spread across the Iraqi desert, relying on scores of arms caches hidden across the region in such sites as schools and mosques.

Perhaps the Fedayeen's biggest success was its ability to intimidate the local and largely anti-Hussein Shi'a population from supporting the invading force. Amazingly, small arms and strong-willed fighters turned out to be far more lethal to American forces that the weapons of mass destruction (WMD) that never materialized. The Fedayeen's unconventional tactics forced the Coalition forces to confront them in the southern cities, the very locales that the "blitz" force had expected to bypass.

Within months, the hints of dirty war that first emerged in Nasiriya and Baghdad became real. U.S. planners had expected an easier and more emphatic repeat of the 1991 Gulf War; this time, the Iraqi dictator would not remain to threaten the United States. Yet, while it only took three weeks to topple Saddam, over 4,000 American troops and countless Iraqi civilians and soldiers died in the ensuing dirty war that took roughly five years to conclude. U.S. commanders and President George W. Bush's administration found themselves in a familiar counterinsurgency dilemma: once we're in, we're in. And, as counterinsurgency theorist David Kilcullen concluded, "the large-scale, high-profile, unilateral, *über-blitzkrieg* manner in which the [U.S.-led] Coalition invaded Iraq (and the inherently strategic concept of the Iraq campaign itself) was deeply flawed."[5]

WEAPONS OF MASS DESTRUCTION

In 1991, President George H. W. Bush directed the U.S.-led multinational coalition that trounced an Iraqi military that many experts claimed was the largest and strongest in the Arab world. Yet, despite easily ejecting Hussein's forces from occupied Kuwait, American commanders and policymakers did not include Hussein's ouster as a priority in the military campaign. Instead, they (not implausibly) assumed that the Iraqi dictator would fall without external pressure, most likely from Shi'ite uprisings in the south, Kurdish minorities in the north near Turkey, or even a "palace coup" against the humiliated leader. Shi'ite communities in the southern portions of Iraq had indeed rebelled against his weakened government after the Gulf War, but Hussein had swiftly retaliated and put down the uprising.

The circumstances of this insurrection had important consequences for the American-led invasion a decade later. After pushing the Iraqis from Kuwait in the Gulf War, President George H. W. Bush had implored Shi'ite factions to rise up against Hussein, but when they did so, the Coalition declined to offer them any assistance. The memory of this failure to provide help led not only to greater animosity toward the Ba'athists but also to a profound distrust of the United States among the Shi'ite Iraqis, who believed that they had been betrayed.⁶

Seven years later, President Bill Clinton's administration attempted to do something about Hussein's pursuit of WMD (including nuclear) programs. Clinton authorized a four-day U.S. bombing campaign in December 1998, the largest attack on Iraq since the end of the Gulf War, in reaction to a standoff over weapons inspections. Known as "Desert Fox," the aerial assault used roughly 415 cruise missiles, more than the 315 launched during the entire Gulf War. An additional 600 bombs were dropped from Air Force B-52s, swing-wing supersonic B-1s, and British bombers.

In the aftermath of the September 11, 2001, terrorist attacks and the subsequent military campaign in Afghanistan, the George W. Bush administration turned its attention to Iraq. Many key administration officials, including Vice President Richard Cheney, Secretary of State Colin Powell, and Deputy Secretary of Defense Paul Wolfowitz, were familiar with the potential threats that Hussein's Iraq posed, having played key roles in the 1991 effort. Now, the younger Bush's administration firmly believed that containment was not working and that action needed to be taken before Hussein used the devastating WMD arsenal he was suspected of having against the United States or its allies. Secretary of Defense Rumsfeld made the administration's assessment clear when he argued that Hussein "wasn't in the box ... he has not been contained.... Their programs are maturing every day.... Diplomacy has been exhausted, almost."⁷ To this end, and according to Bush's National Security Strategy, "We cannot let our enemies strike first.... The overlap between states that sponsor terror and those that pursue WMD compels us to action.... To forestall or prevent such hostile acts by our adversaries, the United States will, if necessary, act preemptively."⁸

The Bush administration's decision to go to war was in part a result of the psychological impact of 9/11 on high-ranking administration officials combined with their existing views about Saddam Hussein's threat. By the summer of 2002, U.S. policy had effectively shifted from "no war with Iraq unless Saddam provokes one" to "war with Iraq in early 2003 unless Saddam capitulates."⁹ The administration's justification for launching a preemptive war against Iraq was predicated on the contention that the intelligence confirming the scale of Hussein's WMD programs was incontrovertible. The National Intelligence Estimate (NIE) entitled "Iraq's

Continuing Programs for Weapons of Mass Destruction" reflected a general consensus within the intelligence community, though many observers and politicians later accused the Bush team of pressuring intelligence analysts to produce conclusions that fit its preconceived ideological notions. The NIE indicated that Iraq possessed WMDs and was "reconstituting" its nuclear program.

Even the widely respected Colin Powell, who had gained great fame as Chairman of the Joint Chiefs of Staff during the Gulf War, went before the United Nations in the lead-up to the war. He stated, "My colleagues, every statement I make today is backed up by sources, solid sources. These are not assertions. What we are giving you are facts and conclusions based on solid intelligence."[10] In the end, 77 senators and 297 of 435 members of the House of Representatives voted in October 2002 to authorize the president to use the necessary military force "to defend the national security of the United States against the continuing threat posed by Iraq."

As the world soon discovered, the intelligence on Saddam Hussein's weapons programs could not have been more wrong. In fact, Hussein had scuttled his programs to expedite satisfactory inspections from UN experts. At the same time, the Iraqi dictator acted as though his regime still had the weapons as a deterrence against external aggressors. But these facts would come to light only after the United States had occupied Iraq.

DE-BA'ATHIFICATION

> An insurgency is a cancer. You can't treat it later. – General Joseph "Fighting Joe" Dunford[11]

With the fall of Baghdad in April of 2003, the American-led force had swept through Iraq and toppled Saddam Hussein's regime in only twenty-one days – a military feat without precedent; it then abruptly found itself occupying a country without a government. What followed the immensely successful invasion – and continues to this day – was a bold experiment in democratization through force of arms and an elaborate transformation from a Sunni Muslim-dominated Ba'athist state to a liberal democracy in the Middle East. But this endeavor has been largely overshadowed by the complex insurgency that sprang up in the early days of the occupation and nearly brought Iraq to its knees a few years later. The United States military, forgetful of the lessons it had learned in its long history of fighting dirty wars, became a police force fighting an elusive enemy in the urban terrain of Baghdad and its environs.

Baghdad destabilized almost immediately. Looters began ransacking government buildings and Ba'ath Party members' residences (most Ba'athists by that time had melted into the countryside, fearing imprisonment by the Coalition or persecution by Iraqi citizens). Coalition forces were instructed not to intervene against criminal activity. Lawlessness filled the vacuum left by Hussein's regime. When asked at a press conference about the significance of the looting, Donald Rumsfeld pithily replied, "Freedom's untidy."

Washington quickly compared the looting to the growing pains of a new democracy. The disorder that began in April 2003 continued and, as foreign policy scholar Gideon Rose wrote, "liberation turned into occupation; local uncertainty turned into insurgency and then civil war." The arrival of the American forces brought an end to the "certainty of political terror" but at the same time unleashed "new, less certain fears."[12]

A telling case of American mismanagement in Iraq was the stubborn insistence of military and civilian officials, particularly Secretary Rumsfeld, that the burgeoning insurrection was not a coordinated insurgency. They dismissed the rising tide of violence as the actions of bandits and the last throes of former regime elements – groups so disparate in their motivations and aims that Rumsfeld did not believe they were part of any organized resistance. Furthermore, Rumsfeld's refusal to acknowledge the existence of an insurgency turned on technicalities: insurgencies were fought against sovereign governments, he contended, and in 2003, Iraq did not yet have one.[13]

Not until the summer of 2003 did a handful of senior leaders begin to admit that they faced a guerrilla-style insurgency in Iraq. Even then, Rumsfeld often rebuked them. In less than two years, with the body counts rising for both American personnel and Iraqi civilians, Rumsfeld was forced to revise his opinion, and he offered his guess that the insurgency in Iraq "could go on for any number of years."[14]

This reluctance to admit certain strategic realities ran contrary to the principle, recurring throughout U.S. counterinsurgency engagements, that statesmen and commanders should understand the type of war they are fighting. Colonel H. R. McMaster, the commanding officer of the Army's 3rd Armored Cavalry Regiment (3rd ACR), admitted, "Militarily, you've got to call it an insurgency, because we have a counterinsurgency doctrine and theory that you want to access."[15] Unfortunately, not only did the Coalition enter Iraq without a coherent strategy for establishing security and starting reconstruction, but the refusal of many high-ranking officials and officers to recognize the existence of an insurgency meant that their subordinates lacked a clear understanding of what their mission was.

Making matters worse, Iraq's infrastructure was in far worse condition than U.S. experts had expected. Most critically, the Ba'athist regime had shut down the electrical grid but Coalition engineers now struggled to get it functioning at preinvasion levels; moreover, two of three sewage treatment plants in Baghdad were in ruins. Bush administration estimates of reconstruction at this point came to around US$1 billion – a fraction of the more than US$20 billion the United States ultimately spent in postinvasion Iraq.

Despite the challenges facing the reconstruction and occupation effort, Secretary Rumsfeld was eager to see U.S. troop levels in the country quickly reduced by two-thirds, to fewer than 50,000. U.S. Army Chief of Staff General Eric Shinseki had earlier told Congress that a force of "several hundred thousand soldiers" would be required to conduct the occupation. Less than a week later, civilian Pentagon official Paul Wolfowitz contradicted Shinseki, claiming before Congress,

some of the higher-end predictions that we have been hearing recently, such as the notion that it will take several hundred thousand U.S. troops to provide stability in post-Saddam Iraq, are wildly off the mark. First, it's hard to conceive that it would take more forces to provide stability in post-Saddam Iraq than it would to conduct the war itself and to secure the surrender of Saddam's security forces and his army. Hard to imagine.[16]

He contended that the occupying force should be substantially smaller than Shinseki's estimate and that the costs would be paid by Iraq's seemingly limitless oil revenues. The Bush administration embraced Wolfowitz's thinking. Despite Wolfowitz's contention, effective counterinsurgency and nation-building have usually required a large commitment of troops, especially because one aim of the mission was to secure the civilian population.

On January 20, 2003, President Bush signed National Security Directive 24, which formulated the Defense Department's authority for overseeing postwar Iraq. The Pentagon chose retired U.S. Army Lieutenant General Jay Garner, who had headed Operation Provide Comfort in the aftermath of the Gulf War, to lead the reconstruction effort. As soon as Garner arrived in Baghdad, Iraqis pleaded with Garner and the Americans to take charge. Yet, within a month, Garner was replaced by L. Paul "Jerry" Bremer III, who was asked to head a new entity called the Coalition Provisional Authority (CPA).

Located in the heavily fortified "Green Zone" section of Baghdad that once housed regime loyalists, the CPA served as an effective "viceroyalty" over occupied Iraq. Bremer was the "viceroy." His mandate was simple yet daunting: run the affairs of Iraq until a new government was in place, after which point, Americans could go home. Journalist Peter Beinart wrote in the aftermath of the war that, unlike Garner, Bremer saw Saddam's regime the way Bush did, "as an ugly skin concealing the pro-American democracy trapped inside."[17]

Bremer certainly saw his newly created position in grand terms, "My new assignment combine[d] some of the vice-regal responsibilities of General Douglas MacArthur, de facto ruler of Imperial Japan after World War II, and of General Lucius Clay, who led the American occupation of defeated Germany. . . . I would be the only paramount authority figure – other than Saddam Hussein – that most Iraqis had ever known."[18] At once Bremer possessed full executive, legislative, and judiciary authority in the Iraqi realm. Ironically, however, he had no direct authority over 98 percent of the official American personnel in Iraq.[19]

Confronted with a daunting task, none of Bremer's tough decisions was as grievously damaging – nor had repercussions as far-reaching and long-lasting – as the summary "de-Ba'athification" of the Iraqi government and the disbanding of the Iraqi Army. These actions were undertaken out of fear that lingering elements of the former regime, if left in power, could subvert the transitional government. While these fears were not entirely irrational, they were not thoroughly considered. By purging the Iraqi government of the Ba'ath Party, the CPA left numerous important positions vacant that would need to be filled. Simultaneously, those Iraqis who were low-level members of the party – often out of necessity, since Ba'ath Party membership was a prerequisite for professional advancement – were also suddenly left unemployed in a state with a barely functioning postinvasion economy.

By dissolving the armed forces, the CPA left tens of thousands of Iraqis jobless, and an entirely new military would have to be constructed to help Coalition forces establish and provide security. Ba'athists who had held government positions as well as the former soldiers were suddenly disenfranchised in the earliest days of Iraq's transition, and the soldiers still possessed military hardware and tactical knowledge. At the time, though, neither the White House nor U.S. Central Command, the regional combatant command with authority over Iraq, soon to be led by U.S. Army Lieutenant General John Abizaid, objected to Bremer's decision, nor did other members of the National Security Council who were briefed.[20] The army had been Hussein's enforcer, so it would be wise to get rid of it and start over from scratch.

Initially there were protests outside of the CPA's headquarters at the Republican Palace in Baghdad. For days, former Ba'athists and Iraqi Army personnel angrily demanded that the CPA return their jobs. By the time Bremer announced plans for a new military to form, the protestors had disappeared. When asked of the whereabouts of the crowds of unemployed men who had once gathered outside the Green Zone, a former Iraqi soldier laughed and said, "They're all insurgents now."[21]

Despite vocal warnings from his own staff, with the mere act of signing his name – removing Ba'athists from government positions and dissolving the army – Bremer likely helped push tens of thousands of Iraqis into the insurgency almost overnight. The Coalition now appeared to the Sunnis and Ba'athists to be their oppressor, not their liberator. Worse yet, the Coalition reinforced long-standing sectarian Sunni-Shi'a friction. (The Sunni [Ba'athists] were in the minority although they had held positions of power – in the army and the government bureaucracy – because of allegiance to Saddam. The Shi'a, who had virtually no presence in the military-governing institutions, made up the majority of the Iraqi population.) The destruction of these key institutions therefore had unmistakable sectarian implications.[22] Had the CPA not humiliated the Ba'athists and deprived them of their jobs, it might be reasonable to speculate, the insurgency would have foundered rather than being dramatically strengthened, and the task of restoring security would not have become so monumental.

IRAQ BEGINS TO UNRAVEL

By the summer of 2003, just a few months after Bremer's fateful decision to disband the Iraqi army, the incipient, shadowy insurgency began to break out in force. The Sunni-dominated sector, often called the Sunni Triangle, to the northwest of Baghdad and incorporating Fallujah, Ramadi, and Anbar provinces, proved to be one of the most active areas of the multi-faceted insurgency. As one journalist put it at the time, "the insurgency didn't begin with an announcement or major event. Rather, it was a change in the weather."[23]

While the insurgency's emergence was subtle, in these early months one spectacular attack stood out: the August 19, 2003, suicide bombing of the UN headquarters in Baghdad. The bomber drove a KAMAZ flatbed truck loaded with military-grade munitions. The cargo exploded in front of the compound's façade, collapsing part of the three-story building, killing twenty-two, including top special UN envoy to Iraq, Vieira de Mello.[24]

The UN attack was followed by a second bombing of UN facilities a month later. The State Department subsequently concluded that Jordanian-born militant Abu Musab al-Zarqawi was behind the attacks.

At the time, UN Security General Kofi Annan referred to the seasoned diplomat Vieira de Mello as "the one person in Iraq we could least afford to lose." The UN abruptly ended its 600-person mission in Iraq, leaving the nascent CPA to deal with the Herculean task of reconstructing the country.

With little centralized leadership, the Sunni insurgency started out with small cells that would target the fledgling provincial government politicians or the thinly dispersed Coalition forces, mostly U.S. soldiers. The standard profile of the Sunni insurgent was "18-year-old with [an] AK-47 and no money." In short, a total of 150,000 American troops were facing an enemy that "had no head, no central nervous system, no hierarchical command and control that could be destroyed."[25]

The early Sunni insurgency was largely driven by unemployed and increasingly desperate Iraqi males vulnerable to calls to join the fight against the occupiers, and these insurgents had access to an enormous glut of weapons and materiel. The initial insurgent attacks were largely "trial and error," yet they increased in frequency and strength as the insurgents found weaknesses in the American ranks and their sophisticated weaponry. The insurgents quickly learned that the IED was by far the most effective weapon against Coalition forces, causing roughly two-thirds of the American casualties. For the next several years, the Coalition and insurgent forces would play a constant game of cat-and-mouse: the insurgents used increasingly complex and lethal IEDs to take out convoys or patrolling American vehicles, while the U.S. forces continued to invent new ways to detect and defuse the bombs.

The Sunni insurgents were most lethal in Anbar province; much of the activity there was spearheaded by foreign jihadists. Americans came to think of Anbar Province as the "Wild West," and foremost among its bandits was Zarqawi, the Islamist who commanded Al Qaeda's forces in Iraq and masterminded the devastating attack on the UN compound. Begun under the name Jama'at al-Tawhid wal-Jihad (Monotheism and Jihad), this network of extremist insurgents gained notoriety for its indiscriminate bombings of civilian targets within Iraq and its publicized executions of Westerners it had managed to capture. Most infamously, in May of 2004 it beheaded American civilian Nicholas Berg, labeling the act a retaliation for U.S. mistreatment of Iraqi prisoners. It later pledged its allegiance to Osama bin Laden and became known as Al Qaeda in Iraq (AQI). It was emboldened by its successes to attempt even more devastating attacks.

One particularly gruesome bombing in September of 2004, at the opening celebration for a water treatment plant in Baghdad, targeted U.S.

soldiers who were passing out candy to Iraqi children. Forty-one Iraqis were killed, including thirty-five children. Al-Zarqawi's group unashamedly claimed responsibility for the attack. It was also widely believed by the Coalition that al-Zarqawi and AQI were responsible for the February 2006 bombing of the al Askari Mosque in Samarra, a revered site for Shi'a Muslims, which drastically accelerated the abysmal cycle of sectarian violence that characterized the war for the next two years.

Al-Zarqawi himself became the most highly valued target in Iraq and was soon the focus of an intense manhunt by the Coalition. A price of $25 million was put on his head, and the U.S. Department of Justice added him to the FBI "Most Wanted Terrorists" list. Videos appeared on the Internet of al-Zarqawi glorifying his struggle, posing with a Belgian-made light machine gun used by American forces, and conspicuously sporting a pair of New Balance tennis shoes. He was the face of America's enemy in Iraq.

Finally, on June 7, 2006, U.S. Air Force F-16C Fighting Falcons, guided onto target by JSOC operatives, dropped precision-guided munitions on a small house north of Baqubah. When the debris settled, al-Zarqawi's body was recovered, along with those of his wife and child and several insurgent leaders. Symbolically, it was an important moment for the American military and the Iraqi people, both of whom had suffered much at the hands of al-Zarqawi and his followers. His death was hailed by the Coalition as a victory and a turning point in the fight against Al Qaeda, but the truth was that it did little to abate the violence that AQI had begun. The death toll in Iraq peaked soon after.

By 2004, Baghdad had erupted as another center of violence. Most harrowing, Shi'ite militias were working with the minister of interior and police forces to create death squads that targeted vulnerable Sunni populations in the capital. Over time, it became clear that the fledgling Shi'ite-led Iraqi government was unwilling to rein in these clandestine groups whose activity further enflamed a nascent civil war and ethnic cleansing in Baghdad.

Complicating the Shi'ite angle was the dogged resilience of Moqtada al-Sadr, the Tehran-backed radical cleric who ordered his followers to revolt against the American occupiers in April 2004. Bremer had ordered one of al-Sadr's newspapers, *Al Hawza*, shut down after it published incendiary materials about the CPA and U.S. military, including a story titled, "Bremer Follows in the Footsteps of Saddam." Al-Sadr's motley militia, the Jaish al-Mahdi (JAM), quickly went on the offensive in the Shi'ite cities of Najaf, Kut, and Kufa, and used thousands of fighters to ambush

U.S. patrols in Sadr City, an enormous Shi'ite slum in Baghdad named for the fiery cleric's revered father. Heavy fighting across the south and in Sadr City continued until early June when a cease-fire was announced.[26]

Then in August, 2,000 JAM fighters seized the shrine of the Imam Ali, a holy site in the southern city of Najaf visited by millions of Shi'ite pilgrims. U.S. commander General George W. Casey eventually ordered his forces to regain the territory from al-Sadr, which occurred after a tense standoff and several weeks of urban fighting. While al-Sadr's revolt was quieted in Najaf, he nonetheless used Iranian funds (which bought weapons such as the infamous "explosively-formed penetrator") to support the now well-equipped JAM, which proved to be a formidable opponent and one more headache for the Coalition in the Shi'ite south and Baghdad. In some instances, though, instead of simply fighting the Coalition forces, the JAM would also fight head-to-head against AQI operatives in bloody confrontations.

THE CAPTURE OF SADDAM HUSSEIN

"Ladies and gentlemen, we got him." These were the words of a euphoric Jerry Bremer in December 2003 at a press conference announcing the capture of Saddam Hussein. Remarkably, though, given the unchecked chaos and violence that would confront the American campaign in Iraq, the capture of Saddam Hussein turned out to be almost irrelevant to the entire war. As part of Operation Red Dawn, around 600 special operations forces from JSOC and conventional troops from the Army's 4th Infantry Division hunted the ousted dictator on a twenty-four-hour search mission led by the hard-charging General Raymond Odierno and Colonel Jim Hickey.

Hussein was discovered near the village of ad-Dawr, about ten miles southeast of the city of Tikrit and not far from Hussein's birthplace. An Iraqi informant had told U.S. troops that an important Iraqi official was hiding there. During an inspection of the suspected location, a soldier noticed a prayer rug over a dirt spot that had recently been swept. This led to the "spider hole" from which the disheveled dictator emerged with his hands up. Hussein's capture led to an immediate yet ephemeral boost in President Bush's approval ratings. The capture, however, did not have nearly the impact on quelling the insurgency that U.S. military and civilian officials had hoped for. On December 30, 2006, Hussein was hanged in a grisly ceremony after a protracted trial in which an Iraqi tribunal court convicted him of crimes against humanity, namely, the 1982 massacre of 148 people in the village of Dujail.

THE BATTLE OF FALLUJAH

Welcome to Chaos. – Marine Captain Doug Zembiec[27]

I come in peace. I didn't bring artillery. But I'm pleading with you, with tears in my eyes: If you fuck with me, I'll kill you all. – Marine General Mattis[28]

In late March 2004, the U.S. Army's 82nd Airborne Division turned over responsibility for the Sunni-majority city of Fallujah in Anbar province to the Marine Corps. Under the 82nd's supervision, Fallujah had been relatively quiet in the year since the invasion. This was an especially sensitive time for the U.S. mission since al-Sadr's Shi'ite uprising was also on the offensive. Yet the situation in Fallujah deteriorated only days after the Marines took over, beginning with a gruesome episode in which four American contractors were ambushed and killed in the city's center. Jubilant mobs then dismembered their bodies and hung them from a nearby bridge. Images of the cheering Iraqis and charred American bodies were broadcast around the world.

Bremer stated that the act would not go unpunished. After being briefed by Rumsfeld, an indignant President Bush approved the plan for an overwhelming attack to seize the city. Some military commanders, however, were more cautious, believing that a hasty attack could prove counterproductive. Nevertheless, Marine General Mattis ordered his men to carry out Operation Vigilant Resolve by taking control of the city and wiping out the insurgent strongholds and weapons caches.

On April 5, the marines encountered heavy resistance from hundreds of insurgents dispersed throughout the city. It took several days of painstaking building-by-building fighting before the marines had finished their sweep of insurgent positions. Calls from the Iraqi government and international capitals and organizations that the U.S. forces were imposing "collective punishment" on the Fallujah residents quickly turned the violent but successful raid into a political issue.[29]

President Bush ordered the marines to halt their operation. During their departure from the city, they left behind a 2,000-man Iraqi-led outfit called the Fallujah Brigade that had the thankless task of ensuring the city's security. Instead of fighting the insurgents, the Fallujah Brigade tended traffic checkpoints and filled other less pressing duties, but even these modest efforts ceased after a few weeks. Over time, the 800 AK-47 rifles, 27 pick-up trucks, and 50 radios the Marines had given to the Brigade found their way to the insurgents.[30]

The back-and-forth decision making in the First Battle of Fallujah apparently led a frustrated General Mattis to quip, echoing Napoleon,

"If you're going to take Vienna, take fucking Vienna."[31] In the ensuing months, the influx of insurgents into the effective sanctuary of Fallujah was so steady that it led some Marines to dub the city the "bomb factory." By the fall, the marines had drafted plans to go into Fallujah a second time with far greater troop numbers and firepower than they'd used in April.

The Second Battle of Fallujah was launched on November 8, a cold, rainy morning. The attacking force comprised 500 Marines, 1,500 U.S. Army soldiers, and 2,000 Iraqi soldiers. For the U.S. military, the Second Battle of Fallujah in November 2004 was cathartic: after months of being unable to retaliate, suffering casualties, and watching the city become a haven for AQI – and, reportedly, even al-Zarqawi himself – soldiers and marines were finally given permission to engage the enemy directly, and they did so zealously.

It was the kind of fight that the U.S. military was designed for. It would allow the forces to display their superiority of arms to the enemy rather than fighting reactively, with one hand tied behind their backs. Whereas there seemed to be little glory or excitement in the endless cycle of foot patrols and policing operations, the takedown of Fallujah was certain to be a true battle. The marines thought of Guadalcanal and Iwo Jima, soldiers remembered Normandy and the Ardennes – names and places that were engraved in the memories and traditions of the American military. Fallujah seemed destined for that pantheon.

Most of Fallujah's citizens fled before the battle after Coalition aircraft dropped leaflets on the city warning them about the impending carnage. Carrying their children and their belongings, they seeped out into the surrounding countryside while thousands of insurgents filled the void, commandeering homes and vehicles in preparation for their struggle against the Americans. An estimated 400 civilians remained at the time of the assault, out of a city of 250,000.

The result was the perfect arena for a climactic showdown between the Coalition and the most dedicated of Iraq's insurgents. With innocent civilians removed from the equation and an impenetrable perimeter thrown up around the city that trapped the insurgents within, America's uncontested artillery and airpower were free to pulverize the city before ground forces moved in.

The U.S. military came down on Fallujah like a sledgehammer. The fighting was ferocious, evoking journalistic comparisons to the marines' battle for Hue City in 1968. It was house-to-house combat at its most brutal. The courage and sophistication of the enemy surprised many Americans, as they had been accustomed to fighting an unorganized rabble. American soldiers in the combat described an enemy capable of mounting ambushes that utilized combined arms of precision rifles, mortars, and rocket-propelled grenades. Insurgents used captured American uniforms and equipment to escape detection. They rigged entire houses with explosives. These building-contained IEDs (BCIEDs) were meant to detonate once an American unit entered the building, collapsing the structure on top of them.

Even more brazen attacks occurred in which insurgents, high on methamphetamines, assaulted American positions en masse. In their drugged state, insurgents were able to withstand numerous hits from American weapons before falling. The intense battle lasted weeks and resulted in the deaths of 2,000 insurgents and 70 Americans, with more than 600 Americans wounded. The fighting was "intense, close, and personal."[32] Marine squads engaged in 200 firefights inside cement rooms, using guns, grenades, and even knives. In three days, the 38 marines in 1st Platoon of Lima Company engaged in 16 firefights, killing 38 insurgents and losing 3 of their own men.

The Fallujah assault left over 2,000 buildings destroyed and 10,000 severely damaged. Amid the rubble, marines encountered 2 car bomb factories, 24 smaller bomb factories, and almost 50 weapons caches. Three buildings held chambers used by Sunni extremists to torture and behead captives. The initial U.S. assessment was that the November battle had broken the back of the insurgency, but like the impact of Hussein's capture, this proved ephemeral. Nonetheless, the massive assault did neutralize Fallujah as an insurgent sanctuary.

But Fallujah, while it was still a major Coalition victory, became tarnished. The overwhelming firepower that the marines and soldiers brought against their opponents, while thoroughly supported by U.S. military doctrine, seemed excessive to much of the rest of the world. Homes, schools, and worse yet, mosques, were damaged and destroyed in the effort to cleanse the city of insurgents and foreign jihadis. In one scene that was aired on news channels across the world, a squad of marines came upon a number of dead insurgents inside a mosque. One of the marines spotted an insurgent whom he was convinced was feigning death to ambush them, so he quickly shot the man lying on the ground. This footage especially drew harsh criticism, and Al-Jazeera displayed it as evidence of American brutality.

The Second Battle of Fallujah became yet another lightning rod for Muslim discontent regarding the war in Iraq even though in many ways, it was the "cleanest" battle that Americans would fight in the midst of a dirty war, thanks to the absence of civilians and the open willingness of the insurgents to fight and die in open battle against them. Fallujah was an island of ferociously intense but still conventional warfare in a vast sea of counterinsurgency.

THE LEGACY OF THE CPA

The U.S occupation of Iraq was not solely about counterinsurgency through combat. On the civilian side there was a multibillion dollar effort to build up the country's decrepit infrastructure and fledgling political and democratic institutions. This was especially true during the CPA's year-long rule of Iraq before it handed over a very tenuous "sovereignty" to an interim Iraqi government. In the days leading up to his final departure from Baghdad in June 2005, Bremer contended that the CPA had put Iraq on a clear path to democracy and a free-market economy through a series of achievements: 2,500 schools had been repaired; three million children had been immunized; local governing councils had been formed in every city and province; and a liberal bill of rights had been written into the interim constitution. But as the *Washington Post*'s Rajiv Chandrasekaran wrote, there was another side to this coin:

> Iraqis saw broken promises. As Bremer prepared to depart, electricity generation remained stuck at around 4,000 megawatts – resulting in less than nine hours of power a day to most Baghdad homes – instead of the 6,000 megawatts he had pledged to provide. The new army had fewer than 4,000 trained soldiers, a third of what he had promised.... Seventy percent of police officers on the street had not received any CPA-funded training. Attacks on American forces and foreign civilians averaged more than forty a day, a threefold increase since January. Assassinations of political leaders and sabotage of the country's electricity infrastructure occurred almost daily.[33]

One of the most widely covered elements of Iraq's frustratingly slow and contentious march toward stability occurred in January 2005 when citizens went to the polls for the first democratic elections in decades. In Baghdad, the Kurdish-dominated north, and the Shi'ite south, the election was a remarkable triumph. Images of elderly women waving fingers stained with purple ink (an anti-fraud measure to show that they had voted) sent a message to the world that Iraqis indeed wanted democracy. It was an especially satisfying moment for the Bush administration as many critics predicted that the attempt to hold an election in such a chaotic environment was a fool's errand. One reason there was far less violence than expected was the three-day curfew that mandated restricted automobile traffic and pedestrian checkpoints.[34]

A less-documented problem, however, was the extremely low voter turnout in the Sunni-dominated areas such as the Sunni Triangle. Local politicians had boycotted the vote to push for a national assembly that would then draft a new constitution. In Ramadi, only six people voted at one polling station; in another city, eight polling stations never opened. As is usually the case in democracy, the results mirrored the turnout. A coalition of Shi'ite parties sponsored by the influential Grand Ayatollah Ali al-Sistani won 48 percent of the vote; two major Kurdish parties gained a combined 26 percent. On the contrary, a Sunni party led by former foreign minister Adnan Pachachi did not receive enough votes to gain a single seat in the legislature. Not surprisingly, when it came time to write the constitution a few months later, Sunnis were generally unhappy with a document they believed was biased against them. What at first glance appeared to bring legitimacy to Iraq's nascent democracy in fact helped to deepen sectarian divisions.

TORTURE AT ABU GHRAIB

One main element in the U.S. military's sagging effort to quell the insurgency and lower levels of violence involved arresting Iraqis and foreigners suspected of being insurgents. For one, U.S. officials believed that taking the suspects off the streets would prevent them from carrying out attacks. More important, though, the roughly 1,000 suspects imprisoned each month would be treasure troves of up-to-the-minute intelligence on insurgent activities and organization. In the first eighteen months of the war, 30,000 to 40,000 Iraqis passed through U.S.-controlled detention prisons. By the end of September 2003, the Abu Ghraib prison, which had been infamous during Hussein's reign, held over 3,500 prisoners. A month later, the number doubled, but there were only 360 American MPs to guard them. In late April 2004, the prison gained global infamy when pictures taken by an abusive guard revealed images of sadistic torture, including one of a hooded detainee with wires tying his hands.

Seventeen officers and soldiers were removed from duty, including one brigadier general and several colonels; seven low-level soldiers were sent to prison. The ensuing investigation revealed that the soldiers had been very poorly prepared for the extremely stressful and chaotic atmosphere at the prison. Yet, while the U.S. military might have meted out justice to the implicated soldiers, the damage done to the image of the U.S. occupation of Iraq was incalculable. The United States claimed to have liberated Iraq, yet the images from Abu Ghraib suggested to many, especially in the Arab world, that the U.S. forces in fact wanted to humiliate and abuse the Iraqi people.

In more utilitarian terms, the Abu Ghraib abuses counted as a serious setback for the Coalition's operations on the ground. American policymakers and commanders were only beginning to understand that the limited-mandate occupation was becoming a full-blown counterinsurgency operation, and that this operation's success would depend in part on the Coalition's ability to win over Iraqi hearts and minds. Much as the atrocities in previous counterinsurgencies, such as the My Lai massacre in Vietnam and the "death squad" executions in El Salvador, had discredited the counterinsurgents' efforts, Abu Ghraib steered sympathies away from the Coalition's mission. The difference this time, though, was that a twenty-four-hour international news cycle and emerging Internet-based social media helped to circulate the images to a global audience. Thus, criticism of the Coalition's efforts came not only from opposition in theater and at home, but from an unprecedentedly global public opinion.

FORCE PROTECTION AND FORWARD OPERATING BASES

The U.S. military's entrenchment in Iraq galvanized a significant portion of the officer corps into a sort of free-thinking intellectual movement that is uncharacteristic of most armies. Battalion, regimental, and division commanders in postinvasion Iraq quickly realized that their troops lacked adequate training for handling the simultaneous challenges of irregular warfare and nation-building, and also that the Coalition as a whole seemed to lack any cohesive long-term strategy for establishing security and ensuring stability in the area of operations. These two corrosive problems were caused not only by an immense doctrinal gap that spanned nearly four decades but also by a vain and stubborn attempt in Washington and among certain key military leaders to play down the violence and disorder that was steadily metastasizing after the fall of Baghdad.

While some commanders adapted their forces to wage the battle of hearts and minds, others withdrew into secure bases to avoid American casualties. Major General David Petraeus, who commanded the Army's 101st Airborne Division (Air Assault) during the march up to Baghdad and through the Coalition's first year of occupation, was quick to implement classic counterinsurgency strategies in the northern city of Mosul and to blend them seamlessly with essential tasks of reconstruction and nation-building. Reportedly, Petraeus effectively ignored the Bush administration's decree to fire the remnants of Saddam's regime, preferring to allow competent officials to remain running the government.[35]

When February 2004 came and the "Screaming Eagles" of the 101st were rotated out of the country, Mosul was a success story amid a dizzying array of Iraqi municipalities for which life was steadily growing bleaker. But this success was quickly extinguished when a Stryker brigade combat team with only one-quarter of the 101st Airborne's light infantry manpower, replaced Petraeus's division. While correlation is no guarantee of causation, it is the case that the Stryker forces disengaged almost entirely from the local population, patrolling in armored vehicles rather than on foot and spurning the governance-oriented strategies that their predecessors had promoted. It is also the case that Mosul spiraled back into chaos within months of Petraeus's departure.

The story repeated itself across the country. U.S. commanders withdrew their forces behind the fortifications of their massive forward operating bases (FOBs) in adherence to a risk-averse doctrine in military thinking known as "force protection." To limit casualties, American personnel were kept within the secure confines of their bases, leading to a rather counterintuitive phenomenon in which combat forces found themselves "commuting to work" each day in convoys from their bases to the towns in their areas of operation. This vacuum of oversight and security allowed insurgents to operate freely, planting IEDs along roads at night. Moreover, while Americans stayed relatively safe inside the FOBs, Iraqi civilians suffered at the hands of the insurgents.

In the same way that the Green Zone became an island within chaotic Baghdad, the American FOBs assumed their own self-contained character. Support personnel involved in logistics, supply, administration, and even intelligence became so ensconced in these fortresses, never going "outside the wire," that combat troops began derisively referring to their more sedentary comrades as "fobbits." Journalist George Packer mentions FOB Speicher, near the northern city of Tal Afar, as being home to 9,000 soldiers, many of whom "seemed to leave the base rarely or not at all: they talked about 'going out,' as if the psychological barrier between them and Iraq had become daunting."[36]

The reliance on FOBs was partly the product of an aversion to casualties and risk that had become ingrained in the U.S. military psyche after Vietnam, and which was reinforced by its ignominious retreat from Somalia in 1993 after the deaths of eighteen soldiers in the trash-strewn streets of Mogadishu. Now, this mindset exposed a critical weakness in its Iraqi counterinsurgency strategy. Said one professor at the Naval Postgraduate School: "It's absurd to think that you can protect the population from armed insurgents without putting your men's lives at risk."[37] An American Special Forces officer echoed the same sentiment, grousing to *Washington Post* writer Thomas Ricks, "What you are seeing here is an unconventional war fought conventionally," meaning with too much emphasis on force protection and not enough on interaction with the local populace.[38]

Indeed, one of the great tensions of U.S. strategy during these years was that the reliance on the FOBs occurred simultaneously with the understanding that greater attention to classical counterinsurgency insights was necessary to rescue this desperate situation. The commanding general in Iraq, General George W. Casey, maintained the FOBs but nonetheless began to more actively seek out "COIN" (the term used by military devotees of counterinsurgency) approaches to quelling the seemingly intractable violence. One signature innovation under Casey's tenure was the establishment in 2005 of a counterinsurgency school at a large U.S. military base at Taji, about thirty miles north of Baghdad. All incoming battalion commanders had to attend a two-week indoctrination before returning to their units.

One of Casey's key advisers on counterinsurgency was Kalev Sepp, a Harvard-trained historian who, as a Special Forces officer, advised two brigades in El Salvador in the 1980s. Sepp produced a short paper that distilled the lessons of fifty-three counterinsurgency campaigns during the twentieth century. The paper identified numerous areas where the U.S.-led effort was coming up short. By the end of 2006, in a clear indication that the strategy for Iraq had now embraced the classical COIN gospel, the U.S. military published the much-discussed *Counterinsurgency Field Manual 3-24*, the most academically influenced field manual in U.S. military history.

"THE LESSON OF TAL AFAR"

In May of 2005, General Casey sent Colonel H. R. McMaster and the 3rd Armored Cavalry Regiment to the embattled city of Tal Afar, a city with a population of 250,000 located 200 miles north of Baghdad and just 40 miles from the Syrian border. U.S. and Iraqi forces had entered the city in 2004, but insurgents subsequently moved in to use it as a base. By the spring of 2005, former regime elements fully controlled the city; they took over schools and mosques and intimidated, kidnapped, or murdered those suspected of cooperating with the Coalition or Iraqi security forces. Insurgents used Tal Afar as a launching base for their suicide-bombing attacks in Mosul, which lay only 40 miles to the east. The insurgents were also able to use their control over Tal Afar to create a sort of ideological sanctuary in which they could brainwash uneducated or unemployed Iraqi youth to oppose American and Iraqi forces.[39] McMaster's daunting task was to clean up Tal Afar.

McMaster routinely distributed classic counterinsurgency texts to prep his subordinates on key lessons such as "every time you treat an Iraqi disrespectfully, you are working for the enemy." McMaster and his soldiers spent the first three months in Tal Afar encircling the city and searching those entering and exiting to cut off the insurgents from their supplies. From May to September, the American regiment and two Iraqi Army brigades exchanged fire with the insurgents on a daily basis.[40] At times, McMaster's soldiers engaged in house-to-house fighting with the insurgents. In September, the joint forces set up twenty-nine small combat outposts every five or six blocks, to be manned by American and Iraqi soldiers. McMaster then went to work on reforming the city's dysfunctional governing institutions, most critically, removing an ineffective police chief and more than 100 of his deputies and replacing them with a more ethnically balanced force of 1,700. U.S. officers were even able to convince critical regional sheiks to cooperate, which resulted in the recruitment of over 1,400 men into the police force.

McMaster also used funds to support a Shi'a-Sunni city council, a novel and risky innovation given the recent sectarian antagonisms. Another large push was to reform the water and electricity departments, whose infrastructure was crippled by war damage and more than twenty years of Ba'athist neglect. But behind each of these programs was a strong military threat. In McMaster's view, "no amount of money or kindness, and no number of infrastructure programs, will facilitate winning over the population if COIN forces cannot provide security to the population."[41] Tal Afar's dramatic transformation from an insurgent stronghold into a relatively pacific provincial city caught the attention of the global media. The *New Yorker*'s George Packer wrote a widely read essay entitled, "The Lesson of Tal Afar." By 2007, there were far more Tal Afar-like operations across Iraq, with outposts in police precincts, neighborhood watches, combined U.S.-Iraqi small unit patrolling, and infrastructure reconstruction, that ultimately helped turn the tide against the insurgency.

THE SUNNI AWAKENING

Over the course of 2006, sheiks throughout Anbar province had made repeated efforts to organize resistance against the foreign AQI fighters who were terrorizing the local Sunni tribal populations. But these efforts were normally brutally suppressed. AQI demanded strict obedience and executed several sheiks to make the point. In one instance, AQI fighters assassinated a prominent Sunni sheik and hid his body from the family for three days so that they were unable to bury him in accordance with Muslim customs. Fury over this offense and others encouraged a small group of Sunni sheiks led by Abdul Sattar Abu Risha to begin to cooperate with Coalition forces against AQI. They called the incipient movement al-Sahwa, or the "Awakening."[42]

The city of Ramadi, located in Anbar province, had begun to spin out of control in early 2004, as hundreds of former Iraqi soldiers sneaked into it to initiate a battle that lasted for over two years and effectively destroyed the city. In June of 2006, Colonel Sean MacFarland arrived as commander of the 1st Brigade Combat Team of the 1st Armored Division tasked with stabilizing and rebuilding Ramadi. In an echo of Tal Afar, MacFarland's troops built combat outposts in neighborhoods to establish control and entice the insurgents into making ill-conceived attacks that would expose them to lethal Coalition firepower.[43]

MacFarland would take control of Ramadi piece by piece. It was a gamble of a strategy that thrust American soldiers into daily firefights for months. In MacFarland's brigade, 95 soldiers were killed and 600 wounded. One battalion lost 25 tanks, trucks, and Bradley fighting vehicles to IEDs and ambushes.[44] Yet, the brigade immediately began reconstruction projects, recruited police, and initiated negotiations that would bring the tribal leaders to the Coalition's side. The tough fighting and painstaking "diplomacy" conducted by MacFarland's forces began to show the Sunni sheiks that they could live free from Al Qaeda's yoke – and that the American and Iraqi forces would not abandon them in the process. AQI excess and American-led COIN innovation helped set the stage for the Awakening in Anbar province to gain traction.

The dynamic Abdul Sattar Abu Risha came from Ramadi, which was a bit ironic since ferocious American firepower there had caused considerable destruction and resentment. Nonetheless, McFarland's nuanced approach to security, population control, and governance helped earn the trust of the sheiks, including Sattar. In fact, it was Sattar who approached MacFarland during a meeting and said, "We are forming an alliance against Al Qaeda. Are you with us?"[45] As two U.S. officers wrote,

"[Sattar's] rallying cry touched a responsive nerve among the population and legitimized a hundred bottom-up partnerships among local leaders and U.S. commanders at the battalion level and below."[46]

The Awakening eventually encompassed 41 mostly Sunni tribes. By the summer of 2007, the movement had driven AQI from Anbar province and killed scores of its top leaders. Violence dropped from 250 killings per month in late 2006 to fewer than 100 by mid 2007. U.S. fatalities in Anbar fell from 43 percent of total casualties in 2006 to 17 percent in 2007. The number of tips to Coalition troops surged, and Sunni recruits for police slots jumped up dramatically. Interestingly, the AQI fighters feared the police more than the army or Coalition soldiers because the police knew the local area and customs – who belonged there and who did not – which made the foreign fighters especially vulnerable.[47]

The Zarqawi-led AQI savagery created its own backlash that diverted Sunni and Shi'a enmity away from the American occupiers and toward the foreign jihadists. So the Coalition was not the only side that made fatal mistakes in Iraq. Sattar was assassinated in September 2007 when someone in his security detail betrayed him for a supposed $1 million payment, which the informant never received. Nonetheless, the "counterinsurgency" against AQI that Sattar had helped create was instrumental in turning the tide of the entire Iraq war. U.S. strategists and commanders came to learn the large role that tribes played in the conflict and that found that success often entailed reaching out to Muslim clerics, tribal sheiks, and village headmen, or *mukhtars*.[48]

THE SURGE

> I give the [U.S.-led surge in 2007] strategy no chance of succeeding. Zero. – Sen. Joseph Biden[49]

By the fall of 2006, there appeared to be a growing sense that the war had shifted in favor of the Coalition. Most important, Sunni tribes and their Awakening had now turned against the foreign jihadists. The war had by no means been won, but it no longer appeared to be the losing cause that it had seemed just a year earlier. However, in the United States the perception continued to grow that the effort in Iraq had come unhinged. In fact, the Democratic Party's decisive victory in the House and Senate elections in November led many in the party to conclude that the vote had been a referendum on Bush's failed Iraq policy.

The Bush administration decided that any successful way forward in Iraq required the Coalition not just to control the population but to protect it. A growing but still contested view inside the administration held that the best way to do this would be through a "surge" of U.S. troops in the most violent and contested locales, including Baghdad.

On January 10, 2007, President Bush used a television address to inform the American people that he planned to send 20,000 additional troops (five battalions) into Iraq and to extend the stay of troops already deployed to create a total surge force of 30,000. This would provide the Iraqi government "the breathing space it needs to make progress ... pass legislation to share oil revenues ... hold provincial elections later this year." In his State of the Union address two weeks later, President Bush expanded on the thinking and expectations behind his decision to send in additional troops:

With Iraqis in the lead, our forces will help secure the city by chasing down the terrorists, insurgents, and the roaming death squads. And in Anbar Province, where al Qaeda terrorists have gathered and local forces have begun showing a willingness to fight them, we're sending an additional 4,000 United States Marines, with orders to find the terrorists and clear them out. We didn't drive al Qaeda out of their safe haven in Afghanistan only to let them set up a new safe haven in a free Iraq.[50]

Yet as the surge got under way in 2007, many back in Washington remained convinced that the war had already been lost and that the surge would only commit more American treasure and toil to a hopeless cause. There had been so much bad news and so many false bursts of optimism that it appeared entirely logical to assume that the surge was at best too little, too late. According to Senate Majority Leader Harry Reid, "This war is lost and the surge is not accomplishing anything as indicated by the extreme violence in Iraq." Instead, Reid and others contended, the United States needed to cut its losses and get out.

When General Petraeus replaced General Casey as head of U.S. ground forces in February 2007, the incoming commander's strategy appeared to come straight out of the COIN manual. Petraeus directed large numbers of U.S. troops to man small joint U.S.-Iraqi outposts in Baghdad, similar to those that had led to success in Tal Afar and Ramadi. Petraeus also emphasized the need for population security and nonmilitary programs that would generate Iraqi trust in the counterinsurgency effort. To quell the shocking violence in Baghdad, Petraeus allocated an American battalion to each of the city's ten districts, something that was only feasible after the White House's decision to increase the U.S. force. Within months, many Marine and some Army units were living among the local populations, patrolling on foot and desperately trying to show that COIN doctrine could win the day in Iraq.[51]

The key innovation in the surge was not simply the addition of extra troops – although that was indispensible – but the expansion of their responsibilities. By operating in small, local groups closely aligned with Iraqi military and police units, the larger forces in Baghdad and its environs, such as Diyala province east of the capital (called the "Wild, Wild East" by soldiers in Baghdad), could deliver the sorts of successes achieved in Tal Afar and Ramadi. The surge brought troops to this insurgent-controlled region for the first time in several years. By March, troops had established a series of joint security stations (JSSs) and combat outposts across the capital, with more being built each week.[52] In the rough neighborhoods directly south of Baghdad, for instance, Coalition forces were also focused on the seemingly mundane tasks of repairing sewage dumps, installing new sidewalks and streetlights, and hiring hundreds of Iraqi civilians to pick up the trash. In a move that critics condemned as "ethnic cleansing," the Coalition separated combatants and neighborhoods by building high walls.

Another key element was the use of "Sons of Iraq" – ad hoc armed forces composed largely of members of the Sunni Awakening – to bolster counterinsurgency efforts. The Sons of Iraq forces identified hundreds of munitions caches that Coalition or Iraqi security forces were unable to discover and remove. They seized loads of weapons, ammunition, and tons of explosives and IED-making material. The intelligence they provided led to the capture of at least five high-value target (HVT) insurgents. Perhaps most critically, though, the Sons of Iraq provided a key link to the local population, enhancing the Coalition forces' ability to build trust, situational awareness, and cooperation.[53]

During these critical months in 2007, Petraeus was constantly out in the conflict zones making contact with Coalition forces and Iraqi politicians and civilians. In a nod to his COIN predecessors T. E. Lawrence and David Galula, Petraeus routinely issued essays that included pithy counterinsurgency maxims such as "Live among the people"; "Pursue the enemy relentlessly"; and "Walk. Move mounted, work dismounted. Stop by, don't drive by. Patrol on foot and engage the population. Situational awareness can only be gained by interacting with the people face-to-face, not separated by ballistic glass."[54] Petraeus firmly believed that Baghdad was the psychological and physical key to the conflict as more than 50 percent of the war had occurred inside the capital since 2006.

A far less visible element of the U.S. strategy was the relentless use of shadowy special operation forces to hunt AQI, JAM, and other insurgent leaders. Under the command of Lieutenant General Stanley McChrystal, special operations forces carried out stealth raids across Iraq that devastated the ranks of an estimated 70 percent of AQI and JAM leadership. Another key element to the eventual turnaround was the slow and inconsistent but ultimately sufficient process of political reconciliation and moderation. In the wake of the Coalition Provisional Authority fiasco, seasoned ambassadors John Negroponte, Zalmay Khalilzad (who had previously been the U.S. envoy in Kabul), and Ryan Crocker all worked tirelessly to cajole disparate and often mistrustful Iraqi political factions to come to various sorts of agreements.

Looking back, it became apparent that one problem with evaluating the surge's effectiveness was the inescapable difficulty of separating correlation from causation. We know that U.S. forces surged troops in under the frenetic guidance of their COIN-inspired military guru General Petreaus, and we also know that Iraq's security situation improved dramatically around roughly this same time. The summer of 2007 witnessed some of the fiercest fighting in this now four-year-long war with more than 100 U.S. soldiers killed in April, May, and June. But then the rate dropped to 25 killed in December. And a year later, in December 2008, only 16 Americans died.[55]

Even so, we will probably never know the true extent to which the surge was successful. To complicate this evaluation, in addition to the directly American-promoted political and military efforts described earlier, there were other surprising developments that helped drive this unfolding and remarkable improvement in the security situation. For one, Sunnis across Iraq recognized that they had lost and that suing for peace was their only means of ensuring survival. Second, the aforementioned walling off of Baghdad into sectarian enclaves had an impact, but the grim reality was that a key share of the decrease in violence was perhaps because Baghdad had already undergone sectarian cleansing by the time the surge happened.[56] Fatefully, for all of his likely successes in Iraq that helped save a doomed American campaign, General Petraeus might have ended up making his own grand mistake: first concluding that U.S.-driven actions drove the positive result in Iraq and then assuming that the same COIN approach would automatically work in Afghanistan.

THE WAR WINDS DOWN

The complex nature of Operation Iraqi Freedom allows many comparisons to be drawn with other dirty wars throughout America's history.

The war in the Philippines after 1898 also began as a conventional operation that quickly descended into guerrilla warfare. A half century later, Vietnam was a conflict that America tried its best to make conventional but that proved to be anything but, and that put tremendous strain on the entire country. In fact, as public opinion began to turn against the Iraq war in 2004, it was indeed popular among critics to liken Iraq to Vietnam, knowing full well the nationwide misery that prevailed during those years. The more Iraq began to resemble an intractable conflict, the more Americans heard terms like "quagmire" in the media. The overarching argument seemed to be that America should only fight clean wars: wars with clear objectives and without moral dilemmas.

One of the great ironies of the Coalition's involvement in Iraq is that in its efforts to appear benevolent upon toppling Saddam Hussein's regime, it unwittingly committed a number of critical mistakes that expedited the country's decline into violence, not only in its responses to the country's lack of security but also in its formation of a transitional government. As one analyst noted, "Iraq's new foreign rulers ... arguably reinforced ethnic and sectarian identities through their misconceptions and resulting actions, especially by the way they went about establishing the institutions of the new state."[57] The Bush team also assumed that the postinvasion phase would be relatively benign – and this was clearly not the case. Instead, the U.S. occupation of Iraq teetered on the brink of a complete disaster. A *Wall Street Journal* correspondent, for example, bleakly wrote from Baghdad in 2004, "Despite President Bush's rosy assessments, Iraq remains a disaster ... a foreign policy bound to haunt the United States for decades to come."[58]

An intelligence failure of enormous portions was behind the fateful decision to launch the Iraq War. Virtually all Western intelligence agencies believed that Saddam Hussein's regime possessed weapons of mass destruction, an assumption that was incorrect. In addition, the Bush team and U.S. military planners failed to realize that Iraq had already mostly fallen apart as a functioning state. For example, when the British engineers and marines seized the "Crown Jewel" of the oil pumping station north of Basra in March 2003, they were appalled to see broken windows, open cesspools, and critical equipment falling to pieces.[59]

Colin Powell once quipped about the Pottery Barn rule in Iraq: "You break it, you own it." Historians will debate whether Iraq would have remained a viable state had the United States not invaded, but Powell's estimation now seems prescient: the American intervention broke Iraq (or, at the very least, precipitated its breakup), and the United States paid for it tremendously in money and lives lost.

When the war began to improve in 2006, planners developed a more formal strategy based on the classic counterinsurgency principles such as protecting the population, marginalizing extremist elements, bolstering the political center, and undertaking joint patrols. Indeed, as the positive results of the surge began to sink in, some military writers began to refer to the years 2004–6 as "BC" (before COIN) and 2007–8 as "AD" (after David). Petraeus certainly played a key role, but so did other "can-do" officers such as Colonels McMaster in Tal Afar and MacFarland in Ramadi, as well as countless others (including Iraqis) who never gained nearly the clout of these three men. Unlike U.S. experiences in Colombia and El Salvador, but certainly like Vietnam and Philippines in the early twentieth century, the experience in Iraq was "large-footprint" COIN. And while the case is noteworthy as an instance of the United States adapting prior experience to a new, unfamiliar, and dirty situation on the ground, its long-term consequences for Iraq and for U.S. counterinsurgency policy are still in the making. Journalists Michael Gordon and Benard Trainor might have summed up the American experience in Iraq best when they wrote in 2013:

The United States had stormed into Iraq in 2003 with extravagant hopes but little understanding. Four years later, it had pulled Iraq back from the precipice of civil war at enormous cost. Generals had been fired and hired. The American military had rediscovered counterinsurgency. Struggling to decipher the labyrinth of sect, religion, and tribe, American commanders and diplomats had cut deals with an assortment of politicians, clerics, militia leaders, and even insurgents. But after the loss of nearly 4,500 American troops and many more Iraqi lives, and the expenditure of more than $800 billion, just what sort of Iraq was the United States military leaving behind?[60]

29

Intermezzo

The Counterinsurgency Field Manual *and Postmodern Insurgencies*

> You are really asking Soldiers and Marines to be prepared each day to be ready for a hand grenade or a handshake.
> – Lt. General David Petraeus[1]

In late 2006, while the counterinsurgency wars in Iraq and Afghanistan were still raging, the U.S. Army and Marine Corps jointly published the seminal *Counterinsurgency Field Manual*. The book's release was much publicized, and it was reportedly downloaded from the Internet more than one million times in the months following publication as friends and enemies across the world were eager to gain insight into how the United States understood irregular warfare – and how these understandings might be applied to the counterinsurgency fight in Iraq in particular.

Notably, most of the new "COIN" (military shorthand for counterinsurgency) doctrine was deeply grounded in the experiences of the Cold War and earlier, especially the seminal influence of counterinsurgency philosopher David Galula. Echoing this, the *Manual* invoked the "counterintuitive" insight – now so familiar as to be obvious – that conventional military approaches in an irregular war are often counterproductive. The manual also used maxims to make these "counterintuitive" points, likely in an intentional response to Mao's *Guerrilla Warfare* and certainly reflecting Galula and other "classical" counterinsurgency thinkers and practitioners who made such points during the Cold War. They included such phrases as "Some of the best weapons for counterinsurgents do not shoot"; "Sometimes doing nothing is the best reaction"; and "The more successful the counterinsurgency is, the less force is used and more risk must be accepted."[2]

The *Field Manual* was not the first codification of counterinsurgency principles in recent years and decades, but it was the first document to elevate these COIN principles to the center of U.S. military doctrine. And for a while after its publication, it appeared as though COIN doctrine was here to stay. Or so it seemed, until the Iraq and Afghanistan wars settled down and the cost of maintaining these "maximalist" and very expensive and lethal counterinsurgency campaigns became clear. According to the *Field Manual*, the "main objective" of any counterinsurgency is to "foster the development of effective governance by a legitimate government." It posits that this development must come through both military and nonmilitary means. Echoing Galula decades earlier, it explains that governments operate through a combination of consent and coercion. Governments characterized as "legitimate" rule through the consent of those governed; those described as "illegitimate" tend to rely on coercion. Citizens of the latter obey the government for fear of the consequences of doing otherwise. Citizens of the former obey voluntarily. The *Field Manual* takes a generally utilitarian view of both concepts. One key way that any government can increase its legitimacy, it argues, is by establishing security for the civilian population. Furthermore, local government forces ultimately need to be central to these efforts for the legitimacy to endure.

The *Field Manual* does not shy away from recognizing the U.S. military's past mistakes in this realm. It quotes General Creighton Abrams, the U.S. Commander in Vietnam in 1971, who recognized that U.S. efforts undermined the South Vietnamese government's legitimacy. "There's very clear evidence ... in some things, that we helped too much," Creighton says. "And we *retarded* the Vietnamese by doing it.... We can't run this thing.... *They've* got to run it. The nearer we get to that the better off *they* are and the better off *we* are." Expectedly, the *Field Manual* then follows with the oft-cited observation from T. E. Lawrence, "Do not try to do too much with your own hands. Better the Arabs do it tolerably than that you do it perfectly. It is their war, and you are to help them, not to win it for them."

When the *Field Manual* came out, many critics noted a potentially damning weakness. It assumed that its politically appealing prescriptions could take the place of aggressive and decisive displays of force to defeat insurgencies. At best, in their view, the *Field Manual* was a "politically correct" document that told the world how the United States should fight a "clean" counterinsurgency. At worst, it was a set of misguided prescriptions whose implementation would fail to defeat insurgents such as those in Iraq and Afghanistan and yield untold American combat casualties. If an insurgent group is willing to inflict endless deaths and destruction to achieve its goals, the skeptics asked, why shouldn't counterinsurgent forces deploy similar force to prevent this outcome?[3] Remarkably, and perhaps revealing its inherently political nature, the *Field Manual* did not explicitly address the counterinsurgent's dilemma: the imperative to win hearts and minds is matched by the inescapable fact that a soldier must also be prepared to kill everyone he meets.

It is a bitter truism that throughout history counterinsurgency has most often been successful when it has used aggressive force against insurgents. Frequently this also entails imposing on civilians measures that severely curtail their rights – collective punishment, forced civilian displacement, and food rationing – not to mention high civilian casualties. A major lesson from these experiences is that prudent civilian-focused counterinsurgency strategies, such as population protection and development, must often be accompanied by a steely resolve to weaken the insurgents' inherent advantages. The *Field Manual* was largely silent on these sorts of issues, which might have muddied the largely "feel-good" nature of its prescriptions.

The *Field Manual*'s publication coincided with the Bush administration's initially controversial but surprisingly successful "surge" in Iraq in 2007. Indeed, the new Iraqi strategy drew heavily on the *Field Manual*'s prescriptions. Its success also helped cement the reputation of General David H. Petraeus as the U.S. military's intellectual author of contemporary counterinsurgency efforts. Now it seemed that perhaps Petraeus and others who promoted this updated and very public manual had found the magic formula for victory in guerrilla warfare.

While the *Field Manual*'s influence continued to grow, many inside the U.S. military and defense policy circles remained unpersuaded by what some called the Petraeus Doctrine. William Odom, a retired three star general who had served as Reagan's director of the National Security Agency (NSA), leveled an oft-cited critique at the *Field Manual*: "There are all kinds of self-appointed experts around Washington. Well, we don't have the right kind of forces; we need counterinsurgency forces; we need smaller forces; a lot of forces – we need them all, and the enemy is not going to conform to your desires. You're going to have to be flexible. Do you want to give up M-1 tanks? I don't. Look what they did to get you to Baghdad."[4] Another critic, West Point professor Colonel Gian Gentile, disputed the conclusion that the surge was responsible for the precipitous drop in violence in Iraq. In Gentile's view, "to think that the reduction in violence was primarily the result of American military action is hubris run amuck [sic]."[5] More broadly, Gentile contended that Petraeus's aggressive pursuit of counterinsurgency was being promoted at the expense of indispensible conventional forces, and that COIN proponents had an unrealistic estimation of the U.S. military's ability to influence the world. Moreover, the *Field Manual*'s oft-cited claim that counterinsurgency was the "graduate level of war" appeared to many military traditionalists as arrogant.

Another concern was that the COIN school's promotion of a "gentler" form of counterinsurgency made it appealing to politicians and others as it appeared to promise all the benefits of antiguerrilla warfare and nation-building without the violence and controversy normally associated with it. As a result, the U.S. military's zealous support for COIN could have the perverse consequence of making the country more inclined to get involved in these dirty wars. Others worried that the *Field Manual*'s contention that insurgencies do not have military solutions would cause the U.S. military to deemphasize "soldiering" and instead stress more "civilian" tasks such as economic and social development.[6] Finally, critics argued, the *Field Manual* wrongly downplayed the reality that counterinsurgencies were bloody affairs.

THE LEGACY OF COIN

One key element of the ongoing debate in the post 9/11 and post-Iraq and Afghanistan context centered on the type of enemy that American forces would confront in upcoming years. According to noted counterinsurgency theorist and practitioner David Kilcullen, the United States and its allies faced a "vanguard of hypermodern, internationally oriented terrorists making use of all the tools of globalization and applying a strategy of transnational guerrilla warfare, while seeking to organize, aggregate, and exploit the local, particular, longstanding grievances of diverse – but usually tribal or traditional – Muslim societal groups."[7] These subjects of terrorism, the "accidental guerrillas" who mobilized for tribal or other reasons, such as when "we [the West] are in their face," seemed bound, for Kilcullen, to cause pain for the United States and other global powers in the years to come. Kilcullen posed the question: if this was in fact the case, then was the United States' approach to counterinsurgency appropriate for the enemy at hand? He argued that it was not and warned that much of what the U.S. military and others learned during the key decades of guerrilla and counterinsurgency warfare at the height of the Cold War in the 1950s and 1960s was still applicable, but that this "tried-and-true" approach must constantly be reappraised.

What was clearly new with respect to these almost exclusively Islamist "postmodern" insurgent movements was that they neither sought nor achieved any practical objective – at least not in the Western estimation. And certainly the tactics of these postmodern jihadists were unlike what past insurgents had attempted. Now, instead of trying to control national territory and win the hearts and minds of guerrilla movements past, these Islamist organizations often had "leaderless resistances" where the manipulation of the global, "24/7" media cycle and online networks mattered more than "liberated territory."

As President Barack Obama announced plans for a dramatic drawdown of the American counterinsurgency campaign in Afghanistan in 2010, it seemed as though the *Field Manual* had already faded into obsolescence. In large part, this was due to the landlocked country's incoherent national identity, which sorely complicated the crucial effort to underpin a legitimate government. And it seemed that following this perceived failure, the *Field Manual* and its counterinsurgency doctrine would be put to rest only a few years after it was unleashed in the midst of the "surge" in the Iraq War. If so, this would not have been the first time that the United States had turned its back on a strategy for fighting dirty wars.

30

Post-9/11 COIN in the Philippines

The attacks of September 11, 2001, pushed President George W. Bush to actively combat terrorist networks around the globe, most visibly in Afghanistan where the fight against the Taliban and Al Qaeda captured the world's attention. At the same time the American military was searching for Osama bin Laden and hunting Taliban insurgents in their isolated mountain strongholds of Afghanistan, the U.S. military initiated a number of smaller-scale operations in a variety of disparate locations that took a more indirect approach toward defeating terrorist groups.

The Philippines – a recurring counterinsurgency battleground ever since the colonial wars at the turn of the twentieth century and the Magsaysay years of the 1950s – would become one example of America's post-9/11 attempts to target the world's murky and lawless areas that nurtured and fueled the spread of global terrorism and insurgency. While the indirect U.S. military effort in the Philippines would receive scant media coverage, it stands as an important but overlooked case of light-footprint counterinsurgency that, in the shadow of the full-scale invasion of Afghanistan, demonstrates the diversity of the American experience with counterinsurgency warfare in the heady moments of the post-9/11 era.

By the time of the September 11 attacks, the southern islands of the Philippines had become a notorious hotbed of insurgency, lawlessness, and ethnic tension. Home to a predominantly Muslim population and located beyond the scope of government influence, the region was plagued by Islamic separatist movements – most notably, the Moro Islamic Liberation Front, active since the 1960s.[1] In the early 1990s, radical members of the group broke away and established Abu Sayyaf, which translates as "Bearer of the Sword."[2] Taking advantage of the permissive environment, Abu Sayyaf began a systematic campaign of bombings, assassinations, and kidnappings for ransom. In the process, they blurred the line between banditry and terrorism and developed a lucrative foothold in the region.[3]

Shortly before 9/11, Abu Sayyaf kidnapped a large group of foreigners that included two American missionaries, causing considerable alarm in Washington. Of particular concern to the Bush administration was Abu Sayyaf's association with a diverse network of Al Qaeda–affiliated terror groups, most notably the Indonesian-based Jemaah Islamiyah. In fact, many of Abu Sayyaf's core leaders – including Abdurrajak Janjalani, the movement's founder, killed by government forces in 1998 – received their baptism of fire in the jihad against the Soviets in Afghanistan in the 1980s.

Later, during the 1990s, Al Qaeda used Southeast Asia to plan and coordinate attacks on Western targets, illustrating both the manner in which terrorist cells operate across national borders and the global scope of modern counterterrorism.[4] Like many other Islamic terrorist cells, Abu Sayyaf did not start as a product of Al Qaeda but instead gradually aligned itself with the movement as part of a broader collection of loosely connected terrorist groups held together by mutual interests and radical Islamic ideology.[5]

In October of 2001, at the same time that American forces were deploying in large numbers to Afghanistan, the Pentagon began to develop an operational plan for dealing with Abu Sayyaf in the Philippines. The Filipino government in Manila, eager to confront its own "bleeding ulcer" of Islamic separatism in the southern regions, welcomed American support. The U.S. military campaign against Abu Sayyaf was referred to as Operation Enduring Freedom-Philippines (OEF-P), highlighting the connection to antiterrorism efforts in Afghanistan. In conjunction with Manila, the United States launched OEF-P to weaken Abu Sayyaf and diminish its presence in the southern Philippines, especially within the island stronghold of Basilan.

The first step, in October 2001, called for an Army Special Forces assessment team, part of U.S. Pacific Command and based in Hawaii, to fly to the Philippines and survey the local situation down to the village level. Once there, they developed intelligence estimates on enemy capabilities, local demographics, and the training needs of Filipino security forces. In this instance, to maintain the lightest of footprints, U.S. forces attempted to work "by, with, and through" their indigenous Filipino counterparts in order to cut off the insurgents from popular support and capture or kill their leadership.[6]

Four months later, the Pentagon dispatched Joint Task Force-510 (JTF-510) to the Philippines to begin conducting conventional and unconventional operations against Abu Sayyaf. Comprising 650 troops, JTF-510 was spearheaded by 160 Special Forces personnel who deployed alongside their Filipino counterparts down to the battalion level near insurgent strongholds. Publicly, the operation was referred to as a live-fire "training exercise," but even such limited engagement garnered criticism from some quarters in the Philippines. The deployment of foreign troops in the Philippines was a controversial subject, given the longstanding and frequently imperialistic nature of U.S. involvement with the country.[7] Nevertheless, with the support of Filipino president Gloria Arroyo and a cap on the number of participating U.S. soldiers, JTF-510 arrived in the Philippines in January 2002 as part of an unfolding counterinsurgency campaign against Abu Sayyaf.

As we have seen in many other instances of counterinsurgency, the garrison mentality of the host government's security forces was the first challenge confronted by American trainers. Such a passive posture often results in the concession of territory and influence to guerrilla forces, allowing them unmitigated access to the local population and solidifying the hold of an insurgency – a mistake made by American forces in both Vietnam and, more recently, in the early days of the Iraq War in 2003.

In the Philippines, aggressive training and the deployment of Special Forces units alongside Filipino troops helped to alleviate this problem. In addition to training, JTF-510 furnished the Filipino Army with intelligence that served as the basis for many of their operations.[8] While progress was not always smooth – in one case, the reluctance of a Filipino general to get out of bed contributed to the failure of a mission – the presence of Abu Sayyaf on Basilan became increasingly tenuous.[9] Members of Abu Sayyaf, after a decade of relatively unchallenged impunity in the southern Philippines, were forced to retreat into hiding or flee to other islands like Jolo. The group's control structure was especially targeted, resulting in the death of Abu Sabaya, a key Abu Sayyaf leader, in June 2002. In another operation, Filipino security forces freed a large group of hostages, including one of the two original American captives.[10]

As well as military-to-military engagement, U.S. forces in the Philippines concentrated on a hearts and minds strategy designed to win over the local population and extend the reach of the Filipino state into previously remote and lawless areas. According to Robert Kaplan, who spent time embedded with U.S. troops in the Philippines while writing *Imperial Grunts: The American Military on the Ground*, the Americans tried to remain in the background during this process as much as possible. He quoted a Special Forces officer: "[The JTF] tried to put some backbone into Manila authorities so they would take better care of their own people. Success meant we couldn't take credit for anything. We had to give credit to the Philippine government. We didn't want credit; that would have ruined the operation."[11]

The humanitarian effort was especially pronounced during the second half of 2002, focusing on medical help, governance, and the improvement of infrastructure. A U.S. Navy Construction Battalion, colloquially known as the "Seabees," repaired bridges and piers while other military units conducted population surveys and built roads. The Americans even funded the construction of several neighborhood mosques.[12] Medical and dental clinics, staffed by Special Forces medics, reached out to the local population. Development projects had military benefits as well; according to Kaplan, "villagers casually volunteered information about the insurgents while their children were being treated for scabies, malaria, meningitis, and having their teeth pulled."[13] The improved security situation also created a safe environment for NGOs and other humanitarian organizations to return to the area, magnifying the benefits of the hearts and minds strategy.[14]

In narrow terms, the American mission in the Philippines in 2002 can be considered a qualified counterinsurgency success story: Abu Sayyaf's leadership structure was dismantled, the group's membership decreased dramatically, and the insurgents were forced to relinquish their grip on Basilan. The training of indigenous security forces – most notably the instruction given to Filipino helicopter pilots, allowing them to fly at night – furthered the country's ability to conduct antiterrorism campaigns independent of U.S. involvement.[15] The central government in Manila reasserted authority over the region at the same time that development and humanitarian assistance returned to the previously dangerous island.

Abu Sayyaf, bloodied but not entirely defeated, continued to conduct low-level criminal activity in the region.[16] In subsequent years, the group began to mount a comeback, as many of the leaders and guerrillas who had initially fled Basilan reemerged on nearby islands to continue kidnapping and extorting. Demonstrating the proven resiliency of insurgent movements, Abu Sayyaf staged a series of bombings across the Philippines in 2004 and 2005, including one on a ferry, that killed more than 100 people.

Despite the relatively quick gains made in 2002, American military support for the Philippines in the form of training and monetary aid would continue as Arroyo's administration grappled with the chaotic southern region of the country. In 2007, the Filipino army struck back at Abu Sayyaf, killing two important emerging leaders: Khaddafy Janjalani and Abu Sulaiman, just days apart. Once again, Abu Sayyaf had been dealt a crippling – but not fatal – blow. The group fragmented, and although Abu Sayyaf was greatly weakened, the group reverted back to banditry and criminal activity.

The resiliency of Abu Sayyaf as a guerrilla movement reveals some important themes concerning the nature of counterinsurgency warfare. While short-term gains are possible, combating the conditions that generate insurgent groups takes more commitment and longer periods of time. In the case of Abu Sayyaf, the group's continued existence owed more to the economic incentives and lawlessness of a region conducive to criminality than to ideological or political dogma. Abu Sayyaf was also only one of several militant groups operating in the southern Philippines, further complicating the challenge faced by the Filipino state.

Given the continued survival of Abu Sayyaf, America's 2002 attempt at counterinsurgency in the Philippines was not an unequivocal success. Even with the support of U.S. trainers, Filipino security forces struggled to land a decisive blow against the insurgency. Securing the island of Basilan proved to be nothing more than a temporary reprieve for the government, as their adversaries were able to disperse and regroup in other parts of the country. At the same time, the partnership between Washington and Manila in 2002 produced undeniable benefits down the road. The quality of leaders, generals, and officers in the Filipino army saw a dramatic improvement in the decade following 9/11. Meanwhile, the increased capability of the Filipino Army helped them to forge a tentative peace agreement with the largest Muslim rebel group in the Philippines, the Moro Islamic Liberation Front, in October 2012.[17]

Given the structural problems that often lead to the formation of militant groups, continued U.S. engagement, especially when limited to training and advising, is not necessarily a sign of failure. In fact, in the summer of 2012 the close military relationship between the Philippines and America resulted in the reopening of two large military bases previously closed in the early 1990s.

As far as counterinsurgencies and dirty wars go, the campaign waged against Abu Sayyaf from 2002 onward was a relatively clean undertaking. The deployment of 650 U.S. soldiers – larger than the 55-man force cap in El Salvador or the restricted troop levels in Colombia during the 1990s – was part of an American-led light-footprint counterinsurgency in the Philippines completely obscured by the U.S. invasion and subsequent occupation of Afghanistan. America's indirect approach, which called for the Filipino security forces to take the leading role in all military operations, differed significantly from U.S. efforts in Afghanistan and Iraq that involved hundreds of thousands of American troops.

While the U.S. campaign in the Philippines in 2002 did not generate headlines, it demonstrated that a hands-off approach to counterinsurgency, followed by continued military cooperation and development programs, could gradually make progress against insurgent groups and eliminate the gray areas that allow such organizations to form in the first place. The Filipino name for OEF-P, *balikatan*, translates as "shoulder-to-shoulder,"[18] revealing the nature of the cooperation between the United States and the Philippines since 2002 and suggesting that the two countries had come full circle since the more paternalistic imperial wars a century earlier.[19]

31

Intermezzo

Afghanistan, Graveyard of Empires

Thirty-one times the size of El Salvador, landlocked Afghanistan traditionally served as a buffer between the Russian tsarist and British empires. The British leaders suffered a bitter defeat during the First Afghan War, 1839 – 42, when they learned that it was much easier to occupy Afghanistan than to conquer it. The conflict ended with the destruction of the British garrison at Kabul, where a column of 16,500 soldiers and civilians fled the city for a garrison at Jalalabad, only 110 miles away. Of that expedition, one member alone made it to Jalalabad safely, although the British did recover some prisoners several months later.[1] It was the worst British defeat until the fall of Singapore a century later.[2] After World War II the British departed Afghanistan, but it was only a matter of time before other interventionist nations, the Soviet Union and United States, respectively, became embroiled in this disputed land.

Under the reign of King Mohammad Zahir Shah, who presided over the country from 1933 until his ouster in 1973, Kabul was a relatively modernizing and liberal capital. A university was open and the press was largely free; many Afghan students traveled abroad and new ideas about how to shape the Afghan state and society were ubiquitous. Communism and radical Islam attracted equal numbers of believers, and the two political movements held the country together in a stable, if ephemeral peace. In 1973, Zahir Shah's cousin and former prime minister Mohammed Daoud overthrew the king in a bloodless coup. Daoud aligned with the communists and launched an undeclared war on Islamic radicals. Yet, when Daoud tried to check the increasingly powerful communists, he was assassinated.

In 1978, the communists seized full power of the central government in Kabul and proceeded to launch a radical program of land redistribution and indoctrination. Within months, under the rule of the diabolical Hafizullah Amin, once a student at Columbia University, the regime killed roughly 12,000 suspected anticommunists – most of them students and members of the intelligentsia – in Kabul alone. Many Islamists fled the country or started isolated, low-intensity guerrilla *jihads* against the communist government. After welcoming the communist coup of 1978, Moscow had become concerned about Amin's delusional effort to "weld the incoherent ethnic-tribal worlds of Afghanistan into a Communist society."[3] Ideologically, the Afghan state that existed under Amin in 1979 was not communist or even socialist, but simply a country ruled by an oligarchy who called themselves communists.

In the final weeks of 1979, and with Amin's regime teetering, Soviet leaders decided to go forward with an invasion modeled on their experience seizing Czechoslovakia in 1968: use Soviet troops to seize control of the capital, remove an unreliable communist regime, and leave a pliant replacement. Moscow optimistically believed that "they would be in and out of Afghanistan almost before anyone noticed." Soviet advisers quietly removed the batteries from Afghan army tanks for "winterization" and gathered up antitank ammunition for "inventory." Soviet commandos then stormed the presidential palace and killed Amin while conventional troops spilled across the border, heading for Kabul. Moscow boldly informed the world that the Afghan government had requested Soviet assistance. In fact, the puppet Revolutionary Council chairman Babrak Karmal made the request from a radio station on the Soviet side of the border, after 20,000 Soviet troops had already crossed into Afghanistan.[4]

After removing Amin, the Soviets rewarded the docile Karmal by making him president. The new ruler was immediately tasked with keeping the splintering Afghan state intact and quelling the country's unfolding instability. Soon after the Soviet invasion began, National Security Advisor Zbigniew Brzezinski apparently sent an ebullient letter to President Carter predicting, "Now we can give the USSR its Vietnam War."[5] Within weeks of the invasion, Brzezinski traveled to Pakistan to discuss a covert action program with General Zia and went to the Afghan border where he was photographed holding a Kalashnikov rifle. Indeed, what the Soviets confidently believed would be a Prague 1968 redux ended up being a deep quagmire.

Karmal was only partly successful in restoring order. In 1986, Moscow replaced him with Mohammad Najibullah, director of KHAD, the

Communist intelligence agency. Najibullah, a notorious organizer of the execution and torture of anticommunists, attempted to moderate the extreme communist policies and rhetoric; he emphasized his Islamic faith and pushed for national reconciliation. Yet his efforts failed in preventing the outbreak of an Islamic insurgency and ferocious Soviet-backed counterinsurgency.

COVERT ACTION IN AFGHANISTAN

Responding to the Soviets' move in Afghanistan, Carter announced a U.S. boycott of the 1980 Moscow Olympics. The administration also canceled wheat sales to Moscow, asked the UN to condemn the invasion, and pushed legislation intended to reintroduce the military draft. Moscow had not anticipated Washington's stern response given that prior U.S. administrations had done next to nothing during the invasions of Hungary in 1956 and Czechoslovakia in 1968. In July 1979 Carter signed the first of the "directives" that allowed for covert assistance to Afghanistan, likely a shipment of venerable Enfield .303 rifles. For the first several years, the CIA attempted to keep its involvement secret. Much of the funding and materiel passed through Pakistan's intelligence service before reaching the Afghan "freedom fighters" who called themselves mujahideen (often translated to mean "those who struggle," or "those who fight jihad"). The CIA largely avoided direct contact with the Afghans in the hope that it could maintain the thinly veiled ruse that it was not funding the guerrillas. Moreover, most of the delivered weapons were made in Warsaw Pact countries, which brought a double advantage, since mujahideen could often use these weapons with ammunition captured from the Soviet or Afghan Army forces.

CIA Director William Casey explained the logic of the American strategy: "Here is the beauty of the Afghan operation. Usually it looks like the big bad Americans are beating up on the natives. Afghanistan is just the reverse. The Russians are beating up on the little guys. We don't make it our war. The Mujahedin have all the motivation they need. All we have to do is give them help, only more of it." At the same time, Pakistan's military dictator, General Zia-ul-Haq, who had seized power in 1977 after deposing standing prime minister Zulfikar Ali Bhutto, strongly agreed with Washington's strategic objective of making the Soviets bleed in Afghanistan. Under Zia's iron rule, Pakistan proved a reliable launching pad for U.S. covert aid, as well as a sanctuary for the poorly armed and fractured mujahideen fighters.

During these same years, the Saudi monarchy saw the jihad in Afghanistan as a fantastic opportunity to export Wahabism – the austere Saudi form of Sunni Islam.[6] The Saudis ended up sending as much aid to the insurgents as did Washington. Prince Turki, head of the Saudi intelligence agency, who collaborated with the CIA and Pakistani operatives, sent to Afghanistan a wealthy Saudi businessman, Osama bin Laden, to organize thousands of poor Arabs from the Middle East and North Africa who were drawn to the Islamist struggle in the landlocked country. Over the decade of the war, an estimated 25,000 Arabs may have passed through Pakistan and Afghanistan. At one point, the CIA weighed whether it should organize volunteer Arab legions to fight in the war, but the notion was soon dismissed as impractical.[7]

By the mid-1980s, the CIA office in Islamabad, Pakistan, was second in size only to the headquarters in Langley, Virginia. The rate of U.S. assistance grew from around $80 million in 1984 to $700 million by 1988, making it the largest covert assistance program since Vietnam. Meanwhile, the motley "coalition" providing said assistance to the Afghan mujahideen had grown to include China, Egypt, Saudi Arabia, Pakistan, and the United Kingdom. Over the course of the war, the coalition poured roughly $5 billion into the country. Scores of Afghan resistance groups formed to accept the military and humanitarian aid. The only thing that united these ethnically, tribally, and linguistically diverse groups was their hatred of the Afghan communists and their Soviet sponsors.

An estimated 80,000 to 150,000 mujahideen were active at any one time during the 1980s. On the other side were roughly 115,000 Soviet troops, along with 30,000 regular Afghan army troops and another 50,000 in other Kabul units. Like their American and NATO successors, the communist forces controlled the cities and large towns, while the mujahideen held the rugged countryside. Echoing the Viet Minh in the lead-up to Dien Bien Phu, the mujahideen supply efforts often consisted of "men carrying backpacks over little-known but dangerous trails."[8] The mujahideen relied on classic guerrilla tactics of mining roads and ambushing convoys. At times they even managed to isolate a city, which required the Soviets to supply the location by aircraft – for years in the case of Khost.

Soviet and Afghan forces began the war using large "sweeps" of the mujahideen-held areas. This usually compelled the guerrillas to fade away into the surrounding hills, accompanied by local villagers. The communist forces, in turn, would be forced to live off the land and to resupply their garrisons with highly vulnerable truck convoys. By and large, the two sides fought to a stalemate through 1985. The outcome very much played into the hands of the mujahideen, who believed that the slow attrition worked to their advantage.

One tactic that gave the Soviets a decisive advantage over the mujahideen early on was the use of helicopter gunships, increasing the number of them fivefold in just a few years. The gunships allowed Soviet units to bring "tank-like" firepower to the remote mountain locales where the mujahideen were located. In 1986, the Soviets were using Mi-24D attack gunships, whose armored bottoms made them almost totally immune to light weapons.

The gunships' superiority diminished considerably by the end of 1986, when, under strong pressure from the U.S. Congress, the CIA began supplying the mujahideen with lightweight and easy to use Stinger missiles that could shoot down the gunships. Interestingly, the Stingers arrived in Afghanistan only a month after Soviet Premier Mikhail Gorbachev's stunning 1986 speech in the Siberian city of Vladivostok where he described the war as a "bleeding wound."[9] In September 1986, mujahideen forces successfully used five Stinger missiles to down three helicopters near the Jalalabad airbase in eastern Afghanistan. Over the next ten months, almost 200 Stingers were used, with roughly three-quarters hitting Soviet aircraft.[10] Soviet losses of helicopter and fighter aircraft were soon running at a rate of 420 to 500 per year. In turn, Soviet commanders sharply reduced the volume of air missions. The Stinger became the symbol of the billions of dollars that Washington covertly funneled to the mujahideen, which tolled the death knell for the Soviet's counterinsurgency war in Afghanistan. Over the course of the war, the CIA provided between 2,000 and 2,500 missiles to Afghan insurgents, some of whom had decidedly anti-American sentiments. As the Soviet war ebbed, President George H. W. Bush and later President Clinton authorized a classified CIA program to spend millions of dollars buying back Stingers, paying from $80,000 to $150,000 per missile.[11]

Moscow's decision to pull out of Afghanistan in 1988 came after a decade of struggling to prop up the puppet regime in Kabul and defeat the mujahideen, all at great cost of treasure and lives lost. Most of the Soviet dirty war was carried out in relative obscurity given press censorship across the Soviet Union and official denials at home and abroad. The Soviets later admitted suffering between 48,000 and 52,000 casualties, including at least 13,000 combat deaths. During the war's first year alone, 1.5 million Afghans became refugees, mostly flooding over the mountain border into Pakistan, where they scraped out a meager life in camps. Out of a population of 16 million, more than 1 million Afghan civilians died. Amazingly, the mujahideen never held a single province during the war.

U.S. policymakers began to forget about Afghanistan following the Soviet Army's withdrawal in early 1989, three years after Gorbachev's "bleeding wound" speech. Within months, the Soviet Union began to unravel as the Cold War came to an end. While Washington turned its attention elsewhere, Afghanistan's bloody war continued as the Afghan communists retained control of the government until they were defeated by mujahideen led by Tajik forces under Burhanuddin Rabbani and his military commander, Ahmad Shah Massoud, three years later.

Interestingly, most observers confidently believed that Najibullah would last only a matter of months after the Soviet departure. Yet, bolstered by continued military aid from Moscow, his regime lasted for an additional three years, in which he succeeded in routing the mujahideen in a key battle for the city of Jalabad. But after the Soviet Union collapsed in 1991, Najibullah's regime was on its own. With supplies low, Afghan army morale dropped and desertions surged. In April 1992, the weary but ebullient mujahideen spilled into the capital city. As one observer recounted the eerie calm associated with the occupation, "It took me some time to realize that the city was calm because the [mujahideen] militias were busy looting government buildings. It took them days to get everything. When they finished, they came after everyone else."[12] Within months, Kabul's electricity, police patrols, and other government services vanished.[13]

THE RISE OF THE TALIBAN

[Right after the Cold War] the United States government decided it had no further interests in Afghanistan. – Steve Coll[14]

Once the communists were defeated, however, the motley assortment of mujahideen began to fight among themselves. Between 1994 and 1996, a group known as the Taliban, made up of rigidly ideological Islamists led by the one-eyed supreme leader Mullah Mohammed Omar, was able to gain control over the national government, despite its inability to defeat the patchwork of Russian- and Iranian-backed Tajik warlords known as the Northern Alliance.[15] The Taliban consisted mainly of theology students and former mujahideen who came from the Pashtun tribes in the east and south of the country. Many of the Taliban's members were drawn from *madrassas*, or Islamic seminaries, created in Afghan refugee camps in

Pakistan during the 1980s. Many ordinary Afghans, of all ethnic stripes, at first supported the Taliban because they expected them to bring peace and order to a war-torn country. But after taking power and effectively controlling 90 percent of the country, the Taliban prevented women from working, closed schools for girls, and executed homosexuals, adulterers, and others suspected of violating Islamic law.[16] The initial admiration or toleration eventually gave way to resignation, submission, and in some cases armed opposition. Moreover, despite their religious fervor, the Taliban generally permitted poppy cultivation and the related opium production. In 1997, almost all Afghan poppy came from areas under Taliban control.[17]

Hoping that these theological students would bring stability to their strategic neighbor, leader Benazir Bhutto's government in Pakistan provided critical aid to the Taliban in their march to power. The Saudis also continued to send funding. Eager to gain support for its ongoing struggle against the Northern Alliance, in 1996 the Taliban provided sanctuary to a Saudi citizen who had recently been forced out of Sudan. Accompanied by his acolytes, his name was Osama bin Laden.

THE RISE OF OSAMA BIN LADEN AND AL QAEDA

Moscow's invasion of Afghanistan in 1979 prompted thousands of young Arab men to travel to Pakistan to prepare for jihad against the Soviet invaders and their puppets in Kabul. Among these Arabs was Osama bin Laden, a Saudi citizen who used his sizable family wealth to recruit men and arms for the anti-Soviet cause. In 1984, bin Laden set up a group called Maktab al-Khidamat (the Services Organization), which funneled money to the Afghan fighters. Two years later, he established an Arab training camp called Al Maasada (the Lion's Den), near the village of Jaji, sixty miles north of Khost, Afghanistan, on the border with Pakistan. The incipient group's theology was a toxic combination of Islamic fanaticism and anti-Soviet guerrilla warfare. From there, his connections with other foreign jihadists led him to establish Al Qaeda (the Base), which would become a global network of organizations aiming to extend and support Islamist struggles around the world. Al Qaeda considered itself a "revolutionary vanguard" working to defend the Islamic world against false prophets and foreign invaders.

Saddam Hussein's invasion of Kuwait and the U.S.-led Operation Desert Storm convinced bin Laden and Al Qaeda to focus increasingly on the United States as the chief threat to their vision of Islam.

Interestingly, bin Laden first offered to send operatives to Saudi Arabia to repel the Iraqi invasion, but the Saudi leaders rejected the offer and instead invited the U.S. military to launch an operation from their soil. This decision infuriated bin Laden and further sharpened his antipathy toward the American presence in sacred Saudi lands.

Bin Laden firmly believed that just as Hezbollah's bombing of the U.S. Marine barracks in Beirut in 1983 had prompted the Reagan administration to withdraw American forces from Lebanon, a hard strike against U.S. assets would precipitate a swift removal of U.S. troops in Saudi Arabia. In 1996, bin Laden declared jihad against the United States, in part because "the presence of the USA Crusader military forces on land, sea and air of the states of the Islamic Gulf is the greatest danger threatening the largest oil reserve in the world." Referring to what he considered an overreaching U.S. foreign policy in the Middle East, bin Laden argued, "The walls of oppression and humiliation cannot be demolished except in a rain of bullets." In 1998, bin Laden called for the murder of Americans as the "individual duty for every Muslim who can do it in any country in which it is possible to do it."[18]

That same year, and in a sharp indication that the terrorist group was expanding its war with the United States beyond the Middle East, bin Laden's organization Al Qaeda bombed the U.S. embassies in Kenya and Tanzania. In August 1998, codenamed Operation Infinite Reach, U.S. cruise missiles targeted four suspected Al Qaeda bases in Afganistan as well as Al-Shifa, a pharmaceutical plant in Khartoum, Sudan, suspected of manufacturing chemical weapons. American officials later admitted that there was never any definite evidence that the Al-Shifa plant produced nerve gas as initially claimed. In the Afghan strikes, the missiles killed an estimated twenty to thirty people but not bin Laden, who had reportedly left the compound a few hours beforehand.[19] Clinton told the American public at the time, "Our mission was clear – to strike at the network of radical groups affiliated with, and funded by, Osama bin Laden, the preeminent organizer and financier of international terrorism in the world today."[20]

In 1999, President Bill Clinton issued an Executive Order declaring that "the actions and policies of the Taliban in Afghanistan to be used as a safe haven and base of operations for Osama bin Laden and the Al Qa'ida organization ... constitute an unusual and extraordinary threat to the national security and foreign policy of the United States."[21] Despite Clinton's desires, and as became tragically apparent following the September 11, 2001, attacks, neither the Clinton nor George W. Bush administrations had understood the full extent of Al Qaeda's threat.

32

The Longest War

America in Afghanistan

In counterinsurgency the population is the prize, and protecting and controlling it is the key activity. The war, therefore, is where the people are: you win or lose it a village at a time, and you secure villages and gain access to the people by controlling valleys, roads, and the heights that overlook them, in that order of priority.

– Counterinsurgency practitioner David Kilcullen[1]

The Americans [in Afghanistan] intended to separate the people from the insurgents. Instead, the insurgents succeeded in separating the people from the Americans.

– War reporter Bing West[2]

[In Afghanistan] we developed a hunter mentality. This was a great place if you're a Marine infantryman.

– U.S. Marine Captain Nikolai Johnson, commander of Kilo Company[3]

On the morning of July 13, 2008, at about 4:20 AM, a force of over 200 insurgents attacked a remote American patrol base near the village of Wanat in the Waigal Valley of Nuristan Province, Afghanistan. The small base was brand-new, its fortifications unfinished. Occupying it was one platoon – thirty-eight soldiers – from the U.S. Army's 2nd Battalion, 173rd Airborne Brigade Combat Team (BCT), augmented by six combat engineers and three U.S. Marines acting as an embedded training team (ETT) for a twenty-four-man detachment of the Afghan National Army. Using combined arms tactics and employing a blistering

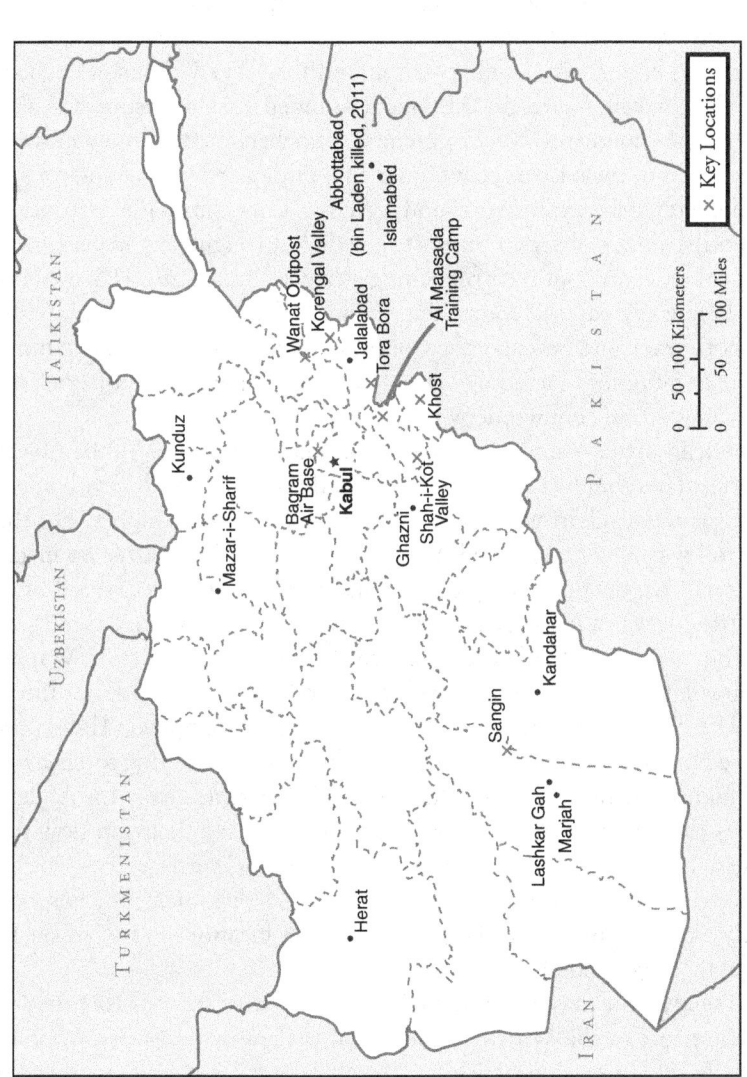

FIGURE 32.1.1. Afghanistan. Map prepared by the University of Wisconsin-Madison Cartography Lab©. Reprinted with permission

array of mortars, light machine guns, rocket-propelled grenades, and snipers, the mostly Taliban fighters battered the American and Afghan forces.

The insurgents navigated through a nearby village to get close to the patrol base and at one point managed to breach the American perimeter. The brunt of the attack targeted the Americans' heavy weapons, quickly neutralizing both their mortar position and their TOW (Tube-launched, Optically tracked, Wire-guided) missile launcher. The insurgents also rendered the Americans' Mk. 19 grenade launchers ineffective by moving close enough to the base to be within the minimum arming distance of the 40-millimeter high-explosive rounds. At the same time, the insurgents isolated the base's observation post, positioned roughly 75 meters from the patrol base, and put their remaining attention on the nine U.S. soldiers there, killing several and compelling the main force at the patrol base to attempt to reach and evacuate the wounded, which in turn led to two more American fatalities, including 1st Lieutenant Jonathan Brostrom, the American platoon commander.

American artillery and air support eventually drove the Taliban back four hours later, but by then 9 Americans had been killed and 27 wounded. Losses for the Taliban were believed to have been much higher, but the death toll was never confirmed. U.S. forces estimated that over 40 insurgents perished, but reportedly only 2 enemy bodies were recovered after the battle.[4] It was a high price to pay for an unfinished patrol base.

Within a week of the battle, American troops withdrew from Wanat. An informal investigation censured the battalion's commanding officer, Colonel Charles Preysler, for leaving the base undersupplied. The report criticized other commanders on the same task force for relying too heavily on a "highly kinetic approach" that alienated Americans from the Afghan civilians they were meant to protect, a factor that may explain how the insurgents were able to infiltrate Wanat before the battle without being detected. A follow-up investigation determined that local officials had directly aided the insurgents by providing them locations in the village to conceal their weapons.[5]

A tragedy that may have helped precipitate this turn of fortune for the U.S. effort in the Waigal Valley took place just one week prior to the battle, when a team of AH-64 Apache attack helicopters engaged and destroyed two speeding pickup trucks following a mortar attack against an American combat outpost. In the aftermath, the bodies found were not those of militants, but of a number of local civilians and health care providers working at a nearby medical clinic. Because

U.S. forces involved believed that insurgents had been in the pickup trucks, the task force was reluctant to apologize or issue condolences to local civilians and families for the strike. According to an exhaustive report on the Battle of Wanat by military historian Douglas Cubbison, Afghans throughout the Waigal Valley were outraged by the incident, and some Afghans connected it with the cooperation later reported between locals and the Taliban during the attack on the Wanat patrol base.[6]

It is doubtful that the average American citizen would know what happened at Wanat, but the battle's significance and its repercussions were not lost on the community of counterinsurgency scholars and practitioners who analyzed after-action reports and media accounts. The complexity and boldness of the Taliban's attack on the patrol base at Wanat signaled to many a growing sophistication in the insurgents' techniques, and a renewed resolve to engage NATO forces in combat.

Most analysts looking at the Battle of Wanat in the context of the greater campaign in Afghanistan concluded that U.S. operations were slipping away from population-centered counterinsurgency strategies. Attacks like this were not just a sign of the Taliban's strengthening but of American forces losing focus.

THE "GOOD WAR"

The deterioration of the conflict in Afghanistan was not foreseen, but it could have been. At first, Operation Enduring Freedom was the "good war." The United States' invasion in late 2001 was precipitated by the worst terrorist attack in history, and military intervention against the Taliban and Al Qaeda enjoyed broad international and domestic support. The initial military action itself was stunning in both its simplicity and effectiveness: small expeditionary forces of U.S. Marines and Army airborne units moved in to seize strategic points such as the airport at Kandahar. Meanwhile, elite teams of CIA officers and Army Special Forces infiltrated key rural areas and made contact with the Northern Alliance, a small rebel army aligned against the Taliban, dazzling their new allies with unseen air strikes and up-to-the-minute intelligence that helped them locate and destroy Taliban forces.

One ten-man CIA team, code-named Jawbreaker, landed in the Panjshir valley north of Kabul on September 26 and met up with Northern Alliance commander Mohammed Fahim. The supervising official, Director of the CIA Counterterrorism Center Cofer Black, was emphatic in his instructions to the CIA team, "I don't want bin Laden and his thugs captured, I want them dead.... I want bin Laden's head shipped back in a box filled with dry ice. I want to be able to show bin Laden's head to the president." Jawbreaker also brought three cardboard boxes filled with $3 million in hundred-dollar bills in order to "influence" potential collaborators.[7]

Led by one Special Forces A-team, ODA-555 (the "Triple Nickel"), the capture of the critical Bagram air base outside Kabul was decisive in the Taliban's precipitous downfall. When ODA-555 arrived at Bagram in late October of that year, the base effectively constituted the front line in the war between the Northern Alliance and the Taliban, the former holding the northern part of the base and the latter the southern part. Utilizing the base's control tower, ODA-555's attached Air Force Combat Controller called in air-strikes that eliminated scores of Taliban soldiers deployed at the base's south end.[8]

The United States and its Afghan allies routed the Taliban less than two months after the insertion of the first Special Forces teams. It was this fast, light campaign utilizing high technology with low-tech unconventional warfare – including the most dramatic use of Army Special Forces since Vietnam – that seemed to vindicate the doctrinal beliefs of policymakers such as Donald Rumsfeld, who then fatefully insisted on a similar approach for the invasion of Iraq two years later.[9] Upon more scrutiny, the initial military actions in Afghanistan were unconventional and innovative, while the "Drive on Baghdad" that began the Iraq War in 2003 could be considered "hyper-conventional." Interestingly, the resurgence of the Taliban and Al Qaeda in Afghanistan focused not on population centers such as the capital city of Kabul but rather on areas where the Afghan government was most easily de-legitimized, in the outer provinces closest to Pakistan where infrastructure and rule of law were most obviously lacking. An especially violent corner of northeastern Afghanistan, the remote and lethal Korengal Valley, played host to numerous brief engagements between insurgents and counterinsurgents, most harrowingly displayed in the documentary film *Restrepo*.[10]

Underestimating Taliban resistance and taking its demise for granted, the United States initially attempted to prosecute this campaign using an "economy of force," helping to ensure that the conflict would drag on far longer than the Bush administration could have imagined in 2001. A look at the allocation of resources to Afghanistan is perhaps most damning. In terms of funding and troop levels, Afghanistan received roughly a quarter of the outlay that Iraq received from the United States. By 2008, after five years of fighting, the Iraq war had cost the United States around $608.3 billion, and Afghanistan over its seven-year slog had cost a mere $162.6 billion.[11] Even in word, American officials seemed focused far more on Iraq, as when Admiral Michael Mullen, then chairman of the Joint Chiefs of Staff, remarked in congressional testimony in December of 2007, "In Afghanistan, we do what we can. In Iraq, we do what we must."[12] Developments in Afghanistan since then turned this logic on its head, as the war in Afghanistan developed into the dominant foreign policy concern of President Barack Obama's first term.

Of course, it would be a mistake to construe funding and troop levels as the surest indicators of attentiveness or potential for success. In its initial stages after 9/11, Operation Enduring Freedom was accomplished with a very light commitment of troops and money, while Operation Iraqi Freedom drained America's coffers for years with very dubious results prior to 2007 and 2008. But there can be little doubt that opening a second front in Iraq drew away critical resources and attention that Afghanistan both needed and deserved.

The war in Afghanistan had four apparently distinct phases: a swift and highly successful invasion in 2001 that toppled the old regime, the transition to a new government while insurgent forces began to coalesce, a period of escalating violence by insurgents against occupying forces, and finally a coordinated counterinsurgency effort led by the United States after admitting the need for a coherent strategy.

By 2011, Afghanistan had already become the United States' longest war. In June of the same year, President Barack Obama announced a significant reduction in the American troop levels in Afghanistan, signaling that the American empire was eager to rid itself of this counterinsurgency and nation-building "ulcer." Almost a year later, in May 2012, Obama's televised address to the American people from Bagram Air Base recognized the undeniable reality that most Americans wanted to end the war: "Many Americans are tired of war. As President, nothing is more wrenching than signing a letter to a family of the fallen, or looking into the eyes of a child who will grow up without a mother or father. I will not keep Americans in harm's way a single day longer than is absolutely required for our national security. But we must finish the job we started in Afghanistan and end this war responsibly."[13] Interestingly, Obama's decision to drastically scale down a campaign that he had previously called a "war of necessity" was done despite the ongoing opposition of most of the involved commanders at the Pentagon and in the field in Afghanistan.[14]

Like all American counterinsurgencies, this was a brand-new operation, and it had to be fought differently than previous operations, though the ability of U.S. forces to apply the lessons of previous conflicts in some cases made the initiatives more successful. However, many of the strategies that succeeded in Iraq were ineffective against an insurgent enemy that had vast resources from opium poppy production and a safe haven in the border areas between Afghanistan and Pakistan. In some ways, Colombia is the closer analogy, but the difference is that in Afghanistan, and contrary to the FARC, the insurgents were often inseparable from the local population: combatants one hour and civilians the next.

THE INVASION OF AFGHANISTAN

On September 11, 2001, bin Laden and a cadre of top Al Qaeda commanders sat in a compound in Khost, listening to the attacks they had planned and coordinated unfold over a BBC radio broadcast. Bin Laden, who had been associated with Afghanistan ever since the mujahideen struggle against the Soviets in the 1980s, had turned to the Taliban-controlled country as a safe haven for himself and his adherents during the 1990s. Almost immediately after the dust cleared on 9/11, U.S. military planners used intelligence linking bin Laden to the Taliban to develop operations for Afghanistan. This included the critical partnership with the Northern Alliance that reinforced the maxim that "the enemy of my enemy is my friend." In an address on October 7, President George W. Bush explained the situation in Afghanistan:

> More than two weeks ago, I gave Taliban leaders a series of clear and specific demands: Close terrorist training camps; hand over leaders of the Al Qaeda network; and return all foreign nationals, including American citizens, unjustly detained in your country. None of these demands were met. And now the Taliban will pay a price. By destroying camps and disrupting communications, we will make it more difficult for the terror network to train new recruits and coordinate their evil plans. Initially, the terrorists may burrow deeper into caves and other entrenched hiding places. Our military action is also designed to clear the way for sustained, comprehensive and relentless operations to drive them out and bring them to justice. At the same time, the oppressed people of Afghanistan will know the generosity of America and our allies. As we strike military targets, we'll also drop food, medicine and supplies to the starving and suffering men and women and children of Afghanistan.[15]

According to the administration, the intervention in Afghanistan would have three distinct, though connected aims: retribution for the Taliban sheltering and supporting a terrorist organization, prevention against future terrorist strikes from Afghan soil, and (at least rhetorical) humanitarianism. The interaction and frequent conflict among these three aims would prove a major source of confusion for the intervening force's mandate. For the George W. Bush administration, the mission's goal was never to engage in "nation-building," which the Bush administration viewed as overly ambitious and unnecessary. As Secretary of Defense Donald Rumsfeld wrote in a memo during the initial stages of the war, in addition to "eliminating" Al Qaeda, the "goal is to terminate the rule of the current Taliban leadership to make an example of them [as state sponsors of terrorism].... Creating a stable, post-Taliban Afghanistan is desirable but not necessarily within the power of the US. The USG [U.S. government] should not allow concerns for stability to paralyze US efforts to oust the Taliban leadership.... Nation-building is *not* our key strategic goal."[16]

Operation Enduring Freedom commenced on October 7, when U.S. and British aircraft and cruise missiles struck Taliban and Al Qaeda targets. Until this point, the Taliban had pinned the Northern Alliance into two mountainous areas of northern Afghanistan and had reduced the force to roughly 12,000 fighters and a militia of almost equal size. Yet the deft use of U.S. airpower consisting of B-52 and B-1B bombers, and F/A-18 fighters hitting Taliban defenses quickly tipped the balance in the Northern Alliance's favor. Accompanied by 350 Army Special Forces and 100 CIA officers, including members of the CIA's elite Special Activities Division, and supported by AC-130 Spectre gunships, the Northern Alliance pushed the Taliban out of Kabul on November 13. The Taliban retreated to Kandahar, their spiritual home, but had to surrender this outpost a month later. Almost overnight, it seemed, the U.S. military had accomplished two of its goals: punishing the Taliban and upending Al Qaeda's sanctuary. And it had done so with a remarkably light footprint.

Many of the defeated Taliban and Al Qaeda fighters fled for the mountains of eastern Afghanistan, while others fled into Pakistan. In December, the United States deployed forces from the 10th Mountain and 101st and 82nd Airborne Divisions to hunt down fleeing Taliban and Al Qaeda militants in the rugged eastern region of Tora Bora. These sweeps, however, failed to yield significant results despite the use of massive firepower to defeat the fleeing enemy. A series of special operations teams, particularly the Army's Delta Force, worked with CIA and British operatives as well as thousands of Afghan soldiers to root out the enemy. U.S. forces called in massive air strikes, including the biggest bomb in the American arsenal – a 15,000-pound CLU-82 Daisy Cutter so big that it had to be dropped with a parachute out of a C-130 transport aircraft.[17]

In March of the following year, the U.S.-driven Coalition launched Operation Anaconda, which airlifted thousands of British, Canadian, Australian, and New Zealand forces into the Shah-i-kot valley and surrounding mountains. The operation resulted in intense combat with insurgents using sniper rifles, machines guns, and man-portable air defense systems (MANPADS). The mountain terrain offered excellent concealment for the Islamist fighters who fought in small units and hid in caves, resulting in eight U.S. troops killed in action in the first four days. Five months later the U.S. military launched Operation Mountain Sweep, with units of the 82nd Airborne division taking the lead. The failure of these missions to meet the objective of annihilating the fleeing enemy proved a harbinger of many more bitter frustrations for the United States and its allies in Afghanistan.

One sobering realization that emerged from these arduous high-altitude campaigns was that both the Taliban's Mullah Omar and Al Qaeda's bin Laden had slipped across the porous border into Pakistan. Accompanied by a coterie of bodyguards, bin Laden likely left Tora Bora sometime in December 2001. CIA agents and Army officers on the ground repeatedly requested an additional battalion of U.S. Army Rangers to block bin Laden's escape, but the Pentagon preferred to rely upon local Afghan forces, and bin Laden slipped to safety.[18] Over most of the next decade, Pakistan proved to be an ideal sanctuary for Taliban and Al Qaeda operatives.

American commanders in the initial years following the Afghanistan campaign lauded what appeared to be an incredible military victory. Indeed, it had required less than 50 days for roughly 300 special operations soldiers and 100 hundred CIA officers to bring down the Taliban. Before Operation Anaconda, remarkably only twelve Americans were killed in Operation Enduring Freedom in the fall of 2001, with only one of these killed by the enemy. Over the next four years, only 259 U.S. fatalities were recorded in the country. According to one heady American general, "We had accomplished in eight weeks what the Russians couldn't accomplish in ten years."[19]

GOVERNANCE AND CORRUPTION IN AFGHANISTAN

Afghanistan is a strong nation, but a weak state. – Afghan diplomat Said Jawad[20]

The Longest War 421

> We fought 11 one year wars [in Afghanistan], where each incoming unit blames the previous one ... there is no continuity, units spend half to three-quarters of the time learning and are usually gone by the time they have figured it out. Generals are even worse – one year tours, half of which are spent back in DC, no real sense of what is happening on the ground. Locals and insurgents learn and adapt but we are always repeating kindergarten. – U.S. intelligence officer[21]

Following an international conference in Bonn, Germany, in December 2001, a provisional government was established for Afghanistan with Hamid Karzai selected as chair of the interim administration. The conference also established the International Security Assistance Force (ISAF) to help bring a lasting peace to the war-torn country. The North Atlantic Treaty Organization (NATO) would take command of ISAF in 2003. Karzai was the leader of a moderate nationalist group who spent most of the Soviet occupation in Pakistan. From this perch, Karzai spent time obtaining foreign funding for the anti-Soviet guerrillas, despite his unease with the Islamic fundamentalism within the mujahideen ranks. With the precipitous fall of the Taliban in late 2001, U.S. forces facilitated Karzai's arrival into Kabul.[22] This new leader immediately became the face of his fractured country. Despite initially seeing him as an indispensable figurehead who would eventually unite a modern and peaceful Afghanistan, the United States and its NATO allies eventually soured on Karzai after continuing allegations of inveterate corruption in his administration.

In theory, a government is a strongly centralized system, with power flowing from the center. In practice in Afghanistan, the central government had limited influence in much of the country outside Kabul.[23] Remarkably, in the years following the Taliban's loss of Kabul, Afghanistan elected a popular president in Karzai and approved a written constitution that codified a representative parliament and supreme court although it had little effect outside the capital.[24] In the 2004 presidential vote, roughly 10.5 million Afghans cast ballots, double what experts predicted given the high incidence of Taliban threats and attacks.

Karzai took around 55 percent of the vote and was inaugurated that December. By the end of 2004, a new cabinet was in place, and Afghanistan's central government appeared to be making progress. But over time many Afghans lost faith in the Karzai government. In 2007, Jabar Shigari, a member of the Afghan Parliament from Ghazni, would articulate the frustration of many Afghans that Karzai's administration had betrayed its country, saying, "We have patiently waited five years for change, for an end to official corruption and abuse of power and for economic development. But we've received nothing."[25] Tragically for Afghanistan, Hamid Karzai was extremely ineffective.

A MULTINATIONAL EFFORT

U.S. military planners knew well that two successive British expeditions in the nineteenth century and the Soviet invasion in the late twentieth century had each ended painfully for the foreign invaders. Thus, and especially after the successes in late 2001, American strategists believed that a light military footprint would help ensure that history did not repeat itself once again.[26] With major combat operations completed in late 2001, the U.S. forces were joined by an additional 12,000 troops from nineteen nations. NATO's ISAF also became a key contributor to the international effort known as the Coalition. Unlike the largely unilateral war in Iraq, the campaign in Afghanistan was a true multinational effort.[27]

Almost from the beginning there were problems with NATO's mission.[28] For starters, in the first decade of the war, NATO had fourteen top commanders in Afghanistan, a dubious number rivaled by the United States' own eight military commanders and seven ambassadors. The initially appealing "lead nation" approach had various NATO contingencies take the lead for specific nation-building areas. Thus, for example, the United States volunteered to helm the creation of the Afghan National Army (ANA), while Germany was responsible for the Afghan National Police, the United Kingdom for counternarcotics, and Italy for the justice system. All in all, the process was a disaster.

A major source of controversy was the refusal of most NATO countries to allow their forces to be used in offensive operations. This resulted in the emergence of a "two-tiered" NATO hierarchy, wherein certain nations (e.g., the United States, the United Kingdom, and the Netherlands) assumed an "authority by merit" over civil and military operations, which brewed resentment among noncombat contingents. This reluctance of some countries to put their soldiers in harm's way was not surprising given that in 2007, 75 percent of German, 70 percent of Italian, and 72 percent of Spanish citizens told pollsters that they did not support the deployment of their troops for combat in Afghanistan.[29]

By 2003, however, the counterinsurgency effort began to shift to a more "population-centered" approach that reflected the growing realization that the U.S.-led international force and its Afghan counterparts were locked in a desperate struggle to win the Afghan people's loyalties away from the Taliban. Once considered a nuisance, the Taliban had used intimidation, illicit drug revenues, theological fervor, and the Coalition's own actions to transform itself into a formidable and highly lethal insurgency. Thus, what was initially a disorganized, retreating enemy had gained momentum in rural Afghanistan and Pakistan as an "insurgent coalition" of ethnic Pashtun nationalists, dispossessed tribes, and Islamic extremists keen to control the Pashtun-majority regions of both countries.

The group aimed to exhaust the occupying enemy and its Afghan lackeys rather than defeat them outright. In this capacity, the Taliban represented a formidable challenge for Coalition forces. The Taliban posed as defenders of remote tribes against central government misrule and neglect in the hope of making the country ungovernable so that the international community would withdraw and leave the illegitimate Kabul regime to its own fate.[30] Ever adaptive, the Taliban was able to exploit Coalition weaknesses by using both traditional guerrilla tactics such as hit-and-run raids, ambushes, and bases in foreign sanctuaries (read Pakistan) and also "postmodern" tactics like suicide bombers and Internet- and social-media-driven propaganda.

"CRAWL, WALK, RUN"

By 2006 the tide appeared to have turned in the Taliban's favor. According to Karzai, "Ridge by ridge and valley by valley, religious zealots who suffered devastating losses in the U.S. invasion that began five years ago ... are surging back into the country's center."[31] Similar to the conditions that allowed Colombia's FARC to endure far longer than it otherwise would have, opium production and trafficking provided the Taliban with critical revenues to fund its insurgency. Exploiting the lack of sizable and effective security forces able to control the population and hamper opium production, the Taliban appeared to have enough resolve and resources to withstand the Coalition indefinitely. By 2005, the Taliban was also improving its tactics by operating in pairs and using snipers, camouflage, and high-powered optics – all unequivocal signs of a growing "professionalism" within its ranks.[32]

In a loud echo of the American counterinsurgency and nation-building campaign in El Salvador two decades earlier, the U.S.-led coalition made the training of Afghan security forces a critical component of its strategy. U.S. and NATO planners reckoned that the only opportunity for exiting this endless and costly counterinsurgency and nation-building campaign would be when the Afghan forces could provide the security necessary to establish the rule of law and deter the Taliban. In November 2003, U.S. officials hired international private security contractors to train Afghan policemen in large numbers. By the end of 2004, 32,000 new policemen had gone through the academy; by mid-2007, 71,000 had graduated. The quality of these new forces, however, was disputable; critics lambasted the private contractors for being "cowboys," more interested in adventures than in creating an effective police force.[33] The training results were often frustrating, leading one U.S. captain to quip, "The people fear the police more than they do the Taliban, and until we can get that fixed, it's going to be a long road."[34]

The Coalition's effort to bolster the ANA had similarly tough going, despite its indispensable part in the counterinsurgency strategy. According to one U.S. trainer, "We began one day at 0730 with 189 students, and by 1000 hours we were down to 111, give or take a few." In some instances, recruits who spoke only Pashto had difficulties because instructions were given through interpreters who only spoke Dari. One big push was to create a healthy well of noncommissioned officers (NCOs) to promote a permanent cadre of professional soldiers among the ranks. As Staff Sergeant George Beck Jr., an American adviser, said in 2008, "It's all about crawl, walk, run. Right now the Afghan army is at a crawl. In a few more years, it will walk and in ten, it will run. Then we can all go home."[35]

The ANA was young and plagued by morale and retention problems, but it remained the only tool that Kabul had against the insurgency. By 2006 the ANA had 63,000 troops in the field and was headed toward a goal of twice that number. Positive developments led former NATO Supreme Allied Commander James L. Jones to testify to the U.S. Congress in 2006 that the ANA was the "most successful pillar" in the reconstruction efforts to date. In July 2007, the ANA reached a milestone when Major General Abdul Khaliq, commander of the 203rd Corps, served as the commanding general during Operation Maiwand in the Taliban stronghold of Andar district in Ghanzi province. The mission aimed to clear insurgents out of Zardulu Pass, a high mountain gap that was critical for transit into and out of the district. Over 1,000 Afghan and 400 U.S. military personnel cleared and held the area. It was the first large-scale operation planned and led by Afghan officers.[36]

The Taliban, however, was not resigned to permitting the ANA to grow unchecked; rather, the Taliban guerrillas exploited the ANA's poor resources by offering almost three times the daily pay for a soldier – up to US$300 per month versus the $80 per month earned by a first-year ANA private. The Taliban often enticed tribesmen and farmers with a variety of offers on a "seasonal basis," including "daily rates" of $10 to $20 per day for joining an attack against Coalition forces, $15 to launch a mortar round into an air base, and $1,000 for killing a government worker or foreigner.

The Australian military scholar and soldier David Kilcullen has described these sorts of episodes as the phenomena of the "accidental guerrilla": the pacific civilians who are somehow caught up in the conflict and become insurgent fighters, or the bored youth who join an insurgent ambush for an afternoon simply to find relief from the monotony of daily existence. And thus the more the United States as a global power fights dirty wars around the world, the more likely there are to be accidental guerrillas. At the height of the Taliban insurgency in 2008, Kilcullen estimated that 90 percent of the insurgent fighters were "reconcilable" and could be convinced to give up the fight, while the remaining 10 percent (or 3,000–4,000 fighters) were hard-core fanatics who could only be dealt with through military force.[37] The accidental guerrilla phenomenon is another example of "blowback" in action: the outcome is the very opposite of what is expected. In this case, the campaigns to defeat guerrillas wound up creating more of them.

A key innovation in the Coalition's counterinsurgency and nation-building strategy occurred with the expansion of Provincial Reconstruction Teams (PRTs). First established in 2002 and led by the United States and NATO, the PRTs' main function was to combine military and civilian resources and personnel to deliver reconstruction, governance, and security to local communities under the auspices of the central government in Kabul. In practice, this entailed the deployment of teams of between 60 and 100 civilian and military personnel to operating bases throughout the country to perform small reconstruction projects. By 2007, NATO had taken command of the dozens of PRTs based throughout the country.

As the PRTs developed on the civilian side, the U.S. and Coalition forces relied upon three different types of military units to attack the insurgents. The first was a combination of special operations forces, or SOF, who focused on direct action raids targeting insurgent leaders, IED makers, and safe houses, and of Army Special Forces, who, in line with their unconventional warfare history, trained and mentored ANA units, especially ANA Commando units. The second component was airpower – transport and assault helicopters and the B-1 bombers, F-18 fighters, and drones that targeted remote insurgent positions. Journalist Bing West estimated that SOF and airpower likely accounted for over 50 percent of the insurgents killed. The final element was the foot soldier, who, often in an advisory role, conducted the indispensable but "monotonous work, patrolling every day, sweltering in the summer and shivering in the winter, all the time knowing the insurgents would get off the first shots."[38] And once more we see how, strategically, counterinsurgents often need to push for an outright victory, while insurgents fight not to lose. But at the tactical level the counterinsurgents almost always concede the tactical initiative to the insurgents. Getting this balancing act right is one of the most difficult issues for a counterinsurgency to reconcile: you need to be everywhere at once while the insurgents only need to find one weak spot to exploit. This sober reality goes a long way in explaining the difficulty of waging a successful counterinsurgency.

Between 2006 and 2009, the Taliban and Al Qaeda had deftly used their sanctuary in Pakistan as a base for raids into Afghanistan. Afghan local governance was not working as hoped, and drug trafficking and related criminal activities were rampant. Operation Enduring Freedom took a back seat for the American media, the public, and even civilian and military leaders. Reports from Afghanistan were sparse, and the death tolls were modest compared to those in Iraq. With the destabilization of Iraq and subsequent Awakening and surge of 2007 in focus, Americans were largely taking for granted that the campaign in Afghanistan was going well. This was a costly mistake. As the cacophony of violence in Iraq waned, reports from Afghanistan became more dire. In the summer of 2006, the Taliban began to focus its military efforts on southern Afghanistan, including Kandahar Province, in surprisingly lethal and effective operations.[39] Over the next two years, the general counterinsurgency and nation-building climate in Afghanistan declined significantly.

OBAMA'S "NECESSARY" WAR

When the Obama administration assumed office in January 2009, there was a growing cry among experts inside and outside the U.S. government that a reinvigorated campaign was necessary to reverse the deteriorating situation in Afghanistan. At the suggestion of defense secretary Robert Gates and the Joint Chiefs of Staff, in June Obama removed the American general running the Afghan War, General David McKiernan, the first firing of a wartime theater commander since President Truman removed General Douglas MacArthur in 1951 for opposing his Korean war policies.[40]

The Obama team quickly replaced him with a publicly anonymous but internally celebrated commander, General Stanley McChrystal, who had run the most clandestine branch of the military, the Joint Special

Operations Command, or JSOC, which controls the United States' "special mission units." JSOC had become legendary in the preceding years for its ferociously lethal nighttime raids in Iraq and Afghanistan. McChrystal was credited with overseeing the successful killing of Abu Musab al-Zarqawi, the head of Al Qaeda in Iraq, while serving in that theater. The tall, gaunt McChrystal lived an ascetic lifestyle, with the much-reported habit of limiting himself to one meal a day, a few hours of sleep a night, and a daily eight-mile run.

As one *New York Times* journalist observed, McChrystal was a "soldier's soldier."[41] Within the tight circles of Special Operations troops, McChrystal was revered for his steely will and legendary willingness to endure the same risks they faced. In 2005, he accompanied a small team of commandos in Iraq on an early dawn raid targeting Abu Musab al-Zarqawi, the leader of Al Qaeda in Iraq. The British and U.S. soldiers soon found themselves overwhelmed by enemy fighters. McChrystal reportedly leaped into a ditch and returned fire at fighters overrunning his position. A day later British commandos presented McChrystal with a certificate that he hung in his Iraq office. "This recognizes that during the period 0230 – 0415 ... while facing hostile fire from enemy forces, LTG Stanley McChrystal was the highest paid rifleman in the United States Army."[42]

President Obama made two other key appointments for his Afghan campaign. Retired Lieutenant General Karl Eikenberry, who had previously served as a commander in Afghanistan, was now sent to run the U.S. embassy in Kabul. The imperious and often maddening Richard Holbrooke, a veteran American diplomat, was tapped to be the State Department's special representative for Afghanistan and Pakistan – in the hope that he would replicate his stunning success in brokering a peace in the Balkans in the 1990s.[43] With his new Afghan team in place, Obama had now raised the number of American forces in Afghanistan to 68,000 from 38,000, hoping that a renewed commitment to this "necessary" dirty war would give the Afghan government and nascent democracy the breathing room it so desperately needed. The perceived success of his predecessor's bold troop "surge" in Iraq undoubtedly influenced the Obama administration.

Soon after arriving in Kabul in June 2009, McChrystal turned his focus to Helmand, a province just to the west of Kandahar. Helmand was home to less than 4 percent of the country's population and some observers openly questioned why the region was now receiving thousands more troops on top of the nearly 11,000 marines already deployed on bases there.⁴⁴ However, McChrystal's military thrust into Helmand was overshadowed by a dubious and highly embarrassing presidential election that took place in Afghanistan over the summer amid stepped up Taliban attacks and credible allegations of pro-Karzai fraud. Once the contested vote was tallied in August, Afghan election officials declared a runoff between President Karzai and his closest opponent, former foreign minister and physician Abdullah Abdullah. Karzai then refused to participate in the second vote, contending that he had already won the election fair and square.

Rattled by this crisis that threatened to further delegitimize the fledgling Afghan government in the eyes of its people, the White House dispatched the chairman of the Senate Foreign Relations Committee, John Kerry, to Kabul to broker an agreement allowing for a second round of elections. Kerry and his European counterparts were finally able to convince Karzai to agree to the second vote, even though Abdullah never participated in what he deemed would be a rigged election.

The Obama administration was now forced to stomach a hastily formed strategy of bolstering an Afghan government led by a dubious democratic figure. One senior administrator lamented to the *New York Times*' David Sanger, "It's hard to say that we are sending your children to fight and die for a guy who steals elections."⁴⁵ Taking a broader view of the American experience in dirty wars, and contrary to the enthusiasm with which George W. Bush embraced him in the early years of the war, Hamid Karzai was decidedly not an effective and legitimate "indigenous" national leader along the lines of the Philippines' Ramón Magsaysay in the 1950s or El Salvador's José Napoleón Duarte in the 1980s, who both proved to be indispensable in those two "successful" American-backed dirty wars.

These sorts of sobering revelations regarding the state of the Karzai government as well as ISAF's own failings helped compel the Obama administration to spend several agonizing months in the fall of 2009 reconsidering the Afghanistan strategy it had only recently unveiled via the McChrystal appointment and related surge in the south. After seven years of toil and billions of dollars spent, the United States and its allies were bogged down in a violent country; public support for the war lagged as Americans began to tire of hearing about more combat deaths, just as had been the case in Iraq in the dark years of 2004–6.

Despite his well-earned reputation as a lethal warrior, McChrystal in his official "COIN guidance" promoted a counterinsurgency effort that divided the political/military effort at an amazing 95/5. That is, McChrystal was attempting to win this dirty war in an unprecedented clean fashion, an approach that weighed down his subordinates with what they believed were incapacitating rules of engagement.[46] Related to this attempt at fighting a clean counterinsurgency, McChrystal also pledged to lower the civilian casualty count down to zero – a virtual impossibility given the grisly reality of this dirty war.[47]

In a classified report that was leaked to the press in September, the incoming McChrystal recommended that an additional 30,000–40,000 more troops were needed to best ensure that this now decade-long war could in fact be won. And the idea was that it could be done by following the general outlines of the COIN doctrine of expansive and patient campaigning that was believed to have been so effective in Iraq. Despite these recommendations from commanders in the field, the Obama White House was not predisposed to sign on to such an open-ended approach given what it increasingly believed was Afghanistan's shrinking political and strategic value. Perhaps most influentially, Vice President Joe Biden – who had long been skeptical about the rationale for sending more troops – contended that the effort should be increasingly confined to what could broadly be considered "counterterrorism" as part of a gradual drawdown of American forces.[48]

In the end, President Obama appeared to split the difference between the maximalist COIN options supported by McChrystal and the Joint Chiefs and Biden's reduced counterterrorism presence by sending additional "surge" troops but sharpening the withdrawal plan. Obama believed that pushing counterinsurgency in some areas and counterterrorism in others was a "hybrid" approach that would help ensure a positive outcome amid drastically reduced goals of what was possible in Afghanistan.

In a televised address to the nation from the U.S. Military Academy at West Point on December 1, 2009, President Obama laid out the broad parameters of his decision to "surge" an additional 30,000 troops into Afghanistan to finish the critical mission of denying Al Qaeda a sanctuary before handing over security responsibilities to a more capable host government. Obama also announced that, despite the surge, American forces would begin a withdrawal after eighteen months. Obama also used the speech to repudiate the increasingly popular critique in the American media that Afghanistan was turning into a replay of Vietnam,

FIGURE 32.2. Lt. Matthew Stuhler visits with Haji Najibullah at his home in western Marjah, Helmand Province, Afghanistan, Sunday, August 1, 2010. Many compounds were empty in the area that was hotly contested between marines and Taliban fighters and Lt. Stuhler visited to offer his support. "I don't want anything. I just want to stay at home, feed my family, and work on my farm," Najibullah said. Photo and permission by Victor J. Blue

There are those who suggest that Afghanistan is another Vietnam. They argue that it cannot be stabilized, and we're better off cutting our losses and rapidly withdrawing. I believe this argument depends on a false reading of history. Unlike Vietnam, we are joined by a broad coalition of 43 nations that recognizes the legitimacy of our action. Unlike Vietnam, we are not facing a broad-based popular insurgency. And most importantly, unlike Vietnam, the American people were viciously attacked from Afghanistan, and remain a target for those same extremists who are plotting along its border. To abandon this area now – and to rely only on efforts against Al Qaeda from a distance – would significantly hamper our ability to keep the pressure on Al Qaeda, and create an unacceptable risk of additional attacks on our homeland and our allies.[49]

Some critics blasted the new strategy for the apparent disconnect between doubling down on the war by sending thousands of more troops, but then immediately announcing an insanely near withdrawal date of summer 2011, which they contended would almost certainly encourage the Taliban and Al Qaeda to wait the Americans out. The Obama administration responded that the 2011 dateline was simply the beginning of a gradual pullout and that the actual level of troop reductions would be determined by the situation on the ground.

Into 2010, most of the surge troops were sent to Afghanistan's southern provinces of Helmand and Kandahar. Involving 15,000 U.S., British, and Afghan troops, the launch of Operation Moshtarak marked the "first salvo" of this new strategy against the Taliban – and by extension a new strategy of sizable military and civilian efforts in the southern provinces.[50] If the

Bush administration's counterinsurgency efforts in Iraq several years earlier had been characterized by "clear, hold, build," then the Obama administration's vision was adjusted to read: "clear, hold, build, and transfer."[51]

One of the first targets for both eliminating the enemy and implementing aggressive public works was Marja, a farming region in Helmand and one of the most productive centers of Taliban-controlled poppy cultivation in the world. According to the new counterinsurgency approach, U.S. Marines and Afghan forces would clear the area so that civilian and military adviser teams could oversee the installation of what in McChrystal's term was "government in a box."

At the outset, the results for what quickly became the biggest military operation since the Afghan war began in 2001 were far from encouraging. This was not good news for McChrystal given that he wanted the Marja mission to be a model of the campaigns that would ensue.[52] It took weeks for the joint force to push the Taliban out of the area's key villages and compounds, and their zone of control, which centered on the Marja bazaar, dwindled almost as soon as they had taken it. At one point during the fighting, a U.S. rocket launcher called HIMARS blew up a compound, killing twelve Afghan civilians. Initial reporting indicated that the usually accurate system had impacted roughly a quarter-mile short of its intended target. Subsequent American-recovered evidence suggested that the compound hit was in fact Taliban-controlled but also had civilians in it. In any case, McChrystal suspended the use of HIMARS pending an investigation. He also ordered his staff to issue a statement apologizing for the killings. McChrystal explained his rationale in a way that could have applied to countless American experiences in dirty wars:

> To some, issuing an apology to Afghans – for whom our soldiers were risking their own lives, often displaying extraordinary "courageous restraint" in the process – symbolized the inherent contradictions in much of the Afghanistan war. Afghans' resentment of mission-critical actions often mystified [American] soldiers and those who sent them to combat. Such an attitude can strike the military as ungrateful. I recognized and respected those feelings and frustrations, but I also knew improving Afghan perceptions was critical to victory.[53]

Echoing Napoleon's lament during the Peninsular War in Spain two centuries earlier, McChrystal called Marja his "bleeding ulcer." After a year, however, American commanders insisted the situation had improved dramatically, with one claiming that it was "safer than Detroit." Observers attributed the improvement in security and local government to the sizable force of 2,000 U.S. marines supported by 700 ANA soldiers and 300 regular police officers.

Perhaps most critical was a program copied from the Awakening councils established in Anbar Province in Iraq. Local leaders from Marja's locales raised teams of up to fifty militia fighters who were expected to repel the Taliban. The locals who organized these teams were paid $150 per man, plus a "start-up fund" of $1,500. While far from perfect (the new money expectedly created new rivalries and jealousies), the councils had the invaluable advantage of being able to identify who was and was not a Taliban outsider. Ironically, the new 800-man force (which cost the Marine Corps an astounding $500,000 every ten days in a poor community of 250,000) was already bigger than the local police force. Back in Kabul, Karzai administration officials expressed concern that such massive irregular forces might transition into illegal warlord groups.[54]

PETRAEUS ENTERS THE FRAY

> You can only take so many killed and wounded before you say, "this cannot continue." We didn't want to destroy Sangin, but there were places that we had to flatten. We had no choice. – Lieutenant Colonel Jason Morris[55]

> We can offer them a way out, we can show them daylight, yeah, but if they don't take it, we'll put them in the fucking grave. – British Army General Graeme Lamb[56]

In June 2010, General McChrystal offered his resignation to President Obama after unflattering remarks from McChrystal and his staff about Vice President Joe Biden and other prominent administration figures were published in *Rolling Stone* magazine.[57] With McChrystal gone, Obama then named General Petraeus to replace the humiliated McChrystal as commander of NATO and American forces in Afghanistan. Attendant with the appointment was the expectation that Petraeus – and at this point his almost messianic promotion of all things counterinsurgency related – would be able to do for Afghanistan what he had done in Iraq. In the first months, he seemed poised to do so, assuming once again the double role of military commander and diplomatic adviser.

The McChrystal affair achieved the effect of elevating the larger issue of whether the United States was winning the war in Afghanistan. Liberal Democrats in Congress, for one, threatened to delay further appropriation to the campaign. Referring to the change from McChrystal to Petraeus, Massachusetts representative Jim McGovern offered, "Same menu, different waiter." On the political right, Republican congressman Ron Paul said,

"That McChrystal thing is just a symptom of what we won't face up to, which is to suggest that it [Afghanistan] is a totally failed policy. If we were on the verge of a great success, do you think we'd fire the general?" Responding to this apparently deteriorating situation, Defense Secretary Robert Gates pleaded for patience, telling the Senate Appropriations Committee: "This is not something where we do ourselves any favors by tearing ourselves up by the roots every week to see if we're growing."[58]

At the same time, U.S. military commanders in Afghanistan began to acknowledge publicly what many of them had long known, that the "classical" counterinsurgency approach of winning hearts and minds through civic works, foot patrols, and low-intensity combat was not working. Remarkably, very few Afghan villagers were even aware of the September 11, 2001, terrorist attacks and why this act drove the massive American campaign in their country. It is very hard to justify a foreign occupation if the local civilians do not understand the event that prompted the invasion. For the United States, the war in Afghanistan was justified by the September 11 attacks, while for local Afghans the Americans were strange, distant soldiers in body armor.[59]

The Taliban and its loose network of insurgents proved too dogged and too vicious, especially against civilian populations. Noted commentators such as the influential Vietnam veteran and combat journalist Bing West pushed the line that the U.S. commanders and politicians needed to realize that Afghanistan could only be won through "hard counterinsurgency." There would be a time for hearts and minds later, but West contended that now the key was to punish these fanatical insurgents and eliminate their ability to intimidate and control the local populations.

For West, the U.S. military's "emphasis upon persuasion through empathy" was illustrated by the U.S. high command's embrace of the author Greg Mortenson and his widely read book, *Three Cups of Tea*. A humanitarian who had funded hundreds of girls' schools in Afghanistan and Pakistan, Mortenson routinely briefed the chairman of the Joint Chiefs of Staff and senior commanders in Afghanistan. In West's view, the military's senior ranks "were determined to see counterinsurgency as 'benevolent nation building,'" an image that appealed to the mainstream press covering the conflict. "We didn't have a war-fighting doctrine for defeating the Taliban. Instead, we had a counterinsurgency doctrine for nation building, much like the Peace Corps on a giant scale."

Continuing his stinging critique, West contended that the new counterinsurgency dogma embodied in General Petraeus's heralded *Field Manual* perplexed soldiers because it confused roles by diminishing the military's core competence: violence. Risk avoidance, for one, had become the "guiding light" at the brigade level. So instead of embracing the "imperial grunts" who fought and killed in places such as the Korengal Valley and were the key to winning this dirty war in Afghanistan, the U.S. military promoted a kind of antiseptic and politically correct counterinsurgency.[60]

By the end of 2010, Petraeus's approach had begun to diverge sharply from the principles of the *Counterinsurgency Field Manual* he helped to create for Iraq, in favor of a strategy journalist David Ignatius has described as "talk and shoot."[61] In short, Petraeus instructed his forces to batter the insurgents while quietly opening channels for them to seek accommodation within local and national governments. The strategy relied heavily on raids and bombings by special operations forces that targeted high-level Taliban leadership. Indeed, a report that Petraeus commissioned showed that 90 percent of effective operations during his command had come from 5 percent of the U.S. force strength.

One notorious feature of this "light-footprint, heavy-impact" approach was the increased use of unmanned aerial vehicle strikes in Pakistan, a move that many analysts censured as illegal as well as deleterious to a U.S.-Pakistan relationship whose good terms were arguably central to mission success in Afghanistan. Petraeus also endorsed Karzai's diplomatic efforts to reach Taliban commanders for reconciliation talks, even helping to open back-channel networks to communicate with the Taliban and push them toward a political solution.[62]

By the end of 2010, the 134,000-strong Afghan army had become one of the country's most respected institutions. It was also far more capable of handling security issues on its own than it had been two years earlier. Afghan and Coalition forces pushed the Taliban out of key areas of Kandahar Province, including Kandahar City. These forces also expanded the security zone around Kabul and continued to interdict insurgents on the border between Afghanistan and Pakistan.

By 2011, Taliban insurgents faced a double threat in what appeared to be a far more effective Afghan security force, as well as widespread national government presence.[63] At the same time, though, the "magic bullet" of training Afghan forces so that they could eventually assume responsibility for their country's security remained mired in problems and controversy. Most glaring were the infamous "green on blue" attacks, the term used for Afghan security attacks on NATO troops. In 2012 alone, and despite ten years and $33 billion to bolster Afghan security forces, more than fifty American and allied soldiers were killed in this manner.[64]

The Longest War

During these violent years, U.S. Marines were achieving operational success through intense close-range firefights and the use of lethal weapons systems not normally associated with the "population-centered" counterinsurgency doctrine. As seen through the battlefield reporting of the *Washington Post*'s Rajiv Chandrasekaran, here is the chilling account of one battle in October 2010 to offer a sense of what this hard-fisted approach looked like:

For the Marines in 3/5's [3rd Battalion of the 5th U.S. Marine Regiment] Kilo Company, their very first patrol led them into the horrors of Sangin. On the afternoon of October 14, 1st Platoon exited its new home, a Spartan outpost in a belt of farmland between the Helmand River and Route 611, the district's main north-south road. Walking single file, scanning the shoulder-high cornfields for signs of insurgents, the platoon set out for a nearby village.

The Marines had not traveled more than 250 yards when the shooting started. First a few pops. Then a volley. And then a fusillade not just from AK-47 rifles but the belt-fed machine guns as well. Pinned down among the corn, the platoon radioed for help. A reinforced machine-gun squad from 2nd Platoon threw on its gear and left the outpost to set up a blocking position so the Marines from 1st could withdraw. But as soon as the backup squad neared the scene, it was ambushed by dozens of insurgents. Within minutes the squad's leader was shot in the leg. The only place his comrades could take cover was an adobe compound to the southwest marked on their maps as Building 3. It was then that those Marines – and soon the rest of Kilo Company – would come to understand why Sangin had become the killing fields of the war in Afghanistan.

As the squad rushed toward the compound, one of the machine gunners stepped on a homemade mine on the southern corner. He was blown into a nearby canal. On the north side of the building, a Marine seeking cover behind a wall was struck by a bomb planted in it. When the squad's medic rushed over to help him, he stepped on a pressure-triggered makeshift bomb. He lost both his legs, and the Marine he sought to save died before the medevac helicopters arrived.

There were so many explosions, so close together, that others in the platoon assumed fellow Marines were firing mortar rounds at the Taliban. Only later would they understand that the sound was from their buddies stepping on mine after mine. ... By the time 1st Platoon and the response squad from 2nd Platoon made it back to their post, they discovered another challenge. They were desperate for more ammunition, but the Taliban had dammed up nearby irrigation canals, flooding the sole dirt road leading to the outpost and rendering it impassable to armored U.S. vehicles. The Marines were eventually forced to wade through the muck on foot, hoisting the ammunition on combat stretchers, under the cover of darkness.[65]

This sort of fighting continued in Sangin for the rest of the year. The Taliban attacks claimed the lives of eight men from Kilo Company, with two dozen wounded, some as double or triple amputees. Yet Kilo

Company continued to fight, sending out almost daily patrols. In short, "their goal was to get in fights and kill as many insurgents as they could."[66] One American officer, Lieutenant Colonel Jason Morris, lost ten Marines within a week of their arrival in Sangin. Morris's conclusion was that the soft side of counterinsurgency that involved reaching out to tribal leaders and rebuilding roads simply did not apply, lamenting: "Sangin was a minefield, and you can't do COIN in a minefield." He told his soldiers that if they were receiving machine gun fire they should respond with rockets. "We need to make a statement," he said.[67]

THE AFGHANISTAN-PAKISTAN BORDER

In July of 2008 there were roughly sixty attacks against Afghan or Coalition forces along the Afghanistan-Pakistan border. In early September 2008, U.S. Navy SEALs launched an assault from Afghanistan into the Pakistani "agency" of South Waziristan (part of the Federally Administered Tribal Areas) against Al Qaeda and the insurgent Haqqani network. In late September, U.S. OH-58 helicopters active near the border took small arms fire from a Pakistani military checkpoint. American cross-border operations infuriated Pakistani officials, including the army's chief of staff, General Ashfaq Parvez Kayani, who contended that the "right to conduct operations against the militants inside our own territory is solely the responsibility of the [Pakistani] armed forces." U.S. commanders were now realizing that no matter what counterinsurgency gains Coalition forces might be making on the Afghan side, the sanctuaries in Pakistan made finishing the task difficult militarily and delicate diplomatically. As one U.S. military intelligence officer revealed, "We recognize the border. They [the insurgents] do not."[68]

The tensions over cross-border incursions would only heighten with the dramatic increase in the use of unmanned aerial vehicles (UAVs, or drones) to strike insurgent positions in Pakistan. The incidence of reported strikes rose from 33 in 2008 to a peak of 118 in 2010, before tapering off to 70 in 2011, as a result of increased scrutiny and questions about the permissibility of deploying lethal force against another state's territory in international law.[69] But drone strikes were small fry compared to the mission that brought the United States one of its most important victories in the war – on the Pakistani side of the border.

Back in August 2010, U.S intelligence analysts reported to President Obama that they had located bin Laden's favorite courier, a man about thirty years old named Abu Ahmed al-Kuwaiti. According to journalist Nicholas Schmidle, the analysts "observed that residents of the compound burned their trash, instead of putting it out for collection, and concluded that the compound lacked a phone or an Internet connection. Kuwaiti and his brother came and went, but another man, living on the third floor, never left. When this third individual did venture outside, he stayed behind the compound's walls. Some analysts speculated that the third man was bin Laden, and the agency dubbed him the Pacer."[70]

In late 2010, President Obama ordered the CIA and U.S. military to consider options for attacking the compound. Six months later, Obama was viewing the real-time footage of the raid, which was being filmed by an unarmed RQ-170 drone hovering more than 15,000 feet above the Pakistani city. Up until this point, Obama's advisers had been divided over the best course of action. Defense Secretary Gates reminded his colleagues that when Eagle Claw – the star-crossed Delta Force operation in 1980 to rescue the U.S. hostages in Iran – was presented to the Carter White House, "they said that was a pretty good idea too."[71]

Gates and U.S. Marine General James Cartwright, the vice chairman of the Joint Chiefs and one of Obama's favored officers, initially pushed the alternative of using B-2 bombers to take out the compound or employing a relatively untested aerial drone to shoot a small missile directly at bin Laden when he would be walking in the compound's courtyard. The problem with the bomb approach, though, was that it would have created giant craters and thus made it virtually impossible to acquire bin Laden's body – the proof necessary to provide that the raid had succeeded in killing its elusive target. In the case of the drone strike, there was fear that even if it succeeded in killing bin Laden, to prove to the world that the Al Qaeda leader had indeed been taken out would be difficult. In the end, though, Obama supported the helicopter-borne raid, an option replete with risks especially as it ensured the involvement of American troops on the ground for a hostile raid inside Pakistan without that government's approval.[72]

"WE GOT HIM"

Go in there and get bin Laden; and if he isn't in there, get the hell out! – Defense Secretary Leon Panetta[73]

Just before midnight on the night of May 1, 2011, two specially modified stealthy MH-60 Black Hawk helicopters took off from Jalalabad Air Field in eastern Afghanistan on a covert operation. Inside the blacked out aircraft were twenty-three U.S. Navy SEALS from Red Squadron Team Six (officially the Naval Special Warfare Development Group, DEVGRU), a Pakistani-American Pashto interpreter, and a highly trained dog – a Belgian Malinois named Cairo.[74] The men in groups like SEAL Team Six, such as Delta Force, had for most of the last decade been routinely deploying to Iraq and Afghanistan for several months at a time. During these months, they would conduct missions (sometimes multiple) almost every night. When deployed, the troops lived mostly sequestered from conventional troops, either at their own forward operating bases or on part of a conventional base that was sealed from the rest. These operatives were roughly ten years older than regular soldiers; most were in their early thirties, veterans of several tours in regular SEAL teams, as opposed to their current status as "black ops."[75] Part of the reason for choosing the SEAL team was that it had successfully conducted around a dozen secret missions inside Pakistan.[76]

The helicopters flew fast and low, navigating the contours of the land with terrain-following radar. Inside the helicopters, each of the SEALs was in full kit: desert camouflage, helmet, night-vision goggles, gloves (for fast roping), and hard knee pads. They were armed with a variety of pistols and automatic rifles outfitted with silencers.[77] After approximately fifteen minutes of flight, the helicopters crossed undetected into Pakistani airspace. For decades, Pakistan's military had maintained a state of high alert against its eastern neighbor, India. Because of this focus, Pakistan's principal air defenses are all pointing east, not west toward Afghanistan. On the Black Hawk's entry into Pakistan, three large Chinook helicopters lifted off from Jalalabad. One flew to a site right inside the border on the Afghan side. The other two proceeded to the staging area north of the small provincial city of Abbottabad via a different route.

The SEAL team's destination was a compound in Abbottabad, a city located about 120 miles from the border with Afghanistan and north of Islamabad, Pakistan's capital. Abbottabad was also the site of Pakistan's premier military academy. The Abbottabad raid was the first serious effort to kill "Crankshaft" – the name that JSOC had given to bin Laden. The intricate plan was disrupted when one of the Black Hawks carrying the assault team hovering over the compound abruptly wheeled, clipping the compound's wall with its tail and suffering a hard but controlled crash. As journalist Mark Bowden, who had written a searing account of the tragic Mogadishu firefight in 1993, chronicled "Here in the first seconds of the mission, they [the Obama administration] had a Black Hawk down."[78] When the first helicopter crashed, the second Black Hawk diverted by landing in a field outside the compound, all of which added an element of improvisation to this unfolding operation.[79] Yet the downed helicopter proved only a minor delay; within seconds the SEALs poured out of both helicopters, both outside and inside the compound.

Before the operation began, the SEALs created a checklist of code words using Native American terms. "Geronimo" was to signal that bin Laden had been located. The SEALs first killed the courier Kuwaiti and other individuals on the premise, including bin Laden's twenty-three-year-old son, Khalid. The original plan called for half the SEALs to rope down through the balcony into the third floor, which would have meant that bin Laden would have been encountered first, not after fifteen minutes of approaching as was the case. The SEALs came up the stairs to the third floor bedroom until one saw a tall, bearded man in a prayer cap and traditional flowing clothes. One of the SEALs entered the compound's third-floor bedroom room and fired his HK416 carbine at bin Laden, striking the Al Qaeda leader in the chest. Another SEAL then shot him in the left eye, reporting on his radio, "For God and country – Geronimo, Geronimo, Geronimo ... Geronimo EKIA [enemy killed in action]." After hearing this in the White House Situation Room, Obama reportedly uttered to no one in particular, "We got him."

Before the SEALs made a hasty departure for Afghan air space after the thirty-eight minutes spent on the ground with no American casualties despite the hard helicopter crash and bin Laden dead, they collected flash drives, CDs, DVDs, and other computer files from bin Laden's media studio. This immediate shift from direct action to intelligence gathering illustrated just how markedly JSOC's "shooters" had changed in the preceding ten years. The intelligence obtained indicated that bin Laden continued to be far more involved in Al Qaeda's operational planning than most intelligence analysts had assumed. His organization had been planning assassination plots against President Obama and the American commander in Afghanistan, General Petraeus. One of the backup Chinooks arrived at the compound to ferry out the operators who were unable to use the ruined Black Hawk. A medic from the Chinook took swabs of blood from bin Laden's body and inserted needles to extract bone marrow for DNA testing. Before departing, SEALs set charges to destroy the damaged Black Hawk. The helicopters then flew north to Kala Dhaka to rendezvous with the second Chinook and refuel the remaining Black Hawk. After twenty-five minutes, they flew to Jalalabad, all without eliciting a response from the Pakistani government. The helicopters landed in Jalalabad at three in the morning local time.[80] The entire operation had taken less than four hours.

Bin Laden's body was flown back into Afghanistan, and then over Pakistani airspace to the U.S.S. *Carl Vinson*, an aircraft carrier sailing in the Arabian Sea. At this point, bin Laden's body was washed, wrapped in a white burial shroud, and slipped inside a bag, fully in accordance with Islamic burial practices, according to U.S. officials. And then from a height of over twenty feet, the corpse was tossed into the waters below.

AMERICA IN AFGHANISTAN

The Taliban are very happy that the foreigners pull out. When the Marines go, war will come back. – Ali Mohhamen Khan, village elder[81]

What takes away from my time is getting all this gear out of here and shutting down the place. We all know that [for the United States] the war is ending. – Marine Lieutenant Mike Breslin[82]

Osama bin Laden's death in Abbottabad in 2011 at the hands of U.S. Navy SEALs deprived the terrorist organization of its commander in chief. But any celebrating that ensued in the months following the daring raid on bin Laden was deflated by the sobering reality that the United States' counter-insurgency campaign in Afghanistan was far from over. This was hammered home in the very early morning of March 11, 2012, when U.S. Army Staff Sergeant Robert Bales massacred seventeen Afghan civilians. After burning eleven of the bodies, he returned to the base, where he was apprehended and subsequently charged and convicted under the U.S. military Uniform Code of Military Justice. The killings echoed an earlier controversial attack in March 2007 in eastern Afghanistan, when marines killed as many as nineteen civilians after a suicide car bomb struck the marines' convoy, wounding one of them.[83]

In June 2010, the war in Afghanistan became the longest war in U.S. history. By this time, more than 3,000 U.S. soldiers and 10,000 Afghan troops had been killed. The Taliban may have lost as many as 20,000 combatants, according to some estimates. All told, it was a bloody and costly conflict. Like each of the dirty wars the United States has been involved in, Afghanistan was a "new" war. The dictates of the particular environment – a widely distributed population, mountainous terrain, a history of government corruption, low government influence in rural areas, and violent ethnic and tribal struggles for power – made it the ideal setting for an insurgency, in many ways similar to previous theaters in Southeast Asia, Central America, and even the North American piedmont almost two and a half centuries earlier.

But other factors made it a totally unfamiliar environment, where the best practices of previous counterinsurgencies did not necessarily apply. Because of their doggedness, endless poppy revenues, and effective safe haven in Pakistan, the Taliban mounted a much stronger and more resilient resistance than did the Sunni insurgency or Al Qaeda in Iraq. Population-centered counterinsurgency efforts such as those that had helped gain the support of the Sunni Awakening were ineffective in areas where the Taliban held military, economic and, in some cases, theological authority over rural populations.

The ability of American and NATO forces to respond to these very different conditions often determined their success or failure. Obama's 2010 surge had a major positive impact on the course of the war, but only when deployed with an "enemy-centered" mandate that largely diverged from the counterinsurgency lessons of "last year's war" in Iraq. All this and more led President Barack Obama to turn Afghanistan into a light-footprint dirty war (e.g., fewer troops, narrower political and military goals, etc.) despite the initial consensus of his military advisers to keep the effort more "maximalist" than had been the approach theretofore.[84] Into his second administration, the president – and the American public as well – continued to believe that ramping down the dirty war in Afghanistan was preferable to the cost of sustained counterinsurgency and nation-building. Yet it remained far from clear exactly what would fill the void left by the departing forces. According to one twenty-nine-year-old Afghan police officer interviewed in Helmand in 2013, "The Taliban are coming back here. Even their women and children are coming back to fight. They are coming to take over the whole country, and I will stay here to fight them until I die."[85] After investing tens of billions of dollars recruiting and training the Afghan forces, Washington had gambled that these 350,000 could maintain order in the midst of the American withdrawal. No one was under the illusion that the future would be perfect. According to Colonel Austin Renforth, who commanded the 7th Marine Regiment combat team in southern Helmand province, the focus of the American troop surge in 2009, "We just want them [Afghan forces] to be a little better than the Taliban."[86] Such lowered expectations are the very nature of dirty wars.

33

The Fall of Muammar Qaddafi, 2011

On the morning of September 12, 2012, the world awoke to shocking news out of Libya: U.S. Ambassador Chris Stevens, head of the American consulate in the provincial coastal city of Benghazi, and three additional American citizens had been killed overnight in a coordinated attack staged by radical Islamic terrorists. The controversy surrounding the incident would continue for months, becoming a key issue of the 2012 presidential campaign and leading to depositions on Capitol Hill and accusations of intelligence failures and even a White House coverup. The uncertainty surrounding the attack was fueled by confusion as to the timeline of the assault, the identity of the perpetrators, and the purpose of the American presence in Benghazi.

Lost amid the furor over the Benghazi attack was the broader issue of America's deep involvement, beginning in 2011, with the bloody and highly controversial effort to overthrow the country's dictator of forty years, Muammar Qaddafi. The harsh lessons of a decade of war in Iraq and Afghanistan helped shape a more hands-off and indirect American approach in Libya, one that relied in large part upon NATO allies to get the job done. In an interesting and telling turn of events, Washington found itself supporting and aiding an insurgency instead of fighting against one – as was the case in Afghanistan and, to a lesser extent, Iraq. While U.S. policy toward Libya showed a desire to escape the "boots-on-the-ground" approach that proved so inconclusive, costly, and polarizing in Iraq and Afghanistan, the Benghazi attacks demonstrated that even a more intentionally hands-off approach to a dirty war was nonetheless fraught with its own set of difficulties and dangers.

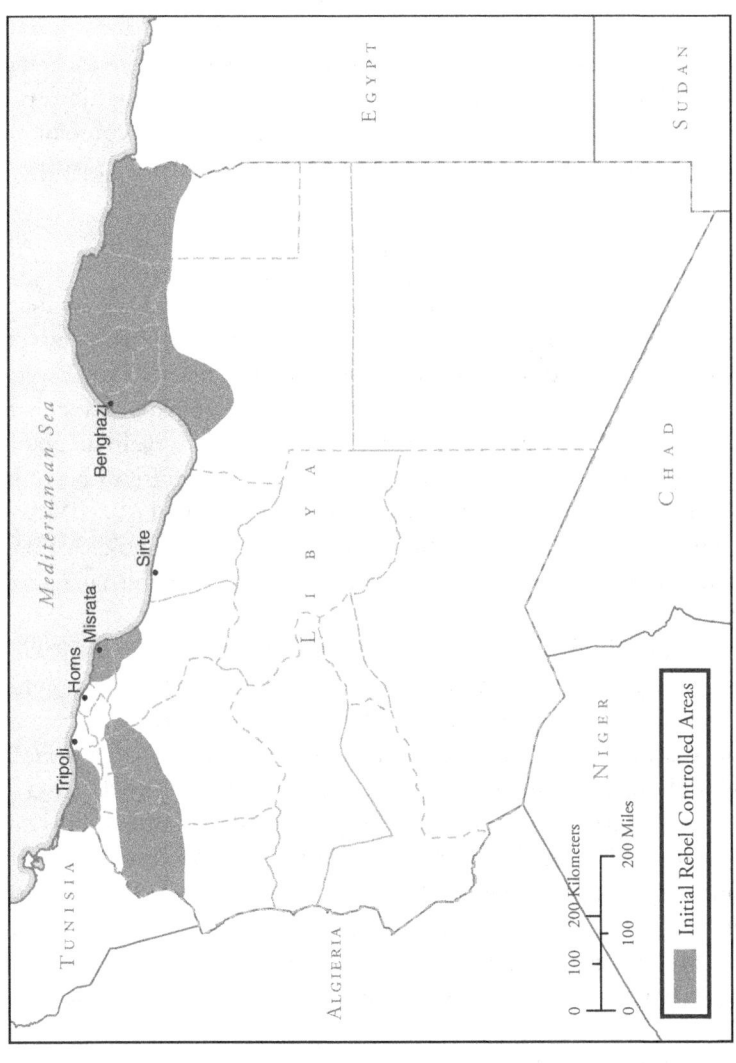

FIGURE 33.1. Libya, 2011. Map prepared by the University of Wisconsin-Madison Cartography Lab©. Reprinted with permission

An insurgency, in most cases, entails an often motley combination of many different actors and moving parts; and once it is unleashed, foreseeing eventual outcomes or controlling events to suit one's purposes can be difficult. This was especially true in Libya, where a spontaneous movement to overthrow a dictator arose in the aftermath of the ultimately successful protests against autocratic regimes in Tunisia and Egypt in 2011 in what came to be known as the Arab Spring. And, at least as far as Barack Obama's administration was concerned, the unfolding case of Libya provided more evidence that trying to aid an insurgency can be as confounding and challenging as attempting to wage an effective counterinsurgency.

QADDAFI IN POWER

Born in 1942, Muammar Qaddafi grew up just as Libya was beginning to escape from its colonial past. In an example of true historical symmetry, he was born outside the desert town of Sirte – the same place where, seventy years later, he would be dragged from a smoking convoy and shot by NATO-supported Libyan rebels. Qaddafi was raised as a Bedouin nomad until the age of eleven, at which point he returned to Sirte to begin his formal education. His first political role model was Gamal Abdel Nasser, the inimitable Egyptian nationalist leader and vocal champion of pan-Arabism who had seized power in 1952 and, in 1956, attempted to nationalize the Suez Canal.[1]

In Libya, Qaddafi began to develop strong feelings against the British-backed government of King Idris. While Libya had achieved nominal independence in 1951, the year that Idris came to power, in practice the country essentially remained a colonial protectorate. Given Qaddafi's strong traditional Bedouin upbringing, subsequent trips to London as part of his military training only exacerbated Qaddafi's antipathy toward the West. Upon his return to Libya, Qaddafi created his own clandestine revolutionary group and named them the Free Officers, in homage to the nationalist organization that had vaulted Nasser to power in neighboring Egypt. The underground movement began slowly, their activities limited to printing newspapers and holding meetings. In 1969, the Free Officers seized power in a bloodless coup while King Idris was out of the country.

Once in power, Qaddafi moved quickly to assert his credentials as an unabashedly nationalist leader, demanding that the British and the Americans remove their military presence from the country. At the same time, he quadrupled Libya's oil revenues by forcing Western oil companies to accept concession terms more favorable to his regime. While these

The Fall of Muammar Qaddafi

actions initially made Qaddafi a hero in the eyes of many ordinary Libyans, they would also signify the beginning of forty-two years of authoritarian rule in Libya and foreshadow Qaddafi's deeply contentious relationship with the West. The twenty-seven-year-old colonel would rule Libya for the remainder of the twentieth century, developing a reputation as an eccentric, unpredictable ruler. In 1969, however, "nothing hinted at the clownish, ranting figure of later years."[2]

QADDAFI AND THE WEST

Over years and decades, Qaddafi used his prodigious oil revenues and political cunning to consolidate his iron grip on power. As with many dictators inebriated by their own power, he gradually came to view himself as the total embodiment of his country, with complete control over the Libyan resources and people. To hold onto power, he played Libya's many tribes against each other, systematically weakening all the country's institutions – including the military – to create a state apparatus that was completely reliant on him. Because of the economic clout generated by Libya's vast oil reserves, Qaddafi was able to sustain an extensive patronage system throughout the country that further solidified his autonomy.

Calling himself "Brother Leader" and "Guide of the Revolution," Qaddafi codified his idea of a perfect society into a governing philosophy named "Jamahiriya," which he translated as "the state of the masses." The Libyan autocrat published his political theories in a work known as the *Green Book*, which covered topics ranging from property rights to gender discrimination. Convinced of his system's innate brilliance, Qaddafi took advantage of every chance to leave his footprint etched on the Libyan nation. He unveiled a new flag and renamed the country the "Socialist People's Libyan Arab Jamahiriyah." The arrival of Fidel Castro in 1977, invited by Qaddafi to speak before the Libyan General People's Congress, touched off street celebrations and military parades.[3]

Despite the fanfare and idealistic rhetoric surrounding the Jamahiriya, Libya never amounted to more than Qaddafi's personal fiefdom and soon settled into a pattern of political repression and harsh authoritarian rule. Student protests were crushed by force, military officers were purged, and public hangings became commonplace. To further increase his stranglehold on the country, Qaddafi organized a cadre of revolutionary supporters into the "Revolutionary Committees Movement," a paramilitary group that quashed dissent and spread fear throughout the country.[4]

At the same time he was moving to dominate the Libyan political landscape, Qaddafi was also making waves abroad – especially for his aggressively outspoken anti-Western stance. He quickly took up the Palestinian cause, allowing Libyan soil to become a meeting point and a refuge for terrorists like the Palestinian Abu Nidal.[5] Qaddafi was an alleged supporter of Black September, the group that abducted and killed eleven Israeli athletes at the 1972 Munich Olympics – an attack that the Libyan ruler praised publicly.[6]

Farther afield, Qaddafi assisted Nicaragua's Sandinista government in the 1980s and supported the Ugandan dictator Idi Amin, even sending 2,500 Libyan troops to help Amin in his war against Tanzania in 1978.[7] Qaddafi's long, complicated, and antagonistic relationship with Great Britain included support for the Irish Republican Army.[8] The list of subversive organizations promoted by Qaddafi continues: Basque separatist movements, the Moro National Liberation Front in the Philippines, and the Italian and Japanese Red Brigades, to name a few.[9]

In the 1970s, Qaddafi's support for various revolutionary groups was mostly limited to rhetoric and financial support. Over time, however, the dictator took on a much more active role in planning attacks against Europe and the United States. In an ominous foreshadowing of the death of Ambassador Stevens, the American embassy in Tripoli was ransacked by Libyan protesters in 1979 in what the ambassador at the time, William Eagleton, described as "a planned military event," not a spontaneous student action, similar to the Iranian takeover of the U.S. embassy in Tehran that same year.[10] The relationship between Libya and the West would continue to deteriorate from there, reaching its lowest point in the 1980s.

"MAD DOG OF THE MIDDLE EAST"

For the Reagan administration in the tense period of the 1980s Cold War, it was bad enough that Qaddafi had his hands in conflicts across Africa and around the world; even worse, Washington feared that Libya, which had purchased much of its military hardware from the Soviet Union, would grow closer to Moscow.[11] Although American fears of a Libyan-Soviet alliance were probably exaggerated, Reagan was convinced that "[Qaddafi] was little more than a Soviet puppet who should be eliminated."[12] From the very beginning of his presidency, Reagan earmarked Qaddafi's regime as a danger to the world community. The United States severed diplomatic ties with the country and the bilateral relationship continued to deteriorate.

The Fall of Muammar Qaddafi 447

This only encouraged Qaddafi to further step up his involvement with anti-Western causes, and he was blamed for a variety of terrorist attacks over the next few years, including the hijacking of an Egyptian airliner in 1985 that killed fifty-nine people. By 1986, Reagan was calling for Qaddafi "to be treated as a pariah in the world community."[13] On April 5, 1986, the bombing of a Berlin nightclub killed two American servicemen and injured seventy-nine others. Suspicion fell on Libya, especially after the U.S. intercepted a number of radio messages between Tripoli and the Libyan embassy in Berlin that seemed to implicate Qaddafi. Reagan responded with lethal force, sending Air Force bombers based in Britain to strike targets in Tripoli and Benghazi, allegedly killing Qaddafi's infant daughter, Hana, and almost killing the Libyan leader himself.[14] The Colonel, however, exacted his revenge two years later in the skies over Lockerbie, Scotland.

In 1988, a bomb was smuggled onto a Pan Am jet bound for New York. The plane had taken off from London carrying mostly Americans, and made it as far as Lockerbie before exploding in mid-air. All 259 passengers were killed, along with eleven people on the ground. The investigation of the crash would lead to two Libyan agents, who in 1991 were charged with conducting the attack. Qaddafi laughed off the allegations and refused to extradite the suspects. The incident further isolated Qaddafi, and in the eyes of the world Libya was now firmly identified as a pariah state. Adding to Libya's seclusion were the first reports, published in 1987, accusing Libya of pursuing weapons of mass destruction.[15] Qaddafi's actions during the 1980s would prompt Reagan to name him the "mad dog of the Middle East."[16]

QADDAFI GIVES UP THE BOMB

While Qaddafi was provoking revolution and violence abroad, he increasingly faced opposition and resentment at home. The Libyan economy, overly reliant on oil exports and damaged by Western sanctions, struggled to fund the country's military expenditures and Qaddafi's lavish patronage system. Internal dissent was also on the rise, and the already paranoid Qaddafi turned even more autocratic and repressive. Show trials, torture, and public executions were a permanent part of Libyan life. The hanging of Sadiq Hamed Shwehdi in 1984 is a good example of both Qaddafi's brutality and his attempts to strike fear into the Libyan people. Shwehdi, charged with terrorism, admitted to joining the "stray dogs" and was forced to kneel and confess his crimes on national television. He was executed in a basketball stadium, surrounded by hundreds of school children forced to watch his body swing from the gallows.[17]

Such repression worsened after 1991, and many observers believed that Qaddafi would lose his grip on power as a result of his domestic troubles. In fact, Qaddafi survived numerous assassinations and at least eight coup attempts. The Colonel held on, but was forced to become more pragmatic in the process. In 1999, Qaddafi finally agreed to hand over the two Libyan suspects in the Lockerbie bombing; they were eventually tried in the Netherlands. Only one, Abdel Basset al Megrahi, was convicted. Qaddafi's reconciliation with the West continued when, in the aftermath of the trial, he pledged to withdraw his support for terrorist groups.[18]

In 2003, Qaddafi, spooked by the U.S. ouster of Saddam Hussein, admitted the extent of Libya's nuclear weapons program and, in return for an end to sanctions, opened the country to inspectors. While the wars in Iraq and Afghanistan seized global attention, beginning in 2003 it appeared that Libya was at last on the path to normalcy. However, the bad blood between Qaddafi and the West would be difficult to overcome: "for the next eight years, the West veered between accepting him back into the world community and holding him at bay, fearing that the new Qaddafi might really be the old Qaddafi."[19]

REVOLUTION

The sequence of events that led to the death of Qaddafi began in Tunisia on December 17, 2010. On that day, a young and unemployed Tunisian named Mohamed Bouazizi staged a public self-immolation after police shut down his unlicensed business. Bouazizi would die of his injuries seventeen days later, but by then the Arab world was aflame with revolution. In what became known as the Arab Spring, public anger and dissatisfaction swept across North Africa and the Middle East, toppling rulers one by one. Tunisia's president was removed from office in January 2011. A month later, the thirty-year rule of Egypt's Hosni Mubarak ended after violent protests and demonstrations. Qaddafi was next in line. The Libyan population had long suffered under his oppressive regime, and, inspired by events elsewhere in North Africa, finally saw their chance to fight back.

Qaddafi took several small steps to prevent a Libyan uprising, lowering food prices in January 2011 and promising better living conditions for his citizens.[20] It was not nearly enough – the Arab Spring had unleashed buried sentiments in Libya that had been building for decades. Beginning

The Fall of Muammar Qaddafi 449

in the first week of February 2011, almost every major city in Libya saw spontaneous protests and marches, initially sparked by people calling for the release of an imprisoned Libyan human rights lawyer.

Unemployment, economic hardship, corruption, and repression fueled the uprising, which involved hundreds of thousands of people and soon grew too large for Qaddafi to contain. His initial response to the revolt was tepid and unorganized: at the same time he was releasing a small number of political prisoners to appease the protesters, he was also sending hired mercenaries from West Africa to contain the crowds. The mercenaries, who even included Chinese and Bangladeshi members, inspired even more anger by, in one episode, firing on unarmed protesters in the early days of the uprising.[21]

The revolution continued to snowball, fostered by a feature that influenced many of the Arab Spring uprisings: the Internet. Social media sites like Twitter and Facebook allowed Libyans to voice their grievances, which soon moved from small complaints to calls for the overthrow of Qaddafi himself. The Colonel, who may have underestimated the force of change sweeping across his country, snapped into action and initiated a severe crackdown. The use of violence by Qaddafi's troops "was so brutal that it seemed clear the intent was not to merely get the protesters off the streets but to terrify them into submission. Early on, a helicopter was used to fire on unarmed civilians."[22] Qaddafi, it seemed, was hell-bent on avoiding the fate that had befallen President Ben Ali in Tunisia and President Mubarak in Egypt.

THE WESTERN RESPONSE

The speed and tenacity of the Arab Spring uprisings caught many observers off guard, and Western governments, while applauding the seemingly democratic transition taking place, were unsure how to react. The situation in Libya differed from the uprisings in Tunisia and Egypt, where leaders were swept from power in rapid fashion. Instead, it was clear that Qaddafi aimed to hold on to power at all costs and that a lengthy conflict might ensue. At the same time, given Qaddafi's difficult history with Europe and Washington, the revolution represented a golden opportunity to remove, once and for all, a longtime enemy of the West.

It became increasingly clear that Qaddafi would not go down without a fight. The Colonel promised to hunt down the rebels "house by house, inch by inch, alleyway by alleyway."[23] Qaddafi's son, Saif, was even more assertive, warning of "rivers of blood" and proclaiming: "we will fight to the last man and woman and bullet. We will not lose Libya.... We will live in Libya and die in Libya."[24] The lines of battle were being drawn: the Qaddafi family and its supporters, including the military, stood resolutely on one side. On the other side, the revolutionaries dug themselves in and prepared to take on the regime. The rebels, although widespread, consolidated their forces around the port city of Benghazi, Libya's second largest city.

One reason for Qaddafi's savage response to the revolt was his unwillingness to believe that the Western powers would intervene in Libya: "with Western troops bogged down in Afghanistan, and with the bitter experience of Iraq not far from the surface, the Colonel assumed that Western governments were in no position to launch an assault against his regime."[25] While extensive military commitments in other parts of the globe undoubtedly complicated the decision to intervene in Libya, ultimately foreign powers would respond and aid the rebels against Qaddafi.

The first steps taken by Western governments were relatively simple. By the end of February, the United States had frozen the assets of Qaddafi, his family, and the Libyan government. A host of European governments followed suit. Additionally, the UN Security Council imposed an arms embargo on Libya and banned international travel by Qaddafi and his officials. The crisis in Libya was also brought to the attention of the International Criminal Court, which prepared to prosecute Qaddafi's ruthless crackdown. After these initial steps failed to halt Qaddafi's forces, however, the situation grew murkier for the Obama administration.

By March 2011, the rebels had been putting up a stern fight but Qaddafi's advantages in weapons and equipment were beginning to bear fruit. Qaddafi's forces surrounded Misrata, a western coastal city originally captured by the rebels on February 24. Constant artillery fire rained down on the revolutionaries, who dug into the rubble of Libya's third-largest city and struggled to hold on. Farther east, Qaddafi's troops approached the rebel capital of Benghazi and threatened to place it under siege as well. Qaddafi had the upper hand and was bearing down swiftly on the rebel positions. For Washington and Europe, it was decision time.

On March 15, Obama and his key advisers assembled in the White House Situation Room to hear a National Security Council briefing on the situation in Libya. The consensus among the intelligence community was that Qaddafi would attack Benghazi within a matter of days, where they expected him "to be at his most brutal."[26] Qaddafi himself did nothing to dispute this notion – by this point, he had taken to referring to his enemies as "rats and vermin."[27] At the time of the meeting, there had already been several weeks of discussion among European and American officials concerning the way forward in Libya. European calls for a no-fly zone were spearheaded by French President Nicolas Sarkozy of France and British Prime Minister David Cameron, both of whom were in favor of sending in NATO planes to protect the rebels from Qaddafi's airstrikes.[28]

Among the higher levels of the U.S. government, the question was whether a Libyan no-fly zone would have any impact on the ground. While Qaddafi did rely on helicopters to support his ground operations, he was estimated to have fewer than forty operational military aircraft.[29] A skeptical Admiral Michael Mullen, chairman of the Joint Chiefs of Staff, advised Barack Obama that the no-fly zone would not work: "This notion that we're going to put some planes in the air to fly over a massacre just doesn't make a lot of sense.... We could feel really good about ourselves, on the right side of history, and the people would still get killed."[30]

The doubts surrounding the no-fly zone caused a great deal of disagreement in Obama's cabinet. Secretary of Defense Robert Gates, for one, opposed military intervention, while others, led by Secretary of State Hillary Clinton, supported it.[31] Beyond the administration, Sarkozy, Cameron, and even the Arab League also voiced their support for a no-fly zone. In the end, it was the "imminent threat" to Libyan civilians that convinced Obama to throw his support behind a limited Western intervention in Libya.[32] Thus, the mission to defeat Qaddafi initially had humanitarian overtones that echoed NATO's involvement in the Balkans in the 1990s. At the same time, Obama was adamant that "we will not, I repeat, we will not deploy any U.S. troops on the ground."[33]

Two days after Obama's March 15 decision to back a no-fly zone, the United Nations passed Security Council Resolution 1973. Five countries – Brazil, India, Russia, China, and, most interestingly, Germany – abstained from the vote. The resolution gave the coalition what amounted to a "free hand" in Libya, granting it permission to use "all necessary measures to protect civilians."[34] On March 19, Operation Odyssey Dawn began in earnest; 120 Tomahawk missiles, fired from several American warships and one British submarine, screeched across the desert sky, striking Qaddafi's command centers and air defense systems. In the following days, American cruise missiles and warplanes turned against Qaddafi's ground forces. The Libyan army was rapidly driven back from Benghazi, giving the rebels "a stronghold and safe haven from which to operate for the rest of the war."[35]

The U.S. military took a leading role in the early days of Operation Odyssey Dawn but had planned all along to gradually take a backseat to the French and the British forces. By the end of March, control of air operations had officially passed from the United States to NATO in what was now referred to as Operation Unified Protection. Contrary to its normal position as the preponderant military power whenever it was involved in this sort of dirty war, America now let other nations take the lead, and missions against Qaddafi were flown almost entirely by non-U.S. coalition aircraft, led mainly by the French and British. As Obama had promised, the United States would limit contribution to "unique capabilities at the front end of the mission to protect Libyan civilians."[36]

Many observers expected Qaddafi's regime to collapse soon after the introduction of NATO air power, but the Colonel proved to be more resilient than anyone had predicted. The rebels were secure in their capital of Benghazi and had a foothold in the Western mountain ranges, but they were still struggling to hold Misrata and found it difficult to make headway elsewhere in the rest of the country.

By this point, several factors were contributing to complicate NATO's mission in Libya. The tenuous coalition, which was spearheaded by NATO but also included some additional participants, had some countries taking on far more of the conflict's military burden than others. Within NATO, there was a great deal of variance in the commitment to the intervention – France and Britain, for example, were firmly in favor, while Italy and Germany, among others, voiced their opposition. Even more problematic, Western leaders seemed unsure of their exact military and political roles and goals in the conflict. Prior to intervention, Obama and several European leaders had called for the ouster of Qaddafi; however, in practice, the no-fly zone was geared toward protecting civilians rather than regime change. This disconnect hampered the war effort, extending the civil war and allowing the conflict to grind into a bloody deadlock.

Other factors also contributed to the impasse. Qaddafi's forces were beginning to disguise themselves as civilians in order to mitigate the effectiveness of coalition airstrikes.[37] At the same time, the "disorganized" and "rag-tag" rebels were unable to take advantage of openings on the battlefield, resulting in a general stalemate across the country. While the intervention had saved the rebel forces, Qaddafi's resolve remained strong and the conflict devolved into a brutal war of attrition.

THE HUNT FOR QADDAFI

While the Obama administration was very publicly taking a backseat to NATO, the extent of American involvement in Libya behind the scenes was deeper than many people realized. As early as March 30, reports were already beginning to emerge of an active CIA role in the conflict.[38] CIA operatives, along with their British counterparts in MI6, were charged with directing airstrikes and identifying targets. More important, they were also responsible for making contact with the rebel forces "to fill in gaps in understanding who their leaders are and the allegiances of the groups opposed to Colonel Qaddafi."[39] Obama also gave the CIA permission to arm the Libyan rebels – a dangerous and bold proposition given the possibility that the weapons might fall into the wrong hands.[40] In late April, U.S. Predator drones began appearing in the Libyan skies, another sign that Washington was expanding the scope of operations in the country.

By the summer of 2011, America and NATO had clearly switched their mission from protecting civilians to hunting Qaddafi. With drones, airstrikes, and covert operations, U.S. forces were essentially engaging in a high-tech manhunt in a manner that echoed the pursuits of Mexico's Pancho Villa and Nicaragua's Sandino a century earlier. The difference in this case, of course, was that instead of hunting a guerrilla leader the Americans were aiding an insurgency to remove a head of state. The CIA increased its efforts to both equip and train the insurgents. Other coalition partners provided similar support, including Britain, France, and Qatar. The training, in particular, had a big effect: the rebel strikes became better coordinated, both tactically and across the country.[41]

The tide was slowly beginning to turn against Qaddafi. By May, Misrata, which had suffered through savage house-to-house fighting for months, was solidly in rebel hands. As the summer wore on, the situation grew even more dire for Qaddafi. The insurgent forces holed up in the western Nafusa Mountains went on the offensive, effectively opening a new front and stretching Qaddafi's forces to the limit.[42] From Benghazi, the battle-hardened revolutionaries pushed steadily westward toward Tripoli, liberating one city at a time. The National Transitional Council (NTC), created by former members of the regime in the early days of the war, asserted itself as an interim ruling body that the revolution could coalesce around. The NTC allowed the rebels to present a united front, especially important given U.S. concerns over the end game in Libya.

As the rebel successes piled up, time grew short for the ruler once known as the Brother Leader. Observers feared that the Colonel would fight for Tripoli at all costs and predicted a bloody siege of the capital that might last for months. There was much surprise, then, when on August 21 the rebel forces faced only token resistance when they entered Tripoli. The NTC moved quickly to consolidate their victory, and celebrations erupted throughout the country. The Colonel's forty-two-year reign was finally at an end. Over the decades, Qaddafi had built a vast array of tributes and monuments to his reign. These were now quickly removed by the revolutionaries, who tore down statues, replaced flags, and defiled portraits of Libya's former ruler.[43] The war, it seemed, was over – but where was Qaddafi?

While the rebels took on the difficult task of governing and rebuilding their country, the hunt for Qaddafi continued. For two months, it appeared that the Colonel had vanished into the desert. On October 21, 2011, the mystery of Qaddafi's whereabouts was finally solved. NTC fighters cornered a convoy of several dozen vehicles just outside the town of Sirte, transporting Qaddafi and approximately one hundred of his remaining bodyguards.[44] A U.S. Predator drone flying overhead fired a missile into the doomed convoy, destroying most of the vehicles and decimating Qaddafi's troops.

Struggling out of his burning vehicle, Qaddafi staggered toward a nearby drainage pipe dug into the side of the road. The group of rebels, surprised to stumble upon Qaddafi in such a fashion, dragged him out of his hiding spot and threw him onto the dirt. Qaddafi appeared confused, repeatedly asking "why are you doing this to me?" As the men hurled insults at the former president, the chaotic scene was interrupted by a gunshot. Despite calls to keep Qaddafi alive, an impassioned revolutionary had fired a single, fatal shot into the left side of Qaddafi's skull. Muammar Qaddafi, Brother Leader, and the "mad dog of the Middle East," had finally met his fate in the desert sands outside his hometown of Sirte, Libya.[45]

LEADING FROM BEHIND

Up until this point, the decision to intervene in Libya appeared to be sound. Without risking American boots on the ground, the United States, with the support of NATO members, had successfully partnered with an insurgency to overthrow a dictator who, because of his involvement with terrorist organizations, had long been a thorn in the side of the Western powers. It seemed a far cry from the huge cost in blood and money spent in Iraq and Afghanistan, and appeared to be a point in favor of light-footprint interventions. It may have taken months to finally catch Qaddafi, but that was the price to pay for keeping American troops out of harm's way in Libya and avoiding another land war in the Middle East. In the short term, at least, the American intervention in Libya appeared to be a success story.

The Fall of Muammar Qaddafi

The worst, however, was yet to come for the Americans. On the morning of September 12, 2012, gunfire erupted outside the U.S. consulate in Benghazi. Initial reports from the scene were inconsistent and contradictory. The media at first latched onto the idea that the attack was a demonstration that had gotten out of hand. As more details emerged, a much darker picture began to materialize: the assault had been planned and coordinated by radical Islamic terrorists, who used mortars, machine guns, and assault rifles to storm the compound. The attack killed Ambassador Chris Stevens and three other American citizens, sending shockwaves throughout the Obama administration. What had seemed like such a success story just days earlier now appeared to be another example of the United States engaging in an unnecessarily dangerous dirty war abroad.

The fallout from the attack was extensive. It became the dominant foreign policy issue of the 2012 presidential election, and the Obama administration suddenly found itself under fire from all sides. The State Department was accused of neglecting diplomatic security, while others pointed to the confusion surrounding the attack as evidence of a government coverup. Depositions and congressional testimony would continue for months, most dramatically when Secretary of State Hillary Clinton appeared before Congress in January 2013 to defend the administration's actions in the aftermath of the tragedy.

While Obama's decision to intervene in Libya may have caused problems at home, it also raised a host of issues abroad. For one, it opened the lid on the growing problem of Al Qaeda in North Africa. On January 16, 2013, militants stormed an Algerian oil refinery and engaged in a four-day standoff with security forces. In the course of the operation, sixty-nine people were killed, at least thirty-nine of them hostages. Seven of the dead were American citizens. Most troubling, reports emerged that the terrorists had obtained their arms from Libya. Even more alarming, several of the Egyptian militants involved in the attack were subsequently linked to the assault that killed Ambassador Stevens. The spillover from Libya was not limited to Algeria; in that same month, over 2,000 French troops arrived in Mali to combat the Al Qaeda safe haven that had surfaced in the lawless north of the country. Taken together, these unintended consequences of the Libyan intervention tempered the initial idea that Libya was an unmitigated success story for the West.

As far as insurgencies go, the American campaign in Libya raises several key issues. The decision to intervene in Libya was not a rash one, and for the most part Washington kept itself at arm's distance from the conflict on the ground. Despite this, America got sucked into the messy aftermath of the Libyan civil war, and many of the region's problems with regard to terrorism still remain.

For America, the experience in Libya followed an unusual script. Instead of engaging in counterinsurgency, the United States found itself aiding an insurgency against a head of state. While it is common to view America as a perpetual counterinsurgent, the fact is that the United States is not exempt from engaging in warfare on the insurgent side when the situation calls for it. The rise of drones, in particular, gave America the option of intervening with the bare minimum of military commitment. At the same time, lowering the risks associated with military intervention might also have lowered the parameters of what makes it acceptable for America to become involved in foreign conflicts. The indirect approach to Libya contrasted significantly with the full-scale campaigns of Iraq and Afghanistan, but each case represented the enormous difficulty in foreseeing the eventual long-term aftermath of military action – even if launched with humanitarian considerations in mind. Like many of the dirty wars recounted in this book, the outcome in Libya was ambiguous and unclear.

34

Intermezzo
JSOC Raids and Drone Strikes

> In Iraq, when we first started [special operations missions], the question was "Where is the enemy?" That was the intelligence question. As we got smarter, we started to ask, "Who is the enemy?" And we thought we were pretty clever. And then we realized that wasn't the right question, and we asked "What's the enemy trying to do?" And it wasn't until we got further along that we said, "Why are they the enemy?"
> – General Stanley McChrystal, interviewed in 2013[1]

On the morning of November 4, 1979, enraged Iranian student protestors began scaling the brick walls of the U.S. embassy compound on Takht-e-Jamshid Avenue in Tehran. Iranian security officials positioned to protect the compound did nothing to block the entering mob. The protestors thus seized the embassy and held hostage more than fifty Americans. The radical university students, including the future president Mahmoud Ahmadinejad, were motivated by a desire to strike a blow against the "Great Satan," but also to help push aside the secular moderate elements who were competing for power since the pro-American shah of shahs, Mohammad Raza Pahlavi, had been ousted earlier in the year. As the blindfolded Americans were led out of the chancery building, a jubilant crowd shouted, God is Great! and Death to America![2]

Over the next several months, American diplomats failed to secure the release of their compatriots, who would not be freed until January 20, 1981, 444 days after their capture and the day that President Jimmy Carter left office and Ronald Reagan was inaugurated. At the same time as the seemingly fruitless talks continued, American military planners hatched a rescue mission code-named Eagle Claw that would use the newly created elite counterterrorism unit, the 1st Special Forces Operational Detachment-Delta, or simply Delta Force. Intense training and planning ensued in the United States, Egypt, and Oman to get the mission ready for action.

President Carter approved the operation in the spring of 1980. On April 24, 1980, U.S. helicopters left the deck of an aircraft carrier headed to a spot outside Tehran, coined Desert One, where fixed-wing aircraft would refuel them before they proceeded to a hiding spot near the city. According to the plan, the following night Delta Force would emerge from the secret location, storm the embassy, free the hostages, and then meet up in a nearby soccer stadium where they would be picked up by the helicopters and flown to an airport that was supposed to have been seized by U.S. Army Rangers.[3] And then onward, out of the country to freedom.

Remarkably, the Delta Force team borrowed helicopters from the Navy used for minesweeping, not covert missions, and the Marine pilots were unused to this special kind of stealthy flying. Due to mechanical failures caused by sandstorms, U.S. operators aborted the mission. And then during the still quiet departure, one helicopter crashed into a four-engine C-130 on the group and both exploded, killing eight American soldiers – five airmen and three marines. The crash immediately ended any hope of keeping the aborted hostage rescue secret. The rescue had failed miserably. And with the Desert One debacle "went Carter's presidency and any realistic hopes for rapprochement with Iran."[4]

The Iran hostage rescue disaster shook the U.S. military to its core and prompted the creation of the Joint Special Operations Command (JSOC) based in Fort Bragg, North Carolina.[5] The ensuing blame focused on the hapless efforts to borrow from the respective service branches unaccustomed to working together. Amazingly, though, the result of one of America's most humiliating military disasters was not to "kill special ops but to expand it." JSOC was formed to integrate elite units from every branch into a lean-and-mean outfit, equipped with vehicles and weapons suited for this highly specialized "special" warfare.

The union brought together the Army's Delta Force, the Air Force's 24th Special Tactics Squadron, and the Navy's Special Warfare Development Group, popularly known as SEAL Team Six, as well as elements of the Army's 75th Ranger Regiment. And because the Eagle Claw mission failed in large part because of air travel failures, the Night Stalkers, the 160th Special Operations Aviation Regiment, was established using the military's most capable helicopter pilots to fly specially designed choppers for special missions. Over the next few decades, JSOC doubled in size to nearly 4,000 men and to its supporters became the country's most celebrated military and intelligence unit, becoming sort of an army within an army. JSOC's reach was global as it operated in secret in scores of countries; it was also relatively free of strict bureaucratic oversight from Washington. By the end of the first decade of the twenty-first century, JSOC had become highly operational, maintaining a frenetic pace of operations, mostly related to the Iraq and Afghanistan campaigns.

Eventual JSOC commander Admiral William McRaven and his men carried out more special operations missions than any such unit in American history. In McRaven's calculation, by the time of the Osama bin Laden raid in 2011 he had been personally involved in thousands of "black" (read clandestine) raids, commanding them remotely or actively. And when it came to the Osama bin Laden raid, one that bore a chilling similarity to the failed Eagle Claw over three decades earlier, McRaven's men had already been hitting similar compounds for a year, at times multiple targets in a single night. For the American commander, "this one [getting bin Laden] was unremarkable.... The layout and location of the compound clearly indicated to him the right way to assault – a small helicopter-borne force."[6]

JSOC SPEAR TIP IN IRAQ

What had been impressive but rudimentary [at the beginning of the Iraq War] was now a relentless counterterrorist machine. – Stanley McChrystal[7]

In the years following the relatively quick and successful overthrow of Saddam Hussein's regime in 2003, Iraq spiraled out of control. A good deal of this horrific violence – much of which was directed at the United States and its allied forces – was driven by Sunni extremist groups, including a new element of Al Qaeda led by Abu Musab al-Zarqawi. His group, Al Qaeda in Iraq, unleashed a campaign of roadside bombs and suicide attacks – intended to kill American soldiers but also Iraqi civilians – all to foment civil war and weaken the American public's appetite for continuing this dirty war in Iraq. In General McChrystal's estimation, al-Zarqawi "had gone from an important but stock jihadist operative slipping through our fingers to the most feared, active, deadly, and controversial Al Qaeda leader."[8] Ultimately, these mass killings (as well as Al Qaeda's other excesses in Iraq, such as forced marriages and bans on alcohol and cigarettes that antagonized many Sunni Iraqis) alienated the Sunni majority that should have been the insurgency's "natural constituency," marking a turning point in the war in favor of the American-backed forces.

During these seemingly dire years for the American-supported counterinsurgency and reconstruction effort in Iraq, JSOC, under the command of General Stanley McChrystal, incessantly battered insurgent Al Qaeda cells with unprecedented ferocity, innovation, and effectiveness. JSOC operatives located Saddam Hussein hiding in a "spider hole" in the final months in 2003. In June 2006, aerially dropped smart bombs, guided onto the target by lasers from on-the-ground JSOC operators, killed al-Zarqawi himself. Impressed observers quickly concluded that McChrystal's successes were among the most significant military achievements of modern times. The American commander called the efforts "collaborative operations" meaning that special operators – teams of elite fighters from every service branch – "operationalized" enormous amounts of data through new computational ability. In one description,

> In the past, after a successful night raid where a member of an insurgent cell was killed or arrested, by morning, or even within a few hours, every critical member of that group would know about it and would have taken evasive action. Information spread quickly. Cell phones would be ditched, computer disks destroyed, bomb-making facilities moved – the bad guys would scatter. But if you could get *inside* that response time – if you could beat their information cycle and learn enough from the first raid through either interrogation or, say scrutinizing a seized cell phone or hard drive – you might be able to launch a new raid or even multiple raids before word of the first one had gotten out.[9]

Back at the command centers, data-competent U.S. military operators would "exploit" the evidence, instantly turning information gathered in raids into broader intelligence networks. Over time, however, the special operations forces themselves were carrying out this process, which allowed them to more effectively turn intelligence into lethal operations. Now evidence recovered in one raid could lead to multiple raids on the very same night. The net effect of this ferocious pace was that JSOC was dismantling insurgent networks before these groups knew what hit them. Writing in his memoir published in 2013, Stanley McChrystal vividly described the atypical characteristics of operators conducting the raids and how Iraqis tended to view them entirely differently:

> The [special forces] were being as sensitive as anyone could be when searching someone else's house. Poise came naturally to them: They were older, in their thirties and forties, and they were seasoned. They did not need to smash things to prove their manhood or to feel powerful. Most were fathers, and that night, as on

the hundreds of raids each went on during the war, they couldn't help but see their own children in the young Iraqis who hid behind their parents' legs.

But the operators' care mattered little to the Iraqis, who never ceased glowering. We were big men, made bigger with body armor, it was one o'clock in the morning, and our searching their home was as humiliating to them as if we had stripped their bodies. They had no way of knowing that we too were fathers; without language, there was no chance even to attempt human connection. I knew we needed to do these raids, but I also knew these searches – on top of the electricity and backed-up sewage and the lack of jobs in a chaotic, post-Saddam Iraq – were producing fury, understandably directed at us.[10]

On one night in September 2007 in western Iraq, a JSOC unit was carrying out one of its "routine" raids on suspected Al Qaeda insurgents, in this case hoping to nab a regional commander who called himself "Muthanna." During the raid the operatives discovered a virtual "Rolodex" of names and numbers that referenced computer files containing photos, travel documents, expense reports, and other key documents for roughly 500 current Al Qaeda recruits. The Sinjar operation revealed that Muthanna was indeed responsible for coordinating the movement of foreign Al Qaeda insurgents and suicide bombers across the close border with Syria.[11] And through the JSOC model, the recovery of this intelligence became the raw material for the ensuing decapitation of al Zarqawi's network that was destroying Iraq – and by extension the American pacification campaign. Indeed, in the year following the Sinjar raid, virtually the entire leadership of the Syrian-based support network for Al Qaeda in Iraq had been destroyed. A single raid inside Syria near the border city of Abu Kamal in October 2008 resulted in the death of the Al Qaeda operative Abu Ghadiya, one of his brothers, and two cousins, all of whom were also insurgent leaders.

FROM KENNEDY'S GREEN BERETS TO OBAMA'S JSOC

After many years of frenetic operations in Iraq, the Afghanistan-Pakistan regions, and elsewhere, JSOC's well-established prowess and track record made it an increasingly attractive military option for American planners and politicians.

As we saw earlier, back in the early 1960s, a young president John Kennedy had been dazzled by the seemingly boundless capabilities of Army Special Forces, something he aggressively enlisted in the unfolding campaigns against communist guerrillas across the globe, including Vietnam.

Half a century later, another young president, Barack Obama, revealed to a journalist that his fateful decision to use special operations forces (often as opposed to a conventional aerial bombing or drone strike) for the bin Laden raid in 2011 stemmed from his confidence in these twenty-first-century imperial grunts: "I just felt as if I'd gotten to known [JSOC commander] McRaven. I had gotten to know the SEALs. I had obviously been monitoring their capacity to carry out night raids in Iraq and Afghanistan. We had mocked up the compound. We had experimented with it. They had run it.... McRaven, he inspires confidence. And I had pressed him hard."[12] Obama continued to elaborate on his view of the new role that special operations forces would play in America's dirty wars, both today and tomorrow:

I think with Special Forces, the dangers [of using them too liberally] are smaller because the human element is still there. Those who are still somebody's dad, somebody's husband, somebody's son. When you send them in, you know they may not come back. And for me at least, as commander in chief, I don't think about that any more causally than I do when I'm sending some green kid off to Kandahar.... I do think that just from a broader military perspective, that we can't overstate what Special Forces can do. Special Forces are well designed to deal with very specific targets in difficult terrain and oftentimes can prevent us from making the bigger strategic mistakes of sending force in, with big footprints and so forth. And so when you're talking about dealing with terrorist networks in failed states, or states that don't have that capacity, you can see that as actually being less intrusive, less dangerous, less problematic for the country involved.[13]

DRONES INTO THE TWENTY-FIRST CENTURY

[Drones give the United States] the ability, with laser-like focus, to eliminate the cancerous tumor called an al-Qaida terrorist while limiting damage to the tissue around it. – John Brennans[14]

Over a two-day period starting on October 13, 2011, the CIA used drone strikes in North Waziristan, Pakistan, to kill some of the sought-after insurgents on the American spy agency's most-wanted list. Those killed included Jan Baz Zadran, the third in command of the shadowy Haqqani network that according to U.S intelligence sources was responsible for numerous attacks on U.S. and allied forces in Afghanistan. Drone attacks the next day nabbed two top Al Qaeda operatives, Abu Miqdad al Masri and Abd al Rahman al Yemeni.

In this same month, Libyan strongman Muammar Qaddafi's time came to an end when his fleeing convoy near the city of Sirte was hit by a missile launched from a Predator drone. Qaddafi survived the strike and jumped

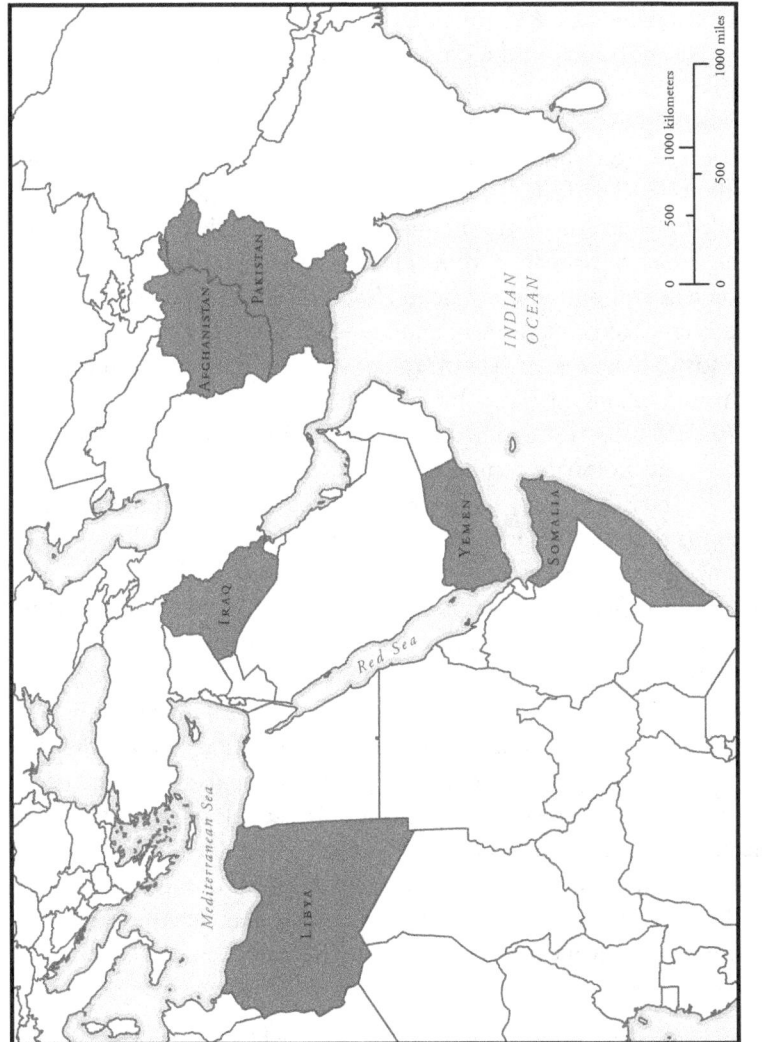

FIGURE 34.1. Countries where American drone strikes occurred, 2003–2012. Map prepared by the University of Wisconsin-Madison Cartography Lab©. Reprinted with permission

into a culvert to hide. Libyan rebels pursued him and, after a brief gun battle, pulled him out, a Kalashnikov in one hand, a pistol in the other. Within an hour, Qaddafi was shot in the head and his body was put on display.

These lethal operations further revealed the extent to which the U.S. government was using UAVs (unmanned aerial vehicles or the more common term, drones) such as the Predator to help fight its dirty wars in the twenty-first century. The Predator drone, for example, was a twenty-seven-foot-long device that could spend a full day in the air at high altitude. The Reaper, a larger and more lethal version of the Predator, could fly up to altitudes of 50,000 feet. The Predator could be configured to carry two laser-guided Hellfire air-to-ground missiles, the multimission Reaper with similar armaments. Launched from at least sixty military and CIA bases in locales such as Djibouti, the Seychelles, and Ethiopia, targets were largely in Afghanistan, Pakistan, Yemen, and Somalia. With its ability to remain airborne for so long, there was little to no warning to the targeted persons on the ground before they were hit.

By 2012, the U.S. Air Force had more drone pilots in training than pilots for fighters and bombers combined.[15] One enormous advantage of the drones as opposed to, say, B-52 strikes of the Rolling Thunder era in Vietnam was that the unmanned devices were infinitely more discriminate in targeting. That is, strikes appeared to better allow the U.S. military and CIA to kill those it wanted and not those it did not want to. At the same time, though, at least one estimate concluded that perhaps 20 percent of fatalities caused by drone strikes were in fact civilians.

Part of the motivation behind the proliferation of drone strikes was that they could allow the U.S. military to maintain its military preponderance around the world without the long, costly, and unpopular wars and occupations that had dominated the past decade.[16] If a couple of generations ago American generals in Vietnam preferred to send "bombs, not boys," their twenty-first-century successors were opting to send "drones, not boys." Indeed, President Obama, for one, believed that it was often preferable to use the precision of drones so America did not have to put special operations forces in the dirty wars of the age. In the words of the American president:

In some of these places [lawless states], the state has only the most tenuous reach into the territory. In other cases, the state lacks the capacity or will to take action. It is also not possible for America to simply deploy a team of Special Forces to capture every terrorist. And even when such an approach may be possible, there are places where it would pose profound risks to our troops and local civilians – where a

Intermezzo: JSOC Raids and Drone Strikes 465

terrorist compound cannot be breached without triggering a firefight with surrounding tribal communities that pose no threat to us, or when putting U.S. boots on the ground may trigger a major international crisis.

Mirroring the political and moral controversies surrounding the burgeoning use of drone strikes, Obama acknowledge the risks associated with such use:

And yet as our fight enters a new phase, America's legitimate claim of self-defense cannot be the end of the discussion. To say a military tactic is legal, or even effective, is not to say it is wise or moral in every instance. For the same human progress that gives us the technology to strike half a world away also demands the discipline to constrain that power – or risk abusing it.[17]

AN AUSTRIAN SKI-MOBILE ENGINE

The drone was not a new technology. Radio-controlled aircraft were used as early as World War II. President John Kennedy's old brother, Joe, was killed on a covert mission when his B-24 plane, designed to fly itself to a German target after Kennedy had bailed out, crashed prematurely. Drones had also been used in Vietnam, and the Israeli military used them successfully over Lebanon's Bekaa Valley in 1982. The CIA purchased several of the Israeli models and turned them over to an American defense contractor for continued development.

Unarmed drones were then used very effectively in the American-led campaign first in Bosnia and then in Kosovo in the 1990s. One Predator precursor, called the Gnat, basically a glider with an Austrian ski-mobile engine, allowed the soldiers a sixty-mile view from a platform that could remain aloft more or less continuously, flown in twelve-hour shifts. Compared to the use of manned aircraft whose mission taxed the pilots, this was a remarkable development. Nonetheless, there were still challenges with this nascent technology. Pilots struggled to fly such a light, awkward plane from satellite-delayed television images. After they pulled on their joysticks, it would take several seconds for the aircraft to respond. There was also no effective way to control ice on the drones' wings. Last, the drone was not stealthy and could be brought down by anti-aircraft fire.[18]

Once the Gnat missions started in the Balkans, they never stopped. Into the twenty-first century, the U.S. Air Force was using the drones in teams, which allowed much greater coverage of targeted areas. In addition, the images did not have to be monitored continually by human operators;

instead, computers, which never got distracted or bored by the complexity or duration of a mission, could monitor the collected data. Then, for example, the movements of a given vehicle could be followed over a region or city for months, or even years, allowing a detailed "map" of a suspect's travels. And adding that map to cell phone calls, American soldiers and spies were gaining a much better sense of the target's connections and habits – that is, his network. Last, improvements in optics allowed for surveillance at such a great distance that the drones could "stand off" well outside the restricted airspace (soldiers reported being able to read a license plate from two miles up) of a country in question, which also appeared to help mitigate potentially embarrassing diplomatic spats.[19]

DRONES, BEACONS, OPERATIVES, AND REPRISALS

In 2012 alone, CIA drone strikes killed hundreds of suspected Islamic militants in the insurgent hubs of North and South Waziristan in northwestern Pakistan, along the Afghan border. Given the drones' chillingly lethal state-of-the-art technology there was little that the insurgents could do to avoid their fate. Yet one significant countermeasure was the dogged search for informers who assisted the CIA by often placing GPS beacons in insurgent compounds to create a twenty-first-century bulls-eye to help ensure that the drone strikes hit their target. The militants' efforts often involved accusing local tribesmen of collaboration and then forcing them to confess into a video camera before their summary execution by hanging or firing squad. The taped confessions were then distributed locally and on the Internet in order to terrify other potential collaborators.

In the Afghan-Pakistan border regions, the insurgents had become obsessed with "patrai," a local word for a tiny metallic device that they believed the CIA used to locate them. In 2009, an Al Qaeda deputy commander published an article with photographs of these devices and warned of their lethality. He was subsequently killed in a drone strike. In 2012, the Taliban distributed a video showing another such device: a tiny electronic circuit board covered in plastic that, when connected to a nine-volt battery, pulsed with an infrared light that acted as a homing device.[20] In this instance, it seemed, the nine-volt batteries revealed a decidedly low-tech element in what was a high-tech dirty war of American drone strikes against suspected terrorists.

35

Conclusion

Nowadays, everyone calls himself a counterinsurgency expert.
— U.S. Special Forces general[1]

Georges Clemenceau is reputed to have said (and perhaps he did) that war was too important to be left to soldiers. Nobody seems to have come forward with the obvious corollary, which is that peace is too precious to be left to politicians. Such aphorisms, while they may delight those who like their thinking supplied for them in tasty capsules, wholly over-simplify the complex problem with which they deal. They can be true, certainly, but at the same time they are nonsense.
— Counterinsurgency expert, 1961[2]

"THE KINDS OF WARS WE MUST MASTER"

When the Iraq War was still raging in 2006, General Petraeus wrote in the U.S. Army's *Military Review* that his forces had learned a tremendous amount in Iraq and Afghanistan about how to fight guerrilla insurgencies, but the United States military needed to continue to learn from those conflicts because "America's overwhelming conventional military superiority makes it unlikely that future enemies will confront us head on." The vaunted American commander conceded that these two insurgencies were not the "wars for which we were best prepared in 2001; however, they are the wars we are fighting and they clearly are the kinds of wars we must master." Petraeus soberly reminded his soldiers that a "liberating force must act quickly, because every Army of liberation has a half-life beyond which it turns into an Army of occupation."[3]

While he referred only to the two major dirty wars that the United States was engaged in at the time, Petraeus could equally have been talking about American involvement in the Philippines after 1898, the chases after Augusto Sandino in Nicaragua in the late 1920s and early 1930s or Pancho Villa in northern Mexico in 1916, or Vietnam sixty years later.

Around the same time that Petraeus offered his reflections, scholar Edward Luttwak described an American society that is "willing to fight wars, that is willing to start wars because of future threats, that is willing to conquer territory or even entire countries and yet... is unwilling to govern what it conquers, even for a few years."[4] In this view, America has been overly willing to engage in dirty wars but has rarely had the stomach to actually carry out the hard-nosed political and military policies necessary to achieve victory.

Whether we see this in the dilemma surrounding the fits and starts of the American siege of the provincial city of Fallujah during the Iraq War, or the debate that raged in the 1980s over whether American advisers in El Salvador should be allowed into combat, throughout its historical experience America's desire to fight cleaner dirty wars has at times made winning more difficult, especially when the real military but not necessarily political answer has been to fight the insurgencies more on their own harsh terms. Compounding this quandary, counterinsurgent operations needed to produce material goods, such as a legitimate and effective government, a dilemma that insurgents did not have to face. In addition, the usual asymmetry of stakes always makes victory that much more elusive: the insurgents are so committed that they are readily willing to die for the cause while American troops are understandably doing their best just to get home alive. In other words, insurgents wage total war whereas U.S. forces, which are actually structured for full-scale war, and the local forces they are backing are fighting a limited war.[5]

> Maybe great nations do not learn lessons, they relearn them. – Peggy Noonan[6]

Some observers have looked at American dirty wars and, drawing especially on the searing Iraq and Afghanistan experiences, have concluded that courageous and effective national leaders, overlapping national interests between "allied" countries, and capable and legitimate governments and security forces are the indispensable elements for any lasting success.[7] For example, scholar Francis Fukuyama wrote in 2011, "In the end no counterinsurgency will ever be won with foreign forces taking the lead. Nor will there ever be an exit for the U.S. from the conflict other than humiliating defeats unless there is an indigenous government and army to eventually carry the burden."[8]

While Fukuyama is right to emphasize the need for strong domestic forces, the very irregular nature of dirty wars ensures that they will be governed by no hard and fast scientific laws. With this intentional intellectual modesty in hand, this book has attempted to fill the gap regarding what we have learned (and often unlearned) during these two and a half centuries of America's experiences with dirty wars.

Not surprisingly, many scholars believe there is a distinct American way of war.[9] It is, in this view, generally characterized by inherent strategic impatience, cultural ignorance, a lack of historical reflection, hypersensitivity to casualties, and obsessive reliance on overwhelming firepower. As we have seen in this survey of the American odyssey in dirty wars, the United States is sometimes guilty on all charges. At the same time, though, the U.S. legacy is far more varied than this depiction. To be sure, in this book we have seen in the experiences of others – the British in the Boer War and Malayan Emergency or the French in Indochina or Algeria – that the United States is not the only global power that has suffered from these cultural defects.

As the foregoing chapters of this book have attempted to make clear, nothing in the American approach to fighting dirty wars is immutable. The nation has had many points of reference for each successive dirty war that it has fought. In some cases, it has applied the experience of the past to great strategic success as we saw in the tough lessons learned in El Salvador that American policymakers applied to Colombia's seemingly intractable narco-conflict a decade later. In other cases, it has failed to apply them, or applied the wrong lessons altogether. The Military Assistance Advisory Groups (MAAGs) that worked relatively successfully in Greece and the Philippines in the 1940s and 1950s, to take one example, were insufficient or ill-suited for the jungles of Vietnam. Similarly, the tenets of the 2006 *Counterinsurgency Field Manual* were ultimately strategically effective in Iraq but were a relatively poor match for the concomitant Afghan conflict.

Perhaps the American nation-building and bandit chasing experiences in the Philippines starting in 1898 provide the most salient examples of the intractable nature of American dirty war endeavors. At once, U.S. politicians and military forces committed excesses or errors that undermined the American effort. At the same time, however, the United States did learn from its mistakes, and its effort at establishing a more inclusive colonial administration was relatively benign compared to the nation-building of other imperial powers at the time.

None of this is somehow to excuse American mistakes or atrocities; on the contrary, our task has been to consider as many of these elements and arguments as possible to develop a fuller sense of this historical legacy – and what might be in store for the United States in its likely future involvement in dirty wars. That dirty wars are unpleasant or might appear to some to be more aberrations than the central focus of America's military history does not mean that we should avoid understanding them, or the United States' involvement in them. Rather, we should hope that the deeper our knowledge of the past goes, the more likely we are to apply its lessons correctly even if we know all too well that this step alone does not ensure success.

IF IT WORKS...

"There are no easy shortcuts to solving problems of revolutionary war. In fact, I would like to close with one last thought, which applies, of course, to everything that is done in the armed forces, but particularly to revolutionary warfare: If it works, it is obsolete."[10] This prescient admonition from Bernard Fall, a veteran of the French Underground during World War II and Indochina in the 1950s, is a fitting reminder about the eternal difficulties of trying to devise any fully satisfying model or prescription for our understanding of irregular warfare. To paraphrase Leo Tolstoy – who opened his epic novel *Anna Karenina*, "Happy families are all alike; every unhappy family is unhappy in its own way" – for America, every dirty war is dirty in its own way.

EPILOGUE

"I Feel More Like a Monster"

He [a U.S. soldier in Iraq] thought of himself as a patriot who had enlisted in the Army for the noblest of reasons: to contribute and to make some kind of difference. Then he punched his first Iraqi in the face, and pushed his first Iraqi down the stairs. Now he was back in the United States, crying and telling his wife, Sascha, "I feel more like a monster."[1]

It is indeed true that in war there are no unwounded soldiers. And America's dirty wars are no exception. The bombs that shred limbs also hammer brains.[2] Post-traumatic stress disorder (or PTSD) is the mental health condition sparked by some type of isolated or sustained psychological terror or by traumatic brain injury, a physiological injury that occurs when the brain is rocked so violently that it collides with the inside of the skull yielding psychological damage.[3]

A decade of dirty war battles in Iraq and Afghanistan wrought enormous psychological damage on American troops. Around two million Americans served in the two wars, many of whom were deployed multiple times. If the many medical studies prove accurate, roughly 500,000 of these servicemen and women will have developed PTSD in varying degrees. Further indicating the degree of post-combat issues, approximately half of the military personnel deployed to these two wars have requested disability benefits from the U.S. government. For comparison, only 21 percent of veterans of the Persian Gulf War in 1991 sought disability.[4]

Many veterans are reluctant to report their condition and instead self-medicate. A study from the U.S. Department of Veteran Affairs (VA) found that veterans suffering from PTSD or depression were about four times more likely than other veterans to have drug or alcohol problems. The VA also reported that on average twenty-two veterans committed suicide each day in 2010.[5]

The cost to the American government of treating PTSD sufferers is already in the multiples of billions; it will be many decades before we know the total cost of PTSD for Iraq and Afghanistan veterans. In September 2013, *The New Yorker* magazine profiled Iraq veteran and PTSD sufferer Nic DeNinno who recalled some of his behavior during his combat tour, which appears psychotic (or deranged) to him today. His graphic memories are a terrifying but necessary reminder of some of the inescapable consequences of the wars that constitute the American experience:

> We used to occupy an Iraqi police station. And every once in a while the Iraqi police would bring in dead bodies, a couple of dead bodies. They'd throw 'em in the back of a truck, bring 'em in, shit like that, and at the time – this was the beginning of my deployment – we'd all run down there and take pictures. You know? And one guy – his head was all bloated and shit, because it had been sitting in raw sewage, you know? And now I can't get those images out of my mind. At the time, though, it was "Yeah, this is cool. This is so cool." I mean, what were we thinking? Why did we even want to go look at that shit? You know ... Horrible, horrible stuff. Us hanging out with dead bodies. At the time, I mean we were rockin' and rollin', we were mean, mean killing machines. Now I look back and I'm, like, God, what were we doing? What were we thinking?[6]

Notes

Chapter 1. Introduction

1. Greg Jaffe, "Petraeus, Not a Hero, but Not a Failure," *Washington Post*, November 30, 2012.
2. Michael Hastings, "The Runaway General," *Rolling Stone*, June 25, 2010, http://www.rollingstone.com/politics/news/the-runaway-general-20100622.
3. Jaffe, "Petraeus, Not a Hero, but Not a Failure."
4. Ibid.
5. For more discussion on the American approach to war, see Dominic Tierney, *How We Fight: Crusades, Quagmires, and the American Way of War*. New York: Little, Brown, 2010, 1–12. Tierney offers the useful framework of the "crusade tradition" where the United States fights in interstate wars. This is contrasted with the other prominent legacy, the "quagmire tradition" where America finds itself conducting "nation-building" (his term for counterinsurgency) in places like Vietnam and Afghanistan.
6. See Thomas G. Paterson, *On Every Front: The Making and the Unmaking of the Cold War*. New York: Norton, 1993.
7. Bales's awards included the Army Commendation Medal, Global War on Terrorism Expeditionary Medal, and Iraq Campaign Medal, and nine others. See "Army Identifies Shooting Suspect," www.defense.gov, retrieved July 23, 2012.
8. At the same time these atrocities came to light, a *New York Times* poll revealed that 69 percent of Americans thought the United States should no longer be at war in Afghanistan, while another poll indicated that a similar number of respondents supported bringing home the troops as soon as possible. After a long and arduous counterinsurgency effort, both numbers indicated that Afghanistan in early 2012 was at least as unpopular as the Iraq war in its worst moments in 2006 and 2007. The polls also followed a number of high-profile killings of American troops by their Afghan partners, a trend that the top American commander in Afghanistan General John R. Allen described to journalists at a Pentagon news conference as "characteristic of this kind of warfare." In irregular conflicts like Afghanistan, where training and professionalizing local security forces is paramount, he warned that "the enemy's going to do all that they can to disrupt both the counterinsurgency operation, but also ... the integrity of the indigenous forces." Without a doubt, the

inherent challenge of these contexts put the members of the U.S. armed forces under considerable mental strain, with Bales's actions in Afghanistan providing the most tragic of reminders. Having pled guilty of killing sixteen Afghans to avoid the death penalty, in August 2013 Bales was sentenced to life in prison without parole. See Graham Bowley and Alissa Rubin, "U.S. Condemns Soldiers with Body Parts," *New York Times*, April 18, 2012; Elizabeth Bumiller and Allison Kopicki, "Support in U.S. for Afghan War Drops Sharply, Poll Finds," *New York Times*, March 26, 2012; Jack Healy, "Soldier Sentenced to Life in without Parole for Killing 16 Afghans," *New York Times*, August 23, 2013.
9. "Congressional Testimony of Mr. John S. Smith," transcript included in the PBS program "The West," http://www.pbs.org/weta/thewest/resources/archives/four/sandcrk.htm#smith (accessed March 28, 2012).
10. Quoted in Stan Hoig, *The Sand Creek Massacre*. Norman: University of Oklahoma Press, 1974, 153.
11. Quoted in Ian F. W. Beckett, *Modern Insurgencies and Counterinsurgencies: Guerrillas and Their Opponents since 1750*. New York: Routledge, 2001.
12. The formal title is the "Convention (III) Relative to the Treatment of Prisoners of War, Geneva, August 12, 1949." The full text can be found at http://www.icrc.org/ihl.nsf/FULL/375 (accessed December 20, 2012).
13. Richard J. Evans, "The Truth about World War II," *New York Review of Books*, October 11, 2012, 52–6; also see Antony Beevor, *The Second World War*. New York: Little, Brown, 2012.
14. http://www.atomicarchive.com/Docs/MED/med_chp10.shtml.
15. Tierney, *How We Fight*, 244.
16. Gideon Rose, *How Wars End*. New York: Simon and Schuster, 2011, 278.
17. Tierney, *How We Fight*, 8.
18. David H. Petraeus, "Learning Counterinsurgency: Observations from Soldiering in Iraq," *Military Review* 86:4 (January/February 2006): 2–12.
19. Gil Gerom, *How Democracies Lose Small Wars: State, Society, and the Failures of France in Algeria, Israel in Lebanon, and the United States in Vietnam*. New York: Cambridge University Press, 2003, 15.
20. Erik Claessen, "Discouraging Hearts and Minds: Democracies and Insurgencies," *Military Review* (May–June 2007): 97–103.
21. Ibid.
22. Colonel John Waghelstein quoted in Lydia Chavez, "The Odds in El Salvador," *New York Times*, July 24, 1983.
23. Russell F. Weigley, *The History of the United States Army*. New York: Macmillan, 1967, 161; also see John D. Waghelstein "What's Wrong in Iraq? Or, Ruminations of a Pachyderm," *Military Review* (January–February 2006): 112–17; Janine A. Davidson, *Lifting the Fog of Peace: How Americans Learned to Fight Modern War*. Ann Arbor: University of Michigan Press, 2010.

Chapter 2. Irregular Warfare 101

1. Quoted in Anthony James Joes, *Resisting Rebellion: The History and Politics of Counterinsurgency*. Lexington: University Press of Kentucky, 2004, 8.

2. Kilcullen, "Counterinsurgency Redux"; for how insurgencies form and end, see Paul Collier, "Rebellion as a Quasi-Criminal Activity," *Journal of Conflict Resolution* 44 (2000): 839–53; James D. Fearon and David D. Laitin, "Ethnicity, Insurgency, and Civil War," *American Political Science Review* 97:1 (February 2003): 75–90.
3. Tierney, *How We Fight*, 14.
4. David Kilcullen, *Counterinsurgency*. New York: Oxford University Press, 2010, x.
5. Ibid., 1.
6. For an excellent discussion of the various definitions of terrorism, see Bruce Hoffman, *Inside Terrorism*. New York: Columbia University Press, 2006, 1–42.
7. Terror is a potent force of any side during warfare. In the London blitz of World War II, the German Luftwaffe traumatized the population of London by its relentless bombing of that city, followed by the unspeakable terror of the V1 and V2 rockets that rained down destruction. When the British government made the decision to target German cities, using incendiary bombs, the United States, as an ally of Britain, took part.

American air commanders considered themselves "precision bombers," which implied that their targets were carefully chosen military installations, although only half of the U.S. Eighth Air Force's payloads were dropped using radar techniques to guide them to a chosen target. And American forces did not shy from using the most lethal weapons available to terrify the enemy population. In the Utah desert, Hollywood set makers and engineers from Standard Oil built two replica working-class neighborhoods, one German and the other Japanese; repeated fire-bombings of the "neighborhoods" led to the development of incendiaries that could punch through stout German roofs. Another devastating device, the M-76 Block Burner, first deployed in March 1944, "spattered incendiary gel in big, burning gobs."

In the end, incendiary devices probably caused as much death and devastation as any other weapon used in World War II. (Allied bombers attacked 131 German cities during the war, leaving 400,000 dead and 7 million homeless.) The destruction of German cities stopped in 1945 simply because there were so few targets left to annihilate. With regard to the Pacific campaign, American planes bombed Tokyo for three years, but the raids of March 10, 1945, were cataclysmic. Walls of flame from the incendiary bombs "sow[ed] the sky with fire": 100,000 people were killed and 16 square miles of the city were destroyed. See Rick Atkinson, *The Guns at Last Light: The War in Western Europe, 1944–45*. New York: Henry Holt, 300–370.
8. Jeffrey Record, *Beating Goliath: Why Insurgencies Win*. Washington, DC: Potomac Books, 2007, 9.
9. Kilcullen, *Counterinsurgency*, 12.
10. John S. Putsay, *Counterinsurgency Warfare*. New York: Free Press, 1965, 23; also see Gerom, *How Democracies Lose Small Wars*, 46.
11. Carl von Clausewitz, quoted in Record, *Beating Goliath*, 131.

12. Jerry, M. Tinker, Andrew R. Molnar, and John D. LeNoir, eds., *Strategies of Revolutionary Warfare*. New Dehli: S. Chand, 1968, 1.
13. Robert Asprey, *War in the Shadows: The Guerrilla in History*. New York: Doubleday, 1975, 1–5.
14. David Rooney, *Guerrilla: Insurgents, Patriots, and Terrorists from Sun Tzu to Bin Laden*. London: Brassey's, 2004, 7.
15. Sun Tzu, *The Art of War*. Mineola, NY: Dover, 2002, 42.
16. Quoted in ibid., 13.
17. Quoted in Joes, *Resisting Rebellion*, 8.
18. Sun Tzu, *The Art of War*, 55.
19. Ibid., 57.
20. Rooney, *Guerrilla*, 30.
21. Edward N. Luttwak, "Dead End: Counterinsurgency Warfare as Military Malpractice," *Harper's Magazine*, February 2007, 33–4; Karl Eikenberry, "The Limits of Counterinsurgency Doctrine in Afghanistan," *Foreign Affairs* (September/October 2013); Gian Gentile, *Wrong Turn: America's Deadly Embrace of Counterinsurgency*. New York: Free Press, 2013.
22. Quoted in Steve Douglas, "Napoleon at the Gates of Baghdad." *Executive Intelligence Review*, April 1, 2005.
23. Tinker, et al., *Strategies of Revolutionary Warfare*, 1.
24. Beckett, *Modern Insurgencies and Counterinsurgencies*, 7.
25. Douglas, "Napoleon at the Gates of Baghdad."
26. Beckett, *Modern Insurgencies and Counterinsurgencies*, 27.
27. Quoted in Douglas, "Napoleon at the Gates of Baghdad."
28. Quoted in ibid.
29. Beatrice Heuser, "Introduction to *On War*," in Carl von Clausewitz, *On War*. New York: Oxford University Press, 2007, viii.
30. Clausewitz, *On War*, 13.
31. Record, *Beating Goliath*, 2.
32. Heuser, "Introduction to *On War*," xxii.
33. Clausewitz, *On War*, 160–1.
34. Ibid., 160–1.
35. Ibid., 184–7.
36. Ibid., 188.
37. Ibid., 186.
38. Ibid., 189–90.
39. Quoted in Heuser, "Introduction to *On War*," viii.
40. C. E. Callwell, *Small Wars: Their Principles and Practice*. Lincoln: University of Nebraska Press, 1996.
41. Quoted in Joes, *Resisting Rebellion*, 8.
42. Beckett, *Modern Insurgencies and Counterinsurgencies*, 32.
43. Quoted in Asprey, *War in the Shadows: The Guerrilla in History*, 224.
44. See Ronald Schaffer, "The 1940s Small Wars Manual and the 'Lessons of History,'" *Military Affairs* 36 (1972): 46–51.

Chapter 3. The American Revolution

1. Quotation written on a display inside the museum at the Visitor Center at Kings Mountain National Military Park, Kings Mountain, South Carolina.
2. Quoted in J. D. Bailey, *Commanders at Kings Mountain*. Greenville, SC: A Press, 1980, 415.
3. Ibid., 42.
4. Ibid., 137.
5. Quoted in Wilma Dykeman, *With Fire and Sword: The Battle of Kings Mountain 1780*. Washington, DC, U.S. Department of the Interior, National Park Service, (pamphlet).
6. "Alexander Chesney's Diary," *The Battle of Kings Mountain: Eyewitness Accounts*, ed. Robert M. Dunkerly. Charleston, SC: History Press, 132.
7. J. David Dameron. *Kings Mountain: The Defeat of the Loyalists, October 7, 1780*. Cambridge, MA: Da Capo Press, 2003, 88.
8. *George Washington: A Collection*, ed. W. B. Allen. Indianapolis, IN: Liberty Classics, 1988, 23.
9. Marshall Smelser, "An Understanding of the American Revolution," *Review of Politics* 38:3 Bicentennial Issue (July, 1976): 31.
10. Dave Richard Palmer, *The Way of the Fox: American Strategy in the War for America, 1775–1783*. Westport, CT: Greenwood, 1975, 97.
11. Ibid., 11.
12. John Richard Alden, *The American Revolution, 1775–1783*. New York: Harper, 1954, 33.
13. Page Smith, *A New Age Now Begins: A People's History of the American Revolution*, vol. 1. New York: McGraw-Hill, 1976, 525.
14. Max Boot, "The Evolution of Irregular War," *Foreign Affairs* (February 2013).
15. Smith, *A New Age Now Begins*, vol. 1, 484.
16. Ibid, 484–6.
17. Ibid, 486.
18. Joseph J. Ellis, *American Creation: Triumphs and Tragedies at the Founding of the Republic*. New York: Alfred A. Knopf, 2007, 838.
19. Smith, *A New Age Now Begins*, vol. 1, 822.
20. Palmer, *The Way of the Fox*, xvii.
21. Ellis, *American Creation*, 61.
22. Alden, *The American Revolution*, 213.
23. Smith, *A New Age Now Begins*, vol. 2. New York: McGraw-Hill, 1976, 1436.
24. Quoted in William Gilmore Simms, *The Life of Francis Marion*. New York, H. G. Langley, 1844, 87.
25. Quoted in Smith, *A New Age Now Begins*, vol. 2, 1437.
26. Quoted in ibid.
27. George Cornwallis, quoted in ibid., 1438.
28. Max Boot, *Invisible Armies: An Epic History of Guerrilla Warfare from Ancient Times to the Present*. New York: Liveright, 2013, 74.
29. Smith, *A New Age Now Begins*, vol. 2, 1454.

Chapter 4. Confederates and Indians

1. James A. Ramage, *Gray Ghost: The Life of Col. John Singleton Mosby*. Lexington: University Press of Kentucky, 1999, 174–5.
2. John J. Tierney Jr., *Chasing Ghosts: Unconventional Warfare in American History*. Washington, DC: Potomac Books, 2006, 53–9.
3. Ibid., 54.
4. John Ellis, *A Short History of Guerrilla Warfare*. New York: St. Martin's Press, 1976, 84.
5. Kevin H. Siepel, *Rebel: The Life and Times of John Singleton Mosby*. New York: St. Martin's Press, 1983, 69.
6. Ibid., 70.
7. Joes, *Resisting Rebellion*, 15.
8. Siepel, *Rebel*, 75.
9. Tierney, *Chasing Ghosts*, 59.
10. Siepel, *Rebel*, 77.
11. Ramage, *Gray Ghost*, 165.
12. Ibid., 165.
13. Robert R. Mackey, *The Uncivil War: Irregular Warfare in the Upper South, 1861–1865*. Norman: University of Oklahoma Press, 2004, 100.
14. Tierney, *Chasing Ghosts*, 54.
15. Quoted in Ellis, *A Short History*, 86; also see Mark Moyar, *A Question of Command: Counterinsurgency from the Civil War to Iraq*. New Haven, CT: Yale University Press, 2009.
16. Ellis, *A Short History*, 88.
17. Lee Kennett, *Marching through Georgia: The Story of Soldiers and Civilians during Sherman's Campaign*. New York: HarperCollins, 1995, 65.
18. Ibid., 12.
19. Mills Lane, *War Is Hell: William T. Sherman's Personal Narrative of His March through Georgia*. Savannah, GA: Beehive Press, 1974, xxi.
20. Kennett, *Marching through Georgia*, 211.
21. Lane, *War Is Hell*, 105.
22. Wilson Angley, Jerry L. Cross, and Michael Hill, *Sherman's March through North Carolina: A Chronology*. Raleigh: North Carolina Division of Archives and History, 1995, 51.
23. Kennett, *Marching through Georgia*, 206.
24. Ibid., 201.
25. Lane, *War Is Hell*, xxi.
26. Angley et al., *Sherman's March through North Carolina*, 57.
27. Thomas A. Britten, *A Brief History of the Seminole-Negro Indian Scouts*. Lewiston, NY: Edwin Mellen Press, 1999, 34.
28. James W. Covington, *The Seminoles of Florida*. Gainesville: University Press of Florida, 1993, 72.
29. David Galula, *Counterinsurgency Warfare: Theory and Practice*. Westport, CT: Praeger Security International, 2006, 4.
30. Ibid., 48.
31. Ibid., 24.

Notes to pages 54–72

32. Robert V. Remini, *Andrew Jackson and His Indian Wars*. New York: Viking, 2001, 275.
33. Covington, *The Seminoles of Florida*, 91.
34. Brent Richards Weisman, *Unconquered People: Florida's Seminole and Miccosukee Indians*. Gainesville: University Press of Florida, 1999, 56.
35. "Florida War." *The National Era*, May 11, 1848.
36. John D. McDermott, *A Guide to the Indian Wars of the West*. Lincoln: University of Nebraska Press, 1998, 49.
37. Ibid., 51.
38. John A. Nagl, *Learning to Eat Soup with a Knife: Counterinsurgency Lessons from Malaya and Vietnam*. Chicago: University of Chicago Press, 2005, 44.
39. McDermott, *A Guide to the Indian Wars*, 55.
40. John Tebbel, *The Compact History of the Indian Wars*. New York: Hawthorn Books, 1966, 256.
41. Nagl, *Learning to Eat Soup with a Knife*, 44.
42. Odie B. Faulk, *The Geronimo Campaign*. New York: Oxford University Press, 1969, 34.
43. Ibid., 132.
44. Larry McMurtry, "The Star Attraction," *New York Review of Books*, January 10, 2013.
45. Faulk, *The Geronimo Campaign*, 152.

Chapter 5. Intermezzo: The Boer War, 1899–1902

1. Thomas Pakenham, *The Boer War*. New York: Random House, 1979, 566.
2. Anthony James Joes. *Resisting Rebellion: The History and Politics of Counterinsurgency*. Lexington: University Press of Kentucky, 2004, 100.
3. Pakenham, *The Boer War*, xiii.
4. Joes, *Resisting Rebellion*.
5. Rooney, *Guerrilla: Insurgents, Patriots, and Terrorists*, 71.
6. Beckett, *Modern Insurgencies and Counterinsurgencies*, 38.
7. Gil Merom, *How Democracies Lose Small Wars: State, Society, and the Failures of France in Algeria, Israel in Lebanon, and the United States in Vietnam*. New York: Cambridge University Press, 2003, 39.
8. Rooney, *Guerrilla: Insurgents, Patriots, and Terrorists*, 82; also see Joes, *Resisting Rebellion*, 100.
9. Pakenham. *The Boer War*, 579.
10. Joes, *Resisting Rebellion*, 106.
11. Quoted in ibid., 107.
12. Pakenham, *The Boer War*, 571.

Chapter 6. America, Aguinaldo, and the Philippines, 1898

1. Quoted in David Haward Bain, *Sitting in Darkness: Americans in the Philippines*. New York: Houghton Mifflin, 1984, 88.

2. Anthony James Joes, "Counterinsurgency in the Philippines, 1898–1954," in Daniel Marston and Carter Malkasian, eds., *Counterinsurgency in Modern Warfare*. London: Osprey, 37–54.
3. Quoted in Bain, *Sitting in Darkness: Americans in the Philippines*, 70.
4. Tierney, *Chasing Ghosts*, 105.
5. Lars Schoultz, *Beneath the United States: A History of U.S. Policy toward Latin America*. Cambridge: Harvard University Press, 1998, 140.
6. Quoted in Leon Wolff, *Little Brown Brother: America's Forgotten Bid for Empire Which Cost 250,000 Lives*. London: Longmans, Green, 1961, 57–58.
7. Robert D. Kaplan, *Imperial Grunts: The American Military on the Ground*. New York: Random House, 2005, 136.
8. Quoted in Stuart Creighton Miller, *Benevolent Assimilation: The American Conquest of the Philippines, 1899–1903*. New Haven, CT: Yale University Press, 1982, 35.
9. Brian Linn, *The U.S. Army and Counterinsurgency in the Philippine War, 1899–1902*. Chapel Hill: University of North Carolina Press, 1989, 5.
10. Ibid., 7.
11. Ibid., 5–10.
12. Quoted in Miller, *Benevolent Assimilation*, 40.
13. Ibid., 42.
14. Linn, *U.S. Army and Counterinsurgency*, 2.
15. Joes, "Counterinsurgency in the Philippines," 44.
16. Linn, *U.S. Army and Counterinsurgency*, 9.
17. Quoted in Miller, *Benevolent Assimilation*, 13.
18. Quoted in ibid., 27.
19. Quoted in ibid., 27.
20. Quoted in ibid., 27.
21. Paul Kramer, "The Water Cure," *New Yorker*, February 25, 2008.
22. Quoted in Miller, *Benevolent Assimilation*, 13.
23. Linn, *U.S. Army and Counterinsurgency*, 12.
24. Ivan Musicant, *The Banana Wars: A History of United States Military Intervention in Latin America from the Spanish-American War to the Invasion of Panama*. New York: Macmillan, 1990, 23.
25. Quoted in Linn, *U.S. Army and Counterinsurgency*, 21.
26. Tierney, *Chasing Ghosts*, 108.
27. Mark Grimsley, "The Philippine War, 1899–1902," http://people.cohums.ohio-state.edu/grimsley1/milhis/phil.htm (accessed 14 August 2008).
28. Linn, *U.S. Army and Counterinsurgency*, 14.
29. Quoted in ibid., 21.
30. William Sexton quoted in Tierney, *Chasing Ghosts*, 111. Original in William Sexton, *Soldiers in the Philippines: A History of the Insurrection*. Washington, DC: Infantry Journal Press, 1944.
31. Joes, "Counterinsurgency in the Philippines," 37–54.
32. Quoted in Wolff, *Little Brown Brother*, 262–63.
33. Quoted in Miller, *Benevolent Assimilation*, 98.
34. Quoted in Linn, *U.S. Army and Counterinsurgency*, 22.
35. Joes, "Counterinsurgency in the Philippines," 37–54.

36. Quoted in "The President Welcomes President Chirac to the White House," *The White House*, November 6, 2001, http://www.whitehouse.gov/news/releases/2001/11/20011106-4.html (accessed 15 August 2008).
37. Quoted in Miller, *Benevolent Assimilation*, 208.
38. Sam C. Sarkesian, *America's Forgotten Wars: The Counterrevolutionary Past and Lessons for the Future*. Westport, CT: Greenwood Press, 1984, 175.
39. Quoted in Bain, *Sitting in Darkness*, 215.
40. Joes, *Resisting Rebellion*, 125.
41. Quoted in Linn, *U.S. Army and Counterinsurgency*, 22.
42. Quoted in Miller, *Benevolent Assimilation*, 267.
43. Quoted in ibid., 69.
44. Kramer, "The Water Cure."
45. Quoted in Joes, "Counterinsurgency in the Philippines," 45.
46. Quoted in Tierney, *Chasing Ghosts*, 126.
47. Sarkesian, *America's Forgotten Wars*, 175–80.
48. Quoted in Tierney, *Chasing Ghosts*, 132.
49. Quoted in Kramer, "The Water Cure."
50. Joes, *Resisting Rebellion*, 149.
51. Max Boot, *The Savage Wars of Peace: Small Wars and the Rise of American Power*. New York: Basic Books, 2002, 55.
52. Kaplan, *Imperial Grunts*, 140.
53. Quoted in Kramer, "The Water Cure."

Chapter 7. Chasing Villa, 1916

1. Frank Tompkins, *Chasing Villa*. Harrisburg, PA: Military Service Publishing, 1934.
2. Candice Millard, *The River of Doubt: Theodore Roosevelt's Darkest Journey*. New York: Anchor, 2005, 87.
3. Boot, *Savage Wars of Peace*, 183.
4. Haldeen Braddy, *The Paradox of Pancho Villa*. El Paso: Texas Western College Press, 1978, 49.
5. Quoted in John S. D. Eisenhower, *Intervention! The United States and the Mexican Revolution, 1913–17*. New York: W. W. Norton, 1993, 217.
6. Rachel St. John, *Line in the Sand: A History of the Western U.S.-Mexico Border*. Princeton, NJ: Princeton University Press, 2011, 132.
7. Tompkins, *Chasing Villa*, 226.
8. Quoted in ibid., 227.
9. Quoted in ibid., 231.
10. Quoted in Eisenhower, *Intervention!*, 235.
11. W. B. Shaw, "Pershing on the Trail," *Review of Reviews* 53 (April 1916): 419–21; Robert S. Thomas and Inez V. Allen, *The Mexican Punitive Expedition under Brigadier General John J. Pershing, United States Army, 1916–1917*. Washington, DC: Department of the Army, Office of the Chief of Military History, War Histories Division, 1954.
12. Quoted in St. John, *Line in the Sand*, 135.
13. Quoted in ibid., 136.

14. Tierney, *Chasing Ghosts*.
15. Haldeen Braddy. *Cock of the Walk: The Legend of Pancho Villa*. Albuquerque: University of New Mexico Press, 1955.
16. Quoted in Eisenhower, *Intervention!*, 253.
17. Quoted in Boot, *Savage Wars of Peace*, 195.
18. Quoted in Eisenhower, *Intervention!*, 236.
19. "The Attack on Our Cavalry at Parral," *Cavalry Journal* 27 (November 1916): 249–53; Edward A. Craig, "The Fight at Carrizal," *Leatherneck* 22 (March 1939): 6, 54–55.
20. Quoted in Eisenhower, *Intervention!*, 289.
21. Eisenhower, *Intervention!*, 299.
22. Quoted in Boot, *Savage Wars of Peace*, 204.

Chapter 8. A Cold Winter in Siberia

1. Boot, *Savage Wars of Peace*, 224.
2. Richard Goldhurst, *The Midnight War: The American Intervention in Russia, 1918–1920*. New York: McGraw-Hill, 1978, 267.
3. Dennis E. Showalter, "Manœuvre Warfare: The Eastern and Western Fronts, 1914–1915," in Hew Strachan, ed., *The Oxford Illustrated History of the First World War*. New York: Oxford University Press, 1998, 46–53.
4. Goldhurst, *The Midnight War*, 193.
5. Robert L. Willett, *Russian Sideshow: America's Undeclared War, 1918–1920*. Washington, DC: Brassey's, 2003, xxi.
6. Ibid., xxii.
7. Joel R. Moore, Harry H. Mead, and Lewis E. Jahns, eds., *The History of the American Expedition Fighting the Bolsheviki: Campaigning in North Russia, 1918–1919*. Detroit, MI: Polar Bear, 1920, 47–50.
8. Peter Kenez, *Civil War in South Russia, 1919–1920: The Defeat of the Whites*. Berkeley: University of California Press, 1977, 19–30.
9. Carol Wilcox Melton, *Between War and Peace: Woodrow Wilson and the American Expeditionary Force in Siberia, 1918–1920*. Macon, GA: Mercer University Press, 2001, 27.
10. Goldhurst, *The Midnight War*, xiv, 13; David S. Foglesong, *America's Secret War against Bolshevism: U.S. Intervention in the Russian Civil War, 1917–1920*. Chapel Hill: University of North Carolina Press, 2001, 11.
11. Betty Miller Unterberger, "American Intervention: A Brake on the Allies?," in Betty Miller Unterberger, ed., *American Intervention in the Russian Civil War*. Lexington, MA: Raytheon Education, 1969, 69–70; Melton, *Between War and Peace*, 16–17.
12. Boot, *The Savage Wars of Peace*, 211.
13. Moore, Mead, and Jahns, *The History of the American Expedition Fighting the Bolsheviki*, 47–50.
14. Melton, *Between War and Peace*, 27.
15. Carl J. Richard, *When the United States Invaded Russia: Woodrow Wilson's Siberian Disaster*. Lanham, MD: Rowman and Littlefield, 2012, 85.
16. Unterberger, "American Intervention," 69–70.

Notes to pages 106–116   483

17. Boot, *The Savage Wars of Peace*, 226–8.
18. Willett, *Russian Sideshow*, 3, 153.
19. Roger Crownover, *The United States Intervention in North Russia–1918, 1919*. Lewiston, NY: Edwin Mellen Press, 2001, 47–8.
20. Moore, Mead, and Jahns, *The History of the American Expedition Fighting the Bolsheviki*, 105–10.
21. Ibid., 105–8.
22. Ibid.
23. Ibid., 289.
24. Andrew J. Birtle, *U.S. Army Counterinsurgency and Contingency Operations Doctrine, 1860–1941*. Washington, DC: Center of Military History–United States Army, 2009, 219–26.
25. Goldhurst, *The Midnight War*, 213.
26. Birtle, *U.S. Army Counterinsurgency and Contingency Operations Doctrine*, 224.
27. Goldhurst, *The Midnight War*, 214.
28. Crownover, *The United States Intervention in North Russia*, 47–8.
29. Foglesong, *America's Secret War*, 220.
30. Goldhurst, *The Midnight War*, xiv.
31. Goldhurst, *The Midnight War*, 268.

Chapter 9. The Banana Wars, 1898–1930s

1. Quoted in Tierney, *Chasing Ghosts*, xv.
2. For an analysis of the rise of American power at this time, see Fareed Zakaria, *From Wealth to Power: The Unusual Origins of America's World Role*. Princeton, NJ: Princeton University Press, 1999.
3. Samuel Flagg Bemis, *The Latin America Policy of the United States: A Historical Interpretation*. New York: Harcourt, Brace, 1943, 129.
4. Ibid., 130.
5. Beckett, *Modern Insurgencies and Counterinsurgencies*.
6. Ibid., 32.
7. Musicant, *The Banana Wars*, 8.
8. David Healy, *Drive to Hegemony: The United States in the Caribbean: 1898–1917*. Madison: University of Wisconsin Press, 1988, 39.
9. For the address, see http://www.mtholyoke.edu/acad/intrel/mkinly2.htm (accessed May 26, 2008).
10. Quoted in Musicant, *The Banana Wars*, 40.
11. "The Teller Amendment," *The Congress of the United States*, in Robert H. Holden and Eric Zolov, eds., *Latin America and the United States: A Documentary History*. Oxford: Oxford University Press, 2000, 72–73.
12. "The Platt Amendment," *The Congress of the United States*, in Robert H. Holden and Eric Zolov, eds., *Latin America and the United States: A Documentary History*. Oxford: Oxford University Press, 2000, 81–82.
13. Theodore Roosevelt, "The Roosevelt Corollary to the Monroe Doctrine," in Robert H. Holden and Eric Zolov, eds., *Latin America and the United States: A Documentary History*. Oxford: Oxford University Press, 2000, 100–102.

14. Quoted in Musicant, *The Banana Wars*, 60.
15. Ibid., 159.
16. Ibid., 161.
17. Quoted in Schoultz, *Beneath the United States*, 232.
18. See Smedley D. Butler, *Old Gimlet Eye: The Adventures of Smedley D. Butler as Told to Lowell Thomas*. New York: Farrar and Rinehart, 1933; "Final Ceremonies in Haiti," *Marine Corps Gazette* 19 (November 1934): 20-1; John A. Gray, "Boucan Carre," *Marine Corps Gazette* 16 (November 1931): 28-32; John A. Gray, "Cul de Sac," *Marine Corps Gazette* 16 (February 1932): 41-4; G. H. Greathouse, "King of the Banana Wars," *Marine Corps Gazette* 44 (June 1960): 28-33; H. W. Snyder, "Butler at Fort Riviere," *Marine Corps Gazette* 64 (November 1980): 83-7; Thomas E. Thrasher, "The Taking of Fort Riviere," *Marine Corps Gazette* 15 (February 1931): 31-3, 64.
19. See Frank L. Bride, "The Gendarmerie d'Haiti," *Marine Corps Gazette* 3 (December 1918): 295-8; "The Carbon Copy Marine Corps," *Leatherneck* 17 (September 1934): 8-9, 48-9; "The Garde D'Haiti," *Leatherneck* 14 (September 1931): 9-11, 53; "The Haitianization of the Garde d'Haiti," *Leatherneck* 14 (March 1931): 12-14, 54; "The Haitian Gendarmerie," *Marine Corps Gazette* 11 (June 1926): 73-81; "History of the Gendarmerie D'Haiti," *Leatherneck* 10 (May, June, September, November 1927): 29; 33; 8; 10.
20. Quoted in Boot, *Savage Wars of Peace*, 167.
21. Quoted in Bemis, *The Latin America Policy of the United States*, 193.
22. Quoted in Boot, *Savage Wars of Peace*, 172-5.
23. Healy, *Drive to Hegemony*, 225.
24. Tierney, *Chasing Ghosts*, 172.
25. Quoted in ibid., 173.
26. Quoted in Musicant, *The Banana Wars*, 223.
27. Quoted in Tierney, *Chasing Ghosts*, 76.
28. Max Boot, *Savage Wars of Peace*, xx.
29. Fred Belton and John Rogers, "Unsung Heroes of the Marine Corps, No. 3," *Leatherneck* 14 (June 1931): 14, 44; John W. Blassingame, "The Press and American Intervention in Haiti and the Dominican Republic, 1904-1920," *Caribbean Studies* 9 (July 1969): 27-43.
30. Senator William Bruce in a 1928 debate about U.S. military activity in Nicaragua.
31. Quoted in Robert H. Holden and Eric Zolov, eds., *Latin America and the United States: A Documentary History*. Oxford: Oxford University Press, 2000, 103-4.
32. Tierney, *Chasing Ghosts*, 168.
33. Quoted in ibid., 167.
34. Boot, *Savage Wars of Peace*, 170-1.
35. W. M. Ancker, "The Imperialistic Mercenaries," *Marine Corps Gazette* 60 (March 1976): 60-2; Edward A. Fellowes, "Training Native Troops in Santo Domingo," *Marine Corps Gazette* 8 (December 1934): 215-33; Rufus

H. Lane, "Civil Government in Santo Domingo in the Early Days of the Military Occupation," *Marine Corps Gazette* 7 (June 1922): 127–46; "The Second Brigade Marines, Santo Domingo, D.R.," *Leatherneck* 7 (August 9, 1924): 1–2; Charles F. Williams, "La Guardia Nacional Dominicana," *Marine Corps Gazette* 3 (September 1918): 195–9.

36. Quoted in Musicant, *The Banana Wars*, 284.
37. See William R. Castle Jr., "Why Marines Are Landed," *Marine Corps Gazette* 19 (August 1934): 16–18; Clyde H. Metcalf, "The Marine Corps and the Changing Caribbean Policy," *Marine Corps Gazette* 21 (November 1937): 27–34, 68–72; Richard Millett, "The State Department's Navy: A History of the Special Service Squadron, 1920–1940," *American Neptune* 35 (April 1975): 118–38; E. W. Sturdevant, "Central America and the Marine Corps," *Marine Corps Gazette* 11 (March 1926): 24–31; John W. Thomas, "With the Special Service Squadron," *Marine Corps Gazette* 12 (June 1927): 76–81.
38. See Robert L. Bullard, "Military Pacification," *Journal of the Military Institution of the United States* 46 (January–February 1910): 1–24; Burgo D. Gill, "Guerrilla Warfare," *Quartermaster Review* 13 (September–October 1933): 27–9; Schaffer, "The 1940 Small Wars Manual and the 'Lessons of History,'" 46–51.
39. Quoted in Musicant, *The Banana Wars*, 55.

Chapter 10. Intermezzo: T. E. Lawrence and the Arab Revolt, 1916–1918

1. T. E. Lawrence, *Seven Pillars of Wisdom: A Triumph*. New York: Doubleday, Doran, 1935.
2. Quoted in Michael Sullivan, "Leadership in Counterinsurgency: A Tale of Two Leaders," *Military Review* 87:5 (September–October 2007): 119.
3. Lawrence, *Seven Pillars of Wisdom*, 188.
4. Jeremy Wilson, *Lawrence of Arabia: The Authorized Biography of T. E. Lawrence*. New York: Atheneum, 1990, 76.
5. Ibid., 95, 106.
6. Ibid., 247.
7. Leslie McLoughlin, *In a Sea of Knowledge: British Arabists in the Twentieth Century*. Reading, UK: Ithaca Press, 2002, 49–50.
8. Ibid., 301–7.
9. Basil Aboul-Enein and Youssef Aboul-Enein, "A Theoretical Explanation of Lawrence of Arabia's Inner Meanings on Guerrilla Warfare," *Small Wars Journal* (July 15, 2011), http://smallwarsjournal.com/jrnl/art/a-theoretical-exploration-of-lawrence-of-arabias-inner-meanings-on-guerrilla-warfare, 4.
10. Hugh Leach, "Lawrence's Strategy and Tactics in the Arab Revolt," *Asian Affairs* 37:3 (November 2006): 339.
11. Lawrence, *Seven Pillars of Wisdom*, 91, 97.
12. Ibid.
13. Aside from his skills and experience as a leader, Lawrence found Faisal an attractive head of the revolt because of his shared view of a unified Arab state

as the insurgency's ultimate end. Faisal promoted a "pan-Arab nationalism" that would transcend sectarian borders – an ideology that concomitantly preceded and emerged from the Arab Revolt itself – seeking to unite Greater Syria, Jordan, and Iraq with the Arabian Peninsula once the territories achieved their independence from the Ottoman Empire. See Nur-eldeen Masalha, "Faisal's Pan-Arabism, 1921–33," *Middle Eastern Studies* 27: 4 (October 1991): 679–93.
14. Sullivan, "Leadership in Counterinsurgency."
15. Wilson, *Lawrence of Arabia*, 364.
16. Lawrence, *Seven Pillars of Wisdom*, 104, 300–301.
17. Ibid., 301.
18. Ibid., 104.
19. Aboul-Enein and Aboul-Enein, "A Theoretical Explanation," 3.
20. Leach, *Lawrence's Strategies and* Tactics, 339.
21. Aboul-Enein and Aboul-Enein, "A Theoretical Explanation," 8.
22. Patricia A. Weitsman, *Dangerous Alliances: Proponents of Peace, Weapons of War*. California: Stanford University Press, 2004, 2; Glenn H. Snyder, "The Security Dilemma in Alliance Politics," *World Politics* 36: 4 (July 1984): 464.
23. These promises were put into writing in such documents as "The Declaration to the Seven Arabs" and the Husayn-McMahon correspondence.
24. Mary C. Wilson, "The Hashemites, the Arab Revolt, and Arab Nationalism," in Rashid Khalidi, Lisa Anderson, Muhammad Muslih, and Reeva S. Simon, eds., *The Origins of Arab Nationalism*. New York: Columbia University Press, 1991, 205.
25. Suleiman Mousa, "A Matter of Principle: King Hussein of the Hijaz and the Arabs of Palestine," *International Journal of Middle East Studies* 9:2 (April 1978): 183–94.
26. Lawrence, *Seven Pillars of Wisdom*, 276.
27. Ibid., 63.
28. Efraim Karsh and Inari Karsh, "Myth in the Desert, or Not the Great Arab Revolt," *Middle East Studies* 33:2 (April 1997): 287.
29. Lawrence, *Seven Pillars of Wisdom*, 25.
30. John C. Hulsman, "Think Again: Lawrence of Arabia," *Foreign Policy* (September 29, 2009), http://www.foreignpolicy.com/articles/2009/09/29/think_again_lawrence_of_arabia?page=0,0 (accessed March 25, 2012).
31. See http://wwi.lib.byu.edu/index.php/The_27_Articles_of_T.E._Lawrence (accessed March 25, 2012).
32. See ibid. (accessed March 12, 2012).
33. Hulsman, "Think Again: Lawrence of Arabia."
34. Dilip Hiro, "The Cost of an Afghan 'Victory,'" *The Nation*, February 15, 1999, http://www.thenation.com/article/cost-afghan-victory?page=0,0 (accessed May 29, 2012).
35. Ibid.
36. Saad Omar Khan, "The Caliphate Question: British Views and Policy toward Pan-Islamic Politics and the End of the Ottoman Empire," *American Journal of Islamic Social Sciences* 24: 4 (2007): 18.

Chapter 11. Chasing Sandino, 1927–1932

1. Quoted in Lester D. Langley, *The Banana Wars: United States Intervention in the Caribbean, 1898–1934.* Lanham, MD: Rowman and Littlefield, 190.
2. Healy, *The Drive to Hegemony*, 155.
3. Quoted in Schoultz, *Beneath the United States*, 261.
4. See Henry L. Stimson, *American Policy in Nicaragua.* New York: Charles Scribner's Sons, 1927; Clarence B. Proctor, "The Nicaraguan Expedition," *Leatherneck* 12 (June 1929): 55–6; Dion Williams, "The Nicaraguan Situation," *Marine Corps Gazette* 15 (November 1930): 55–7; Bullard, "Military Pacification," 1–24; Gill, "Guerrilla Warfare," 27–9.
5. Quoted in Bemis, *Latin America Policy of the United States*, 213; also see Bruce Gundmundsson, "The First of the Banana Wars: U.S. Marines in Nicaragua, 1909–12," in Daniel Marston and Carter Malkasian, eds., *Counterinsurgency in Modern Warfare.* London: Osprey, 2008, 55–69.
6. Quoted in Boot, *Savage Wars of Peace*, 235.
7. Quoted in Karl Bermann, *Under the Big Stick: Nicaragua and the United States since 1848.* Boston: South End Press, 1986, 193
8. Quoted in Robert Kagan, *A Twilight Struggle: American Power and Nicaragua, 1977–1990.* New York: Free Press, 1996, 14.
9. Quoted in Bermann, *Under the Big Stick*, 198.
10. Quoted in Langley, *The Banana Wars*, 189.
11. Quoted in Bermann, *Under the Big Stick*, 198.
12. Quoted in Ivan Musicant, *The Banana Wars: A History of United States Military Intervention in Latin America from the Spanish-American War to the Invasion of Panama.* New York: Macmillan, 1990, 310.
13. Quoted in ibid., 312.
14. Edwin Howard Simmons, *The United States Marines Corps: A History.* Annapolis, MD: U.S. Naval Institute Press, 2003, 115.
15. Boot, *Savage Wars of Peace*, 239.
16. Quoted in Bermann, *Under the Big Stick*, 203.
17. Quoted in Musicant, *The Banana Wars*, 303.
18. Larry Cable, *Conflict of Myths: The Development of American Counterinsurgency Doctrine and the Vietnam War.* New York: New York University Press, 1986, 106.
19. Quoted in Musicant, *The Banana Wars*, 328.
20. Quoted in Tony Lake. *Somoza Falling.* New York: Houghton Mifflin, 1989, 64.
21. Quoted in Bermann, *Under the Big Stick*, 203–4.
22. Quoted in Musicant, *The Banana Wars*, 328.
23. Quoted in Kagan, *A Twilight Struggle*, 17.
24. Quoted in Schoultz, *Beneath the United States*, 268.
25. Quoted in Musicant, *The Banana Wars*, 347.
26. Quoted in ibid., 348.
27. See "Air Operations in Nicaragua," *Leatherneck* 11 (September 1928): 9–51; Joseph L. Baylen, "Sandino: Patriot or Bandi," *Hispanic-American Historical Review* 31 (August 1951): 394–419; J. M. Broderick, "The Science of Jungle

Patrols," *Leatherneck* 16 (August 1933): 56–7; Raymond Lewis Buell, "Getting Out of Central America," *Nation* 135 (July 1932): 32–4; Evans F. Carlson, "The Guardia Nacional de Nicaragua," *Marine Corps Gazette* 21 (August 1937): 7–20.
28. John A. Daniels, "Don't Plan These Battles," *Marine Corps Gazette* 25 (September 1941): 43–6; Robert L. Denig, "Native Officer Corps, Guardia Nacional de Nicaragua," *Marine Corps Gazette* 17 (November 1932): 757; Harold W. Dodds, "American Supervision of the Nicaraguan Election," *Marine Corps Gazette* 14 (June 1929): 117–24; "The Evacuation of Nicaragua," *Leatherneck* 16 (January 1933): 5–7, 47; John A. Gray, "The Second Nicaraguan Campaign," *Marine Corps Gazette* 17 (February 1933): 36–41; Neill Macaulay, "Counterguerrilla Patrolling," *Marine Corps Gazette* 47 (July 1963): 45–8; "The Marines Return from Nicaragua," *Marine Corps Gazette* 17 (February 1933): 23–7; Roger W. Peard, "The Tactics of Bush Warfare," *Infantry Journal* 38 (September–October 1931): 408–15.
29. Quoted in Healy, *The Drive to Hegemony*, 270.
30. Quoted in Nagl, *Learning to Eat Soup with a Knife*, 47.
31. Schaffer, "The 1940 Small Wars Manual," 46–51; U.S. Marines Corps, *Small Wars Manual*. Pavilion, 2004.

Chapter 12. Cold War Counterinsurgencies

1. Quoted in Nagl, *Learning to Eat Soup with a Knife*, 125.
2. Quoted in D. Michael Shafer, *Deadly Paradigms: The Failure of U.S. Counterinsurgency Policy*. Princeton, NJ: Princeton University Press, 1988, 17.
3. Quoted in ibid., 104.
4. Quoted in ibid., 21.
5. Russell Weigley, *The American Way: A History of United States Military Strategy and Policy*. Bloomington: Indiana University Press, 1960, 456–7.
6. Ibid., 456–7.
7. Peter Beinart, *The Icarus Syndrome: A History of American Hubris*. New York: Harper, 2010, 143–4.
8. Quoted in Shafer, *Deadly Paradigms*, 101.
9. Quoted in ibid., 102.
10. Quoted in ibid., 110.
11. See Walt Rostow. "Guerrilla Warfare in the Undeveloped Areas," *Department of State Bulletin*, August 7, 1961.
12. John S. Putsay, *Counterinsurgency Warfare*. New York: Free Press, 1965, 165; also see Julian Paget, *Counterinsurgency Campaigning*. London: Faber and Faber, 1967.

Chapter 13. Intermezzo: Mao Zedong

1. Thomas X. Hammes, *The Sling and the Stone: On War in the 21st Century*. St. Paul, MN: Zenith Press, 2006, 46; Roderick MacFarquhar, "Who Was Mao Zedong?" *New York Review of Books*, October 25, 2012.
2. Beckett, *Modern Insurgencies and Counterinsurgencies*, 71.

Notes to pages 159–171   489

3. Hammes, *The Sling and the Stone*, 45; Boot, *Invisible Armies*, 332.
4. David Rooney, *Guerrilla: Insurgents, Patriots, and Terrorists from Sun Tzu to Bin Laden*. London: Brassey's, 2004, 137.
5. Beckett, *Modern Insurgencies and Counterinsurgencies*, 72.
6. Quoted in Mao Tse-Tung, *Basic Tactics*, 1937. English translation at http://www.marxists.org/reference/archive/mao/selected-works/volume-6/mswv6 _28.htm (accessed 24 January 2009).
7. Quoted in Putsay, *Counterinsurgency Warfare*, 37.
8. Quoted in ibid.
9. Quoted in ibid., 38.
10. Quoted in Beckett, *Modern Insurgencies and Counterinsurgencies*, 75.
11. Jonathan Mirsky, "Tibet: The CIA's Cancelled War," *New York Review of Books*, April 9, 2013.
12. Beinart, *Icarus Syndrome*, 121.
13. Ibid., 127.
14. Quoted in Mark W. Clark, *From the Danube to the Yalu*. New York: Harper and Brothers, 1954, 210–13; also see Mikel Dunham, *Buddha's Warriors: The Story of the CIA-Backed Tibetan Freedom Fighters, the Chinese Invasion, and the Ultimate Fall of Tibet*. New York: Penguin, 2004.
15. Ibid.

Chapter 14. Fighting Communism in Greece

1. Cable, *Conflicts of Myths*, 1.
2. John O. Latrides and Nicholas X. Rixopoulos, "The International Dimensions of the Greek Civil War," *World Policy Journal* 17:1 (Spring 2000): 3–33.
3. Mark, Mazower, *Inside Hitler's Greece*. New Haven, CT: Yale University Press, 1993, 373.
4. Cable, *Conflicts of Myths*, 11.
5. Quoted in Shafer, *Deadly Paradigms*, 178.
6. Quoted in ibid., 177.
7. "Special Message to the Congress on Greece and Turkey: The Truman Doctrine." 12 March 1947. Public Papers of the Presidents of the United States: Harry S. Truman, 1947. Washington, DC: GPO, 1963. The author would like to thank Blair McGraw for her assistance on the Greek Civil War.
8. Quoted in Cable, *Conflicts of Myths*, 15.
9. Quoted in Shafer, *Deadly Paradigms*, 187.
10. Beckett, *Modern Insurgencies and Counterinsurgencies*, 108.
11. Edgar O'Ballance, *The Greek Civil War, 1944–1949*. New York: Praeger, 1966, 153.
12. Quoted in Shafer, *Deadly Paradigms*, 194.
13. Quoted in John O. Iatrides, "George F. Kennan and the Birth of Containment," *World Policy Journal* 22:3 (Fall 2005): 126–45.
14. "An Interview of King Paul of Greece," *U.S. News and World Report*, April 21 1950, 29.

15. David H. Close and Thanos Veremis, "The Military Struggle, 1945–9," in David H. Close, ed., *The Greek Civil War, 1943–1950*. London: Routledge, 1993, 108; also see Timothy J. Lomperis, *From People's War to People's Rule*. Chapel Hill: University of North Carolina Press, 1996.
16. Anthony James Joes, *America and Guerrilla Warfare*. Lexington: University Press of Kentucky, 2000, 186.

Chapter 15. Intermezzo: France in Algeria, 1954–1962

1. Quoted in Peter Paret, *French Revolutionary Warfare from Indochina to Algeria: The Analysis of a Political and Military Doctrine*. New York: Praeger, 1964, 42.
2. Shafer, *Deadly Paradigms*, 135–60.
3. Quoted in ibid., 147.
4. Christopher Cradock and M. L. R. Smith, "No Fixed Values: A Reinterpretation of the Influence of the Theory of *Guerre Révolutionnaire* and the Battle of Algiers, 1956–1957," *Journal of Cold War Studies* 9:4 (Fall 2007): 68–105.
5. Paret, *French Revolutionary Warfare*, 10.
6. Quoted in ibid., 30; also see Bernard B. Fall, *Street without Joy: The French Debacle in Indochina*. Mechanicsburg, PA: Stackpole Books, 1994.
7. Edgar O'Ballance, *The Algerian Insurrection, 1954–62*. Hamden, CT: Archon Books, 1967, 63.
8. John Talbott, *The War without a Name, France in Algeria, 1954–62*. New York: Knopf, 1980.
9. Alistair Horne, *A Savage War of Peace: Algeria 1954–1962*. New York: New York Review of Books, 1977, 4.
10. Talbott, *The War without a Name*, 109–18.
11. Ibid., 112–19.
12. Ibid., 117.
13. Tinker et al., *Strategies of Revolutionary Warfare*.
14. Quoted in Gerom, *How Democracies Lose Small Wars*, 8; Boot, *Invisible Armies*, 370.
15. Beckett, *Modern Insurgencies and Counterinsurgencies*, 163.
16. Quoted in Horne, *A Savage War of Peace*, 195.
17. Quoted in Paret, *French Revolutionary Warfare*, 34.
18. Talbott, *The War without a Name*, 184.
19. Horne, *A Savage War of Peace*, 219–33.
20. Quoted in Paret, *French Revolutionary Warfare*, 67.
21. Quoted in Horne, *A Savage War of Peace*, 230.
22. Ibid., 221.
23. Gerom, *How Democracies Lose Small Wars*, 149.
24. Bernard Fall, *Two Vietnams: A Political and Military Analysis*. Boulder, CO: Westview Press, 1985, 257.
25. Beckett, *Modern Insurgencies and Counterinsurgencies*, 168.

Notes to pages 185–195   491

Chapter 16. Intermezzo: David Galula

1. Daniel Marston and Carter Malkasian, eds., *Counterinsurgency in Modern Warfare*. London: Osprey, 2008.
2. Galula, *Counterinsurgency Warfare*.
3. Thomas E. Ricks, *Fiasco: The American Military Adventure in Iraq*. New York: Penguin, 2006, 266.
4. Quoted in Galula, *Counterinsurgency Warfare*, 4.
5. Quoted in ibid., 50.
6. Quoted in ibid., 61–3.
7. Quoted in ibid., 62; David J. Kilcullen, "Countering Global Insurgency," *Journal of Strategic Studies*, 28:4 (August 2005): 597–617.
8. Quoted in Galula, *Counterinsurgency Warfare*, 52.
9. For a sense of the counterinsurgency thinking at the time, also see William J. Buchanan and Robert A. Hyatt, "Capitalizing on Guerrilla Vulnerabilities," *Military Review* 48 (August 1968): 3–40; William T. Decker, "Anti-Guerrilla Warfare," *Marine Corps Gazette* 30 (August 1951): 22–5.
10. See L. E. Haffner, "Guerrilla War and Common Sense," *Marine Corps Gazette* 46 (June 1962): 20–3; Otto Heilbrunn, "When Counterinsurgents Cannot Win," *Military Review* 49 (October 1969): 36–43; Edward G. Lansdale, "Civic Action Helps Counter the Guerrilla Threat," *Army Information Digest* 17 (June 1962): 50–3.
11. Lewis H. Gann, "Guerrillas and Insurgency: An Interpretative Survey," *Military Review* 46 (March 1966): 44–59; Gustav J. Gillert, "Counterinsurgency," *Military Review* 45 (April 1965): 25–33.
12. Kilcullen, "Counterinsurgency Redux," 111–30.
13. Ibid.
14. Ibid.
15. Ibid.

Chapter 17. Intermezzo: Malaya Emergency, 1948–1960

1. Richard Stubbs, *Hearts and Minds in Guerrilla Warfare: The Malaya Emergency, 1948–1968*. Singapore: Eastern University Press, 2004, 136.
2. Edgar O'Ballance, *Malaya: The Communist Insurgent War, 1948–60*. Hamden, CT: Archon Books, 1966, 114.
3. Thomas E. Willis, "Lessons from the Past: Successful British Counterinsurgency Operations in Malaya, 1948–1960," *Infantry Magazine*, July–August 2005.
4. Robert Jackson, *The Malayan Emergency: The Commonwealth's Wars, 1948–1966*. London: Routledge, 1991, 13.
5. Willis, "Lessons from the Past."
6. O'Ballance, *Malaya: The Communist Insurgent War*, 109.
7. Ibid., 112.
8. Paget, *Counterinsurgency Campaigning*, 61.
9. Sir Gerald Templer, quoted in Cable, *Conflicts of Myths*, 86.
10. Stubbs, *Hearts and Minds in Guerrilla Warfare*, 146.

11. Sullivan, "Leadership in Counterinsurgency."
12. Fifteen years later, Templer referred to this term as "the nauseating phrase I think I invented." See Stubbs, *Hearts and Minds in Guerrilla Warfare*, 1.
13. Moyar, *A Question of Command*, 126.
14. Quoted in Paget. *Counterinsurgency Campaigning*, 71.
15. Quoted in ibid.
16. Quoted in ibid., 68.
17. Cable, *Conflicts of Myths*, 89; also see Anthony Short, *The Communist Insurrection in Malaya, 1948–1960*. New York: Frederick Muller, 1975.
18. Quoted in Paget. *Counterinsurgency Campaigning*, 66.
19. Paget, *Counterinsurgency Campaigning*, 69.
20. Stubbs, *Hearts and Minds in Guerrilla Warfare*.
21. This idea of British learning in Malaya is at the heart of John A. Nagl's thesis in *Learning to Eat Soup with a Knife*, 105; also see Kalev I. Sepp, "Best Practices in Counterinsurgency," *Military Review* (May–June 2005): 8–12.
22. Quoted in Robert Thompson, *Defeating Communist Insurgency: The Lessons of Malaya and Vietnam*. New York: Praeger, 1966, 169.

Chapter 18. Ramón Magsaysay and the Hukbalahap Rebellion in the Philippines, 1946–1956

1. Quoted in Stubbs, *Hearts and Minds in Guerrilla Warfare*, 4.
2. Robert Taber, *War of the Flea: The Classic Study of Guerilla Warfare*. Washington: Potomac Books, 2002, 136.
3. Quoted in Joes, "Counterinsurgency in the Philippines," 37–54.
4. Taber, *War of the Flea*, 136.
5. Benedict J. Kerkvliet, *The Huk Rebellion: A Study of Peasant Revolt in the Philippines*. Berkeley: University of California Press, 1977, 210.
6. Taber, *War of the Flea*, 136.
7. Ibid., 136.
8. Cable, *Conflict of Myths*, 49.
9. Kerkvliet, *The Huk Rebellion*, 190.
10. Tierney, *Chasing Ghosts*, 223.
11. Kerkvliet, *The Huk Rebellion*, 193.
12. Shafer, *Deadly Paradigms*, 205–6.
13. Quoted in ibid., 213.
14. Quoted in ibid., 227.
15. Ibid., 220–30.
16. Carlos P. Romulo and Marvin M Gray, *The Magsaysay Story*. New York: John Day, 1956, 5.
17. Quoted in ibid., 258.
18. Quoted in ibid., 127.
19. Quoted in Shafer, *Deadly Paradigms*, 236; also see Luis Taruc, *He Who Rides the Tiger: The Story of an Asian Guerrilla Leader*. New York: Frederick A. Praeger, 1967; John J. Duffy, "Signpost: Success in the Philippines," *Army* 13 (July 1963): 60–2.

20. Kerkvliet, *The Huk Rebellion*.
21. Richard J. Aldrich, ed., *The Clandestine Cold War in Asia, 1945–65: Western Intelligence, Propaganda and Special Operations*. London: Frank Cass, 2000, 182.
22. Edward G. Lansdale, *In the Midst of Wars: An American's Mission to Southeast Asia*. New York: Harper and Row, 1972, 70.
23. Moyar, *A Question of Command*, 99.
24. Quoted in Lansdale, *In the Midst of Wars*, 86.
25. Beckett, *Modern Insurgencies and Counterinsurgencies*, 105.
26. Tinker, *Strategies of Revolutionary Warfare*.
27. Kerkvliet, *The Huk Rebellion*, 243.
28. Moyar, *A Question of Command*, 101.
29. Quoted in Romulo and Gray, *The Magsaysay Story*, 193.
30. Quoted in Taruc, *He Who Rides the Tiger*, 97.
31. Quoted in Romulo and Gray, *The Magsaysay Story*, 192.

Chapter 19. Vietnam

1. Quoted in Tierney, *Chasing Ghosts*, 237–8.
2. Quoted in Fall, *The Two Vietnams*, 281.
3. Hammes, *The Sling and the Stone*, 222.
4. Ho Chi Minh's speech: http://forum.tayyar.org/f100/ho-chi-minhs-speech-ba-dinh-square-september-2-1945-a-29716/ (accessed 30 January 2009).
5. Paret, *French Revolutionary Warfare*, 16.
6. Fall, *Street without Joy*, 32.
7. Beckett, *Modern Insurgencies and Counterinsurgencies*, 114.
8. Quoted in Phillip Davidson, *Vietnam at War*. Novato, CA: Presidio, 1988, 15.
9. Bernard B. Fall, *Vietnam Witness, 1953–66*. New York: Praeger, 1966, 31.
10. Quoted in ibid., 6.
11. Ibid.
12. Horne, *A Savage War of Peace*, 67.
13. Rene Juillard, *The Battle of Diên Biên Phu*. New York: Harper and Row, 1965.
14. Horne, *A Savage War of Peace*, 67.
15. Fall, *Street without Joy*, 321.
16. Bernard B. Fall, *Hell in a Very Small Place: The Siege of Dien Bien Phu*. Philadelphia: J. B. Lippincott, 1967, 225–78.
17. Fall, *Vietnam Witness*, 225.
18. Alan Brinkley, "Why Were We in Vietnam?" *New York Times*, September 7, 2012.
19. Beckett, *Modern Insurgencies and Counterinsurgencies*, 117; Sarkesian, *America's Forgotten Wars*.
20. W. Scott Thompson and Donaldson D. Frizzell, eds., *The Lessons of Vietnam*. New York: Crane, Russak, 1977, 44.
21. Luttwak, "Dead End," 42.
22. Tierney, *Chasing Ghosts*, 232.
23. Quoted in Sarkesian, *America's Forgotten Wars*, 201.

24. Tierney, *Chasing Ghosts*, 235.
25. Asprey, *War in the Shadows*.
26. Moyar, *A Question of Command*, 136.
27. Neil Sheehan, *A Bright Shining Lie: John Paul Vann and America in Vietnam*. New York: Random House, 1988, 181–5.
28. Logevall, *Embers of War*, 698.
29. Asprey, *War in the Shadows*, 929.
30. Quoted in Logevall, *Embers of War*, 698.
31. Robert W. Komer, *Bureaucracy at War: U.S. Performance in the Vietnam Conflict*. Boulder, CO: Westview Press, 1986, 25.
32. Quoted in Boot, *Savage Wars of Peace*, 288.
33. Quoted in Roger Hilsman, "Foreword" in Võ Nguyên Giáp, *People's War, People's Army*. New York: Praeger, 1962, xvii.
34. Quoted in Tierney, *Chasing Ghosts*, 238.
35. Davidson, *Vietnam at War*.
36. Weigley, *The American Way of War*, 458–9.
37. Fall, *The Two Vietnams*, 339; also see Lansdale, *In the Midst of Wars*.
38. Quoted in Beckett, *Modern Insurgencies and Counterinsurgencies*, 199.
39. Quoted in Shafer, *Deadly Paradigms*, 268.
40. Quoted in Fall, *The Two Vietnams*, 378.
41. Quoted in Beckett, *Modern Insurgencies and Counterinsurgencies*, 199.
42. Quoted in Tierney, *Chasing Ghosts*, 242.
43. Logevall, *Embers of War*, 704.
44. Quoted in Shafer, *Deadly Paradigms*, 273.
45. Quoted in Davidson, *Vietnam at War*, 304.
46. Logevall, *Embers of War*, 706.
47. Thompson and Frizzell, *The Lessons of Vietnam*, 9.
48. Komer, *Bureaucracy at War*.
49. Cable, *Conflict of Myths*, 282.
50. Quoted in Komer, *Bureaucracy at War*, 61.
51. Weigley, *The American Way of War*, 463.
52. Tierney, *Chasing Ghosts*, 242.
53. Fall, *Vietnam Witness*, 304.
54. Adviser Edward Lansdale to a group of U.S. military advisers, 1962, quoted in Logevall, *Embers of War*, 707.
55. Quoted in Jeffrey Record, "The American Way of War: Cultural Barriers to Successful Counterinsurgency," *CATO Policy Analysis*, No. 577, September 1, 2006, 11.
56. Quoted in Boot, *Savage Wars of Peace*, 299.
57. Quoted in Record, "The American Way of War," 11.
58. Moyar, *A Question of Command*, 155.
59. Quoted in Komer, *Bureaucracy at War*, 22.
60. Sepp, "Best Practices in Counterinsurgency," 8–12.
61. Kilcullen, "Countering Global Insurgency"; Ross Coffey, "Revisiting CORDS: The Need for Unity of Effort to Security Victory in Iraq," *Military Review*, March–April 2006, 92–102; Robert M. Cassidy, "Winning the War of the Flea," *Military Review*, September–October 2004, 41–6.

Notes to pages 229–246 495

62. Kilcullen, "Counterinsurgency Redux."
63. Jeffrey Race, *War Comes to Long An: Revolutionary Conflict in a Vietnamese Province*. Berkeley: University of California Press, 1972.
64. Quoted in Beinart, *The Icarus Syndrome*, 180.
65. Ibid.
66. Quoted in Davidson, *Vietnam at War*, 483.
67. Thomas C. Thayer, "Patterns of the French and American Experience in Vietnam," in W. Scott Thompson and Donaldson D. Frizzell, eds., *The Lessons of Vietnam*. New York: Crane, Russak, 1977, 17–38.
68. Lewis Sorley, *A Better War: The Unexamined Victories and Final Tragedy of America's Last Years in Vietnam*. New York: Harcourt, 1999.
69. Komer, *Bureaucracy at War*, 310.
70. Moyar, *A Question of Command*, 163.
71. Quoted in Lewis Sorley, *A Better War*, 327.
72. Ibid.
73. Moyar, *A Question of Command*, 163–4.
74. Davidson, *Vietnam at War*, ix.
75. See Richard Downie, *Learning from Conflict: The U.S. Military in Vietnam, El Salvador, and the Drug War*. Westport, CT: Praeger, 1998; Andrew Krepinevich, *The Army and Vietnam*. Baltimore: Johns Hopkins University Press, 1986.

Chapter 20. From Guatemala, 1954, to Cuba and the Bay of Pigs, 1961

1. Quoted in Hal Brands, *Latin America's Cold War*. Cambridge, MA: Harvard University Press, 2010, 41.
2. Michael Reid, *Forgotten Continent: The Battle for Latin America's Soul*. New Haven, CT: Yale University Press, 2007, 82–6.
3. A thorough history on the U.S. overthrow can be found in Piero Gleijeses, *Shattered Hope: The Guatemalan Revolution and the United States, 1944–1954*. Princeton, NJ: Princeton University Press, 1991.
4. Greg Grandin, *The Last Colonial Massacre*. Chicago: University of Chicago Press, 2011, 59.
5. Brands, *Latin America's Cold War*, 16.
6. Jon Lee Anderson, *Che Guevara: A Revolutionary Life*. New York: Grove Press, 1997, 123.
7. See Charles H. Blake, *Politics in Latin America*. New York: Houghton Mifflin, 2008, 280–5; Reid, *Forgotten Continent*, 81–6.
8. Quoted in Riordan Roett, "Introduction," in Christopher Kojm, ed., *Revolution and Subversion in Latin America: Selected U.S. Intelligence Community Estimative Products, 1947–1987*. Washington, DC: National Intelligence Council, September 2010, xix.
9. Grandin, *The Last Colonial Massacre*, 66.
10. Brands, *Latin America's Cold War*, 17.
11. Ernesto "Che" Guevara, quoted in Grandin, *The Last Colonial Massacre*, 5.
12. Anderson, *Che Guevara*, 126.
13. Ibid., 163.

14. Brands, *Latin America's Cold War*, 17.
15. Beckett, *Modern Insurgencies and Counterinsurgencies*, 168.
16. Julia E. Sweig, *Cuba: What Everyone Needs to Know*. New York: Oxford University Press, 2009, 21.
17. Anderson, *Che Guevara*, 160–75.
18. Boot, *Invisible Armies*, 431.
19. Quoted in Anderson, *Che Guevara*, 245.
20. Sweig, *Cuba*, 37.
21. Daniel F. Solomon, *Breaking Up with Cuba: The Dissolution of Friendly Relations between Washington and Havana, 1956–61*. London: McFarland, 2011, 70–120.
22. Solomon, *Breaking Up with Cuba*, 2011.
23. Ibid., 73–93.
24. Quoted in Anderson, *Che Guevara*, 393–4.
25. Solomon, *Breaking Up with Cuba*, 166; also see Jim Rasenberger, *Brilliant Disaster: JFK, Castro, and America's Doomed Invasion of the Bay of Pigs*. New York: Scribner, 2011, 39–133.
26. An excellent source on U.S.-Cuban relations beginning in 1959 can be found in Robert S. Snyder, "The U.S. and Third World Revolutionary States: Understanding the Breakdown in Relations," *International Studies Quarterly* 43:2 (June 1999): 265–90.
27. Solomon, *Breaking Up with Cuba*, 144.
28. Ibid., 194.
29. Rasenberger, *Brilliant Disaster*, 195.
30. Ibid., 269.
31. David Atlee Phillips, *The Night Watch: 25 Years of Peculiar Service*. New York: Atheneum, 1977, 109. See also Luis Aguilar, ed., *Operation Zapata: The "Ultrasensitive" Report and Testimony of the Board of Inquiry on the Bay of Pigs*. Frederick, MD: University Publications of America, 1981, 28.
32. Rasenberger, *Brilliant Disaster*, 147.
33. Ibid., 227.
34. Quoted in ibid., 62.
35. Brands, *Latin America's Cold War*, 35.
36. Quoted in Rasenberger, *Brilliant Disaster*, 371.
37. Quoted in ibid., 352.
38. Quoted in Brands, *Latin America's Cold War*, 49.
39. Quoted in Rasenberger, *Brilliant Disaster*, 371.

Chapter 21. Guatemala, Post-1963

1. Quoted in Régis Debray, *Strategy for Revolution*. New York: Monthly Review Press, 1970, 113.
2. "Insurgency and Instability in Guatemala." SNIE 82–68, Washington, December 19, 1968, in Christopher Kojm, ed., *Revolution and Subversion in Latin America: Selected U.S. Intelligence Community Estimative Products, 1947–1987*. Washington, DC: National Intelligence Council, September 2010.

Notes to pages 258–270

3. Quoted in Walter LaFeber, *Invevitable Revolutions: The United States in Central America*. New York: W.W. Norton, 1993, 114.
4. Reid, *Forgotten Continent*, 85.
5. Norman Gall, "Slaughter in Guatemala," *New York Review of Books*, November 20, 1971.
6. Quoted in Brian Latell, *Castro's Secrets: The CIA and Cuba's Intelligent Machine*. New York: Palgrave Macmillan, 2012, 73.
7. An excellent survey can be found in Brands, *Latin America's Cold War*.
8. "Insurgency and Instability in Latin America," 193.
9. Author telephone interview with General Fred Woerner, ret., U.S. Army, June 2008.
10. "Memorandum from Viron P. Vaky to the Assistant Secretary of State for Inter-American Affairs, March 29, 1968," *Foreign Relations of the United States, 1964–68*, U.S. Department of State, 1964, vol. 31.
11. Quoted in Brands, *Latin America's Cold War*, 177.
12. Thomas Carothers, *In the Name of Democracy: U.S. Policy toward Latin America in the Reagan Years*. Berkeley: University of California Press, 1991, 59.
13. Quoted in LaFeber, *Invevitable Revolutions*, 114.
14. Brands, *Latin America's Cold War*, 6.
15. "Briefing Book on El Salvador" [Packet of Materials Distributed to Congress and Other Groups on the Eve of Regan's Joint Session Speech on Central America-Cover Memo from McFarlane to Hill Attached], Non-Classified, Report, April 23, 1983. ES03948.
16. Brands, *Latin America's Cold War*, 206.
17. Quoted in Brands, *Latin America's Cold War*, 208.
18. Quoted in Luciano Silva, "The War in El Salvador: A Retrospective," *Strategy Research Project*, U.S. Army War College, Carlisle Barracks, PA (April 15, 1996).
19. Millett, Richard, "Central American Paralysis," *Foreign Policy* 39 (Summer 1980): 99–117.

Chapter 22. Cuba, Post-1963

1. Full text of Kennedy's address at http://www.presidency.ucsb.edu/ws/index.php?pid=8032.
2. Debray, *Strategy for Revolution*; also see Régis Debray, *Revolution in the Revolution?* London: Monthly Review, 1973.
3. Quoted in Sewall Menzel, *Dictators, Drugs, and Revolutions: Cold War Campaigning in Latin America, 1965–1989*. Bloomington, IN: Author House, 2006, 145.
4. Che Guevara, "Message to the Tricontinental: Create Two, Three ... Many Vietnams," first published in English by the Executive Secretariat of the Organization of the Solidarity of the Peoples of Africa, Asia, and Latin America (OSPAAAL), Havana: 1967.
5. Quoted in Menzel, *Dictators, Drugs, and Revolutions*, 145.
6. Quoted in ibid., 148.

7. Beckett, *Modern Insurgencies and Counterinsurgencies*, 173.
8. Brands, *Latin America's Cold War*, 59.
9. "Latin American Reactions to Developments in and with Respect to Cuba," in Christopher Kojm, ed., *Revolution and Subversion in Latin America: Selected U.S. Intelligence Community Estimative Products, 1947–1987*. Washington, DC: National Intelligence Council, September 2010, 39–47.
10. Enrique Krauze, *Redeemers: Ideas and Power in Latin America*. New York: HarperCollins, 2011, 319.
11. Arne Westad, *The Global Cold War*. New York: Cambridge University Press, 2007, 179.
12. Rooney, *Guerrilla*, 217.
13. Anderson, *Che Guevara*, 110–21.
14. Quoted in Henry Butterfield Ryan, *The Fall of Che Guevara: A Story of Soldiers, Spies, and Diplomats*. New York: Oxford University Press, 1998, 8.
15. Quoted in ibid., 41.
16. Quoted in ibid., 80.
17. Quoted in Anderson, *Che Guevara*, 718.
18. Ryan, *The Fall of Che Guevara*, 118.
19. Rooney, *Guerrilla*, 219.
20. Quoted in Ryan, *The Fall of Che Guevara*, 139.
21. Quoted in ibid., 162–5.

Chapter 23. Intermezzo: Che Guevara and Guerrilla Warfare

1. Quoted in Odd Arne Westad, *The Global Cold War*. New York: Cambridge University Press, 2007, 170.
2. Che Guevara, *Guerrilla Warfare*. Lincoln, NE: Univeristy of Nebraska Press, 1998.
3. Quoted in Debray, *Strategy for Revolution*, 42.
4. Che Guevara, *Guerrilla Warfare*, 50.
5. Quoted in Anderson, *Che Guevara*, 398.
6. Guevara, *Guerrilla Warfare*, 50.
7. Putsay, *Counterinsurgency Warfare*, 45.
8. Jorge Castañeda, *Utopia Unarmed: The Latin American Left after the Cold War*. New York: Alfred A. Knopf, 1993, 69.
9. Quoted in Debray, *Strategy for Revolution*, 12.
10. Westad, *The Global Cold War*, 179.

Chapter 24. Carter, Reagan, and the Sandinista Revolution in Nicaragua, 1979–1990

1. Quoted in Kagan, *A Twilight Struggle*, 29.
2. Stephen J. Kinzer, *Blood of Brothers: Life and War in Nicaragua*. Cambridge, MA: Harvard University Press, 2007, 37.
3. Edward Best, *U.S. Policy and Regional Security in Central America*. New York: St. Martin's Press, 1987; Millett, "Central American Paralysis," 99–117.

4. Quoted in Kagan, *A Twilight Struggle*, 30.
5. Best, *U.S. Policy and Regional Security in Central America*, 24.
6. Kent Norsworthy, *Nicaragua: A Country Guide*. Albuquerque, NM: Inter-Hemispheric Education Resource Center, 1989, 1.
7. Quoted in LaFeber, *Invevitable Revolutions*, 222.
8. Kagan, *A Twilight Struggle*, 59.
9. Westad, *The Global Cold War*, 340.
10. Managua Domestic Service, "Sandinistas Issue 'War Communique,'" published in Daily Report. Latin America, FBIS-LAT-78-165, 24 August 1989.
11. Cynthia McClintock, *Revolutionary Movements in Latin America: El Salvador's FMLN and Peru's Shining Path*. Washington, DC: U.S. Institute of Peace, 1998, 217–18.
12. Ibid., 220–1.
13. Jimmy Carter, "University of Notre Dame – Address at Commencement Exercises at the University," May 22, 1977, *The American Presidency Project*, http://www.presidency.ucsb.edu/ws/index.php?pid=7552.
14. Lawrence A. Pezzullo, "Cable: Congressional Presentation on Nicaragua," August 23, 1979, NSA, Nicaragua collection, NI01063.
15. Quoted in Kagan, *A Twilight Struggle*, 51.
16. Ibid., 53.
17. Hammes, *The Sling and the Stone*, 77.
18. Quoted in Lake, *Somoza Falling*, 213.
19. Brands, *Latin America's Cold War*, 186.
20. Quoted in Kagan, *A Twilight Struggle*, 125.
21. Lee H. Hamilton and Daniel K. Inouye, *Report of the Congressional Committees Investigating the Iran-Contra Affair*, Washington, DC: U.S. Government Printing Office, 1987, 483.
22. Quoted in Kagan, *A Twilight Struggle*, 125.
23. Kinzer, *Blood of Brothers*, 41.
24. Ronald W. Reagan, "National Security Decision Directive on Cuba and Central America (NSDD 17)," January 4, 1982, Federation of American Scientists, Intelligence Resource Program, http://www.fas.org/irp/offdocs/nsdd/index.html.
25. Kagan, *A Twilight Struggle*, 203.
26. Peter Kornbluh, "The Covert War," in Thomas W. Walker, ed., *Reagan versus the Sandinistas: The Undeclared War on Nicaragua* (Boulder, CO: Westview, 1987), 22.
27. National Security Council, "Scope of CIA Activities under the Nicaragua Finding," July 12, 1982, NSA, Iran-Contra collection, IC00060.
28. Kagan, *A Twilight Struggle*, 204.
29. Ibid., 726.
30. Permanent Select Committee on Intelligence, "U.S. Intelligence Performance on Central America: Achievements and Selected Instances of Concern," U.S. House of Representatives, Washington, DC: U.S. Government Printing Office, 1982, 3.
31. Kagan, *A Twilight Struggle*, 217.
32. Quoted in Westad, *The Global Cold War*, 343.

33. Quoted in Kagan, *A Twilight Struggle*, 217.
34. Quoted in ibid., 217.
35. Quoted in ibid., 192.
36. Ibid., 194.
37. Ibid., 197.
38. Ibid., 224.
39. Ibid., 250–60.
40. Kinzer, *Blood of Brothers*, 179.
41. Philip Taubman, "U.S. Backing Raids against Nicaragua," *New York Times*, November 2, 1982.
42. U.S. House of Representatives, Congressman Harkin speaking on the Department of Defense Appropriation Bill, 1983, *Congressional Record*, 97th cong., 2nd sess., 1982, 128, no. 21 (December 8, 1982), 29458-9.
43. Kagan, *A Twilight Struggle*, 242.
44. Congressman Boland speaking on the Department of Defense Appropriation Bill, 1983, U.S. House of Representatives, *Congressional Record*, 97th cong., 2nd sess., 1982, 128, no. 21 (December 8, 1982), 29468.
45. Kagan, *A Twilight Struggle*, 240–5.
46. Quoted in ibid., 283.
47. Loren B. Thompson, ed., *Low-Intensity Conflict: The Pattern of Warfare in the Modern World*. Washington, DC: Lexington Books, 1989.
48. Quoted in Kinzer, *Blood of Brothers*, 314.
49. Anthony C. E. Quainton, "Cable: GRN Allegations of Contra Massacre," August 13, 1983, NSA, Nicaragua collection, NI01791.
50. Ibid.
51. American citizen Eugene Hasenfus while in Sandinista captivity, quoted by Peter Kornbluh, "Nicaragua: U.S. Proinsurgency Warfare against the Sandinistas," in Michael T. Klare and Peter Kornbluh, eds., *Low Intensity Warfare: Counterinsurgency, Proinsurgency, and Antiterrorism in the Eighties*. New York: Pantheon, 1988, 140.
52. Quoted in Kinzer, *Blood of Brothers*, 314.
53. http://www.envio.org.ni/articulo/3243.
54. http://www.envio.org.ni/articulo/3243.
55. Andrew Glass, "Eugene Hasenfus Parachutes to Safety, October 5, 1986," *Politico*, October 5, 2011; the pro-Sandinista account can be found at http://www.envio.org.ni/articulo/3243 (accessed May 9, 2012).
56. Kinzer, *Blood of Brothers*, 314; Glenn Garvin, *Everybody Had His Own Gringo*. Washington. DC: Brassey's, 1992, 174.
57. Garvin, *Everybody Had His Own Gringo*, 172, and Kagan, *A Twilight Struggle*, 481.
58. Quoted in Kagan, *A Twilight Struggle*, 488.
59. Johanna Oliver, "The Esquipulas Process: A Central American Paradigm for Resolving Regional Conflict," *Ethnic Studies Report* 17: 2 (July 1999): 149–79. The Arias plan and Esquipulas II evolved out of the earlier Contadora Group that began in January 1983 when foreign ministers of Panama, Colombia, Venezuela, and Mexico met to discuss diplomatic solutions to Central America's wars.

60. Cuban official in Nicaragua quoted in Kagan, *A Twilight Struggle*, 693.
61. Ibid., 668–85.
62. Managua Radio Sandino, "Humberto Ortega on Central American Peace Efforts," published in Daily Report. Latin America, FBIS-LAT-89-227, November 28, 1989.
63. Daniel Siegel and Joy Hackel, "El Salvador: Counterinsurgency Revisited." In Michael T. Klare and Peter Kornbluh, eds., *Low Intensity Warfare: Counterinsurgency: Proinsurgency, and Antiterrorism in the Eighties*. New York: Pantheon, 1988, 112–35.
64. Quoted in Beinart, *The Icarus Syndrome*, 226.

Chapter 25. El Salvador, 1979–1992

1. Westad, *The Global Cold War*, 334.
2. Quoted in Raymond Bonner, *Weakness and Deceit: U.S. Policy and El Salvador*. New York: Times Books, 1984, 47.
3. "The Challenge of Counterinsurgency," *America Abroad* (transcript), October 14, 2006, http://www.americaabroad.org/radio/programs/documentaries/?prog=the_challenge_of_counterinsurgency.
4. Moyar, *A Question of Command*, 173.
5. Mark Danner, *The Massacre at El Mozote*. New York: Vintage, 1993, 26.
6. James L. Buckley, "Reprogramming Proposal for El Salvador," statement before the Subcommittee of Foreign Operations of the House Appropriations Committee, *Official Monthly Record of United States Foreign Policy*, 81:2050 (May 1981).
7. "Military Group Reduction and Richardson Case," Cable San Salvador, April 12, 1977, National Security Archive, El Salvador Document, ES00013.
8. Kagan, *A Twilight Struggle*, 164.
9. Karen DeYoung, "El Salvador: Where Reagan Draws the Line," *Washington Post*, March 9, 1981.
10. "U.S. Assistance to El Salvador – Fact Sheet." Internal Paper, April 1, 1981. ES01512; also see "Background Information on the Security Forces in El Salvador and U.S. Military Assistance" [includes statistics on U.S. Security Assistance], Report, March 1, 1980, ES00477; "U.S. Assistance to El Salvador," Press Briefing, May 18, 1980, ES00631; "Security Assistance to El Salvador," Secret Memorandum, January 8, 1981, ES01153; "Issues under the War Powers and Arms Export Control Acts Raised by U.S. Military Presence in El Salvador," Non-Classified Memorandum, February 23, 1981, ES01385.
11. "U.S. Assistance to El Salvador – Fact Sheet."
12. Loren Jenkins, "From Conquistadores to Comunistas: Why the Killing Will Never End," *Washington Post*, August 16, 1981.
13. Author interview with Gerson Martínez, National Assembly Deputy for the FMLN and former guerrilla leader, San Salvador, July 2008; author interview with Mauricio Gonzalez, director of the Tutela Legal Office of the Archbishop of San Salvador, San Salvador, July 2008.

14. Ana Guadalupe Martínez interviewed in the CNN *Cold War Series* documentary.
15. Karen DeYoung, "El Salvador: A Symbol of World Crisis," *Washington Post*, March 8, 1981.
16. Quoted in Raymond Bonner, "The Agony of El Salvador," *New York Times Magazine*, February 22, 1981.
17. José Napoleón Duarte, *Duarte: My Story*. New York: Putnam, 1986, 115.
18. Paul Heath Hoeffel, "The Eclipse of the Oligarchs," *New York Times Magazine*, September 6, 1981.
19. Quoted in Bonner, *Weakness and Deceit*, 145.
20. "Contact with New Government," State Department cable 270716, October 16, 1979, EL00634.
21. Quoted in Bonner, *Weakness and Deceit*, 13.
22. Archbishop Oscar Romero, *A Shepherd's Diary*, trans. Irene B. Hodges; foreword by Thomas E. Quigley. London: CAFOD, 1993.
23. Quoted in U.S. Institute of Peace, *UN Truth Commission Report*, Washington, DC, 1993,120. The full report is at http://www.usip.org/publications/truth-commission-el-salvador.
24. Author interview with Gerson Martínez, San Salvador, July 2008.
25. *Proceso*, Universidad Centroamericana (San Salvador) Special Archive, author translation, vols. 2–3, 1982.
26. Bonner, *Weakness and Deceit*, 302.
27. Quoted in Carothers, *In the Name of Democracy*, 288.
28. "U.S. Embassy San Salvador, FMLN Threatens Voters, March 5, 1982," NA, SG 59, Entry 5238, "Records Relating to the UN Truth Commission" Box 1.
29. John D. Waghelstein, "El Salvador: Observations and Experiences in Counterinsurgency." U.S. Army War College, Carlisle Barracks, PA, January 1, 1985.
30. "U.S. Embassy San Salvador, FMLN Threatens Voters, March 5, 1982."
31. Colman McCarthy, "Mountains of Sorrow," *Washington Post*, February 14, 1982.
32. Waghelstein, "El Salvador: Observations and Experiences in Counterinsurgency."
33. Quoted in Bonner, *Weakness and Deceit*, 295.
34. Ibid. Also see "Post-Elections Update – 13 April." Confidential Cable San Salvador, April 14, 1982 ES02930; "Coalition Building: Conversations with D'Aubuisson and Barrera" Confidential Cable San Salvador, April 28, 1982, ES02968; "El Salvador since March 28, 1982: The Development of Democracy." Confidential Cable San Salvador, June 1, 1983. ES04035.
35. Carothers, *In the Name of Democracy*, 26.
36. Walter Knut and Philip J. Williams, "The Military and Democratization in El Salvador," *Journal of Interamerican Studies and World Affairs* 35:1 (1993): 39–88.
37. "Embassy San Salvador: Other Reactions to the FDR/FMLN Dialogue Proposal, 01 November 1982," NA, SG 59, Entry 5238, "Records Relating to the UN Truth Commission," Box 1.

38. Confidential author interview with a U.S. State Department official, Washington, DC, March 2011.
39. Warren Hoge, "Salvadoran Rebels Says War Is in 'Definitive Phase,'" *New York Times Magazine*, February 2, 1982.
40. Quoted in Danner, *The Massacre at El Mozote*, 32.
41. John D. Waghelstein, "Military to Military Contacts: Personal Observations – The El Salvador Case," *Low Intensity Conflict and Law Enforcement* 10:2 (Summer 2003); author telephone interview with former Special Forces officer Ed Phillips, August 2011.
42. Quoted in Danner, *The Massacre at El Mozote*, 38.
43. Bonner, *Weakness and Deceit*, 25; Danner, *The Massacre at El Mozote*, 20–38.
44. Moyar, *A Question of Command*, 2009.
45. Norman J. Brozenick, "Small Wars, Big Stakes: Coercion, Persuasion, and Airpower in Counterrevolutionary War," Thesis, School of Advanced Airpower Studies, Air University, June 1998.
46. Quoted in Danner, *The Massacre at El Mozote*, 23
47. Paul P. Cale, "The United States Military Advisory Group in El Salvador, 1979–1992," *Small Wars Journal* (1996), 14–15.
48. Robert D. Ramsey III, "Advising Indigenous Forces: American Advisors in Korea, Vietnam, and El Salvador," Global War on Terrorism Occasional Paper 18. Fort Leavenworth, KS: Combat Studies Institute Press, 2006, 99.
49. Author phone interview with Luis Orlando, former U.S. Army Special Forces soldier, September 30, 2011.
50. Ramsey, "Advising Indigenous Forces."
51. Brigadier General Fred E. Woerner, "Report of the El Salvador Military Strategy Assistance Team," Report, September 12, 1981, ES02030; author telephone interview with Fred Woerner, June 2008; also see "Training of the Salvadoran Military in the United States," Non-Classified, Letter from Powell A. Moore, March 5, 1982, ES02704; "Applicability of Certain U.S. Laws that Pertain to U.S. Military Involvement in El Salvador," Report, July 27, 1982, ES03302.
52. "El Mozote: Lucha por la verdad y la justicia," Tutela Legal del Arzobispado de San Salvador, 2007.
53. Ibid.
54. Danner, *The Massacre at El Mozote*, 77.
55. San Salvador Cable January 1, 1982, NA, SG 59, Entry 5238, Box 19.
56. Also see Raymond Bonner, "Massacre of Hundreds Reported in Salvador Village," *New York Times*, January 27, 1982.
57. "Report on Alleged Massacre," San Salvador Cable, January 1982, NA, SG 59, Entry 5238, Box 19.
58. Quoted in Raymond Bonner, *Weakness and Deceit*, 340.
59. Author email interview with Alma Guillermoprieto, June 2008.
60. See Simon A. Molina, "The Peace Process in El Salvador: 1984–1992," Strategy Research Project. Carlisle Barracks, PA: U.S. Army War College, April 1, 1996; Angel Rabasa et al., "Money in the Bank: Lessons Learned from Past Counterinsurgency (COIN) Operations," Washington, DC:

National Defense Research Institute, RAND Corporation, 2007; Ramsey, "Advising Indigenous Forces"; Alfred R. Barr and Caesar Sereseres, "U.S. Unconventional Warfare Operations and Lessons from Central America, 1980–91," *Low Intensity Conflict and Law Enforcement* 8:2 (Summer 1999): 1–32.
61. Christopher Dickey, "U.S. Advisers Dubious of Effect in Salvador," *Washington Post*, June 7, 1981; John D. Waghelstein "What's Wrong in Iraq? Or, Ruminations of a Pachyderm," *Military Review* (January–February 2006): 112–17.
62. Author telephone interview with James Steele, June 2008.
63. Author telephone interview with John Waghelstein, June 2008.
64. Chavez, "The Odds in El Salvador."
65. Ibid.
66. Skip Thornton, "Thinking about the Tactics of Modern War: The Salvadoran Example," Monograph. Fort Leavenworth, KS: School of Advanced Military Studies, U.S. Army Command and General Staff College, 1988–89; also see Andrew J. Bacevich et al., eds., *American Military Policy in Small Wars: The Case of El Salvador*. Washington, DC: Institute for Policy Analysis, 1988.
67. Waghelstein, "El Salvador: Observations and Experiences."
68. Benjamin C. Schwarz, "American Counterinsurgency Doctrine in El Salvador: The Frustrations of Reform and the Illusions of Nation Building." Santa Monica, CA: RAND Corporation, 1991.
69. Chavez, "The Odds in El Salvador."
70. Schwarz, "American Counterinsurgency Doctrine in El Salvador."
71. Lydia Chavez, "El Salvador," *New York Times*, December 11, 1983.
72. John J. Shea, "Explaining Success and Failure in Counterinsurgency," Thesis, Naval Postgraduate School, Monterey, CA, June 1991.
73. Thornton, "Thinking about the Tactics of Modern War"; Frank Smyth, "Consensus or Crisis? Without Duarte in El Salvador," *Journal of Interamerican Studies and World Affairs* 30:4 (Winter 1988–1989): 29–52.
74. Chavez, "El Salvador."
75. Jochen Hippler, "Low Intensity Warfare: Key Strategy for the Third World Theater," *MERIP Middle East Report* 144 (January–February 1987): 32–38.
76. James LeMoyne, "The Guns of El Salvador," *New York Times*, February 5, 1989.
77. Tommie Sue Montgomery, "Fighting Guerrillas: The United States and Low-Intensity Conflict in El Salvador," *New Political Science* (Fall/Winter 1990): 21–53.
78. Quoted in ibid.; also see "Impact of U.S. Assistance in the 1980s," U.S. General Accounting Office, Report to the Chairman, Committee on Foreign Relations, U.S. Senate, July 1989.
79. *Proceso*, University of Central America, vol. 3, 1987, author translation.
80. "Interim Report of the Speaker's Task Force on El Salvador, April 30, 1990," NA, SG 59, Entry 5238, "Records Relating to the UN Truth Commission" Box 13.

81. Author interview with Kevin Whitaker, U.S. State Department official, Washington, DC, March 25, 2011.
82. *Proceso*, University of Central America, vol. 4, no. 409, 1989.
83. Confidential telephone author interview with former U.S. Army adviser in El Salvador. June 2008.
84. Author interview with Kevin Whitaker.
85. Confidential author interview with U.S. State Department officials, March 26, 2011.
86. Author interview with Gerson Martínez, FMLN member, San Salvador, July 2008, author translation.
87. "The Little War That Will Not Stop," *The Economist*, February 16, 1991.
88. "Cut Away," *The Economist*, October 27, 1990; "Trudging towards Peace," *The Economist*, May 25, 1991; "Safer with a Gun," *The Economist*, September 14, 1991.
89. Author interview with Gerson Martínez, San Salvador, July 2008, author translation; also see Álvaro De Soto and Graciana del Castillo, "Obstacles to Peacebuilding," *Foreign Policy* 94 (Spring 1994): 69–83.
90. "No Deal," *The Economist*, August 11, 1990.

Chapter 26. Dirty Wars after the Cold War

1. John A. Nagl, "Let's Win the Wars We're In," *JFQ*, 1st Quarter 2009.
2. Boot, *Invisible Armies*, 503.
3. Ibid., 503.
4. The Bush administration did not want simply to defeat the Iraqi forces but rather to do so in a way that sent a strong signal to the Middle East and global spectators that the United States was willing to use massive force to achieve its strategic and policy objectives. In hindsight, and as Gideon Rose has written, the Bush administration hoped to strike hard and fast and get the troops home quickly, which meant defining the military objectives narrowly, without considering the full implications of leaving Saddam Hussein in power. Ironically, Rose notes, the administration did not realize that its relatively straightforward "Kuwait" strategy masked a far more complex and messy "Iraq" strategy. Rose, *How Wars End*, 202, 227.

Chapter 27. Colombia

1. Peter De Shazo et al., "Countering Threats to Security and Stability in a Failing State: Lessons from Colombia." Washington, DC: Center for Strategic and International Studies (CSIS), September 2009, 8.
2. Gabriel Marcella, "War without Borders: The Colombia-Ecuador Crisis of 2008," Strategic Studies Institute, U.S. Army War College, December 2008.
3. The foregoing first appeared in Russell Crandall, "Requiem for the FARC?" *Survival* 53:4 (August–September 2011): 233–40. See also Juan Forero, "FARC Computer Files Are Authentic, Interpol Probe Finds," *Washington Post*, May 16, 2008.
4. Thomas R. Pickering, "Anatomy of Plan Colombia," *The American Interest* (November/December 2009): 71–7.

5. For more on this topic see Russell Crandall, *Driven by Drugs: U.S. Policy toward Colombia*. Boulder, CO: Lynne Rienner, 2008, 44–67.
6. Thomas Marks, "A Model Counterinsurgency: Uribe's Colombia vs. FARC," *Military Review* (March–April 2007): 41–55.
7. Colombian Ministry of Defense, "Policy for the Consolidation of Democratic Security," 2008.
8. Marks, "A Model Counterinsurgency"; Thomas A. Marks, "Colombian Army Adaptation to FARC Insurgency," Strategic Studies Army War College (U.S.). Minneapolis: Strategic Studies Institute, U.S. Army War College Command, January 2002– February 14, 2009, http://www.strategic-studiesinstitute.army.mil/pubs/display.cfm?pubid=18.
9. Dennis Rempe, "The Past as Prologue? A History of U.S. Counterinsurgency Policy in Colombia, 1955–66," Strategic Studies Institute: United States Army War College. March 2002.
10. Crandall, "Requiem for the FARC?" 233–40.
11. "Colombian Soldier Wore Red Cross Logo in Hostage Rescue," *New York Times*, July 17, 2008.
12. Crandall, "Requiem for the FARC?"
13. Ibid.
14. Interview with the Narcotics Affairs Sections of the U.S. Embassy in Bogotá, Colombia, December 18, 2008.
15. Alberto Mejía, "Colombia's National Security Strategy, a New "COIN" Approach," 25–6. This document of the Army War College contains figures published by the Colombian government with regard to other economic indicators such as GDP growth, unemployment, hectares of coca, and seizures of Colombian cocaine.
16. Interview with U.S. government contractor representative Brian Reuters, December 17, 2008.
17. Quoted in Marks, "A Model Counterinsurgency."
18. Juan Forero, "Colombia Challenges Rebels with a New Weapon," *Washington Post*, July 10, 2007.
19. For a U.S. government evaluation of the fusion centers, see United States Government Accountability Office, "Plan Colombia: Drug Reduction Goals Were Not Fully Met, but Security Has Improved; U.S. Agencies Need More Detailed Plans for Reducing Assistance" (October 2008): 59–62.
20. United States Government Accountability Office, "Plan Colombia: Drug Reduction Goals Were Not Fully Met."
21. "Presidente Uribe no se lanzaría para una segunda reelección si hay candidato único en el uribismo," *El Tiempo*, January 25, 2009. http://www.eltiempo.com/colombia/politica/presidente-uribe-no-se-lanzaria-para-una-segunda-reeleccion-si-hay-candidato-unico-en-el-uribismo_4773290-1 (accessed January 25, 2009).
22. Government of Colombia, National Administrative Department of Statistics, 2009.
23. Chris Kraul, "Extrajudicial Slayings on Rise in Colombia," *Los Angeles Times*, March 21, 2008.

24. Figures vary depending on source. "Salen 10 oficiales y un suboficial que pasraon por el Batallón La Popa por falsos positivos," *El Tiempo*, January 23, 2009.
25. "Alarmante Incremento de Ejecuciones Extrajudiciales en Colombia," Observando. Boletín no. 6, October 16–31, 2008, http://www.ddhhcolombia.org.co/node/188 (accessed April 14, 2009); see Section II, Part A, Number 2 (p. 12–14) of the Annual Report of the United Nations High Commissioner for Human Rights on the Situation of Human Rights in Colombia. Issued February 28, 2008.
26. See De Shazo, "Countering Threats to Security and Stability."

Chapter 28. Iraq

1. Michael R. Gordon and Bernard E. Trainor, *Cobra II: The Inside Story of the Invasion and Occupation of Iraq*. New York: Pantheon, 2006, xxxi.
2. Nigel Aylwin-Foster, "Changing the Army for Counterinsurgency Operations," *Military Review* (November–December 2005): 9.
3. Bing West, *The Strongest Tribe: War, Politics, and Endgame in Iraq*. New York: Random House, 2008, 5–17.
4. Quoted in Gordon and Trainor, *Cobra II*, 311.
5. David Kilcullen, *The Accidental Guerrilla: Fighting Small Wars in the Midst of a Big One*. New York: Oxford University Press, 2009, 117.
6. Liam Anderson and Gareth Stansfield, *The Future of Iraq: Dictatorship, Democracy, or Division?* New York: Palgrave Macmillan, 2004, 87–90.
7. Quoted in Ricks, *Fiasco*, 94–5.
8. Quoted in ibid., 61; for a detailed discussion of the Bush administration's Iraq strategy and public justification, see Steven Metz, *Iraq and the Evolution of American Strategy*. Washington: Potomac Books, 2008.
9. Rose, *How Wars End*, 241.
10. Quoted in Ricks, *Fiasco*, 90.
11. General Joseph "Fighting Joe" Dunford, U.S. Marines Corps, 2003, quoted in West, *The Strongest Tribe*, 29.
12. Rose, *How Wars End*, 239.
13. George Packer, "The Lesson of Tal Afar," *The New Yorker*, April 10, 2006.
14. http://www.guardian.co.uk/world/2005/jun/27/usa.iraq.
15. Packer, "The Lesson of Tal Afar."
16. Paul Wolfowitz, "The Invasion of Iraq," PBS *Frontline*, February 27, 2003, http://www.pbs.org/wgbh/pages/frontline/shows/invasion/.
17. Beinart, *The Icarus Syndrome*, 361.
18. Quoted in Rose, *How Wars End*, 249.
19. James Dobbins et al., *Occupying Iraq: A History of the Coalition Provisional Authority*. Washington: RAND Corporation, 2009, xiii.
20. Ibid., xxiii.
21. Rajiv Chandrasekaran, *Imperial Life in the Emerald City: Inside Iraq's Green Zone*. New York: Alfred A. Knopf, 2006, 77.
22. International Crisis Group, "The Next Iraqi War?," 8.
23. Ricks, *Fiasco*, 197.

24. Stanley McChrystal, *My Share of the Task: A Memoir*. New York: Penguin, 2013, 107.
25. West, *The Strongest Tribe*, 10.
26. International Crisis Group, "Iraq's Muqtada al-Sadr: Spoiler or Stabiliser?" *Middle East Report* 55 (July 11, 2006).
27. Marine Captain Doug Zembiec, the "Lion of Fallujah," 2004, quoted in West, *Strongest Tribe*, 32. Zembiec was killed by small arms fire while leading a raid in Baghdad on May 11, 2007.
28. Marine General Mattis, quoted in Ricks, *Fiasco*, 313.
29. Moyar, *A Question of Command*, 228.
30. Chandrasekaran, *Imperial Life in the Emerald City*, 277.
31. Quoted in Ricks, *Fiasco*, 342.
32. Ibid., 399.
33. Chandrasekaran, *Imperial Life in the Emerald City*, 288.
34. Ibid., 296–7; Larry Diamond, "Building Democracy after Conflict: Lessons from Iraq," *Journal of Democracy* 16:1 (January 2005): 9–23.
35. Spencer Ackerman, "In the End, Petraeus Really Was That Good," *Wired. com*, August 31, 2011.
36. Packer, "The Lesson of Tal Afar."
37. Ibid.; Max Boot, "Our Enemies Aren't Drinking Lattes," *Los Angeles Times*, July 5, 2006. Also see Robert D. Kaplan, "Think Global, Fight Local," *Opinion Journal*, December 20, 2003.
38. See Thomas E. Ricks, "In Iraq, Military Forgot Lessons of Vietnam," *Washington Post*, July 23, 2006.
39. Chris Gibson, "Battlefield Victories and Strategic Success: The Path Forward in Iraq," *Military Review* (September–October 2006): 47–59.
40. Moyar, *A Question of Command*, 234.
41. Quoted in Gibson, "Battlefield Victories."
42. Andrew W. Koloski and John S. Kolasheski, "Thickening the Lines: Sons of Iraq, a Combat Multiplier," *Military Review* (January–February, 2009).
43. Moyar, *A Question of Command*, 239.
44. Jim Michaels, "An Army Colonel's Gamble Pays Off in Iraq," *USA Today*, May 1, 2007, http://www.usatoday.com/news/world/iraq/2007-04-30-ramadi-colonel_N.htm.
45. Ibid.
46. Koloski and Kolasheski, "Thickening the Lines."
47. Mark F. Cancian, "What Turned the Tide in Anbar?" *Military Review* (March–April 2009); John A. Nagle, "A Better War in Iraq: Learning Counterinsurgency and Making Up for Lost Time," *Armed Forces Journal* (August 2006): 22–8.
48. Michael Eisenstadt, "Tribal Engagement Lessons Learned," *Military Review* (September–October 2007).
49. Senator Joseph Biden, *Charlie Rose Show*, September 2007.
50. http://www.washingtonpost.com/wpdyn/content/article/2007/01/23/AR200 7012301075.html; National Intelligence Council, "Prospects for Iraq's Stability: A Challenging Road Ahead," January 2007.

51. Moyar, *A Question of Command*, 247; also see Mark P. Krieger, "We the People Are Not the Center of Gravity in an Insurgency," *Military Review* (July–August 2007): 96–100; Carl D. Grunow, "Advising Iraqis: Building the Iraqi Army," *Military Review* (July–August 2006): 140–9.
52. Moyar, *A Question of Command*, 247; Dale Kuehl, "Testing Galula in Ameriyah: The People Are the Key," *Military Review* (March–April 2009).
53. Koloski and Kolasheski, "Thickening the Lines."
54. David H. Petraeus, "Multi-National Force-Iraq Commander's Counterinsurgency Guidance," *Military Review* (September–October 2008); also see James R., Crider, "A View from Inside the Surge," *Military Review* (March–April 2009).
55. Boot, *Invisible Armies*, 543.
56. Douglas A. Ollivant, "Countering the New Orthodoxy: Reinterpreting Counterinsurgency in Iraq," New America Foundation National Security Studies Program Policy Paper, June 2011.
57. Ricks, "In Iraq, Military Forgot Lessons of Vietnam."
58. Quoted in Ricks, *Fiasco*, 360.
59. Bing West, "American Military Performance in Iraq," *Military Review* (September–October 2006).
60. Michael R. Gordon and Bernard E. Trainor, *The Endgame: The Inside Story of the Struggle for Iraq, from George W. Bush to Barack Obama*. New York: Pantheon, 4.

Chapter 29. Intermezzo: The *Counterinsurgency Field Manual* and Postmodern Insurgencies

1. Quoted in "The Challenge of Counterinsurgency."
2. United States Army and United States Marine Corps, *Counterinsurgency Field Manual*. Chicago: University of Chicago Press 2007, 47–51.
3. Luttwak, "Dead End," 33–42.
4. Quoted in "The Challenge of Counterinsurgency."
5. Michael Crowley, "COIN Toss: The Cult of Counterinsurgency," *The New Republic*, January 4, 2010; Elisabeth Bumiller, "West Point Is Divided on a War Doctrine's Fate," *New York Times*, May 27, 2012.
6. Ackerman, "In the End, Petraeus Really Was that Good"; Crowley, "COIN Toss"; John Hillen, "Developing a National Counterinsurgency Capability for the War on Terror," *Military Review* (January–February 2007): 8–10.
7. Kilcullen, *The Accidental Guerrilla*, xiv; Kilcullen, "Counterinsurgency Redux"; Kilcullen, "Countering Global Insurgency"; also see Frank G. Hoffman, *Conflict in the 21st Century: The Rise of Hybrid Wars*. Arlington, VA: Potomac Institute for Policy Studies, December 2007; H. R. McMaster, "On War: Lessons to Be Learned," *Survival* 50:1 (February–March 2008): 19–30; Marston and Malkasian, *Counterinsurgency in Modern Warfare*; Neil W. Smith, "Sisyphus and Counterinsurgency," *Small Wars Journal* (September 17, 2008); Kilcullen, *Counterinsurgency*, 30–1.

Chapter 30. Post-9/11 COIN in the Philippines

1. Kaplan, *Imperial Grunts*, 144.
2. Ibid.
3. John Gershman, "Is Southeast Asia the Second Front?" *Foreign Affairs* (July–August 2002): 67.
4. Kaplan, *Imperial Grunts*, 145.
5. Gregory Wilson, "Anatomy of a Successful COIN Operation: OEF-Philippines and the Indirect Approach," *Military Review* (November–December 2006).
6. Kaplan, *Imperial Grunts*, 146.
7. "Hunting Terrorists," *Economist*, January 31, 2002.
8. Kaplan, *Imperial Grunts*, 151.
9. Ibid., 152.
10. The other American hostage, a missionary, was killed in the rescue attempt.
11. Kaplan, *Imperial Grunts*, 165.
12. Ibid., 167.
13. Ibid.
14. Ibid.
15. "Americans Are Going Home," *Economist*, July 11, 2002.
16. Steven, Rogers, "Beyond Abu Sayyaf: The Lessons of Failure in the Philippines," *Foreign Affairs* (January 2004): 15–20.
17. "It Could Be Peace," *Economist*, October 13, 2012.
18. "Hunting Terrorists."
19. Kaplan, *Imperial Grunts*, 135.

Chapter 31. Intermezzo: Afghanistan, Graveyard of Empires

1. Milton Bearden, "Afghanistan, Graveyard of Empires," *Foreign Affairs* (November–December 2001): 17–30.
2. Joes, *America and Guerrilla Warfare*, 279–317.
3. Pankaj Mishra, "The Making of Afghanistan," *New York Review of Books*, November 15, 2001, 18–21.
4. Joes, *America and Guerrilla Warfare*, 283–5.
5. Quoted in Mishra, "The Making of Afghanistan."
6. Ibid.
7. Bearden, "Afghanistan, Graveyard of Empires," 24.
8. Joes, *America and Guerrilla Warfare*, 288.
9. Bearden, "Afghanistan, Graveyard of Empires," 21.
10. Seth G. Jones, *In the Graveyard of Empires: America's War in Afghanistan*. New York: W.W. Norton, 37.
11. Steve Coll, *Ghost Wars: The Secret History of the CIA, Afghanistan, and bin Laden, from the Soviet Invasion to September 10, 2001*. New York: Penguin Press, 2004, 11.
12. Dexter Filkins, "After America," *New Yorker*, July 9, 2012.

13. Daniel Marston, "Lessons in 21st Century Counterinsurgency: Afghanistan, 2001–07," in Daniel Marston and Carter Malkasian, eds., *Counterinsurgency in Modern Warfare*. London: Osprey, 2008.
14. Coll, *Ghost Wars*, 4.
15. Moyar, *A Question of Command*, 191–3.
16. Tim Judah, "With the Northern Alliance," *New York Review of Books*, November 15, 2001.
17. Jones, *In the Graveyard of Empires*, 62.
18. Quoted in Jones, *In the Graveyard of Empires*, 282.
19. Mark Bowden, *The Finish: The Killing of Osama bin Laden*. New York: Atlantic Press, 93.
20. "U.S. Missiles Pound Targets in Afghanistan," CCN.com, August 21, 1998.
21. Quoted in Jones, *In the Graveyard of Empires*, 83.

Chapter 32. The Longest War: America in Afghanistan

1. Kilcullen, *The Accidental Guerrilla*, 73.
2. Bing West, *The Wrong War: Grit, Strategy, and the Way Out of Afghanistan*. New York: Random House, 2011, xxii.
3. Rajiv Chandrasekaran, "In Afghanistan's South, Signs of Progress in Three Districts Signal a Shift," *Washington Post*, April 16, 2011.
4. Kent Harris and Joseph Giordono, "Report Details Attack on GIs in Afghanistan," *Stars and Stripes*, November 9, 2008. Also see Steven Mraz, "Soldiers Recount Deadly Attack on Afghanistan Outpost," *Stars and Stripes*, July 19, 2008.
5. Eric Schmitt, "Afghan Officials Aided an Attack on U.S. Soldiers," *New York Times*, November 4, 2008.
6. See Douglas R. Cubbison's draft written for the U.S. Army's Combat Studies Institute, 2008, 36–40.
7. Max Boot, *War Made New: Techology, Warfare, and the Course of History, 1500 to Today*. New York: Gotham Books, 2006, 368.
8. Kaplan, *Imperial Grunts*, 199.
9. Ibid.
10. See Elizabeth Rubin, "Battle Company Is Out There," *New York Times*, February 24, 2008; also C. J. Chivers, "Turning Tables, U.S. Troops Ambush Taliban with Swift and Lethal Results," *New York Times*, April 16, 2009; also C. J. Chivers, "In Bleak Afghan Outpost, Troops Slog On," *New York Times*, May 14, 2009; Sebastian Junger, "Into the Valley of Death," *Vanity Fair*, January 2008.
11. See Kilcullen, *The Accidental Guerrilla*, 41–3, and Congressional Research Service, *The Cost of Iraq, Afghanistan and Other Global War on Terror Operations since 9/11*, Report for Congress (Washington, DC: Government Printing Office, updated April 11, 2008), 10–12; and Craig Colucci, "Committing to Afghanistan: The Case for Reconstruction and Stabilization in Iraq," *Military Review* (May–June 2007).

12. Ann Scott Tyson, "Gates Criticizes NATO Countries on Afghanistan," *Washington Post*, December 12, 2007, as quoted in Kilcullen, *The Accidental Guerrilla*, 43.
13. "Remarks by President Obama in Address to the Nation from Afghanistan," Bagram Air Base, Afghanistan, May 1, 2012, http://www.whitehouse.gov/the-press-office/2012/05/01/remarks-president-address-nation-afghanistan (accessed May 2, 2012).
14. David Sanger, "Charting Obama's Journey to a Shift on Afghanistan," *New York Times*, May 20, 2012.
15. "President Bush Launches Attack on Afghanistan," ABC News, October 7, 2011.
16. Quoted in Rose, *How Wars End*, 282–3.
17. Boot, *War Made New*, 379.
18. Jones, *In the Graveyard of Empires*, 97.
19. Quoted in Boot, *War Made New*, 382.
20. Said Jawad, Afghan ambassador to the United States, quoted in David W. Barno, "Fighting the 'Other War': Counterinsurgency Strategy in Afghanistan, 2003–05," *Military Review* (September–October 2007).
21. U.S. intelligence officer, interview with author, 2012.
22. Moyar, *A Question of Command*, 194.
23. David K. Spencer, "Afghanistan's Nangarhar Inc.," *Military Review* (July–August 2009).
24. Samuel Chan, "Sentinels of Afghan Democracy: The Afghan National Army," *Military Review* (January–February 2009).
25. Colucci, "Committing to Afghanistan."
26. Moyar, *A Question of Command*, 191–3.
27. Jones, *In the Graveyard of Empires*, 238.
28. Tom Ricks, "Wartime Command Structures: Why Are We so Bad at Designing Effective Ones?" *Foreign Policy*, March 15, 2012.
29. Jones, *In the Graveyard of Empires*, 250.
30. Kilcullen, *The Accidental Guerrilla*, 47–8.
31. Colucci, "Committing to Afghanistan."
32. Kilcullen, *The Accidental Guerrilla*, 55.
33. Moyar, *A Question of Command*, 194–211.
34. Quoted in Chan, "Sentinels of Afghan Democracy."
35. Quoted in ibid.
36. Ibid.
37. Kilcullen, *The Accidental Guerrilla*, 49.
38. West, *The Wrong War*, 138–9.
39. Jones, *In the Graveyard of Empires*, 204.
40. Rajiv Chandrasekaram, *Little America: The War within the War for Afghanistan*. New York: Knopf, 2012, 53.
41. David E. Sanger, *Confront and Conceal: Obama's Secret Wars and Surprising Use of American Power*. New York: Crown, 2012, 21.
42. Greg Jaffe, "McChrystal's Lack of Political Skills Led to Downfall," *Washington Post*, June 24, 2010.
43. Sanger, *Confront and Conceal*, 22.

44. Chandrasekaram, *Little America*, 120.
45. Sanger, *Confront and Conceal*, 25.
46. Fred Kaplan, "The End of the Age of Petraeus," *Foreign Affairs* (January–February 2013): 75–90.
47. See: Sarah Holewinski, "Do Less Harm: Protecting and Compensating Civilians in War," *Foreign Affairs* (January–February 2013).
48. Chandrasekaram, *Little America*, 124.
49. "Remarks by the President in Address to the Nation on the Way Forward in Afghanistan and Pakistan," White House Press Office, December 1, 2009.
50. Chandrasekaram, *Little America*, 11.
51. Sanger, *Confront and Conceal*, 35.
52. Chandrasekaram, *Little America*, 138.
53. McChrystal, *My Share of the Task*, 369.
54. "More Please, Sir," *Economist*, February 26, 2011.
55. Lieutenant Colonel Jason Morris, Helmand Province, October 2010, quoted in Chandrasekaram, *Little America*, 138–40.
56. British Army General Graeme Lamb, quoted in McChrystal, *My Share of the Task*, 246.
57. Hastings, "The Runaway General"; Ahmed Rashid, "The Return of 'The Runaway General,'" *New York Review of Books*, September 27, 2012.
58. Quoted in James Mann, *The Obamians: The Struggle inside the White House to Redefine American Power*. New York: Viking, 2012, 223.
59. Yaroslave Trofimov, "Many Afghans Shrug at 'This Event Foreigners Call 9/11,'" *Wall Street Journal*, September 7, 2011.
60. West, *The Wrong War*, 111.
61. David Ignatius, "Petraeus Rewrites the Playbook in Afghanistan," *Washington Post*, October 19, 2010, A15.
62. Ibid.
63. David M. Rodriquez, "Leaving Afghanistan to the Afghans," *Foreign Affairs* (September–October 2011): 45–53.
64. Matthew Rosenberg, "Training Afghan Allies, with Guard Firmly Up," *New York Times*, September 25, 2012; James Joyner, "The Day We Lost Afghanistan," *National Interest*, September 19, 2012.
65. Chandrasekaran, "In Afghanistan's South."
66. Ibid.; also see Mark Moyar, "The Third War of COIN: Defeating the Taliban in Sangin," *Orbis Operations* (July 2011).
67. Chandrasekaram, *Little America*, 273.
68. Quoted in Jones, *In the Graveyard of Empires*, 308.
69. New America Foundation, Counterterrorism Strategy Initiative, http://counterterrorism.newamerica.net/drones/2011.
70. Nicholas Schmidle, "Getting bin Laden," *The New Yorker*, August 8, 2011.
71. Quoted in Sanger, *Confront and Conceal*, 88.
72. Mann, *The Obamians*, 306.
73. Defense Secretary Leon Panetta's final orders to Joint Special Operations (JSOC) commander William H. McRaven stationed in Jalalabad, Afghanistan; quoted in Bowden, *The Finish*, 220.
74. This section is derived from Schmidle, "Getting bin Laden."

75. Bowden, *The Finish*, 194.
76. Ibid., 210.
77. Ibid., 221.
78. Ibid., 225.
79. Steve Coll, "Dead or Alive," *New York Review of Books*, October 25, 2012.
80. Bowden, *The Finish*, 232–3.
81. Sixty-five-year-old Ali Mohhamen Khan, elder of the Karabay village, Helmand Province, 2013, quoted in Yaroslov Trofimov, "Afghan Forces Set to Soldier On Alone," *Wall Street Journal*, February 4, 2013.
82. Marine Lieutenant Mike Breslin, Helmand Province, 2013, quoted in ibid.
83. Taimoor Shah and Graham Bowley, "U.S. Scrambles to Contain Fury over Attack in Afghanistan," *New York Times*, March 12, 2012.
84. Sanger, "Charting Obama's Journey to a Shift on Afghanistan."
85. Trofimov, "Afghan Forces Set to Soldier On Alone."
86. Ibid.

Chapter 33. The Fall of Muammar Qaddafi, 2011

1. Jon Lee Anderson, "King of Kings: The Last Days of Muammar Qaddafi," *New Yorker*, November 7, 2011.
2. Ibid.
3. Alison Pargeter, *Libya: The Rise and Fall of Qaddafi*, New Haven, CT: Yale University Press, 2012, 93.
4. Ibid., 95.
5. Anderson, "King of Kings."
6. Ibid.
7. Pargeter, *Libya*, 128.
8. Anderson, "King of Kings."
9. Pargeter, *Libya*, 136.
10. Ronald Bruce St. John, *Libya: From Colony to Revolution*. Oxford: Oneworld Publications, 2012, 179.
11. Pargeter, *Libya*, 134–6.
12. Ibid. 137.
13. Ibid. 138.
14. Mann, *The Obamians*, 281.
15. St. John, *Libya: From Colony to Revolution*, 201.
16. Anderson, "King of Kings."
17. Ibid.
18. Ibid.
19. Sanger, *Confront and Conceal*, 337.
20. St. John, *Libya: From Colony to Revolution*, 282.
21. Sanger, *Confront and Conceal*, 337–8.
22. Mann, *The Obamians*, 282–3.
23. Anderson, "King of Kings."
24. Quoted in Pargeter, *Libya*, 228.
25. Ibid. 226.

26. Mann, *The Obamians*, xii.
27. Ibid. 281.
28. Ibid. xi.
29. "The Libya Campaign: Into the Unknown," *Economist*, http://www.econo mist.com/node/18442119 (accessed January 31, 2013).
30. Mann, *The Obamians*, xii.
31. Christopher Chivvis, "Libya and the Future of Liberal Intervention," *Survival: Global Politics and Strategy*, November 30, 2012, 70.
32. Ibid., 71.
33. Mark Thompson, "Target Libya: Odyssey Dawn Begins," *Time*, March 19, 2011, http://nation.time.com/2011/03/19/the-balloon-goes-up-in-libya-with-u-s-in-the-back-seat/ (accessed January 31, 2013).
34. "The Libya Campaign: Into the Unknown."
35. Chivvis, "Libya and the Future of Liberal Intervention," 72.
36. Quoted in Sanger, *Confront and Conceal*, 351.
37. Chivvis, "Libya and the Future of Liberal Intervention," 74.
38. Mark Mazzetti, "CIA Agents in Libya Aid Airstrikes and Meet Rebels," *New York Times*, March 30, 2011, http://www.nytimes.com/2011/03/31/world/africa/31intel.html?_r=2& (accessed January 31, 2013).
39. Ibid.
40. Ibid.
41. Chivvis, "Libya and the Future of Liberal Intervention," 77.
42. Ibid., 77.
43. Anderson, "King of Kings."
44. Ibid.
45. Ibid.

Chapter 34. Intermezzo: JSOC Raids and Drone Strikes

1. "Generation Kill: A Conversation with Stanley McChrystal," *Foreign Affairs* (March–April 2013).
2. Boot, *Invisible Armies*, 482.
3. Bowden, *The Finish*, 100.
4. David Crist, The Twilight War: The Secret History of America's Thirty-Year Conflict with Iran. New York: Penguin, 2012, 31–2.
5. Bowden, *The Finish*, 148, 197.
6. Ibid., 152.
7. McChrystal, *My Share of the Task*, 233.
8. Ibid., 232.
9. Bowden, *The Finish*, 105.
10. McChrystal, *My Share of the Task*, 91.
11. The recovered information also betrayed the fiction that the Al Qaeda fighters were mostly local Iraqis. Instead, these insurgents were overwhelmingly foreign, with large numbers coming from Saudi Arabia as well as Libya, Morocco, Syria, Algeria, Oman, Yemen, Tunisia, Egypt, Jordan, Belgium, France, and the United Kingdom. See Barbara Starr, "Al Qaeda

'Rolodex' Found in Iraq," Cnn.com, November 22, 2007; Bowden, *The Finish*, xi–xii.
12. Quoted in Bowden, *The Finish*, 208.
13. Quoted in ibid., 263.
14. John Brennan, President Barack Obama's counterterrorism and intelligence adviser and CIA director, quoted in Holewinski, "Do Less Harm."
15. P. W. Singer, *Wired for War: The Robotics Revolution and Conflict in the 21st Century*. New York: Penguin, 2009, 217.
16. David, Sanger, *Confront and Conceal*, 243.
17. "Remarks by the President at the National Defense University," May 23, 2013. Full transcript at http://www.whitehouse.gov/the-press-office/2013/05/23/remarks-president-national-defense-university.
18. Coll, *Ghost Wars*, 523.
19. Bowden, *The Finish*, 108–11; Singer, *Wired for War*, 33.
20. Declan Walsh, "Drone War Spurs Militants to Deadly Reprisals," *New York Times*, December 29, 2012.0

Chapter 35. Conclusion

1. Kalev I. Sepp, Review of David Kilcullen, *The Accidental Guerrilla: Fighting Small Wars in the Midst of a Big One*, in *Political Science Quarterly* (Summer 2010): 356–7.
2. Marshall Andrews, foreword to Bernard B. Fall, *Street without Joy: The French Debacle in Indochina*. Mechanicsburg, PA: Stackpole Books, 1994, 9.
3. Petraeus, "Learning"; John Kiszely, "Learning about Counterinsurgency," *Military Review* (March–April 2007): 5–11; Claessen, "Discouraging Hearts and Minds"; Edward N. Luttwak, "Notes on Low-Intensity Conflict," in George Edward Thibault, ed., *Dimensions of Military Strategy*. Washington: National Defense University Press, 1987, 333–42; Gavin Bulloch, "Military Doctrine and Counterinsurgency: A British Perspective," *Parameters*, U.S. Army War College Quarterly (Summer 1996): 4–16; Ike Skelton, "America's Frontier Wars: Lessons for Asymmetric Conflicts," *Military Review* (September–October 2001): 1–10; a seminal work on this issue can be found in Walter Russell Mead's *Special Providence: American Foreign Policy and How It Changed the World*. New York: Routledge, 2002. Also see Thomas G. Mahnken, "The American Way of War in the Twenty-first Century," in Efraim Inbar, ed., *Democracies and Small Wars*. Portland, OR: Frank Cass, 2003, 73–84.
4. Luttwak, "Dead End."
5. Record, "The American Way of War: Cultural Barriers to Successful Counterinsurgency," *Cato Institute Policy Analysis*, No. 77, September 2006.
6. Peggy Noonan, "Can the Republican Party Recover from Iraq?" *Wall Street Journal*, March 21, 2013.
7. See, for example, Moyar, *A Question of Command*.
8. Francis Fukuyama, "Why I Like the Afghan Timetable," *The American Interest* (December 2009); also see Peggy Noonan, "Can the Republican Party Recover from Iraq?" *Wall Street Journal*, March 22, 2013.

9. Record, "The American Way of War."
10. Bernard B. Fall, "The Theory and Practice of Insurgency and Counterinsurgency," *Naval War College Review* (April 1965).

Epilogue: "I Feel More Like a Monster"

1. David Finkel, "The Return: The Traumatized Veterans of Iraq and Afghanistan," *The New Yorker*, September 9, 2013, 36.
2. "The Waiting Wounded," *The Economist*, March 23, 2013.
3. See the Mayo Clinic's definition of PTSD: http://www.mayoclinic.com/health/post-traumatic-stress-disorder/DS00246.
4. "The Waiting Wounded"; Hannah Fischer, *U.S. Military Casualty Statistics: Operation New Dawn, Operation Iraqi Freedom, and Operation Enduring Freedom*. Congressional Research Service, February 2013. http://www.fas.org/sgp/crs/natsec/RS22452.pdf.
5. Ibid.
6. Finkel, "The Return."

Bibliography

Books

Abuza, Zachary. *Balik-Terrorism: The Return of the Abu Sayyaf*. Carlisle, PA: Strategic Studies Institute, 2005.

Aguilar, Luis, ed. *Operation Zapata: The "Ultrasensitive" Report and Testimony of the Board of Inquiry on the Bay of Pigs*. Frederick, MD: University Publications of America, 1981.

Alden, John Richard. *The American Revolution, 1775–1783*. New York: Harper, 1954.

Aldrich, Richard J., ed., with Gary Rawnsley and Ming-Yeh Rawnsley. *The Clandestine Cold War in Asia, 1945–65: Western Intelligence, Propaganda, and Special Operations*. London: Frank Cass, 2000.

Alter, Robert Edmond. *First Comes Courage*. New York: G. P. Putnam's Sons, 1969.

Anderson, Jon Lee. *Che Guevara: A Revolutionary Life*. New York: Grove Press, 1997.

Anderson, Liam and Gareth Stansfield. *The Future of Iraq: Dictatorship, Democracy, or Division?* New York: Palgrave Macmillan, 2004.

Anderson, Scott and John Lee Anderson. *Inside the League: The Shocking Exposé of How Terrorists, Nazis, and Latin American Death Squads Have Infiltrated the World Anti-Communist League*. New York: Dodd, Mead, 1986.

Anderson, Thomas P. *Matanza: El Salvador's Communist Revolt of 1932*. Lincoln: University of Nebraska Press, 1971.

Angley, Wilson et al. *Sherman's March through North Carolina: A Chronology*. Raleigh: North Carolina Division of Archives and History, 1995.

Arendt, Hannah. *On Revolution*. New York: Viking Press, 1962.

On Violence. New York: Harcourt, Brace and World, 1970.

Armstrong, Robert and Janet Shenk. *El Salvador: The Face of Revolution*. 2nd ed. Boston: South End Press, 1982.

Arnson, Cynthia J. *Crossroads: Congress the President, and Central America, 1976–1993*. Second Edition. University Park, PA, Pennsylvania State University, 1993.

El Salvador: A Revolution Confronts the United States. Washington, D.C.: Institute for Policy Studies, 1982.

ed. *Comparative Peace Processes in Latin America*. Washington, DC: Woodrow Wilson Center Press, 1999.

Asprey, Robert B. *War in the Shadows: The Guerrilla in History*. Revised and updated ed. New York: William Morrow, 1994.

Atkinson, Rick. *In the Company of Soldiers: A Chronicle of Combat*. New York: Owl Books, 2005.

Bacevich, A. J., et al. *American Military Policy in Small Wars: The Case of El Salvador. 1988 Special Report, Institute for Foreign Policy Analysis*. Washington, DC: Pergamon Brassey's, 1988.

Bailey, J. D. *Commanders at Kings Mountain*. Greenville, SC: A Press, 1980.

Bain, David Howard. *Sitting in Darkness: Americans in the Philippines*. Boston: Houghton Mifflin, 1984.

Baloyra, Enrique A. *El Salvador in Transition*. Chapel Hill, NC: University of North Carolina Press, 1982.

Barnet, Richard J. *Intervention and Revolution: The United States in the Third World*. New York: World Publishing, 1968.

Barry, Tom. *El Salvador: A Country Guide*. Albuquerque, NM: Inter-Hemispheric Education Resource Center, 1990.

Bates, Robert H. *Prosperity and Violence: The Political Economy of Development*. New York: W.W. Norton, 2001.

Beale, Howard K. *Theodore Roosevelt and the Rise of America to World Power*. Baltimore, MD: Johns Hopkins University Press, 1956.

Beals, Carleton. *Banana Gold*. New York: Arno, 1970.

Beckett, Ian F. W. *Modern Insurgencies and Counterinsurgencies: Guerrillas and Their Opponents since 1750*. New York: Routledge, 2001.

Beede, Benjamin R. *Intervention and Counterinsurgency: An Annotated Bibliography of the Small Wars of the United States, 1898–1984*. New York: Garland, 1985.

Beevor, Antony. *The Second World War*. New York: Little, Brown, 2012.

Beinart, Peter. *The Icarus Syndrome: A History of American Hubris*. New York: Harper, 2010.

Bellavia, David. *House to House: An Epic Memoir of War*. New York: Free Press, 2007.

Bemis, Samuel Flagg. *The Latin America Policy of the United States: A Historical Interpretation*. New York: Harcourt, Brace, 1943.

Bermann, Karl. *Under the Big Stick: Nicaragua and the United States since 1848*. Boston: South End Press, 1986.

Best, Edward. *U.S. Policy and Regional Security in Central America*. New York: St. Martin's Press, 1987.

Binford, Leigh. *The El Mozote Massacre*. Tucson: University of Arizona Press, 1996.

Birtle, Andrew J. *U.S. Army Counterinsurgency and Contingency Operations Doctrine, 1860–1941*. Washington, DC: Center of Military History, 1998.

Blachman, Morris J., William M. Leogrande, and Kenneth Sharpe, eds. *Confronting Revolution: Security through Diplomacy in Central America*. New York: Pantheon, 1986.
Blasier, Cole. *The Hovering Giant: U.S. Responses to Revolutionary Change in Latin America*. Pittsburgh: University of Pittsburgh Press, 1986.
Blaufarb, Douglas S. *The Counterinsurgency Era: U.S. Doctrine and Performance, 1950 to the Present*. New York: Free Press, 1977.
Bonner, Raymond. *Weakness and Deceit: U.S. Policy and El Salvador*. New York: Times Books, 1984.
Book, Max. *Invisible Armies: An Epic History of Guerrilla Warfare from Ancient Times to the Present*. New York: W. W. Norton, 2013.
    The Savage Wars of Peace: Small Wars and the Rise of American Power. New York: Basic Books, 2002.
Boyce, James K. *Economic Policy for Building Peace: The Lessons of El Salvador*. Boulder, CO: Lynne Rienner, 1996.
Braddy, Haldeen. *Cock of the Walk: The Legend of Pancho Villa*. Albuquerque: University of New Mexico Press, 1955.
    The Paradox of Pancho Villa. El Paso: Texas Western College Press, 1978.
Braestrup, Peter. *Big Story: How the American Press and Television Reported and Interpreted the Crisis of Tet 1968 in Vietnam and Washington*. Abridged ed. Novato, CA: Presidio, 1994.
Brands, Hal. *Latin America's Cold War*. Cambridge, MA: Harvard University Press, 2010.
Brands, H. W. *Bound to Empire: The United States and the Philippines*. New York: Oxford University Press, 1992.
Britten, Thomas A. *A Brief History of the Seminole-Negro Indian Scouts*. Lewiston, NY: Edwin Mellen Press, 1999.
Brown, Fred. *History of the Ninth U.S. Infantry, 1799–1909*. Chicago: R. R. Donnelley and Sons, 1909.
Browning, David. *El Salvador: Landscape and Society*. Oxford: Clarendon Press, 1971.
Bruning, John R. *The Devil's Sandbox: With the 2nd Battalion, 162nd Infantry, at War in Iraq*. St. Paul, MN: Zenith Press, 2006.
Bulmer-Thomas, Victor and James Dunkerley, eds. *The United States and Latin America: The New Agenda*. London: Institute of Latin American Studies, 1999.
Butler, Smedley D. *Old Gimlet Eye: The Adventures of Smedley D. Butler as Told to Lowell Thomas*. New York: Farrar and Rinehart, 1933.
Byrne, Hugh. *El Salvador's Civil War: A Study of Revolution*. Boulder, CO: Lynne Reinner, 1996.
Cable, James. *Gunboat Diplomacy: Political Applications of Limited Naval Force*. New York: Praeger, 1971.
Cable, Larry E. *Conflict of Myths: The Development of American Counterinsurgency Doctrine and the Vietnam War*. New York: New York University Press, 1986.

Calder, Bruce J. *The Impact of Intervention: The Dominican Republic during the U.S. Occupation of 1916–1924*. Austin: University of Texas Press, 1984.
Callwell, C. E. *Small Wars: Their Principle and Practice*. 3rd ed. Lincoln: University of Nebraska Press, Bison Books, 1996. 3rd ed. Originally published 1906.
Carothers, Thomas. *In the Name of Democracy: U.S. Policy toward Latin America in the Reagan Years*. Berkeley: University of California Press, 1991.
Carr, Barry and Steve Ellner, eds. *The Latin American Left*. Boulder, CO: Westview Press, 1993.
Castañeda, Jorge G. *Utopia Unarmed: The Latin American Left after the Cold War*. New York: Alfred A. Knopf, 1993.
Chaliand, Gérard, ed. *Guerrilla Strategies: An Historical Anthology from the Long March to Afghanistan*. Berkeley: University of California Press, 1982.
Challener, Richard D. *Admirals, Generals, and American Foreign Policy, 1898–1914*. Princeton, NJ: Princeton University Press, 1973.
Chandrasekaran, Rajiv. *Imperial Life in the Emerald City: Inside Iraq's Green Zone*. New York: Alfred A. Knopf, 2006.
   Little America: The War within the War for Afghanistan. New York: Alfred A. Knopf, 2012.
Chidsey, Donald Barr. *The War in the South: The Carolinas and Georgia in the American Revolution, an Informal History*. New York: Crown, 1969.
Clausewitz, Carl von. *On War*. Translated by Michael Howard and Peter Paret. New York: Oxford University Press, 2007.
Clements, Charles. *Witness to War: An American Doctor in El Salvador*. New York: Bantam Books, 1984.
Clendenen, Clarence C. *Blood on the Border: The United States Army, and the Mexican Irregulars*. New York: Macmillan, 1969.
   The United States and Pancho Villa: A Study in Unconventional Diplomacy. Ithaca, NY: Cornell University Press, 1961.
Close, David H., ed. *The Greek Civil War, 1943–1950: Studies of Polarization*. New York: Routledge, 1993.
Clutterbuck, Richard L. *The Long, Long War: Counterinsurgency in Malaya and Vietnam*. New York: Praeger, 1966.
Cohen, A. S. *Theories of Revolution: An Introduction*. New York: John Wiley, 1975.
Cohen, Warren I. *Empire without Tears: America's Foreign Relations, 1921–1933*. Philadelphia: Temple University Press, 1987.
Colby, William, with James McCargar. *Lost Victory: A Firsthand Account of America's Sixteen-Year Involvement in Vietnam*. Chicago: Contemporary Books, 1989.
Coll, Steve. *Ghost Wars: The Secret History of the CIA, Afghanistan, and bin Laden, from the Soviet Invasion to September 10, 2001*. New York: Penguin Press, 2004
Collins, John M. *America's Small Wars: Lessons for the Future*. Washington, DC: Brasseys, 1991.
Condit, Kenneth W. and Edwin T. Turnbladh. *Hold High the Torch: A History of the 4th Marines*. Washington, DC: Historical Branch, G-3 Division, Headquarters, U.S. Marine Corps, 1960.

Covington, James W. *The Seminoles of Florida*. Gainesville: University Press of Florida, 1993.
Crandall, Russell. *Driven by Drugs: U.S. Policy toward Colombia*. 2nd ed. Boulder, CO: Lynne Rienner, 2008.
Gunboat Democracy: U.S. Interventions in the Dominican Republic, Grenada, and Panama. Lanham, MD: Rowman and Littlefield, 2006.
The United States and Latin America after the Cold War. Cambridge: Cambridge University Press, 2008.
Crownover, Roger. *The United States Intervention in North Russia – 1918, 1919*. Lewiston, NY: Edwin Mellen Press, 2001.
Cullather, Nick. *Illusions of Influence: The Political Economy of United States-Philippines Relations, 1942–1960*. Stanford, CA: Stanford University Press, 1994.
Dameron, J. David. *Kings Mountain: The Defeat of the Loyalists, October 7, 1780*. Cambridge, MA: Da Capo Press, 2003.
Danner, Mark. *The Massacre at El Mozote*. New York: Vintage Books, 1993.
Davidson, Phillip. *Secrets of the Vietnam War*. Novato, CA: Presidio Press, 1990.
Vietnam at War. Novato, CA: Presidio, 1988.
Debray, Régis. *Revolution in the Revolution? Armed Struggle and Political Struggle in Latin America*. New York: Monthly Review Press, 1967.
Strategy for Revolution. New York: Monthly Review Press, 1970.
Denny, Harold Norman. *Dollars for Bullets: The Story of American Rule in Nicaragua*. New York: Dial, 1929.
Dobbins, James et al. *Occupying Iraq: A History of the Coalition Provisional Authority*. Washington, DC: RAND Corporation, 2009.
Downie, Richard. *Learning from Conflict: The U.S. Military in Vietnam, El Salvador, and the Drug War*. Westport, CT: Praeger, 1998.
Drayton, John, *Memoirs of the American Revolution as Relating to the State of South Carolina*, vol. 2 New York: Arno, 1969 (originally printed by A. E. Miller, Charleston, SC in two volumes, 1821).
Duarte, José Napoleón. *Duarte: My Story*. New York: Putnam, 1986.
Dunkerley, James. *Bolivia: Revolution and the Power of History in the Present*. London: Institute for the Study of the Americas, 2007.
The Pacification of Central America. London: Verso, 1994.
Power in the Isthmus. London: Verso, 1988.
Dupuy, Ernest R. and William H. Baumer. *The Little Wars of the United States*. New York: Hawthorn Books, 1968.
Dykeman, Wilma. *With Fire and Sword: The Battle of Kings Mountain 1780*. Washington, DC: U.S. Department of the Interior, National Park Service (pamphlet).
Eisenhower, John S. D. *Intervention: The United States and the Mexican Revolution, 1913–1917*. New York: W. W. Norton, 1993.
Ellis, John. *From the Barrel of a Gun: A History of Guerrilla, Revolutionary, and Counterinsurgency Warfare from the Romans to the Present*. London: Greenhill, 1995.
A Short History of Guerrilla Warfare. New York: St. Martin's Press, 1976.

Ellis, Joseph J. *American Creation: Triumphs and Tragedies at the Founding of the Republic*. New York: Alfred A. Knopf, 2007.
Ellsworth, Henry Allanson. *One Hundred Eighty Landings of United States Marines 1800–1934*. Washington, DC: U.S. Marine Corps, Historical Section, 1934.
Esdaile, Charles. *Fighting Napoleon: Guerrillas, Bandits, and Adventures in Spain, 1808–14*. New Haven, CT: Yale University Press, 2004.
The Peninsular War: A New History. New York: Palgrave Macmillan, 2003.
Esposito, John L. *Unholy War: Terror in the Name of Islam*. New York: Oxford University Press, 2002.
Evans, Ernest. *Wars without Splendor: The U.S. Military and Low-Level Conflict*. Westport, CT: Greenwood, 1987.
Fall, Bernard B. *Hell in a Very Small Place: The Siege of Dien Bien Phu*. Philadelphia: J. B. Lippincott, 1967.
Street without Joy: The French Debacle in Indochina. Mechanicsburg, PA: Stackpole Books, 1994.
Two Vietnams: A Political and Military Analysis. Boulder, CO: Westview Press, 1985.
Vietnam Witness 1953–66. New York: Praeger, 1966.
Faulk, Odie B. *The Geronimo Campaign*. New York: Oxford University Press, 1969.
Fauriol, Georges. *Latin American Insurgencies*. Washington, DC: Georgetown University Center for Strategic and International Studies and National Defense University, 1985.
Feldman, Noah. *After Jihad: America and the Struggle for Islamic Democracy*. New York: Farrar, Straus and Giroux, 2003.
Fick, Nathaniel C. *One Bullet Away: The Making of a Marine Officer*. New York: Houghton Mifflin, 2005.
Fish, Joe and Cristina Sganga. *El Salvador: Testament of Terror*. London: Zed Books, 1988.
Foglesong, David S. *America's Secret War against Bolshevism: U.S. Intervention in the Russian Civil War, 1917–1920*. Chapel Hill: University of North Carolina Press, 2001.
Fuller, Stephen M. and Graham A. Cosmas. *Marines in the Dominican Republic, 1916–1924*. Washington, DC: History and Museums Division, U.S. Marine Corps, 1974.
Funston, Frederick. *Memories of Two Wars: Cuban and Philippine Experiences*. New York: Charles Scribner's Sons, 1911.
Gacek, Christopher M. *The Logic of Force: The Dilemma of Limited War in American Foreign Policy*. New York: Columbia University Press, 1994.
Galula, David. *Counterinsurgency Warfare: Theory and Practice*. Westport, CT: Praeger, 2006.
Gann, Lewis. *Guerillas in History*. Stanford, CA: Hoover University Press, 1971.
Gates, John Morgan. *Schoolbooks and Krags: The United States Army in the Philippines, 1898–1902*. Westport, CT: Greenwood, 1973.
Gentile, Gian. *Wrong Turn: America's Deadly Embrace of Counterinsurgency*. New York: Free Press, 2013.

George Washington: A Collection. Compiled and edited by W. B. Allen. Indianapolis, IN: Liberty Fund, 1988).
Gettlemen, Marvin A. et al. *El Salvador: Central America in the New Cold War.* New York: Grove Press, 1981.
Geraghty, Tony. *The Irish War.* London: Harper Collins, 1998.
Gerolymatos, Andre. *Red Acropolis, Black Terror: The Greek Civil War and the Origins of Soviet-American Rivalry, 1943–1949.* New York: Basic Books, 2004.
Giáp, Võ Nguyên. *People's War, People's Army: The Vietcong Insurrection Manual for Underdeveloped Countries.* Edited by Bernard B. Fall. New York: Praeger, 1962.
Gleijeses, Piero. *Shattered Hope: The Guatemalan Revolution and the United States, 1944–1954.* Princeton, NJ: Princeton University Press, 1991.
Goldhurst, Richard. *The Midnight War: The American Intervention in Russia, 1918–1920.* New York: McGraw-Hill, 1978.
Gordon, Michael R. and Bernard E. Trainor. *Cobra II: The Inside Story of the Invasion and Occupation of Iraq.* New York: Pantheon, 2006.
  The Endgame: The Inside Story of the Struggle for Iraq, from George W. Bush to Barack Obama. New York: Random House, 2012.
Gorriti, Gustavo. *The Shining Path: A History of the Millenarian War in Peru.* Chapel Hill: University of North Carolina Press, 1999.
Graff, Henry F., ed. *American Imperialism and the Philippine Insurrection: Testimony Taken from Hearings in the Philippine Islands before the Senate Committee on the Philippines – 1902.* Boston: Little, Brown, 1969.
Grandin, Greg. *The Last Colonial Massacre.* Chicago: University of Chicago Press, 2011.
Grenier, Yvon. *The Emergence of Insurgency in El Salvador.* Pittsburgh: University of Pittsburgh Press, 1999.
Guevara, Che. *Guerrilla Warfare.* Lincoln: University of Nebraska Press, 1998.
Gunaratna, Rohan. *Inside al-Qaeda: Global Network of Terror.* Berkeley: University of California Press, 2003.
Gurr, Ted Robert. *Why Men Rebel.* Princeton, NJ: Princeton University Press, 1970.
Guzmán, Martín Luís. *The Eagle and the Serpent.* Translated by Harriet de Onís. New York: Alfred A. Knopf, 1930.
Haggerty, Richard A., ed. *El Salvador: A Country Study.* Washington, DC: Federal Research Division, Library of Congress, November, 1988.
Haig, Alexander M. Jr. *Caveat.* New York: Macmillan, 1984.
Haley, P. Edward. *Revolution and Intervention: The Diplomacy of Taft and Wilson with Mexico, 1910–1917.* Cambridge, MA: MIT Press, 1970.
Hammes, Thomas X. *The Sling and the Stone: On War in the 21st Century.* St. Paul, MN: Zenith Press, 2006.
Healy, David. *Drive to Hegemony: The United States in the Caribbean: 1898–1917.* Madison: University of Wisconsin Press, 1988.
  Gunboat Diplomacy in the Wilson Era: The U.S. Navy in Haiti, 1915–1916. Madison: University of Wisconsin Press, 1976.

Hecksher, August. *Woodrow Wilson: A Biography*. New York: Charles Scribner's Sons, 1991.
Hoffman, Frank G. *Conflict in the 21st Century: The Rise of Hybrid Wars*. Arlington, VA: Potomac Institute for Policy Studies, December 2007.
Hoig, Stan. *The Sand Creek Massacre*. Norman: University of Oklahoma Press, 1974.
Holden, Robert H. and Eric Zolov, eds. *Latin America and the United States: A Documentary History*. Oxford: Oxford University Press, 2000
Horne, Alistair. *A Savage War of Peace: Algeria 1954–1962*. New York: Viking Press, 1977.
Jackson, Robert. *The Malayan Emergency: The Commonwealth's Wars, 1948–1966*. London: Routledge, 1991.
James, Daniel. *Che Guevara: A Biography*. New York: Cooper Square Press, 2000.
Joes, Anthony James. *America and Guerrilla Warfare*. Lexington: University Press of Kentucky, 2000.
From the Barrel of a Gun: Armies and Revolutions. Washington, DC: Pergamon-Brassey's, 1986.
Guerrilla Warfare: A Historical, Biographical, and Bibliographical Sourcebook. Westport, CT: Greenwood, 1996.
Resisting Rebellion: The History and Politics of Counterinsurgency. Lexington: University Press of Kentucky, 2004.
ed. *Saving Democracies: U.S. Intervention in Threatened Democratic States*. Westport, CT: Praeger, 1999.
Jones, Howard. *A New Kind of War: America's Global Strategy and the Truman Doctrine in Greece*. New York: Oxford University Press, 1989.
Jones, Seth G. *In the Graveyard of Empires: America's War in Afghanistan*. New York: W. W. Norton, 2009.
Juillard, Rene. *The Battle of Diên Biên Phu*. New York: Harper and Row, 1965.
Kagan, Robert. *A Twilight Struggle: American Power and Nicaragua, 1977–1990*. New York: Free Press, 1996.
Kaplan, Fred. *The Insurgents: David Petraeus and the Plot to Change the American Way of War*. New York: Simon and Schuster, 2013.
Kaplan, Robert D. *Imperial Grunts: The American Military on the Ground*. New York: Random House, 2005.
Karnow, Stanley. *In Our Image: America's Empire in the Philippines*. New York: Random House, 1989.
Kean, Thomas H. et al. *The 9/11 Commission Report: Final Report of the National Commission on Terrorist Attacks upon the United States*. New York: W.W. Norton, Inc., 2004.
Kenez, Peter. *Civil War in South Russia, 1919–1920: The Defeat of the Whites*. Berkeley: University of California Press, 1977.
Kennett, Lee. *Marching through Georgia: The Story of Soldiers and Civilians during Sherman's Campaign*. New York: HarperCollins, 1995.
Kerkvillet, Benedict J. *The Huk Rebellion: A Study of Peasant Revolt in the Philippines*. Berkeley: University of California Press, 1977.
Khalidi, Rashid, Lisa Anderson, Muhammad Muslih, and Reeva S. Simon, eds. *The Origins of Arab Nationalism*. New York: Columbia University Press, 1991.

Kilcullen, David. *The Accidental Guerrilla: Fighting Small Wars in the Midst of a Big One*. New York: Oxford University Press, 2009.
Kinzer, Stephen J. *Blood of Brothers: Life and War in Nicaragua*.Cambridge, MA: Harvard University Press, 2007
Kirkpatrick, Jeane J. *Dictatorships and Double Standards*. New York: Simon and Schuster/ American Enterprise Institute, 1982.
The Reagan Phenomenon. Washington, DC: American Enterprise Institute, 1983.
Klare, Michael T. *War without End: American Planning for the Next Vietnams*. New York: Alfred A. Knopf, 1972.
Klare, Michael T. and Peter Kornbluh, eds. *Low Intensity Warfare: Counterinsurgency, Proinsurgency, and Antiterrorism in the Eighties*. New York: Pantheon Books, 1988.
Knight, Melvin M. *The Americans in Santo Domingo*. New York: Vanguard, 1928.
Kojm, Christopher, ed. *Revolution and Subversion in Latin America: Selected U.S. Intelligence Community Estimative Products, 1947–1987*. Washington, DC: National Intelligence Council, September 2010.
Komer, Robert W. *Bureaucracy at War: U.S. Performance in the Vietnam Conflict*. Boulder, CO: Westview, 1986.
Kornbluh, Peter. "The Covert War." In *Reagan versus the Sandinistas: The Undeclared War on Nicaragua*, edited by Thomas W. Walker. Boulder, CO: Westview, 1987, 21–39.
Krauze, Enrique. *Redeemers: Ideas and Power in Latin America*. New York: HarperCollins, 2011.
Krepinevich, Andrew. *The Army and Vietnam*. Baltimore, MD: Johns Hopkins University Press, 1986.
LaFeber, Walter. *The Cambridge History of American Foreign Relations*. Cambridge: Cambridge University Press, 1993.
Inevitable Revolutions: The United States in Central America. New York: W.W. Norton, 1983.
The New Empire: An Interpretation of American Expansion, 1860–1898. Ithaca, NY: Cornell University Press, 1963.
Lake, Anthony. *Somoza Falling: A Case Study of Washington at Work*. Boston, MA: Houghton Mifflin, 1989.
Lane, Mills. *War Is Hell: William T. Sherman's Personal Narrative of His March through Georgia*. Savannah, GA: Beehive Press, 1974.
Langley, Lester D. *The Banana Wars: United States Intervention in the Caribbean 1898–1934*. Wilmington, DE: Scholarly Resources, 2002.
The United States and the Caribbean in the Twentieth Century. 4th ed. Athens: University of Georgia Press, 1989.
Lansdale, Edward Geary. *In the Midst of Wars: An American's Mission to Southeast Asia*. New York: Harper & Row, 1972.
Latell, Brian. *Castro's Secrets: The CIA and Cuba's Intelligent Machine*. New York: Palgrave Macmillan, 2012.
Lawrence, T. E. *Seven Pillars of Wisdom: A Triumph*. New York: Doubleday, Doran, 1935.
Leebaert, Derek. *To Dare and to Conquer: Special Operations and the Destiny of Nations, from Achilles to Al Qaeda*. New York: Little, Brown, 2006.

Lehrack, Otto J. *No Shining Armor: The Marines at War in Vietnam, an Oral History*. Lawrence: University Press of Kansas, 1992.
Leogrande, William M. *Our Own Backyard: The United States in Central America, 1977–1992*. Chapel Hill: University of North Carolina Press, 1998.
Leonard, Thomas M. *Central America and the United States: The Search for Stability*. Athens: University of Georgia Press, 1991.
Lindo-Fuentes, Héctor, Erik Ching, and Rafael A. Lara-Martínez. *Remembering a Massacre in El Salvador*. Albuquerque: University of New Mexico Press, 2007.
Link, Arthur S. *Wilson: Confusions and Crises, 1915–1916*. Princeton, NJ: Princeton University Press, 1964.
Linn, Brian M. *The Philippine War, 1899–1902*. Lexington: University Press of Kentucky, 2000.
  The U.S. Army and Counterinsurgency in the Philippine War, 1899–1902. Chapel Hill: University of North Carolina Press, 1989.
Logevall, Fredrik. *Embers of War: The Fall of an Empire and the Making of America's Vietnam*. New York: Random House, 2012.
Lomperis, Timothy J. *From People's War to People's Rule*. Chapel Hill: University of North Carolina Press, 1996.
López Vigil, José Ignacio. *Rebel Radio: The Story of El Salvador's Radio Venceremos*. Translated by Mark Fried. Willimantic, CT: Curbstone Press, 1991.
Lowenthal, Abraham F. *The Dominican Intervention*. Cambridge, MA: Harvard University Press, 1991.
  ed. *Exporting Democracy: The United States and Latin America*. Baltimore, MD: Johns Hopkins University Press, 1991.
Lowry, Richard S. *Marines in the Garden of Eden: The True Story of Seven Bloody Days in Iraq*. New York: Berkley Caliber, 2006.
Macaulay, Neill. *The Sandino Affair*. Micanopy, FL: Wacahoota, 1998.
Mackey, Robert R. *The Uncivil War: Irregular Warfare in the Upper South, 1861–1865*. Norman: University of Oklahoma Press, 2004.
Mackinlay, John. *The Insurgent Archipelago*. New York: Columbia University Press, 2010.
Mann, James. *The Obamians: The Struggle inside the White House to Redefine American Power*. New York: Viking Adult, 2012.
Manwaring, Max G. and Court Prisk. *El Salvador at War: An Oral History of Conflict from the 1979 Insurrection to the Present*. Washington, DC: National Defense University Press, 1988.
Mao Tse-Tung. *On Guerrilla Warfare*. Translated by Samuel B. Griffith II. Chicago: University of Illinois Press, 2000.
Marr, Phebe. *Iraq's New Political Map*. Washington, DC: United States Institute of Peace, January 2007.
Marston, Daniel and Carter Malkasian, eds. *Counterinsurgency in Warfare*. London: Osprey, 2008.
Martz, John D., ed. *United States Policy in Latin America: A Quarter Century of Crisis and Challenge, 1961–1986*. Lincoln: University of Nebraska Press, 1988.

Mazower, Mark. *Inside Hitler's Greece*. New Haven, CT: Yale University Press, 1993.
McChrystal, Stanley. *My Share of the Task: A Memoir*. New York: Penguin, 2013.
McClintock, Cynthia. *Revolutionary Movements in Latin America: El Salvador's FMLN, and Peru's Shining Path*. Washington, DC: United States Institute of Peace, 1998.
McCoy, Alfred W. *Policing America's Empire: The United States, the Philippines and the Rise of the Surveillance State*. Madison: University of Wisconsin Press, 2009.
McDermott, John D. *A Guide to the Indian Wars of the West*. Lincoln: University of Nebraska Press, 1998.
McLoughlin, Leslie. *In a Sea of Knowledge: British Arabists in the Twentieth Century*. Reading, UK: Ithaca Press, 2002.
McNamara, Robert S. *In Retrospect: The Tragedy and Lessons of Vietnam*. New York: Times Books, 1995.
McPherson, Alan. *Intimate Ties, Bitter Struggles: The United States and Latin America since 1945*. Washington, DC: Potomac Books, 2006.
Mead, Walter Russell. *Special Providence: American Foreign Policy and How It Changed the World*. New York: Routledge, 2002.
Melton, Carol Wilcox. *Between War and Peace: Woodrow Wilson and the American Expeditionary Force in Siberia, 1918–192*. Macon, GA: Mercer University Press, 2001.
Menzel, Sewall. *Dictators, Drugs, and Revolution: Cold War Campaigning in Latin America 1965–1989*. Bloomington, IN: AuthorHouse, 2006.
Merk, Frederick. *Manifest Destiny and Mission in American History: A Reinterpretation*. New York: Alfred A. Knopf, 1963.
Merom, Gil. *How Democracies Lose Small Wars: State, Society, and the Failures of France in Algeria, Israel in Lebanon, and the United States in Vietnam*. New York: Cambridge University Press, 2003.
Metz, Steven. *Iraq and the Evolution of American Strategy*, Washington, DC: Potomac Books, 2008.
Miller, Stuart Creighton. *Benevolent Assimilation: The America Conquest of the Philippines, 1899–1903*. New Haven, CT: Yale University Press, 1982.
Millett, Allan R. *The Politics of Intervention: The Military Occupation of Cuba, 1906–1909*. Columbus: Ohio State University Press, 1968.
Miscamble, Wilson. *George F. Kennan and the Making of American Foreign Policy, 1947–1950*. Princeton, NJ: Princeton University Press, 1992.
Montgomery, Tommie Sue. *Revolution in El Salvador: From Civil Strife to Civil Peace*. Boulder, CO: Westview Press, 1992.
Moore, Harold G. and Joseph L. Galloway. *We Were Soldiers Once ... and Young: Ia Drang – The Battle That Changed the War in Vietnam*. New York: Random House, 1992.
Moore, Joel R., Harry H. Mead, and Lewis E. Jahns, eds. *The History of the American Expedition Fighting the Bolsheviki: Campaigning in North Russia, 1918–1919*. Detroit, MI: Polar Bear, 1920.
Moultrie, William, *Memoirs of the American Revolution*, New York: Arno, 1968.

Moyar, Mark. *A Question of Command: Counterinsurgency from the Civil War to Iraq.* New Haven, CT: Yale University Press, 2009.
Mullaney, Craig M. *The Unforgiving Minute: A Soldier's Education.* New York: Penguin Press, 2009.
Munro, Dana G. *Intervention and Dollar Diplomacy in the Caribbean, 1900–1921.* Princeton, NJ: Princeton University Press, 1964.
The United States and the Caribbean Republics, 1921–1933. Princeton, NJ: Princeton University Press, 1974.
Musicant, Ivan. *The Banana Wars: A History of United States Military Intervention in Latin America from the Spanish-American War to the Invasion of Panama.* New York: Macmillan, 1990.
Nagl, John A. *Learning to Eat Soup with a Knife: Counterinsurgency Lessons from Malaya and Vietnam.* Chicago: University of Chicago Press, 2005.
Nixon, Richard. *No More Vietnams.* New York: Avon, 1985.
O'Ballance, Edgar. *The Algerian Insurrection, 1954–62.* Hamden, CT: Archon Books, 1967.
The Greek Civil War, 1944–1949. New York: Praeger, 1966.
Malaya: The Communist Insurgent War, 1948–60. Hamden, CT: Archon Books, 1966.
O'Neill, Bard E. *From Revolution to Apocalypse: Insurgency and Terrorism.* Washington, DC: Potomac Books, 2005.
Osgood, Robert Endicott. *Limited War Revisited.* Boulder, CO: Westview Press, 1979.
Paget, Julian. *Counterinsurgency Campaigning.* London: Faber and Faber, 1967.
Pakenham, Thomas. *The Boer War.* New York: Random House, 1979.
Palmer, Bruce Jr. *The Twenty-five Year War: America's Military Role in Vietnam.* New York: Simon and Schuster, 1984.
Palmer, Dave Richard. *The Way of the Fox: American Strategy in the War for America, 1775–1783.* Portsmouth, NH: Greenwood, 1975.
Paret, Peter. *French Revolutionary Warfare from Indochina to Algeria: An Analysis of a Political and Military Doctrine.* New York: Praeger, 1964.
ed. *Makers of Modern Strategy: From Machiavelli to the Nuclear Age.* Princeton, NJ: Princeton University Press, 1986.
Pargeter, Alison. *Libya: The Rise and Fall of Qaddafi.* New Haven, CT: Yale University Press, 2012.
Pastor, Robert A. *Condemned to Repetition: The United States and Nicaragua.* Princeton, NJ: Princeton University Press, 1987.
Not Condemned to Repetition: The United States and Nicaragua. Boulder, CO: Westview Press, 2002.
Whirlpool: U.S. Foreign Policy toward Latin America and the Caribbean. Princeton, NJ: Princeton University Press, 1992.
Paterson, Thomas G. *On Every Front: The Making and the Unmaking of the Cold War.* New York: W. W. Norton, 1993.
Pearce, Jenny. *Under the Eagle: U.S. Interventions in Central America and the Caribbean.* Boston: South End, 1982.
Perkins, Dexter. *A History of the Monroe Doctrine.* Boston: Little, Brown, 1963.

Perkins, Whitney. *The Constraint of Empire: The United States and Caribbean Interventions*. Westport, CT: Greenwood, 1981.
Phillips, David Atlee. *The Night Watch: 25 Years of Peculiar Service*. New York: Atheneum, 1977.
Polk, William R. *Violent Politics: A History of Insurgency, Terrorism, and Guerrilla Warfare from the American Revolution to Iraq*. New York: Harper, 2007.
Pons, Frank Moya. *The Dominican Republic: A National History*. New Rochelle, NY: Hispaniola Books, 1995.
Porch, Douglas. *Counterinsurgency: Exposing the Myths of the New Way of War*. New York: Cambridge University Press, 2013.
Prisk, Courtney E. *The Comandante Speaks: Memoirs of an El Salvadoran Guerilla Leader*. Boulder, CO: Westview Press, 1991.
Putsay, John. S. *Counterinsurgency Warfare*. New York: Free Press, 1965.
Rabe, Stephen G. *Eisenhower and Latin America: The Foreign Policy of Anticommunism*. Chapel Hill: University of North Carolina Press, 1988.
Race, Jeffrey. *War Comes to Long An: Revolutionary Conflict in a Vietnamese Province*. Berkeley: University of California Press, 1972.
Ramírez, Sergio and Robert Edgar Conrad, eds. *Sandino: The Testimony of a Nicaraguan Patriot, 1921–1934*. Princeton, NJ: Princeton University Press, 1990.
Raphael, Ray. *A People's History of the American Revolution: How Common People Shaped the Fight for Independence*. New York: New Press, 2001.
Rasenberger, Jim. *Brilliant Disaster: JFK, Castro, and America's Doomed Invasion of the Bay of Pigs*. New York: Scribner, 2011.
Rashid, Ahmed. *Descent into Chaos: The United States and the Failure of Nation Building in Pakistan, Afghanistan, and Central Asia*. New York: Viking Penguin, 2008.
Record, Jeffrey. *Beating Goliath: Why Insurgencies Win*. Washington, DC: Potomac Books, 2007.
Reid, Michael. *Forgotten Continent: The Battle for Latin America's Soul*. New Haven, CT: Yale University Press, 2007.
Remini, Robert V. *Andrew Jackson and His Indian Wars*. New York: Viking, 2001.
Renda, May A. *Taking Haiti: Military Occupation and the Culture of U.S. Imperialism, 1915–1940*. Chapel Hill: University of North Carolina Press, 2001.
Ressa, Maria A. *Seeds of Terror: An Eyewitness Account of Al-Qaeda's Newest Center of Operations in Southeast Asia*. New York: Free Press, 2003.
Richard, Carl J. *When the United States Invaded Russia: Woodrow Wilson's Siberian Disaster*. Lanham, MD: Rowman and Littlefield, 2012.
Ricks, Thomas E. *Fiasco: The American Military Adventure in Iraq*. New York: Penguin, 2006.
The Gamble: General David Petraeus and the American Military Adventure in Iraq, 2006–2008. New York: Penguin, 2009.
The Generals: American Military Command from World War II to Today. New York: Penguin, 2012.
Robb, John. *Brave New War: The Next Stage of Terrorism and the End of Globalization*. Hoboken, NJ: John Wiley, 2007.
Robinson, Linda. *Tell Me How This Ends: General David Petraeus and the Search for a Way Out of Iraq*. New York: Public Affairs, 2008.

Romero, Archbishop Oscar. *A Shepherd's Diary*. Translated by Irene B. Hodges; foreword by Thomas E. Quigley. London: CAFOD, 1993.
Romulo, Carlos P. and Marvin M. Gray. *The Magsaysay Story*. New York: John Day Company, 1956.
Rooney, David. *Guerrilla: Insurgents, Patriots and Terrorists from Sun Tzu to Bin Laden*. London: Brassey's, 2004.
Rose, Gideon. *How Wars End*. New York: Simon and Schuster, 2011.
Rostow, Walt W. *The Diffusion of Power: An Essay in Recent History*. New York: Macmillan, 1972.
Roth, Russell: *Muddy Glory: America's "Indian Wars" in the Philippines, 1899–1935*. West Hanover, MA: Christopher Publishing House, 1981.
Roy, Jules. *The Battle of Dienbienphu*. New York: Harper and Row, 1963.
Russell, Philip L. *El Salvador in Crisis*. Austin, TX: Colorado River Press, 1984.
Ryan, Henry Butterfield. *The Fall of Che Guevara: A Story of Soldiers, Spies, and Diplomats*. New York: Oxford University Press, 1998.
Sageman, Marc. *Understanding Terror Networks*. Philadelphia: University of Pennsylvania Press, 2004.
Sanger, David E. *Confront and Conceal: Obama's Secret Wars and Surprising Use of American Power*. New York: Crown, 2012
Sarkesian, Sam C. *America's Forgotten Wars: The Counterrevolutionary Past and Lessons for the Future*. Westport, CT: Greenwood Press, 1984.
Schmidt, Hans. *The United States Occupation of Haiti, 1915–1934*. New Brunswick, NJ: Rutgers University Press, 1971.
Schmidt, Steffen W. *El Salvador: America's Next Vietnam?* Salisbury, NC: Documentary Publications, 1983.
Schoonover, Thomas D. *The United States in Central America, 1860–1911: Episodes of Social Imperialism and Imperial Rivalry in the World System*. Durham, NC: Duke University Press, 1991.
Schoultz, Lars. *Beneath the United States: A History of U.S. Policy toward Latin America*. Cambridge, MA: Harvard University Press, 1998.
Sexton, William. *Soldiers in the Philippines: A History of the Insurrection*. Washington, DC: Infantry Journal Press, 1944.
Sexton, William Thaddeus. *Soldiers in the Sun: An Adventure in Imperialism*. Harrisburg, PA: Military Service Publishing, 1939.
Shafer, D. Michael. *Deadly Paradigm: The Failure of U.S. Counterinsurgency Policy*. Princeton, NJ: Princeton University Press, 1988.
Sheehan, Neil. *A Great Shining Lie: John Paul Vann and America in Vietnam*. New York: Random House, 1988.
Short, Anthony. *The Communist Insurrection in Malaya, 1948–1960*. London: Frederick Muller., 1975.
Showalter, Dennis E. "Manœuvre Warfare: The Eastern and Western Fronts, 1914–1915." In *The Oxford Illustrated History of the First World War*, edited by Hew Strachan. New York: Oxford University Press, 1998, 39–53.
Shultz, George P. *Turmoil and Triumph: My Years as Secretary of State*. New York: Charles Scribner's Sons, 1993.

Shy, John and Thomas W. Collier. "Revolutionary War." In *Makers of Modern Strategy: From Machiavelli to the Nuclear Age*, edited by Peter Paret. Princeton, NJ: Princeton University Press, 1986.
Siepel, Kevin H. *Rebel: The Life and Times of John Singleton Mosby*. New York: St. Martin's Press, 1983.
Simms, William Gilmore. *Life of Francis Marion*. New York: H. G. Langley, 1844.
Singer, P. W. *Wired for War: The Robotics Revolution and Conflict in the 21st Century*. New York: Penguin, 2009.
Smith, Gaddis. *The Last Years of the Monroe Doctrine, 1945–1993*. New York: Hill and Wang, 1994.
Smith, Page, *A New Age Now Begins*, vol 1. New York: McGraw-Hill, 1976.
Solomon, Daniel F. *Breaking Up with Cuba: The Dissolution of Friendly Relations between Washington and Havana, 1956–61*. London: McFarland, 2011.
Sorley, Lewis. *A Better War: The Unexamined Victories and Final Tragedy of America's Last Years in Vietnam*. New York: Harvest/HBJ, 2000.
Stanley, William. *The Protection Racket State: Elite Politics, Military Extortion, and Civil War in El Salvador*. Philadelphia: Temple University Press, 1996.
Stern, Steve J., ed. *Shining and Other Paths*. Durham, NC: Duke University Press, 1998.
Stewart, Rory. *The Places in Between*. Orlando, FL: Harcourt, 2004.
The Prince of the Marshes: And Other Occupational Hazards of a Year in Iraq. Orlando, FL: Harcourt, 2006.
Stimson, Henry L. *American Policy in Nicaragua*. New York: Charles Scribner's Sons, 1927.
St.John, Rachel. *Line in the Sand: A History of the Western U.S.-Mexico Border*. Princeton, NJ: Princeton University Press, 2011.
St.John, Ronald Bruce. *Libya: From Colony to Revolution*. Oxford: Oneworld Publications, 2012.
Stubbs, Richard. *Hearts and Minds in Guerrilla Warfare: The Malayan Emergency 1948–1960*. Singapore: Eastern Universities Press, 2004.
Sundaram, Anjali and George Gelber. *A Decade of War: El Salvador Confronts the Future*. London: Catholic Institute for International Relations, 1991.
Sun Tzu. *The Art of War*. Mineola, NY: Dover, 2002.
Sweig, Julia E. *Cuba: What Everyone Needs to Know*. New York: Oxford University Press, 2009.
Taber, Robert. *War of the Flea: The Classic Study of Guerrilla Warfare*. Washington, DC: Potomac Books, 2002.
Talbott, John. *The War without a Name: France in Algeria, 1954–1962*. New York: Alfred A. Knopf, 1980.
Taruc, Luis. *He Who Rides the Tiger: The Story of an Asian Guerrilla Leader*. New York: Frederick A. Praeger, 1967.
Taylor, John M., ed. *The Philippine Insurrection against the United States: A Compilation of Documents*. 5 vols. Pasay City, Philippines: Eugenio Lopez Foundation, 1971–73.
Tebbel, John. *The Compact History of the Indian Wars*. New York: Hawthorn Books, 1966.

Thibault, George Edward, ed. *Dimensions of Military Strategy*. Washington, DC: National Defense University Press, 1987.
Thomas, Lowell. *Woodfill of the Regulars: A True Story of Adventure from the Arctic to the Argonne*. Garden City, NY: Doubleday, Doran, 1929.
Thomas, Robert S. and Inez V. Allen. *The Mexican Punitive Expedition under Brigadier General John J. Pershing, United States Army, 1916–1917*. Washington, DC: Department of the Army, Office of the Chief of Military History, War Histories Division, 1954.
Thompson, Loren B., ed. *Low-Intensity Conflict: The Pattern of Warfare in the Modern World*. Washington, DC: Lexington Books, 1989.
Thompson, Robert. *Defeating Communist Insurgency*. St. Petersburg, FL: Hailer Publishing, 2005.
Defeating Communist Insurgency: The Lessons of Malaya and Vietnam. New York: Praeger, 1966.
Thompson, W. Scott and Donaldson D. Frizzell. *The Lessons of Vietnam*. New York: Crane, Russak, 1977.
Tierney, John J. Jr. *Chasing Ghosts: Unconventional Warfare in American History*. Washington, DC: Potomac Books, 2006.
Tinker, Jerry M. et al., eds. *Strategies of Revolutionary Warfare*. New Dehli: S. Chand, 1968.
Tompkins, Frank. *Chasing Villa: The Story behind the Story of Pershing's Expedition into Mexico*. Harrisburg, PA: Military Service Publishing, 1934.
Trinquier, Robert. *Modern Warfare: A French View of Counterinsurgency*. New York: Praeger, 1964.
Tulchin, Joseph S. and Gary Bland, eds. *Peru in Crisis: Dictatorship or Democracy?* Woodrow Wilson International Center for Scholars. Boulder, CO: Lynne Reinner, 1994.
Tutela Legal. *El Mozote: Lucha por la verdad y la justicia*. Tutela Legal del Arzobispado de San Salvador, 2007.
Twichell, Heath Jr. "Always Outnumbered; Never Outfought." In *Allen: The Biography of an Army Officer 1859–1930*, chapter 6. New Brunswick, NJ: Rutgers University Press, 1974.
Utley, Robert M. *Frontier Regulars: The United States Army and the Indian, 1866–1891*. New York: Macmillan, 1973.
U.S. Department of State. *Foreign Relations of the United States, 1964–68*. Washington, DC: U.S. Government Printing Office.
Villalobos, Joaquín. *El Estado Actual de la Guerra y Sus Perspectivas*. Madrid: Textos Breves, 1986.
Vlavianos, Haris. *Greece, 1941–1949: From Resistance to Civil War – The Strategy of the Greek Communist Party*. New York: St. Martin's Press, 1992.
Walt, Lewis W. *Strange War, Strange Strategy: A General's Report on Vietnam*. New York: Funk and Wagnalls, 1970.
Webre, Stephen. *Jose Napoleon Duarte and the Christian Democratic Party in Salvadoran Politics*. Baton Rouge: Louisiana State University Press, 1979.
Weigley, Russell F. *The History of the United States Army*. New York: Macmillan, 1967.

The American Way: A History of United States Military Strategy and Policy. Bloomington: Indiana University Press, 1960.
Weinberg, Albert K. *Manifest Destiny: A Study of Nationalist Expansionism in American History.* Baltimore, MD: Johns Hopkins University Press, 1935.
Weisman, Brent Richards. *Unconquered People: Florida's Seminole and Miccosukee Indians.* Gainesville: University Press of Florida, 1999.
Weitsman, Patricia A. *Dangerous Alliances: Proponents of Peace, Weapons of War.* Stanford, CA: Stanford University Press, 2004.
Welles, Sumner. *Naboth's Vineyard: The Dominican Republic, 1844–1924.* 2 vols. Mamaroneck, NY: Paul P. Appel, 1966. Reprint of 1926 edition.
West, Bing. *No True Glory: The Battle for Fallujah.* New York: Bantam, 2005.
The Strongest Tribe: War, Politics, and the Endgame in Iraq. New York: Random House, 2008.
The Village. New York: Pocket Books, 1972.
The Wrong War: Grit, Strategy, and the Way out of Afghanistan. New York: Random House, 2011.
Westad, Odd Arne. *The Global Cold War.* New York: Cambridge University Press, 2007.
White, Alastair. *El Salvador.* New York: Praeger, 1973.
Whitfield, Teresa. *Paying the Price: Ignacio Ellacuria and the Murdered Jesuits of El Salvador.* Philadelphia: Temple University Press, 1995.
Wickham-Crowley, Timothy P., *Exploring Revolution: Essays on Latin American Insurgency and Revolutionary Theory.* New York: M. E. Sharpe, 1991.
Guerillas and Revolution in Latin America: A Comparative Study of Insurgents and Regimes since 1956. Princeton, NJ: Princeton University Press, 1992.
Wilcox, Marion. *Harper's History of the War in the Philippines.* New York: Harper and Brothers, 1900.
Willett, Robert L. *Russian Sideshow: America's Undeclared War, 1918–1920.* Washington, DC: Brassey's, 2003.
Wilson, Jeremy. *Lawrence of Arabia: The Authorized Biography of T. E. Lawrence.* New York: Atheneum, 1990.
Wilson, Mary C. "The Hashemites, the Arab Revolt, and Arab Nationalism." In *The Origins of Arab Nationalism*, edited by Rashid Khalidi, Lisa Anderson, Muhammad Muslih, and Reeva S. Simon. New York: Columbia University Press, 1991.
Wilson, Jeremy. *Lawrence of Arabia: The Authorized Biography of T.E. Lawrence.* New York: Atheneum, 1990.
Wittner, Lawrence S. *American Intervention in Greece, 1943–1949.* New York: Columbia University Press, 1982.
Wolfert, Ira. *American Guerrilla in the Philippines.* New York: Simon and Schuster, 1945.
Wolff, Leon. *Little Brown Brother: America's Forgotten Bid for Empire Which Cost 250,000 Lives.* London: Longmans, Green, 1961.

Zakaria, Fareed. *From Wealth to Power: The Unusual Origins of America's World Role*. Princeton, NJ: Princeton University Press, 1999.

Articles

Aizenman, N. C. "Salvadorans Ambushed by Memories in Iraq." *Washington Post*, March 25, 2006.
Aizenman, N. C. and Alejandro Lazo. "Salvadorans See Promise in Candidate." *Washington Post*, June 21, 2008.
Alvarez, Francisco A. "Transition before the Transition: The Case of El Salvador." *Latin American Perspectives* 15:1 (Winter 1988): 78–92.
Ancker, W. M. "The Imperialistic Mercenaries." *Marine Corps Gazette* 60 (March 1976): 60–2.
Anderson, Jon Lee. "King of Kings: The Last Days of Muammar Qaddafi." *New Yorker*, November 7, 2011.
Aylwin-Foster, Nigel. "Changing the Army for Counterinsurgency Operations." *Military Review* (November–December 2005): 2–15.
Baloyra, Enrique A. "Negotiating War in El Salvador: The Politics of Endgame." *Journal of Interamerican Studies and World Affairs* 28:1 (Spring 1986): 123–47.
Barr, Alfred R. and Caesar Sereseres. "U.S. Unconventional Warfare Operations and Lessons from Central America, 1980–91." *Low Intensity Conflict and Law Enforcement* 8:2 (Summer 1999).
Baylen, Joseph L. "Sandino: Patriot or Bandit." *Hispanic-American Historical Review* 31 (August 1951): 394–419.
Bearden, Milton. "Afghanistan, Graveyard of Empires." *Foreign Affairs* (November–December 2001): 17–30.
Belton, Fred and John Rogers. "Unsung Heroes of the Marine Corps – No. 3." *Leatherneck* 14 (June 1931): 14, 44.
Berger, Mark T. and Douglas A. Borer. "The Long War: Insurgency, Counterinsurgency and Collapsing States" *Third World Quarterly* 28:2 (March 2007): 197–215.
Betancourt, Marcelo. "Teníamos militares que no creían en la democracia." Interview with Antonio Morales Erlich, July 9, 2008.
Blassingame, John W. "The Press and American Intervention in Haiti and the Dominican Republic, 1904–1920." *Caribbean Studies* 9 (July 1969): 27–43.
Bonner, Raymond. "The Agony of El Salvador." *New York Times Magazine*, February 22, 1981.
Bride, Frank L. "The Gendarmerie d'Haiti." *Marine Corps Gazette* 3 (December 1918): 295–8.
Broderick, J. M. "The Science of Jungle Patrols." *Leatherneck* 16 (August 1933): 56–7.
Browning, David. "Agrarian Reform in El Salvador." *Journal of Latin American Studies* 15:2 (November 1983): 399–426.
Brozenick, Norman J. "Small Wars, Big Stakes: Coercion, Persuasion, and Airpower in Counterrevolutionary War." Thesis, School of Advanced Airpower Studies, Air University, Maxwell Air Force Base, Montgomery, Alabama, June 1998.
Buchanan, William J. and Robert A. Hyatt. "Capitalizing on Guerrilla Vulnerabilities." *Military Review* 48 (August 1968): 3–40.

Bibliography 537

Buckley, James L. "Reprogramming Proposal for El Salvador." Statement before the Subcommittee of Foreign Operations of the House Appropriations Committee. *Official Monthly Record of United States Foreign Policy* 81:2050 (May 1981).

Buell, Raymond Lewis. "Getting Out of Central America." *Nation* 135 (July 13, 1932): 32-4.

Bullard, Robert L. "Military Pacification." *Journal of the Military Institution of the United States* 46 (January-February 1910): 1-24.

Bulloch, Gavin. "Military Doctrine and Counterinsurgency: A British Perspective." *Parameters*, US Army War College Quarterly (Summer 1996): 4-16.

Cale, Major Paul P. "The United States Military Advisory Group in El Salvador, 1979-1992." CSC 1996. www.smallwarsjournal.com.

Carlson, Evans F. "The Guardia Nacional de Nicaragua." *Marine Corps Gazette* 21 (August 1937): 7-20.

Cassidy, Robert M. "The Long Small War: Indigenous Forces for Counterinsurgency." *Parameters* (Summer 2006): 47-63.

"Back to the Street without Joy: Counterinsurgency Lessons from Vietnam and Other Small Wars." *Parameters* (Summer 2004): 73-83.

"Winning the War of the Flea." *Military Review*, September-October 2004, 41-46.

Castle, William R. Jr. "Why Marines Are Landed." *Marine Corps Gazette* 19 (August 1934): 16-18.

Castleman, James T. "The Columbus Raid." *Cavalry Journal* 27 (April 1917): 490-6.

Cerami, Joseph R. and Jay W. Boggs. "The Interagency and Counterinsurgency Warfare: Stability, Security, Transition and Reconstruction Roles." Strategic Studies Institute, U.S. Army War College, Carlisle Barracks, PA, December 2007.

Childs, Matt D. "An Historical Critique of the Emergence and Evolution of Ernesto Che Guevara's Foco Theory." *Journal of Latin American Studies* 27:3 (October 1995): 593-624.

Chivvis, Christopher. "Libya and the Future of Liberal Intervention," *Survival: Global Politics and Strategy* (November 30, 2012): 69-92.

Coates, Major Robert J. "The United States' Approach to El Salvador." CSC 1991. www.globalsecurity.org.

Coffey, Ross. "Revisiting CORDS: The Need for Unity of Effort to Secure Victory in Iraq." *Military Review* (March-April 2006): 92-102.

Cohen, Eliot et al. "Principles, Imperatives, and Paradoxes of Counterinsurgency." *Military Review* (March-April 2006): 49-53.

Corr, Edwin G. "Societal Transformation for Peace in El Salvador." *Annals of the American Academy of Political and Social Science* 541 (September 1995): 144-56.

Corum, James S. "The Air War in El Salvador." *Airpower Journal* (Summer 1998): 27-44.

"Training Indigenous Forces in Counterinsurgency: A Tale of Two Insurgencies." U.S. Army Strategic Studies Institute, Carlisle Barracks, PA, March 2006.

Cox, Steven J. "Role of SOF in Paramilitary Operations." Thesis. Naval Postgraduate School, Monterey, CA. 1995.

Cradock, Christopher and M. L. R. Smith. "No Fixed Values: A Reinterpretation of the Influence of the Theory of Guerre Révolutionnaire and the Battle of Algiers, 1956-1957." *Journal of Cold War Studies* 9:4 (Fall 2007) 68-105.

Craig, Edward A. "The Fight at Carrizal." *Leatherneck* 22 (March 1939): 6, 54–5.
Crandall, Russell. "Requiem for the FARC?" *Survival: Global Strategy & Policy* 53:4 (August–September 2011): 233–40.
Crane, Conrad. "Avoiding Vietnam: The U.S. Army's Response to Defeat in Southeast Asia." Strategic Studies Institute, Carlisle Barracks, PA, September 2002.
Cruz Rojas, Álvaro. Interviews with Mauricio Funes. *El Mundo*, June 22, 23, 24, 2008.
Daniels, John A. "Don't Plan These Battles." *Marine Corps Gazette* 25 (September 1941): 19–20, 43–6.
Daniels, Josephus. "The Problem of Haiti." *Saturday Evening Post*, July 12, 1930.
Daremblum, Jaime. "Losing El Salvador?" *Weekly Standard online*, June 18, 2008.
De Atkine, Norville. "Why Arabs Lose Wars." *Middle East Review of International Affairs* 4:1 (March 2000): 16–27.
De Shazo, Peter et al. "Countering Threats to Security and Stability in a Failing State: Lessons from Colombia." Center for Strategic and International Studies, Washington, DC, September 2009.
De Soto, Alvaro and Graciana del Castillo. "Obstacles to Peacebuilding." *Foreign Policy* 94 (Spring 1994): 69–83.
Decker, William T. "Anti-Guerrilla Warfare." *Marine Corps Gazette* 30 (August 1951): 22–5.
Denig, Robert L. "Native Officer Corps, Guardia Nacional de Nicaragua." *Marine Corps Gazette* 17 (November 1932): 75–7.
Diamond, Larry. "Building Democracy after Conflict: Lessons from Iraq." *Journal of Democracy* 16:1 (January 2005): 9–23.
Dillon, Sam. "Dateline El Salvador: Crisis Renewed." *Foreign Policy* 73 (Winter 1988–1989): 153–70.
Dodds, Harold W. "American Supervision of the Nicaraguan Election." *Marine Corps Gazette* 14 (June 1929): 117–24.
Dominguez, Jorge I. "Insurgency in Latin America and the Common Defense." *Political Science Quarterly* 101:5 (1986): 807–23.
Donnelly, Thomas and Vance Serchuk. "U.S. Counterinsurgency in Iraq: Lessons from the Philippine War." Washington, DC: American Enterprise Institute for Public Policy Research, November 2003.
Douglas, Steve. "Napoleon at the Gates of Baghdad." *Executive Intelligence Review* (April 2005).
Duffy, John J. "Signpost: Success in the Philippines." *Army* 13 (July 1963): 60–2.
Eikenberry, Karl. "The Limits of Counterinsurgency Doctrine in Afghanistan." *Foreign Affairs* (September/October 2013).
"El Salvador: Economic Reforms and Performance." El Salvador Chamber of Commerce and Industry, April 2008 (Power Point Presentation).
Escobar, Juan B. "El Salvador's Experience in the 1980's and 1990's as a Model of Democratization, Lessons Learned for Strategy in the New World Order." Strategy Research Project, U.S. Army War College, Carlisle Barracks, PA, April 18, 1995.

"Esquipulas II: Procedure for the Establishment of a Firm and Lasting Peace in Central America." Guatemala City, Guatemala, August 7, 1987.
Evans, Richard J. "The Truth about World War II." *New York Review of Books*, October 11, 2012, 52–6.
Fall, Bernard B. "The Theory and Practice of Insurgency and Counterinsurgency." *Naval War College Review* (April 1965).
Farer, Tom J. "Manage the Revolution?" *Foreign Policy* 52 (Autumn 1983): 96–117.
Fellowes, Edward A. "Training Native Troops in Santo Domingo." *Marine Corps Gazette* 8 (December 1934): 215–33.
Fernández Leal, Javier. "Costs of the War in Colombia: A Strategic Vision of the End of the Conflict." U.S. Army War College Strategic Research Project, Carlisle Barracks, PA, March 18, 2005.
Fick, Nathaniel C., Dave J. Kilcullen, John A. Nagl, and Vikram K. Singh. "Tell Me Why We're There? Enduring Interests in Afghanistan (and Pakistan)." Center for a New American Security, Policy Brief, *January* 2009.
Finkel, David. "The Return: The Traumatized Veterans of Iraq and Afghanistan." *New Yorker*, September 9, 2013, 36.
Fischer, Hannah. *U.S. Military Casualty Statistics: Operation New Dawn, Operation Iraqi Freedom, and Operation Enduring Freedom*. Congressional Research Service, February 2013. http://www.fas.org/sgp/crs/natsec/RS22452.pdf.
Fisher, Stewart W. "Human Rights in El Salvador and U.S. Foreign Policy." *Human Rights Quarterly* 4:1 (Spring 1982): 1–38.
Fitz-Simmons, Daniel. "Francis Marion, The 'Swamp Fox': An Anatomy of a Low-Intensity Conflict." *Small Wars and Insurgencies* 6 (1995): 1–16.
Foley, Michael. "Laying the Groundwork: The Struggle for Civil Society in El Salvador. *Journal of Interamerican Studies and World Affairs* 38:1 (Spring 1996): 67–104.
Fukuyama, Francis. "Why I Like the Afghan Timetable." *American Interest* (December 2009).
Gann, Lewis H. "Guerrillas and Insurgency: An Interpretative Survey." *Military Review* 46 (March 1966): 44–59.
Gershman, John. "Is Southeast Asia the Second Front?" *Foreign Affairs* 81:4 (July–August 2002): 60–74.
Gill, Burgo D. "Guerrilla Warfare." *Quartermaster Review* 13 (September–October 1933): 27–9.
Gillert, Gustav J. "Counterinsurgency." *Military Review* 45 (April 1965): 25–33.
Glynn, James F. "El Salvador, Iraq, and Strategic Considerations for Counterinsurgency." U.S. Army War College Strategy Research Project, Carlisle Barracks, PA, March 15, 2008.
Gómez, Leonel et al. "El Salvador: The Current Danger." *Foreign Policy* 43 (Summer 1981): 71–92.
Gray, John A. "Boucan Carre." *Marine Corps Gazette* 16 (November 1931): 28–32.
"The Second Nicaraguan Campaign." *Marine Corps Gazette* 17 (February 1933): 36–41.

Greathouse, G. H. "King of the Banana Wars." *Marine Corps Gazette* 44 (June 1960): 28–33.

Guevara, Che. "Message to the Tricontinental: Create Two, Three ... Many Vietnams." Havana: Executive Secretariat of the Organization of the Solidarity of the Peoples of Africa, Asia, and Latin America, 1967.

Gumz, Jonathan E. "Reframing the Historical Problematic of Insurgency: How the Professional Military Literature Created a New History and Missed the Past." *Journal of Strategic Studies* 32:4 (August 2009): 533–88.

Haffner, L. E. "Guerrilla War and Common Sense." *Marine Corps Gazette* 46 (June 1962): 20–3.

Hammes, Thomas X. "Insurgency: Modern Warfare Evolves into a Fourth Generation." *Strategic Forum*, 214 (January 2005): 1–7.

Heilbrunn, Otto. "When Counterinsurgents Cannot Win." *Military Review* 49 (October 1969): 36–43.

Hernández Pico, Juan. "Peace Is Built of Many Pieces." *Revista Envio* 161 (December 1994).

"Rubén Zamora on the Political Crisis." *Revista Envio* 160 (November 1994).

Hippler, Jochen. "Low Intensity Warfare: Key Strategy for the Third World Theater." *MERIP Middle East Report* 144 (January–February 1987): 32–8.

Hirsh, Michael and John Barry. "The Salvador Option." *Newsweek*, October 16, 2007.

Hoffman, Bruce. "*Insurgency and Counterinsurgency in Iraq.*" Santa Monica, CA: RAND, National Security Research Division, June 2004.

Holewinski, Sarah. "Do Less Harm: Protecting and Compensating Civilians in War." *Foreign Affairs* (January/February 2013).

Hope, Adrian D. "El Salvador Sets the Example for Success." Foreign Area Officer Association, Herndon, VA, 2005. www.faoa.org/journal/Salvador.html.

Hulsman, John C. "Think Again: Lawrence of Arabia." *Foreign Policy* (September 29, 2009).

Iatrides, John O. "George F. Kennan and the Birth of Containment." *World Policy Journal* 22:3 (Fall 2005): 126–45.

International Crisis Group. "Iraq's Muqtada al-Sadr: Spoiler or Stabiliser?" *Middle East Report* 55 (July 11, 2006).

"The Next Iraqi War? Sectarianism and Civil Conflict." *Middle East Report* 52 (February 27, 2006).

Jones, Seth G. "Counterinsurgency in Afghanistan." RAND Counterinsurgency Study, vol. 4. Santa Monica, CA: RAND, 2008.

Judah, Tim. "With the Northern Alliance." *New York Review of Books*, November 15, 2001.

Kagan, Frederick W. "Fighting to Win." American Enterprise Institute for Public Policy Research, Washington, DC, December 2005.

Kaplan, Fred. "The End of the Age of Petraeus." *Foreign Affairs* (January/February 2013): 75–90.

Kaplan, Robert D. "A Colombian Vision for Iraq." Comment, *The Atlantic*, April 30, 2008.

Kaplow, Larry. "The Fight That We Are in Now." *Newsweek*, March 15, 2008.

Karsh, Efraim and Inari Karsh. "Myth in the Desert, or Not the Great Arab Revolt." *Middle East Studies* 33:2 (April 1997): 267–312.
Khan, Saad Omar. "The Caliphate Question: British Views and Policy toward Pan-Islamic Politics and the End of the Ottoman Empire." *American Journal of Islamic Social Sciences* 24:4 (2007): 1–25.
Kilcullen, David. "Complex Warfighting." *Future Land Warfare Branch* (Australian Army), April 2004.
  "Countering Global Insurgency." *Journal of Strategic Studies* 28:4 (August 2005): 597–617.
  "Counterinsurgency Redux." *Survival* 48:4 (December 2006): 111–30.
  "Twenty-Eight Articles: Fundamentals of Company-level Counterinsurgency." *Military Review* 86:3 (May–June 2006): 103–9.
Knut, Walter and Philip J. Williams. "The Military and Democratization in El Salvador." *Journal of Interamerican Studies and World Affairs* 35:1 (1993): 39–88.
Kramer, Paul. "The Water Cure." *New Yorker*, February 25, 2008.
Lane, Rufus H. "Civil Government in Santo Domingo in the Early Days of the Military Occupation." *Marine Corps Gazette* 7 (June 1922): 127–46.
Lansdale, Edward G. "Civic Action Helps Counter the Guerrilla Threat." *Army Information Digest* 17 (June 1962): 50–3.
Latrides, John O. and Nicholas X. Rixopoulos. "The International Dimensions of the Greek Civil War." *World Policy Journal* 17:1 (Spring 2000): 3–33.
Leach, Hugh. "Lawrence's Strategy and Tactics in the Arab Revolt." *Asian Affairs* 37:3 (November 2006): 337–41.
Levitt, Matthew and Michael Jacobson. "Countering Transnational Threats: Terrorism, Narco-Trafficking, and WMD Proliferation." Washington, DC, Washington Institute for Near-East Policy, Policy Focus #92, February 2009.
Link, Arthur. "The Caribbean: Involvement and Intervention." In *Wilson: The Struggle for Neutrality 1914–1915*, chapter 15. Princeton, NJ: Princeton University Press, 1960.
Long, Austin. "Doctrine of Eternal Recurrence: The US Military and Counterinsurgency Doctrine, 1960–1970 and 2003–2006." Washington, DC: RAND, 2008.
Long, David E. "Countering Asymmetrical Conflict in the 21st Century: A Grand Strategic Vision." *Strategic Insights* 7: 3.
López, César Armando. "Civil-Military Relations in El Salvador: Strategic Need for a National Plan." Strategy Research Project, U.S. Army War College, Carlisle Barracks, PA, May 14, 1997.
Luttwak, Edward N. "Dead End: Counterinsurgency Warfare as Military Malpractice." *Harper's Magazine*, February 2007, 33–42.
Maas, Peter. "The Salvadorization of Iraq?" *New York Times Magazine*, May 1, 2005.
  "The Way of the Commandos." *New York Times Magazine*, May 1, 2005.
Macaulay, Neill. "Counterguerrilla Patrolling." *Marine Corps Gazette* 47 (July 1963): 45–8.

Mahoney, Tom. "The Columbus Raid." *Southwest Review* 17 (January 1932): 161–71.
Manwaring, Max G. "Venezuela's Hugo Chávez, Bolivarian Socialism, and Asymmetric Warfare." Strategic Studies Institute, October 2005.
Manwaring, Max G. and Court Prisk. "A Strategic View of Insurgencies: Insights from El Salvador." Institute for National Strategic Studies, McNair Papers, No. 8, May 1990.
Marcella, Gabriel and Donald Schultz. "Colombia's Three Wars: U.S. Strategy at the Crossroads." U.S. Army War College, Carlisle Barracks, PA, 1999.
Martínez, Carlos. "Ese golpe no iba a resolver los problemas del país." Interview with Ana Guadalupe Martínez, El Faro.net, July 9, 2008.
McMaster, H. R. "On War: Lessons to Be Learned." *Survival* 50:1 (February–March 2008): 19–30.
Melara, Rafael. "The Civil-Military Gap in El Salvador." U.S. Army War College Strategy Research Project, Carlisle Barracks, PA, March 30, 2007.
Metcalf, Clyde H. "The Marine Corps and the Changing Caribbean Policy." *Marine Corps Gazette* 21 (November 1937): 27–34, 68–72.
Metz, Steven. "Counterinsurgency: Strategy and the Phoenix of American Capability." Strategic Studies Institute Carlisle, Barracks, PA, 1995.
  "A Flame Kept Burning: Counterinsurgency Support after the Cold War." *Parameters* (Autumn 1995): 31–41.
  "Insurgency and Counterinsurgency in Iraq." *Washington Quarterly* (Winter 2003–4): 25–36.
Meyers, Alan et al. "Community Health Analysis of a 'Repopulated Village' in El Salvador." *Medical Anthropology Quarterly* 3:3 (September 1989): 270–80.
Meyers, Barton. "Defense against Aerial Attack in El Salvador." *Journal of Political and Military Sociology* 22 (Winter 1994): 327–42.
Millett, Richard. "The State Department's Navy: A History of the Special Service Squadron, 1920–1940." *American Neptune* 35 (April 1975): 118–38.
Mishra, Pankaj. "The Making of Afghanistan." *New York Review of Books*, November 15, 2001, 18–21.
Molina, Simon A. "The Peace Process in El Salvador: 1984–1992." Strategy Research Project. U.S. Army War College, Carlisle, PA, April 1996.
Montgomery, Tommie Sue. "Fighting Guerrillas: The United States and Low-Intensity Conflict in El Salvador." *New Political Science* (Fall/Winter 1990): 21–53.
  "Getting to Peace in El Salvador: The Roles of the United Nations Secretariate and ONUSAL." *Interamerican Studies and World Affairs* 37:4 (Winter 1995): 139–72.
Moore, Scott W. "Today It's Gold, Not Purple." *Joint Force Quarterly* (Winter 1998–9): 100–106.
Mousa, Suleiman. "A Matter of Principle: King Hussein of the Hijaz and the Arabs of Palestine." *International Journal of Middle East Studies* 9:2 (April 1978): 183–94.
Nagl, John A. "Let's Win the Wars We're In." *JFQ* (First Quarter 2009).
  "A Better War in Iraq: Learning Counterinsurgency and Making Up for Lost Time." *Armed Forces Journal* (August 2006): 22–8.

Nagl, John. A., Andrew M. Exum, and Ahmed A. Humayun. "A Pathway to Success in Afghanistan: The National Solidarity Program." Center for a New American Security, Policy Brief, March 2009.
Nur-Eldeen Masalha. "Faisal's Pan-Arabism, 1921–33." *Middle Eastern Studies* 27:4 (October 1991): 679–93.
Oliker, Olga. "Iraqi Security Forces: Defining Challenges and Assessing Progress." Testimony presented before the House Armed Services Committee. RAND Corporation, March 2007.
Packer, George. "Knowing the Enemy." *New Yorker*, December 18, 2006.
"The Lesson of Tal Afar." *New Yorker*, April 10, 2006.
Peard, Roger W. "The Tactics of Bush Warfare." *Infantry Journal* 38 (September–October 1931): 408–15.
Petraeus, David H. "Learning Counterinsurgency: Observations from Soldiering in Iraq." *Military Review* (January–February 2006).
Pickering, Thomas R. "Anatomy of Plan Colombia." *The American Interest* (November/December 2009): 71–7.
Proctor, Clarance B. "The Nicaraguan Expedition." *Leatherneck* 12 (June 1929): 8–9, 55–6.
Rabasa, Angel et al. "Money in the Bank: Lessons Learned from Past Counterinsurgency (COIN) Operations." Washington, DC: National Defense Research Institute, RAND Corporation, 2007.
Ramsey, Robert D. III. "Advising Indigenous Forces: American Advisors in Korea, Vietnam, and El Salvador." Global War on Terrorism Occasional Paper 18, Combat Studies Institute Press, Fort Leavenworth, Kansas, 2006.
Record, Jeffrey. "The American Way of War: Cultural Barriers to Successful Counterinsurgency." Policy Analysis Paper No. 577, CATO Institute, Washington, DC, September 1, 2006.
Rennie, Ruth et al. "State Building, Security, and Social Change in Afghanistan: Reflections on a Survey of the Afghan People." The Asia Foundation, San Francisco, December 2008.
Ricks, Thomas E. "In Iraq, Military Forgot Lessons of Vietnam." *Washington Post*, July 23, 2006, A01.
Rodriquez, David M. "Leaving Afghanistan to the Afghans." *Foreign Affairs* (September/October 2011): 45–53.
Rogers, Steven. "Beyond Abu Sayyaf: The Lessons of Failure in the Philippines." *Foreign Affairs* 83:1 (January 2004): 15–20.
Ron, James. "Ideology in Context: Explaining Sendero Luminoso's Tactical Escalation." *Journal of Peace Research* 38:5 (September 2001).
Root, Elihu. "The Real Monroe Doctrine." *American Journal of International Law* 8 (July 1914): 427–42.
Rostow, Walt. "Guerrilla Warfare in the Undeveloped Areas." *Department of State Bulletin*, August 7, 1961.
Schaffer, Ronald. "The 1940 Small Wars Manual and the 'Lessons of History.'" *Military Affairs* 36:2 (April 1972): 46–51.
Schmidle, Nicholas. "Getting bin Laden." *New Yorker*, August 8, 2011.
Schmitt, Eric and Tom Shaker. "U.S. Plan Widens Role in Training Pakistani Forces in Qaeda Battle." *New York Times*, March 2, 2008.

Sepp, Kalev. "Best Practices in Counterinsurgency." *Military Review* (May–June 2005): 8–12.
Shafer, Michael D. "The Unlearned Lessons of Counterinsurgency." *Political Science Quarterly* 103:1 (Spring 1988): 57–80.
Shaw, W. B. "Pershing on the Trail." *Review of Reviews* 53 (April 1916): 419–21.
Shea, John J. "Explaining Success and Failure in Counterinsurgency." Thesis, Naval Postgraduate School, Monterey, CA, June 1991.
Silva, Luciano. "The War in El Salvador: A Retrospective." Research Project, U.S. Army War College, Carlisle Barracks, PA, April 15, 1996.
Smelser, Marshall. "An Understanding of the American Revolution. *Review of Politics* 38: 3, Bicentennial Issue (July 1976).
Smyth, Frank. "Consensus or Crisis? Without Duarte in El Salvador." *Journal of Interamerican Studies and World Affairs* 30:4 (Winter 1988–9): 29–52.
Snyder, Glenn H. "The Security Dilemma in Alliance Politics." *World Politics* 36: 4 (July 1984): 461–95.
Snyder, H. W. "Butler at Fort Riviere." *Marine Corps Gazette* 64 (November 1980): 83–7.
Stahler-Sholk, Richard. "El Salvador's Negotiated Transition: From Low-Intensity Conflict to Low-Intensity Democracy." *Journal of Interamerican Studies and World Affairs* 36:4 (Winter 1994): 1–59.
Studemeister, Margarita S. "El Salvador: Implementation of the Peace Accords." *Peaceworks* 38, United States Institute of Peace (January 2001).
Sturdevant, E. W. "Central America and the Marine Corps." *Marine Corps Gazette* 11 (March 1926): 24–31.
Sullivan, Michael. "Leadership in Counterinsurgency: A Tale of Two Leaders." *Military Review* 87:5 (September–October 2007): 119–23.
Tepperman, Jonathan D. "Salvador in Iraq: Flash Back." Council on Foreign Relations, April 5, 2005.
Thomas, John W. "With the Special Service Squadron." *Marine Corps Gazette* 12 (June 1927): 76–81.
Thornton, Rob. "In the Mosul COIN Fight, Perception often Creates Reality." *Infantry Journal* 96:1 (January–February 2007).
Thornton, Skip. "Thinking about the Tactics of Modern War: The Salvadoran Example." Monograph, School of Advanced Military Studies, U.S. Army Command and General Staff College, Fort Leavenworth, Kansas, 1988–9.
Thrasher, Thomas E. "The Taking of Fort Riviere." *Marine Corps Gazette* 15 (February 1931): 31–3, 64.
Tomes, Robert R. "Relearning Counterinsurgency Warfare." *Parameter* (Spring 2004): 16–28.
Ungo, Guillermo M. "The People's Struggle." *Foreign Policy* (Autumn 1983): 51–63.
"U.S. Embassy San Salvador, FMLN Threatens Voters, March 5, 1982," NA, SG 59, Entry 5238, "Records Relating to the UN Truth Commission," Box 1.
U.S. Institute of Peace, *UN Truth Commission Report*. Washington, DC, 1993.
Valenzuela, Alfred A. and Victor M. Rosello. "Expanding Roles and Mission in the War on Drugs and Terrorism: El Salvador and Colombia." U.S. Army Professional Writing Collection, *Military Review* (March–April 2004).

Villalobos, Joaquín. "A Democratic Revolution for El Salvador." *Foreign Policy* 74 (Spring 1989): 103–22.
Waghelstein, John D. "El Salvador: Observations and Experiences in Counterinsurgency." *US Army War College*, Carlisle Barracks, PA, January 1, 1985.
"Military to Military Contacts: Personal Observations – The El Salvador Case." *Low Intensity Conflict and Law Enforcement* 10:2 (Summer 2003).
"Regulars, Irregulars, and Militia: The American Revolution." *Small Wars and Insurgencies* 6 (1995): 133–58.
"What's Wrong in Iraq? Or, Ruminations of a Pachyderm." *Military Review* (January–February 2006).
"The Waiting Wounded." *The Economist*, March 23, 2013.
Walker, Knut and Philip J. Williams. "The Military and Democratization in El Salvador." *Journal of Interamerican Studies and World Affairs* 35:1 (1993): 39–88.
Weiner, Tim. "Gen. Vang Pao's Last War." *New York Times Magazine*, May 11, 2008.
Weitz, Richard. "Insurgency and Counterinsurgency in Latin America, 1960–1980." *Political Science Quarterly* 101:3 (1986): 397–413.
White, Josh. "Defense Secretary Urges Military to Mold Itself to Fight Iraq-Style Wars." *Washington Post*, May 14, 2008.
Wiktorowicz, Quintan. "The New Global Threat: Transnational Salafis and Jihad." *Middle East Policy* 8:4 (December 2001):18–38.
Willbanks, James H. "Winning the Battle, Losing the War." *New York Times*, March 5, 2008.
Williams, Charles F. "La Guardia Nacional Dominicana." *Marine Corps Gazette* 3 (September 1918): 195–99.
Williams, Dion. "The Nicaraguan Situation." *Marine Corps Gazette* 15 (November 1930): 18–22, 53, 55–7.
Wise, H. D. "Notes on Field Service in Samar." *Infantry Journal* 4 (July 1907): 3–58.
Yingling, Lt. Col. Paul. "A Failure in Generalship." *Armed Forces Journal* (May 2007).

The following military journals were consulted and cited:

Marine Corps Gazette
Leatherneck
Infantry Journal
Military Review
Strategic Review
Infantry Magazine
Small Wars Journal

Primary documents on Central America in the 1980s, and especially for the El Salvador and Nicaragua chapters, included the following:

"El Salvador: War, Peace, and Human Rights, 1980–1994," National Security Archive (NSA), Washington, DC. In the endnotes these documents are listed with the abbreviation ES. Archive information can be obtained at http://www.gwu.edu/~nsarchiv/nsa/publications/elsalvador2/#FOCUS.

"The Iran-Contra Affair, 20 Years On," National Security Archive, Washington, DC. More information can be found at http://www.gwu.edu/~nsarchiv/NSAEBB/NSAEBB210/index.htm).

Proceso. Centro Universitario de Documentación e Información (CUDI).

Universidad Centroamericana José Simeón Cañas (UCA), San Salvador. The CUDI's archives contain the compiled edition of *Proceso* that includes almost every newspaper article published in El Salvador during the war years, 1979–92.

Index

Abdullah, Abdullah, 428
Abrams, Creighton, 232, 394
Abu Ghadiya, 461
Abu Ghraib, 8, 381–2
Abu Sayyaf, 398–402
AC-130 Spectre gunships, 419
Acevedo, Rafael Antonio, 299
Afghanistan: air strikes and, 415–16, 419; Al Qaeda and, 365, 398, 411, 415–16, 418–20, 426–7, 429–30, 436–7, 439; ambush and, 407, 423, 425, 435; Amin and, 405; assassination and, 404, 439; atrocities and, 473n8; Bales massacre and, 4–6, 8, 440, 473n7, 473n8; Battle of Wanat and, 415; bin Laden and, 398, 407, 410–11, 413f, 416, 418, 420, 436–40, 459, 462; border attacks and, 436–7; Britain and, 404, 407, 422; Bush, George W., and, 416, 418–19, 428, 430–1; Carter and, 405–6; Central Intelligence Agency (CIA) and, 365, 406–8, 415–16, 419–20, 437, 464, 466; China and, 407; Clinton and, 411; communism and, 404–9; conventional warfare and, 405, 438; corruption in, 420–2; cost of U.S. war in, 417, 434; counterinsurgency and, 8, 406, 408, 412, 415–18, 422–6, 440–1, 473n8; covert operations and, 405–9, 437–8; Daoud and, 404; democracy and, 427; drones and, 8, 425, 436–7, 464, 466; drugs and, 410, 418, 431, 441; Federally Administered Tribal Areas and, 436; First Afghan War and, 404; Germany and, 421–2; as the "good war," 415–18; governance issues in, 420–2; guerrilla warfare and, 405–7, 410, 421–5, 467; Haqqani network and, 436, 462; historical perspective on, 404; Holbrooke and, 427; insurgency and, 4–5, 8, 406–8, 412–41, 467; intelligence gathering and, 406–7, 415, 418, 421, 436–7, 439; International Security Assistance Force (ISAF) and, 421–2, 428; Iraq and, 416–18, 422, 426–34, 438, 441; Islam and, 404–13, 420–1, 423, 440, 442; Italy and, 422; Jalalabad airbase and, 408, 437; Jawbreaker and, 415–16; jihadists and, 399, 405–7, 410–11; Joint Chiefs of Staff and, 417, 426–7, 433, 438–9; Joint Special Operations Command (JSOC) and, 427–9; Karmal and, 405; Karzai and, 5, 421–3, 428, 432, 434; levels of dirtiness and, 6; light footprint approach and, 419, 434, 441; looting and, 409; loss of life in, 408, 434; Marja mission and, 431–2; McChrystal and, 426–33; media and, 11, 415, 423, 426, 429, 439; morale and, 409, 424; Mortensen and, 433; mujahideen and, 134, 406–9, 418, 421; multinational effort in, 422–3; Najibullah and, 405–6, 409; nation-building and, 417, 419, 422–3, 426, 433, 441, 473n5; NATO and, 4, 407, 415, 421–5, 432, 434, 441; Northern Alliance and, 409–10, 415–16, 418–19; Obama and, 397, 417, 426–32, 436–41; oil and, 411; Operation Enduring

547

Afghanistan (cont.)
Freedom and, 415, 417, 419–20, 426; Operation Moshtarak and, 430–1; opium and, 410, 418, 423; pacification and, 425; Pakistan and, 464; Petraeus and, 1–2, 432–4, 439; poppy cultivation and, 410, 418, 431, 441; propaganda and, 423; Provincial Reconstruction Teams (PRTs) and, 425; public opinion on, 422, 473n8; retreat and, 419, 423; Revolutionary Council and, 405; rule of law and, 416, 424; Rumsfeld and, 419; September 11, 2001, and, 417–18, 433; Shah and, 404; Soviet Union and, 22, 134, 399, 404–10, 418, 420; Sunnis and, 407, 426, 431, 441; Tajik forces and, 409; Taliban and, 134, 189, 365, 398, 409–11, 414–35, 440–1, 466; terrorism and, 411, 415–16, 418–19, 429, 433, 440; torture and, 406; United Kingdom and, 407, 422; U.S. Air Force and, 416; U.S. Army and, 412, 420, 440; U.S. assistance to, 406–7; U.S. invasion of, 418–20; U.S. Marine Corps and, 412, 415, 427, 430f, 431–2, 435–7, 440–1; U.S. Navy and, 436, 438, 440; Waigal Valley attack and, 412, 414–15; warlords and, 2, 409, 432; World War II era and, 404

Afghan National Army (ANA), 424–5, 432
Afghan National Police, 422
Afrikaners, 64
Agency for International Development (AID), 315
Aguinaldo, Emilio: background of, 74; Battle of Manila and, 75–6, 87f; capture of, 86; Dewey and, 74–5, 85; guerrilla warfare and, 74, 79–86; *ilustrados* and, 74, 79–80; nationalist forces of, 74–88; Philippines and, 74–88, 199; *principales* and, 79; Republican Army and, 79–80; runs for President, 86; Spanish bribe of, 74
Ahmadinejad, Mahmoud, 457
Aidid, Mohamed Farrah, 342
Air strikes, 320, 415–16, 419, 453
AK-47 rifles, 297, 299, 366, 374, 377, 435
Alexander the Great, 19
Alfhem (Swedish freighter), 243
Algeria: Armée de Libération Nationale (ALN) and, 178, 182; atrocities and, 177, 180–2, 185; Battle of of Algiers and, 180–2; Casbah and, 179–80; cease-fire in, 183–4; Challe and, 174, 182; communism and, 174–8, 184; counterinsurgency and, 175–84; Foreign Legion and, 211; Front de Libération Nationale (FLN) and, 178–84; Galula and, 185; Gestapo and, 181; *guerre révolutionnaire* and, 175–80, 182; guerrilla warfare and, 176, 180; hostages and, 455; imperialism and, 175, 178; insurgency and, 175–84; intelligence gathering and, 178, 180; Islam and, 177–81; Italy and, 176; Kennedy and, 184; lessons learned from, 469; Marxism and, 176; massacres and, 177; Massu and, 180–3; Morice Line and, 181–2; Nazis and, 177, 180–1; OAS and, 183–4; oil and, 455; pacification and, 182; *pieds-noirs* (immigrants) and, 176–7, 180, 183; psychological warfare and, 176, 179; quadrillage system and, 179, 182; regroupments and, 181; reprisals in, 176–7; revolt in, 176–7; secure borders and, 181–2; Soviet Union and, 174–5; Spain and, 176; terrorism and, 179–80, 183; torture and, 177, 180–2, 185; World War II era and, 174, 183

Al-Jazeera, 379
Al-Kuwaiti, Abu Ahmed, 437
Alliance for Progress, 270
Al Qaeda: Abu Ghadiya and, 461; Afghanistan and, 365, 398, 411, 415–16, 418–20, 426–7, 429–30, 436–7, 439; Al Maasada training camp and, 410; Al-Shifa bombing and, 411; bin Laden and, 61, 374, 398, 407, 410–11, 413f, 416, 418, 420, 436–40, 459, 462; Central Intelligence Agency (CIA) and, 365; classical insurgencies and, 188–9; drones and, 462, 466; foreign personnel of, 515n11; Iraq and, 365, 374–6, 378, 386–90, 441, 459, 461, 515n11; Islam and, 410; Joint Special Operations Command (JSOC) and, 427, 460–1; leaderless resistance and, 188; Libya and, 455; Mali and, 455; Masri and, 462; McChrystal and, 460; Muthanna and, 461; Operation Desert Storm and, 410–11; Pakistan and, 416, 419–20, 426; Philippines and, 399; religious fanaticism and, 188; rise of, 410–11; Sayyaf and, 399; September 11, 2001, attacks and, 4,

12, 62, 94, 134, 343, 350, 361, 368, 398, 411, 418, 433; Syria and, 461; United Kingdom and, 515n11; U.S. embassies and, 411; Yemeni and, 462; Zarqawi and, 373–5, 378, 387, 427, 459–61
Al Qaeda in Iraq (AQI), 374–6, 378, 386–7, 389–90
Al-Sadr, Moqtada, 375–7
Al-Sistani, Ayatollah Ali, 381
Ambush, 154: Afghanistan and, 407, 423, 425, 435; American Revolution and, 36–7, 41; Banana Wars and, 121; El Salvador and, 331; Greece and, 167; Guevara and, 272, 274; Honduras and, 260; Indians and, 56–7, 60; Iraq and, 366, 375–7, 379, 386; Malaya and, 190, 195–6; Nicaragua and, 296; Philippines and, 85; Sandino and, 144, 147
American Institute for Free Labor Development (AIFLD), 315
American Revolution, 3: ambush and, 36–7, 41; American South and, 29–30, 40–4; Battle of Concord and, 34, 37–8; Battle of Cowpens and, 34, 45; Battle of Lexington and, 34; Battle of Princeton and, 33, 38; Battle of Trenton and, 33, 38; Battle of Yorktown and, 45; Breed's Hill and, 38; Britain and, 34–7, 44; Continental Army and, 29–30, 33, 35–40; controlling the countryside and, 40; conventional warfare and, 36–8, 44–5, 49–50; counterinsurgency and, 31, 33, 35, 42–3; covert operations and, 41; decision-making authority and, 34, 36; element of surprise and, 33, 45; flying army and, 44–5; guerrilla warfare and, 33–4, 40, 42; Hessians and, 38; insurgency and, 31, 33–5, 40, 42–5; Kings Mountain and, 31–4, 36, 42, 44; Lincoln and, 29, 44–5; looting and, 32, 40, 43; Loyalists and, 29, 31–3, 35, 37, 41–4; massacres and, 44; morale and, 32, 37, 39; plundering and, 40, 43; propaganda and, 35; psychological warfare and, 35; retreat and, 29, 32, 37–8, 41, 45; summer of 1780 and, 29; swamps and, 41–2; Tories and, 35, 41; unconventional American tactics and, 35–8; Valley Forge winter and, 38–40; Washington, George, and, 32–6, 38–40, 45, 47, 50, 145; Waxhaws Massacre and, 29, 43

American Society of Newspaper Editors, 250–1
Amin, Hafizullah, 405
Amin, Idi, 446
Anaconda strategy, 1–2
Anna Karenina (Tolstoy), 470
Annan, Kofi, 374
Apache attack helicopters, 342, 366, 414
Apache Indians, 55, 56, 58f, 59f, 60–1, 82, 96
Apollo theater, 5
Arab Bulletin, 133
Arab Bureau, 129
Arab League, 451
Arab Revolt: Battle of Yanbu and, 128f; Britain and, 128–35; counterinsurgency and, 127, 134–5; "Declaration to the Seven Arabs, The," and, 486n23; Faisal and, 128–30, 133, 485n13; genie of Arab empire and, 130–3; Germany and, 129; guerrilla warfare and, 131, 133–5; imperialism and, 135; insurgency and, 127–35; Lawrence and, 127–35; looting and, 131; morale and, 131; nation-building and, 134; Ottoman Empire and, 127–35; World War II and, 135
Arab Spring, 444, 448–9
Arana, Carlos, 262
Arapaho, 5, 56–7
Árbenz, Jacobo, 240–4, 246, 252, 255–6, 267, 279
Ardennes, 378
Arellán, John Freddy, 345
Arellán, Oswaldo, 345
Arévalo, Juan José, 240
Argentina, 272, 274, 281, 289
Arias, Desiderio, 123
Arias, Oscar, 300, 333
Armas, Castillo, 243–4, 258
Armée de Libération National (ALN), 178, 182
Armistice Day, 106
Army of the Potomac, 47
Army of the Republic of Vietnam (ARVN), 219–22, 230, 234–5
Arroyo, Gloria, 400
Art of War, The (Sun Tzu), 19, 159
Ashe, John, 44–5
Assassination, 22: Afghanistan and, 404, 439; Banana Wars and, 123; Batista and, 247; Chamorro and, 280, 284, 301; China

Assassination (cont.)
  and, 162; Cristiani, 330–1; Cuba and, 247; Daoud, 404; de Gaulle, 183; El Salvador and, 306, 314–15, 330–1; France and, 183; Guatemala and, 259; Gurney, 190, 195; Iraq and, 380, 386; Kennedy, 223; Libya and, 448; McKinley, 116; Magsaysay, 207; Malaya and, 190, 195; Nicaragua and, 260, 280, 284, 301; Obama and, 439; Péralte, 120–1; Philippines and, 207, 399; Qaddafi and, 448; Romero, 314–15; Sattar, 387; Vietnam and, 220, 229, 235
Asylum, 147, 246
Atrocities: Afghanistan and, 473n8; Algeria and, 182; Banana Wars and, 109, 112, 121, 124; Boer War and, 63, 67, 70–1; Colombia and, 359; death squads and, 259–60 (*see also* Death squads); El Salvador and, 323, 325; Guatemala and, 258, 263–5; human rights and, 8; Indians and, 57; Iraq and, 382; massacres and, 5 (*see also* Massacres); media and, 13; Philippines and, 76, 78, 80, 84–6, 88; rape and, 52, 177, 306, 324; reprisals and, 70; Romans and, 19; Sandino and, 146; torture and, 381–2 (*see also* Torture); United States and, 13, 470, 473n8
Attraction policies, 84, 87
Attrition, 39, 224–9, 408, 452
Australia, 67, 70, 199, 420, 425
Austria-Hungary, 100
Aylwin-Foster, Nigel, 363

B-1 bombers, 425
B-1 swing-wing planes, 368
B-1B bombers, 419
B-2 bombers, 437
B-26 Douglas Invaders, 252–3
B-52 bombers, 368, 419, 464
Ba'aths: de-Ba'athification and, 369–73; Iraq and, 366, 368–73, 385
Bagram Air Base, 417
Baker, Eugene, 6
Baker, James, 288
Bales, Robert, 4–6, 8, 440, 473n7, 473n8
Banana Wars: ambush and, 121; atrocities and, 109, 112, 121, 124; bandits and, 117, 119; *cacos* and, 117–23; communism and, 125, 192–8; conventional warfare and, 112–13, 115, 119; counterinsurgency and, 109, 111, 114, 122, 124, 126; Cuba and, 113–17, 125–6; democracy and, 119–20, 124–5; Dominican Republic and, 109, 110f, 113, 122–5; Germany and, 113, 118, 123; Great White Fleet and, 112; Haiti and, 109, 110f, 112–13, 117–24; imperialism and, 111–12, 116; insurgency and, 109, 111, 113–15, 120–6; Krulak and, 226; Manifest Destiny and, 111; morale and, 123; nation-building and, 109, 112, 117–22; Nicaragua and, 109, 111, 118, 122; pacification and, 109, 115, 122; Platt Amendment and, 115–16; political correctness and, 112; public debate over, 112, 114; *Small Wars Manual* and, 149; U.S. Marine Corps and, 111–13, 118–25; U.S. Navy and, 111–12, 115, 120–1, 123; Wilson and, 111, 113, 118–21, 123
Bandits, 16, 21, 50: Banana Wars and, 117, 119; Catholic Church and, 21; chasing of, 4, 94–9, 145, 469; Greece and, 171–2; Iraq and, 370, 374; Malaya and, 192; Philippines and, 399, 402; Sandino and, 136, 143–6; Villa and, 92–9, 109, 111
Barbarity, 6, 19, 52, 69, 77, 86, 88, 263
Barker, John, 37
Barrientos, René, 272–3
Barrios, Gerardo, 320–1
Basic Tactics (Mao Zedong), 160–1
Basque separatists, 446
Bataan, 73f, 199, 200f
Batista, Fulgencio: Castro and, 15, 246–51, 277, 279, 286, 322; Directorio Revolucionario and, 247–8; fall of, 250–1; País and, 248
Batson, Gregory, 82
Battalion Combat Teams (BCTs), 206
Battle of Algiers, 180–2
Battle of Breed's Hill, 38
Battle of Carrizal, 98
Battle of Celaya, 92
Battle of Concord, 34, 37–8
Battle of Cowpens, 34, 45
Battle of Fallujah, 377–80
Battle of Iwo Jima, 340, 378
Battle of Lexington, 34
Battle of Little Big Horn, 85
Battle of Manila, 75–6, 87f
Battle of Mogadishu, 342

Battle of Ocotal, 143
Battle of Princeton, 33, 38
Battle of Toulgas, 101f
Battle of Trenton, 33, 38
Battle of Wanat, 415
Battle of Waxhaws, 29, 43
Battle of Yanbu, 128f
Battle of Yorktown, 45
Bay of Pigs: Cuba and, 153, 239, 253–7, 261, 269, 289, 295, 299; Kennedy and, 252–5; legacy of, 257; loss of life from, 253–4; mistaken assumption of, 254; as perfect failure, 254; prisoner release and, 256
Beaver float planes, 274
Beck, George, Jr., 424
Beinart, Peter, 372
Bell, J. Franklin, 125–6
Benghazi attacks, 442, 455
Berg, Nicholas, 374
Berlin Wall, 339, 350
Bermer, L. Paul, III, "Jerry," 371–7, 380
Betancourt, Ingrid, 348, 348–9
Betancourt, Rómulo, 251
Bhutto, Benazir, 410
Bhutto, Zulfikar Ali, 406
Bible, 18–19
Biden, Joseph, 387, 432
Bin Laden, Osama: Afghanistan and, 398, 407, 410–11, 413f, 416, 418, 420, 436–40, 459, 462; al-Kuwaiti and, 437; Al Maasada training camp and, 410; Al Qaeda and, 61, 374, 398, 407, 413f, 416, 418, 420, 436–40, 459, 462; Al-Shifa bombing and, 411; Central Intelligence Agency (CIA) and, 415–16, 420, 437; Clinton and, 411; death of, 413f, 437–40; disposal of body of, 440; drones and, 437; Geronimo signal and, 61, 439; Iraq and, 374; Joint Special Operations Command (JSOC) and, 438–9, 459; Kenya embassy bombing and, 411; media studio of, 439; missile strikes against, 411; Obama and, 436–40; Operation Desert Storm and, 410–11; Pakistan and, 61, 410, 420, 437–40; proof of death of, 437, 439; raid on, 437–40; rise of, 410–11; September 11, 2001, and, 418; Taliban and, 410, 418, 420; Tanzania embassy bombing and, 411; Turki and, 407

Bissell, Richard, 243–4, 254–5
Black, Cofer, 415–16
Blackhawk helicopters, 343, 352, 437–9
Black September, 446
Blockhouse system, 64, 67–8, 113, 159, 181
Body counts, 224–6, 370
Boer War, 85, 201: Afrikaners and, 64; atrocities and, 63, 67, 70–1; blockhouse system and, 64, 67–8, 113, 159, 181; breakout of, 65–6; Britain and, 63–71; concentration camps and, 69; conventional warfare and, 66–7; counterinsurgency and, 67, 69; De Wet and, 68; First, 64, 69; gold and, 64–5; guerrilla warfare and, 66–7, 70; insurgency and, 64, 66–70, 93; intelligence collection and, 69; Kitchener and, 63, 67–70; lessons from, 63–4, 469; loss of life from, 63, 71; Roberts and, 63, 66–7; sabotage and, 67; Second, 65–6, 77; Transvaal and, 64–70; Treaty of Vereeniging and, 71; *Uitlanders* and, 65–6
Boland, Edward, 294
Boland-Zablocki amendment, 294, 297, 300
Bolivia: Central Intelligence Agency (CIA) and, 274; communism and, 272; Cuba-inspired insurgencies and, 156, 260–1, 269, 272–6, 281; Green Berets and, 273–5; Guevara and, 261, 269, 272–3, 299; intelligence gathering and, 273; Johnson and, 273; leftists and, 272–3; Marxism and, 275f, 278; paramilitary forces and, 274; U.S. Special Forces Mobile Training Team and, 272–3
Bolsheviks, 101f, 102–7, 157, 186
Bonner, Raymond, 324
Boot, Max, 37
Borge, Tomás, 282, 284, 290
Bosnia, 465
Bowden, Mark, 438, 460
Boyd, Charles T., 98
Braddock, Daniel, 251
Bradley, George, 53
Bradley fighting vehicles, 366, 386
Brazil, 272, 451
Breaker Morant (film), 70
Breslin, Mike, 440
Briggs, Harold, 193–5, 198
Britain: Afghanistan and, 404, 407, 422; Al Qaeda and, 515n11; American Revolution and, 29–45; American South

Britain (cont.)
and, 29–34, 40–4; Anti-Bandit Campaign of, 192–8; Arab Revolt and, 128–35; blockhouse system and, 64, 67–8, 113, 159, 181; Boer War and, 63–71; Galula and, 187; Greece and, 165, 167–8, 172; incendiary bombing and, 475n7; Labor Party and, 69; Libya and, 446–7, 452–3; London blitz and, 475n7; Loyalists and, 29, 31–3, 35, 37, 41–4; Malaya and, 197; mandates and, 129; MI6 and, 453; Napoleon and, 20; Plains of Abraham and, 35; Qaddafi and, 446; Siberia and, 100, 102, 105; Sun Tzu's maxims and, 19; Tin Puncturing Order and, 197; Tories and, 35, 41; Trans–Siberian Railroad and, 105
Brokaw, Tom, 318
Brooke, John R., 115
Brostrom, Jonathan, 414
Bruce, William, 122
Bryan, William Jennings, 81
Brzezinski, Zbigniew, 405
Buford, Abraham, 29, 43
Bummers, 51
Burning at the stake, 22
Bush, George H. W.: Iraq and, 367, 505n4; Nicaragua and, 300–2; Stinger missile buyback and, 408
Bush, George W.: Afghanistan and, 416, 418–19, 428; Colombia and, 334–5; *Counterinsurgency Field Manual* and, 395; Iraq and, 79, 367–72, 377, 380, 383, 387–8, 391, 431; "Mission Accomplished" claim of, 79; National Security Directive 24 and, 371; National Security Strategy and, 368; Operation Vigilant Resolve and, 377; Petraeus and, 383; post-invasion assumptions of, 391; reconstruction costs and, 371; September 11, 2001, and, 94, 350, 368, 398–9, 411; strategies of, 2, 94, 387–8, 416, 418–19, 428, 430–1, 505n4, 507n8; Taliban and, 94, 416; troop surge and, 388; weapons of mass destruction (WMD) and, 367–9; Wolfowitz and, 371
Butler, Smedley, 118–19, 138

C-47 transport aircraft, 274
C-123K cargo plane, 297, 299–300
C-130 transport aircraft, 420

Cabbages and Kings (O. Henry), 139
Cabot, John Moors, 241–2
Cacos, 117–23
Callwell, C. E., 25–6, 188
Cameron, David, 451
Camp Belambay, 4
Campbell, William, 31, 42
Campbell-Bannerman, Henry, 69
Campesinos (peasants), 21–2, 199, 272, 283, 291
Camp Furlong, 89, 92
Camp Hale, 162
Canada, 35, 37, 70, 420
Canales, José Fernando, 297
Cannon, Lee Roy, 138
Cape Colony, 64–6
Cape of Good Hope, 64–70
Caperton, William B., 118, 123
Captain General Gerardo Barrios Military Academy, 320–1
Carpio, Salvador Cayetano, 311
Carranza, Venustiano, 91–5, 98
Carter, Jimmy: Afghanistan and, 405–6; boycotts 1980 Moscow Olympics, 406; Desert One and, 458; Dominican Republic and, 286; El Salvador and, 307–9, 312–13, 361; engagement strategy of, 308; Guatemala and, 263; as hawk, 266, 288, 361; human rights and, 280; Iran hostages and, 437, 457–8; Nicaragua and, 281–2, 285–9, 301–2; strategies of, 263, 280–2, 285–9, 301–2, 307–9, 312–13, 361, 405–6, 437, 457–8
Carthaginians, 19
Cartwright, James, 437
Casas Grandes, 95
Case, Steve, 348
Casey, George W., 376, 384, 388
Casey, William, 295, 406
Castel, Albert, 52
Castro, Fidel: air force of, 252, 254, 256–7; Batista and, 15, 246–51, 277, 279, 286, 322; Bay of Pigs and, 153, 239, 253–7, 261, 269, 289, 295, 299; capture of, 247; Central Intelligence Agency (CIA) and, 153, 239, 252–7, 261, 269, 274, 289, 295, 299; Cuba and, 14, 17, 145, 156, 239, 244–61, 271–2, 274, 276–7, 282, 287, 304, 311, 322, 445; Eisenhower and, 251; El Salvador and, 311; Farabundo Martí National Liberation Front (FMLN) and,

304, 311; first attack of, 246–7; foco theory and, 260–1, 268–9, 272–3, 276–83, 311; Guatemala and, 258, 260–1, 268–9, 272–3; Guevara and, 247, 248, 250; Happy Valley and, 252; Havana rally of, 277; "History Will Absolve Me" speech of, 247; July 26 Movement and, 247–50; Kennedy and, 252; Khrushchev and, 256; Lenin and, 247; longevity advantage and, 17; Mao Zedong and, 247; Martí and, 247; Matthews and, 145, 249; media and, 145, 249–53; missile crisis and, 256; Nixon and, 251; propaganda and, 252–3, 255–6; Qaddafi and, 445; quixotic nature of, 244–50; Radio Rebelde and, 249–50; release of, 247; Sandinistas and, 311; visits United States, 250–1
Castro, Raúl, 246–7, 248, 287
Catholics: bandits and, 21; El Salvador and, 307, 310, 333; Guatemala and, 260; Jesuits and, 291, 312; Nicaragua and, 285, 297; Vietnam and, 217–18
Cazador battalions, 328
Cell phones, 460, 466
Central Intelligence Agency (CIA): Afghanistan and, 365, 406–7, 464, 466; Al Qaeda and, 365; Bay of Pigs and, 153, 239, 253–7, 261, 269, 289, 295, 299; bin Laden and, 415–16, 420, 437; Bissell and, 254–5; Bolivia and, 274; Casey and, 288, 295; Castro and, 153, 239, 252–7, 261, 269, 274, 289, 295, 299; China and, 162–3; Clinton and, 408; Counterterrorism Center and, 415–16; covert operations and, 239, 242, 244, 254–5, 299, 315, 405–9; Cuba and, 153, 239, 251–8, 261, 269, 273–4, 289, 295, 299; drones and, 453, 462–6; Dulles and, 241, 243, 252; Eisenhower and, 241–4; El Salvador and, 315; FSLN and, 283; Greece and, 168; Guatemala and, 239, 242–4, 256, 258, 261–2, 289; guerrilla warfare and, 256, 258; Guevara and, 274; Happy Valley and, 252; Hasenfus and, 299; insurrection and, 244, 253; Jawbreaker and, 415–16; Kennedy and, 255–6; Libya and, 453; Mao Zedong and, 162–3; media campaigns and, 243–4; National Photographic Interpretation Center and, 256; Nicaragua and, 242, 274, 283, 286–91, 294–7, 299; Obama and, 437; Operation Mongoose and, 255–6; Operation PBSUCCESS and, 239–40, 242, 258, 261; Pakistan and, 406–7, 462–4, 466; Petraeus and, 2–3; Philippines and, 202; Phoenix Program and, 228; Project Circus and, 162–3; propaganda and, 243–4, 315; psychological warfare and, 315 (*see also* Psychological warfare); Rodríguez and, 299; Special Activities Division and, 419; Stinger missiles and, 408; Taliban and, 365; Tibet and, 162–3; UCLAs and, 295
Cessnas, 274
Challe, Maurice, 174, 182
Chamberlain, Neville, 302
Chamorro, Edgar, 291
Chamorro, Emiliano, 139
Chamorro, Pedro Joaquín, 280–1, 284
Chamorro, Violeta, 301
Chandrasekaran, Rajiv, 380, 435
Charles IV, King of Spain, 20
Charlie Company, 230–1
Chasing Villa (Tompkins), 89
Chassin, Lionel-Max, 176
Chávez, Hugo, 349
Chavez, Lydia, 329
Cheney, Richard, 368
Cheyenne, 5, 56–7
Chiang Kai-Shek, 159–61, 212
Chicago Daily Tribune, 53
China, 208, 451: Afghanistan and, 407; assassination and, 162; Central Intelligence Agency (CIA) and, 162–3; Chiang Kai-Shek and, 159–61, 212; Cuba and, 248, 276, 279; Guevara and, 278; Japanese invasion of, 159–61; Kennedy and, 154; leftist governments and, 159; Libya and, 449, 451; Long March and, 159, 160f; Malaya and, 192–3; Mao Zedong and, 17, 157–64 (*see also* Mao Zedong); modernization of, 343; Nationalist Party (KMT) and, 157, 159–62; People's Liberation Army (PLA) and, 161–2; Red Army and, 161, 163; Sun Tzu and, 19–20, 159, 161, 188, 278; Sun Yat-sen and, 159; Tibet and, 162–3; Trans-Siberian Railroad and, 105; Vietnam and, 10, 209, 212, 223, 234; warlords and, 19

Index

Chinook helicopters, 438–9
Chivington, John, 5
Chronicle, William, 32
Cienfuegos, Camilo, 250
Civil Operations and Revolutionary Development Support (CORDS), 227–8, 233
Civil War, U.S., 87: Confederates and, 4 (*see also* Confederates); Grant and, 3, 47, 51; guerrilla warfare and, 46–7, 49–50; Jayhawkers and, 49; Merritt and, 75; Missouri insurgency and, 50; morale and, 50–3; Mosby and, 46–50, 66; plundering and, 49, 51; propaganda and, 52; psychology and, 52–3; Sherman's March to the Sea and, 50–3; Union Army and, 46–53, 66, 75, 81
Clark, William, 308
Clarke's Creek, 41
Clausewitz, Carl von, 15, 23–5, 128, 159, 188
Clay, Lucius, 372
Cleveland, Benjamin, 31–2
Clinton, Bill: Afghanistan and, 411; bin Laden and, 411; Central Intelligence Agency (CIA) and, 408; Colombia and, 334–5, 350–2, 356–7; Iraq and, 368; Stinger missile buybacks and, 408; strategies of, 334–5, 351, 368; Taliban and, 411; weapons of mass destruction (WMD) and, 368
Clinton, William Henry (British General), 33, 39–40
Clinton, Hillary, 451, 455
CLU-82 Daisy Cutter bomb, 420
Coalition Provisional Authority (CPA): Iraq and, 371–5, 380–1; legacy of, 380–1
Cody, William F. "Buffalo Bill," 92
COIN: Afghanistan and, 428–9, 436; *Counterinsurgency Field Manual* and, 393–4, 396; guerrilla warfare and, 396–7; Iraq and, 384–6, 388–90, 392; Philippines and, 398–403; *see also* Counterinsurgency
Cold War, 4, 9: Algeria and, 174–84; anticommunism and, 12, 125, 154–6, 163, 201, 205, 218, 242, 291–2, 300, 302, 307, 317f, 332, 405–6; Banana Wars and, 125; Bay of Pigs and, 153, 239, 250–7, 261, 269, 289, 295, 299; Clausewitz and, 25; counterinsurgency and, 153–6; democracy and, 155–6, 319, 330, 339; domino thesis and, 262; El Salvador and, 304–35; Greece and, 156, 165–73; Guatemala and, 239–46, 252–3, 256–8; Kennedy and, 155 (*see also* Kennedy, John F.); Malaya and, 190–8; Mao Zedong and, 154, 157–64; Military Assistance Advisory Groups (MAAGS) and, 155–6; modernization theory and, 155–6; Nicaragua and, 280–304; Philippines and, 153, 156, 199–208; Siberia and, 108; technology and, 344; Vietnam and, 153–4, 219 (*see also* Vietnam)
Coll, Steve, 409
Colombia, 4: alternative crop development and, 356–8; atrocities and, 359; Betancourt and, 348–9; Bush, George W., and, 334–5; Clinton and, 334–5, 350–2, 356–7; counterinsurgency and, 344, 350–1, 355–9, 361; democracy and, 347, 352, 356, 362; drugs and, 342, 347, 349–52, 357f, 358–9, 362; El Nogal bombing and, 345, 350; 52nd Counter-Guerrilla Battalion and, 347; guerrilla warfare and, 345–60; hostages and, 349; human rights and, 350, 358–60; insurgency and, 344–61; intelligence gathering and, 353–6; La Macarena and, 356–8; leftists and, 348–9, 358; levels of dirtiness and, 6; Marxism and, 342, 345, 349–51; massacres and, 347; mayoral corruption and, 347; National Liberation Army (ELN) and, 345–7; nation-building and, 358; Obama and, 334–5; Operation Check and, 349; pacification and, 362; paramilitary forces and, 342, 347, 353, 358–9; Pastrana and, 347–8; Plan Colombia and, 350–2, 356–7; Revolutionary Armed Forces of Colombia (FARC) and, 17, 342, 345–62, 418, 423; shock troops and, 359; Special Forces Groups (SFGs) and, 270–1; terrorism and, 345, 348, 350, 361; Uribe and, 348–50, 352–62; U.S. Air Force and, 353; U.S. Marine Corps and, 353
Colombia Army War College and, 506n15
Colorado Territory, 5
Columbia University, 405
Comanche, 56
Combined Action Platoons (CAPs), 227

Commander of the United States Forces, Military Assistance Command, Vietnam (COMUSMACV), 224
Common Sense, 35
Communism: Afghanistan and, 404–9; Algeria and, 174–8, 184; anticommunism and, 12, 125, 154–6, 163, 201, 205, 218, 242, 291–2, 300, 302, 307, 317f, 332, 405–6; Banana Wars and, 125; Berlin Wall and, 339, 350; Bolivia and, 272; Cold War and, 125, 153–6; Cuba and, 247, 249, 251, 254, 256, 259, 269, 272, 307; El Salvador and, 304, 307; Greece and, 165–73; Guatemala and, 241–6, 256, 259–65, 268; Guevara and, 272, 276; Kennedy and, 239, 254, 270; Malaya and, 192–8; Mao Zedong and, 157–64; Marxism and, 188 (*see also* Marxism); Nicaragua and, 281, 283, 287–91, 294, 300–2, 308, 310–11, 313, 317f, 332–3; Philippines and, 199–202, 205–7; Siberia and, 102, 105; Vietnam and, 99, 154, 198, 208–35, 354, 461
Company N, 144–5
Concentration camps: Algeria and, 181; barbarism of, 69; Boer War and, 64, 67, 69; Cuba and, 69, 113; Philippines and, 69, 78; regroupments and, 181; United States and, 69
Conduct of Anti-Terrorist Operations in Malaya, The (Templer), 196
Confederates, 4: counterinsurgency and, 49–53, 271, 273, 276; guerrilla warfare and, 46–7, 49–50; insurgency and, 46–53; lightweight weapons and, 47; Mosby and, 46–50, 66; propaganda and, 52; Union Army and, 46–53, 66, 75, 81
Congo, 271, 339
Constitutionalists, 91
Contadora Group, 500n59
Continental Army, 29–30, 33, 35–40
Contras: arms of, 296; Boland-Zablocki amendment and, 294, 297, 300; compared to U.S. Founding Fathers, 296–7; conclusion of "endless war" and, 302–3; Cuba and, 293; deaths by, 296; downing of cargo plane and, 297–300; Esquipulas II Accord and, 300; formation of, 291–3; Iran-Contra scandal and, 299–300; Jinotega ambush and, 296; low-intensity conflict and, 294–6; media and, 293–4; Nicaragua and, 282, 291–302; Reagan and, 291–302; UCLAs and, 295; U.S. funding of, 282, 291–302
Conventional warfare: Afghanistan and, 405, 438; American Revolution and, 36–8, 44–5, 49–50; American superiority and, 467; Banana Wars and, 112–13, 115, 119; Boer War and, 66–7; Clausewitz on, 25; *Counterinsurgency Field Manual* and, 26, 393; Cuba and, 255; El Salvador and, 320; Galula and, 186; Greece and, 156, 171, 202; Guevara and, 278; Indians and, 54, 56; ineffectiveness of, 18, 24, 26; Iraq and, 363, 365–6, 376, 380, 391; JSOC and, 462; Korea and, 163; Lawrence and, 129–31; Mao Zedong and, 161; markers of, 7–9, 16–17; Nicaragua and, 295; Philippines and, 78–9, 81, 156, 202, 400; Sandino and, 143; small wars and, 26; Tierney on, 11–12; Vietnam and, 10, 212, 215, 219, 222, 230, 232–3, 235
Conze, Jean-Baptiste, 121
Coolidge, Calvin, 140–1, 144–6
Cooper, William, 299
Cordons system, 201
Cornwallis, Charles, 29, 31, 41, 43, 45
Correa, Rafael, 349
Costa Rica, 251, 274, 300, 333
Counterinsurgency: Afghanistan and, 406, 408, 412, 415–18, 422–6, 440–1, 473n8; Algeria and, 175–84; American Revolution and, 31, 33, 35, 42–3; Arab Revolt and, 127, 134–5; Banana Wars and, 109, 111, 114, 122, 124, 126; Boer War and, 67, 69; Callwell and, 26; civilian population and, 16; classical, 22, 187–9, 328, 384, 393, 433; Cold War and, 153–6; Colombia and, 344, 350–1, 355–9, 361; Confederates and, 49–53; context and, 7; Cuba and, 239, 257, 259, 261–2, 271, 273, 276; defining, 15–17; El Salvador and, 279, 309–10, 315, 320–3, 325, 328–9, 331, 334; experts and, 329, 467; Fukuyama and, 468–9; Galula and, 185–9; Greece and, 164–5, 169–73, 242; Guatemala and, 239–40, 242, 257, 259, 261–8; historical perspective on, 19, 21–3; Indians and, 53–62, 96; Iraq and, 8, 366–7, 370–1, 380–9, 392; JSOC and, 460; Libya and, 444, 456; longevity

Counterinsurgency (cont.)
  advantage and, 17–18; Malaya and, 190, 193, 195–8; Mao Zedong and, 159; Marxism and, 188–9, 240; material goods and, 468; nation-building and, 2–3, 7, 78, 84, 88, 109, 112, 117–22, 134, 149, 221, 309–10, 315, 334, 358, 371, 382–3, 417, 419, 422–6, 433, 441, 469, 473n5; Nicaragua and, 279, 281–2, 293, 295; Panama Canal Zone and, 270; Philippines and, 78–87, 106, 201–2, 206–8, 398–403; by proxy, 6, 207–8, 321–3; repressions and, 61, 81–4, 124, 180, 267, 279, 311–14, 445, 448–9; Sandino and, 143–5; Siberia and, 106–8; superior armies and, 16; Vietnam and, 211, 219–31, 235
Counterinsurgency Field Manual: Bush, George W., and, 395; Callwell and, 26; conventional warfare and, 26, 393; Galula and, 393; guerrilla warfare and, 395, 397; Islam and, 396, 397; Lawrence and, 394; lessons learned from, 469; maximalist campaigns and, 394; past U.S. mistakes and, 394; Petraeus and, 395, 433–4; postmodern insurgencies and, 393–7; risk avoidance and, 434; terrorism and, 396; U.S. Army and, 26, 393; U.S. Marine Corps and, 26, 393; weakness of, 394–5
Counterinsurgency Warfare: Theory and Practice (Galula), 185–6
Covert operations: Afghanistan and, 405–9, 437–8; American Revolution and, 41; capture of bin Laden, 437–8; Central Intelligence Agency (CIA) and, 239, 242, 244, 254–5, 299, 315, 405–9; Cuba and, 239, 252, 254–6, 307; drones and, 465; El Salvador and, 299, 315; Guatemala and, 239, 242, 244; Honduras and, 299; Joint Special Operations Command (JSOC) and, 458–62; Kennedy and, 252, 256; Libya and, 453; Nicaragua and, 289, 291, 294, 299, 302; Nixon and, 252; Pakistan and, 406; Panama and, 270; Reagan and, 289; School of the Americas and, 270–1, 283, 323; Vietnam and, 219, 289
Craft, Letitia, 52
Cristiani, Alfredo, 330–1, 333
Crocker, Ryan, 390
Cronkite, Walter, 231

Crook, George, 57, 58f, 60–1
Cuba, 75: assassination and, 247; Banana Wars and, 113–17, 125–6; Batista and, 15, 246–51, 277, 279, 286, 322; Bay of Pigs and, 153, 239, 253–7, 261, 269, 289, 295, 299; Castro and, 14, 17, 145, 156, 239, 244–61, 271–2, 274, 276–7, 282, 287, 304, 311, 322, 445; Central Intelligence Agency (CIA) and, 153, 239, 251–8, 261, 269, 273–4, 289, 295, 299; China and, 248, 276, 279; communism and, 247, 249, 251, 254, 256, 259, 269, 272, 307; concentration camps and, 69, 113; contras and, 293; conventional warfare and, 255; counterinsurgency and, 239, 257, 259, 261–2; covert operations and, 239, 252, 254–6, 307; democracy and, 249; Dominican Republic and, 260, 269; Eisenhower and, 250–2; foco theory and, 260–1, 268–9, 272–3, 276–83, 311; governance crisis of, 269–70; Green Berets and, 271; Guantanamo Bay, 62; guerrilla warfare and, 130, 156, 248, 256, 258, 260–2, 272–9; Guevara and, 244, 246, 256, 279; imperialism and, 251; insurgency and, 156, 239, 247–9, 256–7, 270–6, 279; insurrection and, 113–16, 246–8, 253, 269, 279, 311; intelligence gathering and, 255, 258, 260, 270–1; Johnson and, 256, 261; Joint Chiefs of Staff and, 252, 254, 256; July 26 Movement and, 247–50; Kennedy and, 156, 239, 252–7, 269–70, 276, 282; leftists and, 239, 246, 251, 259, 279, 282, 289; Marxism and, 156, 257, 262, 266, 270; McKinley and, 114–16; media and, 250–1; Nixon and, 251–2; Operation Mongoose and, 255–6; Orlando and, 322; pacification and, 4, 115; paramilitary forces and, 274; Platt Amendment and, 115–16; propaganda and, 249, 256; psychological warfare and, 256, 270–1; qualified independence of, 116; Radio Rebelde and, 249–50; Reagan and, 302; retreat and, 258; as revolutionary base, 251; Roosevelt and, 116–17, 125; Rough Riders and, 125; Sandinistas and, 284; San Juan Hill and, 125; Soviet Union and, 245f, 252, 255, 269, 276, 279, 288, 302, 333; Spain and, 113–17; swamps and, 253; terrorism and, 249, 259; torture and,

289; University of Havana and, 247; Urrutia and, 250; World War II era and, 249, 252
Cuban Expedition Force, 253
Cuban Missile Crisis, 256
Cubbison, Douglas, 415
Cunningham, William "Bloody Bill," 44
Curtiss JN-3 biplanes, 95, 121
Custer, George, 6, 56
Czechoslovakia, 102–5, 243, 288, 317f, 405–6

Dalton, Roque, 311
Danner, Mark, 306
Daoud, Mohammed, 404
Dargue, Herbert Arthur, 97f
Dari language, 424
D'Aubuisson, Roberto, 314–15, 318–19, 333
Death penalty, 82, 473n8
Death squads: El Salvador and, 306, 314–15, 318, 327, 329–30, 382; Guatemala and, 259–60; Iraq and, 2, 375, 388
Debray, Régis, 269
Deception, 19–20, 126, 366
Decision making, 34, 36, 377–8
De Gaulle, Charles, 174–5, 183–4, 209
De Lattre de Tassigny, Jean, 212
Delta Force, 343, 419, 437–8, 458
De Mello, Vieira, 373–4
Democracy: Afghanistan and, 427; America's image and, 8, 13; Banana Wars and, 119–20, 124–5; Cold War and, 155–6, 319, 330, 339; Colombia and, 347, 352, 356, 362; Cuba and, 249; as destiny of humanity, 155; Dominican Republic and, 125; economic growth and, 155; El Salvador and, 309, 313, 319, 330; Greece and, 168–9; Guatemala and, 240; Haiti and, 119–20, 124; Iraq and, 369–70, 372, 380–1; Kennedy and, 139; Libya and, 444, 448–9; modernization theory and, 155–6; moral imperative of promoting, 111; nation-building and, 119–20, 124; Nicaragua and, 139, 291, 300–1; prosecution challenges and, 76
Democratic Revolutionary Front (FDR), 311–12, 316
Denver News, 122
Desert One, 458

Devía, Edgar, 348–9
Devine, Frank, 313
De Wet, 68
Dewey, George, 72, 74–5, 85
DH-4 biplanes, 142–3
Díaz, Adolfo, 138–42, 148
Diem, Ngo Dinh: Anti-Communist Denunciation Campaign and, 219; ARVN and, 219–22, 230, 234–5; fall of, 223; land reform and, 233; MAAG and, 219; U.S. adviser's opinion of, 219; Vietnam and, 198, 218–25
Dien Bien Phu, 214–17, 407
Directorio Revolucionario, 247–8
Djibouti, 174, 464
Dominican Republic: Arias and, 123; Banana Wars and, 109, 110f, 113, 122–5, 139; Batista and, 250; Carter and, 286; Cuban influence over, 260, 269; democracy and, 125; disorder in, 122–5; Guardia and, 142, 146; Roosevelt's Corollary and, 123; torture and, 124; U.S. withdrawal from, 139; World War I and, 123
Dooly, John, 41–2
Draper, Theodore, 254
Drones: Afghanistan and, 8, 425, 436–7, 466; Al Qaeda and, 462, 466; bin Laden and, 437; Central Intelligence Agency (CIA) and, 453, 462–6; covert operations and, 465; discrimination of, 464–6; Gnat missions and, 465–6; historical perspective on, 465–6; insurgency and, 462, 466; intelligence gathering and, 462–6; Libya and, 453–4, 456, 462, 464; Obama and, 464–5; Pakistan and, 434, 437, 466; Predator, 453–4, 462, 464–5; Qaddafi and, 453–4, 456, 462, 464; Reaper, 464; Somalia and, 464; Taliban and, 466; terrorism and, 464–6; U.S. Air Force and, 462–6; Yemen and, 464
Drugs: Afghanistan and, 410, 418, 423, 431, 441; Colombia and, 342, 347, 349–52, 357f, 358–9, 362; Escobar and, 358–9; Pakistan and, 426; poppy cultivation and, 410, 418, 431, 441; soldiers' use of, 379, 472; Taliban and, 410, 423, 426; war on, 351
Duarte, José Napoleón, 306–7, 309–10, 319, 428

Dulles, Allen, 241, 243, 252
Dulles, John Foster, 214, 217, 241-2
Dumas, Mathieu, 22
Dunford, Joseph "Fighting Joe," 369
Dung, Van Tien, 234
Dunn, William, 52
Dutch East India Company, 64-70

Eagle Claw, 437, 458-9
Easter Offensive, 233-4
Economic Development Corps (EDCOR), 206
Ecuador, 349
Egypt, 153, 407, 444, 447-9, 455, 458, 515n11
Eikenberry, Karl, 427
Eisenhower, Dwight D.: Castro and, 251; Central Intelligence Agency (CIA) and, 241-4; Cuba and, 250-2; Dulles and, 214; Guatemala and, 241-4; Haiti and, 251; military aid levels of, 270; military success of, 3; Panama and, 251; Venezuela and, 251; Vietnam and, 214, 217, 219
Element of surprise, 5, 260: American Revolution and, 33, 36, 38, 45; El Salvador and, 331; Indians and, 54, 61; Libya and, 454; Philippines and, 86; Siberia and, 106; Villa and, 89
Ellis, Joseph J., 39
El Mozote massacre, 305f, 323-6
El Salvador, 3, 14, 83, 85, 340: ambush and, 331; Archbishop Romero and, 312, 314-15; Arias plan and, 300; assassination and, 306, 314-15, 330-1; atrocities and, 323, 325; battles at polls in, 315-19; Boland-Zablocki amendment and, 294; Captain General Gerardo Barrios Military Academy and, 320-1; Carter and, 307-9, 312-13, 361; Central Intelligence Agency (CIA) and, 315; Christian Democratic Party and, 309-10, 315; communism and, 304, 307; conventional warfare and, 320; counterinsurgency and, 279, 309-10, 315, 320-3, 325, 328-9, 331, 334; covert operations and, 299, 315; Cristiani and, 330-1, 333; D'Aubuisson and, 314-15, 318-19, 333; death squads and, 306, 314-15, 318, 327, 329-30, 382; democracy and, 309, 313, 319, 330; Democratic Revolutionary Front (FDR) and, 311-12, 316; Duarte and, 306, 309-10, 313, 315, 319, 428; elections of, 310, 312, 314-16, 318-19; El Mozote massacre and, 323-6; Farabundo Martí National Liberation Front (FMLN) and, 279, 288-91, 301, 304, 306-7, 309, 311-12, 315-19, 322-34, 501n13; final offensive in, 304; foco theory and, 311; Fuerza Armada de El Salvador (ESAF) and, 304, 307, 315-16, 319-32; guerrilla warfare and, 304-7, 310-19, 323-34; human rights and, 307, 309-10, 313-14, 319, 326, 334; imperialism and, 324; insurgency and, 304-12, 315-16, 320-2, 325-34, 468; insurrection and, 291, 306, 311-12, 332; intelligence gathering and, 317f, 327, 334; Iran-Contra scandal and, 299-300; junta of, 306-7, 312-15, 319; JUSMAPG and, 169; leftists and, 306, 310-14, 320, 329; lessons learned from, 468; levels of dirtiness and, 6; Marxism and, 281, 304-7, 309, 317f, 320, 329-30, 333-4, 349, 351; massacres and, 305f, 316, 323-6; media and, 316, 329, 335; morale and, 307, 320, 326; National Guard and, 320, 330; Nationalist Republican Alliance (ARENA) and, 315, 318, 333; nation-building and, 309-10, 315, 334; new government in, 312-13; 1972 elections and, 310; Obama and, 437; Operación Rescate and, 323-6; pacification and, 327, 333; paramilitary forces and, 311, 314, 329; People's Revolutionary Army (ERP) and, 311; Popular Forces of Liberation (FPL) and, 310-11; propaganda and, 324-5; psychological warfare and, 315, 327; Reagan and, 306, 308-9, 315-19, 322, 325, 361; retreat and, 332; Romero and, 306, 314-15; Sandinistas and, 287-303, 307; Soviet Union and, 301, 304, 333; as Spanish Vietnam, 308-10; terrorism and, 307, 315, 325; Ungo and, 310-12; U.S. Army and, 323-4
Embedded training teams (ETTs), 412
Enders, Thomas, 290-1, 313, 315, 325
Enfield rifles, 406
Escobar, 358-9
Esquipulas II Accord, 300
Esso, 251
Estrada, Juan José, 138

Ethiopia, 464
Evacuation, 36, 105, 164, 199, 234–5, 329, 414
Evening Post, 85

F-16C Fighting Falcons, 375
F-18 fighters, 425
F-117 stealth fighters, 342
F/A-18 fighters, 419
Facebook, 360, 449
Fahim, Mohammed, 415–16
Faisal, 128–30, 133, 485n13
FAL automatic rifles, 296
Fall, Bernard, 470
Farabundo Martí National Liberation Front (FMLN), 279: battles at polls and, 315–16; Castro and, 304, 311; death squads and, 306; decline of, 333–4; Democratic Revolutionary Front (FDR) and, 312; El Mozote massacre and, 323–6; El Salvador and, 279, 288–91, 301, 304, 306–7, 309, 311–12, 315–19, 322–34, 501n13; fatal miscalculations of, 306–7; fear of repercussions from joining, 306–7; final agreement with, 332–5; first final offensive of, 304, 306–7; increased strength of, 319; lack of progress of, 304, 306–7; National Plan and, 328–9; Operación Rescate and, 323–6; propaganda and, 324; public favor of, 326–7; Reagan and, 309; second final offensive of, 330–2
FARC Files, The: Venezuela, Ecuador and the Secret Archive of Raúl Reyes (IISS), 349
Fedayeen Saddam, 366–7
Feland, Logan, 144
Ferdinand, Prince of Spain, 20
Ferguson, William, 31–2
Fire-bombings, 475n7
First Aero Squadron, 95
First Afghan War, 404
First Front Army, 159
Figueres, José "Pepe," 251
Floyd, Oliver, 136
Flying army, 44–5
Foch, Ferdinand, 128
Foco theory: Castro and, 260–1, 268–9, 272–3, 276–83, 311; Guevara and, 260–1, 268–9, 272–3, 276–83, 311; Nicaragua and, 280–3; Sandinistas and, 280–3

Fonseca, Carlos, 260, 282
Fontaine, Roger, 304
Foreign Legion, 211
Fort Benning, 321
Fort Bragg, 154, 458
Fort Dade, 55
Fort Lyon, 5
Fort Myers, 3
Fort Rivière, 119
Fort Watson, 41
Forward operating bases (FOBs), 382–4
For Whom the Bell Tolls (Hemingway), 247
Foulois, Benjamin D., 95
Four Freedoms speech, 240
France, 95: Air Force of, 226; Algeria and, 174–84; Al Qaeda and, 515n11; assassination and, 183; de Gaulle and, 174–5, 183–4, 209; Djibouti and, 174; Foch and, 128; 4th Republic and, 182–3; rederick the Great and, 36; *guerre révolutionnaire* and, 175–80, 182, 185, 198; Haiti and, 117; Indochina and, 10, 156, 158f, 174, 176, 185, 189, 198, 209, 211–14, 217, 235, 250, 469–70 (*see also* Vietnam); Libya and, 451–3; Madagascar and, 174; morale and, 22; Morocco and, 174; Napoleon and, 20–4, 50, 56, 64, 377, 431; Plains of Abraham and, 35; *quadrillage* system and, 179, 182; Russian campaign of, 22–4; Sarkozy and, 451; Siberia and, 102, 105; torture and, 177, 180–2, 185; Trans-Siberian Railroad and, 105; Von Steuben and, 39; World War I and, 63, 100; World War II and, 470
Frederick the Great, 36
Free Officers, 444
Free press, 13, 21
Fremont, John C., 49
French Revolution, 186
French Somaliland, 174
French Underground, 470
Frente Sandinista de Liberación Nacional (FSLN), 260, 282–7
Front de Libération Nationale (FLN), 178–84
Fuerza Aérea Revolucionaria (FAR), 252
Fuerza Armada de El Salvador (ESAF): assistance credits and, 322–3; Atlacatl Battalion and, 323–6; battles at polls and, 315–16; conscription by, 320; decline of, 332–5; El Mozote massacre and, 323–6;

Fuerza Armada de El Salvador (ESAF) (cont.)
  El Salvador and, 304, 307, 315–16, 319–32; final agreement with FMLN and, 332–6; incompetence of, 329–32; leadership of, 319–21; National Plan and, 327–9; new joint general staff for, 322; Operación Rescate and, 323–6; Soccer War and, 320; *tanda* culture and, 320–1
Fuerza Democrática Nicaragüense (FDN), 291
Fuerzas Armadas de la República Dominicana, 124
Fukuyama, Francis, 468–9
Funston, Frederick, 86, 93

G-3 rifles, 323
Galula, David, 389: Algeria and, 185; Britain and, 187; classical approach and, 188; conventional warfare and, 186; counterinsurgency and, 185–9; *Counterinsurgency Field Manual* and, 393–4; Greece and, 185; guerrilla warfare and, 186–8; Indochina and, 185, 189; insurgency and, 185–9; intelligence gathering and, 185; Italy and, 185; Marxism and, 185, 187; World War II era and, 186
García, José Guillermo, 327
García, Lucas, 265
Garner, Jay, 371
Gates, Horatio, 29, 43–4
Gates, Robert, 426, 432–3, 437, 451
Gatewood, Charles, 60–1
Geneva Conventions, 7, 154, 217–18, 354
Genocide, 263–5, 313, 324, 342
Gentile, Gian, 395
Germany: Afghanistan and, 421–2; American occupation of, 372; American Revolution and, 38; Arab Revolt and, 129; Armistice Day and, 106; Banana Wars and, 113, 118, 123; Berlin nightclub bombing and, 447; Bonn conference and, 421; Central Forces and, 100, 102; Clausewitz and, 23; fire-bombings and, 475n7; Gestapo and, 181; Greece and, 167; Guatemala and, 259; Hessians and, 38; Libya and, 451–2; Luftwaffe and, 143, 475n7; Malaya and, 195; Mexico and, 91, 98; Nazis and, 18, 165, 167, 171, 177, 180–1; Nicaragua and, 290; Sandino and,
138, 143; Security Council Resolution 1973 and, 451; Siberia and, 100–2, 107; Soviet Union and, 102; World War I and, 100, 107; World War II and, 9, 143, 372, 465, 475n7
Geronimo, 58f, 59f, 60–1, 82
Gestapo, 181
Ghurkas, 197
Giap, Vo Nguyen, 133, 213f: Cuban strategies and, 249–50; Dien Bien Phu and, 214–17; Easter Offensive and, 233–4; Navarre and, 212, 214–17
Gnat missions, 465–6
Goldhurst, Richard, 100
Goldwater, Barry, 295
Good Neighbor Policy, 148
Gorbachev, Mikhail, 408–9
Gordon, Michael, 392
Gorrell, Edgar Staley, 97f
Granma yacht, 248
Grant, Ulysses S., 3, 47, 51
Graves, William S., 106
Grayson, William, 77–8
Great War. *See* World War I era
Great White Fleet, 112
Greece, 3: ambush and, 167; bandits and, 171–2; Britain and, 165, 167–8; Central Intelligence Agency (CIA) and, 168; Civil War of, 167, 172; communism and, 165–73; conventional warfare and, 156, 171, 202; counterinsurgency and, 164–5, 169–73, 207–8, 242; democracy and, 168–9; Galula and, 185; Germany and, 167; guerrilla warfare and, 165, 167, 169–72; insurgency and, 165, 167, 169–72, 242; Johnson and, 173; JUSMAPG and, 169; leftist governments and, 167, 170; lessons learned from, 171–3, 469; National Liberation Front (EAM) and, 165, 167; Nazis and, 165, 167, 171; paramilitary forces and, 167; as pawn, 165, 202; propaganda and, 170; psychological warfare and, 168; Soviet Union and, 169–72; Stalin and, 169–72; terrorism and, 167–8; torture and, 167; Truman Doctrine and, 168–70; United Kingdom and, 172; Vafiadis and, 167–8, 171; White Terror and, 167; World War II era and, 165, 171; Zachariadis and, 171
Greek Communist Party (KKE), 167
Greek Democratic Army (DSE), 167–8

Green Berets, 154–5, 262, 271–5, 331, 461
Green Book (Qaddafi), 445
Greene, Nathanael, 45
Green Zone, 371–3, 383
Groce, Leonard, 138
Grumman HU-16 Albatross flying boats, 164
Guadalcanal, 378
Guam, 76
Guantanamo Bay, 62
Guatemala: Árbenz and, 240–4, 246, 252, 255–6, 267, 279; Arévalo and, 240; assassination and, 259; atrocities and, 258, 263–5; Carter and, 263; Castro and, 258, 260–1; Central Intelligence Agency (CIA) and, 239, 242–4, 256, 258, 261–2, 289; communism and, 241–6, 256, 259–65, 268; counterinsurgency and, 239–40, 242, 257, 259, 261–8; covert operations and, 239, 242, 244; Czech arms and, 243; death squads and, 259–60; Decade of Spring and, 240, 244; democracy and, 240; Eisenhower and, 241–4; enfranchisement and, 240; Esquipulas II Accord and, 300; foco theory and, 260–1, 268–9, 272–3; genocide and, 263–5; Germany and, 259; Green Berets and, 262; guerrilla warfare and, 258–66, 267f; Guevara and, 258, 260–1; human rights and, 263, 265–6; insurgency and, 239, 256–8, 270; insurrection and, 244, 258–9, 269; intelligence gathering and, 262, 264f; land distribution in, 240–1; leftists and, 239, 259; Liberation Army and, 242; Marxism and, 259, 262, 264f, 266, 267f, 281, 288; massacres and, 259, 262, 265; Mayans and, 240, 264–6, 267f; MR-13 and, 258–60; National Revolutionary Union (URNG) and, 265–6; Operation PBSUCCESS and, 239–40, 242, 258, 261; paramilitary forces and, 242, 259, 263; propaganda and, 243–4, 260; psychological warfare and, 242–4; Reagan and, 266; Ríos Montt and, 258, 265–6; scorched-earth policy and, 264–5; Soviet Union and, 241–2, 244; Special Forces Groups (SFGs) and, 270–1; terrorism and, 259; torture and, 263; Truman and, 241, 261; United Fruit Company (UFC) and, 240–2; U.S. Army and, 262; World War II era and, 243, 265; Ydígoras and, 258; Zacapa massacre and, 259, 262
Guatemalan Labor Party (PGT), 259
Guerre révolutionnaire, 175–80, 182, 185, 198
Guerrilla Army of the Poor (EGP), 259, 262, 264f
Guerrilla warfare: Afghanistan and, 405–7, 410, 421–5, 467; Algeria and, 176, 180; American Revolution and, 33–4, 40, 42; Arab Revolt and, 131, 133–5; Boer War and, 66–7, 70; Central Intelligence Agency (CIA) and, 256, 258; charismatic leaders and, 18; Clausewitz and, 25; COIN school and, 396–7; Colombia and, 345–60; Confederates and, 46–7, 49–50; context and, 7–8, 14; *Counterinsurgency Field Manual* and, 395, 397; Cuba and, 130, 156, 248, 256, 258, 260–2, 272–9; defining, 15–17; El Salvador and, 304–7, 310–19, 323–34; French equation of, 176; Galula and, 186–8; Greece and, 165, 167, 169–72; Guatemala and, 258–66, 267f; Guevara and, 20, 130, 277–9; historical perspective on, 18–20; Indians and, 54; Iraq and, 3, 370, 467; JSOC and, 461; Kambas and, 162–3; Kennedy and, 54, 154, 461; Kissinger and, 25; Korea and, 163–4; Lawrence and, 129–30, 133–5; longevity advantage and, 17; Malaya and, 190–4, 196, 198; Mao Zedong and, 20, 54, 154, 157, 159–62, 220, 393; Marxist, 187, 189, 281, 304, 305f, 317f, 333, 343; massive retaliation and, 153; Mexico and, 453; Nicaragua and, 141–4, 147–8, 260, 280–7, 290–3, 296, 300, 453; Petraeus and, 395, 467; Philippines and, 74, 79–86, 199–203, 207, 391, 400–2; pragmatism and, 18; repressions and, 81–4; Sandinista Revolution and, 280–7, 290–3, 296, 300; Sandino and, 141–4, 147–8; Siberia and, 102–13; Spain and, 20, 22–3, 247; Sun Tzu and, 20; technology and, 17; theories on, 25–6; Vietnam and, 14, 212, 215, 218–22, 231, 235
Guerrilla Warfare (Che Guevara), 277
Guerrilla Warfare (Mao Zedong), 160, 220, 393
Guevara, Ángel Aníbal, 265

Guevara, Ernesto "Che," 251: ambush and, 272, 274; Argentina and, 272, 274; background of, 244, 246; Bolivia and, 261, 269, 272–3, 299; capture of, 274; Castro and, 247, 248, 250; Central Intelligence Agency (CIA) and, 274; China and, 278; communism and, 272, 276; conventional warfare and, 278; crisis of Cuban governance and, 269; Cuba and, 244, 246, 256, 279; erratic behavior of, 272; execution of, 274–6; exportation of revolution and, 271–2, 277–9; foco theory and, 260–1, 268–9, 272–3, 276–83, 311; fundamental miscalculation of, 279; Green Berets and, 273–5; Guatemala and, 258, 260–1; guerrilla warfare and, 20, 130, 277–9; imperialism and, 278; Institutional Revolutionary Party (PRI) and, 246; Johnson and, 274–5; Khrushchev and, 256; Mao Zedong and, 278; Marxism and, 257, 275f, 278; morale and, 272; *Second Declaration of Havana* and, 278; social reform and, 279; Sun Tzu and, 278
Guillermoprieto, Alma, 324–5
Gulf of Tonkin resolution, 223–4
Gurkha brigade, 193
Gurney, Henry, 190, 195
Gutiérrez, Abdul, 313
Gwynn, Charles, 186

Habr Gidr militia, 342
Haig, Alexander, 308, 318
Haiti: Banana Wars and, 109, 110f, 112–13, 117–24; *cacos* and, 117–23; Caperton and, 118, 123; Conze and, 121; democracy and, 119–20, 124; Eisenhower and, 251; France and, 117; Guardia and, 142, 146; Jiménez and, 123; Merkel and, 124; nation-building and, 117–22, 124; pacification and, 122; resource drain and, 365; rules of engagement and, 343; Sam and, 117; Treaty of 1815 and, 118; Trujillo and, 124; U.S. withdrawal from, 139; Vásquez and, 124
Hamburger Hill, 232
Hancock, John, 38
Handcock, P. J., 70
Hanging, 447, 466
Hanna, Matthew, 148
Happy Valley operation, 252

Haqqani network, 436, 462
Harcourt, William, 38
Harding, Warren G., 121
Harkin, Tom, 293
Harvey, William, 255
Hasenfus, Eugene, 299, 500n51
Hatfield, G. D., 142
Hatfield, Mark, 330
Hawks: Carter and, 266, 288, 361; Clark and, 308; Dulles and, 217; Haig and, 308; Kirkpatrick and, 308; Reagan and, 266, 302, 306, 308, 361
Hawza, Al (Iraqi newspaper), 375
Hearst, William Randolph, 98
Hebrew scriptures, 18–19
Heflin, J. Thomas, 146
Hemingway, Ernest, 247
Henry, O., 139
Hessians, 38
Hezbollah, 340, 411
Hickey, Jim, 376
High-value targets (HVTs), 389
Hijackings, 447
HIMARS rocket launcher, 431
Hinton, Deane, 318
Hiroshima, 10
Hobhouse, Emily, 69
Ho Chi Minh: American Declaration of Independence and, 209, 211; declares war on France, 211; Dien Bien Phu and, 217; Hanoi attack and, 211; League for the Revolution and Independence of Vietnam and, 211; longevity advantage and, 17; Viet Minh and, 211–19, 407; Vietnam and, 17, 209–19, 407
Ho Chi Minh Trail, 210f, 224
Holbrooke, Richard, 427
Honduras, 305f, 317f: ambush and, 260; Armas and, 243; contras and, 291, 293–4; covert operations and, 299; communism and, 242; ESAF and, 320; FMLN and, 332; Henry, O., and, 139; Sandino and, 140–1, 143; Soccer War and, 320; *tanda* issue and, 321
Hoover, Herbert, 147
Hostages: Algeria and, 455; Colombia and, 349; Dulles and, 217; Indians and, 55; Iran and, 299, 437–8, 457–8; Lebanon and, 299; Philippines and, 400; Sandinista Revolution and, 284
Howard, Oliver O., 51

Index

Huasteca Petroleum Company, 140
Huerta, Victoriano, 91
Hukbalahap: defeat by proxy and, 207–8; growing strength of, 200–1; internal dissension in, 201; lack of external sponsor for, 201; Lansdale and, 205–7; Magsaysay and, 202–8; as pawn, 202; Philippines and, 209; Taruc and, 199, 207; Tenorio and, 206; Truman and, 214
Humanitarianism: Afghanistan and, 419, 433; Algeria and, 179; Colombia and, 349; El Salvador and, 308, 328; Libya and, 451, 456; Nicaragua and, 297; Philippines and, 401; Somalia and, 342–3
Human rights: atrocities and, 8 (*see also* Atrocities); Carter on, 280; championing, 13; Colombia and, 350, 358–60; El Salvador and, 307, 309–10, 313–14, 319, 326, 334; Guatemala and, 263, 265–6; Libya and, 449; Nicaragua and, 281–2, 285–7, 296–7, 302; repressions and, 61, 81–4, 124, 180, 267, 279, 311–14, 445, 448–9
Hungary, 406
Husayn, Sharif, 129
Hussein, Saddam: Ba'athists and, 366; capture of, 376; Fedayeen Saddam and, 366–7; Firdos Square statue of, 366; Iraq and, 12, 341, 363, 366–76, 379, 381, 391, 410, 448, 459–60; Kuwait invasion of, 410–11; massacres and, 376; overthrow of, 366; "shock and awe" campaign against, 363
Hussein, Uday, 366

Idris, King of Libya, 444
Ignatius, David, 434
Ilustrados, 74, 79–80
Imperial Grunts: The American Military on the Ground (Kaplan), 400–1
Imperialism, 11: Algeria and, 175, 178; Arab Revolt and, 135; Banana Wars and, 111–12, 116; Cuba and, 251; El Salvador and, 324; Guevara and, 278; Nicaragua and, 282, 291; Philippines and, 76–7, 81, 84–5, 400; Sandino and, 141, 146, 282
Imperial Policing (Gwynn), 186
Improvised explosive devices (IEDs), 366, 374, 379, 383, 386
Incendiary bombing, 475n7

India, 451
Indians: ambush and, 56–7, 60; American Revolution and, 36; Apache, 55, 56, 58f, 59f, 60–1, 82, 96; Arapaho, 5, 56–7; atrocities and, 57; Baker and, 6; Battle of Little Big Horn and, 85; Cheyenne, 5, 56–7; Comanche, 56; concentration camps and, 69; Confederates and, 46–53; conventional warfare and, 54, 56; counterinsurgency and, 53–62, 96; Crook and, 57, 58f, 60–1; Custer and, 6, 56; Geronimo, 58f, 59f, 60–1, 82; guerrilla warfare and, 54; hostages and, 55; insurgency and, 5–6, 53–62, 96; intelligence collection and, 56; Lakota, 56; lessons from wars with, 61–2; Merritt and, 74; Miskito, 291; morale and, 60; Navajo, 55; pacification and, 3–4; peace groups and, 5–6; political correctness and, 112; propaganda and, 54; Sand Creek massacre and, 5–6, 8, 57; savage West and, 55–61; Seminoles, 53–5, 60–2; Sheridan and, 6; Sioux, 55; swamps and, 54–5, 61; technology and, 57; U.S. Army and, 55–6, 60–1
Indochina: France and, 10, 156, 158f, 174, 176, 185, 189, 198, 209, 211–14, 217, 235, 250, 469–70; Galula and, 185, 189; *guerre révolutionnaire* and, 176, 198; *see also* Vietnam
Influence of Seapower upon History, The (Mahan), 111–12
Institutional Revolutionary Party (PRI), 246
Insurgency: Afghanistan and, 4–5, 8, 406–8, 412–41, 467; Algeria and, 175–84; American Revolution and, 31, 33–5, 40, 42–5; Anaconda strategy and, 1–2; Arab Revolt and, 127–35; Banana Wars and, 109, 111, 113–15, 120–6; Boer War and, 64, 66–70, 93; Callwell and, 26; Clausewitz and, 23–5; Colombia and, 344–61; context and, 7–8, 11; cooperative, 134–5; *Counterinsurgency Field Manual* and, 393–7, 469; Cuba and, 156, 239, 247–9, 256–7, 270–6, 279; defining, 15–17; drones and, 462, 466; El Salvador and, 304–12, 315–16, 320–2, 325–34, 468; Galula and, 185–9; Greece and, 165, 167, 169–72, 242; Guatemala and, 239, 256–68, 270; historical perspective on, 19–23; Indians and, 5–6,

Insurgency (cont.)
53–62, 96; Iraq and, 1–3, 8, 366–89, 392, 467; JSOC and, 460–1; Kennedy and, 155–6, 270; Lebanon and, 340; Libya and, 442, 444, 453–6; longevity advantage and, 17–18; Malaya and, 190–8; Mao Zedong and, 157–9, 162, 164; Marxism and, 342 (see also Marxism); Mexico and, 93; natural constituency and, 460; Nicaragua and, 279, 281–5, 288–96, 300; non-state actors and, 7; Philippines and, 74–5, 78–88, 93, 199–208, 398–403; Sandino and, 143–5, 148; Siberia and, 106–8; Spain and, 23; Taliban and, 2, 4–5; Vietnam and, 211, 213f, 219–31, 235

Insurrection: Arab Revolt and, 131; Callwell and, 26; Central Intelligence Agency (CIA) and, 244, 253; changes in, 16; Clausewitz and, 24; context and, 7; Cuba and, 113–16, 246–8, 253, 269, 279, 311; El Salvador and, 291, 306, 311–12, 332; Guatemala and, 244, 258–9, 269; guerrilla warfare and, 17 (see also Guerrilla warfare); Iraq and, 367, 370; Malaya and, 192, 195; Mao Zedong and, 158; Nicaragua and, 281, 285–6, 291; Philippines and, 74–9, 81, 83, 87–8, 95, 202; Tibet and, 162; Vietnam and, 220

Intelligence gathering, 343: Afghanistan and, 406–7, 415, 418, 421, 436–7, 439; Algeria and, 178, 180; Boer War and, 69; Bolivia and, 273; cell phones and, 460, 466; Colombia and, 353–6; Cuba and, 255, 258, 260, 270–1; drones and, 462–6; El Salvador and, 317f, 327, 334; FARC raid and, 348–9; Galula and, 185; Guantanamo Bay and, 62; Guatemala and, 262, 264f; Indians and, 56; interrogation and, 85, 178, 182, 263, 270–1, 327, 460; Iraq and, 368–9, 381, 383, 389, 391; Joint Special Operations Command (JSOC) and, 457, 459–61; Lawrence and, 129; Libya and, 442, 450; Malaya and, 196; Mao Zedong and, 162, 164; Nicaragua and, 287–90, 293–5; Philippines and, 82, 85, 399–400; Sandino and, 144; School of the Americas and, 270–1, 283, 323; Siberia and, 107; technology and, 62, 343–4, 460, 462–6;

Vietnam and, 215, 220–1, 227–9; see also Central Intelligence Agency (CIA)

International Court of Justice, 295

International Institute for Strategic Studies (IISS), 349

International Military Education and Training Program (IMET), 155

International Security Assistance Force (IASF), 421–2, 428

Internet, 35, 343, 375, 382, 393, 423, 437, 449, 466

Interrogation: psychological warfare and, 85, 178, 182, 263, 270–1, 327, 460; releasing prisoners after, 327; torture and, 85, 178, 182, 263, 270–1, 327, 460; water cure and, 85

Iran: Ahmadinejad and, 457; al-Sadr and, 376; arms sales to, 300; Iran-Iraq War and, 339, 342; Northern Alliance and, 409–10, 415–16, 418–19; Operation Eagle Claw and, 437, 458–9; Pahlavi and, 457; Revolutionary Guard and, 340; Tajik warlords and, 409; terrorism and, 340; U.S. hostages in, 299, 437–8, 446, 457–8

Iran-Contra scandal, 299–300

Iran-Iraq War, 339, 342

Iraq, 3: Abu Ghraib and, 8, 381–2; Afghanistan and, 416–18, 422, 426–34, 438, 441; al Askara Mosque bombing and, 375; Al Qaeda and, 374–6, 378, 386–90, 441, 459, 461, 515n11; ambush and, 366, 375–7, 379, 386; assassination and, 380, 386–7; atrocities and, 382; Ba'aths and, 366, 368–73, 385; Baghdad, 1–2, 128f, 341, 363–6, 380–4, 388–91, 395, 416; bandits and, 370, 374; Battle of Fallujah and, 377–80; bin Laden and, 374; body counts and, 370; Bush, George H. W., and, 367, 505n4; Bush, George W., and, 79, 367–72, 377, 380, 383, 387–8, 391; Clinton and, 368; Coalition forces in, 365–82, 385–91; Coalition Provisional Authority (CPA) and, 371–5, 380–1; conventional warfare and, 363, 365–6, 376, 380, 391; cost of U.S. war in, 417; counterinsurgency and, 8, 366–7, 370–1, 380–9, 392; deaths in, 149; death squads and, 2, 375, 388; decision making and, 377–8; democracy and, 369–70, 372, 380–1; drugs and, 379; failing infrastructure of, 369–76; Fedayeen

Saddam and, 366–7; force protection and, 382–4; forward operating bases and, 382–4; Green Zone and, 371–3, 383; guerrilla warfare and, 3, 370, 467; Hussein and, 12, 341, 363, 366–76, 379, 381, 391, 410, 448, 459–60; IEDs and, 366, 374, 379, 383, 386; insurgency and, 1–2, 8, 366–89, 392, 467; insurrection and, 367, 370; intelligence gathering and, 368–9, 381, 383, 389, 391; Iran-Iraq War and, 339, 342; Islam and, 369, 375, 379, 386–7; JAM and, 375–6, 389–90; jihadists and, 366, 374, 379, 387; Joint Chiefs of Staff and, 369, 375–6; Joint Special Operations Command (JSOC) and, 375–6, 427, 459–61; Kurds and, 364f, 367, 380–1; lessons learned from, 384–5, 468; levels of dirtiness and, 6; looting and, 370; Loyalists and, 371; massacres and, 376; McChrystal and, 457, 459; media and, 11, 341, 382, 385, 391; Muthanna and, 461; National Security Directive 24 and, 371; nation-building and, 371, 382–3; oil and, 371, 388, 391; Operation Vigilant Resolve and, 377; pacification and, 385; paramilitary forces and, 366; Persian Gulf War and, 9, 341–2, 363, 367–71, 471; Petraeus and, 1, 467; psychological warfare and, 368, 383, 389; retreat and, 383; Rumsfeld and, 365, 368, 370–1, 377, 416; Saddam International Airport and, 365; Shi'ites and, 1–2, 364f, 367, 373, 375, 385, 387; "shock and awe" campaign in, 363; Sunnis and, 1–2, 364f, 369, 373–5, 377, 379, 381, 385–90, 441, 459; surge in, 387–90; Tal Afar and, 384–5; Taliban and, 365; terrorism and, 368, 375, 388; torture and, 379, 381–2; U.S. Air Force and, 368, 375; U.S. Army and, 363, 371–2, 377–8; U.S. Marine Corps and, 363, 377–9, 388, 391; weapons of mass destruction (WMD) and, 367–9, 391; winding down of war in, 390–2; Zarqawi and, 373–5, 378, 387

"Iraq's Continuing Programs for Weapons of Mass Destruction" (National Intelligence Estimate (NIE)), 368–9

Irish Republican Army (IRA), 348, 446

Irregular warfare: ambush and, 36–7, 41, 56–7 (*see also* Ambush); assassination and, 22, 116 (*see also* Assassination); atrocities and, 5, 13, 19, 57, 63, 67, 70, 76, 78, 80 (*see also* Atrocities); attrition and, 39, 224–9, 408, 452; blockhouse system and, 64, 67–8, 113, 159, 181; Callwell on, 25–6, 188; categorizing, 9–10; Clausewitz on, 15, 23–5, 128, 159, 188; context and, 7–8; counterinsurgency and, 15–17 (*see also* Counterinsurgency); deception and, 19–20, 126, 366; definitions for, 7–8; element of surprise and, 5, 33, 36, 38, 45, 54, 61, 86, 89, 106, 260, 331, 454; Geneva Conventions and, 7, 154, 217–18, 354; guerrilla warfare and, 15–17 (*see also* Guerrilla warfare); historical perspective on, 18–20; insurgency and, 15–17 (*see also* Insurgency); kidnapping and, 172, 259–60, 296, 310, 348, 359–60, 385, 399, 401; lessons learned from, 467–70; levels of dirtiness and, 6; longevity advantage and, 17–18; mastering, 467–70; morale and, 22, 25, 32, 37, 60, 123, 131, 162, 212, 216, 225, 272, 307, 320, 326, 409, 424; political correctness and, 112, 188, 394, 434; by proxy, 6, 207–8, 321–3; psychology and, 15 (*see also* Psychological warfare); public relations and, 144, 206–7, 242; Punitive Expedition and, 93–9, 109, 112, 121; regular armed forces and, 7; repressions and, 61, 81–4, 124, 180, 267, 279, 311–14, 445, 448–9; rule of law and, 8, 148, 187, 291, 416, 424; scorched-earth strategy and, 42–4, 67, 69–70, 78, 86, 113, 259, 264–7, 309, 325; search-and-destroy missions and, 79, 193, 323, 327; small wars and, 25–6, 40, 74, 125, 136, 149; Sun Tzu on, 19–20, 159, 161, 188, 278; terrorism and, 15–17 (*see also* Terrorism); zeitgeist-like motives and, 10–12; *see also Specific conflict*

Islam: Afghanistan and, 404–13, 420–1, 423, 440, 442; Algeria and, 177, 177–81; Al Qaeda and, 410; Arab Revolt and, 134; bin Laden and, 61, 374, 398, 407, 413f, 416, 418, 420, 436–40, 459, 462; *Counterinsurgency Field Manual* and, 396–7; fanaticism and, 188, 410, 425, 433; fundamentalists and, 421; insurgency

Islam (cont.)
  and, 1 (*see also* Insurgency); Iraq and, 369, 375, 379, 386–7; jihadists and, 340 (*see also* Jihadists); Moro Islamic Liberation Front and, 398, 402, 446; Najibullah and, 406; Philippines and, 398–9, 402, 446; radical, 404, 409, 421; Shi'ite, 1–2, 340, 364f, 367, 373, 375, 385, 387; Sunnis and, 407 (*see also* Sunnis); Taliban and, 409–10, 425, 433; terrorism and, 343–4, 374, 399, 404–13, 420–1, 423, 440, 442, 455, 466
Islamic Jihad, 340
Israel, 339, 360, 446, 465
Italy: Afghanistan and, 422; Algeria and, 176; Galula and, 185; Libya and, 446, 452; Trans-Siberian Railroad and, 105
Iwo Jima, 340, 378

Jackson, Andrew, 54
Jaffe, Greg, 1
Jaish al-Mahdi (JAM), 375–6, 389–90
Jama'at al-Tawhid wal-Jihad, 374
Jamahiriya (state of the masses), 445
Janjalani, Abdurrajak, 399
Janjalani, Khaddafy, 402
Japan: Battle of Iwo Jima and, 340, 378; Chinese invasion by, 159–61; firebombings and, 475n7; Korea and, 163; Libya and, 446; MacArthur and, 372; Malaya and, 190–3; Mao Zedong and, 159–61; nuclear bombing of, 9; occupation of China by, 159–61; Philippines and, 199, 202–3; Trans-Siberian Railroad and, 105; Vietnam and, 211; World War II era and, 9–10, 209, 372; Zelaya and, 138
Jawad, Said, 420
Jawbreaker, 415–16
Jayhawkers, 49
Jefferson Memorial, 251
Jemaah Islamiyah, 399
Jennies, 95, 121
Jericho, 19
Jesuits, 291, 312
Jesup, Thomas Sidney, 55, 60
Jihadists: Afghanistan and, 399, 405–7, 410–11; Iraq and, 366, 374, 379, 387; Islamic Jihad and, 340; postmodern insurgencies and, 397, 399; Zarqawi and, 373–5, 378, 387, 427, 459–61

Jiménez, Juan Isidro, 123
Johnson, Harold K., 226
Johnson, Lyndon B.: Bolivia and, 273; Greece and, 173; Guevara and, 274–5; Operation Mongoose and, 256; Rostow and, 273–5; Vietnam and, 173, 223–6
Johnson, Nikolai, 412
Joint Base Lewis McChord, 4
Joint Chiefs of Staff: Afghanistan and, 417, 426–7, 433, 438–9; Cuba and, 252, 254, 256; Iraq and, 369, 375–6; Kennedy and, 254, 256; Lemnitzer and, 222, 252; Libya and, 451; McKiernan and, 426; Mullen and, 3, 417, 451; Philippines and, 202; Powell and, 340–1, 369; Vietnam and, 222–3
Joint Special Operations Command (JSOC): Afghanistan and, 427–9; Al Qaeda and, 427, 460–1; bin Laden and, 438–9, 459; Black Hawk crash and, 438–9; black raids and, 459; capture of Hussein and, 376; counterinsurgency and, 460; conventional warfare and, 462; covert operations and, 458–62; Delta Force and, 343, 419, 437–8, 458; formation of, 458; Fort Bragg and, 458; global reach of, 459; guerrilla warfare and, 461; increased size of, 459; intelligence gathering and, 457, 459–61; Iran hostages and, 458; Iraq and, 375–6, 427, 459–61; McChrystal and, 427, 460; McRaven and, 459; Muthanna and, 461; Night Stalkers and, 458–9; Obama and, 438–9, 461–2, 464–5; Operation Red Dawn and, 376; pacification and, 461; Pakistan and, 461; reputation of, 427; 75th Ranger Regiment and, 458; Sinjar operation and, 461; Special Warfare Development Group (SEAL Team Six) and, 458; terrorism and, 458–9, 462; 24th Special Tactics Squadron and, 458; Zarqawi, 459–61
Joint security stations (JSSs), 389
Joint task Force-510 (JTF-510), 400
Joint U.S. Military Advisory and Planning Group (JUSMAPG), 169
Jones, James L., 424
Jordan, 373
Joseph, King of Spain, 20
Joshua (biblical leader), 19
Julius Caesar, 15
July 26 Movement, 247–50

Junot, Jean-Andoche, 20
Jupiter missiles, 256

Kabila, Laurent, 271
KAMAZ flatbed truck, 373
Kamba guerrillas, 162–3
Kaplan, Robert, 400–1
Karmal, Babrak, 405
Karzai, Hamid, 5, 421–3, 428, 432, 434
Kassebaum, Nancy, 318
Kayani, Ashfaq Parvez, 436, 462
Kellogg, Frank, 140
Kennan, George, 214
Kennedy, Joe, 465
Kennedy, John F.: Algeria and, 184; Alliance for Progress and, 270; Army Special Forces and, 461; assassination of, 223; Bay of Pigs and, 252–5; Castro and, 252; Central Intelligence Agency (CIA) and, 255–6; China and, 154; communism and, 239, 254, 270; covert operations and, 252, 256; Cuba and, 156, 239, 252–7, 261, 269–70, 276, 282; democracy and, 139, 155; foreign aid and, 155; Green Berets and, 461; guerrilla warfare and, 154, 461; inaugural address of, 269; insurgency and, 155–6, 270; Joint Chiefs of Staff and, 254, 256; Military Assistance Advisory Groups (MAAGS) and, 155–6; modernization theory and, 156; Operation Mongoose and, 255–6; peace revolution strategy and, 270; *Strategy of Peace, The*, and, 252; Vietnam and, 220–3, 226; West Point speech of, 153
Kennedy, Robert, 255, 256
Kerry, John, 428
KHAD, 405–6
Khaliq, Abdul, 424
Khalizad, Zalmay, 390
Khan, Ali Mohhamen, 440, 514n81
Khrushchev, Nikita, 256, 269
Kidnapping, 172, 259–60, 296, 310, 348, 359–60, 385, 399, 401
Kilcullen, David, 396, 412, 425
Kilo Company, 412, 435–6
Kings Mountain, 31–4, 36, 42, 44
Kirkpatrick, Jeane, 288, 308
Kissinger, Henry, 25, 163, 225, 232
KISSSS, 322
Kitchener, Horatio Herbert, 63, 67–70

Knox, Philander, 39, 138
Komer, Robert "Blowtorch Bob," 227–8
Korea, 212: conventional warfare and, 163; guerrilla warfare and, 163–4; Japan and, 163; Truman and, 214
Kosovo, 365, 465
Krag-Jorgenson rifles, 75
Krulak, Victor H., 226
Kuala Lumpur, 196
Kurds, 364f, 367, 380–1
Kuwait, 11, 341, 365, 367–8, 410, 437, 439, 505n4

Labor Party, 69
Lacey, Edward, 32
Lacheroy, Charles, 176
Lake Tsala Apoka, 54
Lakota, 56
Lamb, Graeme, 432
Land-to-the-Tiller program, 233
Lansdale, Edward G., 154, 205–7, 218, 220, 226, 255
Lansing, Robert, 118
Laos, 211, 214–15, 217, 224, 270
Lawrence, T. E., 389: background of, 128–9; British slight of, 133; Clausewitz and, 128; conventional warfare and, 129–31; counterinsurgency and, 127, 134–5; *Counterinsurgency Field Manual* and, 394; depth of understanding Arabs, 127–8; Faisal and, 128–30, 133, 485n13; Foch and, 128; genie of Arab empire and, 130–3; guerrilla warfare and, 129–30, 133–5; intelligence gathering and, 129; Mao Zedong and, 159; *Seven Pillars of Wisdom* and, 127, 212; "27 Articles" and, 133–4; World War I and, 127, 132f
Leach, James, 330
Lebanon, 299, 340, 411, 465
Le Duc, 51–2
Lee, Henry, 41
Lee, Robert E., 39, 48f, 49
Leftists: Bolivia and, 272–3; China and, 159; Colombia and, 348–9, 358; Cuba and, 239, 246, 251, 259, 279, 282, 289; El Salvador and, 306, 310–14, 320, 329; Greece and, 167, 170; Guatemala and, 239, 259; Institutional Revolutionary Party (PRI) and, 246; Mexico and, 147, 246; Nicaragua and, 282, 289, 302

Lenin, 247
"Lesson of Tal Afar, The" (Packer), 385
Liberal Party, 138
Liberation Army, 242
Libya: air strikes and, 453; Al Qaeda and, 455; Arab Spring and, 444, 448–9; Benghazi attack and, 442, 455; Britain and, 446–7, 452–3; Central Intelligence Agency (CIA) and, 453; China and, 449, 451; counterinsurgency and, 444, 456; covert operations and, 453; democracy and, 444, 448–9; drones and, 453–4, 456, 462, 464; economy of, 447; France and, 451–3; Germany and, 451–2; *Green Book* and, 445; hands-off approach in, 442; human rights and, 449; insurgency and, 442, 444, 453–6; intelligence gathering and, 442, 450; Italy and, 446, 452; Jamahiriya philosophy and, 445; Japan and, 446; Joint Chiefs of Staff and, 451; King Idris and, 444; media and, 449, 455; National Transitional Council and, 453–4; NATO and, 442, 444, 451–4; no-fly zone and, 451–2; Obama and, 444, 450–3, 455; oil and, 444–5, 447; Operation Odyssey Dawn and, 451–2; Operation Unified Protection and, 452; paramilitary forces and, 445; patronage system of, 445, 447; public executions and, 447; Qaddafi and, 344, 442–56; Reagan and, 446–7; Revolutionary Committees Movement and, 445; Russia and, 451; Security council Resolution 1973 and, 451; as Socialist People's Libyan Arab Jamahiriyah, 445; Soviet Union and, 446; terrorism and, 442, 446–8, 454–6; torture and, 447; U.S. Air Force and, 447; weapons of mass destruction (WMD) and, 447
Libyan General People's Congress, 445
Light-footprint approach: Afghanistan and, 419, 434, 441; Colombia and, 351; El Salvador and, 322; Greece and, 172; Iraq and, 365; Libya and, 454; Philippines and, 202, 398, 402
Lima Company, 379
Lincoln, Abraham, 51
Lincoln, Benjamin, 29, 45
Lincoln Memorial, 251, 276
Llano operation, 248
Lockerbie, Scotland, 447

Lodge, Henry Cabot, 223
Looting: Afghanistan and, 409; American Revolution and, 32, 40, 43; Arab Revolt and, 131; Iraq and, 370
Los Angeles Times, 5
Loyalists: British, 29, 31–3, 35, 37, 41–4; Iraqi, 371
Luftwaffe, 143, 475n7
Lumumba, Patrice, 271
Luttwak, Edward, 468
Lynch's River, 41

M-16s, 296
M-79 grenade launchers, 296
Macabebes, 82
Macarena, La, 356–8
MacArthur, Arthur, 81–3
MacArthur, Douglas: Bataan and, 199; as de facto ruler of Japan, 372; Mao Zedong and, 163; Philippines and, 199; Truman's removal of, 426
Madagascar, 174
Magaña, Álvaro, 318–19, 327
Magsaysay, Ramón: Diem and, 219; Hukbalahap and, 202–8; Lansdale and, 205–7; lightning visits and, 202–8; Philippines and, 196, 202–8, 219, 355, 398, 428; rural population and, 203, 205; slogans of, 202–8
Mahan, Alfred T., 111–12
Mailed fist, 201
Malaya: ambush and, 190, 195–6; Anti-Bandit Campaign of, 192–8; assassination and, 190, 195; Briggs and, 193–5, 198; Britain and, 197; China and, 192–3; counterinsurgency and, 190, 193, 195–8; Emergency of, 190–8; Germany and, 195; Ghurkas and, 197; guerrilla warfare and, 190–4, 196, 198; Gurkha brigade and, 193; Gurney and, 190, 195; insurgency and, 190–8; insurrection and, 192, 195; intelligence gathering and, 196; Japan and, 190–3; lessons learned from, 469; New Village programs and, 193–7, 221; pacification and, 195; psychological warfare and, 197; retreat and, 190; Templer and, 191f, 195–8; terrorism and, 195–6; Tin Puncturing Order and, 197; World War II era and, 192–3, 195
Malayan People's Anti-Japanese Army (MPAJA), 190, 192

Malayan Races Liberation Army (MRLA), 197–8
Malay Communist Party (MCP), 192, 197–8
Mali, 455
Manifest Destiny, 12, 55, 111
Man-portable air defense systems (MANPADS), 420
Mansfield, 220
Mao Zedong, 209: *Basic Tactics* and, 160–1; Castro and, 247; Central Intelligence Agency (CIA) and, 162–3; Chiang and, 159–61, 212; communism and, 157–64; conventional warfare and, 161; counterinsurgency and, 159; creation of People's Republic of China and, 162; First Front Army and, 159; guerrilla warfare and, 20, 54, 154, 157, 159–62, 220, 393; Guevara and, 278; insurgency and, 157–9, 162, 164; insurrection and, 158; intelligence gathering and, 162, 164; Japan and, 159–61; Lawrence and, 159; leftist governments and, 147; longevity advantage and, 17; MacArthur and, 163; Marxism and, 162, 176; morale and, 162; Nixon and, 163; People's Liberation Army (PLA) and, 161–2; Popular Forces of Liberation (FPL) and, 311; post–World War II tactics of, 157, 161, 163; propaganda and, 161; retreat and, 159; rural population and, 157–9; Soviet Union and, 157; Sun Tzu and, 159, 161; Zhou Enlai and, 159
Marion, Francis ("Swamp Fox"), 33, 41–3
Marshall, George, 3, 168
Marshall Plan, 212
Martí, José, 247
Martial law, 81–2
Martínez, Gerson, 314, 333, 501n13
Marulanda, Manuel, 349, 355f
Marxism: Algeria and, 176; Bolivia and, 275f, 278; Colombia and, 342, 345, 349–51; counterinsurgency and, 188–9, 240; Cuba and, 156, 257, 262, 266, 270; El Salvador and, 281, 304–7, 309, 317f, 320, 329–30, 333–4, 349, 351; Galula and, 185, 187; Guatemala and, 259, 262, 264f, 266, 267f, 281, 288; guerrilla warfare and, 187, 189, 281, 304, 305f, 317f, 333, 343; Guevara and, 257, 275f, 278; Mao Zedong and, 162, 176;

Nicaragua and, 266, 281–2, 285, 287–8, 291; rhetoric of, 342
Mason, George, 34
Mason, William E., 77
Masri, Abu Miqdad al, 462
Massacres: Algeria and, 177; American Revolution and, 29, 43–4; Bales and, 4–6, 8, 440, 473n7, 473n8; Balangiga and, 85; Colombia and, 347; El Mozote, 305f, 323–6; El Salvador and, 305f, 316, 323–6; Guatemala and, 259, 262; Hussein and, 376; Iraq and, 376; My Lai, 229–32, 324, 382; Ninety-Six, South Carolina and, 44; no-fly zones and, 451; Philippines and, 85, 87; public reaction to, 8; Sand Creek and, 5–6, 8, 57; Sétif and, 177; Vietnam and, 229–32, 324, 382; Waxhaws, 29, 43; Zacapa and, 259
Massoud, Ahmad Shah, 409
Massu, Jacques, 180–3
Matthews, Herbert, 145, 249
Mattis, James, 363, 372, 377–8
Mayans, 240, 264–6, 267f
Mayorga, Román, 312
McAuliffe, Dennis P., 286
McCarthy, Colman, 316
McChrystal, Stanley: Afghanistan and, 426–33; Al Qaeda and, 460; Iraq and, 1, 390, 457; JSOC and, 460; Marja mission and, 431–2; military success of, 460; Obama and, 1, 432; reflections of, 460–1; replaced by Petraeus, 1, 432; *Rolling Stone* article and, 1, 432; Zarqawi and, 459
McCormick, Medill, 121
McCoy, Frank, 146
McDowell, Joseph, 31–2
MacFarland, Sean, 386, 392
McGovern, Jim, 432
McKiernan, David, 426
McKinley, William, 76–7, 81, 84, 114–16
McMaster, H. R., 370, 384, 385
McMurtry, Larry, 61
McNamara, Robert, 225, 270
McRaven, William, 459, 462
Media: Afghanistan and, 415, 423, 426, 429, 439; American Society of Newspaper Editors and, 250–1; atrocities and, 13; bin Laden's studio and, 439; Castro and, 145, 249–53; contras and, 293–4; Cuba and, 250–1; El Salvador and, 316, 329, 335;

Media (cont.)
  Facebook, 360, 449; free press and, 13, 21; Internet, 35, 343, 375, 382, 393, 423, 437, 449, 466; Iraq and, 341, 382, 385, 391; Libya and, 449; newspapers, 11, 84, 92, 164, 170, 243, 249, 251–2, 280, 285, 295–7, 316, 318, 324, 326, 329–30, 366, 375, 380, 384–5, 427–8, 435, 444, 472, 473n8; Philippines and, 398; print, 35; propaganda and, 21, 35 (see also Propaganda); radio, 35, 171, 249, 253, 274, 286, 299, 315–16, 323–4, 354, 377, 405, 418, 439, 447; Sandinistas and, 285, 293–4; social, 360, 382, 423, 449; soldier's letters and, 84; television, 35, 251, 315, 318, 388, 448, 465; terrorism and, 397, 415, 439; Twitter, 449; Vietnam and, 229, 233; yellow journalism and, 114
Meese, Edwin, 299
Mein, John Gordon, 259
Melville, Herman, 46
Mena, Luis, 138–9
Mercenaries, 117–18, 138, 243, 271, 449
Merkel, Charles F., 124
Merritt, Wesley, 75, 78
Mexico, 4: Battle of Carrizal and, 98; Battle of Celaya and, 92; Camp Furlong and, 89, 92; Carrancistas and, 96; Carranza and, 91–5, 98; Constitutionalists and, 91; Curtiss JN-3 biplanes and, 95; Germany and, 91, 98; Huerta and, 91; Institutional Revolutionary Party (PRI) and, 246; insurgency and, 93; leftists and, 246; pacification and, 93, 109; Pershing and, 93–9; Punitive Expedition and, 93–9, 109, 112, 121; retreat and, 98; Tompkins and, 89, 92–3, 96; U.S. Navy and, 91; Villa and, 68, 89–100, 109, 111, 113, 118, 136, 453, 468; Wilson and, 89, 89, 91–4, 98, 104
MI6, 453
Mi-8 helicopters, 293
Mi-24D attack gunships, 408
Miles, Nelson A., 60
Military Assistance Advisory Groups (MAAGS), 155–6, 214, 219–20, 270–1, 469
Military Review (U.S. Army), 467
Miller, A. F., 85
Miller, George, 294
Mirsky, Jonathan, 162–3

Miskito Indians, 291
Missouri insurgency, 50
Mk.19 grenade launchers, 414
Modernization theory, 155–6
Molina, Arturo, 310
Moncada, José María, 139–41, 147
Moncadistas, 247
Mondale, Walter, 296
Monterrosa, Domingo, 323
Montiel, Byron, 297
Montojo, Patricio, 72
Morale: Afghanistan and, 409, 424; American Revolution and, 32, 37, 39; Arab Revolt and, 131; Banana Wars and, 123; Clausewitz on, 25; El Salvador and, 307, 320, 326; France and, 22; Guevara and, 272; Indians and, 60; irregular warfare and, 22, 25, 32, 37, 60, 123, 131, 162, 212, 216, 225, 272, 307, 320, 326, 409, 424; Mao Zedong and, 162; Sherman's March to the Sea and, 50–3; Vietnam and, 212, 216, 225
Morant, Harry "Breaker," 70
Morgan, Daniel, 32, 45
Morice Line, 181–2
Morocco, 174, 211
Moro Islamic Liberation Front, 398, 402, 446
Morris, Jason, 432, 436
Mortenson, Greg, 432–3
Mosby, John S. ("Gray Ghost"), 46–50, 66
Movimiento Revolucionario 13 de Noviembre (MR-13), 258–60
Moynihan, Daniel Patrick, 295
Mujahideen, 134, 406–9, 418, 421
Mullen, Michael, 3, 417, 451
Munich Olympics, 446
Mussolini, Benito, 249
Muthanna, 461
My Lai massacre, 229–32, 324, 382

Nagasaki, 10
Najibullah, Mohammad, 405–6, 409
Napalm, 170
Napoleon, 64, 377: Britain and, 20; glory and, 56; Russia and, 22–4; Spain and, 20–3, 50, 431
Nasser, Gamal Abdel, 444
Natal, 66
National Commission for Reconstruction (CONARA), 328

Index   571

National Endowment for Democracy
  (NED), 301
National Intelligence Estimate (NIE), 368–9
Nationalist Party (KMT), 157, 159–62
Nationalist Republican Alliance (ARENA),
  315, 318, 333
National Liberation Army (ELN), 345–7
National Liberation Front (EAM), 165, 167
National Liberation Front for South
  Vietnam (NLF), 218–19
National Revolutionary Union (URNG),
  265–6
National Security Agency (NSA), 395
National Security Council, 169, 289, 299,
  372, 450
National Security Decision Directive 17,
  288–9
National Security Directive 24, 371
National Transitional Council (NTC),
  453–4
Nation-building: Afghanistan and, 417, 419,
  422–3, 426, 433, 441, 473n5; Arab
  Revolt and, 134; Banana Wars and, 109,
  112, 117–22; Colombia and, 358;
  counterinsurgency and, 2–3, 7, 78, 84, 88,
  109, 112, 117–22, 134, 149, 221, 309–10,
  315, 334, 358, 371, 382–3, 417, 419,
  422–3, 426, 433, 441, 469, 473n5;
  democracy and, 119–20, 124; El Salvador
  and, 309–10, 315, 334; Haiti and,
  117–22; Iraq and, 371, 382–3; Philippines
  and, 78, 84, 88, 469; Sandino and, 149;
  Vietnam and, 221, 473n5
Navajo, 55
Navarre, Henri, 212, 214–17
Nazis, 18, 165, 167, 171, 177, 180–1
Negroponte, John, 390
Nelson, Knute, 77
New Anti-Communist Organization, 259
New Deal, 240
Newsweek magazine, 293–4
New Yorker, 385, 472
New York Journal, 98
New York Times, 11, 249, 324, 326,
  329–30, 366, 427–8, 473n8
New Zealand, 420
Nicaragua, 4, 340, 468: ambush and, 296;
  Arias plan and, 300; assassination and,
  260, 280, 284, 301; Banana Wars and,
  109, 111, 118, 122; Bluefields revolt and,
  138; Boland-Zablocki amendment and,
294, 297, 300; Carter and, 281–2, 285–9,
301–2; Central Intelligence Agency (CIA)
and, 242, 274, 283, 286–91, 294–7,
299; Chamorro, Violeta, and, 301;
communism and, 281, 283, 287–91, 294,
300–2, 308, 310–11, 313, 317f, 332–3;
conclusion of "endless war" and, 302–3;
Conservatives and, 138; contras and, 282,
291–302; conventional warfare and, 295;
counterinsurgency and, 279, 281–2, 293,
295; covert operations and, 289, 291,
294, 299, 302; deaths in, 149; democracy
and, 139, 291, 300–1; DH-4 biplanes and,
142–3; Díaz and, 138–42, 148; downing
of cargo plane and, 297–300; Emiliano
Chamorro and, 139; Enders and, 290–1;
Esquipulas II Accord and, 300; Estrada
and, 138; foco theory and, 280–3; FSLN
and, 260, 282–7; Germany and, 290;
Guardia and, 141–4, 146, 148; guerrilla
warfare and, 141–4, 147–8, 260, 280–7,
290–3, 296, 300, 453; human rights and,
281–2, 285–7, 296–7, 302; imperialism
and, 282, 291; institutional violence of,
285; insurgency and, 279, 281–5, 288–96,
300; insurrection and, 281, 285–6, 291;
intelligence gathering and, 287–90,
293–5; Iran-Contra scandal and,
299–300; leftists and, 282, 289, 302;
Liberals and, 138; López Pérez, Rigoberto
and, 260; low-intensity conflict and,
294–6; Managua earthquake and, 283–4;
Marxism and, 266, 281–2, 285, 287–8,
291; Mena and, 138–9; Miskito Indians
and, 291; National Guard and, 280,
283–6, 291, 312; National Palace seizure
and, 284; National Security Decision
Directive 17 and, 288–9; oil and, 295;
pacification and, 302; Panama Canal and,
137–8; paramilitary forces and, 183, 205,
289; Pastora and, 284; Pedro Joaquín
Chamorro assassination and, 280–1, 284;
policy discord and, 288–91; priests and,
285, 291; propaganda and, 243–4, 287;
Provisional Junta of National
Reconciliation and, 286; Reagan and,
282, 288–97, 299–300, 302, 304;
Sandinistas and, 279–304, 306; Sandino
and, 136–49 (*see also* Sandino, Augusto
César); Somoza family and, 253, 260,
280–8, 293, 301, 306, 312; Soviet Union

Nicaragua (cont.)
  and, 290, 293, 301; swamps and, 294;
  torture and, 310; UCLAs and, 295; U.S.
  Air Force and, 252; Zelaya and, 138
Nicaraguan Opposition Union (UNO),
  300–1
Nidal, Abu, 446
Night Stalkers, 458–9
9-to-5 army, 322, 353
Nixon, Richard M.: Castro and, 251; covert
  operations and, 252; Cuba and, 251–2;
  Mao Zedong and, 163; Vietnam and, 225,
  230–4; Watergate scandal and, 289, 299
No-fly zones, 451–2
Normandy, 378
North, Oliver, 299–300
North Atlantic Treaty Organization
  (NATO): Afghanistan and, 4, 407, 415,
  421–5, 432, 434, 441; International
  Security Assistance Force (ISAF) and,
  421–2, 428; Jones and, 424; Libya and,
  442, 444, 451–4; Provincial
  Reconstruction Teams (PRTs) and, 425
Northern Alliance, 409–10, 415–16, 418–19
North Vietnamese Army (NVA), 229–30, 233
Notre Dame University, 310

Obama, Barack: Afghanistan and, 397, 417,
  426–32, 436–41; assassination plots
  against, 439; bin Laden and, 436–40;
  Black Hawk crash and, 438–9; Central
  Intelligence Agency (CIA) and, 437;
  Colombia and, 334–5; drones and, 464–5;
  Joint Special Operations Command
  (JSOC) and, 438–9, 461–2, 464–5; Libya
  and, 444, 450–3, 455; "necessary" war of,
  426–32; replaces McChrystal, 1, 432;
  strategies of, 397, 417, 426–32, 438–9,
  441, 444, 450–3, 455
Ochoa, Arnoldo, 293
ODA-555, 416
Odierno, Raymond, 376
Odom, William, 395
Office of Special Operations, 220
Oil, 475n7: Afghanistan and, 411; Algeria
  and, 455; Iraq and, 371, 388, 391; Libya
  and, 444–5, 447; Nicaragua and, 295
Omar, Mullah Mohammed, 409, 420
I Corps Tactical Zone, 227
On Guerrilla Warfare (Mao Zedong), 54
On War (Clausewitz), 23–5

Operación Rescate, 323–6
Operación Verano, 250
Operation Anaconda, 420
Operation Check, 349
Operation Desert Fox, 368
Operation Desert Storm, 341, 410–11
Operation Eagle Claw, 437, 458–9
Operation Enduring Freedom, 415, 417,
  419–20, 426
Operation Enduring Freedom–Philippines
  (OEF–P), 399, 403
Operation Gothic Serpent, 343
Operation Infinite Research, 411
Operation Iraqi Freedom, 363, 390–1, 417
Operation Linebacker, 234
Operation Maiwand, 424
Operation Mongoose, 255–6
Operation Moshtarak, 430–1
Operation Mountain Sweep, 420
Operation Odyssey Dawn, 451–2
Operation PBSUCCESS, 239–40, 242,
  258, 261
Operation Pocket Money, 234
Operation Provide Comfort, 371
Operation Red Dawn, 376
Operation Rescate, 324
Operation Rolling Thunder, 225, 234, 464
Operation Sodom, 354
Operation Starvation, 194
Operation Unified Protection, 452
Operation Vigilant Resolve, 377
Operation Well-Being, 324
Operation Zapata. *See* Bay of Pigs
Opium, 410, 418, 423, 431, 441
Organisation de l'armée secrete (OAS),
  183–4
Organización Democrática Nacionalista
  (ORDEN), 329
Organization of American States (OAS),
  301, 331
Orlando, Luis, 322
Ortega, Daniel, 287, 290
Ortega, Humberto, 287–8, 290–1, 293, 299,
  301
Otis, John, 78–9, 84
Ottoman Empire, 127–35

Pacer, 437
Pachachi, Adnan, 381
Pacification: Afghanistan and, 425; Algeria
  and, 182; Banana Wars and, 109, 115,

122; Callwell on, 26; Colombia and, 362; Cuba and, 4, 115; Delta Pacification Program and, 221; El Salvador and, 327, 333; global, 11; Haiti and, 122; Indians and, 3–4; Iraq and, 385; JSOC and, 461; Malaya and, 195; Mexico and, 93, 109; Nicaragua and, 302; Philippines and, 4, 74, 77, 79, 81, 83–4, 88, 100; PROVN and, 226; Romans and, 19; Vietnam and, 220–3, 226–33

Packer, George, 383, 385

Pahlavi, Mohammad Raza, 457

País, Frank, 248

Pakistan: Al Qaeda and, 416, 419–20, 426; Bhutto and, 410; bin Laden and, 61, 410, 420, 437–40; border attacks and, 436–7; Brzezinski and, 405; Central Intelligence Agency (CIA) and, 406–7, 462–4, 466; covert operations and, 406; drones and, 434, 437, 462–4, 466; drugs and, 426; Holbrooke and, 427; Iraq and, 379; JSOC and, 461; Mortensen and, 433; opium and, 418; refugees and, 408–10, 419; Soviet Union and, 421; Taliban and, 416, 419–20, 423, 426, 434, 441; Zia and, 405–6

Palestine, 19, 132f

Palestinians, 339, 446

Panama: Canal, 137–8, 270, 323; covert operations and, 270; Eisenhower and, 251; Sandinistas and, 285–6; School of the Americas and, 270–1, 283, 323; *tanda* issue and, 321; U.S. Southern Command and, 286, 328, 330

Pan Am bombing, 447

Panetta, Leon, 437

Paramilitary forces, 7: Algeria and, 183; Bolivia and, 274; Colombia and, 342, 347, 353, 358–9; Cuba and, 274; El Salvador and, 311, 314, 329; Greece and, 167; Guatemala and, 242, 259, 263; Iraq and, 366; Libya and, 445; Nicaragua and, 205, 289; Vietnam and, 218

Pashto language, 424

Pastora, Edén, 284

Pastrana, Andrés, 347–8

Paternalism, 76–7, 112–13, 118, 202, 403

Patrullas de autodefensa civil (self-defense patrols), 266

Paul, Ron, 432–3

Peace Corps, 432–3

Peace groups, 5–6

Pee Dee River, 41

Pentagon: Afghanistan and, 417, 420, 473n8; Green Berets and, 154, 262; Guatemala and, 262; El Salvador and, 321–2, 236–7, 334, 342; Iraq and, 371; Kennedy and, 154; Philippines and, 399–400; San Salvador and, 326–7

People's Anti-Japanese Army. *See* Hukbalahap

People's Liberation Army (China), 161–2

People's Liberation Army (Philippines), 199

People's Revolutionary Army (ERP), 311

Péralte, Charlemagne Masséna, 120–1

Pershing, John J., 3: background of, 93; Curtiss JN-3 biplanes and, 95; Punitive Expedition and, 93–9, 109, 112, 121; Villa and, 93–9

Persian Gulf War, 9, 341–2, 363, 367–71, 471

Petraeus, David: Afghanistan and, 1–2, 432–4, 439; Anaconda strategy and, 1–2; Army's 101st Airborne Division and, 382; assassination plots against, 439; background of, 1; Central Intelligence Agency (CIA) and, 2–3; *Counterinsurgency Field Manual* and, 395, 433–4; grand mistake of, 390; guerrilla warfare and, 395, 467; ignores Bush, 383; Iraq and, 1–3, 382–3, 388–92, 467; *Military Review* article and, 467; military success of, 3; postmodern insurgencies and, 393; reflections of, 393, 467–8; replaces Casey, 388; replaces McChrystal, 1, 432; retirement of, 3; strategies of, 1–2, 383, 388–90, 395–6, 433–4, 439; Stryker brigade and, 383; Taliban and, 2

Petraeus Doctrine, 395

Peurifoy, John, 242

Pezzullo, Lawrence, 285

Philippines, 468: Abu Sayyaf and, 398–9, 398–402; Aguinaldo and, 74–88, 199; ambush and, 85; *americanistas* and, 79; Arroyo and, 400; assassination and, 207, 399; atrocities and, 76, 78, 80, 84–6, 88; attraction policies and, 84, 87; Balangiga massacre and, 85–6; bandits and, 399, 402; Bataan and, 73f, 199, 200f; Battle of Manila and, 75–6, 87f; Central Intelligence Agency (CIA) and, 202;

Philippines (cont.)
communism and, 199–202, 205–7; concentration camps and, 69; containment strategy and, 201–2; conventional warfare and, 78–9, 81, 156, 202, 400; cordons system and, 201; counterinsurgency and, 78–87, 106, 201–2, 206–8, 398–403; Dewey and, 72, 74–5, 85; EDCOR and, 206; guerrilla warfare and, 74, 79–86, 199–203, 207, 391, 400–2; hostages and, 400; Hukbalahap and, 199–209; *ilustrados* and, 74, 79–80; imperialism and, 76–7, 81, 84–5, 400; insurgency and, 74–5, 78–88, 93, 199–208, 398–403; insurrection and, 74–9, 81, 83, 87–8, 95, 202; intelligence gathering and, 82, 85, 399–400; Islam and, 398–9, 402, 446; Japan and, 199, 202–3; Joint Chiefs of Staff and, 202; Joint Task Force-510 and, 400; Jolo, 400; JUSMAPG and, 169; Lansdale and, 205–7; lessons learned from, 469; levels of dirtiness and, 6; Luzon, 73f, 74, 80–1, 84, 199–202; Macabebes, 82; MacArthur and, 81–3, 199; McKinley and, 76–7, 81, 84; Magsaysay and, 196, 202–8, 219, 355, 398, 428; mailed fist campaign and, 201; martial law and, 81–2; massacres and, 85, 87; media and, 398; Merritt and, 74; Mindanao, 73f, 200f, 201–2; Montojo and, 72; Moro Islamic Liberation Front and, 398, 402, 446; nation-building and, 78, 84, 88, 469; Otis and, 78–9, 84; pacification and, 4, 74, 77, 79, 81, 83–4, 88, 100; paternalism and, 76–7; post-9/11 COIN in, 398–403; *principales* and, 79; psychological warfare and, 205; Qaddafi and, 446; Quirino and, 201–2, 205, 207; repressions and, 81–4; Republican Army and, 79–80; retreat and, 79, 206, 400; Roosevelt and, 72, 85–8; Roxas and, 201; Soviet Union and, 202; Spain and, 72, 76–8, 87f, 112–13; swamps and, 89; Taruc and, 199, 207; terrorism and, 398–401; torture and, 85; Treaty of Paris and, 76–7; Truman and, 201–2, 214; U.S. Air Force and, 205; U.S. Army and, 78, 80–4, 111, 114; U.S. Navy and, 74, 401; Vietnam and, 78, 79, 83; World War II era and, 199, 201, 209

Phoenicians, 19
Phoenix Program, 228
Phung Hoang, 228
Pickering, Thomas R., 351
Pied-noirs (immigrants), 176–7, 180, 183
Pillaging, 51, 89
Pinkerton, B. J., 270–1
Plains of Abraham, 35
Plan Colombia, 350–2, 356–7
Platt Amendment, 115–16
Plundering: American Revolution and, 40, 43; Civil War and, 49, 51; Sandino and, 142; Villa and, 89, 92, 94
Pointe, Ali la, 180
Policía Nacional Dominicana, 124
Political correctness, 112, 188, 394, 434
Poppy cultivation, 410, 418, 431, 441
Popular Forces (PF), 228
Popular Forces of Liberation (FPL), 310–11
Post-traumatic stress disorder (PTSD), 5, 471–7
Powell, Colin, 340–3, 368–9, 391
Powell Doctrine, 340–3
Preble, James, 52
Predator drones, 453–4, 462, 464–5
Prensa, La (Nicaraguan newspaper), 280
Preysler, Charles, 414
Principalía, 82
"Program for the Pacification and Long-Term Development of Vietnam, A" (PROVN), 226
Project Circus, 162–3
Propaganda: Afghanistan and, 423; American Revolution and, 35; Castro and, 252–3, 255–6; Central Intelligence Agency (CIA) and, 243–4, 315; Civil War and, 52; Confederates and, 52; Cuba and, 249, 256; El Salvador and, 324–5; Greece and, 170; Guatemala and, 243–4, 260; Indians and, 54; Internet and, 35, 343, 423; labels and, 21; Mao Zedong and, 161; media and, 21, 35; Nicaragua and, 243–4, 287; psychological operations and, 315; rhetoric and, 13, 21, 34, 81, 104, 107, 111, 115, 132, 247, 287, 296, 302, 308, 342, 406, 419, 445–6; Second Battle of Fallujah and, 377–80; Siberia and, 106–7; Spain and, 21; terrorism and, 343; Vietnam and, 218, 220, 228
Provincial Reconstruction Teams (PRTs), 425

Index 575

Proxy approach, 6, 207–8, 321–3
Prussia: Clausewitz and, 15, 23–5, 128, 159, 188; Frederick the Great, 36; Von Steuben and, 39
Psychological warfare, 15: Algeria and, 176, 179; American Revolution and, 35; Anti-Communist Denunciation Campaign and, 219; attraction policies and, 84, 87; Civil War and, 52–3; concentration camps and, 64, 67, 69, 78, 113; Cuba and, 256, 270–1; El Salvador and, 315, 327; Farabundo Martí National Liberation Front (FMLN) and, 326–7; Greece and, 168; Guantanamo Bay and, 62; Guatemala and, 242–4; interrogation and, 85, 178, 182, 263, 270–1, 327, 460; Iraq and, 368, 383, 389; Malaya and, 197; Philippines and, 205; post-traumatic stress disorder (PTSD) and, 5, 471–2; School of the Americas and, 270–1, 283, 323; Sherman's March to the Sea and, 50–3, 61–2; Vietnam and, 235
Public executions, 447
Public relations, 144, 206–7, 242
Puerto Rico, 76
Puller, Louis "Chesty," 144, 227
Punitive Expedition, 93–9, 109, 112, 121
Purple Rose, 259

Qaddafi, Hana, 447
Qaddafi, Muammar, 344: Amin and, 446; background of, 444; Basque separatists and, 446; Bedouin upbringing of, 444; Berlin nightclub bombing and, 447; Black September and, 446; as Brother Leader, 445, 453–4; brutality of, 447–51; Castro and, 445; death of, 444, 454, 464; drones and, 453–4, 456, 462, 464; Egyptian airliner hijacking and, 447; Free Officers and, 444; *Green Book* and, 445; as Guide of the Revolution, 445; hunt for, 452–4; Jamahiriya philosophy of, 445; King Idris and, 444; as "mad dog of the Middle East," 447; Moro National Liberation Front and, 446; Nasser and, 153, 407, 444, 447–9, 455, 458, 515n11; oil companies and, 444–5; Operation Odyssey Dawn and, 451–2; Operation Unified Protection and, 452; Palestinians and, 446; Pan Am bombing and, 447; patronage system of, 445, 447; public executions and, 447; Reagan and, 446–7; Red Brigades and, 446; relationship with the West, 444–6, 449–52; Revolutionary Committees Movement and, 445; Sandinistas and, 446; Security council Resolution 1973 and, 451; terrorism and, 442, 446–8, 454–6
Qaddafi, Saif, 449–50
Qatar, 453
Quadrillage system, 179, 182
Quakers, 31, 45
Quirino, 201–2, 205, 207

Rabbani, Burhanuddin, 409
Radio Rebelde, 249–50
Radio Vencerémos, 324
Ramadier, Paul, 174
Rape, 52, 177, 306, 324
Rasenberger, Jim, 254
Rawlinson, 63
Reagan, Ronald: Boland-Zablocki amendment and, 294, 297, 300; compared to Chamberlain, 302; contras and, 291–2; covert operations and, 289; Cuba and, 302; El Salvador and, 306, 308–9, 315–19, 322, 325, 361; Guatemala and, 266; as hawk, 266, 302, 306, 308, 361; inauguration of, 457; Iran-Contra scandal and, 299–300; Iran hostages and, 457–8; Lebanon and, 411; Libya and, 446–7; National Security Decision Directive 17 and, 288–9; Nicaragua and, 282, 288–97, 299–300, 302, 304; Odom and, 395; Soviet Union and, 302, 304; strategies of, 282, 288–300, 302, 304, 306, 308–9, 315–19, 322, 325, 340, 361, 411, 446–7; "The Uses of Military Power" and, 340
Reaper drones, 464
Rebel Armed Forces (FAR), 259
Red Army (Chinese), 161, 163
Red Army (Russian), 102, 107
Red Brigades, 446
Regional Forces (RF), 228
Reid, Harry, 388
Repressions, 61, 81–4, 124, 180, 267, 279, 311–14, 445, 448–9
Republican Army, 79–80
Retreat, 24–5: Afghanistan and, 419, 423; American Revolution and, 29, 32, 37–8, 41, 45; Cuba and, 258; El Salvador and, 332; Iraq and, 383; Malaya and, 190;

Retreat (cont.)
  Mao Zedong and, 159; Mexico and, 98; Philippines and, 79, 206, 400; Vietnam and, 230
Revolución newspaper, 251
Revolutionary Armed Forces of Colombia (FARC): Betancourt and, 348–9; Chávez and, 349; Colombia and, 17, 342, 345–62, 418, 423; decreased power of, 354–5; despeje (liberated zone) for, 347–9; Devía and, 348; El Nogal bombing and, 350; 52nd Counter-Guerrilla Battalion and, 347; funding of, 349; good-faith negotiations and, 347–8; increasing strength of, 347–8; intelligence gathering on, 348–9; IRA bomb-making teams and, 348; La Macarena and, 356–8; liberated zone for, 347; Marulanda and, 349, 355f; mayoral corruption and, 347; National Liberation Army (ELN) and, 345–7; Operation Check and, 349; Plan Colombia and, 350–2, 356–7; Suárez and, 354–6; Uribe and, 348–50, 352–62; U.S. War on Terror and, 350; visitor's center of, 356
Revolutionary Organization of Armed People (ORPA), 259
Reyes, Raúl, 348–9
Ricks, Thomas, 363, 384
Ridenhour, Ron, 230
Ríos Montt, Efraín, 258, 265–6
Rivera, Rodrigo, 354
Rizopastis newspaper, 170
Roberts, Lord, 19, 63, 66–7
Rochambeau, 45
Rodriguez, Félix, 274, 299
Rolling Stone magazine, 1, 432
Romans, 19, 22
Romero, Carlos Humberto, 306, 312
Romero, Óscar, 312, 314–15
Roosevelt, Franklin Delano, 120, 148, 240, 249
Roosevelt, Theodore: Cuba and, 116–17, 125; Dominican Republic and, 123; Great White Fleet and, 112; Philippines and, 72, 85–8, 111; Rough Riders and, 125; San Juan Hill and, 125
Root, Elihu, 81, 86
Rose, Gideon, 11, 370, 505n4
Rostow, Walt, 155, 221, 273–5
Rough Riders, 125

Royal Marine Commandos, 363
Roxas, 201
RPG-7 grenade launchers, 299
Rule of law, 8, 148, 187, 291, 416, 424
Rules of engagement, 36, 342–3, 429
Rumsfeld, Donald: Afghanistan and, 419; Iraq and, 365, 368, 370–1, 377, 416
Rusk, Dean, 202, 254
Russia: Afghanistan and, 404, 406, 409, 420; Bolsheviks and, 101f, 102–7, 157, 186; Libya and, 451; Napoleon and, 22–4; Red Army and, 102, 107; resurgence of, 343; Security Council Resolution 1973 and, 451; Siberia and, 100–8; Soviet Union and, 22 (*see also* Soviet Union); Trans-Siberian Railroad and, 101f, 103, 105; Triple Entente and, 102; Vladivostok, 101f, 102, 103f, 105, 408

SA-7 surface-to-air missiles, 301
Saadik, Yacef, 179–80
Sabotage, 67, 192, 255, 259–60, 297, 327, 380
Sacasa, Juan, 139–40, 148
Salan, Raoul, 179, 181–3, 212
Sam, Jean Vilbrum Guillaume, 117
Samuel, Herbert, 132f
Sand Creek massacre, 5–6, 8, 57
Sandinistas: anti-Somoza actions and, 280–8, 293, 301, 306, 312; arms shipments to El Salvador and, 287; Boland-Zablocki amendment and, 294, 297, 300; buildup of arms by, 290–1, 293; Bush, George H. W., and, 300–2; Castro and, 311; conclusion of "endless war" and, 302–3; contras and, 282, 291–302; Cuba and, 284, 311; downing of cargo plane by, 297–300; El Salvador and, 287–303, 307; Enders and, 290–1; Esquipulas II Accord and, 300; final offensive of, 286; foco theory and, 280–3; FSLN and, 260, 282–7; guerrilla warfare and, 280–7, 290–3, 296, 300; hostages and, 284; influence of Sandino and, 282–4; Iran-Contra scandal and, 299–300; lost election of, 300–1; low-intensity conflict and, 294–6; Managua earthquake and, 283–4; media and, 285, 293–4; Mi-8 helicopters and, 293; Miskito Indians and, 291; National Palace seizure and, 284; Nicaragua and, 279–304, 306; Ortega

brothers and, 287–8, 291, 293, 299, 301; Pastora and, 284; policy discord and, 288–91; Qaddafi and, 446; Reagan Doctrine and, 296–7; as revolution without frontiers, 284–8; size of, 282; Somoza family and, 280–8, 293, 301; Soviet Union and, 293; Stalin organs and, 293; UCLAs and, 295; universal military conscription and, 293; zones of liberation and, 284

Sandino, Augusto César, 74, 153, 468: ambush and, 144, 147; atrocities and, 146; background of, 140–1; as bandit, 136, 143–6; Battle of Ocotal and, 143; betrayal of, 146–9; conventional warfare and, 143; Corinto-Granada railroad attack and, 148; counterinsurgency and, 143–5; DH-4 biplanes and, 142–3; Díaz and, 141–2, 148; El Chipote and, 143–4; execution of, 282; Germany and, 143; Guardia and, 141–4, 146, 148; imperialism and, 141, 146, 282; insurgency and, 143–5, 148; intelligence gathering and, 144; Moncada and, 141; mythical influence of, 282; nation-building and, 149; Nueva Segovia and, 142; Nicaragua and, 136, 140–9; plundering and, 142; positive depictions of, 145–6; public opinion of, 145–6; Puller and, 227; U.S. Marine Corps and, 136, 140–9; U.S. Navy and, 146–7

Sanger, David, 428
San Juan Hill, 125
Santee River, 41, 43
Santos, Juan Manuel, 354, 359–60
Sarkozy, Nikolas, 451
Sattar Abu Risha, Abdul, 386–7
Saudi Arabia, 297, 300, 407, 410–11, 515n11
Savannah River, 42
Sawyer, Wallace Blaine, 299
Schmidle, Nicholas, 437
School of the Americas, 270–1, 283, 323
Scorched-earth strategy: American Revolution and, 42–4; Banana Wars and, 113; Boer War and, 67, 69–70; El Salvador and, 309, 325; Guatemala and, 259, 264–7; Philippines and, 78, 86; Sherman's March to the Sea and, 50–3
Scott, Mary Means, 93
Scouts, 60, 67, 82, 86

Seabeees, 401
SEALs, 436, 438–40, 458, 462
Search-and-destroy missions, 79, 193, 323, 327
Second Declaration of Havana (Guevara), 278
Second Seminole War, 53–5
Secord, Richard, 299
Sections Administratives Spécialsées (SAS), 179
Seminoles, 53–5, 60–2
Senate Appropriations Committee, 432–3
Senate Foreign Relations Committee, 428
Sepp, Kalev, 384
September 11, 2001, attacks, 4, 12: Afghanistan and, 417–18, 433; American War on Terror and, 134; bin Laden and, 418; Bush, George W., and, 94, 350, 368, 398–9, 411; Guantanamo Bay and, 62; policymakers and, 361, 396; post-9/11 policy and, 361, 396, 398–403, 417–18; Powell Doctrine and, 343; Taliban and, 94, 411
Sétif massacre, 177
Seven Pillars of Wisdom (Lawrence), 127, 212
Seventh-Day Adventists, 141
Sevier, John, 31–2, 42
Sexton, William, 80
Seychelles, 464
Shah, Mohammad Zahir, 404
Shelby, Isaac, 31–2
Shelton, Robert "Pappy," 273
Sheridan, Henry, 6
Sherman, William Tecumseh, 50–3, 57, 61–2
Shi'ites, 2, 340, 364f: control of Finance Ministry by, 1; Iraq and, 367, 373, 375, 385, 387
Shinseki, Eric, 371
Shock troops, 111, 148, 359
Shultz, George, 294, 300
Shwehdi, Sadiq Hamed, 447
Siberia: American Expeditionary Force Siberia and, 105; American North Russian Expeditionary Force and, 106; Battle of Toulgas and, 101f; Bolsheviks and, 101f, 102–7; Britain and, 100, 102, 105; Central Forces and, 100, 102; communism and, 102, 105; counterinsurgency and, 106–8; France and, 102, 105; Germany

Siberia (cont.)
and, 100–2, 107; Gorbachev speech in, 408; guerrilla warfare and, 102–13; insurgency and, 106–8; intelligence gathering and, 107; origins of allied intervention in, 102–4; propaganda and, 106–7; Red Army and, 102, 107; Soviet Union and, 108; Trans-Siberian Railroad and, 101f, 103, 105; U.S. Army and, 106; U.S. Marine Corps and, 103f; Vladivostok and, 101f, 102, 103f, 105, 408; Wilson and, 104–5, 107
Sierra forces, 248
Sierra Madre Mountains, 60, 94–5
Singleton's Mill, 41
Sioux, 55
Slavery, 49–50, 117
Slocum, Henry Warner, 51
Slocum, Herbert J., 92
Small wars, 25–6, 40, 74, 125, 136, 149
Small Wars Manual (U.S. Marines), 149
Smith, Jacob "Hell-Roaring Jack," 85–6
Snow's Island, 41
Soares, João Clemente Baena, 331
Soccer War, 320
Soldiers' letters, 70, 84–5
Somalia, 342–3, 383, 464
Somoza, Anastasio "Tachito," 260, 280–8, 293, 301, 306, 312
Somoza, Luis, 253, 260, 283
Somoza Debayle, Anastasio "Tacho," 148, 242
Sons of Iraq, 389
Soviet Union, 4: Afghanistan and, 22, 134, 399, 404–10, 418, 420; Algeria and, 174–5; Berlin Wall and, 339, 350; Bolsheviks and, 101f, 102–7, 157, 186; boycott of 1980 Moscow Olympics and, 406; canceled wheat to, 406; Cold War and 153–4 (*see also* Cold War); collapse of, 134, 339, 350; Cuba and, 245f, 252, 255, 302, 333; El Salvador and, 301, 304, 333; Germany and, 102; Gorbachev and, 408–9; Greece and, 169–72; Guatemala and, 241–2, 244; Khrushchev and, 256, 269; Libya and, 446; Mao Zedong and, 157; mujahideen and, 134, 406–9, 418, 421; Nicaragua and, 290, 293, 301; Pakistan and, 421; Philippines and, 202; Reagan and, 302, 304; Sandinistas and, 293; Siberia and, 108; Stalin and, 169–72;

Trans-Siberian Railroad and, 101f, 103, 105; Vietnam and, 10, 211–15, 234
Spain, 136: Algeria and, 176; Aguinaldo and, 74; Burgos-Bayonne roadway and, 22; Charles IV and, 20; Civil War of, 247, 249; Cuba and, 113–17; Dewey and, 72, 74; Ferdinand and, 20; guerrilla warfare and, 20, 22–3, 247; insurgency and, 23; irregular warfare and, 19–23; Joseph and, 20, 21; McKinley and, 76–7, 81, 84, 114–16; Napoleon and, 20–3, 431; Philippines and, 72, 76–8, 87f, 112–13; propaganda and, 21; torture and, 22; Treaty of Paris and, 76–7; U.S. declares war on, 72
Special Forces Groups (SFGs), 270–1
Special operation forces (SOFs), 425
Special Services Squadron, 123
Special Warfare Development Group (DEVGRU), 438, 458
Spreading inkblot strategy, 226
Springfield rifles, 75
Stalin, Josef, 169–72
Stalin organs, 293
Standard Oil, 475n7
St. Cyr, Gouvion, 22–3
Steele, James, 326
Stevens, Chris, 442, 455
Stimson, Henry L., 140
Stinger missiles, 408
St. John, Rachel, 94
Stover, 61
Strategy of Peace, The (Kennedy), 252
Stryker brigade, 383
Stuart, 49
Student protests, 445, 457
Stuhler, Matthew, 430f
Suárez, Victor Julio "Mono Jojoy," 354–6
Suez Crisis, 153
Suicide bombers, 2, 373, 385, 423, 461
Sulaiman, Abu, 402
Summer Operation, 250
Sumter, Thomas, 29, 43
Sunnis: Afghanistan and, 407, 426, 431, 441; Awakening of, 386–7, 389, 426, 432, 441; Iraq and, 1–2, 364f, 369, 373–5, 377, 379, 381, 385–90, 441, 459
Sunni Triangle, 381
Sun Tzu, 19–20, 159, 161, 188, 278
Sun Yat-sen, 159

Index

Surprise attacks, 5, 33, 36, 38, 45, 54, 61, 86, 89, 106, 260, 331, 454
Swamps: American Revolution and, 41–2; Cuba and, 253; Indians and, 54–5, 61; Nicaragua and, 294; Philippines and, 89
Syria, 129, 384, 461, 485n13, 515n11

T-55 tanks, 290
Taft, William Howard, 84, 138
Tajik forces, 409
Taliban: Afghanistan and, 134, 189, 365, 398, 409–11, 414–35, 440–1, 466; Afghan National Army (ANA) and, 424–5; Army Special Forces and, 4, 365; bin Laden and, 410, 418; Bush, George W., and, 94, 416; Central Intelligence Agency (CIA) and, 365, 420; Clinton and, 411; drones and, 466; drugs and, 410, 423, 426; farmer payments and, 424–5; highly kinetic approach of, 412, 414; insurgency and, 2, 4–5; Iraq and, 365; Islam and, 409–10, 425, 433; Northern Alliance and, 409–10, 415–16, 418–19; Omar and, 409, 420; Pakistan and, 416, 419–20, 423, 426, 434, 441; Petraeus and, 2; rise of, 409–10; September 11, 2001, and, 94, 411; Waigal Valley attack and, 412, 414–15
Talk-and-shoot strategy, 434
Tanda culture, 320–1
Tanzania, 446
Taruc, Luis, 199, 207
Tarleton, Banastre, 29, 31–2, 41, 43–5
Tarleton's Quarter, 44
Taylor, Maxwell, 221
Technology: cell phones and, 460, 466; Cold War and, 344; Curtiss JN-3 biplanes and, 95; drones and, 8, 425, 453, 462–6; Gnat missions and, 465–6; guerrilla warfare and, 17; Gulf War and, 341–2; Indians and, 57; intelligence gathering and, 62, 343–4, 460, 462–6; Internet, 35, 343, 375, 382, 393, 423, 437, 449, 466; need for restraint in, 465; superiority of American, 57, 62, 341–2, 344, 363, 365, 416, 465–6
Television, 35, 251, 315, 318, 388, 448, 465
Teller Amendment, 115
Templer, Gerald, 191f, 195–8
10E Division Parachutiste (10E DP), 180
Tenorio, Faustino, 206

Terrorism: Afghanistan and, 411, 415–16, 418–19, 429, 433, 440; Algeria and, 179–80, 183; Colombia and, 345, 348, 350, 361; *Counterinsurgency Field Manual* and, 396; Cuba and, 249, 259; defining, 15–17; drones and, 464–6; El Nogal bombing and, 345; El Salvador and, 307, 315, 325; frozen bank accounts and, 62; Greece and, 167–8; Guatemala and, 259; insurgency and, 340 (*see also* Insurgency); Iran and, 340; Iraq and, 368, 375, 388; Islam and, 343–4, 374, 399, 404–13, 420–1, 423, 440, 442, 455, 466; Lebanon and, 340; Libya and, 442, 446–8, 454–6; London blitz and, 475n7; Malaya and, 195–6; media and, 397, 415, 439; Philippines and, 398–401; propaganda and, 343; September 11, 2001, attacks and, 4, 12, 62, 94, 134, 343, 350, 361, 368, 398, 411, 418, 433; suicide bombers and, 2, 373, 385, 423, 461; War on Terror and, 134, 350, 361, 473n7; *see also specific group*
Tet Offensive, 181, 229–32
Texaco, 251
Thieu, Nguyen Van, 233–4
32nd Volunteer Infantry Regiment, 85
Thompson, Robert, 198, 221–2
Three Cups of Tea (Mortenson), 432–3
Tibet, 162–3
Tierney, Dominic, 11–12, 473n5
Tierney, John, 218
Tin Puncturing Order, 197
Tito, 171
Tolstoy, Leo, 470
Tomahawk missiles, 451
Tompkins, Frank, 89, 92–3, 96
Tories, 35, 41
Torture: Abu Ghraib and, 381–2; Afghanistan and, 406; Algeria and, 177, 180–2, 185; burning at the stake, 22; concentration camps and, 64, 67, 69, 78, 113; Cuba and, 289; cutting, 124; Dominican Republic and, 124; El Salvador and, 310; France and, 177, 180–2, 185; Greece and, 167; Guantanamo Bay, 62; Guatemala and, 263; interrogation and, 85, 178, 182, 263, 270–1, 327, 460; Iraq and, 379, 381–2; Libya and, 447; Philippines and, 85; Spain

Torture (cont.)
and, 22; U.S. Marines and, 124; water cure, 85
Trainor, Bernard, 363, 392
Trans-Siberian Railroad, 101f, 103, 105
Transvaal, 64–70
Treaty of Brest-Litovsk, 102
Treaty of Paris, 76–7
Treaty of Vereeniging, 71
Trinquier, Roger, 176
Triple Entente, 102
Trujillo y Molina, Leonidas, 124
Truman, Harry S.: containment strategy and, 201–2; Doctrine of, 168–70; Guatemala and, 241, 261; Hukbalahap and, 214; Philippines and, 201–2, 214; removes MacArthur, 426
Tsongas, Paul, 290
Tube-launched, Optically tracked, Wire-guided (TOW) missile launcher, 414
Turkey, 169, 256, 367
Turki, Prince, 407, 410–11, 515n11
Twitter, 449

U-2 plane, 256
Uitlanders (foreigners), 65–6
Ungo, Guillermo, 310–12
Uniform Code of Military Justice, 440
Unilaterally controlled Latino assets (UCLAs), 295
Union Army: as Bummers, 51; Civil War and, 46–53, 66, 74–5, 81; Merritt and, 74; Sherman's March to the Sea and, 50–3
Union Mountain Department, 49
United Fruit Company (UFC), 240–2
United Nations (UN), 244, 263, 288, 342, 369, 450, 451
United States: Afghanistan and, 8 (*see also* Afghanistan); Alliance for Progress and, 270; American Declaration of Independence and, 35, 209, 211; American Revolution and, 26, 29–45; Armistice Day and, 106; atrocities committed by, 13, 470, 473n8; Banana Wars and, 109–26; boycotts 1980 Moscow Olympics, 406; Civil War and, 46–53, 66, 75, 81; concentration camps and, 69; contra funding by, 282, 291–302; dirty styles of, 13–14; fire-bombings and, 475n7; as "Great Satan," 457; hunt for Sandino by, 140–9; incendiary bombing and, 475n7; Indian Wars and, 53–62; Iraq and, 365–82, 385–91 (*see also* Iraq); KISSSS and, 322; leading-from-behind approach and, 454–6; light-footprint approach and, 172, 202, 322, 351, 365, 398, 402–3, 419, 434, 441, 454; Manifest Destiny and, 12, 55, 111; National Security Decision Directive 17 and, 288–9; NATO and, 4, 407, 415, 421–5, 432, 434, 441–2, 444, 451–4; paternalism and, 76–7, 112–13, 118, 202, 403; Pentagon and, 154, 262, 321–2, 326–7, 334, 342, 371, 399–400, 417, 420, 473n8; Philippines and, 72–88, 199–208, 398–403; Plan Colombia strategy and, 350–2; Powell Doctrine and, 340–3; self-perception of, 11; Siberia and, 100–8; superior technology of, 57, 62, 341–2, 344, 363, 365, 416, 465, 465–6; Trans-Siberian Railroad and, 101f, 103, 105; Vietnam and, 10, 212, 217–27, 232–6; War on Terror and, 134, 350, 361, 473n7
United Task Force (UNITAF), 343
Unmanned aerial vehicles (UAVs). *See* Drones
Uribe, Álvaro: democratic security and, 352–8; paramilitaries and, 358–9; Revolutionary Armed Forces of Colombia (FARC) and, 348–50, 352–62; shock troops and, 359; war tax of, 352
Urrutia, Manuel, 250
Uruguay, 272
U.S. Agency for International Development (USAID), 233
U.S. Air Force, 4: Afghanistan and, 416; B-1s and, 368; B-26 Douglas Invaders and, 252; B-52s and, 368; Colombia and, 353; Combat Controller, 416; drones and, 462–6; F-16C Fighting Falcons and, 375; Iraq and, 368, 375; Libya and, 447; Nicaragua and, 252; Philippines and, 205; precision bombing and, 475n7; 24th Special Tactics Squadron, 458; Vietnam and, 225
U.S. Army, 64: Afghanistan and, 412, 420, 440; Brigade Combat Team (BCT), 412; Center for Special Warfare, 155; Charlie Company, 230–1; *Counterinsurgency Field Manual* and, 26, 393; Delta Force,

Index 581

343, 419, 437–8, 458; 82nd Airborne Division, 3, 377, 419–20; El Salvador and, 323–4; 1st Brigade Combat Team, 386; Green Berets, 154–5, 262, 271–5, 331, 461; Guatemala and, 262; Indians and, 55–6, 60–1; Iran hostage crisis and, 458; Iraq and, 363, 371–2, 377–8; Lincoln and, 51; *Military Review* and, 467; My Lai massacre and, 229–32, 324, 382; 101st Airborne Division, 382–3, 419; 160th Special Operations Aviation Regiment, 458–9; Philippines and, 78, 80–4, 111, 114; Rangers, 274, 420, 458; relocation/expulsion tactics and, 50; 2nd Battalion, 412; Siberia and, 106; Special Forces (SF) and, 4, 14, 154, 221, 229, 261–2, 270, 273, 276, 323, 340, 354, 365, 384, 399–401, 415–16, 419, 425, 458, 460–4, 467; 3rd Armored Cavalry Regiment, 370, 384–5; Vietnam and, 226, 339–40; Villa and, 68, 92, 95, 98–9, 111, 113

U.S. Congress: Afghanistan and, 408, 417, 424, 432; Banana Wars and, 111, 114–16, 123; Bay of Pigs and, 254; Colombia and, 348, 351–2; El Salvador and, 309, 318–19, 321–4, 330; Greece and, 168–70; Guatemala and, 242; Gulf of Tonkin resolution and, 223–4; Iraq and, 371; Libya and, 445, 455; monitoring of military by, 342; Nicaragua and, 284–6, 288, 291–9; Philippines and, 77, 79; Sandino and, 147; Teller Amendment and, 115; Truman Doctrine and, 168–9; Vietnam and, 214, 220, 223, 231, 234–5

U.S. Defense Department, 220, 231, 273, 371
U.S. Department of State, 119
U.S. Department of Veteran Affairs (VA), 471–2
U.S.-Haiti Treaty of 1915, 118
U.S. Marine Corps: Afghanistan and, 412, 415, 427, 430f, 431–2, 435–7, 440–1; Banana Wars and, 111–13, 118–25; Beirut barracks attack and, 340, 411; Colombia and, 353; Company N, 144–5; *Counterinsurgency Field Manual* and, 26, 393; DH-4 biplanes and, 142–3; Iraq and, 363, 377–9, 388, 391; Kilo Company, 412, 435–6; North and, 299; Sandino and, 136–49; Siberia and, 103f; stealth flying and, 458; UNITAF and, 343; Vietnam and, 225–7, 230, 232

U.S. Navy: Afghanistan and, 436, 438, 440; Banana Wars and, 111–12, 115, 120–1, 123; Construction Battalion (Seabees), 401; Great White Fleet and, 112; Iran hostage crisis and, 458; Mahan and, 111–12; Mexico and, 91; Naval Special Warfare Development Group (DEVGRU) and, 438; Philippines and, 74, 401; Sandino and, 146–7; SEALs, 436, 438–40, 458, 462; Special Services Squadron, 123; Special Warfare Development Group, 438, 458; Vietnam and, 223, 234

USS *Carl Vinson*, 440
USS *Eagle*, 118
USS *Maddox*, 223
USS *Maine*, 113–14
USS *Missouri*, 209
USS *Nashville*, 118
USS *Olympia*, 72
U.S. Southern Command, 273, 286, 328, 330
U.S. Special Forces Training Team, 272–3
USS *Washington*, 118

V1 rockets, 475n7
V2 rockets, 475n7
Vafiadis, Markos, 167–8, 171
Vaky, Viron P., 263
Valley Forge, 38–40
Vásquez, Horacio, 124
Vatican, 314
Venezuela, 156, 242, 251, 260, 269, 281, 310, 349, 500n5
Viet Cong (VC): aggressive tactics of, 219; ARVN and, 219–22, 229–30, 234–5; attrition and, 224–9; communism and, 99, 154, 198, 209, 219, 221–35, 354; Easter Offensive and, 233–4; escalating war and, 223–6; pacification and, 220–3, 226–33; Phung Hoang and, 229; Tet Offensive and, 181, 229–32; Vietnamization and, 232–3
Viet Minh, 218–19, 407: base of, 212; Chinese aid to, 212; Dien Bien Phu and, 214–17; Giap and, 133, 212, 213f, 215, 217, 233, 249–50; increased numbers of, 211; pincer encounters and, 211; Soviet assistance to, 212
Vietnam, 3, 391: Anti-Communist Denunciation Campaign and, 219; ARVN and, 219–22, 230, 234–5; assassination and, 220, 229, 235; attrition

Vietnam (cont.)
and, 224–9; B-52 bombers and, 464; body counts and, 224–6; CAPs and, 227; China and, 10, 209, 212, 223, 234; communism and, 99, 154, 198, 208–35, 354, 461; conventional warfare and, 10, 212, 215, 219, 222, 230, 232–3, 235; CORDS and, 227–9, 233; counterinsurgency and, 211, 219–31, 235; covert operations and, 219, 289; deaths in, 149; Democratic Republic of Vietnam (DRV) and, 10, 209, 213f, 217; Diem and, 198, 218–23, 233; Dien Bien Phu and, 214–17; Easter Offensive and, 233–4; Eisenhower and, 214, 217, 219; escalating war in, 223–6; escape from Saigon and, 234–6; Foreign Legion and, 211; Giap and, 133, 212, 213f, 215, 217, 233, 249–50; guerrilla warfare and, 14, 212, 215, 218–22, 231, 235; Gulf of Tonkin resolution and, 223–4; Hamburger Hill and, 232; Ho Chi Minh and, 17, 209, 211, 213f, 217, 219; insurgency and, 211, 213f, 219–31, 235; insurrection and, 220; intelligence gathering and, 215, 220–1, 227–9; Japan and, 211; Johnson and, 173, 223–6; Joint Chiefs of Staff and, 222–3; JUSMAPG and, 169; Kennedy and, 220–3, 226; Land-to-the-Tiller program and, 233; Lansdale and, 218, 220, 226, 255; Laos and, 211, 214–15, 217, 224, 270; lessons learned from, 468, 469; levels of dirtiness and, 6; loss of life in, 231, 235; MAAGs and, 214, 219–20; media and, 11, 229, 233; morale and, 212, 216, 225; My Lai massacre and, 229–32, 324, 382; nation-building and, 221, 473n5; Navarre and, 212, 214–17; Nixon and, 225, 231–4; NLF and, 218–19; North, 10, 209, 217–20, 222–5, 229–31, 233–5; I Corps Tactical Zone and, 227; pacification and, 220–3, 226–33; paramilitary forces and, 218; peace with honor and, 232–3; Philippines and, 78–9, 83; Phoenix Program and, 229; propaganda and, 218, 220, 228; psychological warfare and, 235; public opinion on, 231; Republic of Vietnam (ROV) and, 10; retreat and, 230; South, 145, 154, 213f, 217–36, 394; Soviet Union and, 10, 211–15, 234; spreading inkblot strategy and, 226; Tet Offensive and, 181, 229–32; Thieu and, 233, 233–4; United States and, 212, 217–27, 232–6; U.S. Army and, 226, 339–40; U.S. Marine Corps and, 225–7, 230, 232; U.S. Navy and, 223, 234; Viet Cong (VC) and, 99, 154, 198, 209, 219, 221–35, 354; Viet Minh and, 211–19, 407; Weigley on, 14; Westmoreland and, 224–7, 230–2; World War II era and, 209, 211–12, 215, 224–5

Vietnamization, 232–3
Vilches, Freddy, 299
Villa, Pancho: as bandit, 92–9, 109, 111; Carranza and, 91–5, 98; Cody's Wild West Show and, 92; Constitutionalists and, 91; Curtiss JN-3 biplanes and, 95; elusiveness of, 94–6; lessons learned from, 468; Mexico and, 68, 89–100, 109, 111, 113, 118, 136, 453, 468; Pershing and, 93–9; pillaging and, 89; plundering and, 89, 92, 94; Punitive Expedition and, 93–9, 109, 112, 121; retaliation of, 91; Slocum and, 92; Tompkins and, 89, 92–3, 96; U.S. Army and, 92, 95, 98–9, 111, 113
Villalobos, Joaquín "Atilio," 311
Von Steuben, Baron, 39

Wallace, William, 366
Wall Street Journal, 222
Walt, Lewis, 227
War games, 366
Warlords: Afghanistan and, 2, 409, 432; China and, 19; Somalia and, 342, 342–3
War on Terror, 134, 350, 361, 473n7
Warsaw Pact, 406
Washington, George: American Revolution and, 32–6, 38–40, 45, 47, 50, 145; Valley Forge winter and, 38–40
Washington, John A., 35
Washington Post, 295–6, 316, 318, 324, 366, 380, 384, 435
Water cure, 85
Watergate scandal, 289, 299
Water supplies, 76, 194
Waxhaws Massacre, 29, 43
Wayne, 39
Weapons of mass destruction (WMD), 367–9, 391, 447
Weigley, Russell, 14

Weinberger, Caspar, 308
Welles, Sumner, 124
Wellesley, Arthur (Duke of Wellington), 22–3
West, Bing, 412, 425, 432–3
Westmoreland, William C., 224–7, 230–2
West Point, 57, 153, 395, 429
Weyler, Valeriano, 113
Wheeler, Burton K., 145
White Antelope, 5
White Hand, 259
"White Man's burden." *See* Paternalism
White Terror, 167
Wild West Show, 92
Williams, 32
Wilson, Henry Lane, 91
Wilson, Woodrow: Banana Wars and, 111, 113, 118–21, 123; Mexico and, 89, 91–4, 98, 104; Siberia and, 104–5, 107
Winston, 32
Withlacoochee Cove, 54
Wolfowitz, Paul, 368, 371
World-Herald, 85
World War I era: Armistice Day and, 106; Bolshevik control and, 103; carnage of, 122; Dominican Republic and, 123; Eastern Front and, 102–3; France and, 63, 100; Guevara on, 278; justification of, 108; Lawrence and, 127, 132f; Pershing and, 97f; U.S. belated entry into, 100; Vietnam and, 215; wariness of protracted wars and, 136, 139; Western Front and, 102, 104

World War II era, 136: Afghanistan and, 404; Algeria and, 174, 183; anti-Nazi partisans and, 18; Arab Revolt and, 135; Cold War and, 154; Cuba and, 249; de Gaulle and, 183; fire-bombings and, 475n7; France and, 470; Galula and, 186; Germany and, 9, 143, 372, 465, 475n7; Geronimo signal and, 61; Greece and, 165, 171; Guatemala and, 243, 265; Japan and, 9–10, 209, 372; London blitz and, 475n7; Luftwaffe and, 143, 475n7; Malaya and, 192–3, 195; Mao Zedong's tactics after, 157, 161, 163; Philippines and, 199, 201, 209; South Pacific and, 111; as total war, 9; Vietnam and, 209, 211–12, 224–5

Ydígoras, José Miguel Ramón, 258
Yemen, 129, 462, 464, 515n11
Yemeni, Abd al Rahman al, 462
Yugoslavia, 171

Zacapa massacre, 259, 262
Zachariadis, Nikolaos, 171
Zadran, Jan Baz, 462
Zamora, Rubén, 311
Zarqawi, Abu Musab al, 373–5, 378, 387, 427, 459–61
Zelaya, José Santos, 138
Zhou Enlai, 159
Zia-ul-Haq, 405–6
Zúñiga, Mario, 252–3